COMMUNITY-BASED
CORRECTIONS

ELEVENTH EDITION

LEANNE FIFTAL ALARID

The University of Texas at El Paso

CENGAGE
Learning

Australia • Brazil • Mexico • Singapore • United Kingdom • United States

CENGAGE
Learning®

Community–Based Corrections, Eleventh Edition
Leanne Fiftal Alarid

Product Director: Marta Lee-Perriard

Product Manager: Carolyn Henderson-Meier

Content Developer: Christy Frame

Product Assistant: Valerie Kraus

Marketing Manager: Kara Kindstrom

Art and Cover Direction, Production Management, and Composition: Lumina Datamatics, Inc.

Manufacturing Planner: Judy Inouye

Cover Image: ©Kidstock/First Light

For product information and technology assistance, contact us at
Cengage Learning Customer & Sales Support, 1-800-354-9706

For permission to use material from this text or product,
submit all requests online at **cengage.com/permissions**
Further permissions questions can be emailed to
permissionrequest@cengage.com

Library of Congress Control Number: 2015948053

Student Edition:
ISBN: 978-1-305-63372-8

Loose-leaf Edition:
ISBN: 978-1-305-65941-4

Cengage Learning
20 Channel Center Street
Boston, MA 02210
USA

Cengage Learning is a leading provider of customized learning solutions with employees residing in nearly 40 different countries and sales in more than 125 countries around the world. Find your local representative at **www.cengage.com.**

Cengage Learning products are represented in Canada by Nelson Education, Ltd.

To learn more about Cengage Learning Solutions, visit www.cengage.com. Purchase any of our products at your local college store or at our preferred online store **www.cengagebrain.com.**

Unless otherwise noted, all items are © Cengage Learning

Printed in the United States of America
Print Number: 01   Print Year: 2015

To my students at the University of Texas at El Paso
May you find mucho felicidad y prosperidad in
the pursuit of your American dream.
Leanne Alarid

BRIEF CONTENTS

CONTENTS

Evidence-based practices (EBP) are changing the way that many agencies operate to an acceptance of empirical research and evaluation to determine what improvements can be made for more efficient use of rehabilitation programs and correctional technology. Through the principles of effective correctional intervention, more has been learned about what works with certain types of offenders. There is also a broader array of choices available as alternatives to incarceration than ever before. EBP has caused a dramatic shift in the way that offenders are supervised in the community and prepared for release from prison.

This book operates on two assumptions. First, most people who are diverted from a conviction or who are convicted of a crime are supervised in the community on a form of community-based corrections and not in jail or prison. The second assumption is that while some people should be incarcerated for their crimes, the reality is that few are kept for the remainder of their natural lives. Between 95%–97% of people in jail or prison today will be released at some point and many will undergo a period of community supervision as they transition back to the community. This book examines programs that operate to fit the needs of various types of offenders.

The goal of the eleventh edition of *Community-Based Corrections* is to provide students with a comprehensive and practical guide to EBP and academic research on probation, release from prison, and other community-based alternatives. Community-based correctional programs are based in their historical, philosophical, social, and legal contexts and to integrate real-life practice to the greatest extent possible. Because this book is meant to have practical use, examples of actual community-based programs and procedures are used from various jurisdictions, while at the same time, recognizing that local community corrections programs vary widely.

NEW TO THIS EDITION

This edition features nine new EBP boxes to better feature what programs and techniques work in community-based corrections. The theme for these boxes is entitled "Evidence-Based Practices in Community Corrections." This feature investigates techniques in community corrections supervision and correctional programs that are most effective in reducing recidivism. In Chapter 1, theories relative to community correctional goals were further explained, that include protecting the public through monitoring and specific deterrence theory, rehabilitation through risk, needs, and responsivity theory, and restorative justice. A new chapter opening story was provided on singer, Justin Bieber.

Chapter 2 introduces a new approach to community supervision (and a new glossary term) called criminogenic needs-based supervision that is further discussed in Chapters 5 and 12. The neighborhood-based supervision model is expanded upon in Chapter 2. Chapter 3 contains a new chapter opening story on Lynne Stewart, a former defense attorney who received compassionate release from prison. In the origins of parole section, the reformation contributions of Georg Michael Von Obermaier have been completely rewritten—after finding a more detailed article published in 1937 about his contributions to parole. Two tables were replaced with pie charts showing the same data in aggregated form. One of the tables was each individual state's releasing authority and sentencing structure, and the other was the types of release from prison. The section on medical parole and compassionate release were updated.

Chapter 4 contains a new chapter opening story about the sentencing of Oscar Pistorius, an Olympic and Paralympic athlete who was found culpable in the death of his girlfriend. Figure 4.1 was updated to include names of offenses within federal sentencing guidelines. An improved example of an indeterminate sentence for community corrections was added in Figure 4.4. Chapter 4 also contains updated coverage on the most recent findings related to drug courts and other problem-solving courts.

Chapter 5 is newly titled to: "Case Management Using Risk/Needs/Responsivity" to incorporate more of the RNR research and practices. The chapter also has increased coverage on emergent practices in case planning, strategies, and an expanded section on working with women offenders and gender responsive strategies. Many of these practices, such as risk/needs/responsivity, and motivational interviewing are consistent with EBP. This chapter has a new chapter opening story on Olympic medalist, Michael Phelps and his second DUI arrest. The questionnaire at the end of this chapter was revised to include pertinent information for the Ohio Risk Assessment System.

Chapter 6 contains a new chapter opening story on mixed martial artist, Tito Ortiz. This chapter also has updated coverage for community supervision techniques for drug offenders, offenders with mental illness, and sex offenders. Given that many gang members are juveniles, the section on supervising gang members was moved from Chapter 6 to Chapter 13. Chapter 7 incorporates the most recent and updated literature on revocation and recidivism rates with two new tables and figures.

Chapter 8 has a new chapter opening story about Jesse Jackson Jr. leaving prison for a halfway house. Information on Hannah Chickering, who established the first halfway house for female prisoners and their children, has been added to the history of halfway houses. New evaluations of halfway houses have been added, as well as a new box called: "Who Should get Cognitive-Behavioral Treatment and How Much is Enough?"

Chapter 9 has a new opening story about Torrey Dale Grady and a recently decided U.S. Supreme Court case that could potentially affect post-conviction lifetime electronic monitoring of sex offenders. Chapter 10 also has a new opening story about victim offender mediation after a death caused by texting while driving. The first part of Chapter 10 was updated with new glossary terms, including a new section on procedural justice theory, and rewritten sections on conferencing, reparation boards/victim impact panels, restitution, and fees.

Chapter 11 on reentry has been lengthened and updated to include a new chapter opening story and a brand new section on workforce development and evaluating reentry initiatives with respect to employment outcomes and recidivism. The U.S. map of legal barriers has been updated and a new table of firearms restrictions for convicted offenders has been created. A section on parole and mandatory supervision effectiveness has also been consolidated and summarized at the end.

Chapter 12 has a new chapter opening story on a recent Georgia Supreme Court case on limiting private probation agencies for actions related to nonpayment. The section on probation privatization has been updated, as well as the section on officer training requirements and sample curriculum topics. Chapter 13 opens with discussion on youths caught up in the Baltimore riots that occurred in April of 2015 after the death of Freddie Gray inside a police van. A new section has been added entitled: "Supervising High-Risk Juveniles in the Community." This section includes home visits, youth gang members (section moved from the end of Chapter 6 in 10e) and youths who parole from prison, are among the youths who are likely to recidivate or continue criminal behavior into adulthood. There is updated information on teen/youth courts as approaches for opportunity-focused supervision for working with at-risk juveniles on probation and their families.

In Chapter 14, a new chapter opening story on Mark Wahlberg's recent application for a pardon was discussed. Two boxes were replaced—the technology box in 14.1 was replaced with a box about challenges to implementing EBP. Table 14.1 (restoration of voting rights) was replaced with discussion about legal assistance that law schools can provide former felons who wish to have their rights restored.

Learning Tools

Each chapter opens with a recent human interest story that corresponds to the material in that particular chapter. Each story involves either a highly publicized case, or a well-known person who is serving a community corrections sentence, such as Michael Phelps, Chris Brown, or Justin Beiber. This allows the student to relate to the people in these cases, and help them better understand the material throughout each chapter. Each chapter has learning objectives of noteworthy concepts in a bulleted list format. Key terms are boldfaced in the text, with their accompanying definitions in the margins, and also defined in the glossary at the back of the book. There are 2–3 "Truth or Fiction" feature boxes presented in the margins of most chapters. This feature presents an issue that is commonly perceived in a particular way (such as whether or not criminals can be rehabilitated) and then immediately follows up as to whether that perception is factual or a myth.

The most notable pedagogical teaching tool available in this text allows the students to apply kinesthetic learning and case study methods to examine an arrest report and criminal background check on a created defendant, named Sue Steel. The client information and arrest report is initially presented at the end of Chapter 4. The student can then engage in a mock interview with that client, and prepare a presentence report from that interview. In Chapter 5, the student can score a risk/needs assessment and create an individualized supervision plan for the client. Then, supervision options can be discussed from Chapter 6 through Chapter 11. All of these tools are placed in the appropriate chapters, so students can engage in real-world experiences as they read the text. Each chapter contains the following pedagogical features:

BOXED FEATURES   There are four boxed features running through the text in most chapters. The newest box theme is "Evidence-Based Practices in Community Corrections." This feature investigates techniques in community corrections supervision and correctional programs that are most effective in reducing recidivism. The second box theme is "Technology in Corrections;" that illustrates how advancements in equipment and knowledge about data systems have impacted community corrections supervision. The third box theme is "Corrections Up Close" that investigates a particular topic in more detail as it pertains to the chapter material. The "Field Notes" boxed text features eight different practitioners who write about a different correctional issue from their own perspective.

CHAPTER REVIEW   Each chapter is followed by a bulleted summary list. Discussion questions are included to encourage students to critically think about the material in each chapter. Some discussion questions can be designed as topics for essay questions, exams, or research papers. A listing of websites, videos, and podcasts are available on-line for instructors and students to seek more information on material presented within the chapter.

CASE STUDIES   Each chapter has case studies for in-class discussion or to use as a basis for writing assignments. Each case study provides the student with background information about an offender and requires that the student incorporate a problem-solving skill that was discussed in that chapter, such as and apply them to individual offenders in a similar way to judges, probation officers, and parole board members face on a daily basis.

ANCILLARIES

For the Instructor

MINDTAP FOR CRIMINAL JUSTICE   from Cengage Learning represents a new approach to a highly personalized, online learning platform. A fully online learning solution, MindTap combines all of a student's learning tools—readings, multimedia, activities, and assessments in to a singular Learning Path that guides the student through the curriculum. Instructors personalize the experience by customizing the presentation of these learning tools for their students, allowing instructors to seamlessly introduce their own content into the Learning path via "apps" that integrated into the MindTap platform. Additionally, MindTap provides interoperability with major Learning Management Systems (LMS) via support for industry standards and fosters partnerships with third-party educational application providers to provide a highly collaborative, engaging, and personalized learning experience.

ONLINE INSTRUCTOR'S MANUAL   includes learning objectives, key terms, a detailed chapter outline, a chapter summary, lesson plans, discussion topics, student activities, "What If" scenarios, media tools, and a sample syllabus. The learning objectives are correlated with the discussion topics, student activities, and media tools.

ONLINE TEST BANK   Each chapter's test bank contains questions in multiple-choice, true false, completion, essay, and new critical thinking formats, with a full answer key. The test bank is coded to the learning objectives that appear in the main text, and includes the section in the main text where the answers can be found. Finally, each question in test bank has been carefully reviewed by experienced criminal justice instructors for quality, accuracy, and content coverage.

ONLINE POWERPOINT® LECTURES Helping you make your lectures more engaging while effectively reaching your visually oriented students, these handy Microsoft

PowerPoint slides outline the chapters of the main text in a classroom-ready presentation. The PowerPoint slides are updated to reflect the content and organization of the new edition of the text, are tagged by chapter learning objective, and feature some additional examples and real-world cases for application and discussion.

CENGAGE LEARNING TESTING POWERED BY COGNERO This assessment software is a flexible, online system that allows you to import, edit, and manipulate test bank content from the *Community-Based Corrections* test bank or elsewhere, including your own favorite test questions; create multiple test versions in an instant; and deliver tests from your LMS, your classroom, or wherever you want.

For the Student

MINDTAP FOR CRIMINAL JUSTICE   MindTap Criminal Justice from Cengage Learning represents a new approach to a highly personalized, online learning platform. A fully online learning solution, MindTap combines all of your learning tools—readings, multimedia, activities, and assessments into a singular Learning Path that guides you through the course.

ACKNOWLEDGMENTS

First, I'd like to acknowledge my former co-authors, Paul Cromwell and Rolando del Carmen, who asked me back in 2000 to become a part of this text. While Paul still teaches at the University of South Florida, Rolando is now enjoying a much deserved retirement. I am forever grateful for their mentorship, friendship, and the opportunity to carry on the time honored tradition of what was originally the George G. Killinger and Hazel B. Kerper text in 1976.

I appreciate the professionals who wrote personal "Field Notes" essays that added more personality to the book: Al Alonso, Mark Masterson, Tess Price, Abel Salinas, Denise Bray Hensley, Richard Russell, Eladio Castillo, and Ralph Garza.

I wish to acknowledge reviewers who provided comments on the tenth edition of this text: Samantha Carlo, Miami Dade College; Tom Destito, Metropolitan State University of Denver; Henry Gonzales, University of Houston-Downtown; Elizabeth Grossi, University of Louisville; Thomas Hawley, Eastern Gateway Community College; Alan Johnson, Marian University; Tony Larocca, Kean University; Tom Laughner, American International College; Daniel Osborne, Suffolk Community College; Pamela Simek, Bossier Parish Community College; Lenny Ward, FDU and Mercer County Community College. Reviewers for the ninth edition include: Diane K. Sjuts, Metro Community College; Eric Metchik, Salem State University; Jeb Booth, Salem State University; Shannon Hankhouse, Tarleton State University; Stacy Nonn, Sanford-Brown College; Kevin Dooley, Central New Mexico Community College; and Debra Wicks, Pittsburgh Technical Institute.

Finally, I would be remiss if I didn't acknowledge my students and colleagues who, most of the time without even knowing it, are giving me ideas and providing fresh examples for ways to further improve the text.

Leanne F. Alarid

Part I

Overview and Evolution of Community Corrections

The idea behind community corrections programs is that most offenders can be effectively held accountable for their crimes at the same time that they fulfill legitimate living standards in the community. Most offenders do not pose an imminent danger to themselves or to others and can therefore remain in the community without endangering public safety. Offering correctional options for offenders living in the community confers several benefits.

First, the offender continues to contribute toward individual and familial responsibilities with legitimate employment, paying income taxes, and child support. Second, offenders living in the community are more likely than prison-bound offenders to compensate victims through restitution or to pay back the community through community service. Finally, community corrections programs do not expose offenders to the subculture of violence that exists in many jails and prisons.

Chapter 1 introduces the array of community corrections programs and explains why the study of community corrections is important, including the movement of the field toward evidence-based practices. Chapter 2 chronicles the history of probation from the early 1800s to the present, including a section discussing how supervision philosophy has changed over time, and ends with a description of who is on probation. Chapter 3 examines the history of reentry that began as discretionary parole, which, for violent and habitual offenders, has been replaced by mandatory release. Discretionary parole remains an important decision point in the correctional process, with medical parole becoming the newest issue for the compassionate release of terminally ill prisoners.

An Overview of Community Corrections:
Goals and Evidence-Based Practices

CHAPTER OUTLINE

CHAPTER LEARNING OBJECTIVES

1. Define corrections and its purpose.
2. Explain the role of corrections at each of the three main decision points.
3. Analyze the theories behind correctional goals of punishment and rehabilitation.
4. Explain the importance of evidence-based practices to evaluating effectiveness and achieving correctional goals.

KEY TERMS

community corrections
post-adjudication
pre-adjudication
probation
indeterminate sentencing
determinate sentencing
bail
pretrial supervision
intermediate sanctions
prisoner reentry
prerelease program
parole
specific deterrence theory
rehabilitation
risk/need/responsivity (RNR)
criminogenic needs
restorative justice
participation process model
evidence-based practices (EBP)
net widening
recidivism

I n the last two years, Justin Bieber has seemingly been in the news more often for acting in an aggressive, crude, and disrespectful manner in public than for his singing career. Beginning in July 2013, reports included marijuana use and urinating in a restaurant mop bucket.

A few months later while on tour, Bieber was repeatedly involved in late-night deviance that included nightclub brawls, brothel visits, and allegedly assaulting an individual at a South Korea nightclub. While in Brazil, he vandalized a hotel wall with graffiti and was fined for the damage.

In January 2014, Bieber was pulled over in Miami Beach for drag racing a rented Lamborghini. Bieber failed the field sobriety test and was arrested for driving under the influence (DUI). He also admitted using marijuana and taking prescription medicines. He was charged with driving with an expired driver's license and resisting arrest.

In July 2014, Bieber was placed on two years of probation in California for vandalism (egging a neighbor's house). Part of the probation included five days of community service, completion of 12 weeks of anger management, and victim restitution totaling over $80,000.

A few months later in Ontario, Canada, near his father's home, he was arrested for dangerous driving and assault when his ATV allegedly collided with a photographer's minivan, and Bieber got physical with a paparazzi. Probation officials investigated the case to determine if Bieber's actions violated the conditions of his California probation. As of May 2015, Bieber has remained on probation and has made progress toward his court-ordered conditions.

Considering his prior behaviors and the most recent offense, is it appropriate for Bieber to be back under community supervision or some other type of correctional program?

THE CORRECTIONAL DILEMMA

> "Incarceration reduces crime … but only up to a point. Once the incarceration rate hits a certain level—at the state level this tipping or inflection point appears to be 325 inmates per 100,000 population—crime rates actually increase." (Byrne, 2013, p. 9)

In the United States, nearly 7 million people, equivalent to about 3% of the total adult population, are currently under some form of correctional supervision, which includes those sentenced to prison, jail, or community supervision. Our nation's crime control policies over the past three decades have been driven by the assumption that incarceration reduces crime. Experts estimate that there is only a small reduction at best, especially when compared to other strategies. A 10% increase in the incarceration rate is associated with only between 1% and 4% decrease in the crime rate (Stemen, 2007). On the other hand, more police officers, a decreased unemployment rate, increase in wages, and an increase in citizen education levels have all shown to decrease crime rates at levels greater than what prison can achieve (Byrne, 2013).

Because incarceration as a method of crime reduction is such a costly endeavor, many states have realized that we cannot build our way out of the crime problem. The economic recession of 2008 was a contributing factor to how local and state government thought about reducing correctional costs relative to other costs such as health care, education, and transportation. In 2009, the overall correctional population declined slightly for the first time in 40 years (VERA Institute of Justice, 2010). Most states are continuing to actively reduce the number of people in the corrections system while others are reallocating resources from costly jails and prisons to less costly but effective correctional approaches within the community.

This text focuses exclusively on community-based corrections. **Community corrections** refers to any sanction in which offenders serve all or a portion of their entire sentence in the community. Most community corrections options are **post-adjudication**, which means that the defendant has either pleaded guilty or been found guilty by a judge or jury. After a finding of guilt, the court sentences the defendant, and the corrections system carries out that sentence. Some types of community correctional supervision, however, are **pre-adjudication**, which means that treatment with supervision occurs in the community *prior* to a finding of guilt. Table 1.1 distinguishes these differences.

A community sentence seeks to repair the harm the offender has caused the victim or the community and to reduce the risk of reoffending in the future. Figure 1.1 shows the wide variety of community-based sanctions available, ranging from residential programs (halfway houses, prerelease facilities, and therapeutic communities) to economic sanctions (restitution, fines, and fees) to nonresidential or outpatient options (probation, parole, and electronic monitoring).

The most common form of community supervision is **probation**. Probation is defined as the release of a convicted offender under conditions imposed by a court for a specified period, during which time that court retains authority to modify those conditions or to resentence the offender if he or she violates those

community corrections
A nonincarcerative sanction in which offenders serve all or a portion of their sentence in a community.

post-adjudication
The state in which a defendant has been sentenced by a court after having either pleaded guilty or been found guilty by a judge or jury. Being adjudicated is equivalent to a conviction.

pre-adjudication
The state in which a defendant has not yet pleaded guilty or been found guilty by a judge or jury. Said defendant is either in a pretrial stage or has been offered deferred adjudication.

probation
Community supervision of a convicted offender in lieu of incarceration under conditions imposed by a court for a specified period, during which it retains authority to modify those conditions or to resentence said offender if he or she violates those conditions.

TABLE 1.1 Pre-Adjudication vs. Post-Adjudication Corrections

PRE-ADJUDICATION CORRECTIONS	
Community Corrections	**Institutional Corrections**
Pretrial release	Jail
Pretrial supervision/house arrest	Jail-based work release
Victim–offender mediation	
Diversion/deferred adjudication	
POST-ADJUDICATION CORRECTIONS	
Community Corrections	**Institutional Corrections**
Probation supervision (regular)	Jail
Probation supervision (intensive/specialized)	Prison
Mandatory release or discretionary parole	
Probation or Parole Add-Ons	**Treatment While Incarcerated**
Residential halfway house/prerelease facility	Reentry preparation classes
Residential substance abuse facility	Prison-based therapeutic community
Drug court or mental health court	Psychotropic medications
Outpatient treatment/therapy (substance abuse, parenting, battering/assault, sex offender)	Prison-based cognitive-behavioral therapy
Education/classes (school, life skills, vocational, financial/credit counseling)	Education or vocational opportunities
Electronic monitoring/global positioning	
Day reporting centers	
Community service	
Restitution, fines, fees	
Community reparation boards	

conditions. Probation forms the basis of community supervision, and most of the other sanctions introduced in Figure 1.1 are programs or conditions that can be applied in different combinations to different offenders to achieve individualized results. The American Probation and Parole Association (APPA) was created to bridge these alternatives. As an international policy and educational organization for practitioners who work with adults and juveniles in the field of community corrections, the APPA serves to educate and train members and to develop standards for the discipline.

Table 1.2 shows the latest government statistics on the number of people currently under some form of correctional supervision. There were nearly 4 million offenders on probation and over 853,000 on parole/supervised release, for a total community corrections population of nearly 5 million (Herberman & Bonczar, 2014). Although men account for a disproportionately greater percentage of offenders than women, most women are eligible for a community

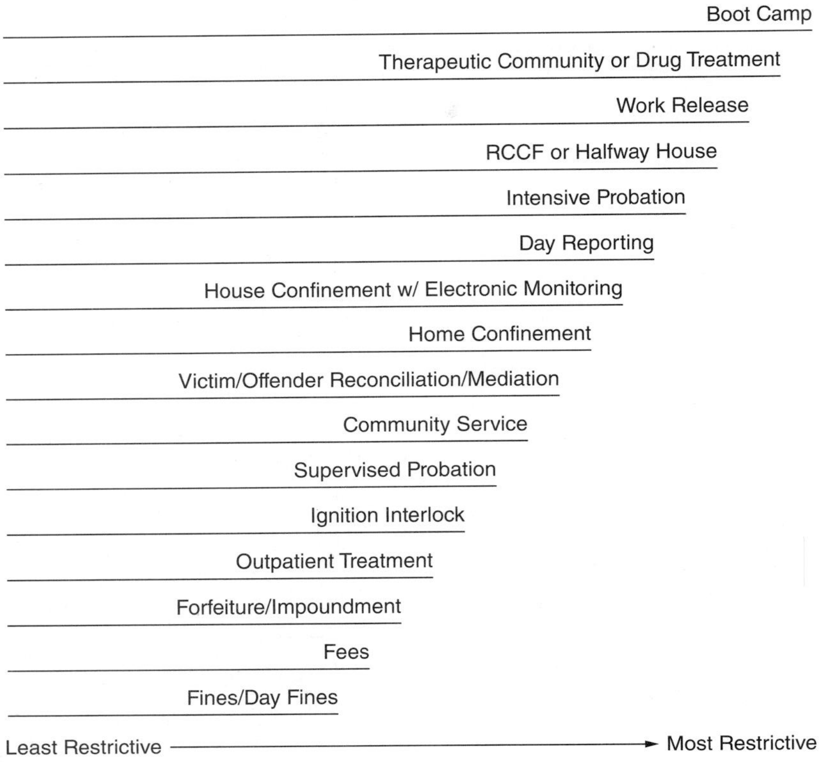
Boot Camp
Therapeutic Community or Drug Treatment
Work Release
RCCF or Halfway House
Intensive Probation
Day Reporting
House Confinement w/ Electronic Monitoring
Home Confinement
Victim/Offender Reconciliation/Mediation
Community Service
Supervised Probation
Ignition Interlock
Outpatient Treatment
Forfeiture/Impoundment
Fees
Fines/Day Fines
Least Restrictive
Most Restrictive

FIGURE 1.1 Community Corrections by Restrictiveness.

Adapted from: Center for Community Corrections (1997). *A Call for Punishments That Make Sense*, p. 37 Washington, DC: Bureau of Justice Assistance. Retrieved from: www.communitycorrectionsworks.org/steve/nccc/punishments.pdf

TRUTH OR FICTION?

Even though the United States has the highest incarceration rate in the world when compared to other countries, probation is still the most common correctional sentence in the United States.

TRUE

FACT: There is more than twice the number of Americans on probation than in all jails and prisons combined. This is because probation includes deferred adjudication, diversion, and post-conviction community sentences.

indeterminate sentencing
A sentencing philosophy that encourages rehabilitation and incorporates a broad sentencing range in which discretionary release is determined by a parole board, based on an offender's remorse, insight into his or her mistakes, involvement in rehabilitation, and readiness to return to society.

corrections sentence because they tend to have shorter criminal histories and commit fewer violent crimes by comparison. Women comprise 24% of probationers, 12% of parolees, and 7% of all prisoners.

There are considerably more male and female offenders under community supervision than those incarcerated in jail and prison. The correctional system carries out the order of the courts, but the variance in the *rate* per 100,000 people is derived from a number of factors that include the nature of each state's sentencing laws, police discretion in responding to criminal behavior, the rate of release from prison, and each agency's probation and parole violation policy. We begin by describing the nature of sentencing, which is distinguished by two basic philosophies: indeterminate and determinate.

Indeterminate Sentencing

From the 1930s to the mid-1970s, **indeterminate sentencing** was the primary sentencing philosophy in the United States. Under this model, judges decided who went to prison, and parole boards decided when offenders were rehabilitated and ready for release on parole. The release date was unknown by an offender and subject to a majority decision of the parole board, which determined whether that offender was making sufficient progress toward rehabilitation and was ready to rejoin the larger society. While incarcerated, offenders were able to enroll in a variety of programs aimed at self-improvement and skill building to demonstrate readiness for the parole board.

TABLE 1.2   Adults on Probation, on Parole, in Jail and in Prison: 1980–2014

Year	Total Estimate in Millions	COMMUNITY SUPERVISION		INCARCERATION	
		Probation	Parole	County Jail	State & Fed Prison
1980	1.84	1,118,097	220,438	182,288	319,598
1982	2.19	1,357,264	224,604	207,853	402,914
1984	2.69	1,740,948	266,992	233,018	448,264
1986	3.24	2,114,621	325,638	272,735	526,436
1988	3.74	2,356,483	407,977	341,893	607,766
1990	4.35	2,670,234	531,407	403,019	743,382
1992	4.76	2,811,611	658,601	441,781	850,566
1994	5.14	2,981,022	690,371	479,800	990,147
1996	5.49	3,164,996	679,733	518,492	1,127,528
1998	6.13	3,670,441	696,385	592,462	1,224,469
2000	6.46	3,839,532	725,527	621,149	1,316,333
2002	6.76	4,024,067	750,934	665,475	1,367,547
2004	7.00	4,151,125	765,819	713,990	1,421,911
2006	7.20	4,237,023	798,202	765,819	1,492,973
2008	7.31	4,270,917	828,169	785,533	1,522,834
2010	7.08	4,055,514	840,676	748,728	1,518,104
2012	7.11	3,942,800	851,200	744,524	1,570,397
2014	7.07	3,910,600	853,200	731,208	1,574,751

Notes: Counts are for December 31 of each year, except for the most recent year (which is as of January 1); jail population counts are for June 30 of each year; jail estimates include convicted prisoners awaiting transfer to prison facilities. Some data have been revised based on the most recently reported counts and may differ from previous estimates.

Sources: All sources for all years of this table were published by the Bureau of Justice Statistics, U.S. Department of Justice in Washington, DC. Most recent estimates from: Carson, E. Ann. 2014. *Prisoners in 2013.* NCJ 247282. Washington, DC: U.S. Department of Justice; Glaze, Lauren E. 2011. *Correctional Population in the United States, 2010,* NCJ 236319. Washington, DC: U.S. Department of Justice; Herberman, Erinn J., and Thomas P. Bonczar. 2014. *Probation and Parole in the United States, 2013,* NCJ 248029. Washington, DC: U.S. Department of Justice; Minton, Todd D., and Daniela Golinelli. 2014. *Jail inmates at midyear 2013—Statistical Tables.* NCJ 245350. Washington, DC: U.S. Department of Justice.

DISCRETIONARY PAROLE AS A RELEASE STRATEGY.   Parole was also used as a back-door strategy for controlling the prison population. When prisons became too crowded, the parole rate increased to make room for incoming prisoners. Under indeterminate sentencing, offenders who did not go to prison were, for the most part, placed on probation. Few intermediate sentencing options existed other than prison or probation. Options that did exist, such as halfway houses and intensive probation, were used infrequently.

Support for indeterminate sentencing declined as people questioned whether prison rehabilitation worked and whether parole boards could accurately determine when offenders were ready for release. This lack of confidence in correctional programming peaked in 1974 with Robert Martinson's publication concluding that "with few and isolated exceptions, the rehabilitative efforts that have been reported so far had no appreciable effect on recidivism" (p. 25). Martinson's findings were poorly stated, criticisms were lodged against the methodology used, and Martinson later recanted those statements. In the complete report published the next year, Douglas Lipton, Robert Martinson, Judith Wilks, et al. (1975) concluded:

> While some treatment programs have had modest successes, it still must be concluded that the field of corrections has not as yet found satisfactory ways to reduce recidivism by significant amounts. (p. 627)

Both of these publications began a national debate about the efficacy of treatment programs. Ironically, the original intent of Martinson's article was to attempt to decrease the use of *prisons* rather than the use of treatment programs, so unbeknownst to his coauthors, Martinson published the solo piece and was ill prepared for the catastrophe that followed. His study was a prelude to one of the most conservative eras in American politics, wherein policy makers were looking for reasons to repudiate the putative liberal rehabilitation policies of previous decades.

In addition to raising questions about rehabilitation, indeterminate sentences created another problem called sentencing disparity. Most indeterminate sentences had a maximum ending date that was far in the future (such as 10 or 20 years) to allow adequate time to rehabilitate. With an unknown or ambiguous release date, nonviolent offenders spent many more years behind bars than their crimes warranted, whereas others—who may have convinced the parole board they were "cured"—were released after only a few years. This issue became a question of fairness and an attempt to reduce sentencing disparity.

Origins of Determinate Sentencing

Given the concerns of potential bias and perceived unfairness in the release decision, many indeterminate sentencing laws were repealed so that offenders convicted of similar crimes would serve roughly equal terms in prison. The American Friends Service committee recommended that sentences be categorized according to severity of crime based on two scales: the harm done by an offense and an offender's culpability. Judgment of the degree of culpability would be based partly on an offender's prior record. Having proposed punishment as the main goal of sentencing, the committee then ruled out prison as punishment for all but the most serious offenses—those in which bodily harm was threatened or done to a victim. The committee proposed alternatives such as periodic imprisonment, increased use of fines, and other lesser sanctions (von Hirsch, 1976).

determinate sentencing
A sentencing philosophy that focuses on consistency for a crime committed, specifying by statute or sentencing guidelines an exact amount or narrow range of time to be served in prison or in a community and mandating a minimum amount of time before an offender is eligible (if at all) for release. Also known as a *presumptive, fixed,* or *mandatory sentence.*

At about the same time, David Fogel (1979) urged a narrowing of sentencing and parole discretion. His work was influential in helping to draft legislative change that became known in various states as **determinate sentencing**. One of his goals was to disconnect release date from prison program participation. He advocated abolishing parole boards and establishing "flat-time" sentencing for each class of felonies.

Maine became the first state to return to determinate sentencing in which the minimum and maximum sentence range was predefined and release was determined by legislative statute. Sentence length was therefore determined by time served rather than by how long it takes for an offender to become rehabilitated. With fewer sentencing options for judges, personal, familial, and environmental variables played less of a role in the sentencing process. The slogan "You do the crime, you do the time" became popular and funding for prison treatment programs diminished. In determinate sentencing, judges had less discretion, and though they are able to deviate slightly (higher or lower) from prescribed sentencing guidelines, they must provide justification for doing so. Parole board decision making was limited in many states to only nonviolent offenders or was abolished altogether (Porter, 2015).

Examples of determinate sentencing policies have included mandatory minimums, truth-in-sentencing, three strikes laws, and sentencing guidelines. All states have adopted some form of mandatory minimum sentencing laws that required violent or repeat offenders to serve a certain percentage of time before release would be considered. For example, truth-in-sentencing laws required that offenders serve at least 85% of their original sentence length before becoming eligible for release (Porter, 2015). Three strikes laws mandate long prison terms for a third felony conviction. Some states require a life sentence for violent third-time felons, while other states count any third felony, whether it is violent or nonviolent.

Sentencing guidelines form a matrix based on an offender's prior criminal record and current conviction, which a judge must follow at the federal level and also in those states where guidelines are mandatory. Some states have guidelines that are only suggestive, although others still have never developed sentencing guidelines. Even though guidelines have decreased sentencing disparity and created accountability for sentencing decisions, most judges have disliked limits on their discretion. Although probation is still allowed at the federal level, federal parole has been replaced by "supervised release" (either mandatory by statute or under the federal sentencing guidelines). Most states, however, have retained aspects of both indeterminate and determinate sentencing structures, examples of which are given in Chapter 4.

THE PARADOX

Correctional policy is in many ways a paradox between economic constraints on what we can afford and shifts in the tide of public perception—that is, in what is important to vocal constituents and public interest groups. Maruna and King (2008) note a shift away from expert-driven decisions in penal policy to one characterized "more explicitly by symbolic and expressive concerns ... [and] emotionalization of public discourse about crime and law" (p. 338). They argue that correctional policy is driven by politics rather than by rationality, and that public opinion is influenced by the media. The media have long been criticized for sensationalizing violence and atypical crimes while downplaying average or common crimes that never result in a prison sentence. The average American citizen, as a result, is only exposed to a very small percentage of the overall crime picture and is less informed than are experts about what should be done in response to crime.

Public Opinion About Community Corrections

Community corrections include alternatives to incarceration and early release from prison. One national public opinion poll indicated that the most well-known community-based corrections were probation, house arrest, and electronic monitoring. Less-familiar options were restorative justice, day reporting, and drug court. The majority of adults thought that alternatives to incarceration were appropriate for nonviolent offenders and/or when a theft was less than $400, and that these methods of supervision did not necessarily decrease public safety. Nearly half (45%) thought that probation and rehabilitation were likely to reduce recidivism for nonserious offenders over prison or jail (Hartney & Marchionna, 2009). Of those who go to prison, it seems that a majority of citizens supported prisons emphasizing rehabilitation, especially reentry services such as housing assistance, mental health, and job training to help prevent future recidivism (Sundt, Vanderhoff, Shaver, Lazzeroni, et al., 2012).

Proposed strategies to increase the level of public support—or at least increase the level of attention for community corrections—include appealing to the public on both a rational and an emotional level. Even though crime policy has shifted to an emotional level as Maruna and King (2008) have noted, with fear and anger driving increased perceptions of punitiveness for some offenses, emotions such as compassion and forgiveness can be equally as powerful as alternatives to prison as individuals and communities heal. Another notion with emotional appeal is that of "redeemability"—that is, convincing the public that offenders can change their ways if given the tools and the means to do so (Maruna & King, 2008, p. 345). But these are only half of the solution. Experts also suggest that the media should present a broader view of issues than just atypical cases. Public opinion research on sentencing preferences demonstrated higher validity when the public was given diverse sentencing options and adequate information, such as program descriptions and detailed knowledge about an offense or an offender.

Prison Is Expensive

The other side of the correctional paradox is that corrections funding source is driven almost completely by public tax dollars. Correctional budgets have been hit hard these last few years, due in part to the most recent economic recession that forced states to cut social programs, initiate hiring freezes, and lay off employees (VERA Inst. Just., 2010). In response to the fiscal crisis, state legislators and correctional administrators have considered the following options:

- Decriminalizing lower-level nonviolent and/or drug felony offenses and reducing them to Class A misdemeanors
- Repealing mandatory minimums
- Using more graduated sanctions in the community
- Increasing discretionary parole rates
- Changing probation and parole policies for responding to violations
- Denying requests to incarcerate for anything but new crimes
- Closing existing housing units within a prison
- Closing existing prisons altogether

There is growing consensus that the use of jail and prison facilities, which are the most expensive option, should be reserved for the most dangerous offenders. At the same time, community-based correctional options should be expanded when regular probation and parole is not enough.

In comparison to prisons, probation and parole agencies garnered about 21 cents of every correctional dollar to supervise the 70% of all people under correctional supervision (Kyckelhahn, 2012). Table 1.3 shows daily costs per person

TABLE 1.3   Daily Cost per Person for Selected Forms of Correctional Supervision

SUPERVISION TYPE	FEDERAL (FY 13–14)	NORTH CAROLINA (FY 11–12)
Prison[a]	$75.25	$76.02
Pretrial detention[a]	$72.67	$60.00
Pretrial community supervision[a]	$8.21	$6.04
Residential community facility[b] or residential substance abuse facility	$60.27	$47.34
Probation	$9.40	$3.57
Intensive probation	$12.10	$15.27
Parole/mandatory Supervised release	$8.10	$3.44
Community service work program	N/R	$1.29
Day reporting	N/R	$24.70
Electronic monitoring/GPS	$10.50	$13.28

Notes: N/R = Cost not reported

[a] = These costs are averaged for supervision of general population offenders. Costs for special needs offenders and those in maximum security institutions are higher.

[b] = The cost of all RCCFs are lower, since a portion is subsidized by the offender.

Sources: North Carolina Department of Public Safety (2012). Cost of supervision ending June 30, 2011. Retrieved from: http://www.doc.state.nc.us/dop/cost/; NC pretrial service estimates at: http://www.jrsa.org/events/conference /presentations-08/Douglas_Yearwood.pdf

Bureau of Prison and U.S. Probation and Pretrial Services costs retrieved from: Oleson, James C., Marie VanNostrand, Christopher T. Lowenkamp, Timothy P. Cadigan, and John Wooldredge. 2014. Pretrial detention choices and federal sentencing. *Federal Probation, 78* (1), 12–18.

Federal electronic monitoring costs retrieved from: http://www.gao.gov/assets/590/588284.pdf

for selected forms of correctional supervision in the federal system compared to North Carolina, a state with moderate living costs. Incarceration is significantly more expensive than community supervision, especially considering that for the latter, the offender shares some of the costs. For example, probationers subsidize annual costs with monthly fees ranging between $40 and $80. Parole, electronic monitoring, day reporting, and residential community correction facilities are all partially subsidized by the offender.

THE ROLE OF CORRECTIONS AT THREE MAJOR DECISION POINTS

The three major decision points in the corrections system—bail, sentencing, and reentry—are guided by formal written laws, codes, and statutes as well as by informal discretion. Discretion is a form of subjective decision making that begins when a victim or witness decides whether or not to report a crime to the police. Some argue that victim discretion plays at least as important a role as formal law. Another decision point early in the process is the arresting decision made by a law enforcement officer. As seen in Figure 1.2, community corrections play a pivotal role at three major decision points that follow an arrest.

FIGURE 1.2
Three Main Decision Points: How Cases Are Referred to Community Corrections.

Adapted from: Center for Community Corrections (1997). *A Call for Punishments That Make Sense*, p. 35. Washington, DC: Bureau of Justice Assistance.

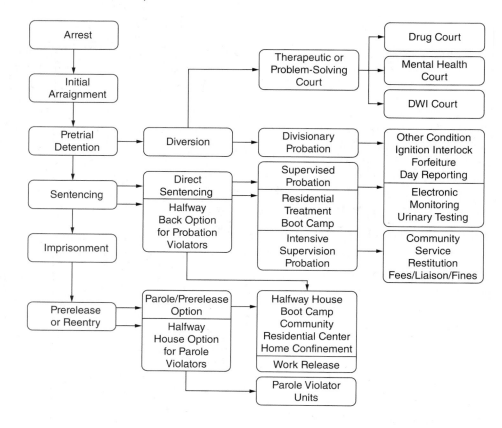

Pretrial and the Bail Decision

After a police officer makes an arrest, the suspect is booked in jail and the prosecutor's office decides whether to charge the suspect with a crime. If the prosecutor chooses not to charge, the suspect is automatically released. If the prosecutor opts to charge, the suspect officially becomes a defendant and goes before a judge, magistrate, or other official authorized to inform the defendant of the charges, determine whether the defendant is requesting appointed counsel, and ascertain whether the defendant is eligible for release from jail. Although most defendants are released on their own recognizance with the promise to appear at their next court date, some defendants must secure their next appearance with **bail**, or monetary payment deposited with the court to ensure their return. When the conditions of the bond have been satisfied, the defendant is released on a bond. Many times, particularly in the federal system, the defendant is released on **pretrial supervision**, which is a form of correctional supervision of a defendant who has not yet been convicted. Forms of pretrial supervision can include client reporting, house arrest, and electronic monitoring. Pretrial supervision has four functions. It:

1. accounts for a defendant's whereabouts to keep the community safe;
2. allows a defendant to prepare for upcoming court appearances;
3. allows a defendant to continue working and supporting dependents; and
4. keeps bed space in a jail available for defendants who may not be eligible for release.

bail
Monetary payment deposited with a court to ensure a defendant's return for the next court date, in exchange for said defendant's release.

pretrial supervision
Court-ordered correctional supervision of a defendant not yet convicted whereby said defendant participates in activities such as reporting, house arrest, and electronic monitoring to ensure appearance at the next court date.

Sentencing Decision

Community corrections agencies and programs perform the important function of implementing the sentence imposed by a judge. At a basic level, a correctional sentence is a social control mechanism for convicted offenders, and it also keeps citizens law abiding through general deterrence. While incarceration serves an important purpose for offenders who are dangerous or who have committed violent crimes, the vast majority of crimes are nonviolent or related to drug use and can be responded to in ways other than imprisonment. Judges and prosecutors need a variety of probationary, or "front-end," punishments from which to choose, and community correction programs offer a diversity of sentencing options.

The community-based punishments shown earlier in Figure 1.1 are known as **intermediate sanctions** because they offer graduated levels of supervision. They provide rewards for positive behavior, with gradually less supervision when offenders achieve and maintain desired program outcomes. Intermediate sanctions can also impose higher levels of surveillance, supervision, and monitoring than probation alone, but they provide less supervision than jail or prison. A full range of sentencing options give judges greater latitude to select punishments that closely fit the circumstances of a crime and the offender. We discuss the sentencing decision in Chapter 4 and then devote six chapters to the forms that community corrections take, beginning with probation and the various graduated residential, monetary, and nonresidential sanctions.

intermediate sanctions
A spectrum of community supervision strategies that varies greatly in terms of supervision level and treatment capacity, ranging from diversion to short-term duration in a residential community facility.

Reentry Decision

Over 45 years ago, the *President's Commission on Law Enforcement and Administration of Justice* (1967) introduced the term *reintegration*. The commission's report stated that

> institutions tend to isolate offenders from society, both physically and psychologically, cutting them off from schools, jobs, families, and other supportive influences and increasing the probability that the label of criminal will be indelibly impressed upon them. The goal of reintegration is likely to be furthered much more readily by working with offenders in the community than by incarceration. (p. 165)

The commission called on the community to provide needed employment and educational opportunities while community correctional workers act as advocates to link offenders to programs and monitor their progress. This goal still holds true today, though instead of *reintegration* we use the term *reentry*. Reentry requires an offender adapting to a community setting to participate in programs that develop legitimate accomplishments and opportunities, although there seems to be less emphasis today on the role of the community in assisting in the offender's return—an issue discussed in greater detail in Chapter 11.

Approximately 95%–97% of prisoners incarcerated today will one day leave prison and rejoin the larger society. A community correction serves an important purpose by assisting prisoners in community reentry after their incarceration. **Prisoner reentry** is any activity or program that prepares former prisoners to live as law-abiding citizens upon their return to the community. Prisoner reentry applies to prisoners released automatically based on mandatory statutes as well as to prisoners released early at a parole board's discretion.

prisoner reentry
Any activity or program conducted to prepare prisoners to return safely to a community and to live as law-abiding citizens.

prerelease program
A program in a minimum-security, community-based or institutional setting for offenders who have spent time in prison and are nearing release. Its focus includes transitioning, securing a job, and reestablishing family connections.

parole
Early privileged release from a penal or correctional institution of a convicted offender, in the continual custody of the state, to serve the remainder of his or her sentence under supervision in a community.

PRERELEASE PROGRAM.   A **prerelease program** is a minimum-security institutional setting for imprisoned offenders who have already spent some time in prison and are nearing release. Prerelease offenders are chosen by corrections officials and transferred to a different type of residential program that offenders can complete in a shorter duration than if they had served their full prison sentence. Prerelease programs are considered more treatment-oriented than prison. Examples of these programs are halfway houses; boot camps; and therapeutic communities that are located inside a prison, separate from the general prisoner population. The purpose of back-end programs, in which participants are diverted from prison, is to save money and prison space while also providing program participants with a specialized treatment regimen. Examples of prerelease programs are discussed in Chapter 8.

PAROLE.   **Parole** is the discretionary release of an offender, under conditions established by the paroling authority, before the expiration of the offender's sentence. Parole is in many ways similar to probation. Both involve supervised release into a community, and the possibility of revocation should the parolee or probationer violate the conditions of release. Although some technical differences do exist, the primary difference is that probation is supervision in the community instead of incarceration, whereas parole is supervised release after a portion of the prison sentence has been served. When the Federal Bureau of Prisons abolished its parole board, prisoners left prison on "supervised release" that was defined by a mandatory provision or by sentencing guidelines rather than by subjectivity (see Chapters 3 and 11 for more coverage of parole and supervised release).

THEORIES BEHIND COMMUNITY CORRECTIONAL GOALS

The field of criminal justice and criminology has a wide variety of different theories that attempt to explain human behavior. Criminological theories explain why people commit crime. These theories include biological determinants, psychological factors, rational choice, lack of conventional bonds to society, social learning, associating with criminal peers, lack of opportunities, breakdown of social norms, and reaction to societal labels. While it is important to understand these theories, most criminal justice majors are required to take a separate class that examines these reasons in detail, so these theories will not be repeated here.

Instead, the theories examined in this text will be directed more toward the goals that community corrections supervision strives toward in carrying out the sentence of the court or the parole board. These goals are protecting the public through recidivism reduction and specific deterrence, rehabilitation through effective treatment, and repairing the harm done to the victim and the overall community. We introduce the theories here and address each in greater detail in future chapters.

Protecting the Public Through Specific Deterrence

Most offenders have shown by their offenses that they cannot easily conform to the norms of society. One of the goals of community-based corrections, therefore, is to help offenders conform to behavioral expectations while keeping public safety in mind. The means by which this goal is reached is based on

specific deterrence theory. Specific deterrence attempts to keep supervised offenders from falling back into old habits and behaviors by supervision, unannounced visits, and letting offenders know in advance what the consequences will be for their actions. This theory assumes that offenders, like all people, consider the costs and benefits of their actions. Provided the consequences for misbehavior are certain and severe enough that the sanctions outweigh the benefits, the offender will refrain from committing technical violations and/or new crimes. This means that courts and paroling authorities must be willing to stand behind their rules and revoke supervision if a new crime is committed (behaviors that constitute probation and parole violations are covered in Chapter 7). Perceptions that offenders have of the likelihood of getting caught, along with the certainty and severity of revocation seems to have an impact on their actions (Pogarsky, 2007).

specific deterrence theory
An offender on community supervision will refrain from committing technical violations and/or new crimes if, after considering the costs and benefits, the consequences for misbehavior are certain and severe enough that the sanctions outweigh the benefits.

Rehabilitation Through Risk/Need/Responsivity

A second goal of community corrections programs is **rehabilitation** or to correct some of the inadequacies of offenders linked to their criminal behavior and continued involvement in the criminal justice system. Some of these problems include, but are not limited to, drug or alcohol addiction, lack of emotional control, inadequate education or vocational training, lack of parenting skills, and mental illness or developmental disability. Correctional treatment, or "programming," is the means by which offenders can receive assistance for their problems to reduce further criminal behavior. An underlying assumption of rehabilitation is that behavioral change is possible. Offenders should have an opportunity to change, and they must have a genuine desire to change—to complete the mental, emotional, and sometimes spiritual work to promote a personal transformation. Individual motivation is an important point, because some offenders are not yet ready to change or do not respond to treatment, but may be ready later.

rehabilitation
A primary goal of the corrections system, and the process in which offenders are exposed to treatment programs and skills training in order to change their thinking processes and behaviors.

The basis of effective rehabilitation is the theory of **risk/need/responsivity (RNR)** initially proposed by Andrews, Bonta, and Hoge (1990). RNR suggests that rehabilitation efforts are most effective when they focus on treating high-risk offenders (and leaving low-risk offenders alone), and when they match correctional interventions with **criminogenic needs**, which are any problem or deficit that is directly related to criminal behavior. The third principle is responsivity, and it addresses the most conducive therapeutic environment to achieve the maximum amount of learning and change. A responsive environment addresses the unique learning styles and characteristics of offenders, which differ according to gender, marital status, and education level. Using cognitive-behavioral treatment for a long enough duration—three to nine months—is ideal. Using RNR in the intended way has a significantly greater effect on reducing recidivism than programs that do not adhere to these standards (Bourgon & Bonta, 2014).

risk/need/responsivity
A theory of rehabilitation that suggests focusing on treating high-risk offenders, matching correctional interventions with criminogenic needs, and implementing treatment according to offenders' learning styles and personal characteristics.

criminogenic needs
Problems, habits, or deficits that are directly related to an individual's involvement in criminal behavior.

One final point about offering rehabilitation in a community setting: Oftentimes offenders are more likely to receive treatment under a community corrections sentence than in prison. This is partly because prison is less than an ideal setting for rehabilitation to occur. Another reason is a financial one. Programs in prison are 100% taxpayer-funded, while community-based programs are subsidized by offenders who pay for services as clients. Even as correctional budgets have tightened and in-prison treatment programs have been trimmed, taxpayers are bearing less of the cost for offender treatment in the community.

restorative justice
Various sentencing philosophies and practices that emphasize an offender's taking of responsibility to repair harm done to a victim and to a surrounding community, including forms of victim-offender mediation, reparation panels, circle sentencing, and monetary sanctions.

Healing the Victim and Community Through Restorative Justice

Community-based sanctions provide offenders opportunities to repay their victims and their communities. A different philosophy of justice emerged in the 1970s known as **restorative justice**. Restorative justice is centered on the victims of crimes throughout the criminal process and emphasizes the responsibility of offenders to repair the injustice they have caused their victims (Umbreit & Armour, 2010).

When a crime is committed, the offender harms both the individual victim and the community at large. Through a variety of techniques such as community boards, mediation, and face-to-face meetings with victims, restorative justice attempts to strengthen community life by drawing on victim compassion, and on the strengths that offenders bring (Umbreit & Armour, 2010). Local volunteers and the faith community agree to mentor or assist in the supervision of an offender's reparation. The offender is not publicly shamed or humiliated, but must repair the damage through community service, providing victim restitution, and participating in victim impact panels and other educational programs.

Restorative justice is most effective for nonviolent crimes committed by juveniles or first-time adult felony offenders, in part, because the victim is compensated for property losses. What many victims may not realize is that although incarcerating offenders for property crime will provide a loss of temporary freedom for the offender, the victim will rarely, if ever, be compensated. When given a choice between compensation and incarceration, most people would rather be compensated for a property crime than demand the offender be incarcerated. At this time, however, restorative justice is less likely to be endorsed for violent crimes. Community-based corrections programs that guide restorative justice processes are discussed in Chapter 10.

In sum, community correction programs are important because its sanctions provide options for individuals who have committed a crime but do not pose a serious threat to community safety. Community-based corrections seek to sanction offenders through punishment while also attempting to improve individual life circumstances. Decreasing risk, increasing rehabilitation, and restoring justice are important aspects of changing offenders' attitudes and behaviors, leading to the prevention of criminal behavior. Community corrections also serve to ease institutional crowding in jails and prisons by drawing from the population of convicted offenders those predicted to be less risk to the outside community.

participation process model
An integrated theory of community supervision that suggests that offender compliance and active participation, along with officer supervision strategies of communication, casework, and leverage are necessary to achieve offender accountability, offender risk/need reduction, and public safety. Change is mediated by offender motivation, parental/significant other support, and officer-client relationship quality.

An Integrated Theory of Community Supervision: The Participation Process Model

To more comprehensively explain how community supervision practices can influence a successful outcome, Craig Schwalbe (2012) interviewed probation officers about what they do and proposed what might be the first attempt at developing an integrated theory of how probation works. He called this theory the **participation process model**. Participation process assumes at a basic level that offender *compliance* and active *participation* are integral to the offender's own success on community supervision. Without these two elements, there will be no successful outcome, and of course, for youth, parental compliance and participation is also important. Second, participation process theory suggests that the three goals of community supervision are offender accountability, offender risk/need reduction, and public safety, which is consistent with deterrence and RNR theories discussed earlier. Third, probation and parole officers use strategies such as communication, casework, and leverage to achieve goals. Communication includes listening, clarifying expectations, giving praise/encouragement for desirable behavior, and confronting offenders for undesirable behavior. Casework strategies include assessing problems, establishing long-range goals, and assisting the client with implementing steps to meet these goals. Leverage is "aversive sanctions, either applied or threatened, that are imposed by the courts and probation officers as a consequence for rule-violating behavior" (Schwalbe, 2012, p. 193). These strategies will be discussed further in Chapter 5. Finally, the change process is mediated by the amount of motivation the offender has, the level of parental support or the degree of positive support from a significant other, and the quality of the officer–client relationship. Schwalbe (2012) believes that the theory is still a work in progress and hopes that through further testing of hypotheses (the probation strategies and mediators), this will lead to development of increasing successful client outcomes through increased completion rates and reduced recidivism.

EVIDENCE-BASED PRACTICES IN COMMUNITY CORRECTIONS

Insofar as community corrections serve to meet correctional goals of offender accountability, specific deterrence, and rehabilitation, many of today's strategies use **evidence-based practices (EBP)**, which means that only the best-known practices or interventions for which there is consistent and solid scientific evidence of success, are used. Assessment must show that such practices work to meet intended outcomes and are open to periodic measurement, evaluation, and dissemination of interventions. EBP is used in a number of fields, including medicine, education, social work, mental health, and criminal justice. Within the criminal justice system, EBP is used in police departments, courts, and correctional departments.

evidence-based practices Correctional programs and techniques shown through systematically evaluated research studies to be most effective with offenders.

EBP is not based on intuition, speculation, anecdotal evidence, or tradition (e.g., "that's the way we've always done it around here"). Rather, EBP is grounded in empirical data and research in studying what works. The idea behind EBP in corrections is that agencies use only the most successful programs. The best programs are those that are effective in changing offender behavior—whether that behavior is reducing technical violations or rearrest, increasing the number of drug-free days, or increasing the number of days an offender is employed while on supervision. Each goal must be measured empirically—meaning that data collected need to be scientifically sound, valid, and reliable.

Evaluating Effectiveness

For citizens to view community corrections as the preferred punishment option, agency leaders need to be open about research and program evaluations. To measure both the process of going through a program and the impact a program has had after its completion, it is necessary to conduct and report empirical research in a way that makes sense to the average citizen.

It is important to determine the methodological rigor and sophistication of the research to know what does and does not work. The research must be able to identify for which type of offenders and under what conditions the treatment best works. When evaluating the effectiveness of a program, the most rigorous design compares offenders who are randomly selected to receive a *treatment* (e.g., home visits on probation) compared to random assignments to a *control* group (those on regular probation). Then the two groups could be compared on a number of outcome measures. This ideal situation is hard to come by in reality because sentencing guidelines prevent such comparison groups, and many judges cannot be persuaded to randomly assign offenders to programs. When random assignment is not possible, the control group can be matched as closely as possible to the treatment group according to demographic characteristics to attempt to isolate the effects of the treatment as much as possible. Since offenders are sentenced to multiple programs, it is often difficult to isolate one treatment effect from another and to evaluate which program has had the intended effect.

A final difficulty with evaluating the effectiveness of intermediate sanctions is determining the outcome. Do the participants have reduced recidivism compared to the control group? Do the participants use less illicit drugs? Does the program save money? Are participants diverted from probation (a front-end strategy) or kept from returning to prison (a back-end strategy)? Suppose the only two sentencing choices for the control group were probation or prison. The intermediate sanction (the program to be measured)—which targets criminals who would have gone to prison anyway but are being given one last chance—takes on more serious offenders than if it had recruited offenders who were not prison-bound. Intermediate sanctions would be an increased penalty for offenders who would otherwise have been sentenced to probation had that intermediate sanction not existed. This is called **net widening**, or "widening the net," and it usually results in a cost increase instead of a cost savings. We revisit the net-widening issue throughout the book when we apply this term to diversion, boot camps, and intensive supervision probation.

net widening
Using stiffer punishment or excessive control for offenders who would ordinarily be sentenced to a lesser sanction.

recidivism
A return to criminal behavior, variously defined in one of three ways: rearrest; reconviction; or reincarceration.

Outcome Measures in Evaluation

The most commonly used measure of program or treatment effectiveness is the rate of **recidivism**. Recidivism is defined as a repetition of or return to criminal behavior, measured in one of three ways: rearrest, reconviction, or reincarceration. Some studies differentiate a return to criminal behavior via a new crime, from technical violations committed while under community supervision. Other studies lump violations and crimes together as a single category. Bear in mind that researchers define recidivism in a variety of ways; hence there are no universally accepted means by which to measure it.

Recidivism as the primary (or sometimes the only) outcome measure has caused concern among criminal justice researchers. Reasons for not including other outcome measures are that programs keep poor records of those or that available measures are buried within an officer's handwritten notes deep within offender files. As more programs collect data electronically, data become easier to collect and measure.

Other variables of importance will, of course, depend on the type of program being evaluated. Variables that can be measured during supervision include: the number of days employed; the amount of restitution collected compared to the amount ordered; the percent of fines and/or fees collected; the number of community service hours performed; the number of clients enrolled in school; the number of drug-free days; the types of treatment programs completed; and the number of times clients attended each treatment program. The type of termination—that is, whether a client completed supervision successfully or unsuccessfully—is critical. The number and types of technical violations and/or new arrests are vital measures, particularly for unsuccessful clients. Finally, effectiveness can also be measured based on the impacts that community corrections programs have in reducing institutional crowding and on incurring total cost savings.

Community corrections programs have been encouraged to develop EBP that incorporate sound diagnostic and classification testing of risks and needs as well as cognitive-behavioral treatment paired with community supervision techniques, all of which we discuss later in the text.

SUMMARY

- Community corrections provide many options for individuals who have committed a crime but do not pose a serious threat to community safety.

- Community-based corrections seek to sanction offenders through punishment while also attempting to improve individual life circumstances. Specific deterrence, rehabilitation, and restorative justice are important components in changing offenders' attitudes and behaviors, leading to the prevention of criminal behavior.

- Community corrections also serve to ease institutional crowding in jails and prisons by drawing from the population of convicted offenders those predicted to be less risk to the outside community.

- Indeterminate sentencing and determinate sentencing are the two main sentencing philosophies. Most states ultimately use both philosophies (determinate for violent crimes and indeterminate for nonviolent), but are predominately one or the other.

- Corrections play a role at three major decision points in the criminal justice system: pretrial and bail, sentencing, and reentry.

- The participation process model suggests that offender compliance and active participation, along with officer supervision strategies of communication, casework, and leverage are necessary to achieve offender accountability, offender risk/need reduction, and public safety. Change is mediated by offender motivation, parental/significant other support, and officer-client relationship quality.

- Providing a range of community-based sanctions allows a rewarding of positive behavior by increasing freedom and a punishing of negative behavior by increasing the sanction.

- Evidence-based practices (EBP) offer steps to further professionalize and transform the image of community-based corrections as the method of choice for lasting offender change.

- The effectiveness of community supervision programs depends on the following factors: how recidivism is defined and how long after supervision it is measured; how other outcome variables are measured during supervision; whether there is a comparison group; how the groups are selected; and whether net widening has occurred.

DISCUSSION QUESTIONS

1. What do you believe is the primary purpose of community-based corrections?

2. Other than the factors mentioned in the book, what other factors may have contributed to growth in the correctional system?

3. What does a *continuum of sanctions* mean in the sentencing process? If you were a judge, how would you apply this continuum?

4. Of the various community corrections goals, which one do you believe to be the most important and why? Which one is used the least and why?

5. Will evidence-based practices be just another passing fad?

6. To measure the effectiveness of community corrections, are there any other outcome measures (other than those discussed) that could be used?

WEBSITES, VIDEOS, AND PODCASTS

Websites

American Probation and Parole Association
http://www.appa-net.org/

National Center on Institutions and Alternatives
www.ncianet.org

The Corrections Connection
www.corrections.com

Fortune Society
http://fortunesociety.org

Videos/Podcasts

Adult Community Corrections Monroe County—Part 1
This video discusses the Department's mission, cost savings, and public perceptions of community corrections services in Monroe County, Indiana (5:25 minutes)
http://www.youtube.com/watch?v=HJnHy9BFKhk

Community Corrections as an Alternative to Incarceration
(Length: 6 minutes) This video explains why community correction is the most cost-effective alternative to incarceration and best at integrating offenders back into the community.
https://www.youtube.com/watch?v=iG5EgPBgpe8

Rural Community Corrections Officers Go the Extra Mile
(Length: 5 minutes) This video discusses the differences and difficulties of being a community corrections agent in a rural area.
https://www.youtube.com/watch?v=tulrFzHZXH0

Evidence-Based Practices in Community Corrections with Dr. Edward Latessa.
(Length: 1 hour, 20 minutes) This video introduces evidence-based practices with respect to parole and probation, reentry programs, and community-based programs.
https://www.youtube.com/watch?v=8dz36WOmg-8

CASE STUDY EXERCISES

Organizations and Associations Related to Community Corrections

In this chapter, we discussed the importance of garnering public support for alternatives to prison. Assume you are a staff member who works for a state legislator and you have been assigned to examine organizations and interest groups affiliated with community-based corrections such as the American Probation and Parole Association (APPA). Report back to the legislator the APPA's position on other topics. Find other interest groups that advocate the expansion of various community-based alternatives.

CASE A: Looking Further into the APPA
The APPA is an international organization that provides education and training for community corrections practitioners and supervisors. The APPA establishes standards in all areas of community supervision, including restitution, electronic monitoring, pretrial, conditional early release, and issues related to prisons. Go to **http://www.appa-net.org** and click on *About APPA* and then on *Where we stand*—this area shows position statements, resolutions, and position papers.

Research three different topics and the position the APPA has taken on these issues. Report your findings to the legislator and discuss whether they are politically feasible in today's economic climate.

CASE B: Researching Other Community Corrections Advocacy Groups
The APPA is only one of several organizations that serve a similar purpose for community corrections advocacy. Other organizations include:

- American Correctional Association (**http://www.aca.org**);
- National Association of Pretrial Services Agencies (**http://www.napsa.org/**) and
- International Community Corrections Association (**http://iccalive.org/icca/**)

Look up one of the three organizations above and compare and contrast it to the APPA from Case A. Which organization—the APPA or another organization—would you most likely recommend to the legislator for its practicality in its approach to alternatives to incarceration, and why?

How Probation Developed: Chronicling Its Past and Present

Dave Kotinsky/Getty Images

CHAPTER OUTLINE

Chapter Learning Objectives

1. Recall the social and legal history of probation in England and the United States.
2. Discuss the founders of probation.
3. Restate how supervision philosophies have changed in the United States.
4. Describe how probation is now organized and operates.
5. Examine how community corrections acts help implement local community supervision programs.
6. Characterize how probation supervision styles have changed over time.

Key Terms

amercement
security
motion to quash
suspended sentence
laid on file
John Augustus
parole
parens patriae
diversion
community corrections acts
casework
brokerage of services
community resource management team model
justice model
neighborhood-based supervision
criminogenic needs-based supervision
split sentence

A ctress Amanda Bynes, aged 29, has attracted quite a bit of media and law enforcement attention in the last few years, which has resulted in her being placed on probation. Beginning in April 2012, Amanda was arrested for driving under the influence (DUI) when her BMW sideswiped a Los Angeles sheriff's car. Bynes allegedly refused to take a Breathalyzer or drug test at the scene of the accident and was immediately taken into custody. Bynes was released on her own recognizance.

Later that same year, Bynes rear-ended a driver in Los Angeles, causing $800 worth of damage. According to police reports, the other driver stated Bynes said she saw no problem with the car, and drove away without exchanging insurance information or allowing time for police to respond to the accident.

On September 4, 2012, Bynes was charged with a third automobile collision. As a result, Bynes's driver's license was suspended. The judge dismissed the two counts of hit-and-run misdemeanor offenses after Bynes agreed to pay the drivers for damages (California allows defendants to resolve misdemeanors with civil settlements). Bynes received three years of probation for the DUI back in April. While on probation, Bynes was also ordered to pay a fine and to complete alcohol education classes.

In 2013, an arrest for possession of drug paraphernalia was dismissed. In July 2013, Amanda Bynes was admitted to a psychiatric facility for 4 months, and a judge granted her parents control over the actress's finances. After her release, no news surfaced until September 2014, when Amanda Bynes was arrested for her second DUI. One month later, the actress allegedly tweeted that she was bipolar, and that she was physically and sexually abused by her father. Although the tweets have since disappeared, these allegations and prior behavior raise concerns about the actress's father, along with Bynes's need for attention, self-medication of drugs and alcohol, and overall mental health.

What would be the best course of action for probationer Amanda Bynes when she goes before the judge for her second DUI?

PRECURSORS TO AMERICAN PROBATION

Probation, as it is known and practiced today, evolved out of ancient precedents in England and the United States devised to avoid the mechanical application of the harsh penal codes of the day. Early British criminal law, which was dominated by the objectives of retribution and punishment, imposed rigid and severe penalties on offenders. The usual punishments were corporal: branding, flogging, mutilation, and execution. Capital punishment was commonly inflicted on children and animals as well as men and women. At the time of Henry VIII's reign in the sixteenth century, for instance, more than 200 crimes were punishable by death, many of them relatively minor offenses against property.

Methods used to determine guilt—what today is called criminal procedure—also put the accused in danger. Trial might be by combat between the accused and the accuser, or a person's innocence might be determined by whether he or she sank when bound and thrown into a deep pond—the theory being that the pure water would reject wrongdoers. Thus, the choice was to drown as an innocent person or to survive the drowning only to be otherwise executed. Sometimes the offender could elect to be tried "by God," which involved undergoing some painful and frequently life-threatening ordeal, or "by country," a form of trial by jury for which the accused first had to pay an **amercement** to the king. The accepted premise was that the purpose of criminal law was not to deter or rehabilitate but to bring about justice for a past act deemed harmful to the society.

Early legal practices in the United States were distinct from British common law in a number of ways. First, **security** was a fee paid to the State as collateral for a promise of good behavior. Much like the modern practice of bail, security for good behavior allowed the accused to go free in certain cases either before or after conviction.

Massachusetts's judges also often granted a **motion to quash** after judgment, using any minor technicality or the slightest error in the proceedings to free the defendant in cases in which they thought the statutory penalties inhumane. Some early forms of bail had the effect of suspending final action on a case, although the chief use of bail then (as now) was for the purpose of ensuring appearance for trial.

All of these methods had the common objective of mitigating punishment by relieving selected offenders from the full effects of the legally prescribed penalties that substantial segments of the community, including many judges, viewed as excessive and inappropriate to their offenses. They were precursors to probation as it is known today. The procedure most closely related to modern probation, however, is the **suspended sentence**.

Procedures Related to Modern Probation

Commonwealth v. Chase (1831) is often cited as an early example of how a suspended sentence works when the defendant gets into trouble again. Judge Peter Oxenbridge Thacher found the defendant, Jerusha Chase, guilty of theft, but suspended the imposition of sentence, and ruled that the defendant be released and her indictment **laid on file** as long as she did not get into trouble again. The effect was that the first case was laid to rest without either dismissal or final judgment. When Jerusha Chase got into trouble again, the judge imposed the first sentence for the original theft. This practice came to be used in Massachusetts as a means of avoiding a final conviction of young and minor offenders in the hope that they would avoid further criminal behavior.

amercement
A monetary penalty imposed arbitrarily at the discretion of a court for an offense.

security
A recognizance or bond given a court by a defendant before or after conviction, conditioned on his or her being "on good behavior" or on keeping the peace for a prescribed period.

motion to quash
An oral or written request that a court repeal, nullify, or overturn a decision, usually made during or after a trial.

suspended sentence
An order of a court after a verdict, finding, or plea of guilty that suspends or postpones an imposition or execution of sentence during a period of good behavior.

laid on file
When an indictment is held in abeyance with neither dismissal nor final conviction, in cases in which the judge wishes to defer adjudication or suspend the sentence.

Today, a suspended sentence is a court order that postpones the sentence contingent on the good behavior of the offender, but is revoked or terminated if the offender committed a new crime. Handing down suspended sentences and calling it "probation" was a common practice in the federal courts. In *Ex parte United States* (1916) a case known as the "Killits case," Judge Killits refused to vacate a suspended sentence even when the victim did not wish to prosecute. This case went all the way to the U.S. Supreme Court, and in 1916 the Court held that federal courts had no power to suspend indefinitely the imposition or execution of a sentence (*Ex parte United States*, 1916). This aspect—the recognition of legislative authority to grant the power of indefinite suspension to the courts—made probation as now defined, statutory practice. The Supreme Court, as a remedy to an indefinite suspension, suggested probation legislation. In 1984, the Federal Sentencing Reform Act recognized probation as a bona fide sentence (18 U.S.C.A. 3561).

The Founders of Probation

Volunteers and philanthropists were instrumental in the development and acceptance of probation in practice long before probation became law. The development of the probation idea can be credited to two cofounding individuals: John Augustus and Matthew Davenport Hill.

John Augustus
A Boston bootmaker who was the founder of probation in the United States.

JOHN AUGUSTUS   The credit for founding adult probation in the United States is reserved for **John Augustus** (1784–1859). While Augustus's work can be more accurately described as the first pretrial supervision officer, his efforts at pretrial supervision later expanded into the use of probation for both pretrial and post-conviction purposes. Augustus owned a shoe manufacturing company on the west side of Boston. His business prospered, and he owned a number of residences, one of which is now the Jonathan Harrington House, which faces the Lexington Common. Augustus was a member of the Washington Total Abstinence Society (Moreland, 1941). Its members pledged to abstain from alcohol and to treat alcoholics with kindness and understanding rather than punishment. Discovering that the same people were being repeatedly arrested and detained in jail for public intoxication, Augustus (and other abstinence members) interviewed first-time defendants before their court appearance and bailed out those who would most likely change their habits and return to court. Augustus's home became a refuge for the newly bailed defendants until their next court appearance. Augustus described the scene in his own words:

> In the month of August 1841, I was in court one morning when the door communicating with the lock-room was opened and an officer entered, followed by a ragged and wretched looking man, who took his seat upon the bench allotted to prisoners. I imagined from the man's appearance that his offence was that of yielding to his appetite for intoxicating drinks, and in a few moments I found that my suspicions were correct, for the clerk read the complaint, in which the man was charged with being a common drunkard. The case was clearly made out, but before sentence had been passed, I conversed with him a few moments, and found that he was not yet past all hope and reformation, although his appearance and his looks precluded a belief in the minds of others that he would ever become a man again. He told me that if he could be saved from the House of Correction, he never again would taste intoxicating liquors; there was such an earnestness in that tone, and a look expressive of firm resolve, that I determined to aid him; I bailed him, by permission of the Court. He was ordered

to appear for sentence in three weeks from that time. He signed the pledge and became a sober man; at the expiration of this period of probation, I accompanied him into the courtroom; his whole appearance was changed and no one, not even the scrutinizing officers, could have believed that he was the same person who less than a month before, had stood trembling on the prisoner's stand. The Judge expressed himself much pleased with the account we gave of the man, and instead of the usual penalty—imprisonment in the House of Correction—he fined him one cent and costs, amounting in all to $3.76, which was immediately paid. The man continued industrious and sober, and without doubt has been, by this treatment, saved from a drunkard's grave. (1852, pp. 4–5)

The efforts of the Washington Total Abstinence Society were praised by Peter Oxenbridge Thacher and other local judges. John Augustus became the most well-known of the members because not only did he post bail of $30 per person to ensure the next court appearance, he also paid the fine and court costs for indigent defendants. Private philanthropists donated money so the volunteer efforts could continue.

By 1846, Augustus's generosity caused his shoemaking business to go under and he was forced to close his shop. For the next 15 years until his death in 1859, Augustus pursued philanthropy full-time—dedicated to helping men, women, and children, despite great opposition from police officers who thought that the accused deserved jail, jailers who lost money on every defendant that was released, and from people in the community who thought he was trying to profit from offenders. According to court records, Augustus assisted 1,946 people who paid $2,418 in fines and court costs, and he made himself liable for a total

John Augustus owned a shoe factory similar to this one, in which he employed pretrial defendants to work until their next court date.

Hulton-Deutsch Collection/Historical/Corbis

of $99,464 for bail (Augustus, 1852/1972). Although most of the bail money was refunded, there were reportedly only 10 defendants who got into trouble again.

Other than the abstinence society, colleagues of John Augustus included John Murray Spear, who served as a "voluntary public defender, lecturer, and traveler, a tract distributor, and a worker with discharged prisoners" (Lindner & Savarese, 1984b, p. 5). The settlement movement, a group of university students and professors, was prominent in the establishment of probation in New York. The University Settlement was a grassroots social reform organization that advocated for the poor people of the community, including those on probation. In protest of materialism, industrialization, and widening gaps between social classes, settlement residents lived and worked in the poorest sections of the city and resolved to teach and learn from the local residents (Lindner & Savarese, 1984c, 1984d).

In 1878, almost 20 years after the death of John Augustus, adult probation in Massachusetts was sanctified by statute. A law was passed authorizing the mayor of Boston to appoint a paid probation, who was also a member of the police force to serve in the Boston criminal courts. Three years later, the law was changed so the probation officer reported to the prison commissioner. Due to continuing corruption, the law was revised again to disallow police officers from becoming probation officers (Panzarella, 2002). Statewide probation did not begin until 1891 when a statute transferred the power of appointment over to the courts and made such appointments mandatory instead of permissive. For the first time, the probation officer was recognized as an official salaried agent of the court.

MATTHEW DAVENPORT HILL   Matthew Davenport Hill was less known in the United States, but he deserves equal credit alongside John Augustus as a cofounder of probation. Hill laid the foundation for probation in England, where he lived and worked. Born to Reverend Thomas Wright Hill in 1792 and the eldest of eight children, Matthew Davenport Hill was a member of a family intimately involved in politics and the movement for social change (Lindner, 2007). While in Parliament, Hill was deeply concerned with equality for all people and worked toward ending the transportation of English convicts, among other causes. According to criminal justice historian Charles Lindner:

> His contribution to helping develop a probation system may have evolved from his early experiences as a lawyer, during which time he witnessed a number of cases in which young offenders were sentenced to a term of imprisonment of only one day ... [Hill] also required that there be persons willing to act as guardians of the young offender. (Lindner, 2007, p. 40)

The guardians were required to report back to Hill on the juveniles' behavior. Police had the power to enforce the court reporting process and to provide social service assistance. Hill kept court records of offenders' behavior, which included early accounts of recidivism measured by reconviction rates. Apparently, over a 12-year period, 80 offenders out of 417 were reconvicted, many because they returned to similar circumstances that contributed to crimes in the first place (Lindner, 2007, p. 40). Hill was a close personal friend of a number of other justice reformers, including Jeremy Bentham; Sir Robert Peel; Dr. Enoch Wines, a prison reformer; and Captain Alexander Maconochie (discussed in the next chapter as influential in the development of **parole**). Matthew Davenport Hill died in 1872 at the age of 80.

TRUTH OR FICTION?

John Augustus was America's first professional probation officer.

FICTION

FACT: John Augustus' actions most closely resembled *bail bonding and pretrial supervision.* While Augustus is likely America's first volunteer pretrial supervision officer, he reformed defendants at his home, but was never officially recognized as a probation officer. Edward Savage, a former Chief of police in Boston, was appointed as the first paid probation officer in the United States after probation legislation was passed in 1878, nearly two decades after Augustus's death.

parole

Early privileged release from a penal or correctional institution of a convicted offender, in the continual custody of the state, to serve the remainder of his or her sentence under supervision in a community.

Development of Federal Probation

Historical accounts of federal probation suggest that federal judges were extremely resistant to enacting probation legislation. Between 1909 and 1925, 34 unsuccessful attempts were made to pass a law authorizing federal judges to grant probation. Because prohibitionists were afraid that judges would place violators of the Volstead Act (the Prohibition Amendment) on probation (Evjen, 1975), through their intense lobbying they convinced judges not to support probation. The bill was finally passed in 1925 and sent to President Coolidge, who as former governor of Massachusetts, understood how probation worked. Because probation in Massachusetts had been successful for nearly five decades, Coolidge had no problem signing the National Probation Act. The act authorized each federal district court to appoint one salaried probation officer with an annual income of $2,600.

Between 1927 and 1930, eight probation officers were required to pass the civil service examination. In 1930, the original law was amended to empower judges to appoint without reference to the civil service list, and the limitation of one officer to each district was removed. At the same time, the Parole Act was amended to give community supervision officers field supervision responsibility for federal parolees and probationers. Thus the average number of people supervised by one officer was 400 offenders. Officers relied heavily on as many as 700 volunteers (Evjen, 1975).

Between 1930 and 1940, the Federal Bureau of Prisons (FBP) administered the federal probation system, and Colonel Joel R. Moore became the first federal probation supervisor. The number of officers increased from eight to 233, but the appointments remained largely political.

By 1940, the U.S. probation system had increased so dramatically that the administration of probation was moved from the FBP to the Administrative Office of the U.S. Courts. The era from 1940 to 1950 was concentrated on initial qualifications, standardized manuals, and in-service training. Initial qualifications for federal probation officers stipulated that they be at least 25 years old but preferably 30–45 years of age, have a baccalaureate degree, possess two years of experience in social work, and be mature, intelligent, of good moral character, patient, and energetic (Evjen, 1975). In 1984, the Comprehensive Crime Control Act abolished federal parole and brought all supervised prison releasees under the auspices of federal probation. Federal probation was administered as an appendage of the federal courts, where it remains today. Contemporary probation serves an important purpose as explained by the American Probation and Parole Association in Box 2.1.

History of Juvenile Probation and the Juvenile Court

From the 1700s to the early 1800s, children were disciplined and punished for crimes informally by parents and other adults in the community. Most children contributed to the family income, but there were no formal mechanisms to care for children who were left homeless or whose parents had died. Between 1817 and the mid-1840s, middle-class female reformers, or "child savers," institutionalized runaway or neglected children in houses of refuge to provide them with a family environment, but the good intentions of the child savers were not fully realized in practice. Although some institutions were humane, most children were further exploited for labor, abused, and victimized.

To protect children from this exploitation, the New York Children's Aid Society shipped children to farmers in the West to keep them from being committed

TRUTH OR FICTION?

Federal probation officers supervise both probationers and prisoners released into the community.

TRUE

FACT: Federal probation officers primarily oversee former prisoners on supervised release (83%) and only a small number of probationers (15.8%).

BOX 2.1 **COMMUNITY CORRECTIONS UP CLOSE**

What Is the Purpose of Probation?

The purpose of probation is to assist in reducing the incidence and impact of crime by probationers in the community. The core services of probation are to provide pre-sentence investigation and reports to the court, to help develop appropriate court dispositions for adult offenders and juvenile delinquents, and to supervise those people placed on probation. Probation departments in fulfilling their purpose may also provide a broad range of services including, but not limited to, crime and delinquency prevention, victim restitution programs, and intern or volunteer programs.

Position

The mission of probation is to protect the public interest and safety by reducing the incidence and impact of crime by probationers. This role is accomplished by:

- assisting the courts in decision making through the probation report and in the enforcement of court orders;
- providing services and programs that afford opportunities for offenders to become more law-abiding;
- providing and cooperating in programs and activities for the prevention of crime and delinquency;
- furthering the administration of fair and individualized justice.

Probation is premised upon the following beliefs:

- Society has a right to be protected from persons who cause its members harm, regardless of the reasons for such harm. It is the right of every citizen to be free from fear of harm to person and property. Belief in the necessity of law to an orderly society demands commitment to support it. Probation accepts this responsibility and views itself as an instrument for both control and treatment, appropriate to some, but not all offenders. The wise use of authority derived from law adds strength and stability to its efforts.
- Offenders have rights deserving of protection. Freedom and democracy require fair and individualized due process of law in adjudicating and sentencing the offender.
- Victims of crime have rights deserving of protection. In its humanitarian tradition, probation recognizes that prosecution of the offender is but a part of the responsibility of the criminal justice system. The victim of criminal activity may suffer

loss of property, emotional problems, or physical disability. Probation thus commits itself to advocacy for the needs and interests of crime victims.
- Human beings are capable of change. Belief in the individual's capability for behavioral change leads probation practitioners to a commitment to the reintegration of the offender into the community. The possibility for constructive change of behavior is based on the recognition and acceptance of the principle of individual responsibility. Much of probation practice focuses on identifying and making available those services and programs that will best afford offenders an opportunity to become responsible, law-abiding citizens.
- Not all offenders have the same capacity or willingness to benefit from measures designed to produce law-abiding citizens. Probation practitioners recognize the variations among individuals. The present offense, the degree of risk to the community, and the potential for change can be assessed only in the context of the offender's individual history and experience.
- Intervention in an offender's life should be the minimal amount needed to protect society and promote law-abiding behavior. Probation subscribes to the principle of intervening in an offender's life only to the extent necessary. Where further intervention appears unwarranted, criminal justice system involvement should be terminated. Where needed intervention can best be provided by an agency outside the system, the offender should be diverted from the system to that agency.
- *Punishment.* Probation philosophy does not accept the concept of retributive punishment. Punishment as a corrective measure is supported and used in those instances in which it is felt that aversive measures may positively alter the offender's behavior when other measures may not. Even corrective punishment, however, should be used cautiously and judiciously in view of its highly unpredictable impact. It can be recognized that a conditional sentence in the community is, in and of itself, a punishment. It is less harsh and drastic than a prison term but more controlling and punitive than release without supervision.
- Incarceration may be destructive and should be imposed only when necessary. Probation practi-

(Continues)

BOX 2.1	COMMUNITY CORRECTIONS UP CLOSE *(continued)*

tioners acknowledge society's right to protect itself and support the incarceration of offenders whose behavior constitutes a danger to the public through rejection of social or court mandates. Incarceration can also be an appropriate element of a probation program to emphasize the consequences of criminal behavior and thus effect constructive behavioral change. However, institutions should be humane and required to adhere to the highest standards.

- Where public safety is not compromised, society and most offenders are best served through community correctional programs. Most offenders should be provided services within the community in which they are expected to demonstrate acceptable behavior. Community correctional programs generally are cost effective, and they allow offenders to remain with their families while paying taxes and, where applicable, restitution to victims.

For Discussion: How has probation changed since 1997, when the original position statement was written?

Source: American Probation and Parole Association. 1997. "Appa Position Statement: Probation." Available at: http://www.appa-net .org/eweb/DynamicPage.aspx?Site=APPA_2&WebCode=IB _PositionStatements Reprinted with permission.

---

to a house of refuge. In 1890, the Children's Aid Society of Pennsylvania offered to place in foster homes delinquents who would otherwise be sent to reform school. Known as *placing out*, this practice was an early form of juvenile probation (Mennel, 1973).

The Illinois Juvenile Court Act of 1899 legally established a juvenile system that was different from the adult system to stop the exploitation of children. The court was anchored in the belief that a child's behavior was the product of a poor family background and surroundings. It operated informally, was civil in nature, and was geared toward rehabilitation. The juvenile courts were created in part, to respond to abused children and homeless children living on the streets. Since they were more informal and less mired by legal obstacles, juvenile courts could intervene at an earlier point in time well before a conviction. Some considered them more efficient and effective to deal with social problems without abiding by criminal procedure and due process rights. Lucy Flower, wife of a prominent Chicago attorney, helped create juvenile probation services in Illinois. She obtained support from the Chicago Bar Association to draft and pass the necessary legislation to provide a separate court and detention system that was different from the adult system (Lindner & Savarese, 1984b).

By 1925, 46 states, three territories, and the District of Columbia had juvenile courts (Mennel, 1973). Two concepts that formed the backbone of the original juvenile justice system were a recognition that the level of mental intent over one's actions for youth is different than that for adults, and that the State might have to intervene as a protector in the child's best interest. Juvenile probation was formed under English common law and the doctrine of **parens patriae**, which is a Latin term for the doctrine that "the State is parent" and therefore serves as guardian of juveniles who might not be able to fend for themselves. The State intervened as a substitute parent in an attempt to act in the best interests of a child by using four principles. First, the court appointed a guardian to care for a child. The second principle was that parents of offenders must be held responsible for their children's wrongdoing. Third, no matter what offense children had committed, placing them in jail was inappropriate. The fourth principle stated that removing children from their parents and sending them even to an industrial school should be avoided, and

parens patriae
Latin term meaning that the government acts as a "substitute parent" and allows the courts to intervene in cases in which children, through no fault of their own, have been neglected and/or are dependent and in which it is in their best interest that a guardian be appointed for them.

that when it [a child] is allowed to return home it should be under probation, subject to the guidance and friendly interest of the probation officer, the representative of the court. To raise the age of criminal responsibility from seven or ten to sixteen or eighteen without providing for an efficient system of probation, would indeed be disastrous. Probation is, in fact, the keynote of juvenile court legislation. (Mack, 1909, p. 162–163)

Mack further related:

Whenever juvenile courts have been established, a system of probation has been provided for, and even where as yet the juvenile court system has not been fully developed, some steps have been taken to substitute probation for imprisonment of the juvenile offender. What they need, more than anything else, is kindly assistance; and the aim of the court, appointing a probation officer for the child, is to have the child and the parents feel, not so much the power, as the friendly interest of the State; to show them that the object of the court is to help them to train the child right, and therefore the probation officers must be men and women fitted for these tasks. (p. 163)

A detailed discussion of the contemporary juvenile court and other types of community corrections for juveniles is found in Chapter 13. For now, we return to a discussion of early probation laws in the adult system at the time when probation first began in the northeastern region of the United States.

Early Probation Legislation in Other States

New York's probation law allowed police officers to be probation officers, but one of the two positions was occupied by three different University Settlement members (Lindner & Savarese, 1984d). Later probation legislation in other states included a provision that the probation officer not be an active member of the regular police force. Although probation officers were allowed, most legislation did not provide money for salaried positions. This omission was deliberate because probation legislation would not have passed at all if there were costs attached (Lindner & Savarese, 1984a). Thus probation workers began as volunteers, paid from private donations, or they were municipal workers and other court officers who supervised probationers in addition to their regular jobs.

PROBATION TODAY

diversion
An alternative program to traditional criminal sentencing or juvenile justice adjudication that provides first-time offenders with a chance or addresses unique treatment needs, with a successful completion resulting in a dismissal of current charges. Also known as *deferred adjudication*.

When probation first began as a way to mitigate harsh English law, the courts first used probation as a way to suspend a prison sentence, or to offer an alternative to prison. Today, probation is used in the same way as it was originally intended, except there are now two ways in which it is used. Probation can be a sentence in itself where a defendant is convicted but on probation, or probation can be used even earlier in the process as a form of pretrial supervision.

Deferred Adjudication/Diversion

Before the defendant is convicted or pleads guilty, (s)he may be offered **diversion** (also known as *deferred adjudication*), which is the chance to avoid a criminal record completely. If the defendant completes the terms of supervision and stays out of trouble for two to five years, the charges are dismissed and there is no official conviction.

A defendant's situation and offense must qualify for this alternative to traditional criminal sentencing. In considering which factors are important in an attorney's decision to recommend diversion, a defendant's probation or parole history, mental health, substance abuse history, community ties, and evaluative needs are all viewed as relevant by both prosecutor and defense. A defendant's adult criminal record, gang affiliation, the official version of the offense, and pending cases are all ranked significantly higher in a diversion decision by prosecutors than by defense attorneys (Alarid & Montemayor, 2010b).

Defendants whose situations qualify for diversion might be juveniles or first-time felons, persons charged with certain offenses, or offenders with mental health problems. Diversion enables offenders to avoid the criminal label or deviant stigma that results from a conviction. It can help first-time offenders who do not pose a risk to public safety and who, upon completion of their program, are unlikely to return to criminal behavior. Persons with special needs, such as mental illness, who have also committed minor offenses are better suited for rehabilitative functions like medication stabilization and counseling (Castillo & Alarid, 2011). Offenses that qualify for diversion typically include theft, possession of controlled substances, driving while intoxicated, domestic assault, and prostitution (Alarid & Montemayor, 2010b). While diversion is used frequently by county and local prosecutors, diversion is not used as often in the federal system.

Probation Departments: County or State?

After Massachusetts, Vermont was the second state to pass a probation statute, adopting a *county* plan of organization in 1898. Each county judge was given the power to appoint a probation officer to serve all the courts in the county. On the other hand, Rhode Island in 1899 adopted a statewide and state-controlled probation system. Initial probation legislation followed either Vermont's local organizational pattern or Rhode Island's state organizational pattern.

Over time, changes have occurred in the way that probation departments are structured. Smaller, more localized departments have found themselves at a disadvantage when trying to compete fiscally with larger agencies, such as state prisons and county jails. Larger agencies have funds to send lobbyists to the state capitol during key budget times. For that reason, many adult probation and parole departments have merged. It has been only recently that some probation departments have combined adult and juvenile probation services. Table 2.1 shows how probation and parole agencies are structured in every state—whether it is county or State, and whether the branch of government is judicial or executive. About half of all states administer adult and juvenile systems separately. However, juvenile and adult probation services are fully integrated in at least 10 states and are partially integrated in select jurisdictions in another six states (Krauth & Linke, 1999). This table may be helpful to consult when it comes time to look for employment in probation or parole—a probation department that is structured by the county will advertise its jobs on the county or local website, while a state parole department will advertise on the state government website.

TABLE 2.1 Looking for a Job? Consider the Organizational Structure of Adult and Juvenile Probation/Parole

	ADULT		JUVENILE	
STATE	Level/Branch	Combined or Separate Adult Probation & Parole	Level/Branch	Combined or Separate Juvenile w/Adult
Alabama	State/Executive	Combined	County/Judicial	Separate
Alaska	State/Executive	Combined	State/Executive	Separate
Arizona	County/Judicial	Both	County/Judicial	Both
Arkansas	State/Executive	Combined	County/Judicial	Separate
California	County/Judicial	Separate	County/Judicial	Combined
Colorado	State/Judicial	Separate	County/Judicial	Combined
Connecticut	State/Judicial	Separate	State/Judicial	Separate
Delaware	State/Executive	Combined	State/Executive	Separate
Florida	State/Executive	Combined	State/Executive	Separate
Georgia	State/Executive	Separate	Mixed/Exec. & Judicial	Separate
Hawaii	State/Judicial	Separate	State/Judicial	Separate
Idaho	State/Executive	Combined	County/Judicial	Separate
Illinois	County/Judicial	Separate	County/Judicial	Combined
Indiana	County/Judicial	Separate	County/Judicial	Combined
Iowa	County/Executive	Combined	State/Judicial	Separate
Kansas	State/Judicial	Separate	County/Judicial	Combined
Kentucky	State/Executive	Combined	State/Executive	Separate
Louisiana	State/Executive	Combined	Mixed/Exec. & Judicial	Separate
Maine	State/Executive	Separate	State/Executive	Separate
Maryland	State/Executive	Combined	State/Executive	Separate
Massachusetts	State/Judicial	Separate	State/Judicial	Separate
Michigan	State/Executive	Combined	County/Judicial	Both
Minnesota	Mixed/Exec. &Judicial	Both	Mixed/Exec. & Judicial	Separate
Mississippi	State/Executive	Combined	Mixed/Exec. & Judicial	Separate
Missouri	State/Executive	Combined	Mixed/Exec. & Judicial	Separate
Montana	State/Executive	Combined	State/Judicial	Separate
Nebraska	State/Judicial	Separate	State/Judicial	Combined
Nevada	State/Executive	Combined	County/Judicial	Separate
New Hampshire	State/Executive	Combined	State/Executive	Separate
New Jersey	State/Judicial	Separate	State/Judicial	Combined
New Mexico	State/Executive	Combined	State/Executive	Separate
New York	County/Executive	Separate	County/Executive	Combined
North Carolina	State/Executive	Combined	State/Executive	Separate
North Dakota	State/Executive	Combined	State/Exec. & Judicial	Separate
Ohio	Mixed/Exec. & Judicial	Both	County/Exec. & Judicial	Both
Oklahoma	State/Executive	Combined	Mixed/Exec. & Judicial	Separate
Oregon	County/Executive	Combined	Mixed/Executive	Both
Pennsylvania	Mixed/Exec. & Judicial	Both	County/Judicial	Both
Rhode Island	State/Executive	Combined	State/Executive	Separate

(Continues)

TABLE 2.1 Looking for a Job? Consider the Organizational Structure of Adult and Juvenile Probation/Parole (*Continued*)

		ADULT		JUVENILE
STATE	Level/Branch	Combined or Separate Adult Probation & Parole	Level/Branch	Combined or Separate Juvenile w/Adult
South Carolina	State/Executive	Combined	State/Executive	Separate
South Dakota	State/Judicial	Separate	State/Judicial	Combined
Tennessee	State/Executive	Separate	Mixed/Exec. & Judicial	Separate
Texas	County/Judicial	Combined	State/Judicial	Both
Utah	State/Executive	Combined	State/Judicial	Separate
Vermont	State/Executive	Combined	State/Executive	Separate
Virginia	State/Executive	Combined	Mixed/Exec. & Judicial	Separate
Washington	State/Executive	Combined	County/Exec. & Judicial	Separate
West Virginia	County/Judicial	Separate	State/Judicial	Combined
Wisconsin	State/Executive	Combined	County/Exec. & Judicial	Separate
Wyoming	State/Executive	Combined	Mixed/Exec. & Judicial	Separate

Notes: Executive = Administered under the executive branch of government.
Judicial = Administered under the courts/judicial branch.

Source: Krauth, Barbara and Linke, Larry. 1999. *State Organizational Structures for Delivering Adult Probation Services.* Longmont, CO: LIS, Inc. for the National Institute of Corrections, U.S. Department of Justice.

Community Corrections Acts

Community corrections acts (**CCAs**) is a contractual agreement that assures county government that it will receive state funding to support its programs. State-run departments and programs do not need CCAs—only those departments that are operated locally or through private agencies need funding assurance and the opportunity to develop programs to fit their needs. For example, Ohio and North Carolina developed day reporting centers, whereas Iowa and Indiana developed victim-offender dialogue meetings. Jurisdictions that want to initiate a new program, such as a drug court or mental health court, must agree to contribute matching funds. Oregon is a good example of a CCA that shares characteristics found in other state agreements, such as how the money will be used and whether it may contract with private agencies (see Box 2.2). Note that Oregon's act includes a provision for a monthly fee while under supervision, so that offenders help subsidize their own costs to taxpayers.

community corrections acts
Formal written agreement between a state government and local entities that funds counties to implement and operate community corrections programs on a local level.

COMMUNITY SUPERVISION MODELS OVER TIME

As probation departments were developed within the courts, they created stability for correctional supervision in the community as a primary alternative to incarceration. This section reviews how probation and parole supervision has changed since the early 1900s to the present.

BOX 2.2 OREGON COMMUNITY CORRECTIONS ACT

423.475. The Legislative Assembly Finds and Declares That:

(1) Passage by the voters of Chapter 2, Oregon Laws 1995, has created mandatory minimum penalties for certain violent offenses, and the probable effect thereof will be a significant increase in the demands placed on state-secure facilities.

(2) The State recognizes that it is in a better position than counties to assume responsibility for serious violent offenders and career property offenders.

(3) Counties are willing, in the context of a partnership with the State, to assume responsibility for felony offenders sentenced to a term of incarceration of 12 months or less.

(4) Under the terms of the partnership agreement, the State agrees to provide adequate funding to the counties if the counties agree to assume responsibility of those offenders.

423.505 Legislative Policy on Program Funding.

Because counties are in the best position for the management, oversight and administration of local criminal justice matters, and for determining local resource priorities, it is the legislative policy of this State to establish an ongoing partnership between the State and counties and to finance with appropriations from the General Fund statewide community correction programs on a continuing basis.

The intended purposes of the Community Corrections Partnership Act are to:

(1) Provide appropriate sentencing and sanctioning options including incarceration, community supervision, and services;

(2) Provide improved local services for persons charged with criminal offenses with the goal of reducing the occurrence of repeat criminal offenses;

(3) Promote local control and management of community corrections programs;

(4) Promote the use of the most effective criminal sanctions necessary to protect public safety, administer punishment to the offender, and rehabilitate the offender;

(5) Enhance, increase and support the State and county partnership in the management of offenders; and

(6) Enhance, increase, and encourage a greater role for local government and the local criminal justice system in the planning and implementation of local public safety policies.

423.520: The Department of Corrections shall make grants to assist counties in the implementation and operation of community corrections programs. The department shall require recipients of the grants to cooperate in the collection and sharing of data necessary to evaluate the effect of community corrections programs on future criminal conduct. [1977 c.412 §5; 1987 c.320 §221; 1995 c.423 §3; 1997 c.433 §10]

(1) The county may contract with public or private agencies including, but not limited to, other counties, cities, special districts and public or private agencies for the provision of services to offenders. [1977 c.412 §13; 1987 c.320 §224; 1989 c.613 §2; 1995 c.423 §7]

423.570: Monthly Fee Payable by Person on Supervised Release; Use Payment as Condition of Release; Waiver.

(1) A person sentenced to probation or placed by an authority on parole, post-prison supervision or other form of release, subject to supervision by a community corrections program established under ORS 423.500 to 423.560, shall be required to pay a monthly fee to offset costs of supervising.

(2) The fee shall be determined and fixed by the releasing authority but shall be at least $25.

(3) Fees are payable one month following the commencement of supervision and at one-month intervals thereafter. Each county shall retain the fee to be used for funding of its community corrections programs.

Discussion: According to Oregon's community corrections act, is it possible for monthly fees to be used to improve county-level probation departments?

Source: Oregon Legislative Assembly, Legislative Counsel Committee. Adapted from the 2009 Oregon Revised Statutes, Chapter 423—Corrections and Crime Control Administration and Programs.

Casework Model: 1900–1970

When probation began, the supervision process was oriented toward **casework**, providing therapeutic services to probationers or parolees (often referred to as clients) to assist them in living productively in the community. Probation and parole officers frequently viewed themselves as "caseworkers," or social workers, and the term "agent of change" was a popular description of their role. The literature on probation and parole supervision during this period was replete with medical and psychiatric terminology, such as *treatment* and *diagnosis*. Casework placed stress on creating therapeutic relationships with clients through counseling and directly assisting in behavior modification. Probation and parole officers were thus viewed as social workers engaged in therapeutic relationships with "clients."

casework
A community-supervision philosophy that allows an officer to create therapeutic relationships with clients through counseling and behavior modification, assisting them in living productively in a community.

Brokerage of Services Model: 1971–1981

In the early 1970s, the casework approach began to break down. Many services needed by probationers and parolees could be more readily and effectively provided by specialized community agencies that handled mental health, employment, housing, education, private welfare, and other services. This alternative strategy for delivering probation and parole services was referred to as the **brokerage of services** approach. "Service broker" officers did not consider themselves agents of change as in the casework approach. Instead, they attempted to find the appropriate community agency to which they could refer the client. Thus an unemployed parolee might be referred to vocational rehabilitation services, employment counseling, or the state employment office. Instead of attempting to counsel a probationer with emotional problems, the service-broker officer would locate agencies and refer the probationer to staff skilled in working with problems faced by the client. In this supervision strategy, developing linkages between clients and appropriate agencies was considered one of the probation or parole officer's most important tasks.

brokerage of services
Supervision that involves identifying the needs of probationers or parolees and referring them to an appropriate community agency.

Closely allied to the brokerage approach was the **community resource management team model**. Individual probation and parole officers became specialists by developing skills and linkages with community agencies in one or two areas. For example, one officer might be designated a drug abuse specialist and another, an employment specialist, whereas a third developed expertise with female offenders. This approach recognized that the diverse needs of the probation or parole caseload could not be adequately satisfied by one individual. Thus the caseload was "pooled," and the probationer might be assisted not by one officer but by several.

community resource management team model (CRMT)
A supervision model in which probation or parole officers develop skills and linkages with community agencies in one or two areas only. Supervision under this model is a team effort, each officer utilizing his or her skills and linkages to assist an offender.

Justice Model: 1982–2000

By the mid-1980s, the **justice model** dominated probation and parole supervision. The justice model advocated an escalated system of sanctions corresponding to the social harm resulting from an offense and an offender's culpability. The justice model regarded a sentence of probation not as an alternative to imprisonment but as a valid sanction in itself. The public tends to regard probation established as an alternative to incarceration as an expression of leniency. The justice philosophy regarded probation as a separate, distinct sanction requiring penalties that are graduated in severity and duration according to the seriousness of a crime.

justice model
A correctional practice based on the concept of just desserts and evenhanded punishment. The justice model calls for fairness in criminal sentencing so that all people convicted of a similar offense receive a like sentence. This model of corrections relies on determinate sentencing and/ or abolition of parole.

Advocates of the justice model considered practices of counseling, surveillance, and reporting to accomplish very little and to have minimal impact on recidivism. They favored probation that consists of monitoring court orders for victim restitution or community service and that ensures an imposed deprivation of liberty is carried out. Thus, this model primarily assisted offenders in complying with supervision conditions. Other services such as mental health counseling and alcohol and drug treatment are available but are brokered through social agencies in the community.

Neighborhood-Based Supervision Model: 2001–Present

neighborhood-based supervision
A supervision strategy that emphasizes public safety, accountability, partnerships with other community agencies, and beat supervision.

criminogenic needs-based supervision
A community supervision style emphasizing motivational interviewing and meaningful professional relationships between clients and officers in a dual role as a therapeutic change agent and an enforcer.

A philosophical change unfolded in 2000 as probation officers had mobile technology to supervise out in the field, and spend less time in the office. Supervision needed to become more efficient, and probation officers needed to learn more about the communities in which probationers resided. A supervision strategy known as **neighborhood-based supervision (NBS)** evolved where probation officers supervised their caseload according to zip code, so that the probation officer stayed in a small area, and did not drive all over the city to conduct visits. With NBS, probation officers could be more visible to the community and act as street "boundary spanners" between the corrections system and community police, treatment providers, and faith-based practitioners (Lutze, 2014, p. 18). Being a boundary spanner means more than just supervision within the confines of the probation or parole agency—it requires community supervision officers to fully understand and interact with community leaders, values and desires so that they can truly provide a safe community according to the definitions of what that means for that community. Working with the community also requires officers to be able to identify legitimate opportunities for offenders as well as locations or establishments that may contribute to deviant opportunities (Lutze, 2014).

Criminogenic Needs-Based Supervision Model: 2012–Present

Alongside NBS, a new philosophy called **criminogenic needs-based supervision** emerged in probation and parole that replaced the justice model in the way that offenders are classified, supervised, and treated. This paradigm shift requires community supervision officers and supervisors to think and operate differently from the earlier justice model (Lowenkamp, Holsinger, Robinson, & Cullen, 2012). This style requires that the officer return to establishing meaningful and professional relationships with their clients in a blended dual role as a therapeutic change agent and as an enforcer. In Chapter 5, we discuss how both models—the neighborhood-based and the criminogenic needs-based supervision—are implemented together.

WHO IS ON PROBATION?

Table 2.2 shows characteristics of probationers supervised by county and state departments. Women on probation have been increasing over time, from 21% of all probationers in 1995 to 25% in 2013. Still, 3 out of 4 adult probationers are men. The race/ethnic group composition for probationers varies by region of the country, but on average, more than half (54%) of probationers are white,

TABLE 2.2 Characteristics of Adults on Probation Over Time

	1995	2000	2013
Gender			
Male	79%	78%	75%
Female	21	22	25
Race/Ethnicity			
White	53	54	54
Black	31	31	30
Hispanic	14	13	14
American Indian/Alaska Native	1	1	1
Asian/Pacific Islander	1	1	1
How Probation was Imposed by Courts			
Conviction/Direct imposition	48	56	54
Sentence suspended	32	32	35
Split sentence	15	11	9
Other	4	1	2
Status of Probation Supervision			
Active	79	76	69
Inactive (on probation, but not reporting)	8	9	6
Absconded	9	9	9
Supervised out of state	2	3	3
Warrant status	*	*	9
All other	2	3	5
Type of Offense			
Felony	54	52	55
Misdemeanor	44	46	43
Other infractions	2	2	2
Most Serious Offense			
Violent	*	*	19
Property	*	*	29
Drug law violation	*	24	25
Public order/DWI	16	18	17
Other	84	52	10
Adults Leaving Probation			
Successful completion	62	60	66
Returned to incarceration	21	15	15
Absconded[a]	*	3	3
Technical violations[a]	*	11	11
Death	1	1	1
Other	16	11	3

Notes: *Not measured. [a]In 1995 absconder and technical violators were included under "other."

Sources: Bonczar, Thomas P. 1997. *Characteristics of adults on probation, 1995.* Washington, DC: U.S. Department of Justice; Herberman, Erinn J., and Thomas P. Bonczar. 2014. *Probation and parole in the United States, 2013,* NCJ 248029. Washington, DC: U.S. Department of Justice, Bureau of Justice Statistics.

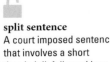

split sentence
A court imposed sentence that involves a short time in jail, followed by a longer period of probation. Also known as *shock incarceration*.

30% are African-American, 14% are of Hispanic origin, and two percent are either Native American or Asian/Pacific Islander. About 54% of probationers in the United States have a direct sentence to probation, 35% have some type of suspended sentence (such as diversion), and 9% have a **split sentence** (a short time in jail, followed by a longer period of probation). The vast majority of probationers have been sentenced for a drug violation, or for property offenses, with 18% of probationers sentenced for a violent offense.

Over the last three decades, felony probationers as a population have begun to resemble parolees (who are described the next chapter). People on probation have more lengthy criminal histories and serious offenses of conviction now than they did in the past. For example, about 30% of all probationers had two or more previous convictions and another 20% had at least one prior conviction. Of those with prior convictions, one out of every four was convicted of a violent crime. Probationers have also gotten older, with the greatest growth in the 25–44 age range and a decline in offenders aged 18–24 (Auerhahn, 2007). As we progress into the future, it is predicted that more and more probation and parole departments will not only combine to supervise offenders more efficiently, but will supervise them in similar ways according to risk posed. The history of parole comprises the next chapter, to which we now turn.

SUMMARY

- In the American colonies where English law prevailed, distinct American practices developed. Precursors to American probation included security for good behavior, laying on file, and suspension of imposition of sentence. American judges exercised discretion to reduce the severity of punishment in cases that warranted leniency.

- An increasing awareness that prisons were not accomplishing their stated purpose of reforming the offender and that suspension of sentence without supervision was not a satisfactory alternative brought about the development of probation as it is known today.

- Upon the foundation laid by judges, volunteers, and the University Settlement movement, John Augustus brought about the practice of probation as it is known today.

- The concept that crimes committed by children should be dealt with differently than crimes committed by adults, with special courts and special facilities for juveniles, was formalized by the creation of the first juvenile court in Illinois in 1899.

- Diversion focuses on offenders who voluntarily agree to enter a contractual agreement with the courts and a probation office where they are supervised in the community.

- Upon completion of a period of diversion supervision, an offender will not have a formal record of conviction. If an offender on diversion supervision does not comply with the conditions, a formal sentence ensues.

- Probation organizational patterns have little uniformity throughout the United States.
  - Probation services may be combined with parole or kept separate.
  - Adult and juvenile probation may be combined or kept entirely separate.
  - Probation may be administered by the executive branch of government or by the judiciary.

- Community corrections acts (CCAs) provide state funding to local probation agencies for development of a wide range of community supervision and treatment programs.

- The varied approaches to community supervision that characterize the eras of probation over time are: casework, brokerage of services, justice model, neighborhood-based and criminogenic needs-based supervision.

DISCUSSION QUESTIONS

1. What was the significance of the decision in *Commonwealth v. Chase*?

2. How did the Killits case later impact probation?

3. How did John Augustus and Matthew Davenport Hill create support for probation as we know it today?

4. Argue for or against the following proposition: Diversion/deferred adjudication should be completely abolished as an option for defendants.

5. Are probation departments better off if controlled locally or by the state?

6. What does a typical probationer look like, in terms of demographics, offense committed, and success rate?

7. How has the concept of supervision changed over the past century? What factors have brought about these changes?

8. Which model of supervision do you view as most effective for use today?

 ## WEBSITES, VIDEOS, AND PODCASTS

Websites

History of US Probation Office
http://www.uscourts.gov/FederalCourts /ProbationPretrialServices/History.aspx
http://www.nmcourt.fed.us/web/PBDOCS /pbindex2.html

History of New York Corrections, N.Y. Corrections Society
http://www.correctionhistory.org/

Hampshire Probation Service, United Kingdom
http://www.hampshire-probation.gov.uk

Federal Probation
http://www.uscourts.gov/library/fpcontents.html

Videos/Podcasts

The Probation Service: Looking back, looking forward

(Length: 3 minutes) A brief look at the history of the Probation Service and to the future development of the Probation Service in Ireland
https://www.youtube.com/watch?v=igLfGnllExY

Community-Based Corrections—The Front Line: Keeping Minnesota Safe

(Length: 2 minutes) Provides a description of what the community-based corrections agents do and how they make sure the offenders are complying with restrictions. https://www.youtube .com/watch?v=xjKMy60-1Ds

Deferred Adjudication Compared to Probation in Colorado

(Length: 2 minutes) A Denver attorney describes what it means to have a deferred judgment. https://www.youtube.com/watch?v=tdou7mijupk

CASE STUDY EXERCISES

The Diversion Decision

This chapter discussed appropriate candidates for diversion. You are tasked with deciding whether each case below should or should not be diverted and why. If the case should be diverted, then you believe the defendant should be given a chance to avoid conviction. If you believe the case should not be diverted, you then believe the defendant should be convicted and sentenced by the court. You must justify your decision in writing.

Case A: Defendant Smith, Possession of Ecstasy

Defendant Smith has been arrested for possession of Ecstasy—enough for two hits. Smith has no criminal history and has been employed as a laborer with a construction company for two years, excluding a brief layoff period. He has a good work record with the company. He admits that he uses alcohol and had been drinking and using Ecstasy the night of the offense. Smith has used marijuana and cocaine but indicates that all usage was in the past rather than recent. He lives by himself; he has never been married and has one child from a previous relationship. He is two months behind on his child-support payments and does not see his child very often. Smith's defense attorney argues that his client has never been in any form of mental-health counseling, substance-abuse treatment, or counseling, and that he would agree to go to drug court as a diversionary measure. The State's attorney is opposed to drug court for Defendant Smith because of the type of drug—Ecstasy. The police have recently been trying to rid the streets of the supply of Ecstasy and believe that Smith may be somehow tied to a major Ecstasy drug ring in the area, but they need more time to prove the allegations, which right now are "shaky" at best.

Case B: Defendant Thompson, Reckless Injury to a Person

Defendant Thompson has been arrested for a felony crime— "throwing objects from an overpass"—that resulted in injury to a passenger of a vehicle. Thompson is a 19-year-old college freshman. He and another college friend had prepared shredded paper in their school colors for a homecoming football game. While walking across an overpass over the interstate highway, he and another student decided to throw some of the shredded paper, which was held in black plastic trash bags.

They proceeded to cut open a bag and pour the paper down on the vehicles. When they cut into a second bag and poured the contents onto the passing vehicles, they were unaware that a brick had been put into the bag for weight. The brick struck the windshield of a vehicle, causing the windshield to break and chip; a piece of the glass flew into the eye of the victim, causing permanent loss of vision.

Defendant Thompson has a prior misdemeanor for theft when he was 17, for which he received a one-year diversionary sentence, which he completed just six months ago. He is not employed and is a full-time college student. He makes passing grades and has not had any student violations at the university. He denies any illegal drug usage and admitted to drinking in the past, but he denies drinking at all since his prior misdemeanor arrest. Thompson's attorney proposes to the court diversion once again: Thompson will continue to attend school, and he will participate in community service by helping the victim and her family at their farm without pay. The State's attorney is adamantly opposed to diversion insofar as this is Thompson's second arrest in less than two years. Due to the seriousness of the victim's injuries, the State's attorney feels this offense should become part of the court record. The district attorney believes that diversion would trivialize the victim's injuries and appeals to you not to grant diversion.

History of Parole and Mandatory Release

ZUMA Press, Inc. / Alamy

CHAPTER OUTLINE

CHAPTER LEARNING OBJECTIVES

1. Explain how transport and ticket-of-leave influenced the development of parole, including how parole was inspired by Alexander Maconochie on Norfolk Island.

2. Discuss how parole was subsequently implemented by Walter Crofton in Ireland and Zebulon R. Brockway in New York's Elmira Reformatory.

3. Identify the reasons why discretionary parole was replaced by mandatory release in many states.

4. Describe the demographic characteristics of parolees today.

5. Argue the pros and cons of medical parole.

KEY TERMS

mandatory release
discretionary release
expiration
parole d'honneur
Alexander Maconochie
marks system
Norfolk Island
transportation
ticket-of-leave
Sir Walter Crofton
Irish system
Zebulon R. Brockway
medical model
just deserts
justice model
medical parole

In 2005, defense attorney Lynne Stewart was convicted at age 64 for helping her client, Sheik Omar Abdel Rahman, communicate from prison to his terrorist group in Egypt, via a reporter in Cairo. Stewart's client was serving a life sentence for a 1995 conviction for organizing a plot to blow up landmarks in New York City—a plot that was not carried out. In 2006, Stewart was sentenced to 28 months in federal prison, and was disbarred from practicing law. She was, however, allowed time to seek cancer treatments before she began her sentence in 2009. Following her sentencing hearing, Stewart made statements to the media that implied that she will have no problem serving her sentence, and that she would do her actions all over again.

Based on those comments, the judge was forced to reconsider his sentence. With Stewart's seeming lack of remorse and failure to appreciate the severity of her actions, she was resentenced to 10 years in federal prison. Stewart contended that her post sentencing statements should not have been used against her, but a panel of three appeals judges disagreed and let the 10-year sentence stand.

While in prison, Stewart's health diminished rapidly and her cancer returned. By 2013, Stewart's stage IV breast cancer had metastasized to her lungs and bones, and she was moved to the Federal Medical Center prison in Carswell, Texas. A motion was filed by prosecutors and the Federal Bureau of Prisons requesting that Stewart's sentence be reduced so that she could be released because she had already served four years in prison; doctors had confirmed that she had terminal and incurable cancer, and her release posed a minimal re-offense risk. U.S. District Judge Koetl agreed and granted a motion for compassionate release. On December 31, 2013, Lynne Stewart, age 74, was released from prison to be with her family and seek medical attention at a local cancer center (Ferrigno & Sanchez, 2014).

Do you agree with Judge Koetl's decision? Why or why not?

INTRODUCTION

Most prisoners who reenter the community do so under some type of supervised release. With over 850,000 state and federal prisoners currently under supervision across the country, many will complete supervision within two years (Herberman & Bonczar, 2014). There are two types of post-prison supervision: discretionary and mandatory release. Individuals on **mandatory release** enter the community automatically at the expiration of their maximum term minus credited time off for good behavior. Mandatory release is decided by legislative statute and is tied to determinate sentences. In contrast to mandatory release, individuals released on **discretionary release** enter the community because members of a parole board have decided that the prisoner has earned the privilege of being released early from prison while still remaining under supervision of an indeterminate sentence.

Parole entails the conditional release of a convicted offender from a correctional institution, under the continued custody of the state, to serve the remainder of his or her sentence under supervision in the community. Historically, parole referred only to discretionary release. But as you will see in this chapter, as laws and release methods have changed, parole has become a broader concept incorporating both mandatory and discretionary supervision. Parolees on both mandatory release and discretionary release are supervised by a parole officer and adhere to similar conditions. If these conditions are not followed, either the mandatory or discretionary type of parolee can be returned to prison for the remainder of a sentence.

A third way that a prisoner leaves prison is by being released free and clear through sentence **expiration**, whereby the prisoner serves 100% of his or her sentence behind bars and there is no post-prison supervision. According to Figure 3.1, almost half (48%) of prisoners are released under mandatory supervision, about 29% under discretionary parole boards, and 23% of releasees literally walk freely out the door with no further obligations or supervision. Over time, mandatory and expiration release has increased, whereas prisoners leaving prison on discretionary parole board release has lessened.

mandatory release
Conditional release to a community under a determinate sentence that is automatic at the expiration of a minimum term of sentence, minus any credited time off for good behavior.

discretionary release
Conditional release because members of a parole board have decided that a prisoner has earned the privilege while still remaining under supervision of an indeterminate sentence.

expiration
A form of release from prison after 100% of the sentence has been served behind bars and there is no post prison supervision.

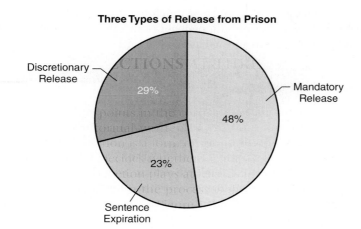

Three Types of Release from Prison

Discretionary Release — 29%
Mandatory Release — 48%
Sentence Expiration — 23%

FIGURE 3.1
Three Types of Release from Prison.

Sources: Herberman, Erinn J., and Thomas P. Bonczar. 2014. *Probation and Parole in the United States, 2013* (NCJ 248029), Washington, DC: U.S. Department of Justice; Carson, E. Ann. 2014. *Prisoners in 2013* (NCJ 247282), Washington, DC: U.S. Department of Justice (for the sentence expiration releases).

THE ORIGINS OF PAROLE

parole d'honneur
French for *word of honor*, from which the English word *parole* is derived.

The English word *parole* is derived from the French **parole d'honneur**, meaning "word of honor." The French seem to prefer the term *conditional liberation* to the one borrowed from their language. In 1791, during the French Revolution, the Comte de Mirabeau (Honoré-Gabriel Rigueti) published a report based on the concept of reformation, which emphasized the principles of labor, segregation, rewards under a mark system, conditional liberation, and aid on discharge. Another Frenchman, Bonneville de Marsangy, public prosecutor of Versailles, published a book in 1847 in which he discussed conditional liberation, police supervision of discharged convicts, aid upon discharge, and rehabilitation. This book was distributed by the government to the members of both chambers of Parliament (Wines, 1919).

The credit for putting parole into practice originated simultaneously with three European prison administrators: a Spaniard named Manuel Montesiños; a German named Georg Michael Von Obermaier; and an Englishman named Alexander Maconochie.

Manuel Montesiños

In 1835, Colonel Manuel Montesiños was appointed governor of the prison at Valencia, Spain, which held about 1,500 convicts. He organized the institution using military-type discipline, and also encouraged prisoner vocational training and education. The novelty of his plan was that although there were practically no officers to watch the prisoners, they nevertheless made few, if any, attempts to escape. Each prisoner could earn a one-third reduction in the term of his sentence through good behavior and positive accomplishments. The number of prisoner recommitments while Montesiños was governor was significantly reduced. Despite all his efforts, the law that allowed this program was subsequently repealed, and Montesiños ultimately resigned. He drew the following conclusions from his experiment:

> Self-respect is one of the most powerful sentiments of the human mind, since it is the most personal; and he who will not condescend, in some degree, according to circumstances, to flattery of it, will never attain his object by any amount of chastisement; the effect of ill treatment being to irritate rather than to correct, and thus turn from reform instead of attracting to it. The moral object of penal establishments should not be so much to inflict punishment as to correct, to receive men idle and ill-intentioned and return them to society, if possible, honest and industrious citizens. (Wines, 1919, p. 194)

Georg Michael von Obermaier

Georg Michael von Obermaier, a prison warden between 1830 and 1862, was also known for reforming a number of Bavarian prisons and suggesting that prison aid societies supervise inmates when released. von Obermaier began as a soldier and experienced inhumane treatment first hand when he was captured as a prisoner of war (POW) in Russia for one year during the War of 1812. After the war ended, he worked as an accountant and tax collector. A prison riot broke out in the small town in which he resided, and coincidentally von Obermaier played a significant and courageous role in ending the riot (Hoefer, 1937).

This incident gave him notoriety and subsequent appointment as prison warden. In an era where harsh punishment was driven by hopes of deterrence, his principles of reformation and early release were considered radical at the time. Reformation included abolition of corporal punishment, substituting the ball and chain with education, and appointing the inmates with leadership abilities to help monitor the larger prisoner population. von Obermaier also garnered government support to authorize that inmates released early be supervised by prison aid societies:

> These societies enlisted volunteer work of the community to supervise and care for the released prisoners morally and economically, provide work for them and protect their families, and particularly their children, against social and economic ostracism. They cooperated with police and parishes as well as among themselves. (Hoefer, 1937, p. 45)

Alexander Maconochie

Chief credit for developing parole however, goes to **Alexander Maconochie**, who was in charge of the English penal colony on Norfolk Island. In 1837, Maconochie, a retired British naval captain and professor of geography, proposed a **marks system** whereby the duration of a sentence would be determined not by time but by a prisoner's industry and good conduct. Daily tallies or "marks" would be credited to prisoners in accordance with their behavior and the amount of labor they performed. As prisoners evidenced good behavior and work ethic, their freedom and privileges gradually increased. Marks were deducted for negative behavior. Maconochie's system allowed prisoners to move from strict imprisonment, to labor in work gangs, through conditional release around the island, and finally to complete restoration of liberty (Morris, 2002).

Alexander Maconochie
A British naval captain who served as governor of the penal colony on Norfolk Island, off the coast of Australia. He instituted a system of early release that was the forerunner of modern parole. Maconochie is known as the *father of parole.*

marks system
A system of human motivation organized by Alexander Maconochie that granted credits for good behavior and hard work and took away marks for negative behavior. Convicts used the credits or marks to purchase either goods or time (a reduction in sentence).

Norfolk Island was the destination where English convicts who were disciplinary problems were sent. This view is the way the former penal colony looks today.

Michael S. Yamashita/Documentary Value/Corbis

Norfolk Island
A notorious British "supermax" penal colony a thousand miles off the coast of Australia that housed the most incorrigible prisoners.

transportation
The forced exile of convicted criminals. England transported convicted criminals to the American colonies until the Revolutionary War and afterwards to Australia.

ticket-of-leave
A license or permit given to a convict as a reward for good conduct that allowed him or her to go at large and work before expiration of sentence, subject to certain restrictions and revocable upon subsequent misconduct. A forerunner of parole.

NORFOLK ISLAND. Maconochie was given an opportunity to test his marks system in 1840 when he was appointed superintendent of the notorious penal colony on **Norfolk Island**, 1,000 miles off the eastern coast of Australia. Norfolk Island was known to have 2,000 of the most incorrigible convicts; they had been sent there from other prisons in Britain and Ireland because they had committed crimes of violence while incarcerated. Within a span of four years, Maconochie's humane system transformed prisoners' horrific lives into ones of peaceful, orderly existence. Maconochie discontinued flogging and chain gangs and introduced adequate food, health care, disciplinary hearings, and reading material (Morris, 2002).

Despite his successes, many influential colonists in Australia who believed that convicts should be kept in irons and flogged saw Maconochie's treatment of prisoners as radical and lobbied the governor for the reformer's dismissal. The governor was torn between his hope that Maconochie's experiment would succeed and his fear of the political power of the colonists who opposed the project. Maconochie was dismissed in 1844, and his experiment came to an abrupt end. As free settlers in Australia increased in number, they protested the use of the country as a repository for prisoners. In 1867, transport of prisoners from England to Australia was terminated (Morris, 2002).

The years following saw an outbreak of crime and prison riots in England, conditions that were attributed to poor prison administration and a lack of supervision of recently released prisoners. The British public thus came to regard prison releasees as a menace to public safety. A royal commission was appointed to investigate the situation, and a report resulted in policemen becoming responsible for supervising released prisoners. Later a number of prisoner aid societies, supported in part by the government, were established.

BOX 3.1   **COMMUNITY CORRECTIONS UP CLOSE**

Banishing English Prisoners to the United States and Australia

Transportation of English criminals to North America began with a 1597 law that allowed the banishment of dangerous criminals as a partial solution to the poor economic conditions and widespread unemployment in England. Felons who could physically work were transported by private contractors to distant lands to help grow food, some of which was transported back to England. The government paid private contractors a fee for each prisoner who arrived alive. Upon arrival, prisoners were sold as indentured servants to the highest bidder. In exchange, transported convicts were granted a stay of execution for as long as they remained out of trouble.

The Revolutionary War of 1776 brought an end to the practice of transporting criminals to America, but the public demand in England for the transportation of convicts rose. England turned its attention to transporting its prisoners to mainland Australia and Norfolk Island, with the first shipload arriving in 1788. In contrast with the transport of prisoners to the American colonies, the British government incurred all expenses of transportation to and maintenance in Australia, and the prisoners remained under government control instead of being indentured. As of 1811, prisoners were eligible to receive a **ticket-of-leave** after they had served a specified amount of time. (For example, those serving a seven-year sentence became eligible for a ticket-of-leave after four years, and those serving life sentences became eligible for such after eight years.)

Other than England, what other countries were involved in the transport of prisoners?

Sir Walter Crofton and the Irish System

Sir Walter Crofton, who studied Maconochie's innovations on Norfolk Island, became the administrator of the Irish prison system in 1854. Crofton adopted the use of the marks system inside prison. Under his administration, the **Irish system** became renowned for its three levels: strict imprisonment, indeterminate sentence, and ticket-of-leave. Each prisoner's classification was determined by the marks he or she had earned for good conduct and achievement in industry and education, a concept borrowed from Maconochie's experience on Norfolk Island.

Sir Walter Crofton
An Irish prison reformer who established an early system of parole based on Alexander Maconochie's experiments with a mark system.

Irish System

Developed in Ireland by Sir Walter Crofton, the Irish system involved graduated levels of institutional control leading up to release under conditions similar to modern parole. The American penitentiaries were partially based on the Irish system. The ticket-of-leave system was different from the one in England. The general written conditions of the Irish ticket-of-leave were supplemented with instructions designed for closer supervision and control and thus resembled the conditions of parole in the United States today. Ticket-of-leave men and women residing in rural areas were under police supervision, but a civilian employee called the "inspector of released prisoners" supervised those living in Dublin. The inspector had the responsibility of securing employment for the ticket-of-leave person, visiting his or her residence, and verifying employment. The Irish system of ticket-of-leave had the confidence and support of the public and of convicted criminals.

Irish system
Developed in Ireland by Sir Walter Crofton, a system that involved graduated levels of institutional control leading up to release under conditions similar to modern parole. American penitentiaries are partially based on the Irish system.

Parole was later applied to prisoners of war as part of Articles 10, 11, and 12 of the 1949 Geneva Convention. A parole agreement in this context is a promise that prisoners of war give their captors that they will not escape or bear arms. If a country authorizes military members to use parole, captors may choose to free a POW under certain conditions bound by the POW's word of honor. Although parole is authorized by some countries in the world, the United States does not allow any member of the armed services to enter into a parole agreement.

THE DEVELOPMENT OF PAROLE IN THE UNITED STATES

In the United States, parole was first tried in New York at Elmira Reformatory in 1876. Federal parole began in 1910 but was not formalized until 1930 under the U.S. attorney general's office. In 1950, because of an increased prison population in the federal system, the parole board was placed under the Justice Department.

Four Justifications of Parole

Parole in the United States developed for four main reasons: (a) a reward for good conduct in prison; (b) aiding supervision of the parolee; (c) imposition of the indeterminate sentence; and (d) reduction in the rising cost of incarceration.

REWARD FOR GOOD PRISON CONDUCT.   The first legal recognition in the United States of shortening a term of imprisonment as a reward for good conduct was by way of an 1817 good time law in New York. Good time was rewarded with one day subtracted off a prisoner's sentence for each day in which there were no reports of misconduct.

TRUTH OR FICTION?

Reducing a prisoner's sentence for good behavior is unnecessary and shortens the length of stay too much.

FICTION

FACT: The use of "good time" is a necessary behavioral management tool favored by correctional administrators as a way to regulate behavior of prisoners while incarcerated. Without good time, there is no privilege with which to reward an offender for positive behavior and to withhold for negative behavior. It is also useful to increase good time for all prisoners across the board when institutions become too crowded, which means that good time can be earned faster in crowded prisons.

POST-RELEASE SUPERVISION. Volunteers and prison society members originally supervised those released from prison in a model similar to that developed by Georg Michael Von Obermaier. For example, the Philadelphia Society for Alleviating the Miseries of Public Prisons recognized the importance of caring for released prisoners as early as 1822. In 1851, the society appointed two agents to assist prisoners discharged from the Philadelphia County prison and the penitentiary. The first public employees paid to assist released prisoners were appointed by the state of Massachusetts in 1845, among others.

RELEASE FROM AN INDETERMINATE SENTENCE. By 1865, American penal reformers were well aware of the reforms achieved by the conditional release programs of the Irish system. As a result, an indeterminate sentence law was adopted in 1876 in New York with the help of prison superintendent **Zebulon R. Brockway**. The system established at Elmira included grading inmates on their conduct and achievement, compulsory education, and careful selection for parole. Volunteer citizens, known as guardians, supervised the parolees. A condition of parole was that parolees report to their guardian on the first day of each month. Written reports were submitted to the prison institution after being signed by a parolee's employer and guardian. By 1944, every U.S. jurisdiction had adopted some form of parole release and indeterminate sentencing.

REDUCING THE COST OF INCARCERATION. Parole may have been initiated in the U.S. primarily for economic reasons. For about one century between the 1840s and 1940s, American prisons were self-supported entirely by convict labor. Many southern penitentiaries turned a huge profit from convict labor by leasing their convicts to private companies. The private companies benefited because they paid the prison less than they otherwise would have had to pay nonincarcerated workers for hard labor such as building railroads, manufacturing goods to sell on the open market, and growing crops. Prison administrators pocketed the money, given that the prisoners did not get paid. Most prisoners worked long hours "under the gun" in remote prison camps miles away from the main prison unit (Walker, 1988).

Private companies liked the idea of using convict labor so much that its use began to affect the employment rate of "free world" people (i.e., those who were not prisoners). Organized labor unions outside of prison began to apply pressure to limit private companies' use of convict labor. Due to the high unemployment rate during the Great Depression, legislation was passed to limit convict labor only to goods that could be sold to government agencies. Because of this legislation, prisoners in remote prison camps had to be relocated to a prison unit where they would be behind bars and work within the walls. More prisons had to be constructed to make space for these incoming prisoners. The profits decreased, and for the first time taxpayers began to bear some of the cost of incarceration (Walker, 1988). Not long after legislation was passed that limited convict labor to prison walls, the notion of parole became more accepted.

The Medical Model: 1930–1960

Parole was seen as a major adjunct to the rehabilitation philosophy that dominated American corrections from the 1930s through the 1960s. This rehabilitative ideal, called the **medical model**, assumed that criminal behavior had its roots in environmental and psychosocial aspects of an offender's life and that these

Zebulon R. Brockway
An American prison reformer who introduced modern correctional methods, including parole, to Elmira Reformatory in New York in 1876.

medical model
The concept that, given proper care and treatment, criminals can be cured to become productive, law-abiding citizens. This approach suggests that people commit crimes because of influences beyond their control, such as poverty, injustice, and racism.

behaviors could be corrected. This meant that every offender must be dealt with on an individual basis to determine the causes of his or her criminal behavior.

Under the old punitive model of corrections, the question was "What did (s)he do?" The medical model was more concerned with "Why did (s)he do it, and what can be done to improve the situation?" According to this model, if prison staff could diagnose and treat "badness," then a lawbreaker should be released when "cured." The mechanisms for accomplishing this release were the indeterminate sentence and parole. The release decision was thus shared between the court, which set a minimum and a maximum period of incarceration, and the correctional system. The parole board's responsibility was to determine the optimal release time at which an inmate was ready to reenter the community as a responsible citizen.

The medical model assumed that correctional specialists had the ability to diagnose an offender's problems and to develop a means of curing those problems. Because one cannot know at the time of diagnosis how long it will take to effect a cure, the indeterminate sentence made it possible, in theory at least, to confine an offender only as long as necessary and to follow up that confinement with community supervision.

Various parole boards came under attack by critics who claimed that parole release failed to produce the desired lasting changes in offenders' behavior and attitudes. Other critics pointed out that future behavior was difficult to accurately predict.

From Discretionary Parole to Mandatory Release

The correctional system's inability to reduce recidivism, rehabilitate offenders, or make predictive judgments about offenders' future behavior brought about public disillusionment, disappointment, and resentment. Concern also arose that wide and unfair disparities existed in sentencing based on an offender's race/ethnicity, socioeconomic status, and place of conviction. As you read in Chapter 1, the pendulum shifted in the 1970s from a rehabilitative focus on the offender (via indeterminate sentencing), to the **just deserts** or **justice model**'s emphasis on the severity of the crime (inherent in determinate sentencing).

just deserts
The concept that the goal of corrections should be to punish offenders because they deserve to be punished and that punishment should be commensurate with the seriousness of an offense.

With parole boards abolished or their releasing authority limited in about 20 states (Hughes, Wilson, & Beck, 2001), "parole" was split into either "discretionary release" (by a parole board) or "mandatory release" (by statute). Currently, only about 29% of prisoners are released via discretionary release, whereas mandatory release numbers have increased (Herberman & Bonczar 2014).

Under discretionary release, offenders reentered society when correctional authorities and board members believed they were ready or thought they had improved their lives enough to earn the privilege to be released. This meant that offenders had to show they had a reentry plan and that they knew how they were going to stay out of trouble. Under mandatory release, offenders are released no matter how many disciplinary reports they have had or how they acted while incarcerated. Thus, many offenders under mandatory release may be less prepared for the transition and may not have the right kind of social support when they go home.

justice model
A correctional practice based on the concept of just deserts and evenhanded punishment. The justice model calls for fairness in criminal sentencing so that all people convicted of a similar offense receive a like sentence. This model of corrections relies on determinate sentencing and/or abolition of parole.

PAROLE TODAY

Figure 3.2 shows the sentencing philosophies of states throughout the United States. Nearly half (45%) of all states, practice both indeterminate and determinate sentencing, depending on the type of offense. These states have a releasing authority of some kind.

FIGURE 3.2
Predominate Sentencing
Practices Across the United
States

Source: Adapted from percentages
provided by: "Association
of Paroling Authorities
International. 2008. *International
Survey of Paroling and Releasing
Authorities.* Available at: http://
www.apaintl.org/resources/
documents/surveys/exec_
summary.pdf

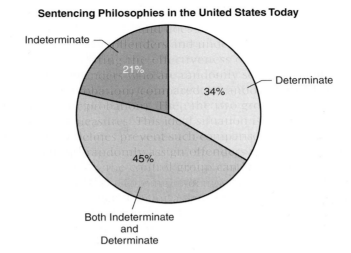

Sentencing Philosophies in the United States Today

Indeterminate — 21%

Determinate — 34%

Both Indeterminate
and
Determinate — 45%

About one-third of the states, such as Arizona, Arkansas, Florida, Illinois, Indiana, Kansas, Maine, New Mexico, Virginia, and Wisconsin have a determinate sentencing structure that also limits the discretion of parole boards for felonies. A small number of states (21%) have maintained full parole board discretion and an indeterminate sentencing structure. These states include Alabama, Iowa, Massachusetts, Nevada, New Hampshire, New Jersey, Pennsylvania, Utah, and Vermont.

States that limit parole boards' power of release require that prisoners serve a flat minimum or some proportion of their maximum sentence before becoming eligible for parole. Other jurisdictions that retained discretionary release have established guidelines to reduce and structure release decision making. Both the American Probation and Parole Association and the Association of Paroling Authorities favor retaining parole boards as an important correctional institution tool. Arguments in favor of discretionary release include:

- Parole boards can impose prisoner participation in treatment programs as incentives for release; with automatic release, however, there are no incentives for prisoners to better themselves while behind bars.
- Objective assessments and parole guidelines have greatly improved parole board decision making.
- Victims can attend parole board hearings to convince the board not to release their offender, but victims have no say in mandatory or automatic release situations.
- Abolishing discretionary release does not mean that prisoners will serve their full sentence; it does not prevent prisoners from release, and it does not necessarily increase public safety (Burke, 2011).

Joan Petersilia agrees: "While abolishing parole [discretionary release] may make good politics, it contributes to bad correctional practices—and ultimately, less public safety .... The public doesn't understand the tremendous power that is lost when parole is abandoned" (Petersilia, 2000, p. 32). Discretionary parole is far from completely disappearing from the correctional scene. Growth in the sheer number of releasees is expected in the future when prisoners complete the minimum terms of their sentences.

Characteristics of Parolees

As you learned earlier, about three out of four prisoners are released from prison on some form of community supervision. However, the rate of release varies by region. The southern region of the United States has the highest incarceration rates, yet the lowest parole rates. The northeastern region shows the opposite situation—a higher rate of parole and a lower rate of incarceration per 100,000 residents (Herberman & Bonczar, 2014).

Table 3.1 shows how parolee characteristics have changed over time. Most parolees are men, but females now make-up 12% of offenders on parole. Parolees typically serve between one and two years of time under post-prison supervision, with about 6% serving parole in another state than the one in which the crime was committed. Parole success rates are lower than those for probation, with about 44% of all parolees successfully completing their parole term. About 3 out of 10 parolees are removed from parole for too many rule violations, and 1 out of 10 for commission of a new crime, attesting to how difficult it is for parolees to transition once they have been imprisoned (Herberman & Bonczar, 2014).

TABLE 3.1   Characteristics of Adult Parolees over Time

	1995	2000	2013
Gender			
Male	90	88	88
Female	10	12	12
Race/Ethnicity			
White	34	38	43
Black	45	40	38
Hispanic	21	21	17
All Others	1	1	2
Status of Supervision			
Active	78	83	84
Inactive (on parole, but not actively reporting to an officer)	11	4	5
Absconded	6	7	6
Supervised out of state/other	4	6	5
Adults Leaving Parole			
Successful completion	45	43	62
Returned to incarceration	41	42	30
With new sentence/additional time	12	11	9
To finish remaining sentence	29	31	21
Absconded/other unsuccessful	10	11	3
Transferred/deported	3	3	4
Death	1	1	1

Sources: Glaze, Lauren E. 2001. *Probation and Parole in the United States, 2000,* NCJ 188208. Washington, DC: U.S. Department of Justice, Bureau of Justice Statistics; Herberman, Erinn J., and Thomas P. Bonczar. 2014. *Probation and Parole in the United States, 2013,* NCJ 248029. Washington, DC: U.S. Department of Justice.

FIGURE 3.3

Conviction Offense for State vs. Federal Prisoners on Parole/Supervised Release

Source: Herberman, Erinn J. and Thomas P. Bonczar. 2014. *Probation and Parole in the United States, 2013*, NCJ 248029. Washington, DC: U.S Department of Justice; U.S. Courts. 2013. *U.S. Court Statistics* (September 30). Accessed at: http://www.uscourts. gov/uscouts/statistics/judicial business/2013/appendices /E03Sep13.pdf

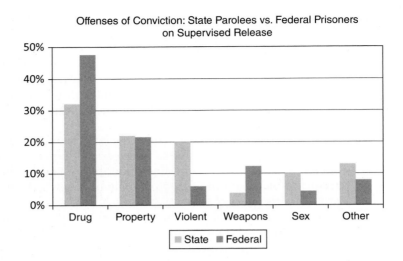

Another interesting characteristic of adults on supervised parole or release is the offense of conviction that led to their initial incarceration. Figure 3.3 shows the difference between state prisoners and federal prisoners, in the type of offenses they commit. You might note that there is a higher percent of violent and sex offenders in state prisons than in federal prisons. However, federal prisons house a greater percentage of drug offenders, who are higher level traffickers and distributors. State prisons house lower-level drug offenders convicted of possession and sales. The types of property offenses are also different; state parolees did time for larceny, burglary, and motor vehicle theft. Federal offenders tended to commit white-collar offenses such as fraud, bribery, money laundering, and extortion. The "Other" crime category in Figure 3.3 consists mainly of driving while intoxicated at the state level, and immigration-related offenses at the federal level.

Contemporary Functions of Parole

In offering a gradual transition from prison to the community, parole continues to aid in reintegration and to reduce recidivism by helping ex-offenders become gainfully employed so they can later support themselves. However, parole officers are under greater scrutiny than previously to protect the public from released offenders by:

1. enforcing restrictions and controls on parolees in the community;
2. providing services that help parolees integrate into a noncriminal lifestyle; and
3. increasing the public's level of confidence in the effectiveness and responsiveness of parole services.

Some argue that parole has changed essentially from being a tolerant force for reintegration to merely an enforcement of the law with a low tolerance for mistakes. This shift in focus may be one reason why revocation rates remain so high.

PRISON POPULATION CONTROL.   Parole has served as the "back doorkeeper" of America's prisons, often operating as a safety valve to relieve crowded institutions. Some states have given legislative authority and directives to their parole boards to control prison population when necessary. Others have done so

TRUTH OR **FICTION?**

All criminals are bad and dangerous people.

FICTION

FACT: Of people who are engaged in criminal behavior, most commit nonviolent and petty offenses. Most criminals have made a series of bad decisions, but for the most part, are not dangerous to the safety of others. Of the criminals in state prisons who commit felonies, an estimated 30% have harmed another person with a sexual or violent offense (Herberman & Bonczar, 2014).

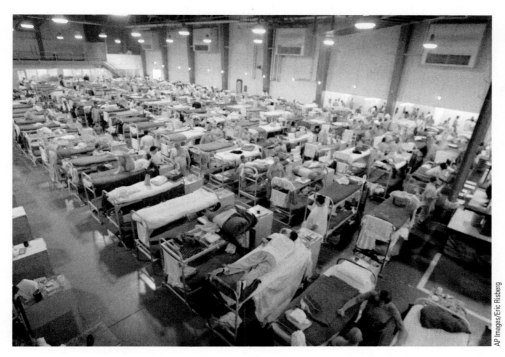

One contemporary function of early prison release is population control of crowded prisons so they don't become like this gymnasium in San Quentin State Prison, California.

AP Images/Eric Risberg

through informal agreements among the governor, the director of corrections, and the legislature or state sentencing commission. California was under court order to decrease their prison population out of necessity. Prison populations had risen to levels that threatened correctional authorities' ability to deliver adequate medical and mental health care, and the U.S. Supreme Court intervened (*Brown v. Plata*, 2011). Known as "Public Safety Realignment," the Supreme Court mandated that California decrease its prison population to 137% of design capacity. This meant a reduction of the prison population from approximately 150,000 inmates to no more than 110,000 by 2015.

MEDICAL PAROLE.   The Bureau of Prisons estimated that over $40,000 is spent just on health care for one prisoner per year (U.S. Department of Justice, 2013). With the high cost of health care and the increased graying of America's prisoners, discussion has centered on the necessity for increasing the rate of **medical parole** as an option for elderly and/or terminally ill prisoners who are no longer a public safety risk. Each prisoner on medical parole is typically required to have either a medical condition that is terminal, that permanently limits them from movement, or that could be treated less expensively in a community treatment facility than in a prison.

A slightly modified version of medical parole in the Federal Bureau of Prisons is called "compassionate release." A federal judge can later reduce a federal prisoner's sentence for "extraordinary and compelling" circumstances. This means that the request can be based on either medical or nonmedical conditions that could not reasonably have been foreseen at the time of sentencing. This was the circumstances that led to the release of former defense attorney, Lynne Stewart, in the chapter opening story.

Releasing terminally ill prisoners to a community hospice to live out their remaining months is not that widely implemented despite repeated arguments showing hospice care to be a cost-effective and humane treatment for inmates

medical parole
Otherwise known as compassionate release, a prisoner's conditional release from prison to the community if (s)he has a terminal illness or needs long-term medical care and does not pose an undue risk to public safety.

and their families (Berry, 2009; Rikard & Rosenberg, 2007). The Bureau of Prisons found that 5 out of 142 federal inmates under compassionate release were rearrested within three years, representing a low recidivism rate of 3.5% compared to 41.0% in the overall prisoner population (U.S. Department of Justice, 2013). A similar low rate was reported in Oklahoma, where only 2 out of 135 medically paroled prisoners were rearrested (Savage, 2013).

Roughly two-thirds of prison systems and nearly half of all city or county jails have a medical parole policy, but only a small number are released nationwide, in part because the policies are too restrictive or there is no effective mechanism by which prisoners can routinely be considered for release. If released, some states require that the releasee must agree to the use of electronic monitoring, regular visits from the parole officer, and to remain in a halfway house or other medically suitable placement under the care of a physician.

The use of medical parole has recently attracted new interest as states examine ways to cut medical costs and decrease the number of prisoners. The case study at the end of this chapter allows you to further consider the issue of compassionate release.

SUMMARY

- Parole has its origins in the work of penal reformers in Germany, Spain, and France as well as that of Alexander Maconochie on Norfolk Island. Prison reformer Zebulon R. Brockway studied Maconochie's work and implemented his ideas in the United States.

- Steadily increasing crime rates, a perceived failure of rehabilitation programs, and the perception that parole boards were incapable of making predictive judgments about offenders' future behavior caused the replacement of the medical rehabilitation model and indeterminate sentencing philosophies of the 1930s with the justice model and determinate sentencing in the 1970s.

- Parole is divided into discretionary release and mandatory release. Under discretionary release,

when correctional authorities believe offenders have improved their lives enough to earn the privilege to be released, they reenter society. Under mandatory release, which has steadily increased, offenders are released regardless of disciplinary reports or their behavior while incarcerated.

- Currently, 23% of all people released from prison do not receive any post-prison supervision.

- The purpose of parole is to ease crowded facilities, to provide behavioral incentive while incarcerated, to save money, and to reintegrate offenders.

- Medical parole or compassionate release is a way to control medical costs and allow low-risk inmates to live out their remaining days with their families on a structured release plan.

DISCUSSION QUESTIONS

1. Why did England transport convicts to America and Australia? What was the connection between transportation and parole?

2. What was the significance of Alexander Maconochie's approach to prison administration upon the behavior of the convicts?

3. Why was Maconochie dismissed from Norfolk Island despite his success?

4. How did parole develop in the United States? Be sure to include in your explanation discussions of the Irish system and the indeterminate sentence.

5. What role does parole play in the twenty-first century?

6. What are the pros and cons of discretionary parole and mandatory release?

7. How do you feel about the use of medical parole?

WEBSITES, VIDEOS, AND PODCASTS

Websites

History of parole in Alabama
http://www.pardons.state.al.us

History of parole in Texas
http://www.tdcj.state.tx.us/divisions/parole/parole_history.html

History of parole in Utah
http://bop.utah.gov/board-top-public-menu/history-top-public-menu.html

Videos/Podcasts

History of Women in Prison and Parole
A 1956 movie about the history of women in prison and parole in Corona, CA.
http://www.youtube.com/watch?v=Z9c1IrD2N8s

The Benefits of Parole
(Length: 4:21 minutes) David Park speaks with former inmate Xavier McElrath-Bey about his time in a youth prison and how he stopped the cycle of recidivism.
https://www.youtube.com/watch?v=gCf5U21jvuM

Utah Board of Pardons and Parole
(Length: 2:49 minutes) A woman goes before the Utah parole board while in prison for burglary and kidnapping, and finds out the Board's decision.
https://www.youtube.com/watch?v=fUOuk1mKLJc

Medical Parole
This is an interview with Bob, who has coordinated medical parole in Oklahoma. The podcast defines, explains, and discusses medical parole.
http://www.corrections.com/system/podcast/file/34/media_20021217.mp3

CASE STUDY EXERCISES

Should Terminally Ill and/or Elderly Prisoners Be Medically Paroled?

Assume that you are part of a committee that evaluates medical parole prisoners with various documented medical diagnoses. A prisoner has met the minimum requirements on time served for parole, but your job is to determine, based on two factors, whether he or she should be released early on medical parole while still remaining under community supervision:

1. That he or she is no longer a risk to public safety if released into the community.

2. That he or she has a verifiable terminal medical condition OR a permanent medical condition that limits movement OR a medical condition that could be treated less expensively in a community treatment facility instead of a prison.

CASE A: Tony, Terminal Illness and in for Murder

Tony has served 40 years in prison for a highly publicized murder case that he committed when he was 20 years old. He has been a model inmate, compiling few disciplinary reports while incarcerated. He was a clerk in the law library until about five years ago, when he had to quit his job because he was diagnosed with a brain tumor. The tumor was cancerous, so he received chemotherapy and radiation for two years, but that did not completely stop the cancer from spreading throughout his body. Now at age 62 Tony is bedridden, breathes and eats through a tube, and takes pain medication

to ease his suffering. He has been deemed not to be a danger to anyone. It costs the state $1,000 per day just to keep Tony locked up, whereas a community hospice could provide the same medical care for $500 per day. However, his case was a high-profile murder case, and the victim's survivors said they will never forgive Tony, nor will they give up fighting for him to stay in prison until he dies, no matter what the cost.

CASE B: William, Elderly and in Prison for Motor Vehicle Theft and Reckless Endangerment

William, a career criminal, has a long rap sheet consisting of at least five felony crimes and over two dozen misdemeanors, mostly drug-related and property offenses. In his life, he has spent more time institutionalized than out in the free world. He was arrested on his latest felony when he was 60 years old. Although he pleaded guilty to motor vehicle theft, he said that he mistook the car for his own and didn't mean to steal it—his eyesight was bad. Now at age 75, he has served 15 years out of his 20-year sentence, and is ready to turn over a new leaf. William is tired of institutions—his health is not what it used to be. He does not have a terminal illness, but he is diabetic and has heart problems. Due to diabetes, William's left foot was amputated and he is blind in one eye. He is not capable of working, but he can get around pretty well in a wheelchair. Given that he was insured and suffered no serious losses, the victim in the case has no problem with William's release.

Part II

Evidence-Based Community Correctional Supervision and Treatment

This section focuses on the techniques of evidence-based correctional practice that are important in community supervision. In explaining these practices, two other decision points are discussed in Chapter 4: pretrial release/supervision and the sentencing decision. Chapter 4 also introduces how the presentence investigation report aids judges prior to sentencing. Students will learn how to conduct an interview and assemble a presentence report.

Chapter 5 is the foundation chapter in evidence-based practice in the community supervision and treatment of probationers and parolees. Some of these techniques include the assessment of risk and needs and developing strategies through the case treatment plan. Students will learn how to write a case treatment plan. Using cognitive behavioral treatment and focusing on criminogenic needs is critical for high-risk clients and offenders with special needs. Chapter 6 discusses various types of unique needs, such as clients with substance abuse problems, clients with mental health problems, and sex offenders. Chapter 7 discusses what happens when community conditions need to be modified or terminated on either probation or parole. This chapter also details who the most likely offenders are to recidivate and how recidivism rates can be reduced.

Sentencing, and the Presentence Investigation Report

Chapter 4

Herman Verwey/Foto24/Gallo Images/Getty Images

CHAPTER LEARNING OBJECTIVES

1. Distinguish the differences among pretrial release, pretrial supervision, and diversion.

2. Explain the factors involved in a decision to release pretrial defendants from detention.

3. Define the legal factors in granting community sentences.

4. Explain the purpose and contents of a presentence investigation report.

5. Summarize the legal issues and criticisms regarding the presentence investigation report.

KEY TERMS

pretrial release
recognizance
delegated release authority
surety
pretrial supervision
failure to appear (FTA)
sentencing
reflective justice
presumptive sentencing grids
sentencing commission
presentence investigation (PSI) report
post-sentence report
presentence investigation
victim impact statement
collateral contacts
disclosure
harmless error
hearsay
standard conditions
special conditions
scarlet letter conditions

At the 2012 Olympics, Oscar Pistorius from South Africa became the world's first double amputee sprinter to compete with two prosthetic legs made of carbon fiber. Although he did not medal in the Olympics, he broke records and medaled in the Paralympic Games. He became famously known around the world as "Blade Runner" or the "Fastest Man on No Legs."

What many people may not have known was that Pistorius carried a firearm, and he was a jealous and short-tempered man when it came to his private life and his girlfriend, Reeva Steenkamp. In January 2013, he was accused of "reckless endangerment" when he discharged a loaded gun in a public restaurant. A few weeks later, while at home on Valentine's Day, Pistorius shot his 9 mm gun four times through a locked bathroom door at what he thought was an intruder. The "intruder" ended up to be his girlfriend who had gotten up in the middle of the night to use the bathroom, and now lay dead. In September 2014, Oscar Pistorius was found guilty of "culpable homicide" in the death of Reeva Steenkamp, but his actions were *not* premeditated or deliberate.

One month later, during the sentencing hearing, the Judge considered a sentence that would be perceived by the public as fair and just, and at the same time, one that provided closure to the victim's family. South Africa has an indeterminate sentencing structure, in that there is no minimum required sentence, and no requirement of prison. The maximum time Pistorius could potentially receive would have been 15 years, so the judge had much leeway. The Judge ultimately decided a sentence of five years in prison for the death, and a three-year suspended sentence for the restaurant incident. According to South African law, Pistorius will be eligible after 10 months (August 2015) for early release from prison on house arrest for the remaining four years.

Do you think the sentence was fair and just under the circumstances? Why or why not?

INTRODUCTION

Many misdemeanor offenders and some low-level felony offenders are issued a citation or summons for their next court appearance. Offenders who are arrested typically spend a night in a city jail or holding cell and are released the next day. If a suspect is expected to stay longer in a local jail, he or she is interviewed by a bail commissioner or magistrate who will make decisions about the bond or the terms on which the defendant will be released from jail, if at all. A release decision takes place between 24 and 72 hours following arrest. Most people who are accused of a crime do not need to be held in jail while waiting for their next court date, insofar as holding them disrupts their employment, their family life, and their ability to prepare for and aid in their own defense (Miyashiro, 2008). Still, about 64% of felony defendants were held in confinement until their case was completed (Cohen, 2012).

PRETRIAL SERVICES

Pretrial services is an agency that assists the court in deciding whom to release and whom to detain based on validated assessment instruments and a pretrial interview of the defendant. During the interview, the defendant is not required to answer any questions about the pending crime, nor is the pretrial services officer allowed to consider the weight of the evidence against the defendant. Pretrial services also helps ensure that defendants appear at their next court date (VanNostrand & Crime and Justice Institute, 2007). Ultimately, a defendant's case will likely result in one of four options: dismissal, diversion, conviction as a result of a plea agreement, or the defendant pleads not guilty and requests a trial. We discuss pretrial release and pretrial supervision more closely below.

   Pretrial release is defined as a defendant's release from jail while awaiting his or her next court appearance. The pretrial release decision is one of the first decisions made following an arrest in order that defendants who qualify can be released to the community prior to their next court date. Pretrial release allows defendants who have not yet been convicted an opportunity to live and work as productive citizens until their next scheduled court date.

pretrial release
While preparing for the next scheduled court appearance following arrest, a defendant's release into a community as an alternative to detention.

History of Pretrial Release

Early research indicated that being detained during the pretrial process was a disadvantage to a defendant's sentencing outcome. Consequently, release became an option, and bail was offered as a way to guarantee a defendant's return to court. However, people most likely to be detained at the time could not afford bail because they were impoverished. The situation inspired the Manhattan Bail Project as the first opportunity for defendants to be granted release on recognizance (ROR) before their next scheduled court date. This in turn led to the Federal Bail Reform Act of 1966, which established guidelines on appropriate bail amounts and alternatives to detention for those unable to afford bail. The act was a reminder that the law favors release, unless there is a substantial risk that a defendant may not appear at the next court hearing. Pretrial programs became so successful that within two decades more than 200 cities had developed such programs. Growing concern about the risks posed by some pretrial defendants led to the passage of a second Bail Reform Act in 1984 that included the safety of the public as an important criterion in a decision to detain a pretrial defendant. When this act was challenged in the courts, the U.S. Supreme Court upheld the act, affirming that pretrial detention served not for punishment but for high-risk defendants who posed a threat to themselves or to others (*U.S. v. Salerno,* 1987). Recent research determined that a defendant's ties to the community, long thought to make a difference, were not at all useful in predicting a defendant's risk or likelihood of appearing in court (Cadigan, Johnson, & Lowenkamp, 2012).

Cadigan and Lowenkamp (2011) compared two groups of defendants who were convicted, sent to prison, and released on post conviction supervision. One group was released from jail following arrest and the other group was detained in jail prior to a conviction. Defendants at low and medium risk who were incarcerated during the pretrial period were twice as likely to be arrested following a prison term than defendants of the same risk level who were released into the community at pretrial (Cadigan & Lowenkamp, 2011). The detention decision did not seem to matter for high-risk defendants who failed at about the same rate regardless of whether they were detained or released following arrest. So while pretrial detention can serve an important purpose for high-risk individuals, if not used properly for the right reasons, pretrial detention can significantly disadvantage defendants, making it more likely that detained defendants will be sentenced to prison, and have longer sentence lengths when compared to federal defendants who were granted release (Oleson, Lowenkamp, Wooldredge, VanNostrand, & Cadigan, 2014).

Decision to Detain or Release

Both state and federal pretrial services recommend the least restrictive option available to a court, taking into consideration the safety of a community and a defendant's likelihood of reappearance in court. To make the best possible decision, a pretrial assessment tool was developed by Lowenkamp, Lemke, and Latessa (2008) as a part of the Ohio Risk Assessment System (ORAS). The

A Judge listens to a recently arrested defendant before deciding whether the defendant should be released prior to her next court date

© wavebreakmedia/Shutterstock.com

failure to appear
A situation in which a defendant does not attend a scheduled court hearing.

delegated release authority
Statutory authority that allows pretrial services officers to release a defendant before an initial court appearance in front of a judge.

assessment, shown in Figure 4.1, was validated and is publicly available to any agency to predict new arrests and future incidents of **failure to appear** (FTA) in court. Its items include defendant's age at first arrest, number of times the defendant has failed to appear in court over the past two years, number of jail incarcerations, employment status at arrest, self-reported use of illegal drugs, and stability of residence (Lowenkamp, Lemke, & Latessa, 2008; Latessa et al., 2009).

The federal system uses a similar instrument called the "Pretrial Services Risk Assessment" (known as the PTRA) that has been validated, but could still use further improvements (Cadigan, Johnson, & Lowenkamp, 2012). Quantitative instruments like ORAS and the PTRA can assist pretrial service officers in recommending detention with no release or **delegated release authority**, which allows pretrial services officers to release defendants before an initial court appearance.

FIGURE 4.1

OHIO RISK ASSESSMENT SYSTEM: PRETRIAL ASSESSMENT TOOL (ORAS-PAT)

Name: _____   Date of Assessment: _____

Case#: _____   Name of Assessor: _____

Pretrial Items   **Verified**

1.1 Age at First Arrest
        0 = 33 or older
        1 = Under 33

1.2 Number of Failure-to-Appear Warrants Past 24 Months
        0 = None
        1 = One Warrant for FTA
        2 = Two or more FTA Warrants

1.3 Three or More Prior Jail Incarcerations
        0 = No
        1 = Yes

1.4 Employed at the Time of Arrest
        0 = Yes, Full-time
        1 = Yes, Part-time
        2 = Not employed

1.5 Residential Stability
        0 = Lived at Current Residence Past Six Months
        1 = Not Lived at Same Residence

1.6 Illegal Drug Use During Past Six Month
        0 = No
        1 = Yes

1.7 Severe Drug Use Problem
        0 = No
        1 = Yes

                                                        Total Score:

(Continues)

FIGURE 4.1 *(Continued)*

Scores	Rating	% of Failures	% of Failure to Appear	% of New Arrest
0–2	Low	5%	5%	0%
3–5	Moderate	18%	12%	7%
6+	High	29%	15%	17%

Please State Reason if Professional Override:

Other Areas of Concern. Check all that Apply:

_____Low Intelligence*
_____Physical Handicap
_____Reading and Writing Limitations*
_____Mental Health Issues*
_____No Desire to Change/Participate in Programs*
_____Transportation
_____Child Care
_____Child Care
_____Language
_____Ethnicity
_____Cultural Barriers
_____History of Abuse/Neglect
_____Interpersonal Anxiety
_____Other _____

*If these items are checked it is strongly recommended that further assessment be conducted to determine level or severity.
Source: Latessa, Edward, Paula Smith, Richard Lemke, Matthew Makarias, and Christopher Lowenkamp, 2009. *Creation and Validation of the Ohio Risk Assessment System: Final Report.* Cincinnati, OH: University of Cincinnati, Center for Criminal Justice, Research, pp. 49–50. Reproduced with permission. In the Public Domain.

TYPES OF BONDS   Once a judge decides whether to detain or to release, the next decision is under what conditions (if any) a defendant is to be released. This requires setting a bond or bail amount according to offense severity. Table 4.1 identifies four ways a defendant can be released. Unsecured bonds do not require any money up front and only require the full bond amount if a defendant refuses to appear. ROR requires only a signed agreement by a defendant that he or she will appear, and is also known as a "personal recognizance" or "PR bond." If a defendant with an ROR fails to attend the next hearing, there is no bond amount to pay, but a warrant is still issued for that defendant's arrest.

Secured bonds require cash or property assets deposited directly with a court for the full bond amount before the defendant is released. A secured bond assures the court that the defendant will appear, and when the defendant does appear, the deposited amount is returned to the defendant. If the defendant does not have the financial ability to secure his or her own release, the defendant may use a bond company, which is also known as a **surety**. The bond company deposits the entire bail amount with the court on behalf of the defendant, and charges the defendant a nonrefundable fee of 15% and 20% of

TABLE 4.1 Types of Pretrial Release

Release Type	Definition
Unsecured Bond	Defendant pays no money to the court but is liable for the full bail amount if s/he fails to appear
Release on recognizance	Defendant signs an agreement to appear; no money is paid or owed to the court for FTA
Cash/property collateral	Defendant deposits bail amount in cash or property collateral with court; money is returned after court dates; bond is forfeited for FTA
Surety bond	Use of a bail bond company wherein the bail company is liable if the defendant FTA; bail company charges a fee for securing the bond

Source: Cohen, Thomas H. 2012. *Pretrial release and misconduct in federal district courts, 2008–2010.* NCJ 239243. Washington, DC: U.S. Department of Justice.

the bail amount. When the defendant appears in court, the bond company is refunded the entire amount.

WHY ARE MORE DEFENDANTS BEING DETAINED? Pretrial detention rates have been steadily *increasing* in the federal system and now comprise over 70% of defendants who are detained during the pretrial process, while less than 30% are released. In contrast, average detention rates for state courts have remained consistent at about 40% of defendants (Cohen, 2012). One explanation might be an increase in immigration cases that necessitate detention if a defendant cannot show community ties and might be a flight risk. With immigration cases, the FTA rate is a little bit higher than that for other crimes (4.3% for immigration offenses vs. 2.8% for violent crimes), but the likelihood of committing a new crime on

Bail Bond companies help provide the means of release for pretrial detainees who do not have the money to pay the full bail amount.

Marmaduke St. John/Alamy

release is less (2.3% for immigration offenses vs. 6.9% for weapons-related offenses). Researchers are hinting at a possibility of racial disparity in federal pretrial decision making (Byrne & Stowell, 2007).

Another explanation of rising pretrial detention rates is that as individual situations have changed, that has increased the measure defendants received. For example, fewer defendants are employed—31% of defendants today compared with 57% in 1987. Also, more defendants are transient. For example, in 1987, two-thirds of defendants lived in the same area for five years or more. Today that rate has diminished to one third of defendants, leading one to question whether the pretrial decision favors release (Cadigan, 2007). One consistent finding about pretrial detention is that defendants who were detained during the pretrial process were more likely to be sentenced to prison, and have longer sentence lengths when compared to federal defendants who were granted release, after controlling for offense severity and criminal history score (Oleson et al., 2014). Another consistent trend is that most pretrial defendants, whether they are detained or not, appear in court and do not commit new offenses, suggesting an overuse of pretrial detention in the federal system (Byrne & Stowell, 2007).

Solutions to the reduced use of pretrial detention and/or high bond amounts include having an attorney to present facts in favor of the defendant so that the judge may be convinced to lower the bond schedule or remove it altogether. Defendants have the right to request an attorney at the time when the type of bond and bond amount is set (*Rothgery v. Gillespie County,* 2008). Another solution is for county jails to offer information to newly booked inmates about bail bondsmen fees and methods of payment, along with other ways of bonding out besides the use of a bail bond company. Jail inmates are not allowed to keep their cell phones while incarcerated, so they are unable to look up numbers of family or friends that could help them post bond (Levin, 2012). With approval of a new risk prediction instrument discussed above, along with the ability to request an attorney at the hearing, the pretrial detention trend should decrease and bond schedules become more precise in the future.

Pretrial Supervision

Once a decision has been made to release a defendant, **pretrial supervision** can be ordered as a condition of the bond. A pretrial services officer is designated by the courts to assume supervision until a case has been resolved. Most federal offenders who are released pretrial have conditions to follow for six to seven months until sentencing.

In the state system, for every 100 defendants evaluated, only 20% received pretrial supervision. Clients on pretrial supervision were required to call in weekly until their scheduled court date, comply with curfew, submit to drug testing, maintain employment, and avoid contact with victims and any witnesses who might have to testify. Individuals who tended not to follow these conditions had previously failed to appear in court and had a previous criminal history measured by arrests and convictions (Bechtel, Lowenkamp & Holsinger, 2011). A more recent study of a similar population found that pretrial supervision failures had a substance abuse problem, were younger in age, had dropped out of high school, and had at least one prior FTA or escape on their record (Fennessy & Huss, 2013).

pretrial supervision
Court-ordered correctional supervision of a defendant not yet convicted whereby said defendant participates in activities such as reporting, house arrest, and electronic monitoring to ensure appearance at the next court date.

diversion
An alternative program to traditional criminal sentencing or juvenile justice adjudication that provides first-time offenders with a chance or addresses unique treatment needs, with a successful completion resulting in a dismissal of current charges. Also known as deferred adjudication.

When a defendant is not in compliance with pretrial supervision conditions, 89% of programs will give that defendant a warning the first time. Most programs will report the second act of noncompliance to a court with a recommendation for specific action, such as increasing telephone contact with said defendant. More serious acts of noncompliance, such as absconding or a rearrest, can result in a court's issuance of a bench warrant, the detention of a suspect, or bail revocation.

One thing is certain—random drug testing and providing services during the pretrial process may increase the likelihood of technical rule violations, but do not increase the likelihood of court appearances nor do they decrease new offenses (Byrne & Stowell, 2007; VanNostrand & Crime & Justice Institute, 2007).

FAILURE TO APPEAR   The purpose of pretrial supervision is to ensure that a defendant appears for court and that the public is safe while that defendant is out on bond. Defendants who failed to appear (FTA) did not attend their scheduled court date and seemed most likely to flee the day before their trial or sentencing hearing, or just prior to surrendering themselves for incarceration (Henry, 2007).

Diversion

Thus far we have talked about pretrial release and supervision under the assumption that an offender has been released on bond under a certain set of supervisory conditions. Another option during the pretrial process is diversion or deferred adjudication (initially discussed in Chapter 2). Recall that when a defendant successfully completes the terms of diversion and so long as the defendant stays out of trouble for two to five years following diversion, the charges are dismissed and there is no official conviction. For this reason, **diversion** is a type of pretrial supervision. However, the main difference between the two is that diversion completion results in no criminal record because a person is considered low risk, whereas pretrial supervision as part of a surety bond may still result in a criminal conviction (given that supervision was necessary before conviction insofar as a defendant was considered high risk). Box 4.1 discusses whether diversion is more effective than probation in reducing later recidivism rates.

BOX 4.1   **EVIDENCE-BASED PRACTICES IN COMMUNITY CORRECTIONS**

Does Youth Diversion Work?

Diversion offers individuals who have made an isolated bad decision, a second chance at keeping a criminal incident off their record, as long as they never get into trouble again. Diversion can be accomplished with youth and adults in one of two ways: either a simple judicial warning and release without supervision, or it can involve supervision coupled with some

sort of treatment intervention. But some people have been left wondering which form of diversion may be more effective, and whether diversion actually has its intended effect of reducing future criminal behavior.

The warn and release diversion programs seemed to work the best with low-risk youth, while diversion supervision with a treatment intervention component worked the best for medium-risk youth (Schwalbe, Gearing, MacKenzie, Brewer, & Ibrahim, 2012). This finding is consistent with one principle of evidence-based practices: The higher risk an individual poses, the more intense the intervention strategy needed (we examine how "risk" is calculated in the next chapter).

Wilson and Hoge (2012) examined a matched sample of low- and medium-risk youth who received diversion with intervention and compared them to youth who received traditional probation supervision. The diversion intervention program was developed specifically around the risk/needs/responsivity model discussed in Chapter 1 where the youths' criminogenic needs were treated. The researchers found that the intervention diversion program for medium-risk

youth reduced recidivism more effectively than traditional probation. The youths with greatest reduction in recidivism were the ones who completed the diversion. Diverted youths who only partially completed the diversion program actually had higher recidivism than youths on probation, leading researchers to believe that the key factor was the *completion* of the diversion programs, not the act of being on diversion that led to the reduction (Wilson and Hoge, 2012).

Sources: Schwalbe, C. S., Gearing, R. E., MacKenzie, M. J., Brewer, K. B., and Ibrahim, R. 2012. A meta-analysis of experimental studies of diversion programs for juvenile offenders. *Clinical Psychology Review,* 32, 26–33; Wilson, Holly A., and Robert D. Hoge. 2012. Diverting our attention to what works: Evaluating the effectiveness of a youth diversion program. *Youth Violence and Juvenile Justice,* 11 (4): 313–331.

SENTENCING

Sentencing has long been considered the most difficult decision in the criminal justice process. **Sentencing** can be defined as a post-conviction stage in which a defendant is brought before a court for formal judgment pronounced by a judge. The judge is influenced by a presentence investigator's report as well as by the wishes of prosecutor and defense attorney. Sentencing demands choosing among a number of alternatives and considering issues of public safety, rehabilitation, deterrence, and retribution. The philosophy behind community sentences argues that an offender can better learn how to live productively in a community by remaining in free society under supervision than by being transferred to the setting of a jail or prison.

sentencing
The post-conviction stage, in which a defendant is brought before a court for formal judgment pronounced by a judge.

Factors That Affect Granting a Community Sentence

A judge's decision to allow a defendant to serve a community corrections sentence depends on the offender's eligibility by law for a community corrections sentence, which is defined largely by the current offense and the prior record. In addition to legal requirements, the judge considers the defendant's ability to meet those conditions and the availability of space and resources in community-based programs. Judges engage in a process of **reflective justice**, which means that each individual case is considered in terms of "its subjectivities, harms, wrongs, and contexts, and then measured against concepts such as oppression, freedom, dignity, and equality" (Hudson, 2006, p. 39). In reflective justice, judges use a presentence investigation (PSI) report (discussed later in the chapter) to examine the economic stability of a defendant, family ties, marital status, employment length, and drug abuse history. Judges also take into account whether a case was plea bargained or brought to trial and the amount of media attention generated that may affect public opinion.

reflective justice
A form of justice whereby each defendant's case is considered by a judge, parole board, or a decision-making authority according to its subjectivities, harms, wrongs, and contexts, then measured against concepts such as oppression, freedom, dignity, and equality.

Determinate Sentencing Examples

Recall our discussion in Chapter 1 about the difference between determinate and indeterminate sentencing. The goals of determinate sentencing include reducing or eliminating perceived sentencing disparity, increasing judicial accountability for sentences, increasing punishments for violent offenders, and providing a basis for population projections and resource allocation. To help meet these goals, sentencing guidelines have been constructed in about half of all states based on severity of offense and an offender's prior criminal history.

presumptive sentencing grids
A statutorily determined sentence that judges are obligated to use. Any deviations (mitigating or aggravating circumstances) must be provided in writing and may be subject to appellate court review.

With **presumptive sentencing grids**, judges are obligated to use guidelines from which they may not deviate without providing written reasons as to why they have chosen to do so. **Sentencing commissions** monitor how sentencing guidelines and judicial departures are used and make sentencing recommendations to a legislature. These departures may also be subject to appellate court review. North Carolina, Pennsylvania, and Washington states have "structured presumptive sentencing zones"; that is, they have integrated intermediate sanctions directly into both their felony and misdemeanor sentencing guidelines. Violent offenders in these states receive lengthier prison sentences than do nonviolent offenders, who can receive intermediate sanctions or other forms of community-based or even restorative justice sanctions. We present two different sentencing guidelines—the federal sentencing table and the North Carolina sentencing guidelines.

sentencing commission
A governing body that monitors the use of sentencing guidelines and departures from recommended sentences.

UNITED STATES SENTENCING GUIDELINES   The original United States Sentencing Guidelines set narrow, mandatory ranges of punishment based on the current offense or plea, an offender's prior criminal history, and the established facts that, if proven by a preponderance of evidence, could potentially increase an offender's sentence above the range in the Guidelines. If a prosecutor could show aggravating facts to a sentencing judge, a court would be obligated to enhance a punishment even further. *U.S. v. Booker* (2005) ruled this practice unconstitutional, but two distinct majority opinions followed. One said that to enhance a punishment, a defendant had to admit to aggravating circumstances or a prosecutor had to prove guilt to a jury beyond a reasonable doubt. The second majority opinion said the Guidelines should be advisory rather than mandatory. This served once again to give federal judges discretion in sentencing.

The federal sentencing guidelines were most recently updated in 2012 and are shown in Figure 4.2. The first eight offenses are misdemeanors and eligible for one year of probation without any period of confinement. The next four are low-level felonies and are eligible for combining residential community corrections or home confinement with probation for between one and five years. Offenses within Rows 13 and below are not eligible for probation, so a prison term must be served.

The criminal history categories are listed in each column. The intersection between the current offense row and the criminal history score determines the range in months. The criminal history score is determined by adding together three subtotals:

Subtotal 1: Add (a) **three** points for each prior sentence of imprisonment exceeding one year and one month; (b) **two** points for each prior sentence of imprisonment of at least 60 days not counted in (a); (c) and **one** point for each prior sentence not counted in (a) or (b), up to a total of **four** points for this subsection.

Subtotal 2: Add (d) **two** points if a defendant committed the instance of offense while under any criminal justice sentence, including probation, parole, supervised release, imprisonment, work release, or escape status.

Subtotal 3: Add (e) **one** point for each prior sentence resulting from conviction of a crime of violence that did not receive any points under (a), (b), or (c) above because such sentence was counted as a single sentence, up to a total of three points for this subsection.

There are countless exceptions to the point system, so for full instructions visit Chapter 4, Part A of the Sentencing Guidelines Manual at: http://www.ussc .gov/Guidelines/2010_guidelines/Manual_HTML/Chapter_4.htm

FIGURE 4.2   Federal Sentencing Table (in months of imprisonment)

Criminal History Category (Point)

Offense	I (0 or 1)	II (2 or 3)	III (4, 5, 6)	IV (7, 8, 9)	V (10, 11, 12)
Lying Tax returns	0–6	0–6	0–6	0–6	0–6
Fish/game/wildlife	0–6	0–6	0–6	0–6	0–6
Traffick taxable property/customs	0–6	0–6	0–6	0–6	2–8
Trespass/destruction Fed land/property	0–6	0–6	0–6	2–8	4–10
Larceny/Embezzlement	0–6	0–6	1–7	4–10	6–12
Possession of Controlled Substance	0–6	1–7	2–8	6–12	9–15
Assault; Tax Evasion; Escape	0–6	2–8	4–10	8–14	12–18
Theft; Commercial Bribery	0–6	4–10	6–12	10–16	15–21
Blackmail/Extortion	4–10	6–12	8–14	12–18	18–24
Gambling/Animal Fights	6–12	8–14	10–16	15–21	21–27
Intercept private communication	8–14	10–16	12–18	18–24	24–30
Obstruct election by fraud/deceit	10–16	12–18	15–21	21–27	27–33
Possession prison contraband	12–18	15–21	18–24	24–30	30–37
Fraud/forgery	15–21	18–24	21–27	27–33	33–41
Invol/Negligent manslaughter	18–24	21–27	24–30	30–37	37–46
Sale/transportation drug paraphernalia	21–27	24–30	27–33	33–41	41–51
5–10 kg Marijuana; 5–10 g Heroin/PCP; 50–100 mg LSD	24–30	27–33	30–37	37–46	46–57
Bribery Public Official; Perjury	27–33	30–37	33–41	41–51	51–63
50–100 g Cocaine; 10–20 g Heroin; 10–20 kg Marijuana	30–37	33–41	37–46	46–57	57–71
Robbery/Bank robbery	33–41	37–46	41–51	51–63	63–78
100–200 g Cocaine; 20–40 g Heroin; 20–40 kg Marijuana	37–46	41–51	46–57	57–71	70–87
Abusive Sexual Contact	41–51	46–57	51–63	63–78	77–96
Extortion	46–57	51–63	57–71	70–87	84–105
>200 g Cocaine; > 40 g Heroin; > 40 kg Marijuana	51–63	57–71	63–78	77–96	92–115
Mishandling Toxic Waste/Pollutants	57–71	63–78	70–87	84–105	100–125
Tampering Consumer Products	63–78	70–87	78–97	92–115	110–137
Arson	70–87	78–97	87–108	100–125	120–150
Smuggle/Transport Aliens	78–97	87–108	97–121	110–137	130–162
Unlawful Possess Firearms	87–108	97–121	108–135	121–151	140–175
Manufact Methamphet	97–121	108–135	121–151	135–168	151–188
Sexual Exploitation Minor	108–135	121–151	135–168	151–188	168–210
Kidnapping	121–151	135–168	151–188	168–210	188–235
Murder for Hire	135–168	151–188	168–210	188–235	210–262
Conspiracy Commit Murder	151–188	168–210	188–235	210–262	235–293
Gathering Top Secret Info	168–210	188–235	210–262	235–293	262–327

(Continues)

FIGURE 4.2 Criminal History Category (Points) *(Continued)*

Offense	I (0 or 1)	II (2 or 3)	III (4, 5, 6)	IV (7, 8, 9)	V (10, 11, 12)
Manufact Large Quantities of Drugs	188–235	210–262	235–293	262–327	292–365
Sexual Abuse	210–262	235–293	262–327	292–365	324–405
Human Traffick Minors/Pornography	235–293	262–327	292–365	324–405	360–life
Second Degree Murder	262–327	292–365	324–405	360–life	360–life
Poss/Distrib Nuclear/chemical weapons biological toxins	292–365	324–405	360–life	360–life	360–life
Treason	324–405	360–life	360–life	360–life	360–life
Manuf/Import/Drugs RICO	360–life	360–life	360–life	360–life	360–life
First Degree Murder	life	life	life	life	life

Source: U.S. Sentencing Commission. 2010. Federal Sentencing Guidelines Manual Chapter 5, Part A, p. 401. Available at: http://www.ussc.gov/Guidelines/2012_Guidelines/Manual_PDF/

The shading indicates the offenses (together with criminal history) that are eligible for probation and residential community corrections.

NORTH CAROLINA SENTENCING GUIDELINES How do you increase sentence lengths for only the most serious offenses without building new prisons? North Carolina has done so by incarcerating only the most serious offenders—so that violent prisoners must serve 100% of their time in prison without early release. Violent offenders must also serve an automatic nine-month post-release community supervision, whereas sex offenders serve five years of community supervision after prison. So far this sounds like what many states did, except that sentencing guidelines in many states did not authorize community options. The difference between North Carolina and other states can be seen in the former's sentencing grid, which allows more classes of crimes to be eligible for community-based corrections and builds that expectation right into the grid (see Figure 4.3). As a result, sentence lengths for violent offenders increased, but the percentage of sentenced offenders going to prison decreased. The state instead increased its use of pretrial release programs, work release, day-reporting centers, and community substance abuse treatment programs for drug and nonviolent offenders.

Sentence type is listed for each class of crimes. North Carolina's sentencing grid (see Figure 4.3) has three types of sentences: (1) jail or prison *(prison)*; (2) residential intermediate sanctions or intensive supervision such as boot camps and day reporting *(CC)*; and (3) nonresidential community options *(probation)*, which can include probation, community drug treatment, community service, restitution, and fines. Prior record points are calculated as follows: one point per Class 1 or A1 misdemeanor; two points per property or drug felony; four points for each voluntary or involuntary manslaughter; six points for kidnapping or robbery or second-degree murder; nine points for each rape; and ten points for each first-degree murder.

Within each class of crimes, you will also see an aggravating sentence, a presumptive sentence, and a mitigating sentence. A sentence may not deviate from a presumptive one except in a predefined list of aggravating and mitigating circumstances. For example, if there was a firearm used in a crime (an aggravating circumstance), 60 months are added to the minimum. If "substantial assistance" is rendered for helping a prosecutor arrest or

FIGURE 4.3 North Carolina Felony Sentencing Grid (numbers represent months)

OFFENSE CLASS / CURRENT FELONY CRIME CLASS		PRIOR RECORD LEVEL					
		I 0 Pts	II 1–4 Pts	III 5–8 Pts	IV 9–14 Pts	V 15–18 Pts	VI 19+ Points
Class A: Murder		Death or Life Without Parole ONLY					
Class B1: Agg Sexual Battery	Sentence Type Aggravating	Prison 240–300	Prison 288–360	Prison 336–420	Prison 384–480	Prison Life Without Parole	Prison Life without Parole
Agg Child Molestation Rape, Agg Sodomy	Presumptive Mitigating	192–240 144–192	230–288 173–230	269–336 202–269	307–384 230–307	346–433 260–346	384–480 288–384
Class B2: Second deg. Murder	Sentence Type Aggravating Presumptive Mitigating	Prison 135–169 108–135 81–108	Prison 163–204 130–163 98–130	Prison 193–238 152–190 114–152	Prison 216–270 173–216 130–173	Prison 243–304 194–243 146–194	Prison 270–338 216–270 162–216
Class C: Kidnapping Second deg. Rape Agg Assault	Sentence Type Aggravating Presumptive Mitigating	Prison 63–79 50–63 38–50	Prison 86–108 69–86 52–69	Prison 100–125 80–100 60–80	Prison 115–144 92–115 69–92	Prison 130–162 104–130 78–104	Prison 145–181 116–145 87–116
Class D: Armed Robbery Burglary First Degree Arson	Sentence Type Aggravating Presumptive Mitigating	Prison 55–69 44–55 33–44	Prison 66–82 53–66 40–53	Prison 89–111 71–89 53–71	Prison 101–126 81–101 61–81	Prison 115–144 92–115 69–92	Prison 126–158 101–126 76–101
Class E: Child Molestation Drug Trafficking Drug Manuf/Selling	Sentence Type Aggravating Presumptive Mitigating	CC or Prison 25–31 20–25 15–20	CC or Prison 29–36 23–29 17–23	Prison 34–42 27–34 20–27	Prison 46–58 37–46 28–37	Prison 53–66 42–53 32–42	Prison 59–74 47–59 35–47
Class F: Involun. Manslaughter Att Rape, Incest, Cocaine 200–400 g	Sentence Type Aggravating Presumptive Mitigating	CC or Prison 16–20 13–16 10–13	CC or Prison 19–24 15–19 11–15	Res CC or Prison 21–26 17–21 13–17	Prison 25–31 20–25 15–20	Prison 34–42 27–34 20–27	Prison 39–49 31–39 23–31
Class G: Second Degree Arson Robbery; Unlawful Carrying of a Weapon	Sentence Type Aggravating Presumptive Mitigating	CC or Prison 13–16 10–13 8–10	CC or Prison 15–19 12–15 9–12	CC or Prison 16–20 13–16 10–13	CC or Prison 20–25 16–20 12–16	Prison 21–26 17–21 13–17	Prison 29–36 23–29 17–23
Class H: Forgery, Theft Sale/Distribution LSD or Cocaine	Sentence Type Aggravating Presumptive Mitigating	Probation or CC 6–8 5–6 4–6	CC 8–10 6–8 4–6	CC or Prison 10–12 8–10 6–8	CC or Prison 11–14 9–11 7–9	CC or Prison 15–19 12–15 9–12	Prison 20–25 16–20 12–16
Class I: Poss Control. Sub Bad Checks Agg Stalking	Sentence Type Aggravating Presumptive Mitigating	Probation 6–8 4–6 3–4	Probation CC 6–8 4–6 3–4	CC 6–8 5–6 4–5	CC or Prison 8–10 6–8 4–6	CC or Prison 9–11 7–9 5–7	CC or Prison 10–12 8–10 6–8

Note: For each Crime class, a "sentence type" directs the judge to: "prison" (jail or prison); "CC" (any residential community correction program), or "probation" (which includes nonresidential and economic options). Then the judge selects the presumptive row, unless aggravating or mitigating circumstances warrant a deviation.

Sources: North Carolina Sentencing and Policy Advisory Commission, Structured Sentencing for Felonies—Training and Reference Manual. (Raleigh: North Source: North Carolina Sentencing and Policy Advisory Commission, 1994.)

prosecute other criminals, judges may reduce or even suspend a mandatory sentence for drug defendants (a mitigating situation). Only sentences may be appealed in which a deviation occurred based on an aggravating or mitigating circumstance, or if a prior record score was miscalculated. Other states that have used this same approach have been effective in differentiating the type of offenders sent to prison from those who serve time in the community. Any modifications of the grid must also show how such changes would impact the current number of prison beds or community resources.

Indeterminate Sentencing Example

Many states continue to use an indeterminate sentencing structure that provides for more judicial discretion on type of sentence (prison vs. community-based options). Such sentencing also allows for consideration of early release by a parole board after a minimum term has been met. In Figure 4.4, you will

FIGURE 4.4 Indeterminate Sentencing Example

OFFENSE CATEGORY	COMMUNITY SUPERVISION (CS) TERM	SANCTIONS AND ALTERNATIVES
FIRST DEGREE FELONY • 5 to 99 Years or Life • Up to $10,000 Fine	• Finding of Guilt 5–10 Years • Deferred Up to 10 Years	**CUSTODY SANCTIONS** • 1st, 2nd, & 3rd Degree Felonies; Up to 180 Days in Jail; Condition of CS • State Jail Felonies; Up to 90 Days in Jail; Condition of CS • 90–180 Days Up Front Condition • 90–365 Days Up Front Condition; Drug Delivery • 60–120 Days ID TDCJ 3g Offense Granted CS by a Jury
SECOND DEGREE FELONY • 2 to 20 Years Confinement • Up To $10,000 Fine	• Finding of Guilt 2–10 Years • Deferred Up to 10 Years	**REVOCATION CUSTODY ALTERNATIVES** • 1st, 2nd & 3rd Degree Felonies, Up to 180 Days in Jail; Condition of CS • Original and Alternative Sanctions Cannot Exceed 180 Days • State Jail Felonies; 90–180 Days in State Jail; Condition of CS
THIRD DEGREE FELONY • 2 to 10 Years Confinement • Up To $10,000 Fine	• Finding of Guilt 2–10 Years • Deferred Up to 10 Years	**ADDITIONAL FINE ALTERNATIVES** • State Jail, 1st, 2nd, & 3rd Degree Felonies • The Court on Finding of a Violation Can Increase the Fine up to the Statutory Maximum for the Offense
STATE JAIL FELONY • 180 Days to 2 Years Confinement • Up to $10,000 Fine • Convict as a SJ Felony, Punish as a Class A Misdemeanor • Reduce and Punish as a Class A Misdemeanor	• Finding of Guilt 2–5 Years • Deferred Up to 10 Years • Mandatory Community Supervision for Defendants with No Prior Felony Convictions for State Jail Offenses	**TERM EXTENSION ALTERNATIVES** • Up to 10 Years Total **SUBSTANCE ABUSE INTERVENTION/ RELAPSE ALTERNATIVES** • Treatment for Outpatient or Residential • Treatment for State Jail Controlled Substance Cases • Placement on a Specialized Caseload **ADDITIONAL COMMUNITY SERVICE ALTERNATIVES** • To Retire Unpaid Financial Obligations Alleged in a Motion to Revoke • To Sanction Technical Violations

(Continues)

FIGURE 4.4 Indeterminate Sentencing Example (*Continued*)

OFFENSE CATEGORY	COMMUNITY SUPERVISION (CS) TERM	SANCTIONS AND ALTERNATIVES
Class A Misdemeanor • Confinement in County Jail Not to Exceed 1 Year and/ or Fine Up to $4,000	Up to 2 Years	**CUSTODY SANCTIONS** • Up to 30 Days in Jail **REVOCATION CUSTODY ALTERNATIVES** • Up to 30 Days in Jail as a Condition of CS • Original and Subsequent Sanction Cannot Exceed 30 Days
Class B Misdemeanor • Confinement in County Jail Not to Exceed 180 Days and/or Fine Up to $2,000	Up to 2 Years	**ADDITIONAL FINE ALTERNATIVES** • Up to the Statutory Maximum for the Offense **EXTENSION ALTERNATIVES** • Up to 3 Years If/When Extension is Added to Original CS Term • If Fine, Court Costs and Restitution are Unpaid an Additional 2 Years Can Be Imposed for a Total of 5 Years CS from Date of Imposition of CS
Class C Misdemeanor • No Jail Confinement; Fine Up to $500	Not Subject to Community Supervision	**SUBSTANCE ABUSE INTERVENTION/ RELAPSE ALTERNATIVES** • Amend Conditions of CS Consistent with Options for Treatment Referrals for Outpatient or Residential • Placement Specialized Caseload **ADDITIONAL COMMUNITY SERVICE** • To Retire Unpaid Financial Obligations Alleged in a Motion to Revoke • To Sanction Technical Violations;

COMMENTS: No Deferred Adjudication for DUI, Intoxication Manslaughter, Indecency with a Child, Sexual Assault, Agg. Sexual Assault; No community supervision for Murder, Capital Murder, Indecency w/a Child, Agg Kidnapping, Agg Sexual Assault, Agg Robbery, Sexual Assault

Source: TDCJ Community Justice Assistance Division. 2003. *Texas Intermediate Sanctions Bench Manual.* Austin, Texas. Available at: http://www.tdcj .state.tx.us/cjad

see the punishments determined for each category of crimes listed in the very first column. The first column begins with misdemeanors and then graduates to felony crimes, ending with capital felonies at the bottom. In each instance, there is a sentence length and a fine listed, but judges are not limited to incarceration only—community options are available in most every crime class except for offenders who have repeated a felony and in death penalty or capital crime cases.

THE PRESENTENCE INVESTIGATION (PSI) REPORT

presentence investigation (PSI) report
A report submitted to a court before sentencing describing the nature of an offense, offender characteristics, criminal history, loss to victim, and sentencing recommendations.

Prior to a judicial sentencing decision, many probation departments provide a judge with a **presentence investigation (PSI) report**. The PSI is a document prepared by a probation officer to aid judges in a felony sentencing decision or in a case of offenders who have violated probation and are facing a potential incarceration sentence. The PSI is also used by prosecutors, defense attorneys, parole boards, and probation or parole officers in carrying out tasks and making decisions. Although U.S. probation officers are involved in both case supervision and in conducting a small number of PSIs per month, most state and local probation agencies separate investigative from supervisory duties. One way that this is done is by designating some probation officers only to conduct PSIs and write PSIs and other officers to supervise cases.

Purposes of the PSI Report

The primary purpose of a PSI report is for a probation officer to provide a judge with timely, relevant, and accurate information to make a rational sentencing decision. Probation officers are not seeking to change a judge's mind—they are merely attempting to summarize a case and to provide supporting evidence.

The PSI describes the nature of an offense, offender characteristics, criminal history, loss to a victim, and sentencing recommendations. In juvenile court, a judge is furnished with a social history, or predispositional report, prior to a disposition hearing. Presentence reports are seldom used in sentencing for misdemeanor crimes. The PSI has been used for felony sentencing since the early 1900s and was declared by the U.S. Supreme Court to be a valid instrument in 1949 (*Williams v. New York*). Other than for sentencing recommendations, the PSI report has other uses:

- It assists jails and prisons in suggesting types of institutional programming that would fit an offender's needs while incarcerated.
- Paroling authorities can compare a defendant's version of an offense at the time of arrest to that determined by a parole board hearing.
- It assists in making community supervision caseload assignments.
- It serves a basis for writing a client treatment or program plan.

About 64% of all felony cases nationwide included a PSI prior to sentencing. About half of all states require a PSI in all felony cases, whereas a PSI is discretionary in 16 states and nonexistent in about 10 states. In the federal system, PSIs have increased in significance because federal probation officers are considered experts on federal sentencing guidelines. In one year alone in the federal system, federal probation officers wrote 65,156 presentence and post-sentence reports and completed 52,047 collateral PSIs and an additional 27,117 prerelease investigations of military defendants (U.S. Department of Justice, 2005).

A **post-sentence report** may be written after a defendant has pleaded guilty and waived a presentence report, when a court proceeds directly to sentencing. In such cases, the post-sentence report serves to aid a probation or parole officer in supervision efforts during probation, parole, or release and to assist a prison system in classification, programming, and release planning.

post-sentence report
After a defendant has pleaded guilty and been sentenced, a report written by a probation officer in order to aid probation and parole officers in supervision, classification, and program plans.

With the introduction of sentencing guidelines, sentencing has become less discretionary, with the result that the importance of the PSI has declined in some states. For example, in 10 states in which sentencing guidelines are used, probation officers no longer write presentence reports. Instead, they complete a guidelines worksheet and calculate a presumptive sentence.

Contents of the PSI Report

For jurisdictions that conduct a PSI, probation officers are guided in their **presentence investigation** to understand the causes of an offender's antisocial behavior and to clinically evaluate his or her potential for change. By learning about the character of the person under consideration and the external influences that surrounded him or her, an offender-based PSI suggests alternatives for sentencing beyond incarceration that are specific to that offender. The sentencing court is also concerned with an offender's culpability in an offense, whether anyone was injured, whether a firearm was used, the extent of loss to the victim(s), and other aspects of an offense. Secondary information about an offender is considered relevant, such as prior criminal record, employment history, family ties, health, and drug use. Instruction on how to conduct and write a presentence report for a client is provided in Case Study 3 at the end of this chapter.

presentence investigation
An investigation undertaken by a probation officer for the purpose of gathering and analyzing information to complete a report for a court.

In jurisdictions in which a court uses sentencing guidelines to determine appropriate sentences, the emphasis of a PSI is on applying particular guidelines to the facts of a case. This means that all presentence reports should be factually accurate, objective, nonjudgmental, and ideally verified by a presentence officer. The report's length and content should be appropriate to the seriousness of an offense. The greater the consequences of a judgment, the more likely a court or a subsequent decision-making body will need more information.

Probation officers have often noted that judges only skimmed their lengthy reports and skipped to the end where a sentence was recommended. In response to this reality, some jurisdictions have moved to shortened versions of the PSI that focus only on certain relevant variables. In some cases, such brief versions of a PSI are presented to a court in a fill-in-the-blanks format. This practice places a duty on a probation officer to present the most critical information in a concise yet complete manner. Other reports are open-ended and in paragraph format, analogous to an essay.

Federal and some state presentence reports also require a **victim impact statement**. The use of victim impact statements stems from a renewed interest in victims' rights and in mitigating the harm an offender has caused. A victim impact statement such as the one provided in Box 4.2, identifies the relationship (if any) between the victim and offender and specifies the emotional and psychological toll that the offense has taken on the victim and the victim's family. For violent offenses, the judge is informed about any physical injury the victim may have suffered, whether the victim sought medical attention, whether he or she endured physical rehabilitation, and the permanency of the injuries. A breakdown of the victim's financial costs not covered by a victim compensation fund is also provided. At times, victims may even state their wishes as to what they think should be done with the offender. While many victims may wish to exact some sort of revenge, what should happen if and when a victim requests leniency for the offender?

victim impact statement
A written account by a victim as to how a crime has taken a toll physically, emotionally, financially, and/or psychologically on said victim and victim's family. Victim impact statements are considered by many states at the time of sentencing and at parole-board hearings.

| BOX 4.2 | A SAMPLE VICTIM IMPACT STATEMENT |

A male defendant, age 34, was charged with Assault First Degree, two counts of Assault Second Degree, Armed Criminal Action, Kidnapping, two counts of Burglary, and Felonious Restraint. The male defendant followed the female victim when she moved from South Carolina to Missouri. They had two boys together, now ages 8 and 10. Based on the defendant's previous arrests for domestic violence in South Carolina, the victim obtained a full order of protection upon arriving in Missouri, with the court giving her full custody of their children and prohibiting defendant from having any contact with her. She chose not to list her residence because she was attempting to keep that information confidential. She did allow for defendant to call their sons on weekends; however, she indicated that he never called to speak to their children.

On Valentine's Day, defendant broke into victim's apartment, ripped out the lining of her couch, and hid inside of it. Upon her arrival home with their sons, he woke up (he had fallen asleep waiting for her). When she sat on the couch, he popped out of it and began to assault her. She was beaten severely around her face, arms, and stomach area. The entire assault was in front of their two sons. Finally, she was able to get to a gun, which she kept loaded in her bedroom closet. He managed to rip the gun from her hands, and he shot her point blank in the forehead. The victim survived the attack and attempted murder.

She gave the following victim impact statement at the sentencing hearing:

> In front of our boys, you tried to kill their mother. It has always been about you. I had to move six states away from you, to another time zone, and it wasn't far enough. You have cost me two jobs and a lifetime of self-esteem. The bullet is lodged in my forehead. Would you like to feel it? You put it there. I know that it wasn't smart of me to have a loaded gun in my house with two young children. Does everyone see now what choice I had? I didn't have any choices. You made all of my decisions for me. I told you that I wanted to live near my family again someday. I did not take the children away from you, and I did not move for any man. Although, that is what you want to believe. Even though I have $100,000 dollars in medical expenses to pay, the State was only able to cover $15,000, I would rather be stuck with that debt, than stuck with you. Tell me again that you will pay for my hospital bills as long as I don't testify against you. Well, you always said that you wanted to live in Missouri, congratulations, now you have your chance.

Question for discussion: How much weight should the victim impact statement have on the PSI?

Source: State of Missouri v. Anthony Williams CR2000-00704.

Preparing the PSI Report

Preparing the PSI report requires many important skills, including interviewing, investigating, and writing. A probation officer's responsibility is to gather the facts about the offense and the offender, verify the information received, and present it in an organized and objective format.

Preferred practice is to conduct a PSI and prepare a presentence report after adjudication of guilt but before a sentencing hearing. A PSI should not be undertaken until after a finding of guilt because none of the material in a presentence report is admissible at trial or during plea negotiation, and an investigation represents an invasion of privacy. Exceptions to this rule are allowed when a defendant's attorney consents to preparation of a report before conviction and plea. When this happens, it is called a *pre-plea report*. Attorneys are generally not open to receiving a pre-plea or pre-arraignment document instead of a regular PSI (Alarid & Montemayor, 2010a).

A Probation Officer Interviews an Offender to Prepare a PSI Before the Sentencing Hearing

Denise Hager/Catchlight Visual Services / Alamy

PSI Interview and Verification

The first task in preparing any type of PSI report is to interview a newly convicted offender regarding his or her criminal history, education, employment, physical and emotional health, family, and other relevant data. An officer also uses this time to develop an initial sense of the offender's character, personality, needs, and problems. This meeting usually occurs in the probation officer's office or, if the defendant has not been released on bail, in jail. In some cases the initial interview takes place at the defendant's home, which provides the officer an opportunity to observe the offender's home environment and thus offers an additional dimension to his or her understanding of the defendant. The officer interviews the defendant's family and friends, the arresting police officer, the victim and/or victim's family, and the defendant's present employer or school officials, all of whom are known as **collateral contacts**.

Following the initial interview, the probation officer verifies as much of the information as possible through criminal justice agencies, employers, credit reporting services, medical doctors, and schools. Documents such as arrest reports, plea agreements, previous probation/parole records, and even treatment records are used. Many of these records are protected by state and federal privacy laws and obtaining them may require the defendant's written permission for release.

The probation officer is interested in information that might influence the sentencing decision but that is omitted during the trial, particularly any aggravating or mitigating circumstances. When obtaining information from any source—particularly from relatives, friends, acquaintances, and employers—the probation officer must be careful to distinguish facts from conclusions. As a general rule, the report should contain only information the probation officer knows to be accurate. In some cases, information may be presented that the officer has been unable to verify. When this happens, the officer should clearly denote the information as "unconfirmed" or "unverified."

collateral contacts
Verification of a probationer or parolee's situation and whereabouts by means of an officer's speaking with a third party who knows the offender personally (such as a family member, friend, or employer).

In writing the evaluative summary, probation officers must use their analytical ability, diagnostic skills, and understanding of human behavior. They must bring into focus the kind of person that is before the court, the basic factors that landed the person in trouble, and the special assistance the defendant needs for resolving those difficulties. Part of the evaluative summary should discuss the defendant's probability of risk to the community, the amount of harm the defendant caused the victim and/or community, the defendant's ability to pay restitution and court fines, and the defendant's need for treatment.

The Sentence Recommendation

A probation officer's recommended sentence to a judge largely depends on the sentencing guideline system or statutory equivalent. It is important to note that officers recommend a sentence type but not a sentence length. Probation officers were consistent in their sentence recommendations in about 70% of cases that advocated for intermediate sanctions. However, probation officers more often recommended intermediate sanctions to impose a harsher sentence than probation than as an alternative to prison, a practice that suggests "net widening" (Homant & DeMercurio, 2009). The researchers buttressed this evidence by finding that, in cases in which intermediate sanctions were recommended first, if a judge did not agree with this course, then an officer would recommend probation as a second choice. If intermediate sanctions were truly an alternative to prison, then prison would have been the second choice after probation.

An appropriate use of sentencing guidelines reduced sentencing disparity such that prior criminal record and offense severity were the most important predictors of sentencing outcomes, but attorneys and the judge collectively affected the sentence a defendant received (Haynes, Ruback, & Cusick, 2010). Alarid and Montemayor (2010a) found that legal factors such as a defendant's criminal history, previous times on probation and parole, pending cases, and police version of an offense were more important to attorneys than extra-legal factors. Important extra-legal factors for both prosecutors and defense attorneys included social support system, mental health issues, and substance abuses. Although legal factors can be used to control sentencing disparity, practitioners also found that extra-legal factors were valuable aids in identifying treatment intervention services.

Legal Issues Concerning the PSI Report

Various legal concerns about the PSI have been raised on appeal in the courts and are each briefly addressed.

disclosure
The right of a defendant to read and refute information in a presentence investigation report prior to sentencing.

DOES A DEFENDANT HAVE THE RIGHT TO DISCLOSURE OF THE PSI?   **Disclosure** is an opportunity for a defendant (and/or a defendant's attorney) to view a draft of the presentence report. The U.S. Supreme Court held that there is no denial of due process when a court does not disclose a PSI's contents to a defendant or give a defendant an opportunity to rebut them (*Williams v. New York*, 1949; *Williams v. Oklahoma*, 1959). A defendant may have such a right, however, if disclosure is required by state law. Despite the Supreme Court ruling, federal defendants are provided an opportunity to view a PSI draft at least 35 days prior to sentencing, and then are given 14 days to refute any statements prior to final report submission to federal court. A PSI is not, however, a public document, so disclosure is limited to the defendant, the defendant's attorney, and the prosecutor. To safe-guard information that victims and witnesses provide that they fear might be used by an offender to retaliate, the federal system requires withholding various parts of a PSI from a defendant when:

- disclosure might disrupt rehabilitation of that defendant (such as psychiatric reports addressing future dangerousness);
- information was obtained on a promise of confidentiality; and
- harm might result to that defendant or to any other person from such disclosure.

In sum, federal rules represent an intermediate position between complete disclosure and complete secrecy.

ARE INACCURACIES IN A PSI REPORT LEGAL GROUNDS FOR RESENTENCING?   Disclosure policies attempt to minimize errors in the final PSI submitted to a court. Two federal circuit courts ruled that detected inaccuracies in a PSI are not grounds for automatic revocation of the sentence imposed (*United States v. Lockhart*, 1995; *United States v. Riviera*, 1996), provided only **harmless error** exists—meaning the error would not have affected the sentencing outcome. If the inaccuracies would have changed a sentencing outcome, a defendant has the burden of establishing that an error was harmful. The remedy entails vacating an original sentence and remanding a harmful error case to a trial court to prepare a new PSI report prior to resentencing.

harmless error
One or more types of error made in the pretrial and/or trial process that does not change the outcome of a case.

WHAT ABOUT OTHER RULES OF CRIMINAL PROCEDURE?   Once a defendant has pled guilty or been convicted, it is important that a judge be given every opportunity to obtain relevant information during sentencing without rigid adherence to rules of evidence. Thus, different types of information that are not allowed in a trial proceeding are allowed in a PSI. This includes evidence obtained or seized illegally by police and **hearsay**. In addition, during a PSI interview, defendants do not have the same rights that they otherwise would when they are presumed to be innocent, such as the right to have an attorney present or being given their *Miranda* warnings prior to the interview. A defendant generally does not possess a Sixth Amendment right to have an attorney present during a PSI interview, according to the Tenth Circuit Court (*United States v. Gordon*, 1993; *United States v. Washington*, 1993). The rationale is that guilt has already been determined; hence, an adversarial situation that requires the assistance of a lawyer is absent. However, a Massachusetts court disagreed, saying that a defendant has a right to counsel at a presentence interview because this interview has "due process implications with respect to a defendant's interest in a fair and even-handed sentence proceeding" (*Commonwealth of Massachusetts v. Talbot*, 2005).

hearsay
Information offered as a truthful assertion that does not come from personal knowledge but rather from a third party.

COMMUNITY CORRECTION CONDITIONS

Authority to impose conditions of a community corrections sentence is vested with the courts. Although conditions may be recommended by a presentence investigator or probation officer, only a judge has final say regarding what an offender is obligated to do. In general, there are two types of conditions: standard and special.

BOX 4.3   STANDARD CONDITIONS OF SUPERVISION

The defendant must report to the probation office within 48 hours. The defendant/probationer shall:

1. not commit another Federal, State, or local crime;
2. not unlawfully possess a controlled substance, refrain from any unlawful use of a controlled substance and submit to drug tests as determined by the court or probation officer;
3. pay restitution and/or a fine if imposed by the court;
4. submit to the collection of a DNA sample as directed;
5. work conscientiously at suitable employment or pursue conscientiously a course of study or vocational training that will equip defendant for suitable employment;
6. refrain from associating with any person engaged in criminal activity and/or convicted of a felony offense unless granted permission in advance by the probation officer;
7. refrain from excessive use of alcohol, or any use of a narcotic drug or other controlled substance without a prescription by a licensed medical practitioner; shall not frequent places where controlled substances are being sold or used;
8. refrain from possessing a firearm or other dangerous weapon if the conviction is for a felony or if a firearm or other weapon was used in the course of the current offense;
9. undergo alcohol/substance abuse treatment if the court has reason to believe the defendant is in need of such treatment;
10. undergo psychiatric or psychological treatment if the court has reason to believe

the defendant is in need of mental health treatment;

11. remain within the specified geographic area, unless granted permission to leave by the court or a probation officer;
12. report to a probation officer as directed by the court or the probation officer;
13. permit a probation officer to visit him at his home or elsewhere and shall permit confiscation of any contraband observed in plain view by the probation officer;
14. answer truthfully all inquiries by a probation officer;
15. notify the probation officer at least 10 days prior to any change in residence or employment;
16. notify the probation officer with 72 hours if arrested or if questioned by a law enforcement officer;
17. comply with the terms of any court order requiring child support payments by the defendant for the support and maintenance of one or more children and the parent with whom the child is living;
18. provide the probation officer with any requested financial information; obtain permission before opening new lines of credit;
19. shall not enter into any agreement to act as an informer without advance permission of the court.

Adapted from: U.S. Sentencing Commission. 2010. *Federal Sentencing Guidelines Manual,* Chapter 5, Part A, p. 401. Available at: http://www.ussc.gov/Guidelines/2010_guidelines/Manual_HTML/Chapter_5.htm

standard conditions
Probation or parole conditions imposed on all offenders regardless of the offense.

special conditions
Probation or parole conditions tailored to fit the offense and/or needs of an offender.

Standard Conditions

Standard conditions are imposed on all community sentences in a jurisdiction, regardless of the offense committed. Standard conditions (also called mandatory conditions) are either prescribed by law or set by court or agency practice.

Box 4.3 shows examples of **standard conditions** of federal and state probation.

Special Conditions

Special conditions are additional stipulations tailored to fit the problems and needs of an offender. Most special conditions are related to the offense of conviction, but they should be related to the offender's overall rehabilitation so they can include problems during previous offenses as well. As such, a judge imposes them consistent with the crime committed or the offender's deficits in skill or ability. For example, a defendant may be required to:

- attend literacy classes if he or she does not know how to read or write;
- obtain a GED if he or she did not finish high school;
- participate in drug or alcohol treatment if he or she is addicted;
- attend parenting classes if there are issues with dependent children;
- pay victim restitution if damage was caused;
- refrain from entering designated areas if the offense involves crimes against children; and
- seek mental health treatment if he or she suffers from mental dysfunction.

LIMITATIONS OF SPECIAL CONDITIONS   Special conditions of community supervision should be clearly stated without ambiguity, be reasonable so that a probationer can comply, and must either protect society or rehabilitate an offender. The definition of "clearly stated" and "reasonable" and relationship to offense of conviction depends on an offender's circumstances and is decided on a case-by-case basis. For example, requiring an employed offender with a good salary to pay $500 each month in restitution may be reasonable, but the same condition would be unreasonable if imposed on an indigent probationer with a sixth-grade education. Another example is that a probationer cannot be ordered to attend sex offender treatment for a nonsexual offense (*State v. Bourrie*, 2003). In an interesting twist, a probationer who has never had a drinking problem and whose crime is unrelated to use of alcohol can still be ordered to refrain from the use of alcohol. The Federal Court of Appeals held that a trial court could require that a defendant totally abstain from using alcohol during probation because in this case the defendant's *family* living at the same residence had an active history of alcohol abuse and the defendant had a serious problem with illegal drugs (*United States v. Thurlow*, 1995).

scarlet letter conditions
A condition of community supervision that attempts to invoke shame in an offender by requiring him or her to publicly proclaim guilt.

   Scarlet letter conditions of community supervision attempt to invoke shame in an offender by requiring him or her to publicly proclaim guilt. For shaming to have maximum effectiveness, the offender must belong to a community and/or group in which public knowledge of a crime would temporarily compromise the offender's social standing. The punishment must be communicated to the offender's group or larger community, which must temporarily withdraw or shun him or her. The most important aspect of shaming, is there must be some way that the offender can regain social status in his or her community.

   Shaming punishments have been challenged in the courts. Jurisdictions that have upheld scarlet letter or shaming conditions have done so on deterrence grounds. While at least one court held that shaming conditions do not violate the Eighth Amendment prohibition against cruel and unusual punishment, state courts are in disagreement as to whether scarlet letter conditions serve a legitimate purpose for probation, citing that they are not reasonably related to a defendant's rehabilitation which is in violation of many state constitutions (see Box 4.4).

| BOX 4.4 | **COMMUNITY CORRECTIONS UP CLOSE** |

Is Public Shaming Reasonable or Unconstitutional?

A married couple in Houston was convicted of felony theft in 2010. But they didn't target just anyone. Eloise Mireles and her husband Daniel stole $250,000 from the crime victims fund in the course of Mrs. Mireles employment. Both were sentenced to perform community service and to post a sign outside their home that read: "The occupants of this residence, Daniel and Eloise Mireles, are convicted thieves." In addition, every weekend for the next six years, Daniel must walk in front of an upscale mall holding a similar sign describing what they did (Roth, 2010). See video of this at: http://www.youtube.com/watch?v=c1_DaXpETa8

In Illinois, a trial court ordered a probationer to erect at his home a 4 × 8 sign with 8 high lettering that read "Warning! A Violent Felon Lives Here. Enter at Your Own Risk!" Upon appeal, the Illinois Supreme Court found the purpose of this sign was to inflict humiliation on the probationer (*People v. Meyer*, 1997). The court further noted that the statutory provisions for probation in Illinois did not include humiliation as a punishment. Thus, the court disallowed this condi-

tion. These situations leave open the question to the U.S. Supreme Court as to whether a state legislature can amend its laws and authorize a trial court to impose a scarlet letter condition.

The practice of shaming or scarlet-letter sanctions is meant to *briefly* stigmatize offenders publicly so that punishment affects an offender's dignity. Other examples of shaming sentences that have been used include public apologies, obligating offenders to place a bumper sticker on their car or a sign on their front yard acknowledging what they did. In an analysis of the constitutionality of scarlet-letter sanctions, their duration should be short and should not endanger an offender's safety in any way. Currently, no empirical evidence exists on the effectiveness of shaming punishments.

Sources: People v. Meyer, 176 Ill. 2d 372, 680 N.E. 315 (1997); Roth, Tanya (2010). Thief sentenced to hold shaming sign for 6 years. Available at: http://blogs.findlaw.com/legally_weird/2010/10/thief-sentenced-to-hold-shaming-sign-for-6-years.html

SUMMARY

- Pretrial services consist of pretrial release from jail and pretrial supervision of defendants as a condition of their release.

- After controlling for offense severity and criminal history score, defendants who were detained during the pretrial process were more likely to be sentenced to prison, and have longer sentence lengths when compared to federal defendants who were granted release—making pretrial detention a significant disadvantage for the defendant.

- Pretrial supervision and bonds ensure that a defendant appears in court and the defendant refrains from further deviance and criminal activity while the case is being processed in court.

- Granting a community sentence to an individual offender depends primarily on severity of current offense and prior criminal history in a determinate sentencing structure.

- Indeterminate sentencing can also consider individual circumstances of the offender, level of remorse, the risk the offender poses, and the interest to the victim and society.

- The use of sentencing guidelines has reduced some sentencing inequality, but at the expense of reducing judicial discretion.

- The PSI report is a document written by a probation officer to aid a judge in an indeterminate sentence—to expose individual factors that will mitigate for or against successful community supervision.

- A PSI is also later used in community supervision and/or the parole board release decisions.

- Legal issues in a PSI include: an offender has an opportunity to refute information contained in the PSI, hearsay evidence is allowed, and the presentence interview does not require Miranda warnings or the presence of an attorney.

- Community supervision conditions are both standard (imposed on all probationers) and special conditions (tailored to fit an offender and offense).
- Scarlet letter or public shaming is controversial because they are not reasonably related to a defendant's rehabilitation, which violates many state constitutions.
- Jurisdictions that have upheld shaming say it can deter and does not violate the Eighth Amendment of the U.S. Constitution.

DISCUSSION QUESTIONS

1. What kinds of individuals do you think are best suited for pretrial release?

2. What rate of FTA is acceptable to you? How can FTAs be further reduced?

3. How can bail be made more affordable for indigent offenders who cannot afford to bond out of jail?

4. What should be the purpose of sentencing for first-time felony offenders? What about for repeat offenders?

5. Is it more important that sentences be consistent for all offenders of a similar class of crimes or that sentences be adapted to the characteristics and needs of each offender?

6. Argue for or against the proposition that probation conditions should be left solely to the discretion of judges and should not be prescribed by law.

7. What are the limitations on the power of courts to impose conditions? Why are these limitations important?

8. Given the time and effort it takes to complete a PSI interview and report, is the effort worth it? Why or why not?

9. How have sentencing guidelines affected the content of a PSI report?

10. What is the purpose of a victim impact statement in a PSI report? What factors have brought about the use of this statement?

11. What factor(s) might explain why probation officers' recommendations are so highly correlated with actual sentences imposed by judges?

 ## WEBSITES, VIDEOS, AND PODCASTS

Websites

San Francisco Pretrial Diversion Project, Inc.
http://www.sfpretrial.com/community.html

Louisiana (Baton Rouge) Parish Attorney Pretrial Diversion Division
http://brgov.com/dept/parishattorney/pretrial.htm

Families Against Mandatory Minimums
http://www.famm.org

U.S. Sentencing Commission
http://www.ussc.gov

Kansas Guidelines for the Presentence Investigation Report
http://kansasstatutes.lesterama.org/Chapter_21/Article_47/21-4714.html

Colorado Attorney Advice for Offenders Regarding the PSI
http://www.hmichaelsteinberg.com/thepresentencereport.htm

Conditions of Probation in Alaska
http://touchngo.com/lglcntr/akstats/Statutes/Title12/Chapter55/Section100.htm

Intensive Probation Conditions in Arizona
http://www.superiorcourt.maricopa.gov/AdultProbation/AdultProbationInformation/Supervision/IntensiveProbationSupervision.asp

Terms and Conditions of Probation in Indiana
http://www.in-map.net/counties/BENTON/probation/terms.html

Videos/Podcasts

What is the criminal sentencing process?
(Length: 1 minute) Talks about what the sentencing process looks like and gives the punishment options. https://www.youtube.com/watch?v=2_6upP-kM9E

What is a pre-sentence investigation report for?
(Length: 1:45 minutes) An Odessa Criminal Defense Attorney gives an overview of what the pre-sentence investigation process is like. https://www.youtube.com/watch?v=ncbHoFiLuYY

Presentencing in Ohio
This video is a brief explanation of how presentencing is used in Ohio. http://www.youtube.com/watch?v=O6yVkj9gf2g

Presentence investigation report discussed by DWI lawyer
In this video a lawyer discusses what PSI is and why it is important in court. http://www.youtube.com/watch?v=8-vSySwLJLs

Special Needs Offenders: Women Offenders and Their Children: **United States v. Jones.**
Federal Judicial Center presents a panel discussion of PSI issues related to the case of United States v. Jones. http://www.youtube.com/watch?v=yXZkfH8ypbU

Special Needs Offenders: Women Offenders and Their Children: **United States v. Thomas.**
The Federal Judicial Center presents a panel discussion of PSI issues related to United States v. Thomas. http://www.youtube.com/watch?v=UDkBd1O3fuw&feature=relmfu

CASE STUDY EXERCISE NO. 1

The Sentencing Decision

The following two cases assume that a judge has granted probation. Discuss which probation conditions would be appropriate and an appropriate length for the term of probation supervision.

CASE A

Defendant Green devised a scheme to pass fictitious payroll checks. He recruited other individuals to pass the fictitious checks in exchange for money. Mr. Green opened a bank account using a fictitious check he had produced. He then produced additional fictitious payroll checks using the bank's logo, routing number, and account number. He recruited individuals from homeless shelters who had valid identification. Upon receiving checks from Mr. Green, the individuals went to area stores to pass the fictitious payroll checks. Mr. Green gave a portion of the money to the individual passing the check and kept the remainder. When his residence was searched subsequent to his arrest for the offense, an electronic typewriter, 29 payroll checks matching those previously passed, a computer, marijuana, and drug paraphernalia were confiscated. Upon further examination of the computer, evidence of payroll check counterfeiting was discovered on it. Nine retail stores were victimized in the offense because they had cashed the payroll checks. A total loss of $14,503 was determined through documentation and investigation.

Mr. Green's prior criminal history includes a conviction for misdemeanor possession of marijuana and disorderly conduct. He was raised in a two-parent home. Neither of his parents has a criminal record, and it appears they provided their son with appropriate structure and discipline. Mr. Green revealed that he has used marijuana for the past 12 years. He is currently 28 years of age. He has a high school diploma and a sporadic work history. His personal finances reveal his only asset to be an automobile valued at $4,500. He has four credit card accounts. Two of the accounts are current with combined balances of $670. The other two accounts are in collection status and their balances total $6,210. The defendant is eligible for not less than one nor more than five years probation by statute.

CASE B

Police officers stopped Defendant Tuff after they observed his vehicle stopping and starting at an accelerated speed. They subsequently arrested him on several charges.

Police observed Mr. Tuff's vehicle accelerate at an unsafe speed after stopping at a yield sign. Mr. Tuff's vehicle had come to a stop at the yield sign, although there was no traffic requiring a stop. Police stopped Mr. Tuff. They smelled alcohol on Mr. Tuff, and a breath test showed he had a blood alcohol content of 0.16 (twice the legal limit of 0.08). Mr. Tuff was arrested. Found on his person were a 0.38 caliber handgun and a small amount of marijuana. An open container of beer was inside the vehicle. Police reports reveal Mr. Tuff became angry and violent during the arrest. He had to be placed in restraints.

Mr. Tuff was convicted of driving under the influence (DUI), Transporting an Open Container, and Carrying a Concealed Weapon. All were misdemeanor charges. Mr. Tuff has a prior arrest for Disorderly Conduct. The prior offense involved police responding to a disturbance at which shots had been fired. Upon arrival, officers saw the defendant throw a pistol up onto a roof. He was chased and appeared to be intoxicated when apprehended. Mr. Tuff told officers he had called police because someone had shot at his home. Mr. Tuff was irate, shouting profanities and screaming that he was going to kill someone. When attempts to calm him were unsuccessful, Mr. Tuff was taken into custody and charged with Disorderly Conduct.

Defendant Tuff is 21 years of age. His parents were divorced when he was born. At the age of six, he began living with his maternal grandparents because his mother worked nights at a tavern. Mr. Tuff reports going to a Job Corps when he was 16 years old. He was terminated early from the two-year program with the Job Corps after assaulting a security guard for not being allowed a pass into town. Mr. Tuff has been employed as a laborer for three different firms. The longest term of employment in any of the positions was eight months. He was terminated from two of the positions due to absenteeism. He states he resigned from the third job due to personal problems with his spouse and a dispute with his employer over pay. Mr. Tuff completed one year of high school before the Job Corps. He completed his GED as a condition of a previous term of probation.

Mr. Tuff states he was referred for anger management classes when in junior high school. He acknowledged he has had prior thoughts of suicide and on one occasion played Russian roulette. On another occasion he tried to shoot himself in the head and pulled the trigger; however, a friend pulled the gun away, causing the bullet to miss him. He states he was "depressed with life" at the time. He explains he does not currently feel a desire to commit suicide and does not desire counseling. Mr. Tuff began using marijuana when he was in high school. He has also reported use of crack cocaine and methamphetamine. A urine specimen submitted by him during the presentence phase revealed the use of marijuana.

The defendant was married two years ago. He has a daughter. The marriage lasted only a short period of time, and Mr. Tuff states the couple has been separated for more than a year. He does not have contact with his wife or child and is court-ordered to pay $250 monthly in child support. His personal finances reveal his only reported asset to be a pickup he estimates as valued at $8,000. His only outstanding debt is $3,600 in child support owed to the county in which his daughter resides. The defendant is eligible for not more than five years probation by statute.

CASE STUDY EXERCISE NO. 2

Sample Federal Presentence Investigation Report

Below you will find an example of a federal PSI report in which all names and places are fictitious. After reading the report, you may wish to discuss the case in class or use the information below to construct your own electronic PSIR in a fillable PDF file. See: http://www.txnp.uscourts.gov/sites/default/files/files/txnproform1a.pdf

IN THE UNITED STATES DISTRICT COURT FOR THE WESTERN DISTRICT OF ATLANTIS,
United States vs. Frank Jones

Docket No. CR 14-002-01-KGG

Prepared for:	The Honorable Kelly G. Green, U.S. District Judge
Prepared by:	Craig T. Doe, U.S. Probation Officer

	Breaker Bay, Atlantis (123) 111-1111
Assistant U.S. Attorney	Mrs. Sharon Duncan
Defense Counsel	Mr. Arthur Goodfellow
Sentence date:	June 5, 2014
Offense:	Tax Evasion (26 U.S.C. § 7201)
Release status:	$50,000 personal recognizance bond with pretrial supervision (no pretrial custody)
Related cases:	Nancy Oscar CR 14-002-25; Vincent St. James CR 14-005-48
Date report prepared:	5/15/14
Date revised:	5/25/14

Identifying Data:

Date of birth:	3/19/81
Race:	Caucasian
Sex:	Male
S. S. #:	222-22-2222
FBI #:	2BR22-32B14CX
Education:	B.S., Marketing

Dependents:	two
Citizenship:	United States
Legal address:	1430 Bird Avenue, Breaker Bay, AT 10101
Aliases:	None
Tattoos:	None
Gang affiliation:	None known

PART A. THE OFFENSE

Charge(s) and Conviction(s)

1. Frank Jones was named in a three-count indictment filed by a Western District of Atlantis grand jury on November 1, 2013. Counts one through three charge that the defendant attempted to evade income tax due and owed by him and his wife for calendar years 2010, 2011, and 2012, in violation of 26 U.S.C. § 7201. On November 15, 2013, superseding information was filed by the United States Attorney's Office in the Western District of Atlantis. The information charges that on October 15, 2012, Mr. Jones evaded income tax due and owed by him and his wife for the calendar year 2012 by writing a check to the American Medisearch Organization in the amount of $20,000, for which he received 90% back in cash, and by filing a false tax return in which he deducted as a charitable contribution the entire amount of $20,000, in violation of 26 U.S.C. § 7201.

2. On November 21, 2013, Mr. Jones was released on his own recognizance and was ordered to report to the Pretrial Services Agency. On December 1, 2013, in accordance with the terms of a written plea agreement, the defendant pleaded guilty as charged. Mr. Jones is scheduled to be sentenced on June 5, 2014.

3. According to his supervising pretrial services officer, Mr. Jones made satisfactory adjustment while under pretrial services supervision and reported as directed. Additionally, Mr. Jones maintained employment, and there were no substance-related issues with the defendant.

The Official Version

1. The American Medisearch Organization (AMO) is a not-for-profit national corporation that supervises fungus research. Across the country, the AMO derives its funds from 50 charter divisions, which are separately incorporated not-for-profit organizations. Atlantis Division, Inc. of the AMO is located in Breaker Bay, Atlantis. In late 2012 the AMO began to raise funds through an annual fall dinner-dance called Casino Night.

2. Nancy Oscar began employment with the AMO in 2009 as a field services representative. Ms. Oscar, who created the dinner-dance fund-raising event, was responsible for the fund-raising activities of the AMO. Three schemes developed from the dinner-dance, all of which were aimed at enabling various "contributors" to inflate or falsify their "charitable" donations that they would then report and deduct on personal, corporate, partnership, or private foundation federal income tax returns.

3. At the dinner-dance, which was usually held in October, guests were permitted to write checks, payable to the AMO, to purchase gambling chips. Ten percent of the value of each check was retained by the AMO as a donation, but 90% was returned to the contributor in the form of gambling chips.

4. Although the AMO raised money from other fund-raising events, its major source of income was from the annual dinner-dance. Over the years the number of people attending the dinner-dance increased, the amount of advance check cashing increased, the amount of checks written for gambling chips increased, and the amount of money raised for the AMO increased. In 2009, the organization raised $73,000, whereas in 2012 the organization raised $360,000.

5. This scheme was in essence a check-cashing operation, allowing contributors to draw on checks to the AMO several weeks before the dinner-dance affair.

6. After the checks cleared the account, Ms. Oscar and other employees at her direction arranged for the bank to ship cash to the dinner-dance site. Ms. Oscar and some of the officers and members of the AMO then met in rooms at the dinner-dance site where they placed the cash in envelopes in amounts corresponding to 90% of the face value of the checks sent in advance of the dinner-dance by the contributors. Ms. Oscar also arranged for additional cash to be available at the dinner-dance for those members who chose to redeem their chips for cash. The scheme was able to continue and flourish not only because of the greed of the so-called

contributors but also due to Ms. Oscar's book-keeping methods.

7. In support of their income tax submissions, contributors often attached to their tax returns copies of the fraudulent checks they had written to the AMO, and during routine audits they furnished original copies of these fraudulent checks to agents of the Internal Revenue Service (IRS), thus directly or indirectly misrepresenting the full amount of the checks as charitable contributions to the AMO.

8. Over the years the number of participants in this scheme substantially increased from 120 in 2007 to approximately 650 in 2009, according to available records, the federal government has sought prosecution of only those contributors who participated in the various kickback schemes and filed fraudulent tax returns when the total amount of their checks written to the AMO was $30,000 or more over several years, or $20,000 in one given year. To date, the government has prosecuted Nancy Oscar, who was the organizer and creator of this scheme. She recently pleaded guilty to a three-count indictment charging her with mail fraud, income tax evasion, and wire fraud along with five "contributors"—namely, the defendant Frank Jones together with Samuel James, Brian McDonald, Vincent St. James, and Donald Goodman. In total, the government expects to obtain indictments of approximately 30 additional contributors. Although the value of the checks written to the AMO varied from contributor to contributor, the check writers are equally culpable.

9. Frank Jones participated in this false deduction scheme involving the Atlantis division of the AMO and filed fraudulent income tax returns for the years 2010, 2011, and 2012. During each of these years Mr. Jones made contributions of $20,000, but he received 90% of the contribution (or $18,000) back in cash or in gambling chips, some of which he gambled with but the majority of which he redeemed for cash. However, on each of his individual income tax returns, filed jointly with his wife, Mr. Jones deducted the full amount of $20,000 as a charitable contribution, even though he was only entitled to deduct $2,000 in each tax year, which represents the 10% retained by the Atlantis Medisearch Organization as a contribution.

Victim Impact Statement

The IRS is the victim. In each tax year of 2010, 2011, and 2012, Frank Jones deducted $20,000 as a charitable contribution from his taxable income, when in fact he was only entitled to deduct a total of $2,000 as a charitable contribution during each tax year. As a result, Mr. Jones underreported his taxable income by $54,000. According to the results of an IRS audit, Mr. Jones had outstanding tax liabilities, not including interest and penalties, in the amount of $27,000.

Adjustment for Defendant's Acceptance of Responsibility

1. During an interview with IRS agents, Mr. Jones readily admitted his involvement in this offense. He explained that he had falsely claimed the charitable deductions on his personal tax returns because everyone else who attended the dinner-dance was claiming the deductions.

2. Mr. Jones added that his involvement in this offense has had an adverse effect on his career and in retrospect he never envisioned the potential impact such wrongdoing would have on his life. He expressed feelings of both embarrassment and regret, and assumes full responsibility for his criminal conduct, as supported by his recent tax payment to the IRS in the amount of $27,000. Mr. Jones indicates that he will immediately pay the balance of his tax liabilities once the IRS has assessed interest and penalties.

Offense Level Computation

1. In this offense, the total amount of evaded taxes is $27,000. According to USSG. §2T4.1(D), the base offense level for tax losses of more than $12,500 but less than $30,000 is computed as Level 12.

PART B. THE DEFENDANT'S CRIMINAL HISTORY
Juvenile Adjudications

None.

Criminal History Computation

A check with the FBI and local police authorities reveals no prior convictions for Frank Jones. Therefore, Mr. Jones has a criminal history score of zero. According to the sentencing table (Chapter 5, Part A), 0 to 1 criminal history points establish a criminal history category of I.

PART C. OFFENDER CHARACTERISTICS: Personal and Family Data

Frank Samuel Jones was born on March 19, 1981, in Breaker Bay, Atlantis, to the union of Samuel and Patricia Jones. Mr. Jones is an only child and was raised by his parents in the Upper River section of Breaker Bay in an upper middle-class socioeconomic setting. Mr. Jones has fond memories of his developmental years, indicating that he was reared according to Roman Catholic traditions by concerned, loving parents who emphasized hard work, respect, and honesty.

The defendant's father was a partner in the Atlantis Tallow Company, a refinery and exporting company that manufactured tallow, the main ingredient in soap. When the defendant was in his senior year of high school, his father became critically ill with tuberculosis and was not expected to recover. Mr. Jones worked at his father's company and managed to finish high school with decent grades. According to the defendant, his father died following a massive heart attack. While reporting a positive relationship with his father, Mr. Jones advised us that he had felt much closer to his mother who is still living.

Mr. Jones married Nancy Lipson Smith. This union produced two children—Frank, Jr., and Melissa, ages six and eight, respectively. For the past five years, the defendant and his family have resided in a rather upper-class area in Breaker Bay. A home investigation found this five-bedroom bi-level, ranch-style home to be impeccably maintained.

Mrs. Jones describes her marriage in harmonious terms and states that the defendant is a kind, considerate, and devoted husband and father. Mr. Jones, for the most part, is a private person and has suffered embarrassment as a result of the publicity in this case. The defendant's wife believes that her husband's actions "were not very well thought out," adding that "he never thinks about the impact his actions may have on his life or family." Mrs. Jones considers the defendant's conduct in this offense as an isolated incident contrary to his otherwise "law-abiding lifestyle." According to Mrs. Jones, her husband has been described by his children as a "workaholic," but he never allows himself to neglect the needs or concerns of his family.

Physical Condition

The defendant is 5′10″ tall and weighs 180 pounds. He has brown eyes and slightly graying short brown hair. Mr. Jones described his overall physical health as excellent.

Mental and Emotional Health

The defendant states that he has never been seen by a psychiatrist and describes his overall mental and emotional health as good. We have no information to suggest otherwise. Mr. Jones was polite and cooperative during the presentence process and presented himself as a professional and soft-spoken businessman, voicing normal stress and concerns affiliated with pending legal difficulties.

Substance Abuse

Mr. Jones states that he rarely drinks alcohol and has never used narcotics. A urine specimen collected by the probation officer tested negative for illicit drug use.

Education and Vocational Skills

The defendant earned a Bachelor of Science degree in marketing. This was confirmed by the registrar's office at Atlantis University.

Employment Record

For the last five years, Mr. Jones has been employed by Greater Life Securities, Inc., in Breaker Bay, where he earns approximately $80,000 a year. Prior to that he was employed by Marshall, Jones, and LaBelle Securities. Mr. Jones also worked at his father's business for several years following high school until he was able to sell it to investors.

Financial Condition: Ability to Pay

A review of the defendant's amended personal income tax returns for 2010 through 2012 (which now reflect the $57,000 in additional income previously reported as charitable deductions) reveals that he earned approximately $121,000 adjusted gross income.

Equity in Other Assets: 1701 Seagull Lane, Breaker Bay, Atlantis (family residence), $280,000

Unsecured debts: auto loan, $17,000; credit cards, −$3,000

Monthly cash flow: $4,500

Based on the defendant's financial condition, he has the ability to pay a fine within the guideline range.

PART D. SENTENCING OPTIONS

Based on an offense level of 12 and a criminal history category of I, the guideline range of imprisonment, if warranted, is 10 to 16 months. The defendant is eligible for a term of probation in this offense, pursuant to 18 U.S.C. § 3561(a). The authorized term for a felony is not less than one nor more than five years, pursuant to 18 U.S.C. § 3561(c)(1).

Impact of Plea Agreement

Under the plea agreement, Mr. Jones has entered a plea to one count of tax evasion, in return for the dismissal of two other tax evasion counts.

Fine

According to USSG §5E1.2(c)(3), the minimum fine for this offense is $3,000 and the maximum fine for this offense is $30,000.

Restitution

Pursuant to 18 U.S.C. § 3663, restitution may be ordered. Restitution of $62,500 shall be ordered. ($57,000 + interest and penalties = $62,500) to be paid the IRS, and can be forwarded to the following address:

Internal Revenue Service
Attention: Uncle Sam Claim
111 IRS Tower
Breaker Bay, Atlantis 11111

PART E: FACTORS THAT MAY WARRANT DEPARTURE

The probation officer has no information concerning the offense or the offender that would warrant a departure from the prescribed sentencing guidelines.

PART F: SENTENCING RECOMMENDATION U.S. DISTRICT COURT FOR THE WESTERN DISTRICT OF ATLANTIS DOCKET. # CR 05-002-01-KGG

Total Offense Level 12
Criminal History Category: I

Frank Jones is a successful businessman who appears to be a situational offender, having been motivated by opportunistic greed. Although his acceptance of responsibility and remorse are reflected in the guideline calculation, a sentence within the guideline range is recommended. As such, a split sentence of five months in a federal community correctional facility followed by five months of home confinement as a condition of supervised release is the recommended sentence to reflect the seriousness of the defendant's conduct and to provide just punishment. The defendant earns a considerable income and is employed with a reputable commodities firm. In view of Mr. Jones's financial profile, restitution of $62,500 and a fine of $20,000 in addition to the $100 penalty assessment are also recommended to be paid immediately. Inasmuch as he does not appear to pose a risk to the community or to be in need of correctional treatment, the minimum term of supervised release of two years will be sufficient. Since the defendant will owe interest and penalties to the IRS as soon as they are calculated, it is recommended that collection of these monies be a condition of supervised release. A restriction against incurring any new debts until the criminal sanctions are paid is an additional recommended condition. Disclosure of financial information is also recommended. As this is a felony conviction, Mr. Jones must submit to DNA testing. Within 72 hours of sentencing, the defendant shall report in person to the Atlantis Federal Community Corrections Center, 123 Willow Lane. While on supervised release the defendant shall not commit any federal, state, or local crimes, and he shall be prohibited from possessing a firearm and all controlled substances. He shall comply with the standard conditions of supervised release as recommended.

Respectfully submitted,

Craig T. Doe, U.S. Probation Officer

Source: Adapted from: Administrative Office of the U.S. Courts. 2006. *The presentence investigation report*, Publication 107. Washington, DC: U.S. Department of Justice. Available at: www.fd.org/pdf_lib/publication%20107.pdf

---

CASE STUDY EXERCISE NO. 3: CLIENT SUE STEEL

Instructions on How to Conduct a Presentence Interview and Write a Presentence Investigation Report

Create a client named Sue Steel OR your instructor can create a mock interview in which the class interviews a client named Sue Steel. The 10-part section below is a bit different from that of the federal PSI, but it includes all the necessary information that you would find representing a state-level PSI.

Before the PSI Interview

You can prepare your own questions to ask the client or use the 50-question sample assessment interview at the back of Chapter 5. Read the instructions on how to complete and score the interview questions. Most of the questions you'll need to complete the PSI are already addressed, except for:

- "How many times have you moved around in the last 12 months?"
- "What percentage of the time have you been employed in the last 12 months?"

Tips on Conducting a Presentence Interview

You have one class period to ask questions of the defendant. The goal of a PSI is to gain a breadth of information from the defendant on behalf of the judge. To meet this goal, here are five tips:

1. Ask questions in a clear and objective way—you may need to restate a question if the defendant does not understand jargon or certain words.

2. Avoid showing bias or judgment about the defendant's responses. Your job is to get the

defendant's point of view. You are to avoid pointing fingers, criticizing, or pushing for what you think is the truth.

3. Pay attention to your own emotions and/or reactions and try not to let those show—that is the mark of a true professional.

4. If the defendant provides a response that you question or if the response directly conflicts with other information you already have, make note of this difference (e.g., the defendant self-reports that he is not in a gang, but PO notices that defendant had a tattoo on his forearm that "seems to resemble a tattoo of the Mexican Mafia or that is commonly thought of as a gang tattoo."). Document both of these differences in your PSI.

5. For every section of your PSI, make note of the information SOURCE—it will be primarily an official report (arrest/conviction data), a self-report (from the defendant), or a collateral report (from a third party other than the defendant).

After the Presentence Interview, Complete the PSI Report

Use the interview of the defendant, along with the following information, to assemble the PSI report: the arrest report, prosecutor information, criminal background check, and interviews with victims, witnesses, and others who know the defendant (collateral interviews).

Construct the PSI in outline or bulleted format using the same 10-part headings and subheadings—*the more detailed and complete,* the better. Be sure to include everything asked for and include HOW you received the information (e.g., Self-report during the PSI interview? Official records? Collateral interview? Your direct observations?). If information is not readily available for an area, you need to say so—do not leave blank.

PSI Format

TO: Judge Name (Your instructor)
FROM: Probation Officer Name (Your name)
RE: Defendant's Name, Case Numbers

1. Defendant's Personal Characteristics
   - Name and aliases
   - Case numbers
   - Gender
   - Date of birth
   - Education level
   - Employment history and skills
   - Vocational skills
   - Military service
   - Mental health history (any psychotropic medications?)
   - Physical health (major illnesses, current prescription meds)
   - Drug history, dependence, and/or current addiction
   - Known gang affiliations and/or tattoos

2. Current Offense
   - Facts of the crime *verbatim* from the police report (best to use it as is, rather than paraphrasing)
   - Initial charge(s) and final plea agreement or conviction(s)
   - Defendant's version of the offense and circumstances leading up to it
   - Accomplices and/or role in current offense
   - Defendant's acceptance of responsibility for crime

3. Defendant's Prior Criminal History
   - Juvenile adjudications (case numbers, offense type, dates, and dispositions)
   - Adult diversions or convictions (case numbers, offense type, dates, and dispositions)
   - Previous time spent in custody
   - Pending charges or outstanding warrants

4. Family History and Background
   - Family of origin (parents, upbringing, siblings)
   - Criminal history of family members
   - Marital status (evidence of domestic violence or abuse?)
   - Dependent children
   - Current family ties and responsibilities (e.g., child support?)
   - Stable living arrangements

5. Victim Impact Statement: Use the victim impact statement and the collateral interviews provided (verbatim) in this book OR (if your instructor says) contact victims and request statements or interviews.
   - Any statements made by the victim to police or the probation officer
   - The type of harm done to the victim as a result of the offense (physical, emotional, psychological, financial, property)
   - The monetary amount of the victim's loss

6. Collateral Information from People Who Knew the Defendant
   - Former employers
   - Former educators and teachers
   - Former probation or parole officers

- Former neighbors
- Interviews with family members

7. Fines and Restitution: Use the victim impact statement to estimate loss and use the defendant's monthly bills and/or what he or she makes in wages to estimate what could be paid each month.
   - Mandatory and recommended restitution and/or fines to be assessed against the defendant
   - Defendant's ability to pay restitution and fines
   - Does defendant have any other debts (credit card debt, auto loans, mortgage, etc.)?

8. Determinate Sentencing Options
   - Using Figure 4.3 (North Carolina sentencing grid): Figure the prior criminal history score. Then figure the presumptive sentence for EACH charge separately. State the sentencing type (jail/prison, CC [community corrections], or probation) and what is most suitable for this defendant.
   - Using Figure 4.3 (North Carolina sentencing grid): Decide whether there are mitigating or aggravating circumstances that warrant departure from the presumptive sentence. In other words, are there any situations, characteristics of the defendant, or things you want the judge to know about prior to sentencing to either mitigate (go easier) or aggravate (go tougher) what the sentencing grid says (in your Part 8)?

9. Indeterminate Sentencing Options
   - Using Figure 4.4 (the indeterminate sentencing table): Figure the client's sentence and compare with your results from the North Carolina sentencing grid.

10. Summary Sentencing Recommendation to the Court
    - Summarize the main points from Sections 1–9. Do not present any new information—just the highlights should be used as a justification.

ENCLOSED DOCUMENTS YOU WILL NEED TO COMPLETE THE PSI:

Police Arrest Report:

Officer Briggs responded to a disturbance call at JCPenney at Anytown Mall at 3:15 P.M. on April 12, 2015. The call was placed by Mall Security Officer Washington at 2:53 P.M. Officer Briggs interviewed the JCPenney clerk who had notified mall security. The clerk said that Defendant Steel became agitated and irate because the clerk refused to accept her check without proper identification. As Steel angrily tried to leave the mall, she was approached for questioning by private security. One of the private security officers happened to notice a "shiny metal object" in her waistband that appeared to be a weapon of some sort. Private security conducted a frisk and recovered a 0.38 caliber weapon from her waistband and a book of checks for "Lisa L. Griswald" when she was arrested. Private security detained Steel at the mall until police arrived. Defendant booked in county jail at 4:25 P.M.

Officer Briggs phoned the bank and the victim. Bank research conducted the next business day on this account revealed that four checks were written to retail stores that totaled $975 over a period of three days. The signature of all four checks did not match the signature on file at the bank. The four checks were written out of order—in different numerical sequence from the rest of the checks in the account.

Victim Lisa Griswald confirms never receiving said checks in the mail, and confirms that she did not write these checks nor authorize anyone else to sign checks on her account.

NCIC Criminal Background Check

NAME:	Steel	Sue	M.	White	Female
DOB: 01/05/85		SS# 123-45-6789		FBI: 98765US43	

Aliases:	Harris, Cherlyn	DOB: 6/30/85
	Steel, Suzanne	DOB: 3/20/81
1679		S. Madison Anytown, TX 78999

Prints on file

Finger Print Class:	PO	PI	09	CO	18
	15	PM	12	23	19

Adult Arrest Record:
2010 MISD 123—Theft by Deception. Bench warrant issued.
2008CV 5967422496—Credit Card Abuse. Disposition unknown.
2004CV 283845067—Simple Felony Fraud. Probation completed after 14 months.
Juvenile Arrest Record:
2002JV 16412345—Juvenile records sealed.

Information from the Prosecutor

The prosecutor has reviewed the case and has decided that enough evidence exists in the police report to charge Defendant Steel with two felonies, and those felonies fall under the North Carolina Sentencing Grid:

Forgery   Class "I" Felony   Case #: 2015CV 993564
(pled down from a Class "H" felony)
Unlawful Carrying of a Firearm During Commission of a Felony
                Class "G" Felony   Case #: 2015CV 993565

Court Fee Schedule

Fees that the offender might be asked to pay, depending on the sentence imposed:

$40–$75 per month	Outpatient Treatment (assuming once per week)
$60 per month	Probation
$400 per month	Residential Community Corrections Facility (work release or halfway house)
No charge	Inpatient Substance Abuse Treatment
$8 per test	Drug and/or Alcohol Tests (urinalysis)
$75 per session	Diagnostic Testing (severity of mental illness, substance abuse)
$15 per month	Electronic Monitoring (radio frequency land-line)
$100 per month	Electronic Monitoring (global positioning system)

Fines (Court Costs)

$40 per offense	General State Victim Compensation Fund
$100–$500	Court Operations (depending on complexity of investigations and hearings)
$20 per sample	Provide a DNA Sample

Victim Impact Statement

Lisa Griswald made the following statement to the prosecutor:

"Ms. Steel is a neighbor that lives down my street. I have said "hi" to her once or twice but never expected that she would be the kind of person to do anything like this. I was just shocked when the police called me. Although the bank knows that I didn't write the checks, my checking account is still short $975.00 which is a lot of money for me to lose in one month. That is nearly all I have—now I am unable to cover my rent and pay my utility bills. I may be able to work something out with some of the companies under the circumstances, but I am not sure if my landlord will go for it. If I could just get my money back, that's all I want. I don't know what I'm going to do."

Interview with former employers:

Mrs. Juanita Medina, the defendant's most recent employer, was contacted by phone to verify that Sue Steel was employed at a janitorial service cleaning office buildings. Steel worked at this firm prior to detention in this case. Mrs. Medina was willing to rehire Steel upon her release from custody because her "work habits were good." Her employer is aware of her conviction and supervision. No other job history could be verified.

Interview with neighbors:

One neighbor, who wishes to remain anonymous, says he remembered the defendant as "quiet and kept to herself."

Interviews with family members:

Defendant's sister (Mary Sparks) has one child of her own and has agreed for Steel to reside with her if Steel is granted community supervision. The home was checked, and it seems to be acceptable and close to a bus route. Defendant Steel has one dependent child, who is currently in the temporary custody of her mother. Steel's mother could not be reached despite repeated calls. Defendant's father is reportedly deceased.

Case Management Using Risk/Needs/Responsivity

Chapter 5

Heinz Kluetmeier/Getty Images

CHAPTER OUTLINE

CHAPTER LEARNING OBJECTIVES

1. Identify the importance of assessment in identifying risk and needs.

2. Describe techniques that lead to defining the level of supervision and development of a treatment plan.

3. List the principles of effective correctional intervention in offender treatment.

4. Explain the similarities and differences of supervising female offenders in the community.

5. Understand how offenders are supervised when they want to go to a different jurisdiction than where their crime was committed.

KEY TERMS

assessment
risk
criminogenic needs
static factors
dynamic factors
supervision
surveillance
field contact
caseload
principles of effective intervention
cognitive-behavioral therapy
motivational interviewing
chronos
staffing
gender-specific programming
Interstate Compact
sending state
receiving state

Michael Phelps is considered to be one of the greatest Olympic athletes in history. Having amassed 18 medals in four Olympic competitions, he hopes to qualify for his fifth Olympics in Brazil in August 2016. But it seems that his continued dependency on alcohol threatens that dream. Beginning in 2004, Phelps was arrested for driving under the influence (DUI), which was later pled down to a lesser charge of driving while intoxicated. He was sentenced to 18 months of probation and court-ordered to talk to high school students about the dangers of drinking alcohol. He completed the first probation successfully.

In 2009, a photograph showing Phelps using a marijuana pipe at a party caused Phelps to get suspended from USA swimming for three months, and it caused Kellogg Company to drop him as one of his sponsors. Although it caused significant embarrassment, Phelps was never criminally charged for that incident.

In September 2014, Phelps was pulled over in his car by Baltimore police for going 84 mph in a 45 mph zone, and for crossing double lines on an interstate. A sobriety test revealed that Phelps was driving with a blood alcohol content level of 0.14. Following this second arrest, USA Swimming immediately suspended Phelps from competing for six months, which included missing the 2015 World Championships in Russia. Phelps later pled guilty to DUI. Prior to his sentence, Phelps voluntarily agreed to complete a 45-day inpatient alcohol treatment program in Arizona during the summer of 2014. In December 2014, the judge sentenced Phelps to one year in jail, but suspended the jail sentence as long as Phelps successfully completes 18 months of probation, continues to attend aftercare treatment, and attends weekly Alcoholics Anonymous meetings until June 2016.

Considering what you know about Michael Phelps's behavior, identify possible criminogenic needs. Do you think the alcohol treatment program and Alcoholics Anonymous meetings will be enough to encourage a permanent behavior change?

IDENTIFYING RISKS AND CRIMINOGENIC NEEDS

Community corrections departments serve both a supervisory and rehabilitative function in the criminal justice system. In this chapter, we first discuss the importance of assessment and how risks and needs are identified. Then we discuss the importance of evidence-based correctional practices (EBPs) in case treatment planning, supervision, cognitive-behavioral treatment, and responsivity of offenders. This chapter applies to both probation and parole case management insofar as the mechanics of the **supervision** process and the conditions are similar. In many states and in the federal system, officers supervise a mix of both probationers and parolees.

Each new client under community supervision must first be interviewed. The earliest offender interviews used anecdotal information to make subjective decisions. Professional judgment and intuition yielded inconsistencies in how each person was interviewed, and this method was oftentimes extremely time consuming, making comparisons among cases difficult. Over the years, probation and parole jurisdictions developed risk prediction scales to measure the statistical probability that offenders would commit new crimes or violate conditions of supervision. Research indicated that *objective* actuarial prediction models, if used by a trained officer, were more reliable and efficient than subjective judgments.

Objective Risk and Needs Assessments

Objective **assessment** scales are the best way for a supervising officer to identify the recidivism risks posed by an offender, identifying criminogenic needs requiring intervention, and selecting the appropriate supervision and treatment strategies for that particular individual (Lowenkamp, Holsinger, Robinson, & Cullen, 2012). Assessments use a structured interview to provide supervision officers a measure of a probationer/parolee's **risk**, or the likelihood that the offender will engage in future criminal activity. Risks that are related to recidivism include prior criminal record, associating with criminal friends, antisocial attitudes/values, and lack of self control or problem-solving skills. An assessment also helps to identify **criminogenic needs** that are either the root causes to and/or directly related to a particular individual's criminal behavior. Such treatment needs include drug or alcohol abuse, mental illness, anger management, and skill deficiencies. Programs and approaches that focus on other needs that are unrelated to crime have little impact on changing future criminal behavior.

Assessments that are better at predicting recidivism seem to include both static and dynamic factors. **Static factors** are variables that do not change or have already occurred in the past, such as gender, number of arrests and convictions. **Dynamic factors**, on the other hand, are variables that do change and are the most valuable in measuring both negative and positive offender change over time. Dynamic factors can include family/marital relationships, peers, school/work, emotional control/impulsivity, financial situation, leisure/recreational activities, and attitude. However, not all dynamic factors will be influenced in the same way for each and every person with treatment exposure. Needs that are only weakly related to criminal behavior, and thus *not* criminogenic, include low self-esteem, physical health, medical needs, and anxiety.

Given that the purpose of an assessment instrument is to differentiate offenders by low, medium, and high risk/needs, a good assessment instrument can correctly do this significantly better than chance. Two different instruments,

supervision
The oversight that a probation or parole officer exercises over those in his or her custody.

assessment
Structured interview of an offender using a validated quantitative instrument that identifies an offender's risk of recidivism and criminogenic needs to address during treatment.

risk
A measure of an offender's propensity to commit further criminal activity that also indicates the level of community supervision required.

criminogenic needs
Problems, habits, or deficits that are directly related to an individual's involvement in criminal behavior.

static factors
Correlates of the likelihood of recidivism that, once they are set, cannot be changed (such as age at first arrest, number of convictions, and so forth).

dynamic factors
Correlates of the likelihood of recidivism that can be changed through treatment and rehabilitation (drug and alcohol abuse, anger management, quality of family relationships, and so forth).

the Ohio Risk Assessment System (ORAS), and the Level of Service Inventory-Revised (LSI-R) seem better able to distinguish levels of risk/needs than their predecessors, and are discussed below.

The LSI-R is a 54-item scale that assigns a numerical value to many of the same factors identified in a presentence report. An officer completes the LSI-R by interviewing an offender and scoring one point for every affirmative answer. The LSI-R has been validated for use with male and female adult offenders and some juvenile offender populations (Manchak, Skeem, Douglas, & Siranosian, 2009; Vose, Lowenkamp, Smith, & Cullen, 2009). The risk score of the LSI-R can accurately predict future criminal activity to the extent that the higher a risk score, the more likely an offender will recidivate (Lowenkamp & Bechtel, 2007). For this reason, high-risk offenders should receive the bulk of treatment services to counteract that risk. A meta-analysis of 47 different studies of the LSI-R shows that it accurately targets high-risk clients who are at greatest need of intervention, but that it more accurately predicts adult men and is less accurate at predicting recidivism for female offenders (Vose, Cullen, & Smith, 2008). There is a fourth generation risk and needs assessment called the LSI Case Management Inventory that integrates assessment with case planning (VanBenschoten, 2008) to better link risk and needs to a treatment plan.

The ORAS is the first comprehensive assessment in the public domain that can be used at pretrial, during community supervision, and there is even an assessment for the reentry process following a prison term (Latessa et al., 2010). The ORAS pretrial assessment was introduced in Chapter 4. Figure 5.1 illustrates the community supervision assessment of the ORAS. Once an offender is initially assessed, additional assessment tools have been validated for specific types of problems. For example, valid assessment tools are available that look deeper into cognitive thinking distortions, clinical assessments further examine various types of mental health problems, and a substance abuse assessment looks more into what type of addiction is a serious problem (Lowenkamp et al., 2012).

FIGURE 5.1

OHIO RISK ASSESSMENT SYSTEM: COMMUNITY SUPERVISION TOOL (ORAS-CST)	
Name: _____	Date of Assessment: _____
Case#: _____	Name of Assessor: _____

1.0 CRIMINAL HISTORY:

1.1 Most Serious Arrest Under Age 18   [   ]

    0 = None

    1 = Yes, Misdemeanor

    2 = Yes, Felony

1.2 Number of Prior Adult Felony Convictions   [   ]

    0 = None

    1 = One or Two

    2 = Three or more

(Continues)

FIGURE 5.1 *(Continued)*

1.3 Prior Sentence as Adult to a Jail or Secure Correctional Facility   ☐
      0 = No
      1 = Yes

1.4 Received Official Misconduct While Incarcerated as Adult   ☐
      0 = No
      1 = Yes

1.5 Prior Sentence to Probation as an Adult   ☐
      0 = No
      1 = Yes

1.6 Community Supervision Ever Been Revoked for Technical
    Violation as Adult   ☐
      0 = No
      1 = Yes

          Total Score in Criminal History: ☐

2.0 EDUCATION, EMPLOYMENT, AND FINANCIAL SITUATION:

2.1 Highest Education   ☐
      0 = High School Graduate or Higher
      1 = Less than High School or GED

2.2 Ever Suspended or Expelled from School   ☐
      0 = No
      1 = Yes

2.3 Employed at the Time of Arrest   ☐
      0 = Yes
      1 = No

2.4 Currently Employed   ☐
      0 = Yes, Full-time, Disabled, or Retired
      1 = Not Employed or Employed Part-time

2.5 Better Use of Time   ☐
      0 = No, Most Time Structured
      1 = Yes, Lots of Free Time

2.6 Current Financial Situation   ☐
      0 = Good
      1 = Poor

      Total Score in Education, Employment, Financial: ☐

(Continues)

FIGURE 5.1 *(Continued)*

3.0 FAMILY AND SOCIAL SUPPORT

3.1 Parents Have Criminal Record

    0 = No

    1 = Yes

3.2 Currently Satisfied with Current Marital or Equivalent Situation

    0 = Yes

    1 = No

3.3 Emotional and Personal Support Available from Family or Others

    0 = Strong Support

    1 = None or Weak Support

3.4 Level of Satisfaction with Current Level of Support
    from Family or Others

    0 = Very Satisfied

    1 = Not Satisfied

3.5 Stability of Residence

    0 = Stable

    1 = Not Stable

Total Score on Family and Social Support:

4.0 NEIGHBORHOOD PROBLEMS

4.1 High Crime Area

    0 = No

    1 = Yes

4.2 Drugs Readily Available in Neighborhood

    0 = No, Generally Not Available

    1 = Yes, Somewhat Available

    2 = Yes, Easily Available

Total Score in Neighborhood Problems:

5.0 SUBSTANCE USE

5.1 Age First Began Regularly Using Alcohol

    0 = 17 or Older

    1 = Under Age 17

5.2 Longest Period of Abstinence from Alcohol

    0 = Six Months or Longer

    1 = Less than Six Months

(Continues)

FIGURE 5.1 *(Continued)*

5.3 Offender Ever Used Illegal Drugs ⬜

    0 = No

    1 = Yes

5.4 Drug Use Caused Legal Problems ⬜

    0 = None

    1 = One Time

    2 = Two or More Times

5.5 Drug Use Caused Problems with Employment ⬜

    0 = No

    1 = Yes

Total Score for Substance Use: ⬜

6.0 PEER ASSOCIATIONS

6.1 Criminal Friends ⬜

    0 = None

    1 = Some

    2 = Majority

6.2 Contact with Criminal Peers ⬜

    0 = No Contact with Criminal Peers

    1 = At Risk of Contacting Criminal Peers

    2 = Contacts or Actively Seeks Out Criminal Peers

6.3 Gang Membership ⬜

    0 = No, Never

    1 = Yes, but Not Current

    2 = Yes, Current

6.4 Criminal Activities ⬜

    0 = Strong Identification with Prosocial Activities

    1 = Mixture of Pro- and Antisocial Activities

    2 = Strong Identification with Criminal Activities

Total Score for Peer Associations: ⬜

7.0 CRIMINAL ATTITUDES AND BEHAVIORAL PATTERNS

For the Following Items Please Rate the Offender:

7.1 Criminal Pride ⬜

    0 = No Pride in Criminal Behavior

    1 = Some Pride

    2 = A Lot of Pride

(Continues)

FIGURE 5.1 *(Continued)*

7.2 Expresses Concern About Others' Misfortunes

      0 = Concerned About Others

      1 = Limited Concern

      2 = No Real Concern for Others

7.3 Feels Lack of Control Over Events

      0 = Controls Events

      1 = Sometimes Lacks Control

      2 = Generally Lacks Control

7.4 Sees No Problem in Telling Lies

      0 = No

      1 = Yes

7.5 Engages in Risk Taking Behavior

      0 = Rarely Takes Risks

      1 = Sometimes Takes Risks

      2 = Generally Takes Risks

7.6 Walks Away from a Fight

      0 = Yes

      1 = Sometimes

      2 = Rarely

7.7 Believes in "Do Unto Others Before They Do Unto You"

      0 = Disagree

      1 = Sometimes

      2 = Agrees

Total Score Criminal Attitudes and Behavioral Patterns:

TOTAL SCORE:

Risk Categories for MALES			Risk Categories for FEMALES		
Scores	Rating	Percent of Failures	Scores	Rating	Percent of Failures
0–14	Low	9%	0–14	Low	7%
15–23	Moderate	34%	15–21	Moderate	23%
24–33	High	58%	22–28	High	40%
34+	Very High	70%	29+	Very High	50%

(Continues)

FIGURE 5.1 *(Continued)*

Domain Levels					
1.0 Criminal History			**2.0 Education, Employment, and Financial Situation**		
	Score	Failure		Score	Failure
_____	Low (0–3)	27%	_____	Low (0–1)	21%
	Med (4–6)	46%		Med (4–6)	37%
	High (7–8)	53%		High (7–8)	55%
3.0 Family and Social Support			**4.0 Neighborhood Problems**		
	Score	Failure		Score	Failure
_____	Low (0–1)	32%	_____	Low (0)	17%
	Med (2–3)	41%		Med (1)	35%
	High (4–5)	48%		High (2–3)	45%
5.0 Substance Use			**6.0 Peer Associations**		
	Score	Failure		Score	Failure
_____	Low (0–2)	27%	_____	Low (0–1)	21%
	Med (3–4)	40%		Med (2–4)	43%
	High (5–6)	45%		High (5–8)	64%
7.0 Criminal Attitudes and Behavioral Patterns					
	Score	Failure			
_____	Low (0–3)	24%			
	Med (4–8)	44%			
	High (9–13)	59%			

The ORAS is in the Public Domain. The assessment was reproduced with permission.

Source: Latessa, Edward, Paula Smith, Richard Lemke, Matthew Makarios, and Christopher Lowenkamp. 2009. Creation and Validation of the Ohio Risk Assessment System: Final Report. Cincinnati, OH: University of Cincinnati, Center for Criminal Justice Research, pp. 51–54.

Other sources of information that can be used to identify treatment needs include a presentence report, prison disciplinary records, a prerelease plan, physical or medical health evaluations, records of drug or alcohol abuse and other related criminal conduct, financial history, and residential history. Because federal presentence investigations (PSIs) are so detailed, they capture most of the information in the risk and needs assessment of the LSI-R. In these cases, case managers use the LSI-R to gauge honesty (or consistency) by comparing client responses to the PSI and the LSI-R. The importance of carefully gathering and evaluating an offender's history cannot be overstated, for past behavior is at present the best predictor we have of future behavior. Box 5.1 provides examples of open-ended questions that are important during an initial client interview. A more structured interview, which can be found at the back of this chapter following the case study, is an alternative interview that contains 50 more specific questions to ask an offender.

BOX 5.1   SAMPLE COMMUNITY SUPERVISION INTAKE INTERVIEW

- Full name, including any aliases
- Address/phone/e-mail
- Number of address changes in the past year
- Religious denomination preference
- Are you a military veteran?

Current/Instant Offense

- What was/were your offense(s) of conviction?
- What is the length of your sentence? Is it deferred or regular?

Prior Record

- Do you have a juvenile record?
- How old were you when you committed your first offense?
- What previous convictions do you have on your adult record?
- Do you have any pending charges or court dates?

Education and Training

- What is your education level?
- Did you finish high school? If not, do you have a GED?
- Do you have any certificates or special vocational training?

Employment

- What was your last job? Rate of pay? Reason for leaving?
- What was your longest period of employment?
- What was your longest period of unemployment?

Marital Status and Children

- Have you ever been married? Legally married or common law? To whom?
- Names/ages/father or mother of children?
- Do you retain custody? If not, who does?

- With whom do your children live?
- Are your children involved with juvenile probation or protective services?

Family of Origin

- Describe your relationship with your parents/in-laws/siblings.
- Do you have other relatives involved with the criminal justice system?

Finances

- Describe your credit history/finances/current debts.
- Are you receiving Aid to Families with Dependent Children/food stamps/social security/Medicare/child support?

Medical and Mental Health

- Do you have a history of medical conditions (including pregnancies, surgeries, miscarriages, and abortions)?
- Are you having any medical problems right now?
- Are you taking any medications?
- Have you ever experimented with any illegal drugs?
- When was the last time you used any illegal drug? What was it and how often?
- Do you use alcohol? How recently? How often?
- Did you ever seek treatment for substance abuse?
- Have you ever suffered from depression?
- Have you ever tried to commit suicide? Were you hospitalized?
- Have you ever sought mental health treatment or been diagnosed with a mental illness?
- Have you ever been physically or sexually abused or involved in an abusive relationship?
- Have you ever received treatment or rehabilitation for anything else? If so, for what?

THE SUPERVISION COMPONENT

Neighborhood-based supervision allows probation and parole officers to leave their department and conduct field visits. In recent years, case assignment has been made according to where offenders live within the community, such as within certain street boundaries or within a single zip code. Supervising offenders, according to zip code, allows probation and parole officers to more efficiently visit offenders in a smaller area (as opposed to driving across the entire city), and at the same time, develop solid community partnerships with police, treatment providers, and faith-based organizations.

Visits and Field Contacts

A **field contact** is considered to be the most time consuming but is also the most valuable type of face-to-face contact. In a field contact, an officer visits an offender's home or place of employment to monitor progress. Probation and parole officers can conduct warrantless searches of probationers' homes based on a "reasonable suspicion" of criminal activity (*United States v. Knights,* 2001). Reasonable suspicion is a lower standard of proof than "probable cause," which is needed for most residence searches. However, the U.S. Supreme Court has held that a probationer has a diminished expectation of privacy while on probation.

Collateral contacts (a term introduced in Chapter 4), are also valuable for an officer to contact third parties that have direct contact with the offender, such as employers, teachers, and/or relatives to verify that each offender is adhering to probation conditions. Field contacts are scheduled according to specialized mapping software programmed for use in probation and parole agencies (see Box 5.2). Laptops and tablets with Internet capabilities are used to retrieve GPS coordinates of offenders, retrieve client information from protected databases, and schedule client appointments with the same level of security they enjoy at their physical office. A voice recognition feature can help document visits and generate reports needed for case management and upcoming court dates.

field contact
An officer's personal visit to an offender's home or place of employment for the purpose of monitoring progress under supervision.

| BOX 5.2 | **TECHNOLOGY IN CORRECTIONS** | |

Field Visits Using GIS Mapping

Geographic information system (GIS) mapping uses computer software to obtain a full picture of where probationers live in relation to other nearby locations such as schools and alcohol establishments. Available data include the number of police calls for service, the number and location of orders of protection, and access to treatment venues from probationers' residences. An officer who supervises an entire caseload of offenders in the same area can achieve a higher level of field **surveillance** than an officer who must drive all over a city. GIS technology can also overlay information on bus routes, employer locations, locations of alcohol establishments, and schools to determine feasibility of probationer success and how travel time can be minimized when probationers move from one location to another. This technology gives probation officers more details about their jurisdiction or the "beat" in which their clients live, and information can be shared with police depart-

ments, who already use GIS to locate suspects and investigate new crimes.

GIS technology is also helpful for supervisors when assigning new clients to a caseload. A supervisor can examine where an offender lives and assign offenders in the same neighborhood to the same officer, such as in neighborhood-based supervision. In this way, officers can supervise their caseload in a small area of town, where they are more likely to visit them in the neighborhood rather than driving haphazardly all over town. Using GIS mapping, routes from one house to the next can be planned for a series of home visits. The possibilities of GIS applications for corrections are still being discovered and linked to other agencies within the broader criminal justice system.

Source: Karuppannan, Jaishankar. (2005). Mapping and corrections: Management of offenders with geographic information systems. *Corrections Compendium 30* (1), 7–9, 31–33.

Levels of Supervision

One of the principles of effective supervision entails differentiating offenders who need closer supervision from those who require less supervision. Risk variables determine the level of supervision required by an offender. Although various names are used, there are typically three or four levels of supervision. A three-level supervision refers to maximum, medium, and minimum supervision, whereas a four-level probation system like that found in Table 5.1 refers to maximum (sex offenders), high, standard, and administrative supervision. The idea behind defining these supervision levels is also to distribute a fair workload or caseload to every officer based not only on the number of clients, but on the time that each client is predicted to take. A **caseload** is defined as the number of individuals or cases one probation or parole officer can supervise effectively based on the supervision level. In practice, caseloads vary widely because not every offender requires the same amount of supervision (Lutze, 2014).

At the lowest level of supervision, there may be no requirement that a probationer personally visit or contact a probation officer. Rather, the probationer may be required to call in and leave a message on a voice-recorded line, or mail-in a verification of address and employment. This level of supervision is known as administrative supervision and in California as banked probation. Over 60% of all Los Angeles probationers were tracked solely by computer and had no contact with an officer (see Box 5.3). Administrative probation is for offenders who have committed minor crimes, who have satisfied their financial obligations, or have been in compliance for two years and can be transferred down to this level.

caseload
The number of individuals or cases for which one probation or parole officer is responsible.

TABLE 5.1   Differences for Each Supervision Level

Supervision Level	Minimum Monthly Contacts	Maximum Caseload Cap	Percent on Each Level
Maximum	4	40	3.4%
High	2	80	8.3%
Standard	1	250	46.5%
Administrative	0	No Cap	41.8%

BOX 5.3   **TECHNOLOGY IN CORRECTIONS**

Do Virtual and Mobile Check-ins Count as "Supervision"?

In the past, officers used to spend most of their day in their offices responding to calls and receiving visits from probationers. But with caseload sizes growing larger and increased pressure on officers to more closely supervise high-risk offenders, low-risk probationers in some states never actually see their probation officer. Instead, they check in using centrally located kiosk machines that are equipped with a camera like an ATM. Once logged in using their fingerprint as their password, the kiosk is interactive and has a touch screen to allow offenders on probation or parole to receive and send personal messages back and forth to their supervising officer at any time of day. The machine can be set up anywhere that is monitored, such as in a lobby of a police station or in a 24-hour grocery store. Offenders use kiosks to notify their probation officer of a change of address or employment and be asked questions in turn, to which they can type a response. Kiosks

(Continues)

BOX 5.3   **TECHNOLOGY IN CORRECTIONS** *(Continued)*

also store information on bus routes, job postings, and schedules for services such as treatment programs, employment offices, and driver's license bureaus.

For offenders in remote areas or probationers who cannot afford telephones, special pagers are provided in lieu of a kiosk that allow a supervision officer to beep a client with a directive, such as to call the officer immediately or to submit a urine sample within a designated period of time. Clients do not know the number to their personal pagers, so no one else can beep them with personal calls. Kiosk-style supervision

doesn't appear to compromise public safety in any way, yet clients seem to comply and prefer checking in at their convenience over having to appear at a specified time and place (Wilson, Naro, & Austin, 2007). One thing is for sure—with less time spent on low-risk clients, probation and parole—officers can then spend more time out in the field meeting their higher-risk clients in person.

Question for discussion: What might some problems be, if any, with the use of kiosks to replace face-to-face supervision for low-risk offenders?

Reporting kiosks, such as this one in New York, are more common in public areas or in police stations to allow nonviolent and low-risk offenders the convenience of checking in with their probation officer.

Joel Gordon

Regular or standard probation supervision includes a wide variety of contact types. For example, Offender A on medium supervision may expect two face-to-face contacts per month and verification of residence and employment once every 12 months. Offender B on medium supervision may only have one

principles of effective intervention
Eight treatment standards that, if practiced, have been shown to reduce recidivism below that of other methods and that constitute the theory behind evidence-based correctional practices.

quarterly face-to-face contact but weekly mail-in and quarterly home visits. The frequency and intensity of contacts increase with the supervision level, such that an offender on the highest level can expect one weekly face-to-face or field contact, one monthly collateral contact, verification of residence and employment every three months, and a criminal history check every 12 months.

IMPLEMENTING THE CASE TREATMENT PLAN

One central idea that holds true throughout this text is that no matter what forms or level of community supervision, effective supervision must involve some sort of treatment component and/or referrals to outside resources to help offenders. After reviewing court-ordered conditions of probation, assessing an offender's risk of recidivism, and determining treatment needs, an officer selects appropriate strategies for addressing them. In other words, an officer develops a case treatment plan, which is an individualized written document that clarifies how each court-ordered condition is to be fulfilled by offender and supervising officer in the context of the risks and needs posed (Bosker, Witteman, & Hermanns, 2013). A case treatment plan includes the main goals the offender will work on during probation/parole, how the offender must go about meeting those goals, the strengths that the offender has to draw upon, and how the officer can help the offender collaborate toward meeting those goals (Fortune, Ward, & Willis, 2012). Once completed, the case treatment plan is signed by both parties. Progress on the case plan is reviewed during each appointment and can be modified as circumstances change. Along with reducing opportunities for crime, a case treatment plan should ideally be directed toward removing or reducing barriers that could result in recidivism as well as assisting an offender in positive behavioral change, which may involve placement in a treatment program.

The Principles of Effective Correctional Intervention

For the last few decades, researchers and treatment specialists have sought to figure out what type of treatment is most effective with which types of offenders. Gendreau (1996) initially published the **principles of effective intervention**, a theoretical perspective of EBPs that is currently considered the basis by which correctional treatment programs should operate. There are a total of eight principles, which indicate that treatment services should:

1. be intensive, occupying 40%–70% of each day for three to nine months;
2. contain cognitive-behavioral components to prepare the mind for behavioral change;
3. match program level with client aptitudes or propensities according to gender, age, cultural background, and risk level, so that higher-risk clients make greater strides;
4. offer positive reinforcements that exceed punishments by a ratio of 4:1;
5. require minimum education and experience levels for staff;
6. teach clients to replace criminal networks with prosocial ones;
7. provide relapse prevention and aftercare; and
8. evaluate the program and assess its compliance to the previous seven principles by using the Correctional Program Assessment Inventory (CPAI). The CPAI is really not a concern for readers of this text, as it is a checklist for researchers to ensure each program has met the criteria for staff and program quality.

Many agencies, such as the Federal Probation District in Hawaii and jurisdictions in Maryland, embrace these principles as they discover the true meaning of EBPs (see Davidson, Crawford, & Kerwood, 2008; Taxman, 2008), which in turn see the value in collecting data that will later be important to an evaluation.

Cognitive-Behavioral Therapy

One of the principles of correctional intervention is the use of **cognitive-behavioral therapy** (CBT) with offenders. CBT, an effective method for helping a person to change, has two components. The cognitive component focuses on replacing self-defeating thought patterns with motivating and empowering thoughts. Once the individual recognizes a cycle of negativity, they must learn to stop that behavior immediately. The behavioral component teaches an individual to replace harmful and inappropriate behaviors with new habits and legitimate skill sets. CBT is used to quit habitual behaviors such as smoking, drinking, or drug use, and to change harmful thinking patterns such as those linked to criminality. Box 5.4 discusses six different types of CBT used with offenders.

cognitive-behavioral therapy
A therapeutic intervention for helping a person to change that is a blend of two types of therapies—cognitive therapy of the mind and behavioral change of the body.

| BOX 5.4 | **EVIDENCE-BASED PRACTICES IN COMMUNITY CORRECTIONS** | |

Six Examples of Cognitive-Behavioral Therapy for Offenders

Cognitive-behavioral programs are a general category of therapy programs that have been shown through research to be effective, particularly for people who are resistant to change. The cognitive component focuses on reducing thinking errors that many offenders may have, such as blaming others, seeing themselves as victims, harboring self-hatred, among other problems. Reducing thinking errors is important to prepare the mind for behavioral change. The behavioral component links self-destructive mental processes to harmful acting out. These therapy modules are delivered in group sessions for six to twelve offenders by a trained group facilitator. Six examples of cognitive-behavioral treatment for offenders include:

1. *Moral Reconation Therapy (MRT).* Developed by Little and Robinson in 1985, this 32-hour CBT program helps to develop a positive identity and higher stages of moral reasoning through giving testimonies. MRT is a group therapy and is based on an assumption that people who have moral development skills are less likely to repeat criminal behavior. MRT is useful for offenders during residential treatment and particularly for offenders who need to learn how to think more abstractly and to share another

person's perspective. When used with probationers and parolees, MRT reduced recidivism by nearly two-thirds between 6 and 24 months (Little, 2005).

2. *Reasoning and Rehabilitation* (R&R). Developed in the mid-1980s by Ross and Fabiano, this 70-hour program (35 sessions of 2 hours each) includes modules such as cognitive problem-solving, self-control, critical reasoning, values enhancement, emotional control, and victim awareness.

3. *Thinking for a Change* (T4C). Developed in the mid-1990s by Bush, Glick, and Taymans and adopted for use and dissemination by the National Institute of Corrections, this program consists of 22 lessons lasting one to two hours each. It is classified as a cognitive restructuring program in which offenders examine their attitudes, beliefs, and thinking patterns so they can fully consider the consequences of their actions. Change is sought through social skills and problem-solving techniques, and two sessions per week is considered an optimal dosage.

4. *Strategies for Self-Improvement and Change* (SSC). This year-long program was developed by Wanberg and Milkman for adult substance abusers engaged in a long-term community treatment

(Continues)

BOX 5.4	EVIDENCE-BASED PRACTICES IN COMMUNITY CORRECTIONS *(Continued)*

program. The therapy examines thoughts and behavior patterns that contribute to substance abuse, emphasizing commitment to change and taking responsibility for oneself.

5. *Relapse Prevention Therapy* (RPT). After intensive residential treatment, RPT is a good aftercare program that follows the SSC program discussed above. RPT is also good for relapse prevention of any obsessive thoughts and/or compulsive or habitual behavior. RPT, developed in 2000 by Parks and Marlatt, teaches coping skills when habitual thoughts resurface.

6. *Aggression Replacement Training* (ART). For youth and adult offenders with anger management problems, this therapy uses cognitive-behavioral techniques to recognize and appropriately handle anger. Developed by Goldstein and Glick in the mid-1990s, this is a 30-hour program.

Source: Hansen, Chris. (2008). Cognitive-behavioral interventions: Where they come from and what they do. *Federal Probation, 72* (2), 43–49.

CBT helps an offender replace both unhealthy thinking processes and criminal behavior with a sense of responsibility, empathy, and prosocial behavior. One CBT program called *Thinking for a Change* was evaluated over one year using treatment and control groups of medium- to high-risk offenders in stable mental health who were neither substance abusers nor sex offenders. Although technical violation rates and rates of rearrest were not significantly different between the two groups, the treatment group had better interpersonal problem-solving skills compared to the control group (those not involved in the treatment regimen) (Golden, Gatchel, & Cahill, 2006). Cognitive-behavioral treatment programs that followed the principles of effective correctional intervention had a significantly greater reduction in recidivism (25%) than correctional treatment programs that did not follow these principles.

Employment Assistance

Employment is likely the single most important element in preventing recidivism for adult probationers and parolees. The positive effect of continuous employment seems to reduce recidivism well beyond the correctional supervision period (Van der Geest, Bijleveld, & Blokland, 2011). Not only does employment provide financial support for an offender and his or her family, but it is also crucial for establishing and maintaining self-esteem and personal dignity—qualities seen by most seasoned probation and parole officers as essential for success. However, finding and maintaining employment is not simple. Offenders are often the last to be hired and the first to be terminated. Many of them are unskilled, and many have poor work habits. Some are barred from employment in their chosen fields as a result of regulatory and licensing laws that preclude the hiring of people with a criminal conviction. (We discuss these issues in Chapter 14.)

Because of the critical relationship between success under parole or probation supervision and meaningful employment, probation and parole officers must assess the employment status of each person under their supervision and work with him or her to land a job. Many require vocational or job-readiness training before they can seek employment. Ideally these services are obtained from external agencies and organizations such as state employment offices and vocational network services. For example, a workforce development program in Delaware offered paid vocational training, job counseling, and job referrals to agencies

The foundation of supervision is getting into the field to meet with clients in their own neighborhoods.

Andrew Ramey/PhotoEdit

with pre-established relationships. Once an individual's skills and abilities are assessed, the individual is matched with a job, while undergoing vocational training to meet long-term goals. Involvement in the Delaware workforce program significantly reduced recidivism for offenders who participated (15% revocation or rearrest rate) compared with a matched group of probationers from other districts (26% revocation or rearrest) who did not participate (Visher, Smolter, & O'Connell, 2010).

Developing Prosocial Networks

Informal social controls such as provided by family members and community agencies are also significant resources that officers can access to help probationers develop prosocial behaviors. Neighborhood-based supervision uses family and community support techniques to aid in supervision, and this activity spanned beyond the boundaries of the agency office (Lutze, 2014). As discussed in Chapter 2, being a boundary spanner requires community supervision officers to fully understand community values and be able to interact with businesses and social service agencies to identify legitimate employment opportunities, and resources to help offenders. It is also extremely helpful for officers to know locations and establishments that may contribute to possible deviant opportunities, where the offender is instructed not to be (Lutze, 2014).

chronos
A chronological account of detailed notes written by a probation or parole officer and organized by date, about any client contact and/ or case information that becomes a permanent part of the offender's case file.

Officers spent about 20% of the time on office visits and counseling, 20% on home and field visits, 20% of their time on investigations/court appearances (presentence investigations, technical violations, revocations), and about one-third of their time on administrative paperwork to keep track of their offender's behavior and of their own responses (DeMichele, 2007). Read one federal probation officer's view in Box 5.5 about a typical day on the job, and see whether you are able to determine which activities are supervision functions, which are oriented toward counseling/treatment, which are investigatory/court appearances, and which are examples of tracking these activities through paperwork.

| BOX 5.5 | **FIELD NOTES** | |

A Day in the Life of a Federal Probation Officer

It's Tuesday, and I've got my work cut out for me on this cold January day in rural West Texas. On the way in to work, I mentally review the upcoming scheduled events for the day: 8:30 A.M. meet with assistant U.S. attorney regarding a probation revocation hearing on John D.; 9:00 A.M. revocation hearing in Judge B.'s court—contested; thereafter, head for the small towns to do field supervision and collateral work. This will be an overnighter, so I'll be back in the office on Thursday—another court day.

I'm almost at the office, but I first need to make a quick stop at Joe R.'s to collect a urinalysis (UA). He's been out a month now and seems to be doing all right. He's working, home is stable, and the UA will address the primary supervision issue in this case—history of drug abuse. I'm almost done with writing his supervision plan which may include drug treatment in the community. Time will tell; but for right now random UAs will do. Well, I caught Joe before he left for work, and things seem solid. The wife seemed happy, the job is stable, and there was no problem with the UA. It's going to be a great day! On to the office.

Oops, I spoke too soon: I just got a call: David S. got arrested for DWI [driving while intoxicated]—he's still locked up at County. I'll swing by the county jail after John D.'s revocation hearing.

John D. is contesting his revocation. That's fine; five dirty UAs and failure to participate in drug treatment will get you every time. The supervision file is well documented, and I'm prepared to testify as to chain of custody on the dirty UAs. Our contract provider was subpoenaed and will testify on the failure to participate violation. We're in Judge B.'s court, and the assistant U.S. attorney tells me the defendant has decided to plead true and throw himself on the mercy of the court—good

luck. Sure enough, the judge revokes John D.'s probation and sentences him to 24 months' custody. John takes it all right, but his mother doesn't. If he had taken the judge's advice and "lived at the foot of the cross," he'd still be on probation—instead, he's locked up, and his mother is crying in court. It's always harder on the family. I'll talk to her—maybe it will help. John couldn't do it on the street, so maybe he will get the help he needs inside. The FCI [federal correctional institution] in Fort Worth has an excellent treatment program—I'll tell her that and maybe she will feel better.

Well, it's mid-morning and time to hit the road. Fort Stockton is 100 miles away, but I've got to stop at the county jail on the way out of town. I've got my government vehicle, cell phone, pepper spray, sidearm, and laptop in case I have time for **chronos**.

At the county lockup David S., who was arrested for DWI advises he really only "had a couple" and "forgot" he was supposed to abstain completely from alcohol (yeah right!). When I return, I'll get the police report, staff the case with the boss, and decide what type of action to take. David has been on supervision for over a year and has done exceptionally well. Graduated sanctions may be in order, and if so, I'll ask the court to place him in a halfway house with an outpatient alcohol treatment.

On the road again to Fort Stockton to check in with the sheriff—he knows everything that is going on in his county; go by our drug contractor's office and visit with the therapist regarding Mary J.; go by the county clerk's office and finish this collateral request out of the Northern District; and conduct home inspections on Bob S. and Joe R. Talk about time management—the boss will love this! Sheriff B. is in a great mood, and he says all my people have been behaving themselves. At

(Continues)

BOX 5.5	**FIELD NOTES** *(Continued)*

the drug treatment facility the contractor gives me a good report on Mary J. She's keeping all her appointments and has not had any dirty UAs. Her participation in treatment is good, and her mother has also attended a couple of counseling sessions. Great report!

The county clerk was busy, but she did have the judgments I called ahead about—that was quick and easy, not like the last time I had to wait for two hours to find the court papers.

Well, I've arrived at Bob S.'s house. I think I'll drive past and around the block—just in case. Everything looks cool, and his car is in front, so he should be home. Bob was surprised to see me, advising it was his day off since the day before he had pulled a double shift on the oil rig. Oil field work is steady, but the cold weather is hard, and it shows on Bob's face. The wife seems to be doing well, and the house is neat and clean. Things look solid, but I know better than to start bragging. This offender has a history of drug violations, which presents certain risk control issues. Risk control issues never go away!

At Joe R.'s no one comes to the door, but I think I heard someone inside. I leave my card, drive around the block, and call Joe on the cellular phone. It amazes me how sneaky I can get when I have to. Sure enough, Joe's girlfriend answers the phone and advises Joe is still at work. Work is 15 miles out of town at a ranch, so I'll try to catch him first thing in the morning.

I'm running a little ahead of schedule, so I'll stop by and see Mary J. She should be home from work; if she's not, her mother will be, and she'll let me know how her daughter is really doing. The supervision issues here are enforcing court-ordered sanctions and drug treatment. Sure enough, Mary J. is there and seems to be doing really well. She gives me her community service hours documentation and discusses her progress in the drug treatment program. Her mother is obviously very satisfied with her daughter's progress and is a good supervision resource to me.

Before I check into the motel, I check my voice mail and texts. David S. called to advise that he bonded out of jail. I call him back and set up an appointment for him to come on Thursday. We'll staff him at that time. I'm glad now that I brought the laptop—I can catch up on some chronos. Since I lucked out and saw all the people I needed to, I won't need to go out tonight. What a day—win a few, lose a few.

The next morning comes early, and I catch breakfast before I hit the road. I figure, I'll work my way back to the office and try to catch Joe R. at the ranch before he gets busy. I'm positive that his girlfriend told him I was by the house, so he should be expecting me. I'm not quite comfortable with this offender because he does have some violence in his background. Therefore, officer safety and risk control are my primary supervision issues. As I drive up to the ranch headquarters, I can see my man out by the horse corral. He seems surprised to see me. We visit, and he convinces me he is making a "good hand." I try not to be too obvious, but I'm looking for any signs of contraband or a weapon. Nothing is obvious, although Joe just seems to be nervous. As I drive back down the road to the main gate, I call the Border Patrol sector headquarters and check in with the duty agent. Joe is clean as far as they know, but they agree to drive by the ranch in the next few days and let me know.

Well, I'm almost home, and it's a beautiful day. In fact, it looks like it will warm up. The only pressing issue I know of is the **staffing** on David S., some court paperwork to file, and the continuous upkeep on the chronos. You know what, I really do love this job!

Questions for Discussion: Within this one day, which activities are surveillance functions and which are oriented toward treatment? How does the probation officer use collateral contacts to help gain information about his clients?

Source: The author, Richard V. Russell, was a U.S. probation officer for the Western District of Texas. He is now retired. Reprinted with permission.

WORKING WITH FEMALE OFFENDERS

Although female probationers originate from all walks of life, many have typical backgrounds. Women under community supervision have typically entered the criminal justice system because of a crime they committed alongside a male partner (boyfriend, husband, or brother) or else if acting alone, out of financial

staffing
A bi-monthly meeting of key staff members to discuss the progress and/or outcomes of probationers or parolees on a particular caseload or who are enrolled in a specific community corrections program.

need (Alarid & Wright, 2014). The typical female probationer or parolee has not completed high school and lacks requisite skills for employment above the minimum wage. Added to this is the sheer fact that women are primary caretakers of dependent children, and in many households, adult women are also the head of the household. Three out of four women in the criminal justice system have dependent children. The low wages and reality of children mean that many women are living below the poverty line with little perceived means and opportunity to change their situation (van Wormer, 2010).

Early Pathways to Women's Criminality

There is a disproportionate number of women who have been physically or sexually abused and/or neglected as children. The abuse oftentimes continues into adulthood through male partners and is sometimes passed on to children as women remain in a submissive and dependent role. Although more women than in the past may act in leadership crime roles, far more of them serve in secondary, traditional roles. Early experiences of abuse and disempowerment later affect a woman's self-esteem, emotional and mental states, and rate of substance abuse, all of which are linked as various pathways to crime (Alarid & Wright, 2014). Because many women define themselves by their relationships rather than by their careers, they tend to seek partners who will provide them with what they feel they deserve.

This link between early experiences and criminality is noteworthy because ordinarily women typically are more at risk of harming themselves than of harming others. All else being equal, women generally pose less risk than men do to the community at large. This is partially due to the way that risk is currently defined by assessment instruments.

Practitioners who have worked with both sexes have noted that women under supervision seem more open to sharing their feelings and thoughts than men, in part because women value relationships and the establishment of rapport to further them. Men under supervision, on the other hand, value independence and tend to withhold information (not always intentionally) because they have been socialized not to share their problems with others (Malloch & McIvor, 2011). As a result, officers and treatment providers view female offenders as having more needs than men, when women are just more open about their problems than men.

Motivational Interviewing and Establishing Rapport

Unstructured and informal styles of officer and client contact will reportedly establish trust and openness, regardless of the officer's gender. However, some women who may have been victimized, abused, or marginalized by men, preferred to be supervised by a female officer because they felt that another woman was more likely to understand their situation (Malloch & McIvor, 2011). Supervising a woman involves an ability to listen, empathize with, and be nonjudgmental about her past, while simultaneously aiding her in changing her victim mentality to become more responsible and empowered. **Motivational interviewing** is an evidence-based practice that is used by probation and parole officers to overcome difficulties that many women offenders face in the change process. This relational style of promoting empathy and listening

motivational interviewing
A communication style in which a community-supervision officer creates a positive climate of sincerity and understanding that assists an offender in the process of change.

Case management involves a balance between helping offenders get through their supervision, and communicating the consequences of their actions.

Bob Daemmrich / PhotoEdit

helps to establish mutual respect and trust to address the complex issues that women face. This style helps women offenders to feel empowered to build or strengthen their personal resources across a variety of domains such as family, work, and personal (van Wormer, 2010). Other asset-building approaches to change includes rewarding offenders with oral or written praise, certificates of completion, vouchers with small monetary rewards, or special privileges that encourage certain positive behaviors. Although removing privileges for negative behavior would be expected, simultaneously incorporating a reward system can motivate a probationer to change (Alexander, VanBenschoten, & Walters, 2008).

Gender-Specific Programming

Men on probation outnumber female offenders by a ratio of 3:1. Most assessments, supervision techniques, and treatment programs have therefore been developed to serve the largest group in terms of their backgrounds, risk level, and individual needs. While some of the strategies for men may also work fine for women, some of the gender differences discussed above that are unique for most women have been quite slow to develop. Other strategies, called **gender-specific programming**, require a deeper understanding of finer gender distinctions to formulate an approach that works better with women offenders. These strategies are discussed in Box 5.6.

| BOX 5.6 | **EVIDENCE-BASED PRACTICES IN COMMUNITY CORRECTIONS** | |

Explaining the Principle of Responsivity

The risk/needs/responsivity model is the most effective for offender assessment and treatment. This section better explains the third principle in the RNR model, the responsivity principle. Responsivity suggests that treatment will be more effective when certain offender characteristics are considered, so knowing more about the offender's attributes that may either limit or facilitate learning is important so that a learning environment is created to match the clients (Bourgon & Bonta, 2014). One of those factors may be the number of survival needs that an offender has, such as food, housing, safety, and unemployment that must be addressed first, but that may limit a person's ability to get the most of a treatment program (Taxman, 2014).

Gender-specific or gender-responsive programming with women offenders is a concrete example of responsivity because the treatment not only holistically addresses the topic areas and *life circumstances that most pertain to girls and women, but also how the treatment is delivered* is different. For example, childhood sexual victimization and/or substance abuse, which are common amongst women offenders, are more effective when they are addressed in a single-sex treatment environment with just women clients. This is important for a number of reasons: first, females may have been socialized at a very young age to ignore their own needs, and instead put their needs secondary to

males. Women in the criminal justice system are more likely to have suffered traumatic experiences at the hands of men that have placed women solely in sexualized and submissive interactions that they come to view themselves primarily as sexual dependent beings (van Wormer, 2010).

Treatment responsivity for women would also suggest that nonconfrontational therapy modalities work best for female offenders, particularly when the focus is on structural circumstances that were related to offending, rather than the offending behavior itself. Females may respond better when the therapy is connected to improving their relationships. At the same time, modalities of teaching women how to be independent, assertive, and how to establish healthy relationship boundaries may better alleviate issues of domestic violence, sexual abuse, mental health, low self-esteem, deficient educational opportunities, and substance abuse (Dalley, 2014).

Responsivity can be applied more broadly to many other groups of offenders, such as how best to teach offenders with learning disabilities. Another approach may be how to integrate culturally-relevant values and practices into treatment modalities that better fit an individual's family or community context, such as Native Americans who are supervised on tribal reservations (Melton, Cobb, Lindsey, Colgan, & Melton, 2014).

SUPERVISION OUTSIDE THE STATE

Interstate Compact
An agreement signed by all states and U.S. territories that allows for the supervision of parolees and probationers across state lines.

In the early 1930s, a probationer or parolee had to be supervised in the same state in which he or she was convicted. That practice was not feasible because offenders may have committed their crime in a different county or state from where they live, or could not move for better opportunities if life circumstances changed. As a result, the **Interstate Compact** was developed in 1937 by 25 states that agreed to supervise adult probationers and parolees for each other. By 1951, the Interstate Compact had been ratified by all states including the Virgin Islands. Interstate Compacts for juveniles were established in 1955 to provide for the return of juvenile runaways, escapees, and absconders as well as for cooperative supervision of juvenile probationers and parolees.

In more recent times, a national commission called the Interstate Commission for Adult Offender Supervision (ICAOS) was formed. One compact administrator from each state meets annually to ensure that supervision remains uniform and rules are modified if needed. The state compact administrator is responsible for communicating changes throughout the state, but everything is centralized on the Internet. Currently, there are over 115,000 offenders in the United States being supervised via interstate compact, most often for drug offenses, secondly for property crimes (burglary, larceny, fraud, forgery, and stolen property), and third for assault or robbery (http://www.interstatecompact.org).

Eligibility for the Interstate Compact

Each compact has a **sending state** (where the crime and sentence occurred) and a **receiving state** (the state that undertakes community supervision). The sending state determines the actual sentence and length of time served. The receiving state determines all standard and special conditions while under parole or probation supervision, which must be similar to other offenders within that receiving state. Figure 5.2 illustrates how the interstate compact works with two possible scenarios: prison or probation.

Offenders must fall into one of the following situations to seek approval:

- The offender is already a resident of the receiving state;
- The offender desires to live with relatives who are residents of the receiving state and agree to having the offender live with them;
- The offender, or a member of an offender's immediate family, received an employment transfer;
- The offender, or a member of an offender's immediate family, is transferred/relocated because of military orders (http://www.interstatecompact.org).

sending state
Under the interstate compact, the U.S. state in which a conviction is based.

receiving state
Under the interstate compact, the state that undertakes a supervision.

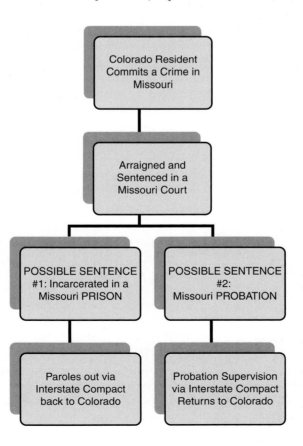

FIGURE 5.2 How Interstate Supervision Works

Interstate compacts are discretionary, and are approved by each receiving state on a case-by-case basis. An offender can be transferred either at the beginning of a probation or parole term, or, if sudden life circumstances change, in the middle of supervision as long as at least 90 days remain on the sentence.

About 7 out of 10 transfer requests are approved. When this happens, the receiving state agrees to provide "courtesy supervision" at the same level that it gives to its own cases. The receiving state informs the sending state on a quarterly basis of a probationer's progress. Roughly one-third of all interstate offenders incurred at least one reportable violation every year. While most "reportable violations" are if an offender has a large number of technical violations, it could also be absconding from supervision (discussed in detail in Chapter 7) or a new arrest/conviction.

Revocation and Extradition

The sending state retains ultimate authority to modify the conditions of probation, to revoke probation, and to terminate probation. A probation or parole violator may be incarcerated in the receiving state, at the expense of the sending state, while awaiting transfer (known as "retaking"). A sending state is expected to pick up and transport their own probationer or parolee back to the original jurisdiction to face the court or parole board. The pick-up may be done without going through extradition proceedings. It is also generally held that a sending state must retake all violent offenders. For nonviolent offenders, the sending state has discretion to determine upon what basis a violator may be returned. The main problem with retakes is that most states have limited resources for extradition. Offenders may wait for months in a county jail in the receiving state, in which case, many sending states merely terminate supervision in the receiving state after some time has been served, to avoid extradition costs.

The receiving state is obligated to surrender a probationer unless a new criminal charge is pending against the individual in the receiving state. In such a case, the probationer cannot be retaken by the sending state until he or she has answered the charges and has served their time for the new offense.

SUMMARY

- Techniques of effective case management include risk and needs assessments, developing a treatment plan, linking with cognitive-behavioral treatment, motivational interviewing, and principles of correctional intervention.

- The highest priority is placed on identifying risks that would likely jeopardize public safety if not addressed. At the same time, a priority is placed on identifying needs that, if not addressed, will likely lead to a return to criminal behavior.

- All forms of community supervision must involve some sort of treatment component and/or referrals to outside resources to help offenders. The treatment case plan help offenders achieve goals and assists the officer in following up with the appropriate level of supervision and treatment.

- Adequate supervision must focus on all phases of offenders' lives, including family issues and relations with the community in which they live and work.

- Working with female offenders requires knowing about the potential pathways to crime invoked by domestic violence, sexual and physical abuse, mental illness, lack of educational opportunities and skills, and substance abuse problems. Supervising women entails empathizing with their pasts while simultaneously aiding them in changing their victim mentality to become more responsible and empowered.

- Interstate compacts are written agreements between two agencies that allow probationers and parolees to be supervised in a state other than the place of conviction.

DISCUSSION QUESTIONS

1. Argue for the use of neighborhood-based supervision of probation over traditional methods. In what situations might NBS be most useful?

2. How does officer assessment of client needs in education, employment, treatment, and so on help develop a program plan? How much should a client be expected to do while under supervision?

3. Discuss the use of various risk prediction scales. How might risk assessment best be used in community supervision?

4. Discuss the concept of caseload and workload computation. Why might workload be a better method of allocating probation or parole officer resources?

5. How might interstate compact supervision be more helpful for an offender than local supervision? How might interstate supervision be more difficult for an offender?

 ## WEBSITES, VIDEOS, AND PODCASTS

Websites

Case Management and Risk Assessment
http://www.justiceconcepts.com

Applying EBP to Offender Supervision
http://nicic.gov/Library/024046

"Thinking for a Change" Lesson Plans—An Example of a Cognitive-Behavioral Program
http://nicic.gov/Library/025533

Motivational Interviewing
http://www.motivationalinterviewing.org

Evidence-Based Practices That Work in Florida
http://www.dc.state.fl.us/pub/recidivismWSIPP/index.html

Videos/Podcasts

Role-playing Scenarios on Video: Two PO/Offender Contact Sessions (24 minutes)
http://www.nicic.org/library/022005

Using Random Forest Risk Prediction in the Philadelphia Probation Department
This 9 minute video interviews Geoff Barnes and Jordan Hyatt about a new way of predicting risk for adult probationers. http://nij.ncjrs.gov/multimedia/video-barnes-hyatt.htm

Solutions in Corrections: Using Evidence-Based Knowledge
A 7-part NIJ sponsored video of Dr. Edward Latessa of the University of Cincinnati, about evidence-based practices in community supervision. http://nij.ncjrs.gov/multimedia/video-latessa.htm

What Works in Offender Supervision
An NIJ sponsored audio recording with a three-member panel led by Marlene Beckham, about effective practices in community supervision. http://nij.ncjrs.gov/multimedia/audio-nijconf2009-offender-supervision.htm
http:/nij.ncjrs.gov/multimedia/audio-nijconf2009-offender-supervision.htm

Female Offenders
The podcast interviews Ashley McSwain, executive director of Our Place D.C., and Dr. Willa Butler of Court Services and Offender Supervision Agency, discussing how both organizations are meeting the unique needs of female offenders.
http://www.corrections.com/system/podcast/file/120/CSOSA123.mp3__audio_mpeg_Object_.mp3

Monroe County, Indiana, Adult Community Corrections (Part 2)
(Length: 9 minutes) Part 2 discusses specific programs at five different risk levels, such as community service, Level 1 work release, Level 2–3 electronic monitoring, Level 4 curfew and GPS, and Level 5 daily reporting.
http://www.youtube.com/watch?v=w5pIo9P9o5o&feature=related

Probation Officers
(Length: 2 minutes) This video shows how probation officers assist offenders on probation or parole through formulating a rehabilitation plan and administering drug and alcohol tests. https://www.youtube.com/watch?v=aDrKiZKQF_o

CASE STUDY EXERCISES

Classification and Supervision in Probation and Parole

There are two new clients in your caseload. Below is the information you have received on each person. Using the Classification Instruments (Figure 5.1 in this chapter), complete the following:

1. Assess the risks and needs posed by the offender.

2. If you're able to interview the offender, use the Sample 50 question Interview at the end of this chapter. If an interview is not possible, consider the factors that have placed the client at risk and which factors are related to the offense.

3. Choose the top three to four problems to develop goals that the client should strive to achieve and action items of what the client needs to do to reach each goal. Then complete the "program plan" part of the assignment.

CASE A: Thomas User, Possession of Methamphetamine

Thomas User, age 20, has been placed on probation for possession of methamphetamine and Ecstasy. There were no known victims in the current offense. Police reports indicate that Mr. User was stopped by a police cruiser because he had been standing on the same corner for hours. An outer pat search revealed that he had eight tablets confirmed by drug testing to be Ecstasy and that he had enough methamphetamine for up to 12 hits.

Mr. User has two previous misdemeanor convictions as a juvenile, one for possession of paint huffing material and one as a minor in possession of alcoholic beverages. He has one misdemeanor conviction as an adult for menacing in the second degree.

Mr. User has remained in the same rental house with two roommates for the last three years—the roommates seem neutral influences at this point. He has been employed at a fast-food restaurant for seven months out of the last 12 months. The rest of the time, Mr. User says, he sold and used drugs. He drinks alcohol "recreationally on occasion," but alcohol does not seem to be related to his offense. He has a drug habit that is related to his arrest, but he has not yet been assessed for drug treatment. It is unclear how motivated he is to attend a treatment program.

Mr. User has an IQ of 68, which defines him as developmentally disabled, but he has no signs of mental illness. He is a high school dropout, having only completed the tenth grade. He does not have his GED. He reports himself in good physical health and has mentioned he has been sexually abused in the past by a former boyfriend, for which he

wants to be tested for HIV. You notice that he seems underweight, and he has two teeth missing.

Mr. User is single and not in any relationship right now, although he shares his living expenses with his two roommates. He reports that he has fathered one child, but he does not know the whereabouts of the child or the mother. The child is approximately three years of age, and there is no claim by the mother for child support.

CASE B: Maria Diaz, Identity Theft

Maria Diaz has been placed under community supervision for identity theft. She pleaded guilty to stealing the identities of 14 different victims from her employer's protected database, opening up accounts in their names and charging merchandise in small amounts, averaging $500 per victim, stealing an estimated grand total of around $7,000 in merchandise. She says that she has had significant financial difficulties and has filed for bankruptcy. Ms. Diaz is 25 years of age, divorced, and has no known juvenile arrest or adjudication history. As an adult, she had one prior forgery charge for which she was originally placed on probation (which was revoked for technical violations), and assigned to a halfway house for nine months, where she successfully completed her supervision.

Ms. Diaz has a high school diploma, and she has a transient job history. Moving from one minimum wage job to another, her employed time in the last year is estimated to be 50%. She was ordered to pay $7,000 in restitution for her current offense. She has not yet made any payments toward her restitution. Her divorce was finalized one year ago, and her ex-husband is nine months behind on child support payments. Because of her financial situation, she currently lives with her boyfriend, who is allegedly an undocumented immigrant from Mexico. She says that he "is unpredictable ... I never know if he'll be home at night or if he'll call and want me to bail him out of jail."

Because of her boyfriend's unstable situation, Ms. Diaz reports moving back and forth between her sister's house and her boyfriend's address, having lived at two different addresses in the past year. She has one dependent child living with her who is 10 years old. Mother and daughter both report good medical health, and there is no evidence indicating otherwise. There is also no evidence that alcohol or drug use was related to the current offense, and Ms. Diaz has never attended drug treatment. Her motivation to start restitution payments is low and her attitude is a bit problematic, but it is hoped that Ms. Diaz's resistance will change with motivational interviewing and job training. There is no evidence of developmental disability, sexual dysfunction, or emotional problems, and Ms. Diaz does not report being on any medications for mental or physical problems.

SAMPLE CLIENT INTERVIEW QUESTIONS

Column One: Questions to Ask Client The interview takes an average of 60 minutes. Use a natural, open conversational style of interviewing that is comfortable for both you and the probationer. If the offender presents some important or interesting information requiring follow-up, feel free to probe before returning to the structured sequence.

Column Two: The Client's Response
Choose one multiple choice response that best represents what the client is saying.

Questions to Ask Client	(Circle One Choice that Best Represents Offender's Response, unless Marked)

1. How did you get involved in the current offense? (*or if client denies*) What did the police say that you did?	1. Motivation for committing the offense:
	  a. Emotional (e.g., drug use, anger, assault, sex offense)
	  b. To get money (theft, selling drugs)
	  c. Both emotional and material

2. Was there anyone else involved?	2. Acceptance of responsibility for current offense/level of remorse:
	  a. Admits committing the offense and is remorseful
	  b. Admits committing the offense but emphasizes excuses (influence by friends, drinking, etc.)
	  c. Denies committing the offense

3. How old were you when you first had to go to court? What were/was the hearing(s) for? Any as a juvenile?	3. **a.** 14 or younger
	  b. 15–17
	  c. 18–22
	  d. 23 or older

4. What prior offenses have you been convicted of as an adult?	4. **a.** No priors
	  b. Mainly misdemeanors
	  c. Mainly felonies

5. Have you ever spent time on probation? (If so, tell me about those times and whether you were revoked or completed.)	5. **a.** None/first offense
	  b. One year or less
	  c. Over one year; up to three years
	  d. Over three years

6. Have you ever been in detention, jail or prison? Can you tell me about those times?	6. **a.** None
	  b. One
	  c. Two or more

7. Did you ever receive a disciplinary report while you were in detention or jail?	7. **a.** No **b.** Yes

8. Were you alone or with others when you get into trouble?	8. **a.** Alone
	  b. No consistent pattern
	  c. With accomplices

9. Now we want to ask you about your use of alcohol and drugs. How old were you when you began to use alcohol regularly?	9. **a.** Under 17
	  b. 18–20
	  c. 21 and over
	  d. Doesn't drink alcohol

Questions to Ask Client	(Circle One Choice that Best Represents Offender's Response, unless Marked)
10. Have you ever used illegal drugs? (*if so, tell me about this*)	10. **a.** Experimental drug user **b.** Moderate drug user—recommend further evaluation **c.** Severe drug user **d.** Doesn't use drugs
11. What is the longest period of time that you have been abstinent from alcohol or drugs?	11. **a.** Less than six months **b.** Longer than six months
12. Were you drinking or on drugs when you committed your offenses?	12. Percent of offenses committed while drinking/on drugs. **a.** Never **b.** 50% or less **c.** Over 50%
13. Has your alcohol or drug use ever caused problems with your employment?	13. **a.** No **b.** Yes
14. Are drugs readily available in your neighborhood?	14. **a.** No **b.** Yes
15. Let's talk about school. How far did you go in school? (*if you didn't graduate why not?*)	15. Probationer's school performance **a.** No problems **b.** Learning problems **c.** Lack of interest, behavior or other problems
16. Were you ever suspended or expelled from school?	16. **a.** No **b.** Yes
17. Now, I'd like to know about your work history. Start with the first one and work toward the present, What kind of jobs have you had and how long did you work at each place?	17. Primary vocation **a.** Unskilled labor **b.** Semi-skilled labor **c.** Skilled/Degree required **d.** No employment history
18. Do you feel that you have a very structured day where everything is scheduled or do you tend to have lots of free time?	18. **a.** Structured **b.** Free time
19. How do you spend your free time (e.g., with prosocial activities, hanging out.)	19. **a.** Mostly prosocial activities **b.** Mixture of prosocial and criminal activities **c.** Mostly criminal activities
20. Would you say that you are proud of any of your criminal activities?	20. **a.** No **b.** Yes
21. If you did something wrong as a teenager, how did your parents handle it?	21. **a.** Verbal or privilege withdrawal **b.** Permissive (let do as he/she pleased) **c.** Physical
22. While you were growing up, did either parent have a history of: criminal record, psychiatric hospitalizations, drinking problems, drug use, or use of violence in the home?	22. Parent problems (*circle all that apply*) **a.** Criminal Record **b.** Psychiatric hospitalization **c.** Drinking problems or Drug Use **d.** Domestic violence
23. How do you get along with your father now?	23. **a.** Close **b.** Mixed or neutral **c.** Not close
24. How do you get along with your mother now?	24. **a.** Close **b.** Mixed or neutral **c.** Not close

Questions to Ask Client

(Circle One Choice that Best Represents Offender's Response, unless Marked)

25. How do you get along with your brothers and sisters?

25.
a. Close
b. Neutral or mixed
c. Not close
d. No siblings

26. Have any of your siblings (including half/step siblings) ever been arrested?

26.
a. None
b. Some
c. Most
d. Not applicable

27. Are you satisfied with the level of family support that you have now?

27.
a. No
b. Yes

28. **Now I'd like to ask you about your intimate relationships.** What is your current marital status?

28.
a. Never married
b. Separated or Divorced
c. Married (Includes common-law)
d. Widowed

29. In your intimate relationship, who tends to make the decisions and have control?

29. Probationer generally:
a. Dominates
b. Has a plutonic/balanced relationship
c. Is nonassertive or dominated

30. Have you ever been abused by someone you cared about as an adult?

30. Abuse in Adult Relationships
a. Physical
b. Emotional
c. Sexual

31. How many of your significant others have been in trouble with the law, or have involved you in lawbreaking behavior?

31.
a. Essentially noncriminal
b. Mixed
c. Mostly criminal

32. Are you satisfied with the level of support that you are getting from your significant other?

32.
a. No
b. Yes
c. No significant other

33. If you have children, tell me their names, ages, and where they are living.

33.
a. No children
b. Names/ages: _____

34. **Now I'd like to ask you about your friendships.** How many of your friends been in trouble with the law?

34.
a. Essentially noncriminal
b. Mixed
c. Mostly criminal

35. How much contact do you have with your friends who have been in trouble with the law?

35.
a. No contact
b. Possible risk of contacting criminal peers
c. Active contact with criminal peers

36. Do you have any ties to gang members?

36.
a. No gang ties
b. Yes, but not currently
c. Current gang ties

37. When someone you know is in need, how likely are you to help them?

37.
a. Concerned about others
b. Limited concern
c. No real concern for others

38. When someone else tries to engage you in a physical fight, how do you respond?

38.
a. Walk away/avoid
b. Depends on the situation
c. Will stay to fight

39. Do you feel like you have control over events in your life?

39.
a. Yes, I have control
b. Sometimes I lack control
c. No, I have very little control

Questions to Ask Client	(Circle One Choice that Best Represents Offender's Response, unless Marked)
40. How often do you engage in risk taking behaviors?	40. **a.** Rarely takes risks **b.** Sometimes takes risks **c.** Generally takes risks
41. Do you see a problem in telling lies?	41. **a.** Telling lies is a problem **b.** Telling lies is not a problem
42. Do you believe in the saying "Do unto others before they do unto you?"	42. **a.** No, I disagree **b.** Sometimes **c.** Yes, I agree
43. Do you currently have any major medical problem (something that keeps bothering you, or something you should see a doctor about)?	43. Physical Health for age **a.** Excellent—very few complaints **b.** Average/good—some problems **c.** Poor/chronic health problems
44. Have you ever been treated for drug or alcohol use? OR psychological problems?	44. Psychological or treatment issues (circle as many as apply): **a.** Inpatient or outpatient drug/alcohol treatment **b.** Individual/group counseling for _____ **c.** Prior psychiatric hospitalization **d.** No problems
45. Do you live in a high crime neighborhood?	45. **a.** No **b.** Yes
46. How many times have you moved around in the last 12 months?	46. **a.** None **b.** Once **c.** Two or more times
47. Aside from your legal problems, what is the biggest problem in your life right now?	47. What does the probationer view as his/her most important problem area right now? **a.** Personal **b.** Relationships **c.** Vocational/Educational (including employment) **d.** Financial
48. How do you expect this problem to work out?	48. Attitude toward solving problems: **a.** Optimistic; expects to succeed **b.** Unclear **c.** Pessimistic; expects to fail
49. What goals do you have for the future? What are your plans for achieving these goals?	49. Future Plans **a.** Unrealistic goals or No goals **b.** Short-term goals (can be fulfilled within six months) **c.** Realistic, long-term goals (beyond six months)
50. What do you expect to get from probation if the judge agrees that you are eligible for it?	50. Probationer's general expectations about supervision **a.** No effect **b.** Monetary, counseling, or program help **c.** Hopes supervision will keep him/her out of trouble **d.** Negative expectations **e.** Mixed or unclear expectations

Sources in the public domain: Latessa, Edward J., Richard Lemke, Matthew Makarios, Paula Smith, and Christopher T. Lowenkamp. 2010. *The creation and validation of the Ohio Risk Assessment System: Final report.* Cincinnati, OH: University of Cincinnati, Center for Criminal Justice Research; Ohio Risk Assessment System National Institute of Corrections (n.d.). *Classification in probation and parole: A model system approach—A supplemental report: The Client Management Classification System.* Washington, DC: U.S. Government Printing Office.

Prioritizing Problems

Instructions: After you have conducted your interview, examine the first column of the table below. Choose three or four areas that are your client's priority problem areas that are most directly related to previous and current legal trouble.

Area	Rank Order Top 3–4 Problem Areas Related to Crime
Education/learning	
Mental health	
Employment record	
Vocational skills	
Financial management	
Residential stability	
Family history	
Interpersonal skills	
Companions/Peers	
Intimate marital relationships	
Drugs & alcohol	

DEVELOP THE CLIENT'S PROGRAM PLAN

Problem Statement: Using the top three or four problems identified in the table above, restate each problem area more specifically as to WHY or HOW that area is a problem for THAT client. *You need one problem statement for each problem area identified.*

Long-Range Goal: After each problem statement, develop one long range goal that the client will strive to achieve.

Probationer Action Item to Meet Goal: Develop two–three step-by-step instructions (like a roadmap) for the probationer to achieve to reach each long-term goal. Include dates or deadlines by which the client needs to complete each item.

Officer Action Item to Meet Goal: Think of at least one thing a supervision officer needs to do to help the client achieve his or her long-term goal for each of the problem areas.

Problem Statement #1:

Long-range Goal for Problem #1:

_____

_____

Probationer Action Item A to Meet Goal 1:

_____

_____

_____

_____

Probationer Action Item B to Meet Goal 1:

_____

_____

_____

_____

Probationer Action Item C to Meet Goal 1:

_____

_____

_____

_____

Officer Action Plan to Help Client Reach Goal 1:

_____

_____

_____

Problem Statement #2:

_____

Long-range Goal for Problem #2:

_____

_____

Probationer Action Item A to Meet Goal 2:

_____

_____

_____

_____

Probationer Action Item B to Meet Goal 2:

_____

_____

_____

_____

Probationer Action Item C to Meet Goal 2:

_____

_____

_____

_____

Officer Action Plan to Help Client Reach Goal 2:

_____

_____

_____

Problem Statement #3:

_____

_____

Long-range Goal for Problem #3:

_____

_____

Probationer Action Item A to Meet Goal 3:

_____

_____

_____

_____

Probationer Action Item B to Meet Goal 3:

_____

_____

_____

_____

Probationer Action Item C to Meet Goal 3:

_____

_____

_____

_____

Officer Action Plan to Help Client Reach Goal 3:

_____

_____

_____

Problem Statement #4:

_____

Long-range Goal for Problem #4:

_____

Probationer Action Item A to Meet Goal 4:

_____

_____

_____

Probationer Action Item B to Meet Goal 4:

_____

_____

_____

Probationer Action Item C to Meet Goal 4:

_____

_____

_____

Officer Action Plan to Help Client Reach Goal 4:

_____

_____

_____

_____

Signed/Dated,

_____   _____

Client   Supervising Officer

Supervision and Treatment for Offenders with Special Needs

CHAPTER LEARNING OBJECTIVES

1. Understand how intensive supervision differs from regular probation or parole supervision.

2. Identify various treatment options for drug-addicted offenders, such as drug court and therapeutic communities (TCs).

3. Analyze the issues inherent in the supervision and treatment of offenders with mental illness.

4. Describe the characteristics of a mental health court and a veterans' court.

5. List the specific strategies that are used for supervising and treating sex offenders in the community.

KEY TERMS

intensive supervision probation/parole (ISP)
relapse
Antabuse
drug courts
therapeutic communities (TCs)
retention rates
mental health courts
penile plethysmograph
child safety zones

Jacob Christopher "Tito" Ortiz, a 40-year old mixed martial artist, held the Ultimate Fighting Championship (UFC) for the light-heavyweight weight class from 2000 to 2003. Ortiz is open about his history of drug use and juvenile delinquency early in his life, including growing up around his parents' addiction to heroin. He escaped his own addiction to methamphetamines by competing in wrestling before building his amateur and professional fighting careers and coaching the 11th season of the television series, *The Ultimate Fighter*.

In April 2010, Ortiz was arrested for domestic violence, but was not formally charged in the incident. In January 2014, Los Angeles police responded to the scene where Ortiz had crashed his Porsche into a concrete Interstate median when he was returning home from a party. The fighter's blood alcohol level was 0.12. On April 30, 2014, Ortiz pled "no contest" to the driving under the influence (DUI) charges and received three years of probation, undisclosed fines, and was court-ordered to attend an alcohol education program.

Given Tito Ortiz's current age, drug use history, and the fact that this is his first DUI, would you consider him a special needs offender? Why or why not? What sort of treatment plan would you suggest?

INTENSIVE SUPERVISION AND SPECIALIZED CASELOADS

Standard probation and parole techniques provide sufficient monitoring for most sentenced offenders, but there are some offenders who have different needs or who need a more intensive form of monitoring and treatment. **Intensive supervision probation/parole** (ISP) is an enhanced form of supervision that subjects offenders to closer surveillance, more conditions to follow, and more treatment exposure than that to which regular probationers and parolees are subjected. Using smaller caseload sizes to keep tighter control on each offender, ISP initially emerged under an assumption that increased contact and surveillance would deter offenders from committing crimes. Although smaller caseloads certainly provided increased surveillance and control, more rules and contact visits did not deter offenders. Instead, watching offenders more closely allowed officers to detect significantly *more* technical violations and crimes, and this led to a higher revocation rate. One of the important lessons learned early on was that increased community supervision without the use of treatment programs is not effective and does not necessarily promote a safer community. Treatment access and helping offenders learn how to reduce criminal opportunities is just as important as the supervision component (Miller, 2014).

Important changes were introduced to save ISP from extinction, many of which emerged from evidence-based practices. First, high-risk offenders were chosen for close supervision with intensive cognitive-behavioral treatment to significantly lower recidivism. Second, change was treated as a process, and offenders were allowed a certain degree of noncompliance to complete a program. Third, direct contact with an offender in the form of personal visits and phone contact increased the chances of program completion. The important measure is not so much trying to catch offenders for every last technical violation, but to

intensive supervision probation/parole (ISP)
A form of probation that stresses intensive monitoring, close supervision, and offender control.

Mikael Karlsson/Alamy

Offenders on specialized caseloads must meet frequently with their supervision officer to discuss their progress.

focus on certain patterns of technical violations that may be related to reducing rates of rearrest for new crimes. High-risk offenders who were exposed to appropriate services to address criminogenic needs had fewer new crimes and rearrests (Paparozzi & Gendreau, 2005).

ISP is also referred to in the field as "specialized caseloads." The use of specialized caseloads means that a supervising officer becomes an expert in working with a particular subpopulation of offenders based on a particular criminogenic need or type of offense. About 10%–15% of probationers and parolees are eligible for inclusion on a specialized caseload. The specialized caseloads we discuss in this chapter consist of offenders who are addicted to drugs and alcohol, offenders with a mental illness, and offenders convicted of a sex offense.

OFFENDERS WHO ARE ADDICTED TO DRUGS AND ALCOHOL

Over half of offenders serving community correction sentences were either under the influence of drugs or alcohol during the commission of their crime, or substance abuse contributed in some way to their crime. Drug use ranges widely from methamphetamine, pharmaceuticals, and hallucinogens that have been around for decades, to newer manufactured synthetic or designer drugs such as K2, Spice, and N-bombe. Crack cocaine and heroin addiction is most likely tied to criminal behavior above many other types of drugs. Continued drug use on probation or parole is also a common reason for revocation. Treatment for drug use is more helpful and effective than punishment alone, but the quality of treatment varies widely and according to the severity of the problem. Figure 6.1 shows the various forms that drug treatment can take, from drug education classes to the most intensive long-term therapeutic communities (TCs). Being fully committed to treatment goals, bonding with treatment counselors, and interacting with other clients during treatment only enhances the benefits of treatment.

FIGURE 6.1
Substance Abuse Treatment Modalities: From Least to Most Intensive

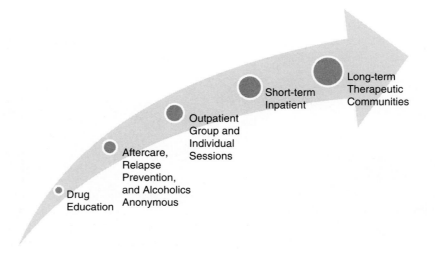

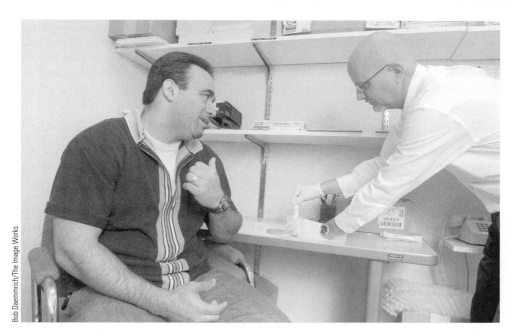

Drug and alcohol testing is common while on probation supervision.

Bob Daemmrich/The Image Works

According to Steiner (2004), obstacles that probation and parole officers face in the supervision of offenders with substance abuse problems include:

- assigning quality drug treatment programs to trained staff;
- ability to refer clients to a community-based program (due to lack of space availability);
- limited ability to keep clients in mandatory treatment; and
- relapse after intensive treatment ends (events, thought patterns, or stressful situations can trigger substance use).

Because of these challenges, a supervision style called a *treatment retention model* was proposed for parole officers. The model recommends that drug treatment begin for offenders while they are incarcerated and that, when they are released from prison, a cognitive-behavioral relapse prevention program retains offenders in treatment throughout the reentry and parole period (Steiner, 2004). Relapse prevention attempts to maintain the changes brought about during the treatment process through applying coping skills to stressful situations. If former addicts begin to **relapse** (return to drug use) while under supervision, Steiner argues for graduated sanctions tailored to a treatment plan rather than revocation to prison. In this section, we discuss general supervision and treatment strategies that probation and parole officers use with clients who have a problem with drugs or alcohol.

relapse
When an offender with a substance abuse problem returns to abusing alcohol and/or drugs.

Prescription Medications That Decrease Cravings

One supervision tool consists of monitoring a prescription medication that helps offenders stay away from drugs or alcohol. For example, alcoholics take **Antabuse**, a prescription medication that negatively reacts with their system if they ingest alcohol. Clients on Antabuse must take this medication every two to three days under the watchful eyes of staff, who administer the medication in

Antabuse
A prescription medication that causes someone to experience severe nausea and sickness if mixed or ingested with alcohol.

community clinics or in day reporting centers. Medications such as Methadone or Buprenorphine are administered to clients with addictions to heroin or other opiate-based drugs. Naltrexone is an opiate antagonist that blocks opiate access to brain receptors. These substances must be used over a long period of time to decrease severe drug dependency.

Drug Courts

drug courts
A diversion program for drug addicts in which a judge, prosecutor, and probation officer play proactive roles and monitor the progress of clients through weekly visits to a courtroom, using a process of graduated sanctions.

Drug courts are a proactive way for a court judge, prosecutor, and defense attorney to work with a treatment provider in monitoring and treating people with substance abuse problems. The idea of drug courts began in 1989 in Dade County, Florida, under an assumption that outpatient treatment interventions with first-time drug offenders or low-level drug users were more likely to curb future drug use than administering community sanctions without treatment. A second assumption was that the sooner a treatment intervention began after arrest, the less time an offender might spend in jail in a negative environment where drug use could continue. Currently, there are over 2,000 adult and nearly 500 juvenile drug courts in existence in the United States (Shaffer, 2011). There are also family drug courts that target parents with substance abuse problems who are in danger of losing custody of their children due to drug use.

The drug court concept is much different from traditional criminal courts. The judge, prosecutor, defense attorney, and probation officer all work together with a treatment provider to allow more informal and direct interaction. The entire team monitors the progress of each client for one year via court hearings every 2–4 weeks. Promoting the idea of a drug court from within the criminal justice system is sometimes politically difficult to navigate with practitioners who are trained in traditional courtroom practices, as Judge Alonso's *Field Notes* essay attests (see Box 6.1).

ELIGIBILITY FOR DRUG COURT. Drug courts are specifically for nonviolent drug offenders with at least a moderate substance abuse problem. The offenders may be misdemeanants or felons, and they must voluntarily agree to participate. An initial substance abuse assessment determines eligibility for program participation (Alarid, Montemayor, & Dannhaus, 2012). About half of drug courts are pre-adjudication, which means that upon successful completion of a drug court program, charges are dismissed. Post-adjudication drug courts usually mean that following a plea of guilty the sentence remains, but the defendant stays out of jail. If pre-adjudication offenders withdraw or are terminated from a program without successful completion, they are charged and tried for the original offense and sentenced accordingly.

Drug court treatment is one year in length and is based on a four-phase or levels system. Phase 1 typically begins with the most intensive number of hours—either full-time inpatient treatment—or 12 hours of outpatient treatment per week. Treatment often involves detoxification through acupuncture, group/individual counseling, and drug testing through saliva samples, urine screenings, and retina testing (pupillometer technology). Progression into the next phase occurs when the client is ready and as a way to reward appropriate behavior. As a client progresses through a program and reaches benchmarks of success (such as sobriety or keeping a job for a fixed number of days), the levels gradually taper down to less intensive outpatient treatment. Phase 4 is the final phase that must be completed before graduation.

BOX 6.1	**FIELD NOTES**	

What Were the Challenges and Rewards You Faced Introducing the Concept of Drug Courts?

As a judge handling criminal cases, I was frustrated at the large number of probationers testing positive for alcohol and illegal drugs. While working on my Masters at the National Judicial College, I shared my frustration with one of my professors. He introduced me to drug courts and their existence in many cities. That year, I returned home and began implementing the rudimentary steps of drug courts following the 10 key components. Because this was a new concept in our jurisdiction, I was met with incredible resistance from probation officers, defense attorneys, and the district attorney's office. Even our legislators informed me that this was a rehabilitative program not supported by the public. The public, they said, supported the "tough on crime, lock them up and throw away the key" concept.

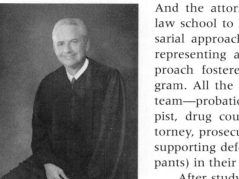

My first obstacle was the opposition of our 10 probation officers who had been trained on being "tough." In a traditional court, if a defendant tested positive for illegal drugs, in most cases, they recommended revocation and incarceration. If a judge ordered treatment instead of jail, the judge was considered weak and ineffective. One of the probation officers even asked to be transferred out of my court.

Our district attorney's office would not agree to pretrial diversion and did not buy into the non adversarial approach of drug courts. The DA advised me their prosecutors were not "social workers."

And the attorneys, who were trained in law school to be advocates for the adversarial approach, also had a difficult time representing a client within a team approach fostered by the drug court program. All the members in the drug court team—probation officer, treatment therapist, drug court coordinator, defense attorney, prosecutor—work together toward supporting defendants (drug court participants) in their recovery.

After studying the drug court program and reading the research, I knew drug court was the best program we had in our criminal justice system in addressing nonvoilent drug abusers and alcoholics. I realized the answer to all resistance was to educate all members on drug courts, including our county-elected officials and state legislators.

A federal grant provided for drug court training for ten people, and we became certified by the National Drug Court Institute. Slowly, attitudes began to change. The next challenge was communication with the program participants. Team members had to learn the technique of "motivational interviewing," a non confrontational, non argument, and sympathetic approach. Each participant is treated with fairness, dignity, and respect. Some personnel changes had to take place. In my 40-year professional career in criminal law and 15 years as a judge, drug courts are the one program that changes lives, saves money, and lowers crime. It is the most satisfying work I have done in my legal career.

Holding someone longer in a phase is used as a sanction if clients miss too many treatment sessions and/or court dates. With any addiction, relapse is expected, but participants are also responsible for preventing relapse from becoming a pattern. Clients who relapse might have to repeat certain segments of a program, and repeated relapses may mean short-term incarceration, or even program failure. Judges intervene before a pattern of technical violations occurs, as with regular probation, and the treatment team collaborates with drug treatment specialists.

With juvenile drug courts, parental participation is also required in all court hearings (once every two weeks) and weekly family treatment sessions. Parents are expected to consistently enforce all court orders and help with sobriety at home through being good role models and helping their child practice new cognitive thinking skills (Alarid et al., 2012). With family drug courts, adult parents with dependent children are the targeted clients. Family drug courts help parents become self sufficient, emotionally stable, and teach them to be effective parents so as to regain custody of their children.

GENDER-RESPONSIVE STRATEGIES. Treatment approaches for substance abuse should vary according to why clients abuse drugs and how they can best be helped. For example, research shows that women use drugs to cope with traumatic situations, such as domestic violence, mental illness, sexual abuse, and physical abuse. In this manner, women are likely to self-medicate alone and need to be drawn out of the despair they feel. Women also use substances to maintain a relationship with a significant other who also uses them (Guydish et al., 2011; Messina, Calhoun, & Warda, 2012).

To best help clients during the treatment process, drug court programs also vary by gender. Programs for women tend to concentrate on stressful and abusive situations leading to drug use, while treatment programs for men are more effective if they emphasize the problems caused by alcohol and drug abuse. Men tend to abuse substances in a more social and public context than women do, which involves establishing or maintaining a reputation or gaining a sense of control. Men have better completion rates, perhaps because drug courts have been modeled to better address their needs, patterns, and reasons for drinking (Messina, Calhoun, & Warda, 2012).

As a result, gender-specific drug court programs have evolved that separate women from men. Programs for women can be directed more specifically at traumatic significant relationships, parenting issues, and domestic violence. Supervision of female probationers is more effective if they engage children and significant others in recovery. At the same time, using programs that empower women to feel more competent will help them achieve independence. Women who were exposed to gender-specific treatment modalities did better than in a mixed-gender environment (Messina et al., 2012).

EVALUATING DRUG COURTS. A meta-analysis of drug courts found that drug courts reduced recidivism by 37% to 50% for participants compared to non participants (Eggers, MacKenzie, Mitchell, & Wilson, 2012; Gottfredson, Kearley, Najaka, & Rocha, 2007). Drug courts that served nonvoilent adult offenders with moderate addictions fared better than those of different client characteristics, such as juveniles.

Juvenile drug courts have smaller reductions than adult drug courts in general. Juvenile participants who had positive and active support from their parents throughout the phases of the program were more likely to complete drug court than were youths whose parents were less supportive (Alarid et al., 2012). Access to other community services, program size, police practices, prosecutor decisions, program duration, and violation policies affected the recidivism rate as well. According to Bouffard and Richardson (2007), drug courts seemed to be more effective with methamphetamine users than among alcohol offenders who had been convicted of DWI (see Box 6.2).

In sum, the drug court model is more effective when it targets nonvoilent offenders and individuals who are genuinely motivated to change. Tied to that, gender-responsive techniques help women respond to drug court treatment

BOX 6.2 **COMMUNITY CORRECTIONS UP CLOSE**

Does DWI Court Work with Repeat DWI Offenders?

Every year in the United States, about 1.5 million people are arrested for DWI. While many are first-time offenders, a small number of people are chronic repeat DWI offenders that are responsible for 80% of all drunk driving incidents (DeMichele & Lowe, 2011).

DWI courts were established to address the seeming disregard for the law and unwillingness to change their behavior behind the wheel. DWI courts allow offenders to have their criminal records expunged after successful completion so there is quite a bit at stake. Modeled after drug courts, DWI courts use daily journals, alcohol counseling, and allow participants to have input so that they feel more connected to the program staff, and this helped most participants. According to one person,

> The program gave me a new, positive outlook on life. For the better, it helped me to have organization and responsibility which helped me keep on track. Also, it helped me to start a sober lifestyle. In the past, my plans revolved around drinking. Now, it revolves around achievement and enjoying life. (Narag, Maxwell, & Lee, 2013, p. 237)

Some participants found it difficult to be under supervision and treatment where they felt they had little control, such as one participant who ended up not finishing:

> First of all, the environment is not conducive to honesty as they assume the clients to be extremely[sic] alcoholics. They do not differentiate between people with different drinking patterns. Secondly, the clinician/counselor enjoys her control and abuses power; the counseling program is not about recovery but rather the counselor's enforcing her will on clients. (Narag, Maxwell, & Lee, 2013, p. 242)

A recent risk assessment that differentiates first-time DWI from habitual DWI offenders found that those with multiple DWIs tended to be nonvoilent, middle-aged Caucasian males who were employed, but were more defiant, more likely to have dropped out of high school, and more likely to be emotionally unstable when compared to first-time DWI offenders (DeMichele & Lowe, 2011).

Sources: DeMichele, Matthew and Nathan C. Lowe. 2011. DWI recidivism: Risk implications for community supervision. *Federal Probation 75*(3): 19–24; Narag, Raymund E., Maxwell, Sheila Royo, and Lee, Byung. 2013. A phenomenological approach to assessing a DUI/DWI program. *International Journal of Offender Therapy and Comparative Criminology 57*(2): 229–250.

(Messina, Calhoun, & Warda, 2012). Finally, the structure of the program matters most when it has enough leverage to hold clients accountable, possesses capable staff, and is long enough in duration to adequately help fully with the change process. It seems that leverage is more powerful with pre-adjudication clients who can complete drug court without a conviction than having a drug court for clients who have already been convicted (Shaffer, 2011).

Therapeutic Communities

When outpatient treatment is not enough, offenders on probation or parole who have more severe addictions require an inpatient residential treatment facility, such as a residential drug treatment center or therapeutic community. **Therapeutic communities** (TCs) focus on long-term treatment of alcoholism and drug addiction and abstinence from substances for criminal offenders. This section addresses TCs in the community. TCs are generally better suited for long-term polydrug addictions (addiction to more than one kind of drug for an extensive period of time), whereas drug courts are geared toward moderate addiction. Helping an individual through change is a process that entails stumbling blocks.

therapeutic communities (TCs)
Residential community facilities specifically targeted to drug-addict and alcoholic offenders and/or drug addicts amenable to treatment.

TABLE 6.1 Comparing Therapeutic Communities and Drug Courts

Characteristic	Therapeutic Community	Drug Court
Initial Point of Intervention	**Post-Adjudication Only**	**Pre-Adjudication or Post-Adjudication**
Type of program	Residential/inpatient	Nonresidential/outpatient
Where located	Community or prison	Community only
Average length of stay	32 weeks	45 weeks
Voluntary	Yes	Yes
Percent of waking hours devoted to treatment and self-improvement	100%	20%–25%
People involved in defendant's progress	TC counselor, TC former addicts, TC peers in program	Judge, prosecutor, public defender, probation officer/case manager, treatment provider
Who imposes rewards and sanctions	TC participants/peers (confrontational)	Judge (nonadversarial collaborative)
Treatment and monitoring forms	Group, confrontation, individual counseling, community meetings, drug testing, shaming, extra chores	Group counseling, individual counseling, drug testing, acupuncture, community service, case management visits

Source: Bhati, Avinash S., John K. Roman, and Aaron Chalfin. 2008. *To treat or not to treat: Evidence on the prospects of expanding treatment to drug involved offenders.* NCJ 222908. Washington, DC: U.S. Department of Justice.

Thus a typical TC provides six to nine months of residential drug and alcohol treatment, with a period of aftercare as an offender transitions from a therapeutic environment to dealing with the stressors of daily life. Table 6.1 summarizes the differences between TCs and drug courts.

THE THERAPEUTIC COMMUNITY ENVIRONMENT. TC candidates are thoroughly screened for suitability and readiness for treatment. If accepted, offenders with a substance abuse problem must be motivated to adhere to all rules and participate in all activities required by a TC program. A TC environment is considered a supportive surrogate family, except that physical fighting and sexual relations are not allowed. Each day in a TC is highly structured and disciplined. Clients have daily cleaning chores within the facility and hours of peer group sessions in which the attitudes and behavior of each resident are confronted. The goal of these sessions is to tear down the defense mechanisms and excuses that addicts adopt when using drugs as a response to a desire or stressor. The sessions attempt to resocialize clients to new thoughts, attitudes, and behavioral choices in all areas of their lives (with family, friends, work, leisure time, spirituality, etc.). Other types of counseling focus on self-worth, self-discipline, and respect for authority. There is little idle time, for even free personal time is used for some type of intellectual or creative self-improvement.

The TC is also the only type of program that is largely peer-operated and peer-enforced. Although there might be a free-world staff contact person, a group is run by residents, who earn various leadership roles based on a level's hierarchy, and they enforce the TC rules. Clients who graduate from a program are transferred to outpatient treatment while still remaining on probation or parole, depending on their initial status. Abel Salinas, manager of a community-based, residential substance abuse treatment facility (SATF), provides insight into the rewards and challenges of working with probationers who have substance abuse problems (see Box 6.3).

| BOX 6.3 | **FIELD NOTES** |

When working with offenders who have difficulties with substance abuse, what are the most rewarding long-term and short-term aspects? What are the greatest challenges and how do you and your staff attempt to overcome them?

There are many rewarding aspects that result from working with substance abusers. However, the single most rewarding aspect that I can see is the improvement in the quality of life for, not just the offender who successfully completes treatment, but for the immediate and extended family as well. Too many times, children and spouses suffer the residual effect of a drug user's inability to maintain employment, effectively communicate problems to their significant others, and serve as role models to children who seek the support and guidance of adult users. Children who witness this learned behavior often times fall into the same lifestyle as their using parents, and the cycle continues.

By helping to repair one person, the domino effect of ruined lives and extreme hardships for families can be stopped or broken, and in some situations, even reversed. Seeing a former offender who spent time in the drug and alcohol treatment facility at a local grocery store, while putting gas in their car, or at a movie theater, and having them tell you that they have removed themselves from their drug-using lifestyle and are well on their way to improving their family relationships and employment status is nothing short of gratifying.

A very rewarding short-term aspect are those offenders who come into the program who, although not entirely excited to be here, nonetheless appear to have their stress level lowered somewhat by their new structured and therapeutic environment. This is often the complete opposite of the chaotic and deceitful environment that they've left, where the threat of violence, arrest, and looking over their shoulder is the norm.

Abel Salinas
Former Residential Treatment Facility Manager

Courtesy of Leanne Fiftal Alarid

The single greatest challenge in residential services can be described as the career criminal vs. the drug abuser. The drug abuser readily admits a problem, wants help, understands the negative consequences of their drug abuse, but still feels a strong desire to use drugs. This is where the treatment staff, probation officers, and security personnel intervene to assist the individual, using cognitive behavioral therapy and motivational interviewing techniques.

On the other hand, the career criminal does not admit a problem, does not want help for a drug problem, does not understand the negative consequences of their drug abuse or drug dealing, does not have any desire to stop their anti social behavior, and sees treatment as only a way of avoiding a lengthy jail or prison term. Their only desire is to get back into the community and neighborhoods and continue their lifestyle. This clash of attitudes and beliefs between the career criminal and drug abuser is probably one of the most challenging aspects to deal with in residential services. Although the career criminal, in my opinion, represents only a small minority of the entire population, their manipulation of well-intentioned residents, staff, and counselors can have a detrimental impact on many of the residents.

We try our best to overcome this constant push and pull by singling out the career criminals and offering them more intensive treatment, while paying special attention to their criminogenic needs. Good quality communication between security staff, counselors, and probation officers keeps us on our toes and lessens the chances of falling for the manipulative ways of the career criminal.

retention rates
The combined total of successful program completers and active program enrollees compared to the total number admitted to drug court.

CHALLENGES OF THE TC. One of largest challenges for TCs to overcome is a low program completion rate. Treatment programs should expect failures and relapses, but during the first 30 days between 25% and 85% of new residents drop out. Efforts are needed either to improve **retention rates** (perhaps by redefining *success* and *failure*) or to better screen applicants' motivation to participate. For the first 30 days, new residents need to be more thoroughly educated about the treatment process, and they might need confidence building before being confronted in group therapy.

A second challenge concerns the use of shaming and humiliation with clients who misbehave or fail to participate. Examples include "PT" (extra chores or duties), wearing a dunce cap or a sign (stating the infraction) around the facility for a specified period of time, or shaving one's head. Some of the methods of punishment for disobedience have been criticized for their ineffectiveness in changing behavior.

TYPES AND USES OF THERAPEUTIC COMMUNITIES. A community-based TC is designed for clients who have often failed in other community programs such as from halfway houses, probation, or parole due use of alcohol or illegal substances. Residential drug and alcohol treatment programs are also used as diversion from prison. For example, a community-based SATF is for nonvoilent felony men and women probationers. A SATF provides an alternative to jail or prison provided there are no behavioral or mental health problems. Like with drug court, a SATF has a phase system that first consists of offenders recognizing the extent of their problem and motivating them for change. Then, through individual and group counseling, they are exposed to cognitive restructuring techniques to change negative feelings and thinking patterns that act as a predisposition to substance use. The client then establishes life goals and explores other areas such as relationships, spirituality, nutrition, HIV/AIDS education, and GED preparation. Depending upon an individual's motivation, treatment could be shortened or extended from 90 to 180 days (Alarid & Webster, 2013). Then clients enter an aftercare program in which they live at home and report to a probation officer. This is important because transition from residential living to community living is seen as a prime opportunity for relapse. Probation officers continue to work with treatment facility staff to review clients' progress (Alarid & Webster, 2013).

Sometimes TC programs are used as a transition step for clients who graduate from prison-based TCs or other types of drug treatment programs while behind bars. For example, women in California with drug problems can attend a drug treatment program and then, upon their release, be transferred to a residential program in the community to grapple with issues of relapse and possible temptations.

EVALUATIONS OF THERAPEUTIC COMMUNITIES. Offenders who participate in community-based residential treatment programs are often in the last program available before jail or prison (Perez, 2009). The pressure to succeed can cause significant stress, and clients are also at high risk for relapse and recidivism because making the transition from a structured environment directly to their home in the community, even when under probation and parole supervision, poses challenges (Sung, 2011). An interesting look at the effect of treatment interventions on specific problems showed that not all risks and needs affect people in the same way. While limiting exposure to antisocial family members helped decrease probationer drug use, treatment interventions did not change antisocial cognitions or thinking processes significantly (Wooditch, Tang, & Taxman, 2014). This may be because of the type of intervention was not affecting cognitive distortions or because thinking patterns take longer to change than behavior (Helmond, Overbeek, Brugman, & Gibbs, 2015).

Overall evaluations of residential treatment have found that it reduces future criminal behavior and future drug use, particularly for those who are accepting of program norms and protocols (Sung, 2011). For those who complete it, residential drug treatment is more effective than outpatient treatment (Levin, 2011). Participants who do not complete treatment are vulnerable to relapse, which is fairly common for offenders with drug and alcohol addictions.

SUPERVISING OFFENDERS WHO ARE MENTALLY ILL

A disproportionately large number of people with mental health issues come to the attention of the criminal justice system. Due to the deinstitutionalization of the mentally ill and the lack of community mental health providers to serve clients without health insurance, indigent people with mental illnesses have limited resources to avoid drawing attention to themselves. As a result, jails and prisons have become the largest mental health institutions in the country. Yet correctional institutions are stressful and overcrowded places that in turn exacerbate mental conditions (Slate, Buffington-Vollum, & Johnson, 2013). Also, the cost of confining an inmate being treated for a severe mental illness to special housing is 2.5 times greater than for an inmate not on psychotropic medication. It is for this reason that most offenders with mental illness qualify for community correctional supervision.

It is estimated that about 16% of all probationers have general mental health needs and between 5% and 10% of parolees have serious mental illnesses that require medication and therapy (Slate, Buffington-Vollum, & Johnson, 2013). The Council of State Governments (2008, p. 2) reported that "nearly two-thirds of boys and three-quarters of girls detained in juvenile facilities were found to have at least one psychiatric disorder, with approximately 25% of these juveniles experiencing disorders so severe that their ability to function was significantly impaired." Although a small number of offenders with mental illnesses need to be separated from the rest of society, incarceration is overly stressful and not the best situation for stabilizing the majority of mentally ill individuals, who are better served in the community.

Supervising offenders with mental illnesses poses a special challenge because most correctional supervision officers do not have training in mental health or in psychiatric disorders. Having a base level of knowledge about various forms of mental illness and the laws pertaining to the treatment of mental illness is very important when working with offenders. Here are some of the basics: Most people with severe mental illnesses are not violent or dangerous; they simply need help getting to a psychiatrist; becoming stabilized on medication; and meeting their basic needs for safety, food, and permanent housing. The long-term challenge is to convince offenders with mental illness to remain on medication even when they report feeling better. People with severe mental disorders who go off their medications may eventually find themselves in jail or on probation because they eventually draw attention to themselves in two possible ways. Some self-medicate with illegal drugs or turn to criminal activities to support a habit

FIGURE 6.2
Five Community-Based
Programs That Integrate
Counseling for Offenders
with Mental Illnesses

and are turned away from a resource-depleted mental health system. There are also some severely mentally ill people who are not stabilized on medication and who may act out in deviant ways, though they are not necessarily violent or dangerous (Slate, Buffington-Vollum, & Johnson, 2013). Figure 6.2 identifies community-based responses to offenders with mental illnesses, including mental health courts, veterans' courts, specialized caseloads, outpatient clinics, and residential treatment.

Mental Health Courts

mental health courts
A diversion program for mentally ill defendants in which a judge, prosecutor, and probation officer play proactive roles and monitor the progress of clients through weekly visits to a courtroom.

Many of the people suffering from mental illnesses who come to the attention of the criminal justice system are appropriate candidates for a diversion program, from which they can obtain linkages to medication and counseling services. Mental health courts began in 1997 for this purpose. Like drug courts discussed in the previous section, **mental health courts** use a team problem-solving approach, in lieu of traditional case processing, to supervise and treat mentally ill offenders in the community. Participants are initially identified during the jail booking process through mental health screening or assessment. For example, a jail diversion coordinator receives an instant message when a client with certain criteria is booked in jail. Within 24 hours, the diversion coordinator notifies the courts that an eligible diversion case should be considered (Redlich, Liu, Steadman, Callahan, & Robbins, 2012). Eligibility criteria are long-term Axis I disorders that, as defined by the current version of the *Diagnostic and Statistical Manual of Mental Disorders*, have affected daily functioning, such as schizophrenia, anxiety or obsessive–compulsive disorder, bipolar disorder, and severe depression. Participants must be competent and able to voluntarily participate on their own. The eligible Axis I disorders do not include substance abuse as a primary diagnosis. However, even though an Axis I disorder must be an offender's primary problem, substance abuse is frequently a secondary diagnosis. Offenders with a mental illness who also have

Barry Lewis/Alamy

Offenders with mental illness receive counseling and medication monitoring by a service provider who in turn communicates client progress with the community supervision officer.

a substance abuse problem—a large proportion of this population—are treated simultaneously for both conditions (Redlich et al., 2012).

Another way of identifying appropriateness for the diversion program bypasses the preapproval of a prosecutor, relying instead on mental health specialists along with a jail medical screener to make a group decision that is then presented to a court for final approval. Once a judge agrees, the group creates a transition plan while an eligible offender stabilizes on medications in jail, separated from the regular inmate population (Rubin, Alarid, & Lopez, 2014).

Once a participant is accepted into a mental health court program, a mental health court team deals with each offender. A typical mental health court team is comprised of a judge, prosecutor, defense attorney, mental health providers, and a pretrial services officer with specialized training in mental health (Slate, Buffington-Vollum, & Johnson, 2013). Defense attorneys assist offenders who are unable to fully understand their circumstances because of their psychiatric disorder and possible chemical dependence. The same team members meet with each participant twice a month in a status hearing to discuss progress in the program. The status hearing takes place in a courtroom whose daily docket is specifically for mental health court clients. Prior to each status hearing, team members "staff" each individual situation, which means they meet as a group without a participant present to update and share information. Each team comes to a decision on which actions to take at the next status hearing—whether to increase or decrease medication, treatment exposure, and sanctions, to graduate a participant to the next level, or to in some way reward him or her with a gift certificate. Specially trained probation officers have smaller caseloads that use a special case management style specific to the needs and challenges that people with mental illnesses face.

The more successful mental health courts have a solid community partnership with an availability of services addressing homelessness, transportation needs, and medication stability. Outcome evaluations of various courts have found that participants in mental health courts received fewer new charges and arrests. However, it took nearly twice as long for a diverted client to start mental health court treatment after arrest than a similar client who was convicted through the traditional criminal courts (Redlich et al., 2012). Once a client enters mental health court, they seemed to receive services at a higher rate compared to individuals who were court-ordered through a traditional process to undergo treatment (Council of State Governments, 2008).

Veterans' Courts

About one in five military service members who returned from overseas had some level of post-traumatic stress disorder (PTSD) or major depression that can result in suicide. PTSD is a type of mental illness that frequently causes memory loss, blackouts, and a reliving of horrific scenes that can lead to panic attacks, anger, depression, and substance abuse. Less than half of those affected will ever seek mental health treatment or counseling, due in part to the stigma that mental illness has and the fact that symptoms of PTSD may not occur right away (Thompson & Gibbs, 2012).

Within a year after he was discharged and returned home, former Marine Jonathon Wheeler had such intense panic attacks that he was unable to work. For the next five years, his behavior became worse rather than better. He drank alcohol, used drugs, and exhibited violent behavior in front of his wife and two children before an arrest landed him in jail facing a possible conviction. A few months after the arrest, he agreed to go to counseling, where he was diagnosed with PTSD. Cases like Mr. Wheeler's can now be handled in an alternative court called veteran's court, which allows military service members a diversionary alternative to criminal conviction if they comply with required counseling and medication and agree to permanently stop alcohol and drug use (Mador, 2010).

Although most military personnel never come in contact with the criminal justice system, about 6.3% of arrestees are military veterans. Of the military personnel who are arrested, about 22% have been diagnosed or treated for a substance abuse problem and 34% have been diagnosed or treated for some type of mental disorder—most commonly for PTSD (White, Mulvey, Fox, & Choate, 2012). The Department of Veterans Affairs (VA) acknowledged that options need to be provided for treatment and close supervision of such cases to ensure stability with medication and satisfaction of basic needs for food, clothing, and shelter. The earliest veterans' courts were opened in 2004 in Anchorage, Alaska, and in 2008 in Buffalo, New York (Berenson, 2010). They have since expanded to over 22 jurisdictions in the United States, particularly in areas with a disproportionately high number of vets. For example, a court was established in 2011 in San Antonio, Texas, which is home to over 160,000 veterans, of whom 11,000 (less than 7%) have experienced combat.

Most veterans' courts require, first, that an individual has been honorably discharged from the military, which is also a prerequisite for obtaining the VA benefits that help fund these courts. Although veterans can obtain help through the VA at any time provided their mental illness or traumatic brain injury is directly connected to combat, a veterans' court intervenes once a misdemeanor has been committed. Veterans' court participants agree to undergo weekly drug testing and treatment through the VA Health Care Network, as needed for their individual situation (Russell, 2009). Some courts also assign a court-approved

BOX 6.4	**EVIDENCE-BASED PRACTICES IN COMMUNITY CORRECTIONS**

How Can Officers Reinforce Positive Behavior for Offenders Under Their Supervision?

Community supervision takes many forms, and can involve probation and parole officers working as partners with various treatment providers and problem-solving courts. Licensed counselors and therapists deliver the treatment, whereas the probation and parole officers ensure compliance with the court-ordered conditions. New research indicates that officers who become more aware of these various treatment modalities and integrate positive incentives into the supervision process will help reinforce treatment and encourage even more change. The possibilities of incentives range widely, and have been divided into three categories: incentives at the discretion of an individual officer, incentives needing supervisory approval, and incentives needing court or parole board approval.

Positive incentives that an individual officer can use may include a later curfew time for a special event or a temporary reduced reporting requirement, which may be either one less time an offender must see his or her officer, or by temporarily changing the mode of reporting to call-in. Positive recognition during reporting appointments can include encouragement, verbal recognition for accomplishments, giving the offender a completion certificate, or affirmation letter. If warranted in certain situations, reference letter from an employer, or a school helps in this endeavor.

Some rewards for good behavior need supervisory approval, and they include decreasing community service hours, or permanently reducing reporting requirements. Incentives that would require involvement of a supervisor may include providing verbal praise, a monthly bus pass, or a clothing voucher at a second-hand store. Judges in problem-solving courts use verbal praise, written recommendation letters, and recognition ceremonies during supervision. They have been known to ask offenders to speak at mental health court graduations, or at life skills classes. Incentives needing court or parole board approval include the officer recommending later curfew times or doing away with curfew altogether, decreased drug testing, and the ultimate recommendation: early termination from supervision.

---

mentor to provide a participant with a positive support system and to help him or her with resolving problems. As with all problem-solving courts, veterans' court also employs a system of incentives for compliance and sanctions for noncompliance, similar to that discussed in Box 6.4. Once conditions are met, an offense is expunged from an individual's criminal record. Early evaluations of participants have shown a low recidivism rate (Russell, 2009).

Specialized Mental Health Probation Caseloads

Another response to supervising offenders with mental illness is by means of a specially trained caseload officer specializing in mental health issues (Castillo & Alarid, 2011). When traditional probation caseloads were compared with specialized caseloads, 90 supervisors drawn from a nationwide sample of 25 probation departments reported training in mental health issues and a reduced caseload number as the two biggest differences (Skeem, Emke-Francis, & Eno Louden, 2006). Such training gave probation officers a more empathetic understanding of various mental imbalances, enabling them to recognize mental deterioration before a situation reached the point of no return. Training also helped officers to understand psychological resistance and to learn how to gain the trust and compliance necessary to work with this population. Specialized caseload size was less than half that for traditional probation—averaging 48 clients compared with 130—allowing officers on specialized caseloads a style of case management with an enhanced focus on both treatment and supervision (Skeem et al., 2006).

Maintaining a positive working relationship with treatment providers was important for these specialized probation officers. The two greatest challenges found in working with mentally ill probationers were coordinating treatment and ensuring compliance with medication and counseling sessions. Mentally ill individuals tend to behave in a noncompliant manner more often than do probationers in traditional caseloads (Babchuk, Lurigio, Canada, & Epperson, 2012). Consequently problem-solving strategies and court appearances were used much more often than revocation to address noncompliance. It is recommended that community officers who work with offenders with mental illnesses be:

> patient and flexible, have a basic knowledge of mental health disorders, and be particularly skilled in firm yet non-confrontational communication strategies . . . monitoring compliance with any medication regimen and detecting signs that may indicate that the defendant is a danger to others or disoriented . . . pay attention to signs of withdrawal (such as poor hygiene, disorganization within a household or drastic changes in physical appearance) . . . [and] establish a collateral network that includes treatment providers and individuals who are in daily contact with the defendant and thus in the best position to observe early signs of deteriorating and/or dangerous behavior. (Administrative Office of the U.S. Courts, 2007, Chapter V, p. 17)

Outpatient Community Clinics

Outpatient community clinics allow mentally impaired offenders who are not a danger to themselves or others a chance to avoid the harmful incarcerative environment, while improving independent functioning and continuing an ongoing treatment regimen. Outpatient community clinics as a form of diversion appears most successful when services begin immediately following arrest or following residential treatment as a part of a continuum of care. For example, one outpatient treatment clinic serves clients who have been arrested for a misdemeanor offense, who are eligible for a personal recognizance bond, and who have been diagnosed with a mental disorder. Referrals thus come within the first 48 hours after arrest from pretrial staff, magistrate judges, or law enforcement officers. The client must also voluntarily express interest to receive mental health treatment. Once approved for release on recognizance, a law enforcement officer will drive the client directly from detention to the outpatient clinic for an initial psychiatric evaluation by the clinic psychiatrist. The program serves up to 55 clients for 3–12 months with medications and helps them remember to attend their next court date and pay all court fines, if ordered. A licensed cognitive-behavioral therapist and two case managers are on staff (Rubin, Alarid, & Lopez, 2014). Outpatient clinics reduced the likelihood of future arrests for offenders with mental illnesses compared to one year before, because compliance with psychotropic medication is more likely to lead to longer term stability.

Based on this discussion, we recommend that mental health services be strongly connected with criminal justice agencies. Examples of programs with such criminal justice collaborations are those in Milwaukee; Wisconsin; and Multnomah County, Oregon. Further, it is necessary to continually educate workers in criminal justice about mental health issues, such as through a standardized training curriculum for probation and parole officers. A model program in New York incorporates elements of crisis intervention and recognizes signs of mental disorder (Slate, Buffington-Vollum, & Johnson, 2013).

Community-Based Residential Facilities for Mentally Ill Offenders

An inpatient residential facility is an alternative to a jail setting for offenders who need more structure and treatment intervention but are not yet ready to be released to outpatient services, probation, or parole. For example, Castillo and Alarid (2011) studied a 60-bed community-based facility for clients with one or more major mental disorders who were admitted by a court order and who had high-risk and needs scores. Since the facility opened in 2004, it has served 750 high-risk probationers with counseling and medication stabilization. Mentally ill offenders are then transferred to probation within three to six months to a specialized caseload for one year. The study uncovered the role of alcohol in the lives of mentally ill offenders. Specifically, offenders with an alcohol problem were more likely to recidivate earlier and be rearrested for a violent offense than were mentally ill offenders who did not have a problem with alcohol (Castillo & Alarid, 2011).

SUPERVISING SEX OFFENDERS

The term "sex offense" refers to sexual acts against a victim's will, and includes a wide range of behaviors ranging from exposing oneself in a public place (a misdemeanor) to rape (a felony). Some sex offenders are aggressive and violent, whereas others are passive and use more subtle techniques to gain compliance from their victims. In any case, sexual acts against children are included in the definition because it is assumed that children are unable to give consent. Sex offenders are a heterogeneous group, and some target children whereas others exclusively victimize adults. Child molesters are more likely to have been victimized as children by someone else, whereas offenders convicted of sexual assault evince anger management problems and chemical dependency (Alexander, 2010). In any case, whether child molester, incest offender, or rapist, a perpetrator is more likely to "groom" victims with whom he or she is already familiar.

People might be surprised to find out that there are more convicted sex offenders under conditional supervision in their community than are incarcerated. However, the period of supervision for sex offenders is significantly longer than it is for other types of offenders. Sex offenders generally have lower recidivism rates than other types of offenders, but they are strongly feared and regarded with enormous disdain by the public. Public contempt and political pressures have caused more laws to be passed that regulate sex offenders—perhaps more than any other type of offender, with the exception of death row prisoners. These laws include mandatory treatment, polygraphs, increased supervision, public notification, and the possibility of civil commitment and/or chemical castration.

Supervising sex offenders thus takes an extraordinary amount of training, time, and resources to find suitable housing, conduct home and employment visits, and monitor sex offenders to satisfy rising community expectations. Probation and parole officers in sex offender units are specially trained in the area of sex offenses and in recognizing secrecy, manipulation, and deceit. Some officers even recognize that offenders on their own caseload will use the same grooming techniques that they use to establish a relationship with their victims. One officer shares how grooming happens:

> Well, more times than not they call for things they don't need to be calling for. Just seems like they are checking up on *me* to see if I am really involved in their case [and to see] what they can get away with as well . . . Because they're trying

TRUTH OR **FICTION?**

Most sex offenders are eligible for community supervision.

TRUE

FACT: Over half of all sex offenders are supervised in the community—either their entire sentence or the last part after their prison term. The category of sex offenders comprises a wide range of both misdemeanor and felony offenders.

to create a relationship between me and them . . . they will start asking questions about what I am doing this weekend . . . or something about my family.
(Severson & Pettus-Davis, 2013, p. 12)

In the offender's mind, people are to be manipulated to get them to think a certain way or to behave how the offender wants them to behave whether it is a victim
or a supervising probation or parole officer. Part of "the game" that offenders engage
in is to assure their officer that they are being compliant and everything is "fine."

Payne and DeMichele (2008) discuss how to work with sex offenders without
compromising an officer's own mental health. The main way is to separate such
persons from what they have done. Working with sex offenders does not mean
condoning their behavior. The mark of a true professional is an ability to supervise
and help a person who has behaved badly, while viewing the individual in a nonjudgmental way, all the while being careful not to get emotionally involved, manipulated or conned. The second way is to have a healthy outlet to reduce stress and
secondary trauma that may accompany the job (Severson & Pettus-Davis, 2013).

Sex Offender Treatment

Sex offenders are typically court-mandated to undergo intensive treatment specific to the type of sex offense. Sex offender treatment programs use multiple reg-
imens that include cognitive-behavioral therapy to address thinking errors and
victim minimization, polygraph tests to detect deception, and aversive conditioning to alter inappropriate sexual interests. Aggressive rapists require an entirely
different treatment approach based on anger management than more passive pe-
dophiles, who focus on attachment issues, emotional loneliness, social skills, and
assertiveness training. The assumption about inappropriate sexual behaviors is
that there is no "cure" in the medical sense, but offenders can learn through cognitive behavioral therapy how to control their urges, reduce arousal levels, and
replace them with appropriate behaviors.

Decisions in court cases have raised interesting legal issues involving treatment
programs for sex offenders. One consideration is that sex offender treatment requires offenders to admit their guilt. If the crime is denied, then the offender will
not be allowed to participate in treatment. Failure to participate in a treatment
program is a violation of probation or parole and a legitimate reason for revocation.
A Connecticut appellate court noted that an offender must be informed in advance
that denial of guilt will ultimately result in revocation (*State v. Faraday*, 2002).

Another issue that has surfaced during sex offender treatment is that an offender must acknowledge all prior sex offenses. In *McKune v. Lile* (2002), the U.S.
Supreme Court held that a sex offender treatment program did not violate the
Fifth Amendment's privilege against self-incrimination when it required that offenders acknowledge past crimes, insofar as doing so was the beginning of rehabilitation and acceptance of responsibility for their actions. According to the
Supreme Court, acknowledging past crimes even if the State offers no immunity
and could then potentially prosecute for them is different from the right to invoke
Fifth Amendment protection in the face of criminal prosecution by the State.

POLYGRAPH TESTS.   Polygraph tests have been recognized as a tool to reduce the
secrecy and deceit that sex offenders typically use with their victims and with supervising probation officers. Many sex offenders are motivated by gaining power
over their victims in a calculating way that minimizes detection. As a result, some

jurisdictions require that sex offenders, when initially placed under community supervision, submit to a baseline polygraph examination that explores previous sexual behaviors and current deviant thoughts. Compared to a nonpolygraphed sex offender group, polygraphed sex offenders "reported many more victims, far less history of being sexually abused themselves, and a much higher incidence of having [sexually] offended as juveniles" (Hindman & Peters, 2001, p. 10). If used properly, the baseline test can then be shared with treatment providers to measure treatment progress.

The other purpose of polygraphs is for supervision purposes throughout probation/parole. If a polygraph given during supervision indicates possible deception, the officer then may be able to increase the level of supervision if department policy concurs. However, a deceptive polygraph, by itself, cannot be used as a basis for filing a revocation (Vance, 2011). Also, a probation/parole officer can only use information related to the instant offense (the crime for which the offender has already been convicted). The officer may not threaten an offender with revocation for refusal to answer any follow up questions that may potentially incriminate then in a different offense that may have occurred during supervision (Vance, 2011). The best recourse here is to refer a potential new offense to police for investigation.

PENILE PLETHYSMOGRAPH.   A **penile plethysmograph** is used as treatment to identify the gender and ages of victims to whom a sex offender is attracted. The device is used for assessment to measure erectile responses in male sex offenders to determine level of sexual arousal. This device also tracks how treatment is progressing and whether a different approach needs to be used. A sex offender may not contest a penile plethysmograph as a probation or parole condition. The Seventh Circuit Court of Appeals upheld submission to a penile plethysmograph as a parole condition for a Michigan inmate convicted in federal court of kidnapping and allegedly molesting a six-year-old boy before attempting to drown him (*Walrath v. Getty*, 1995). The offender in this case objected to the condition, saying that it was fundamentally unfair and therefore denied him due process. His parole was revoked. On appeal, the Seventh Circuit ruled that "the Commission may impose or modify other conditions of parole so long as they are reasonably related to the nature of the circumstances of the offense and the history and characteristics of the parolee."

Therapy can be supplemented with prescribed hormones called medro oxyprogesterone acetate, otherwise known as Depo-Provera. Depo-Provera changes hormone levels to decrease sexual urges and increase responsiveness to treatment. These medications are also known as antiandrogens or selective serotonin reuptake inhibitors because they change the hormone balance in the brain to help decrease sexual urges (Payne & DeMichele, 2008).

penile plethysmograph
A device that measures erectile responses in male sex offenders to determine level of sexual arousal to various types of stimuli. This device is used for assessment and treatment purposes.

Containment Supervision Approach

Supervising sex offenders in the community involves more frequent contacts and more frequent searches than with other offenders. This is because the majority of sex offenses are planned acts committed when opportunities arise. A "containment approach" was first recommended by English et al. (1996) and remains the guiding model today:

- two to four face-to-face contacts between officer and probationer per month;
- two probationer home-and-computer searches per month;
- thorough mental health evaluation;

TABLE 6.2 Risk Factors Related to Sex Offending

Slow-Changing Risk Factors	Sudden Risk Factors
Deviant sexual arousal	Sexual preoccupation
Loneliness	Emotional collapse
Impulsivity	Lack of social support systems
Intimacy conflicts and deficits	Victim access
Pro-rape/pro-molester attitudes	Use of drugs or alcohol
Ineffective problem solving	Noncompliance with supervision

Source: Pimentel, Roger, and Jon Muller. 2010. The containment approach to managing defendants charged with sex offenses. *Federal Probation 74*(2): 24–26.

- weekly cognitive-behavioral group therapy and individual counseling;
- regular staffings with treatment provider and polygraph examiner; and
- sharing of information on a regular basis between probation officers and treatment providers.

Home visits are conducted at strategic times to reduce the opportunity that an offender might have access to victims. For example, home visits are conducted on Halloween for sex offenders who had child victims. The average home visit took about 30 minutes—7 minutes inside the home and about 20 minutes driving between each home (Alexander, 2014).

Table 6.2 identifies factors related to the likelihood of future sexual offending. Sex offenders who are most at risk of recidivism are increasingly monitored using global positioning systems (GPS) technology. One study found that paroled sex offenders on GPS were *less* likely to commit new offenses than sex offenders supervised on traditional parole, which is a good indication that GPS is effective for its increased cost (Bulman, 2013). Of the states that use GPS to monitor sex offenders; 10 require lifetime monitoring of the highest-risk sex offenders (Armstrong & Freeman, 2011). How GPS technology works is discussed in more detail in Chapter 9.

Sex offenders must provide blood and saliva samples to create a DNA (deoxyribonucleic acid) bank. This condition was initially challenged as violating parolees' right against unreasonable searches and seizures. The Tenth Circuit Court of Appeals upheld the ruling because of the significance of DNA evidence in solving sex offenses, the minimal intrusion on an inmate's right to privacy, and a parolee's diminished constitutional rights (*Boling v. Romer*, 1996). Other special conditions required of sex offenders might include prohibition of any pornography, restricting Internet access to certain chat rooms and websites, prohibition of patronizing sex-oriented businesses, and exclusion from **child safety zones**. Monitoring a parolee's home computer and limiting their access to Internet sites is discussed in Box 6.5.

child safety zones
A condition of probation or parole whereby the offender is not allowed within a certain range of places where children typically congregate such as schools, day care centers, and playgrounds.

Sex Offender Registration Laws

Sex offender registration statutes stemming from Megan's Law in 1996 assist police in investigating sex crimes and allow the public to know the identities and locations of convicted sex offenders in their area. Registration is required through the National Sex Offender Public Website (http://www.nsopw.gov), operated by

| BOX 6.5 | TECHNOLOGY IN CORRECTIONS | |

How Are Internet Activities of Sex Offenders Monitored?

With the increase in wireless capabilities in public places and across entire cities, access to the Internet is widespread, and it is virtually impossible to prohibit use as part of probation or parole conditions. Officers have instead allowed offenders to use the Internet, but courts have upheld the right of officers to examine and control the type of Internet sites offenders visit. Officers with specialized caseloads of offenders for whom the Internet should be monitored can obtain software called *Field Search* that allows them to visit an offender's home and conduct a search of a computer hard drive for URLs linked to unauthorized sites (e.g., pornography sites for offenders convicted of a sexual offense). The software is so thorough that it detects deleted web addresses visited during a specific period of time—either since an officer's last visit or since the

hard drive was first installed. It can be set to detect websites, images, videos, zipped files, browser histories, cookies, and password-protected files on any type of computer. Even those addresses deleted by so-called wiping software that claims to erase websites off a computer can be detected, and date- and time-stamped as to the last time a file or image was opened. When unauthorized addresses are detected, an offender takes a polygraph test to corroborate the findings. The results of the software scan together with a failed polygraph test can be used as evidence for an officer to request a change in the terms of supervision or to terminate the supervision altogether.

Source: National Law Enforcement and Corrections Technology Center. 2009. Field Search. *TechBeat* (Winter). Accessed May 15, 2011: http://www.justnet.org

the U.S. Department of Justice. The registry includes names, addresses, dates of birth, convictions, fingerprints, places of employment, ages and genders of victims, completion of sex offender treatment, and a recent photo. By law all sex offenders on probation and parole are required to register, with each state varying on how long sex offenders remain on the registry.

The database organizes sex offenders into three risk tiers. Tier 1 offenders are considered the lowest risk because they are responsive to treatment and are employed. Tier 1 offenders must include a photo depending on the state and require an offender to update information once per year. Tier 2 offenders are considered moderate risk and must update their whereabouts every six months. Tier 3 offenders are considered at highest risk of committing another sexual offense either because they have refused treatment, they have denied their offense, or they lack remorse for their victims. As a result, Tier 3 offenders must update their whereabouts every three months, and some states require that offenders remain on the registry for the rest of their lives. Failure to register and update information is a felony.

There are about 728,000 convicted sex offenders throughout the United States, of whom 100,000 are estimated to be still missing from the registry (Wolf, 2011). States that fail to comply with federal regulations risk losing federal funding, but many states say that it costs them more money to comply than the funding they would lose by not tracking sex offenders according to federal regulations. In the federal system, any federal sex offense that occurred after 1998 or any military conviction for a sex crime after 1997 must be registered. Moreover, registered offenders are not just adults. In Texas, for example, 8.5% of all sex offenders were juveniles, most of whom were considered higher risks than many of the adults due to having committed more sex crimes total and more sex crimes of an aggravated nature (Craun & Kernsmith, 2006).

When legally challenged, the U.S. Supreme Court said that the public posting of a sex offender registry does not violate the due process clause of the Fourteenth Amendment (*Connecticut Department of Public Safety et al. v. Doe*, 2003). Connecticut law required sex offenders to register for 10 years, but those convicted of sexually violent offenses must register for life. The offender in this case alleged that this law was unfair because he was no longer "currently sexually dangerous," and therefore the law violated his due process rights. The Court disagreed, ruling that the law is constitutional, even if no prior opportunity is given to prove that the defendant is not dangerous. Cases have also argued unsuccessfully that registration violates an offender's right to privacy, saying that disclosure of information serves a public safety function that supersedes an offender's right to privacy.

In another case, also decided that same year, the Court said that a sex offender registration and notification law does not violate the ex post facto clause of the Constitution (*Smith v. Doe*, 2003). In this case, the Alaska Sex Offender Registration Act was retroactive, meaning it applied to offenders who were convicted before the law was passed. Defendants challenged its constitutionality, saying its retroactive application violated the ex post facto clause of the Constitution. The Court upheld the Alaska law, saying that the Alaska Offender Act regulates rather than punishes; therefore, its retroactive application does not violate the ex post facto clause. This is a significant decision because some states (such as Missouri) have retroactively applied the law to sex offenses going back as far as 1979. Critics of this decision contend that registries have had a significant negative impact on sex offenders' ability to find a place to live, work, and reintegrate back into the community.

Community Notification Laws

Community notification statutes make information about sex offenders available upon request to individuals, or else they authorize or require probation and parole departments, law enforcement agencies, or prosecutor offices to disseminate information about released offenders to the community at large. Notification statutes are a secondary way of informing the public of who is a sex offender, under an assumption that the registration process overlooks some offenders.

Sex offenders are believed to pose different levels of risk to a community, depending on the nature and prevalence of their crimes as well as their choices of victims. As with the registry there are three tiers of risk in community notification, with each tier having its own set of notification procedures. The third tier permits or requires proactive dissemination (knocking on doors, flyers, etc.), whereas the other lower tiers permit information dissemination only in response to individuals who seek out that information. Notifying a community about the presence of sex offenders is fraught with disparity, making this practice problematic (Shaffer & Miethe, 2011).

Sex offender registration and community notification laws are thus put in place to regulate sex offenders and to increase public safety, particularly to protect children. How have these policies affected the community? When parents are notified of a high-risk sex offender in their neighborhood, they report taking action to ensure that their own children receive more protection against sexual victimization (Bandy, 2011). However, studies have consistently found that most citizens do not report taking protective measures when they have been notified of a high-risk sex offender in their neighborhood (Anderson & Sample, 2008; Bandy, 2011). In fact, citizens reported feeling more fearful rather than safer with knowledge of where an offender lived. These policies still seem to concentrate on strangers (a condition that, in reality, characterizes only 7% of all sex offenses against children) and draw attention away from the more than nine out of ten perpetrators who are related to or already known to children (Alexander, 2010).

Critics of policies regulating sex offenders argue that these are founded on faulty assumptions about sex offending, such as that sex offenders prey only on children and are strangers to their victims. In fact, sex offenders vary widely in their behavior toward and choice of victims, to whom many of them are related or at least acquainted with in some way. In the following sections, we discuss two more restrictions of sex offenders: residency restrictions and possible civil commitments.

Residency Restrictions

Residency restrictions prohibit sex offenders from living within 1,000–2,500 feet of areas in which children are likely to be present. Offenders who would otherwise depend on living with a family member are often homeless or forced to move to areas that are far away from work, treatment services, and family support—elements necessary to reduce recidivism. These added restrictions caused additional stress and contributed to recidivism rather than lowered sexual offending behavior (Levenson, 2008). In addition, sex offenders required to register for life are unable to live in public housing, which reduces their housing options even further. In Ohio, the locations of 1,095 sex offenders were spatially mapped in relation to the 345 schools in the area. Researchers found that 45% of sex offenders in their sample were living within 1,000 feet of school property (Grubesic, Mack, & Murray, 2007). In this particular county, half of all residents lived within 1,000 feet of a school, so adhering to policy reduced housing choices by 50%. In more densely populated counties, the percentage is likely higher.

The invasiveness of such policies upon offenders, all in the interest of public safety, has not significantly altered the self-protective behavior of citizens, though there is some evidence the public has taken measures to protect children from high-risk sex offenders residing nearby (Bandy, 2011). However, restricting where sex offenders *live* has not been shown to decrease recidivism because the sex offender's residence is not the place where most motivated offenders cultivate and groom their targets (Zandbergen, Levenson, & Hart, 2010). What seems more effective with sex offenders may be enacting child-safety and no loitering zones instead of residency restrictions. Allowing sex offenders the opportunity to work, complete treatment programs and having a place to live with a positive social support system can only help decrease recidivism.

> **TRUTH OR FICTION?**
>
> Areas where registered sex offenders live will also have more sex offenses.
>
> **FICTION**
>
> **FACT:** The number of registered sex offenders in a particular area is independent of the number of reported sex offenses in that same area. Sex offender registries inform the public about convicted sex offenders, but does not predict level of safety from sex offenders (Stucky & Ottensmann, 2014).

SUMMARY

- ISP programs are most effective if they operate with close supervision and cognitive-behavioral treatment intervention.

- Drug court is a type of diversion program that integrates substance abuse treatment with a coordinated and ongoing interactive team that includes judges, prosecutors, and probation officers.

- Mental health courts and veterans' courts are organizationally similar to other problem-solving courts except that they work with offenders who are mentally ill and/or are veterans, and they link to a variety of community service providers.

- TCs use peer support and cognitive-behavioral interventions to help individuals overcome addiction to drugs and to prevent relapse episodes so they can maintain a life of sobriety.

- Sex offenders are a heterogenous group that engages in a wide variety of deceptive and manipulative behaviors to lure chosen victims.

- All sex offenders need intensive specialized treatment and intensive supervision (a containment approach), but some molesters need medications to control their hormonal balance.
- Supervision includes ongoing home visits, Internet restrictions, restrictions on residency and

leisure time, monitoring of offenders' associations, collaboration with treatment providers, and the engagement of polygraph experts.

- Sex offender registration and community notification statutes are for the regulation of sex offenders and for public safety—not for punishment.

DISCUSSION QUESTIONS

1. How does intensive supervision differ from regular probation or parole supervision?

2. Are drug courts a good idea for higher-level drug dealers?

3. How many chances in drug court should be given to drug-addicted offenders (i.e., how much leeway and for which types of offenses) before they are considered to have "failed" the program? Would your response be different for drug-addicted offenders in a therapeutic community?

4. Is a therapeutic community more or less effective for achieving sobriety than a drug court? Why?

5. What are the issues concerning the treatment of offenders with mental illness?

6. Should mental health courts be expanded for juveniles with mental illness? Why or why not?

7. What specific strategies are most effective for working with sex offenders in a community?

8. Does community notification of sex offenders increase public safety? Why or why not?

9. Is requiring sex offenders to register good public policy? Why or why not?

10. What types of offenders could benefit from specialized caseloads, other than the ones mentioned in this chapter?

 ## WEBSITES, VIDEOS, AND PODCASTS

Websites

National Drug Court Resource Center
   http://ndcrc.org

National Drug Court Institute
   http://www.ndci.org/ndci-home/

SAMHSA's National Registry of Evidence-Based Programs and Practices
   http://nrepp.samhsa.gov/

Adult Drug Court Research to Practice Initiative
   http://research2practice.org

Judge David L. Bazelon Center for Mental Health Law
   http://www.bazelon.org

Policy on Mental Health Courts
   http://www.youthlaw.org/policy/advocacy/juvenile_mental_health_court_initiative/

The Criminal Justice/Mental Health Consensus Project
   http://www.consensusproject.org

Shared Services: Defendants with Mental Illnesses
   http://www.criminaljustice.ny.gov/opca/shared_mentally_ill.htm

Veterans' Court Clearinghouse, National Association of Drug Court Professionals
   http://www.nadcp.org/learn/veterans-treatment-court-clearinghouse

National Center for Post-Traumatic Stress Disorder, Veterans Affairs
   http://www.ptsd.va.gov

Sex Offender Risk and Needs Assessment (Canada)
   http://www.csc-scc.gc.ca/text/pblct/forum/e091/e091g-eng.shtml

U.S. Dept of Justice Sex Offender Public Website
http://www.nsopw.gov

Association for the Treatment of Sexual Abusers
http://www.atsa.com

Center for Sex Offender Management
http://www.csom.org

Training Curriculum for Supervising Sex Offenders in the Community
http://www.nicic.org/library/017636

Videos/Podcasts
Drug Court: Personal Story
http://www.youtube.com/watch?v=Cf1pRLwCP4o

This video is a look at the drug court graduates and staff from across New York State through history, statistics, and personal stories.

NJ Court Clips: Drug Court
(Length: 3:13 minutes) Examines the New Jersey Drug Court Program. https://www.youtube.com/watch?v= DpiR9b7rcUE

Alternative Sentencing Policies for Drug Offenders
This five-part audio recording, sponsored by NIJ, examines drug treatment in lieu of incarceration for drug offenders in Kansas. http://nij.ncjrs.gov/multimedia/audio-nijconf2009-alternative-sentencing.htm

Responding to High Rates of Substance Abuse Failure Among Probationers
(Length: 3 minutes) An NIJ sponsored interview with Dan O'Connell of the University of Delaware, about Delaware's Decide Your Time program. http://nij.ncjrs.gov/multimedia/video-nijconf2010-oconnell.htm

The Released
(Length: 54 minutes) A PBS Frontline documentary about offenders with mental illnesses. http://www.pbs.org/wgbh/pages/frontline/released

Short Videos About Offenders With Mental Illnesses
(Length: varies between 4 and 9 minutes) A PBS sponsored series of shorter documentaries about individual offenders with mental illnesses such as one that goes inside a mental health court and another depicts a release from jail to a group home. http://www.pbs.org/wgbh/pages/frontline/criminal-justice

Tailoring Policies for Effective Sex Offender Reentry into Communities
(Length: 3 minutes) An NIJ sponsored interview with Alisa Klein, of the Association for the Treatment of Sex Abusers, about reentry policies for sex offenders in the community. http://nij.ncjrs.gov/multimedia/video-nijconf2010-klein.htm

King County Mental Health Court
(Length: 6 minutes) A look inside one of King County's therapeutic courts for offenders with mental illness. https://www.youtube.com/watch?v=DFIDmuevXQQ

For Mentally Ill Defendants, A Different Kind of Court
(Length: 8 minutes) Adam Reilly went inside the Boston Mental Health Court to find out how it works. https://www.youtube.com/watch?v=O-ym4b9m4PU

Mental Health Court: Part 1, 2, 3
http://www.youtube.com/watch?v =tPAopiYqDds http://www.youtube.com/watch?v=0vfu60kOSOk&feature=related http://www.youtube.com/watch?v =kd4-CU6M-YE&feature=related

This three-part series discusses various aspects of mental health courts. It comprises an educational video series.

CASE STUDY EXERCISES

Which Supervision Conditions Are Pertinent to These Sex Offenders?

The specific conditions pertaining to sex offenders have received attention in recent years. For each case below, which additional conditions should be imposed on the offender in terms of his or her offense, and what challenges of community supervision does each case present?

Assume that conditions for sex offenders include one or more of the following:

- No contact with any minor child (including offender's minor children) if victim of sexual crime was a minor, or no contact with minors at all even if the victim was of adult age.
- Contact with minor children approved only if parole officer approves another supervising adult to be present at time of contact.
- No possession of sexually explicit material—written, audio, or visual.
- If the offense involved the use of the Internet or a computer, cannot have a personal computer and cannot work where access to Internet is allowed, or in some jurisdictions can have no computer access at all even if offense did not involve computer usage.
- Notification to neighbors and employers of offender's sexual offense history and supervision status.
- Mandatory participation in sexual offender treatment or aftercare programs.
- Mandatory routine polygraph exams as part of treatment or supervision.
- If offense involved filming or pictures of victims, no camera or video equipment access allowed.
- Cannot work in any employment that would allow access to children or victim-aged groups; cannot be self-employed.
- Cannot live within a certain distance of schools, playgrounds, public parks, or other places where minors congregate.

CASE A: Parolee Steven, Sexual Assault of a Minor

Steven is serving a 5- to 15-year sentence for Sexual Assault of a Minor. He has served seven and one-half years of his sentence, which is five years beyond the minimum time to be served. Because he has three prior convictions for similar offenses, he does not have to be released until he has served 10 years of his sentence. Steven spent time in prison for two of the three prior offenses against minors. Each time he was released, he successfully completed the release period of parole supervision. All of his victims have been his grandchildren; family members are strongly opposed to his release and fear he will commit similar acts upon release. Steven has completed a sexual offender treatment program during this incarceration; he always refused to participate in treatment during prior incarcerations. The prognosis by the treatment counselor is guarded but indicates that Steven has worked hard on learning his offending triggers and knows whom to avoid if released. He has not had any rule violations while incarcerated and has accounting skills. He will be released under the supervision of a parole officer to a community where none of his family reside and does not want contact with his family. He has been accepted into a halfway house program and plans on attending community-based sexual offender aftercare groups.

CASE B: Parolee Gloria, Lewd Sexual Conduct and Sexual Contact with a Minor

Gloria has been paroled after serving three years of her nine-year sentence for Lewd Sexual Conduct and Sexual Contact with a Minor. She was 27 years old at the time of the offense, and her victim was 16. Currently Gloria is 30 years old; her victim is now 19 years of age and enrolled as a full-time college student in another state. This is Gloria's first felony offense, and she has no history of offending behavior under community supervision. Gloria agreed to complete a sex offender treatment program during her incarceration but claimed during her counseling sessions that she and her victim loved each other and that sexual relations were consensual. Gloria still reports feelings for him, but the victim's family wishes to have no contact with Gloria. However, at this time no one knows how the victim feels about the relationship because his most recent contact information was unavailable when the field officer performed her investigations. The field officer did find out that Gloria's former employer would not accept her back in her former occupation as a registered nurse despite Gloria's statements that the institution would. Gloria wishes to parole back to the same house she lived in when arrested. She has one male child, aged 13, who has been staying with Gloria's mother over the last three years.

CASE C: Probationer Jonas, Indecent Sexual Behavior with a Minor

Jonas has been placed on probation for indecent sexual behavior with a five-year-old boy. This is his first felony offense, with two prior misdemeanor offenses as an adult—one count of indecent exposure and one count of misdemeanor theft. Jonas is now 20 years of age and lives with his maternal aunt, who was his guardian from when he was the age of 12 until he turned 18. Jonas has never been to prison.

Jonas suffered emotional and sexual abuse from his stepfather and mother for the first six years of his life, when he became known to Social Services investigating his case. This investigation resulted in his stepfather being charged with Indecency with a Child, and Jonas was placed in foster care. While in foster care over the next several years, Jonas was adjudicated numerous times for fire setting and cruelty to animals, for which he was finally sent to juvenile detention. While in detention at the age of 12, he tried to hurt himself and was removed to a padded cell for further assessment. Testing revealed that Jonas had attention deficit hyperactivity disorder and he was prescribed Ritalin. He remained out of the system from the age of 12 until the age of 18, when he was arrested for indecent exposure.

His IQ was recently assessed using the Wechsler Abbreviated Scale of Intelligence (WASI test) and estimated to be 70 (verbal IQ was 72 and performance IQ 73). His current communicative and daily living skills are equivalent to that of an eight-year-old boy, and his socialization domain is equivalent to that of a seven-year-old. He has a reduced capacity to learn new information and to solve problems. He has a fourth-grade education and cannot read very well. He has not yet registered as a sex offender in the state. The PSI recommends some form of cognitive-behavioral treatment.

Community Supervision Modification and Revocation

Chapter 7

The Washington Post/Getty Images

CHAPTER OUTLINE

CHAPTER LEARNING OBJECTIVES

1. Identify how probation and parole conditions are modified and under what circumstances.

2. List progressive sanctions options that probation and parole officers have available before filing or reporting revocations to the court or parole board.

3. Analyze the legal rights and options probationers and parolees have during the revocation process.

4. Discuss offender demographic and situational factors that increase the chances of succeeding on probation and parole.

KEY TERMS

early termination
revocation
law violations
technical violations
absconder
preliminary hearing
final revocation hearing
due process
preponderance of evidence

Chris Brown has many identities: a singer, songwriter, dancer, and a former probationer. In February 2009, Brown punched recording star Rihanna in the face. Rihanna was hospitalized and Brown pled guilty to felony assault. In August 2009, Brown was sentenced to five years of probation, 1,400 hours of community service, and to attend one year of domestic violence counseling. The presiding judge also issued a restraining order that required Brown to remain away from Rihanna.

By February 2011, the judge modified the restraining order to allow Chris Brown to be near Rihanna, provided that he does not annoy, harass, or conduct surveillance on his ex-girlfriend. The judge praised Brown for his progress on probation and spoke positively regarding his participation in domestic violence counseling.

In June 2012, Brown tested positive for marijuana. However, the judge did not revoke the performer's probation because drug tests were never a part of his original probation. Brown went before the judge again in 2013, where the judge modified his probation supervision so that he could complete 90 days of inpatient anger management. The modification was based on an arrest in October 2013 for felony assault when Brown punched a man outside his hotel when the man "photo bombed" a picture that Brown agreed to take with two female fans. Brown broke the man's nose, so the victim pressed charges. Brown allegedly was thrown out of one anger management facility for throwing a rock at his own mom's vehicle and then was dismissed from a second rehabilitation facility when he had an inappropriate relationship with a female staff member. He spent 10 weeks in the county jail for failure to complete treatment and was released back onto to probation in June 2014. He was diagnosed as having bipolar disorder. Between August 2014 and January 2015, Brown was present during incidents where people were injured from gunfire, including a party that Brown hosted where music producer Suge Knight was shot and a San Jose nightclub incident where five people were injured from gunfire. While Brown did not directly participate in either shooting, his probation officer was concerned that Brown's pattern of behavior was counterproductive to probation success. Meanwhile, Brown completed his community service, so that by his next court hearing on March 20, 2015, the judge successfully terminated Chris Brown's probation.

Question for discussion: Over the last six years, there were a number of modifications, failures, and successes. In the end, how would you classify this case, and why?

INTRODUCTION

Once an offender is on community supervision, the court or parole board relies on the probation and parole officer to keep track of an individual offender's progress or lack of progress with the court order. This chapter examines how, when, and why the length and terms of a probation or parole term would be changed, extended, terminated early, or revoked. Probation and parole officer decision making is influenced first by the severity of offender behavior, the intensity of the supervision, and also by agency policy and laws that guide discretion. You learned from previous chapters how officer discretion is guided by principles of rehabilitation in the best interest of the offender and also by the principles of social control for the good of the public. Each officer identifies with varying techniques and uses of power by which they gain compliance from offenders (Steiner, Hester, Makarios, & Travis, 2012). Each officer has differing abilities to detect violations and an individual tolerance level for when to use graduated sanctions or file a revocation (Grattet, Lin, & Petersilia, 2011). We begin with compliant offenders who have fulfilled their payment obligations and have shown their ability to continue to abide by conditions. In such cases, shortening a term or easing restrictions can be used as a reward or applied after a minimum amount of time has been served.

Early Termination for Good Behavior

early termination
Termination of probation at any time during a probation period or after some time has been served.

Community supervision officers (CSOs) supervising probationers or parolees in some jurisdictions can apply on behalf of their clients for **early termination**. In many jurisdictions, probation officers can apply to the courts after a client has satisfactorily served two years or one-third of their probation term, whichever is less. In other jurisdictions, offenders can earn "time credits" based on positive behavior that shortens the period at which they can become eligible for early termination. For example, 15–30 days can be credited for full payment of court costs or fines. Between 30 and 90 days can be credited if an offender completes a treatment program or earns a high school diploma or equivalency certificate. Although an officer initially recommends early termination, the actual authority to terminate early rests with a parole board for state parolees and with a judge for county-level probationers. In federal court, a judge may:

> terminate a term of probation previously ordered and discharge the defendant at any time in the case of a misdemeanor or an infraction or at any time after the expiration of one year of probation in the case of a felony, if it is satisfied that such action is warranted by the conduct of the defendant and the interest of justice. (*Federal Rules of Criminal Procedure*, Title 18, Chapter 227, Article 3564)

Early termination does not appear to increase the risk of recidivism after supervision ends. A recent study showed that after three years the rearrest rate was 14.4% for probationers who were granted early termination, compared with 16.2% of a matched group who served the full term of probation (Baber & Johnson, 2013). The rate of successful termination of local- and state-level probation varies greatly by jurisdiction. A national average estimates that between 60% and 70% of state probationers and 49%–57% of parolees successfully complete supervision. At the federal level, the rate of success is higher, with over 80% of federal probationers terminating probation successfully with no violations (see Figure 7.1).

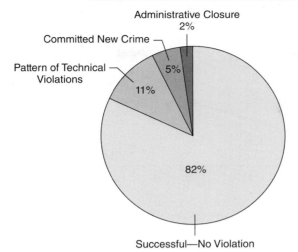

Reason for Federal Probation Termination

Administrative Closure 2%

Committed New Crime 5%

Pattern of Technical Violations 11%

82%

Successful—No Violation

FIGURE 7.1
Federal Probation Outcomes

Source: U.S. Department of Justice. 2008. *Compendium of Federal Justice Statistics.* Washington, DC: U.S. Department of Justice.

Conversely, a resistant offender is someone either not making sufficient progress or involved in new criminal behavior. Violations or serious misbehavior can cause a period of supervision to be extended, additional conditions imposed, or a recommendation for **revocation** of community supervision. When considering modifying or revoking probation, the courts assess the risk an offender poses to a community, whether the change will increase compliance, and whether the change will better serve the needs of the offender at the present time. When prison is invoked, either by a judge who resentences offenders to prison or by a parole board that returns parolees back to prison, bed space is needed to make room. Figure 7.2 shows how revocations of parole have increased over time until they peaked at 35% of all prison admissions in 2000. A change in departmental policies occurred that decreased the reasons for which offenders could be sent back to prison, and mandated that probation and parole departments work with offenders using in-house progressive techniques. Prison admissions for revocations have decreased since 2009 as a result of this policy change that is discussed later in this chapter (Grattet et al., 2011; White, Mellow, Englander, & Ruffinengo, 2011).

revocation
The process of hearings that results when a probationer is noncompliant with a current level of probation. Revocation results either in modifying probation conditions to a more intensive supervision level or a complete elimination of probation, with a sentence to a residential community facility, jail, or prison.

TYPES OF VIOLATIONS

Revocation of community supervision is generally triggered in two ways: law violations and technical violations. A **law violation** occurs if an offender is rearrested for another misdemeanor or felony crime. By contrast, a **technical violation** is a pattern of infractions that breaches conditions of probation or parole. When considering all revocations as a whole, rates vary widely by jurisdiction.

law violations
When an offender commits a new misdemeanor or felony while being supervised on probation or parole for another offense.

Law Violations

As we discussed in Chapter 1, the rate of recidivism of course measures an offender's return to criminal behavior, but it largely depends on a number of factors, including:

technical violations
Multiple violations that breach one or more noncriminal conditions of probation.

FIGURE 7.2
Percentage Who Enter State
Prison Because of Parole
Revocation: 1930 to Present

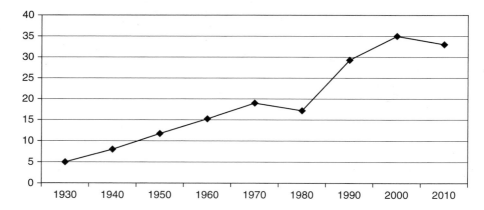

Sources from 1980 and earlier can be found in earlier editions of this book. Sources for 1990 and beyond: Robyn L. Cohen. 1995. *Probation and Parole Violators in State Prison, 1991*. Washington, DC: Bureau of Justice Statistics; Joan Petersilia. 2000b. When prisoners return to the community: Political, economic, and social consequences. In *Sentencing and Corrections: Issues for the 21st Century* [paper 9 from the Executive Sessions on Sentencing and Corrections]. Washington, DC: U.S. Department of Justice. West, Heather C., William J. Sabol, and Sarah J. Greenman. 2010. *Prisoners in 2009*. Washington, DC: Bureau of Justice Statistics.

1. how recidivism is defined (i.e., by rearrest, conviction, parole revocation, return to prison);
2. duration of time that subjects were studied (the longer the period of time subjects were followed, the higher recidivism rate);
3. size of sample studied (a larger sample will yield a wider variance in recidivism than a smaller sample); and
4. decision-making style and behavior of probation officers, judges, and parole boards.

The type of law violation varies from minor misdemeanors to serious felony crimes. Even if an offender is guilty of a new crime, however, revocation is not automatic. Instead it is left to the discretion of a court or parole board. In misdemeanor and drug use or possession cases, most offenders will have their probation or parole revoked but will not be prosecuted for the new crime. In more serious felony offenses, revocation for the new crime may result in a period of incarceration, along with a second conviction for the new charge. Even if evidence for a new offense doesn't meet "guilty beyond a reasonable doubt," the standard of proof for revocation is only "preponderance of the evidence"—a lower standard of proof that is sufficient to revoke, though not sufficient enough to be added to one's criminal record. If more evidence surfaces later such that an offender is tried for the crime that led to revocation, that is not considered double jeopardy because revocation is merely an administrative and not a criminal proceeding, even if it results in incarceration.

In general, state parolees tend to be revoked more often for new crimes than probationers or even federal prisoners. Parolee re-incarceration rates have varied over the years between 25% and 48% (Vito, Higgins, & Tewksbury, 2012), although the numbers of those reincarcerated for technical violations have declined considerably in the last few years. While new crimes comprised about 60%–70% of all parole revocations, federal offenders who were revoked committed a new felony crime in 36% of cases and a misdemeanor offense only 7% of the time (Administrative Office of the US Courts, 2012).

Technical Violations

The remaining 57% of federal offenders who were revoked have committed no crimes, but instead have committed a series of technical violations, which are violations of supervision rules or conditions (Administrative Office of the US Courts, 2012). Unlike new crimes, which are clearer as to when a revocation should be filed, technical violations allow for more officer discretion and a tendency for inconsistent responses between officers and jurisdictions. As a result, technical violation revocations can be used for reasons unrelated to public safety, such as by officers reducing their workload. Officers with higher caseloads of offenders were more likely to support revocations sooner than were officers with lower caseload sizes (Kerbs, Jones, & Jolley, 2009). This finding may be a tolerance issue—a reaction to job stress as a result of being overworked.

The most common types of technical violations are shown in Table 7.1, and they are clearly related to drug use, failure to complete drug treatment, and failing to report, likely due to the offender's fear that they will not be able to pass a drug screening.

As a general rule, probation is not revoked for occasional violations of technical conditions, but for an ongoing pattern of infractions after other options have been tried such as verbal warnings, written reprimands, increasing reporting requirements, increasing rate of drug tests, and adding home visits. Because incarceration results in high costs, revocation should be a last resort in handling offenders with a pattern of technical violations. Box 7.1 discusses

TABLE 7.1   Revocation Reasons Among Parole Versus Probation Violators

Reason for Revocation	National (Parole)	California (Parole)	National (Probation)	Illinois (Probation)
Arrest/Conviction for New Offense	70%	60%	16%	10%
Drug-Related Violations				
Positive test for drug use	8%	12%	27%	22%
Possession of drug(s)	7%	9%	N/R	N/R
Failure to report for drug testing	2%	5%	10%	34%
Failure to complete alcohol/drug treatment	2%	1%	20%	9%
Absconders	22%	27%	19%	3%
Other Technical Violations	18%	21%	9%	23%

Note: Detail for parolees adds to more than 100% because some inmates have had more than one violation of parole.
N/R = Data for drug possession was not reported.
Source: adapted from Hughes, Timothy A., Wilson, Doris James, and Beck, Allen J. 2001. *Trends in State Parole, 1990–2000.* Washington, DC: U.S. Department of Justice, Bureau of Justice Statistics, p. 14; Peggy B. Burke. 1997. *Policy-driven responses to probation and parole violations.* Washington, DC: U.S. Department of Justice, National Institute of Corrections. Gray, M. Kevin, Monique Fields, and Sheila Royo Maxwell. 2001. Examining probation violations: Who, what and when. *Crime and Delinquency* 47(4): 537–557.

| BOX 7.1 | # EVIDENCE BASED PRACTICES IN COMMUNITY CORRECTIONS |

Do Swift and Certain Sanctions Work for Probationers Who Evade Drug Testing?

Under traditional community supervision, offenders receive advance notice that they must provide a drug test. This also allows them the potential to schedule their drug use around the test, or even to avoid the drug screening altogether. Offenders who used drugs while under supervision also failed to make their scheduled appointments, which resulted in a long time before an officer could schedule a court date to determine whether revocation is appropriate. A new program was launched by a Hawaii prosecutor that sought to increase compliance and reduce the costs incurred by revocation. The Hawaii Opportunity Probation with Enforcement program (better known as HOPE) required that offenders enter HOPE only if they have violated probation by missing a drug test or failing to undergo treatment.

Once in HOPE, a formal warning is delivered immediately in open court by a judge, and offenders are issued a color code (e.g., blue, red, green). Every day, probationers call a hotline to learn the color assigned for that day. If their color has been chosen, they have until 2:00 P.M. that same day to provide a urine sample. Failure to drug test results in a few days in jail, with probation resuming upon release. In such a case, probation is not revoked but modified by an officer to allow the judge to issue a bench warrant to authorize an arrest and jail booking for two to three days. With each incident of noncompliance, jail days increase. As behavior improves, drug tests become less frequent.

At a cost of $1,000 per person, the first evaluation by Hawken and Kleiman (2009) indicated that HOPE participants had significantly fewer positive drug tests, less skipped appointments, and reduced revocations and rearrests than a comparison group. As a result of the large group differences, jurisdictions all over the country quickly adopted the approach without waiting to see whether these effects lasted beyond the supervision period and if these results could be replicated elsewhere.

Skeptics of the HOPE program question the long-term effects of specific deterrence, most notably how such large differences are found without a treatment intervention (Duriez, Cullen, & Manchak, 2014). They question whether the popularity of the program is a dangerous shift away from rehabilitation, which has garnered strong empirical support, to one advocating for certain and swift sanctions that has historically less support. Replication studies of other HOPE sites in Clackamas County, Oregon; Essex County, Massachusetts; Saline County, Arkansas; and Tarrant County, Texas, conducted by Pam Lattimore and Doris MacKenzie, should be available in the near future.

Source: Hawken, A. and M. Kleiman. 2009. *Managing drug involved probationers with swift and certain sanctions: Evaluating Hawaii's HOPE.* Washington, DC: U.S. Department of Justice. Available at: http://www.nij.gov/topics/corrections/community/drug-offenders/hawaii-hope.htm

an evidence-based program aimed at reducing drug use for drug offenders who resist urine screenings and treatment while under community supervision.

Absconding from Community Supervision

absconder
An offender under community supervision who, without prior permission, escapes or flees the jurisdiction he or she is required to stay within.

Other than drug use, another surprisingly frequent technical violation is absconding from supervision. Absconding is listed in some jurisdictions as a new criminal offense. An **absconder** is defined as an offender under community supervision who, without prior permission, escapes or flees the jurisdiction he or she is required to stay within. Official nationwide estimates have reported that 12% of all parolees and about 18% of probationers abscond from supervision (Glaze, Bonczar & Zhang, 2010; Levin, 2008a). The absconding rate of clients at restitution centers was even higher, likely in part to restitution centers accepting clients who have recently been released from prison, but may be staying at the center for up to two years. With more extensive felony criminal histories and longer periods of supervision, with more stringent conditions than regular parole, absconding is more likely.

Offenders who abscond are uncertain about what their CSO will do once he or she discovers a violation, and that uncertainty translates into fear of losing their freedom. Most absconders stop reporting out of fear; they do not trust or understand the system well enough to predict the outcome of their actions. In highly charged emotional states, offenders drop all responsibilities and release building pressures to escape without thinking about the serious consequences. Ironically, any violations that trigger an escape are usually less serious than an escape charge itself, which affects an offender for the remainder of a sentence and shadows any future convictions. For such persons, reasons for absconding range from drug use to financial difficulty to needing to leave a state to visit a dying relative. Most absconders are just interested in avoiding detection. A smaller category of absconders have committed one or more serious crimes while under community supervision. If their recent criminal behavior is serious enough, they know they may never get out of prison again, so they continue to commit crimes until they are caught. This type of absconder is more likely to appear on a wanted list and may be a threat to community safety.

Because of the large number of absconders every year, most states take a passive approach to locating and apprehending fugitives. When an offender absconds from supervision, a warrant is filed with local, state, or national crime information systems. Ironically, many absconders never leave their state and can later be located by searching public utility records or through a routine traffic stop.

A community supervision officer conducts a home visit to check on an absconded probationer.

Modesto Bee/ZUMA Press

IN-HOUSE PROGRESSIVE SANCTION OPTIONS BEFORE FILING A REVOCATION

Progressive sanctions are in-house approaches that take place when an offender shows initial signs of resistance or when technical violations first start. A CSO, in conjunction with a supervisor's advice or approval, is encouraged to use in-house options prior to filing a formal revocation. Through these progressive interventions, an officer attempts to gain compliance via oral or written reprimands, staffings, motivational interviewing techniques, or directives (Taylor & Martin, 2006). Interventions and additional conditions are limited to that set in policy so that CSOs are not overstepping their bounds by imposing conditions above that of the court or parole board.

Offering more in-house options and decision matrices for minor technical violations will likely reduce revocation filings and incarceration responses (Kerbs, Jones, & Jolley, 2009). An example of these guidelines is found in Table 7.2. Once a response range has been determined, with or without

TABLE 7.2   Probation Violation Decision Guidelines

Decision-Making Level	Probation Violation Type[a]	Possible Responses Level to Probationer
Probation Officer	Failure to report	Verbal warning/reprimand
	Making false statements	Case staffing
	Violating curfew	Home visit 1 7-day curfew
	Changing residence/jobs w/o permission	Loss of travel
	Failure to pay restitution	Community service: 1–8 hrs.
	Failure to perform community service	Increase reporting
	Drug use/positive drug test	Increase drug testing
		Probationer sign waiver
Supervisor Staffing	Failure to test for drugs or take Antabuse	Drug treatment
	Failure to participate in drug treatment	Increase supervision level
	Possession of contraband	Community service: 20–40 hrs.
	Failing to register as a sex offender	Curfew (up to 30 days)
	Repeated curfew violations	Curfew (up to 30 days)
	Second positive drug test	Drug treatment
	Repeated failure to report	Increase supervision level
Court Hearing	Third positive drug test	Residential treatment
	Possession of weapons	Boot camp
	Absconding after 60 days	Electronic monitoring
	Denying access to searches	Intensive probation
	Committing new offense	Jail or prison
	Threatening victim	Day reporting center
	Deliberate pattern of noncompliance	Extension of probation

Note: [a]Response also depends on level of risk probationer poses.

Source: Carter, Madeline M. (Ed.). 2001. *Responding to Parole and Probation Violations: A Handbook to Guide Local Policy Development.* Prepared for the National Institute of Corrections, U.S. Department of Justice (Washington, DC), pp. 54, 75.

a second opinion from a supervisor, CSOs can choose from a variety of responses, depending on what they feel is appropriate for each particular case. The State of Ohio has perfected its matrix to include supervision risk and needs levels and factors known to increase risk of recidivism in the sanctions imposed. While progressive sanctions by themselves, did not reduce recidivism, the way that officers used the sanctions, and added treatment options allowed the officers to more expediently and better fine tune services with each individual offender's problem over what the court or parole board could accomplish (Martin & Van Dine, 2008).

Some agencies have an offender sign a waiver that he or she agrees to modified sanctions in lieu of going to court and thus waives the right to a court hearing. This waiver is kept on file to show a court the avenues tried before a probation officer requested a formal revocation proceeding. According to Jones and Kerbs (2007), most officers preferred to use in-house intervention techniques with probationers who made little to no effort to find employment, who failed to report, did not appear for community service work, or upon the first positive alco-sensor test, indicating an offender has ingested a substance with alcohol. Supervisory strategies to reduce occurrence of technical violations include a sound assessment and case treatment plan, as discussed in Chapter 5 (Sachwald, Eley, & Taxman, 2006), intervention by a specially trained "technical violation" unit officer, reduction in the number of cases each officer supervises (Hill, 2006), and the use of out-of-custody hearings (Andrews & Janes, 2006).

REVOCATION PROCEDURES

When in-house strategies have been exhausted, yet are still not being followed by an offender, a CSO recommends revocation. Revocation procedures are governed by a combination of constitutional rules, state law, and agency policy. Revocation proceedings begin with a violation report prepared by a supervision officer when enough information has been collected in chronological notes to document a pattern of technical violations or when a new crime has been discovered. In Box 7.2, Ralph Garza discusses the steps that CSOs go through to file a warrant and a revocation. He stresses that offenders are given multiple chances and that incarceration is used only as a last resort after all other graduated sanctions have been tried.

Predefined agency policy determines whether offenders will be picked up off the streets and have to wait in jail for their revocation hearing or whether they may remain free until their hearing. Arrest for a technical violation or arrest for a new crime does not automatically mean that supervision will be revoked—it just means that an officer can incarcerate an offender and request that a court conduct a revocation hearing. Federal law contains the following provision for federal probationers:

> If there is probable cause to believe that a probationer or a person on supervised release has violated a condition of his probation or release, he may be arrested, and upon arrest, shall be taken without unnecessary delay before the court having jurisdiction over him. A probation officer may make such an arrest wherever the probationer or releasee is found, and may make the arrest without a warrant. (Title 18 U.S.C. sec. 3606)

BOX 7.2 **FIELD NOTES**

How Do Parole Officers Respond to Parole Violators and Absconders?

When the officer suspects that a parolee has absconded or violated supervision, the parole officer first visits the last known residence. If there is no response at the parolee's home, then the officer reviews the local county jail bookings to determine if the parolee was arrested. Provided the parolee is not in local custody, the parole officer searches the state and national crime information centers. Then the officer calls local hospitals to determine if the offender was admitted for an illness or injury. Finally, the officer will call the local morgue and verify that the offender is not dead in the parolee's county of residence. After the parole officer has exhausted all possibilities, he or she completes a violation report and requests that a warrant be issued.

Ralph Garza

Fugitive or absconder violations are time intensive for officers. When a parolee is arrested for a new offense, another series of investigations begins. First, the officer must determine if anyone was killed or injured and if the offender in custody? If the parolee is in custody, this may explain why the offender could not be found and could not report. Please keep in mind that while the parole officer is dealing with one parolee, there are still 80 to 85 other parolees still on supervision that demand the officer's attention.

The parole officer will also deal with nonfield assaults. This is when the victim does not, will not, or cannot go to the police and file a police report against the parolee. The parole officer attempts to gather as much evidence as possible without coercion, so that if a warrant is later issued against the parolee for the assault, then the evidence presented by the victim could result in a parole revocation for that offender.

Parolees with criminal charges are monitored by reviewing their upcoming court dates and cases. The officer will examine the parolee's case and note any changes or comments in an offender information database. If charges are pending against the parolee, then any parole hearings are held in abeyance until the pending charges are adjudicated. The Warrant Section of the Texas Parole Division issues approximately 150 warrants a day, which is about 3,000 per month. A parolee with a warrant is not automatically returned to prison. Those offenders that either have a parole hearing or waive their hearing may be continued on supervision, transferred to an intermediate punishment facility, or revoked. Given the overcrowding in county jails and prison units, the parole officer must exercise every possible means to keep the parolee reporting and out of jail through a series of graduated sanctions. The graduated sanctions most often utilized are: warnings/admonishments, increased control, increased monitoring/programming, and modifying the special conditions pending approval by a parole panel. Warnings and admonishments consist of compliance counseling, written reprimands, and case conferences. Compliance counseling is providing guidance to the releasee to follow the rules of supervision. It is meant as a first level nonthreatening sanction. A case conference means a meeting occurs between the parolee, parole officer, and unit supervisor to discuss the violation(s).

The next level of sanctions is for the officer to reclassify the parolee at a higher supervision level for increased control. For example, a minimum supervision parolee requires a home visit every six months. If that parolee has not reported or has not attended his substance abuse treatment, the officer can increase to "intensive" where the parolee will receive a home visit every month until compliance is attained. Another increase control device is having the parolee report to the District Resource Center (similar to a day reporting center), which means now the offender has to find a ride, arrive on time, and participate in substance abuse meetings for two hours. The third level involves getting the parole panel to modify the conditions. If all else fails, the last stop is back to prison.

BOX 7.3	**COMMUNITY CORRECTIONS UP CLOSE**

When Are Warrants Needed to Search Offenders on Community Supervision?

In Chapter 4, you learned that evidence obtained or seized illegally by police cannot be used to convict, but hearsay and/or illegally obtained evidence can be mentioned in the presentence investigation report. This is because when the PSI has been written, the offender has already been convicted. This line of reasoning is also applied to revocation. In parole revocation hearings (*Pennsylvania Board of Probation and Parole v. Scott,* 1998) and probation revocation hearings (*State v. Pizel,* 1999), the court ruled that illegally obtained evidence may also be used during revocation hearings. This is the case for two reasons: First, a revocation hearing is an administrative hearing that has a lower burden of proof—reasonable suspicion—than criminal court prosecutions that require the presence of probable cause. Second, probation/parole officers are allowed to search probationers and parolees' cars or homes without a search warrant if reasonable grounds exist to believe contraband is present (*Griffin v. Wisconsin,* 1987) or that a probationer has engaged in criminal activity (*United States v. Knights,* 2001). An offender on community supervision must agree to warrantless searches as specified in their conditions. As long as it is specified in the parole agreement ahead of time, a parolee can even be subjected to a warrantless search at any time for any reason (with or without probable cause) by any police officer. The warrantless search of a parolee who was independently searched by a police officer was upheld in *Samson v. California* (2006) because he had this condition in his parole agreement. His parole was subsequently revoked for the contraband found during the search.

Information is collected in a variety of ways, such as via searches, home visits, collateral contacts, and drug tests. Box 7.3 discusses the issue of whether search warrants are required by probation and parole officers.

Warrants and Citations

The violation process is depicted in Figure 7.3 as a series of decision points. After a CSO discovers a violation and investigates, agency policy defines whether an offender is arrested immediately or is issued a citation or summons to appear at a revocation hearing and kept under supervision. When an arrest warrant is issued, a parolee is detained in a county jail until the revocation hearing. Although the process and options are the same, the decision as to whether to revoke parole resides with a parole board and with a judge to revoke probation.

Most violators enter the jail-booking process by a warrant, but that means that a jail bed is occupied until the revocation hearing process ends. The time it takes to revoke varies by jurisdiction according to case backlog and whether an offender openly admits the allegations. The time from violation detection by an officer to disposition by a parole board or a court averaged between six and eight weeks. The federal system requires that revocation hearings be held within 90 days from the time an offender is taken into custody (*U.S. Parole Commission,* 2006). To save jail space for individuals who are a true threat to public safety, more jurisdictions are turning to citations in place of automatic warrants for violators waiting for revocation hearings. If a violation was violent or if an offender might abscond, then he or she must wait behind bars until a revocation hearing. For most offenders who violate, a citation allows them to continue working to support dependents while at the same time preparing for a possible jail or prison term.

FIGURE 7.3
The Revocation Process

Adapted from: New York State Division of Paroles Office of Policy Analysis and Information. 1993. Overview of the parole revocation process in New York in *Reclaiming Offender Accountability: Intermediate Sanctions for Probation and Parole Violators*, Rhine, Edward E. (Ed.). Laurel, MD: American Correctional Association, 41.

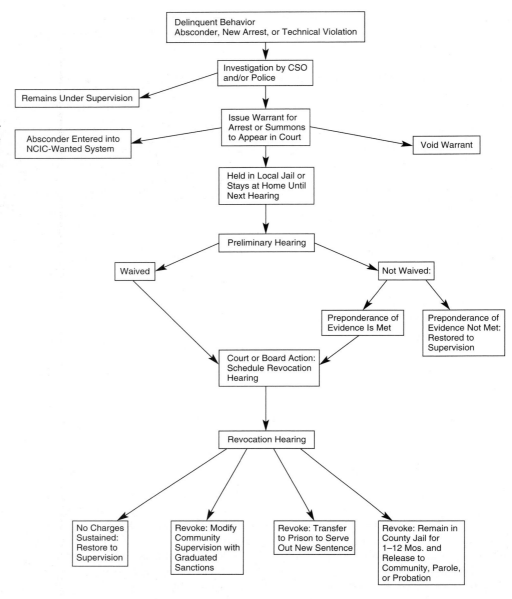

preliminary hearing
An inquiry conducted to determine whether there is probable cause that an offender has committed a probation or parole violation.

final revocation hearing
A due-process hearing that must be conducted before probation or parole can be revoked.

Two-Stage Process

As depicted in Figure 7.3, offenders are entitled to a two-stage hearing consisting of a **preliminary hearing** and a **final revocation hearing.** A preliminary, or show cause, hearing is a recorded hearing to determine whether a preponderance of the evidence exists to believe a violation has occurred. If a preponderance of the evidence exists, a revocation hearing is scheduled and later held separately. If a standard of proof is not met, charges are dismissed. Many jurisdictions, in an effort to speed up the process, allow offenders to waive a preliminary hearing. This is known in the federal system as an expedited revocation, which accounts for almost half of all revocations (Hoffman & Beck, 2005). An expedited revocation requires a parole violator to admit wrongdoing and waive a right to a revocation hearing before the U.S. Parole Commission, and does not allow a right to appeal a revocation decision.

Although most revocation decisions are discretionary, some jurisdictions explicitly mandate automatic revocation and resentencing for some behaviors. In the federal system, instances of mandatory revocation include: (a) commission of any crime of violence or facilitation of sexual contact against a child under the age of 16; (b) possession of a firearm; (c) possession of a controlled substance or positive drug test; and (d) refusal to comply with drug testing.

In discretionary matters, offenders who wish to contest accusations or to retain a right to appeal must wait in jail for a formal revocation hearing. Two studies indicate that discretionary revocation decisions are difficult to predict. Hoffman and Beck (2005) compared the outcomes of cases in which offenders agreed to expedite revocation with case outcomes for the same charge of offenders who waited for a formal hearing. About 38.5% of offenders who waited for a formal revocation received the same decision as expeditors, whereas 31% received a more lenient decision and 30% received a harsher decision.

In a second example in another jurisdiction, 42% of offenders whose case went in front of a judge had their probation conditions modified or extended by a court for noncompliance, and 54% went to some sort of intermediate residential facility, jail, or prison (Stickels, 2007).

Although revocation may not always result in imprisonment in many state and local jurisdictions, imprisonment is mandatory in the federal system if an offender is revoked. Table 7.3 shows the number of months of imprisonment that revoked federal offenders must serve, depending on their original offense of conviction and their original criminal history score. Offenders originally convicted of a Class A felony serve the same amount of time regardless of whether their new revocation was for a new crime or technical violations. For all others, there are three violation grades or levels of severity of revocation behavior that determine the number of months served. For example, let's say Nadine was originally convicted of Possession of a Controlled Substance and her original criminal history category defined by her prior record was II. Nadine was sentenced to probation. While on probation she committed a series of technical violations (positive drug

TABLE 7.3   Number of Imprisonment Months for Federal Revocations

Original Conviction	ORIGINAL CRIMINAL HISTORY CATEGORY AT INITIAL SENTENCING					
	I	II	III	IV	V	VI
Class A Felony						
Any new crime or technical violations	24–30	27–33	30–37	37–46	46–57	51–63
Class B Felony and Below						
New crime	12–18	15–21	18–24	24–30	30–37	33–41
Serious technical violations	4–10	6–12	8–14	12–18	18–24	21–27
Less serious technical violations	3–9	4–10	5–11	6–12	7–13	8–14

Source: U.S. Bureau of Prisons. 2008. *Guidelines Manual* (November 1, 2008). Section 7B1.4, p. 488.

tests) defined as serious technical violations. According to Table 7.3, Nadine must serve between six and twelve months, as long as the number of months in the table does not exceed her original sentence length.

An example of a state that has mandatory probation revocation rules is Michigan. In Michigan, mandatory revocation is imposed on juveniles who have been "waived" to adult probation supervision and who subsequently commit a new misdemeanor or felony crime while under supervision. In such a case, the new crime runs concurrent with the original offense—that is, the length of supervision for the new charge cannot exceed the term left of the original charge, but probation must be revoked.

LEGAL ISSUES REGARDING REVOCATION HEARINGS

A probation or parole revocation is an administrative hearing that is closer to a civil proceeding because it is seen as an extension of an existing sentence (*Hampton v. State*, 2001). As such, neither is governed by the same rules as in formal criminal trials. Given that legal rights at time of revocation are virtually identical, the rights afforded in probation revocation proceedings are extended to parole revocations and vice versa. The result of a revocation hearing is not a conviction, but a finding of "revoked" or the offender continues on probation or parole.

Rights for Which Offenders Qualify

During a revocation proceeding, offenders are entitled to certain rights prior to revocation of probation. These rights were granted by the U.S. Supreme Court to parolees (*Morrissey v. Brewer*, 1972) and probationers (*Gagnon v. Scarpelli*, 1973), arguably the two most important parole and probation cases ever decided. Gerald Scarpelli was on probation for a felony when he was arrested for burglary. He admitted involvement in the burglary but later claimed his admission was coerced and therefore invalid. His probation was revoked without a hearing and without a lawyer present. After serving three years of his sentence, Scarpelli sought release, saying that his **due process** rights were violated because he did not obtain a right to a hearing and a right to a lawyer during the hearing. The court extended the same due process rights to probationers that parolees were afforded one year earlier in *Morrissey v. Brewer*. Both probationers and parolees were entitled to the following due process rights before and during revocation hearings:

1. written notice of alleged violation;
2. disclosure of the evidence of violation;
3. an opportunity to be heard in person and to present evidence and witnesses;
4. a right to confront and cross-examine adverse witnesses;
5. a right to judgment by a detached and neutral hearing body; and
6. a written statement of reasons for revocation, including evidence used in arriving at that decision.

Rights Limited to Offenders

In revocation proceedings, an offender is not constitutionally entitled to a jury (*People v. Price*, 1960) nor to a speedy trial. In some states, however, the law provides for a jury hearing in juvenile cases. A probationer or parolee is not entitled

due process
A recognition that laws must be applied in a fair and equal manner. Fundamental fairness.

to the Fifth Amendment privilege against self-incrimination (*Perry v. State*, 2001). Remaining silent at a revocation hearing might prejudice the outcome against a defendant, but testifying at a revocation hearing can be used as evidence at a later criminal trial unless a probationer (or parolee) has been given immunity for what he or she says at the revocation.

Probationers are generally not entitled to a court-appointed lawyer during revocation proceedings unless they appear incapable of speaking for themselves (*Gagnon v. Scarpelli*, 1973). Given the fact that inarticulate people must voice their need for counsel to obtain legal assistance, indigence is used as a proxy, with some states routinely providing counsel to indigent probationers in revocation proceedings.

Level of Proof and Evidence Required

Most courts require that evidence be collected to satisfy **preponderance of the evidence** as the standard for revocation (*United States v. McCormick*, 1995), which is evidence that convinces a judge that a probationer violated the terms of his or her probation. If the state presents proof of a condition violation, a probationer has the burden of presenting evidence to meet and/or overcome prima facie proof (*State v. Graham*, 2001). Preponderance of the evidence is approximately the same amount of evidence as that required to make an arrest (probable cause). However, one court case (*Benton v. State*, 2003) said that arrest for a crime by itself is not enough to revoke probation, but probation may be revoked for an "indictment" by a grand jury (*Newsom v. State*, 2004) or for a conviction by a judge or jury. Interestingly, parole revocation is permissible even if charges are later dismissed (*Reyes v. Tate*, 2001). So it seems that whether a lower burden of proof than preponderance of the evidence (such as reasonable grounds or reasonable suspicion) would suffice for revocation is being addressed by lower courts, but this has yet to be addressed by the U.S. Supreme Court.

preponderance of evidence A level of proof used in a probation revocation administrative hearing by which a judge decides guilt, based on which side presents more convincing evidence and its probable truth or accuracy, and not necessarily on amount of evidence.

The testimony of a CSO is crucial at a revocation proceeding. Whether such testimony—unsupported by any other evidence—is sufficient to revoke varies by state. For example, a probationer's admission to a probation officer was sufficient to support a revocation and eliminates the need on the part of the government to present proof of violation (*Fields v. State*, 2002).

Most states admit hearsay evidence during revocation, but some do not. Reliable hearsay evidence (statements offered by a witness based upon what someone else has told the witness and not upon personal knowledge or observation) may be admitted in a parole (or probation) revocation hearing (*Belk v. Purkett*, 1994). A yes answer to any of the three questions below signifies that hearsay is reliable and therefore may be admitted as evidence in a revocation proceeding:

1. Is the information corroborated by a parolee's own statements or other testimony at a hearing?
2. Does the information fit within one of the many exceptions to the hearsay rule?
3. Does the information have other substantial indicia of reliability?

Other Revocation Situations

Other situations include whether offenders can be revoked for not fulfilling financial commitments, juvenile probation revocations, and credit for time served on probation or parole.

REVOCATION FOR AN INABILITY TO PAY?   Violating an offender for failure to keep current on payments largely depends on whether the behavior was willful and intentional. For example, a probationer can be revoked for refusal to pay monthly fees, restitution, or fines. An indigent probationer cannot be revoked if he or she is unable to pay a fine or restitution, provided that probationer was not responsible for failure to pay, such as getting laid off from a job (*Bearden v. Georgia*, 1983). The probationer, however, has the burden of showing that the inability to pay was not willful. In other words, a defendant has to show effort and desire to fulfill financial obligations (*State v. Gropper*, 1995).

On the other hand, the courts will allow revocation, even in cases in which an offender is not at fault (i.e., there is no willful violation), if it can be shown that not revoking is a risk to public safety. For example, offenders under community supervision for predatory sex offenses were not able to complete mandatory sex offender treatment programs because none were available in their community. After finding no better alternatives, the court supported incarceration over allowing these offenders to remain in the community without treatment (*People v. Colabello*, 1997).

TIME ON PROBATION OR PAROLE IS USUALLY NOT CREDITED IF REVOKED   If probation is revoked and an offender goes to prison, most courts have ruled that time served on probation or parole is not credited toward a sentence in the same way that incarceration time in jail or prison would be (*Bruggeman v. State*, 1996). However, a federal court and now a Florida statute permit a court options to credit none, some, or all time spent under supervised release toward a sentence (*United States v. Pettus*, 2002; *Summers v. State*, 2002). Generally a parolee whose parole has been revoked may be paroled again, but the revoked parolee must remain in prison for a specified time before becoming eligible for another parole.

As long as an offender abides by the terms of parole (or probation), he or she will minimally receive credit on a sentence as straight time—that is, without the benefit of good time credits. In other states, a parolee may receive reductions for good behavior while on parole.

TRUTH OR FICTION?

When probationers and parolees are revoked for breaking the rules, it means that parole and probation don't work.

FICTION

FACT: A revocation decision due to technical violations is complicated by an offender's situation, which rules are broken and why, agency policy on technical violations, officer discretion, and judicial discretion, and has little to do with the overall effectiveness of community supervision.

WHEN COMMUNITY SUPERVISION ENDS

As we have seen so far, violations during probation or parole supervision are influenced primarily by how closely the offender is supervised, officer discretion, and agency policy on technical violations. The research with respect to supervision officer experience and likelihood to file a revocation is mixed. While one study found that federal officers with more experience and more education were more likely to file revocations (Baber & Motivans, 2013), a study of California officers found the exact opposite conclusion (Grattet et al., 2011). With both studies, however, the more closely an offender is supervised, the more likely that an officer will detect technical violations. But does this mean that this person actually poses a public safety risk?

Recidivism and Offender Characteristics

Table 7.4 shows characteristics of federal probationers who have completed probation successfully and unsuccessfully. Female offenders, those over the age of 30, with shorter criminal histories, and without serious drug abuse and mental illness problems were the most likely to succeed. Also, offenders who possessed skills that allowed them to maintain employment, those who were high school graduates, and those who completed treatment programs were less likely to become recidivists (Baber & Motivans, 2013; Steiner, Makarios, Travis, & Meade, 2012). Conventional ties and positive social support from friends and family significantly certainly do contribute to success. On the other hand, being young, being unmarried, having previous convictions, and lacking emotional maturity contributed to higher failure rates.

TABLE 7.4 Characteristics of Federal Probationers Terminating Supervision

		PERCENT TERMINATING SUPERVISION WITH:			
Characteristic	Number of Probation Terminations	Successful Completion	Committed New Crime	Technical Violation	Admin. Closure
Gender					
Male	10,781	81.2%	5.9%	10.9%	2.0%
Female	4,915	84.6%	4.4%	9.5%	1.5%
Race					
White	10,598	84.0%	5.3%	9.0%	1.7%
African-American	3,935	78.1%	6.1%	13.6%	2.2%
American Indian	428	64.7%	4.9%	28.3%	2.1%
Asian/Pacific Islander	492	92.5%	2.7%	4.2%	0.6%
Ethnicity					
Hispanic	2,818	80.8%	8.3%	9.9%	1.0%
Non-Hispanic	12,602	82.6%	4.8%	10.6%	2.0%
Age					
16–18 years	114	67.5%	7.9%	22.8%	1.8%
19–20 years	567	61.6%	11.3%	26.0%	1.1%
21–30 years	4,762	76.3%	7.5%	14.7%	1.5%
31–40 years	4,105	82.5%	6.0%	10.2%	1.3%
41 and over	6,166	89.0%	2.7%	5.8%	2.5%
Education					
Less than High School	3,642	76.2%	7.8%	14.2%	1.6%
High School Graduate	5,254	81.4%	5.2%	11.8%	1.6%
Some College	3,538	86.8%	3.7%	7.5%	2.0%
College Graduate	1,878	92.9%	1.9%	2.9%	2.3%
Drug Abuse					
None	12,664	92.6%	2.4%	3.7%	1.3%
Drug History	1,691	84.5%	4.0%	9.0%	2.5%
GROUP TOTAL	15,721	82.3%	5.4%	10.5%	1.8%

Note: Each termination was counted separately. Technical violations and terminations for new crimes are shown only if supervision terminated with incarceration or removal from active supervision for reason of a violation. The data exclude corporate offenders.

(a) Technical violations range widely from drug use, escape, quitting a job without permission, not reporting, and other probation conditions

Source: U.S. Department of Justice. 2008. *Compendium of Federal Justice Statistics, 2004.* Washington, DC: U.S. Department of Justice.

Time to Revocation

The research that has been done on probation and parole failure has indicated that the first three months are clearly the most vulnerable time—not only after release from prison, but also when probation starts as the time period when revocation for technical violations are most likely for up to one-third of probationers or parolees (Grattet et al., 2011; Johnson, 2014). After the first 24 months, the recidivism rates begin to level off between years 2 and year 5. Probationers who committed a new crime seemed to violate later in the probationary period, but they were also more likely to be unemployed, to have a prior criminal history, to be on probation for an assaultive offense, and to have a pattern of technical violations.

Probationers generally present less of a recidivism risk than parolees because probationers commit significantly fewer new crimes. The data in Figure 7.4 certainly support that probationers were more likely to complete supervision successfully than were parolees (both on discretionary parole and under mandatory parole supervision), no matter of which type of crime they had been convicted. Also, parolees who were convicted of property, drug, and public order crimes were more likely to succeed than were offenders who went to prison for violent crimes, weapons, or immigration offenses (Steiner, Makarios, Travis, & Meade, 2012).

Recidivism Rates of Released Prisoners over Time

Over 400,000 prisoners released in 30 different states were tracked for up to five years in what is the largest national study of its kind. As depicted in Figure 7.4, researchers documented the time from release to the first arrest, and then whether that arrest generated a conviction. The "return to prison" variable was prisoners who were readmitted to prison for either a new crime or technical violations. For example, 67.8% were rearrested for a new offense and nearly half were returned to prison within the three-year period (Durose, Cooper, & Snyder, 2014). With the exception of prisoners who were initially convicted of robbery, property offenders (burglary, larceny, and motor vehicle theft) had higher rates of rearrest than offenders convicted of violent crimes (Grattet et al., 2011). Some of

FIGURE 7.4
Probation vs. Parole: Federal Revocations (Both Technical and New Crime) Separated by Original Conviction

Source: U.S. Department of Justice. 2008. *Compendium of Federal Justice Statistics.* Washington, DC: U.S. Department of Justice.

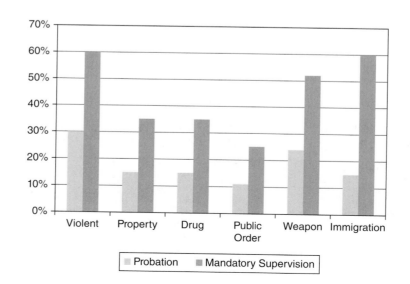

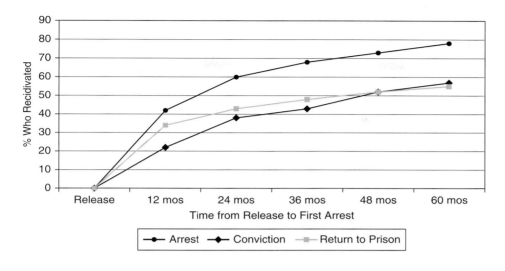

FIGURE 7.5 Recidivism Over five years of Prisoners Released in 30 States

Source: Durose, Matthew R., Alexia D. Cooper, and Howard N. Snyder. 2014. *Recidivism of Prisoners Released in 30 States in 2005: Patterns From 2005 to 2010.* NCJ 244205. Washington, DC: U.S. Department of Justice.

these differences stem from the fact that the crimes with the highest recidivism are motivated by the need for money. Other types of crimes, such as murder or rape are indeed serious, but are tied more to emotions than to profit. State prisoners who did recidivate tended to be male, African-American, and most were between 25 and 39 years of age. The more extensive the offender's criminal history, the greater the likelihood of parole failure (Durose, Cooper, & Snyder, 2014).

Why Have Revocation Rates Increased?

With the increase in rate of violations in recent years, research has been undertaken to discover the underlying causes of parole and probation revocations. One reason involves a lower threshold for behavior tolerated before revocation occurs (White, Mellow, Englander, & Ruffinengo, 2011). Second, an increase in the average number of offenders that each officer supervises causes more stress and offers less face-to-face contact. Officers spend less quality time with offenders and more time on rule enforcement and paperwork. A third reason is that parolees and probationers alike have more parole conditions imposed and thus more ways to violate. A probationer/parolee has an average of 19 conditions to follow, ranging from 10 to 24 (Travis & Stacey, 2010). An increased number of conditions means that offenders experience more pressure to perform and to try to meet all those conditions. Fourth, with advances in drug testing technology, more drug use is now detected. Finally, with increased use of electronic monitoring in parole and probation, more hardened offenders tend to be placed in a community so as to avoid institutional overcrowding.

An increase in revocation rates puts pressure on a number of other components in the criminal justice system. For example, parole and probation officers must devote more of their time to revocation paperwork and less time to supervising other offenders in their caseload who are functioning satisfactorily. Furthermore, while probation and parole revocators are awaiting hearings, revocation drains court resources, parole board resources, and county jail bed space. As a result, some solutions to decreasing revocation that we've discussed in this chapter include using more in-house progressive sanctions, decreasing the number of rules that offenders are expected to follow, imposing conditions according to risk level and type of crime, and heavily rewarding treatment completion and providing incentives for completion of financial obligations.

TRUTH OR **FICTION?**

Probationers and parolees are given too many chances.

FICTION

FACT: Revoking probation and parole makes sense if an offender commits a new crime. Revocation due solely to not following the rules is more complicated and should depend on if the pattern of violations is linked to a return to criminal behavior. Otherwise, graduated sanctions and the use of other tools while remaining on probation or parole is more effective.

Alternatives to Incarceration for Technical Violations

Incarcerating probationers for technical violations when they don't follow the rules is an extremely costly option for taxpayers. Many states recognize this and have developed progressive sanctions for technical violations and incentives for successful completion. For example, Delaware's Probation Reform Law not only shortened a term of probation to no longer than two years, but technical violators could be placed on work release or in probation violation centers for up to five days per violation, not to exceed 10 days per calendar year (Sentencing Accountability Commission & the Statistical Analysis Center, 2005). Michigan, Kentucky, and New Jersey created technical violator programs that are residential halfway house-style programs where offenders can be sent for intensive programming for up to 90 days. Most offenders are referred to these programs by probation and parole officers. An evaluation of New Jersey's "Halfway Back" intermediate sanction therapeutic program matched technical violators who were referred and completed the program with eligible technical violators that did not go through the program. While the Halfway Back residents had slightly fewer new arrests over 18 months than the comparison group, the two groups did not significantly differ in amount of time that elapsed until their first arrest. The program's biggest strength was that it saved $1.3 million in incarceration costs that would have been incurred for every 100 technical violators who had gone to jail as a response to revocation (White et al., 2011). Another option might be to decrease the number of standard conditions, so that low-risk offenders have only a small number of conditions that apply to them the most.

For higher risk parolees, though, it is recommended that community-based sanctions be administered with certainty and in a swift manner to be more effective in reducing the chance of recidivism before it happens (Steiner, Makarios, Travis, & Meade, 2012). The future of community supervision entails examining patterns of behavior that reliably indicate when a parolee has become too much of a public safety risk to remain in a community. Prediction research into the causes of recidivism and subsequent revocation would be invaluable in equipping a parole officer with the tools necessary for supervision. Recall our earlier discussion of classification and risk and needs assessment instruments in Chapter 5. It is interesting to note that many of the same variables that initially classify offenders also can predict post-release behavior on parole, which might lead us to a deeper understanding of why some offenders succeed and some do not.

SUMMARY

- Offenders who are doing well on supervision and have fulfilled their obligations should be rewarded by early termination.

- Offenders who are misbehaving may have committed a new crime and/or a series of technical violations of conditions.

- In-house progressive sanctions, guided by a decision matrix, should be used to respond to violations with

certainty and swiftness for most effective results, and prior to recommending revocation.

- A decision to revoke for noncompliance is initially recommended by a supervision officer but is empowered at judicial discretion for probationers and at parole board discretion for parolees.

- Time served in a community is not credited as jail or prison time if supervision is revoked.

- Probationers and parolees must be given due process rights, including notice of charges, right to confront witnesses, and right to present evidence in their favor.
- Offenders do not have a constitutional right to an attorney, but one is provided if competency is an issue. There is typically no right to appeal a revocation, but about half of the states, by law or agency policy, allow parolees this option.
- The increase in the revocation rate is due to a lower tolerance rate in the way offenders are monitored; there are more conditions to follow/violate, and less time is spent on treatment and reentry concerns (due to a higher caseload per officer).

DISCUSSION QUESTIONS

1. Should early termination of probation be given as a good behavior incentive or should probationers serve their entire term regardless of behavior? What are the advantages and disadvantages of each approach?

2. If you were a CSO and your client refused to report or check in, how many times (or how long) would it take before you filed a revocation with the courts?

3. If you were a CSO and your client could not find a job, what steps would you take to help this person? At what point would you consider taking him or her back to court to request a modification in conditions or revocation for not having a job? Defend your answer.

4. If you were a CSO and your client admitted to using drugs and said that her drug test would come back positive, what would you do?

5. How might motivational interviewing techniques factor into unresponsive client behavior?

6. Which type of technical violation do you perceive as the worst kind, and why?

7. In a decision to revoke probation, what are implications for the probationer, the probation officer, and the community? Are these the same or different with a parolee?

8. Do the revocation procedures in place now provide due process for offenders? What, if anything, might be lacking?

9. Is the "preponderance of the evidence" standard of proof too low, and should a different standard be used for revocation? If so, should the new standard require more or less evidence?

10. How does revocation contribute to jail crowding? What alternatives could be tried to remedy this problem?

11. If you were an offender under post-prison parole supervision accused of a series of technical violations (three times that you didn't report and one positive urine screening for cocaine) for which you were guilty, would you request expedited revocation procedures or a hearing? Justify your answer.

 ## WEBSITES, VIDEOS, AND PODCASTS

Websites
U.S. Parole Commission Rules and Procedures Manual
http://www.usdoj.gov/uspc/rules_procedures /rulesmanual.htm

Iowa Code for Parole Revocations
https://www.legis.iowa.gov/DOCS/ACO/IAC /LINC/Chapter.205.11.pdf

Videos/Podcasts
Lawyer Discusses Probation Violations in Florida

(Length: 3:23 minutes) A central Florida Criminal Defense Attorney discusses what a violation of probation is and possible consequences
https://www.youtube.com/watch?v=9v-QfzhQCBU

Probation violation hearings in Nevada
(Length: 2 minutes) Las Vegas criminal defense attorney explains how probation violation hearings work.
https://www.youtube.com/watch?v=99YfNiaNi38

Violation of Probation in Florida

Attorney Deidra Sibley, of Allen & Arcadier in Melbourne, Florida, discusses violation of probation.

http://www.youtube.com/watch?v=Z_hnUY3ikQQ

Probation Violation Hearing

Mark Provenza, former Lorain City Law Director, at a probation violation hearing with Judge Patrick Carroll at Lakewood Municipal Court

http://www.youtube.com/watch?v=CXWMfl WmA7o

Testing What Works in Probation: The HOPE Program

This five-part segment sponsored by NIJ, interviews Eric Martin about the original HOPE program in Hawaii.

http://nij.ncjrs.gov/multimedia/video-martin.htm

CASE STUDY EXERCISES

Modification and Termination

In the following two cases, list the violations of supervision that are applicable. What decision would you make in each case? Your choices are: (a) modification and retention under community supervision; (b) modification with some other graduated sanction; or (c) revocation and return to jail or prison. Pick one response for each case and fully justify your decision.

CASE A: Probationer Conner, Possession of an Explosive Device

Probationer Conner is under supervision for Possession of an Explosive Device, which was an undetonated homemade bomb. Mr. Conner has three years of college education (major in physics) and reportedly has an IQ of 125. Given his particularly eccentric behavior during pretrial, the special conditions of his supervision require that he obtain a comprehensive mental health diagnosis. Shortly after Mr. Conner's supervision term begins, he tests positive for marijuana use. When confronted by his probation officer, he admits to using marijuana. However, he states that he uses marijuana to self-medicate because it helps calm him, and he feels that he would commit violent acts if he were to cease its use. At this point Mr. Conner is not undergoing substance abuse treatment nor has he been court-ordered to do so. The probation officer reminds Mr. Conner of a condition of supervision that he neither use nor possess illegal drugs and advises him that his use of illegal substances cannot be allowed, adding that the sentencing court would be advised of any violation.

The probation officer immediately refers Mr. Conner for a psychiatric evaluation to determine whether he would benefit from psychotropic medication. The psychiatrist diagnoses him with **Bipolar Affective Disorder**, Type II, and

prescribes Depakote, which takes up to two weeks to take effect. However, this medication requires regular lab work to evaluate its effectiveness. Mr. Conner fails to attend his next appointment with the psychiatrist, so you are unsure as to whether he is taking his Depakote medication regularly. Results of a urine specimen taken from him a week after his evaluation by the psychiatrist reveal trace amounts of Depakote but also that Mr. Conner has used both marijuana and methamphetamine. What should you as the probation officer do next?

CASE B: Parolee York, Aggravated Assault

Parolee York was convicted and sent to prison for two years for aggravated assault. She has a history of violent behavior and anger management issues. She has no known drug nor alcohol problems and until recently was a dishwasher at Joe's Pancake House. She has been under parole supervision with you for the last five months and for a time was reporting regularly. Special conditions of Ms. York's supervision require she complete anger management classes by the end of her term, which is supposed to end in seven months if all goes well. Anger management treatment takes three months, and the program has a waiting list of clients who are court-ordered to attend treatment. Ms. York had repeatedly stated she would undergo an anger management assessment but just never has. When you call to verify employment at the restaurant, her employer says that she quit coming three weeks ago and has been replaced by another dishwasher.

Now two weeks have gone by since you called Joe's Pancake House and still no sign of Ms. York. She won't return your phone calls. She missed her regular appointment with you this afternoon. You called the jail to see whether she had been picked up, but police have had no contact with her. What should you do next?

Part III

Enhancements and Graduated Sanctions

With the push toward decreasing jail and prison populations, intermediate community sanctions have become more popular for offenders in which regular probation or parole may be too lenient, but jail and prison is not an option. Chapter 8 considers residential programs, in which offenders must live away from home and inside a facility within the community while completing their sentence. Residential programs include halfway houses, work release, and correctional boot camps. Chapter 9 explores nonresidential community corrections programs in which the offender resides at home while participating in the program under a strict set of rules and curfews. Nonresidential programs include house arrest, electronic monitoring, and day reporting centers.

Finally, Chapter 10 discusses sanctions tied to restorative justice and economic sources. Restorative justice is a philosophy that underscores the need for offenders to acknowledge their crime and agree to repair the harm done to their victims and to the surrounding community. Forms of restorative justice include victim-offender mediation, family group conferencing, reparation boards, and sentencing circles. Community service, restitution, and fines are economic sanctions that can be used as tools to accomplish objectives in appropriate cases.

Residential Community Supervision Programs

AP Images/Patrick Semansky

CHAPTER OUTLINE

CHAPTER LEARNING OBJECTIVES

1. Describe the purpose of residential community correctional facilities.

2. Discuss the effectiveness of residential community correctional programs for medium- and high-risk offenders.

3. Compare and contrast halfway houses, shock incarceration, and work release programs.

KEY TERMS

intermediate sanctions
halfway house
residential community correctional facilities (rccfs)
work release
restitution center
work ethic camp
shock incarceration
boot camp

Former U.S. Representative Jesse Jackson Jr. who served as a Congressman from 1995 until 2012, is the son of Reverend Jesse Jackson, is married, and has two kids. Just before Jackson Jr.'s sudden resignation from Congress, he reportedly was being treated for bipolar disorder and was being investigated for spending $750,000 of campaign contributions on personal goods and services, such as electronics, watches, furniture, and restaurant dinners, among other things. Jackson pled guilty to the charges in 2013 and was sentenced to 30 months in federal prison and to perform 500 hours of community service. He began serving his time on October 29, 2013, at a prison in Butner, North Carolina and then was transferred to a federal prison camp in Montgomery, Alabama. While incarcerated, Jackson completed substance abuse treatment and earned good time (54 days per year). After 18 months, he was released in March 2015 to serve the remaining time in a halfway house in Washington DC (Rousseau, 2015). This halfway house collects 25% of Jackson's income for rent, so Jackson, like all other residents there, is expected to find full-time employment within two weeks of arrival. He is expected to remain at the halfway house until September 2015, whereby he may be considered to return home and be under supervised release (similar to parole) until 2018.

Question for discussion: Is a six-month stay in the halfway house enough time for Jesse Jackson Jr. to transition from federal prison to supervised release? Why or why not?

intermediate sanctions
A spectrum of community supervision strategies that vary greatly in terms of supervision level and treatment capacity, ranging from diversion to short-term duration in a residential community facility.

halfway house
The oldest and most common type of community residential facility for probationers or parolees who require a more structured setting than would be available if living independently.

residential community correctional facilities (RCCFs)
A community sanction in which a convicted offender lives at a corrections facility and must be employed, but can leave said facility for a limited purpose and duration if preapproved. Examples include halfway houses, prerelease centers, restitution centers, drug-treatment facilities, and work-release centers.

INTRODUCTION

Regular probation supervision is adequate for misdemeanor and felony offenders who pose a minimum or medium risk of recidivism. However, offenders who are eligible for community supervision but who may not require 24-hour supervision like that provided by jail or prison are ideal candidates for intermediate sanctions. We introduced the term **intermediate sanctions** in Chapter 1 as a community-based sentence that provides more freedom than prison but less freedom than traditional probation and parole. There are both residential and nonresidential options. This chapter addresses residential programs that require offenders to live in a facility but allow them to remain in the community, where they have access to more treatment services. Sometimes a sentence to a residential facility is preceded by a short stay in jail for a few weeks or months. Though they are known by multiple names, the three residential programs discussed here are: (a) halfway houses, (b) work release programs, and (c) correctional boot camps.

RESIDENTIAL COMMUNITY CORRECTIONAL FACILITIES/ HALFWAY HOUSES

Halfway houses are residential facilities for probationers and parolees who require a more structured setting than would be available from living independently. Halfway houses are staffed 24 hours a day, seven days a week for various types of offenders and are also known as community corrections centers (CCCs) or **residential community correctional facilities (RCCFs)**. The term *halfway house* was the original term used because of the two groups of clients accepted: the halfway out's and the halfway in's (see Figure 8.1).

Because of their diversity, it is difficult to know the precise number of halfway houses. The last known nationwide count of local facilities estimated over 600 facilities housing nearly 19,500 offenders. Of this number, over 90% of facilities are privately owned and operated, and less than 10% are operated by the Department of Corrections. The number of inmates living in RCCFs represents 4.4% of the total inmate population in the United States, at an average cost per day of around $45 per offender. Alaska, Iowa, Montana, and Wyoming are the

FIGURE 8.1
Different Types of Halfway House Clients

Halfway OUT
- **Prerelease:** Minimum-custody prisoners who anticipate receiving parole within the next year
- **Parolees:** Prisoners who earned parole, but require more assistance and supervision with reentry

Halfway IN
- **Probation Violators:** High-risk/high-need probationers
- **Parole Violators** Graduated sanction or last stop before prison

Source: © 2017 Cengage Learning

most avid users of RCCFs, which house about 14% of their total inmate populations. In the federal system, there are over 8,000 federal inmates in CCCs (Sabol & Couture, 2008).

History of Halfway Houses

The concept of the halfway house has been traced back to the early 1800s in England and Ireland. In the United States, the halfway house idea originated at a time when most penitentiaries still practiced a Pennsylvania-style system of solitude and complete silence. Because prisoners were locked in their cells all day and were not allowed to interact with each other, halfway houses originated as a way to help prisoners transition back to normal social life (Keller & Alper, 1970).

As penitentiaries transformed from the solitude of the Pennsylvania system to the silent interaction of the Auburn, or "congregate" system, prisoners were allowed to work outside of their cells. State support for halfway houses was still lacking, so private, nonprofit organizations opened halfway houses for the first time to provide a place for prisoners to live after release from prison.

For example, in 1845 the Isaac T. Hopper Home opened to accept Sing Sing prisoners in New York City. The building, now considered a historical landmark, is still a functioning residential facility for women and is the oldest halfway house still in operation. In 1864, the Temporary Asylum for Discharged Female Prisoners (renamed in 1910 as the Dedham Temporary House for Women and Children) opened in Massachusetts by Hannah Chickering in an effort to help women released from the Dedham County Jail. Halfway houses for women received less opposition than facilities for men due to an underlying belief that female prisoners did not associate for the purpose of conversing about criminal activity. Female ex-prisoners were believed to establish support systems that contributed to their own rehabilitation. At that time, halfway houses were operated by faith-based and charitable organizations, which offered food and shelter to ex-prisoners but did not provide treatment services.

By the end of the nineteenth century, private halfway houses opened in eight other states. Criminal justice officials, such as law enforcement officers and corrections administrators, remained opposed to halfway houses, and funds for them dwindled; with the Great Depression of the 1930s, many were forced to close. Only a few halfway houses including the Dedham Temporary House and Pittsburgh's The Parting of the Ways, remained open (Keller & Alper, 1970).

In the 1950s, private halfway houses were viewed in a new light. Concern about crime and high-parole revocation rates prompted halfway houses to assume a role beyond offering food and shelter. They provided transition services to prisoners, becoming involved in both drug treatment and correctional supervision. In addition to being less expensive than prison, halfway houses protected the community insofar as residents were more closely monitored than were traditional parolees.

In the 1960s, halfway houses became more visible when Congress appropriated funds for the first time to open federal-level halfway houses. The Safe Streets Act of 1968 established a source of funding for halfway house expansion throughout the 1970s. A meeting of a newly formed group called the International Halfway House Association was held in Chicago in 1964. This private nonprofit policy organization, which later changed its name to the International Community Corrections Association, currently seeks to improve community corrections policy all over the world. The organization, serving 1,000 individual members, now represents 250 private corrections agencies operating approximately 1,500 programs (International Community Corrections Association, 2015).

Private halfway houses have since found a permanent niche in the corrections market providing alternatives to imprisonment and creating an outlet for prison crowding. In the last few years, for example, many females in California's prisoner population have been transferred to private community correctional facilities following court mandates to decrease the number of prisoners (Schultz, 2007).

Program Components

Each halfway house is unique in structure, treatment programs offered, and type of clients it serves. For example, New Jersey has 16 accredited halfway houses that provide substance abuse counseling to prisoners who first complete a prison-based therapeutic community. Each client spends between three and eighteen months (Hamilton & Campbell, 2013). Private halfway houses can choose which clients they wish to accept on a contractual basis. Their prison case manager or probation officer refers offenders who are eligible for placement. The government pays a facility a specified amount per day per offender, and the offender is expected to assist in the per diem payment. In a hypothetical example, if it costs $65 per day per offender to operate a residential halfway house, state or federal correctional departments pay the halfway house about $48.75 per day per offender, and each client is charged about 25% of the cost, or $16.25 per day. Each facility has a different per-day cost, depending on how many in-house programs are offered.

Most RCCFs and CCCs do not have surrounding property fences or any locks on the doors. Residents, who may leave a facility at any time to work at a verified job, must obey the following rules:

- Live in one's facility
- Be employed (or be working part time and going to school)
- Keep current on rent (offender is charged per daily stay to subsidize cost to taxpayers)
- Be preapproved to leave one's facility for reasons other than work

Leaving one's facility other than for work, school, rehabilitation, or medical attention depends on good behavior and is limited to a certain duration, purpose, and curfew. When not at work, residents maintain their facility through assigned chores and perform court-ordered community service, as well as attend any classes or counseling sessions that their case manager mandates. Most halfway houses require residents to submit to regular drug testing and breathalyzers.

LEVELS SYSTEM: A FORM OF BEHAVIOR MODIFICATION.   Increased freedom for residents must be earned and is based on good behavior, amount of time spent in the program, and their financial situation. Most halfway house programs offer some kind of behavior modification program called a levels system, in which the bottom level is the most restricted; the top level grants more freedom away from the halfway house and more privileges.

For example, a halfway house in Denver has a five-level system where residents move from Level 5 up to Level 1. New residents start on Level 5, in which a hold is placed on them (they cannot leave the facility) until their case manager has completed the intake process. Once intake is complete, residents move to

Level 4, in which they remain until they obtain a job and catch up on their rent. Level-4 residents are allowed passes to attend treatment (Alcoholics Anonymous and Narcotics Anonymous) and are given one 4-hour pass per week to attend church (outside of leaving for work). Each level has its own curfew, which is not applicable to residents who work evenings or nights. In addition to treatment and passes for places of religious or spiritual worship, Level-3 residents may take one daytime pass of no longer than 8 hours, with a curfew of 10:00 P.M. Level-2 residents have Level-3 privileges but with a later curfew of 11:59 P.M.

At Level 1, residents must be caught up on all restitution, community service, and rent. They must have $200 in savings. Level-1 residents have a weekday curfew of 11:59 P.M. but can take weekend passes, from Friday to Sunday, to visit preapproved friends and family. Level-1 residents can own an insured car and have driving privileges, whereas all other residents must depend on someone else for a ride or must take a bus. All residents, regardless of their level, must produce receipts and verification that an approved destination was visited. Passes are allowed to visit a verified address of a family member or for 4 hours at a time to see a movie or to go shopping. Some programs require residents to spend a certain number of days (e.g., two weeks) on each level before advancing to the next level.

TRANSITIONING OUT.   Upon program completion of the residential phase, released clients are assigned to either a probation or parole officer in an appropriate jurisdiction. Some RCCFs have "aftercare" programs in which successful residential clients move out of the halfway house to live at home but continue to return periodically for drug testing, to attend group treatment, and to visit an RCCF nonresidential case manager who functions just like a probation or parole officer.

Residents who successfully completed an RCCF program have reported experiencing a greater internal locus of control. Released clients have found that RCCFs assisted them with readjustment from prison, finding a better job, and abstaining from drugs and alcohol while allowing them to financially assist their families and to develop closer family relations than when in prison.

Staff Perspectives About Supervision and Treatment

Two types of staff work at a halfway house. One group of staff, called "client managers," are primarily involved in activities that are security-oriented and keep track of offender's whereabouts. The second group of staff are case managers who take care of treatment and rehabilitation. The job of a halfway house case manager has been described as similar to that of a probation and parole officer, in the sense that the counselor must be able to administer rehabilitation and supervision, except that the case manager's office is less than 50 yards from where each client lives. The author of this book, Leanne Alarid, worked at a halfway house in Denver, Colorado. She describes her job responsibilities working as both a client manager and a case manager:

> I began working as a member of the client management staff, involved in security and physical accountability for nearly 90 men and women. In this capacity, I conducted population counts, pat searched people and their belongings for contraband, signed clients in and out of the facility, dispensed medications and Antabuse, and administered breathalyzers and urinalyses. When an opportunity to work as a case manager became available, I transferred within the facility from the security-oriented job to one oriented around treatment. In this

position, I assessed my client's needs and risks, devised individual program plans to meet each of their needs, and assisted my clients with adjustment problems they experienced while in the program. I documented their progress and helped them meet their court-ordered conditions, from helping them find a job to referring them for a psychological assessment. If the need arose, I had to make recommendations for revocation to the court or parole board. Once per week, I taught drug and alcohol treatment classes. Once per month, I prepared prerelease plans and attended parole board hearings. If I had to choose between the security and treatment sides, I would say I enjoyed the case management side more because I could use the principles of rehabilitation that I learned in college and actually see the change process in action.

At the same time, there was mutual distrust between residents and staff, and a code of secrecy was maintained, particularly with the offenders who came out of prison. Most staff experienced a degree of role conflict, which was coming to terms with supervision and treatment goals. Alarid explains:

> When I moved from being a client manager involved in control and security issues to case management, I found I experienced more role conflict as a case manager because that position made the initial recommendation for revocation. The most effective case managers were the ones who could balance the two sides and who believed in both. However, some counselors were lopsided in that they invested heavily in treatment issues but could not bring themselves to put someone in jail who posed a liability risk to the community. No one ever likes sending someone back to prison, but you have to be willing to switch hats pretty readily from helping someone out one day and having to revoke them the next. The most valuable thing I learned through all this was to treat people with fairness, consistency, and respect, and to see the human side of the person, and not just define them by the criminal behavior that brought them into the facility.

The best way to deal with the perceived chasm between the two philosophies is to embrace both of them and accept that a more balanced approach is the most effective way (Whetzel et al., 2011).

RCCFs for Female Offenders

Most female offenders have been convicted of misdemeanors or felonies that constitute either nonviolent property or drug crimes. Examples of typical offenses committed by women include theft, fraud, shoplifting, prostitution, and possession of a controlled substance. Since most female felons do not pose a threat to the community, they do not require prison sentences and are ideal candidates for community placement. One type of placement developed especially for women arrested for prostitution is a Women's Recovery Center in Minnesota (see Box 8.1).

Given that many female offenders also have problems with drugs and/or alcohol, and that many are mothers of at least one child under the age of 18, RCCFs that address gender-specific issues have grown. There are more than 65 residential treatment programs and another 70 programs resembling halfway houses for women to live with their children while they are serving a residential community sentence. Studies indicate that children of offenders suffer emotionally, developmentally, and economically when their parents go to prison. Children of incarcerated parents stand a greater chance of following in the footsteps

BOX 8.1	COMMUNITY CORRECTIONS UP CLOSE

Dealing with the Root Causes of Prostitution

"I had been through so much abuse that I honestly believed that I was not worth anything, and it really didn't matter if I got high because nobody gave a damn anyways."—Sheila Ayala, graduate of the Magdalene Program (Neff, 2006).

In Nashville, Tennessee, Reverend Becca Stevens started "Magdalene" as a grassroots nonprofit outreach program for women involved in prostitution (Neff, 2006). Ramsey County in St. Paul, Minnesota, opened a 12-bed program called the "Women's Recovery Center" with funding from the Minnesota legislature (Nelson, 2004). Both centers are a diversion option at the front end or a postrelease option for female prisoners who have a genuine desire to get out of prostitution. Both programs address the root causes of prostitution, which are childhood and young adult physical and sexual abuse, drug dependency, and mental health issues resulting from abuse, including post-traumatic stress, depression, and low self-esteem. Women in the two programs learn to understand how sexuality formed a large part of their identity and how drug use masked a painful past. For

example, Clemmie is a Magdalene client who reported that since she was six years old, her mother allowed other adult men to molest her sister and her. "At that time [as a teenager], we got introduced with an older guy that had told me about how I can make money off of selling my body, and it was like 'off to the races' because I know I can do this. . . . I already know what the mens want." A program resident learns the difference between unequal male–female relationships (such as that of an abusive pimp who feeds her drug habit), in comparison with relating to others in a more equal way. Most important, she discovers self-worth and sobriety, which along with learning about opportunities for housing, legitimate employment, and health care teach her how to build a stable life to regain full parental rights of her children. The St. Paul program reports an 80% success rate; the Tennessee program success rate is unknown (Neff, 2006; Nelson, 2004).

Sources: Neff, Tom. 2006. *Chances: The women of Magdalene.* Video: The Documentary Channel; Nelson, William F. 2004. Prostitution: A community solution alternative. *Corrections Today* (October): 88–91.

of their parents by becoming involved in the juvenile justice system at an early age. Because the mother is still the primary caregiver in the majority of families, the effect of incarcerating mothers who have dependent children is pronounced. The question then becomes: How can female offenders be punished or sanctioned without punishing their children?

JOHN CRAINE HOUSE.   The John Craine House, located in Indianapolis, Indiana, is designed specifically for female offenders convicted of misdemeanors or nonviolent felony offenses who are caretakers of preschool-aged children. The program teaches the women to be emotionally and economically independent as a preventive intervention for their children. As only one of six programs in the country, Craine House serves six women and up to eight children at one time who stay between five and six months. (http://www.crainehouse.org)

The goals for the Craine House are to provide a safe, nurturing environment; help women achieve economic and emotional independence; promote the preservation of mother–child relationships; and prevent potential delinquency of the offenders' children. The Craine House resembles a halfway house in the sense that women pay for part of the program cost through an expectation of employment. Staff assesses the needs of each woman and formulates an individualized treatment plan. However, this facility seems to provide much more individualized and specialized attention than do typical halfway houses, not only for offenders' needs but also for their children. The Craine House offers job seeking skills, educational and/or job placement, parenting classes, substance abuse treatment, and monthly budgeting. The program has a licensed day care specialist on-site to enable the women to work in the community. Out of over 500 women who have been through the program in the last 36 years of program operation, the recidivism rate of incurring a new charge after leaving is 20%, which is lower than other offender populations. (For a 6-minute video about the Craine House, see: http://www.youtube.com/watch?v=0mZ4M3dCuGQ)

Do RCCFs Work?

RCCF programs are measured by their integrity, or quality of services provided that follow the principles of evidence-based practices. Halfway houses across Ohio exhibited a wide variety in quality of program characteristics, such as staff training, client positive reinforcement, timely use of standardized assessments, and other items related to EBP. RCCFs located in disadvantaged areas were of lower quality than those facilities located in more affluent and less transient areas (Wright et al., 2013).

Programs have also been evaluated by examining their success or failure rates as well as by comparing recidivism rates of halfway house residents. Given that most RCCFs emphasize working and paying rent, stable employment and substance abuse counseling are keys to successful program completion along with keeping current on restitution and child support. Within a five-year period, about 13% of halfway house clients had committed a new crime and were returned to prison, while 37% had completed the program successfully and stayed completely out of trouble. About half the clients committed too many technical violations to complete successfully (Hamilton & Campbell, 2013). In a later study of over 13,000 parolees, half of whom went to one of 18 halfway houses and the other matched comparison did not, halfway house clients had significantly less revocations for technical violations. However, the rates of rearrest, reconviction, and reincarceration for new crimes were not different between the two groups (Hamilton & Campbell, 2014). While the authors did not find any treatment effect that interacted with risk level, the treatment dosage was not specified. Box 8.2 examines just how much cognitive-behavioral treatment is enough for what level of risk.

WORK RELEASE PROGRAMS

work release
A program in which offenders who reside in a facility (a community facility, jail, or prison) are released into a community solely to work or attend education classes, or both.

Work release may be considered both a type of institutional corrections and a community corrections program, given that offenders reside in a county jail but are released into the community for a short duration every day to work, attend education classes, or both. Work release controls institutional crowding and simultaneously provides an offender with an opportunity to retain employment, which is the most important factor in reintegration success and in reducing recidivism. The first documented use of work release was in Vermont in the early 1900s, with work release legislation first introduced in the state of Washington in 1913. The federal system and all states have authorized work release programs since the mid-1970s, primarily for minimum-security inmates who already have employment and are within six to nine months of being released from a jail or a prison.

| BOX 8.2 | EVIDENCE-BASED PRACTICES IN COMMUNITY CORRECTIONS |

Who Should Get Cognitive-Behavioral Treatment and How Much Is Enough?

We know that cognitive-behavioral therapy is the most effective type of therapy for offenders. But, should this therapy apply equally to all offenders? To answer this question, data from 7,306 RCCF clients were compared with 5,801 parolees to analyze success rates and recidivism rates of low-risk versus high-risk clients so that there were four groups. In both low-risk groups, parolees had lower recidivism rates than RCCF clients. However, for high-risk individuals in both groups, high-risk RCCF clients were more successful than high-risk parolees. The researchers concluded that the CBT that halfway house clients experienced was more effective with high-risk adult offenders than with low-risk offenders (Lowenkamp & Latessa, 2005). Research in that same jurisdiction found similar results with high-risk youths (Lowenkamp et al., 2010).

To answer the question about how much treatment is enough, Sperber and colleagues (2013) examined new crimes and technical violations together with all three risk levels (low, medium, and high) and compared them with the amount of treatment each person completed. The researchers found that:

Of particular importance is that the largest reduction in recidivism from dosage occurs for the group of high-risk offenders who received the highest levels of dosage. That is, the recidivism rate for high-risk offenders moves from 81% to 57% when treatment hours are increased from 100 to 199 hours to 200 or more hours. This indicates a reduction of 24 points in the percentage of offenders who recidivated for those who received the highest level of dosage. (p. 345)

In summary then, given the existence of scare resources, while increasing the dosage will reduce recidivism for all risk levels, cognitive-behavioral treatments for high-risk offenders will have the greatest effect on recidivism reduction, especially when high-risk offenders have been exposed to at least 200 hours of CBT treatment. Low-risk offenders simply don't need much supervision or treatment at all—low intensity supervision for low-risk offenders (Barnes et al., 2010).

Inmate selection for work release programs are at the discretion of jail or prison administrators in 37 states and of judges in 11 states. Work release eligibility varies greatly, from misdemeanants and those serving county jail time, all the way to nonviolent prisoners who qualify for minimum custody, who have good behavior reports, and are within one year of release (Daly et al., 2009). Statutes typically limit violent and sex offenders from participating in work release. Work release programs originate from a jail or a community-based facility.

Jail-/Prison-Based Work Release

The traditional use of work release is much more restrictive than a halfway house environment because offenders in the former case are not allowed to leave a facility for any other reason than work and school. This type of release is for a specified purpose and for a specific duration.

The definition of work release varies greatly, however. A strict definition of work release can include defendants or convicted offenders who spend a portion of their time in jail and a portion of their time working in the community. If a broader definition is used, work release can include traditional work release, weekender programs, and some pretrial programs.

Statistics indicate that for jails nationwide, 7,369 offenders were on traditional work release. If the broader definition is used, an additional 10,473 offenders on a weekender program and 11,148 on some sort of other pretrial supervision might be added (Sabol & Minton, 2008). These numbers can also be substantiated by other state Department of Corrections websites. Some states, like Ohio and Washington, are avid users of work release for between 20% and 23% of prisoners (Daly et al., 2009).

A weekend jail program entails reporting to jail only on weekends (e.g., reporting in by 7:00 P.M. Friday and staying until Sunday at 7:00 P.M.) but living and working regularly during the week. Work release participants are employed in public works and community service projects in eight states, but most states allow clients on work release to hold regular jobs in private businesses. Earnings of work release inmates are collected by a jail or prison agency. Box 8.3 discusses the use of iris recognition to better ensure that the correct offenders exit jail each day for work release.

The two basic types of traditional work release, which are unsupervised and supervised, are:

- An offender on unsupervised work release would, for example, be incarcerated in jail from 6:00 P.M. until 6:30 A.M., whereby every morning the offender is released out the door to catch a bus to go to work. After leaving work at 5:00 P.M., the offender has 60 minutes to return to jail each evening. Offenders in this program must submit paycheck stubs and/or documentation of hours worked to account for their time.
- An offender on supervised work release would also spend the same number of hours in jail but would leave with a group in a county-owned van to go to a temporary or permanent work site for the day. The group would be accompanied by at least one deputy officer and would return together in the evening.

For both unsupervised and supervised work release, offenders who leave a work site or do not return on time will have a warrant issued for their arrest.

BOX 8.3　**TECHNOLOGY IN COMMUNITY CORRECTIONS**

"The Eyes Have It": Iris Recognition for Work Releasees

Given the daily releases and reentries of work release inmates from jail, it is possible that staff could mistakenly authorize the reentry of a different person or, worse yet, allow the release of a wrong person. As a result some jails, such as the Pinal County jail have turned to iris recognition technology to reduce identification errors, especially when people have a similar look or share the same name. Unlike fingerprints, which can fade or change over one's life as a result of injuries or scarring, the iris tissue remains the same. Today's technology allows five times the number of comparison points using iris scanning instead of fingerprints, making iris recognition technology more accurate. Furthermore, on a single individual the left iris is different from the right, making the combination of the two irises unique. The iris image is initially captured on a high-resolution digital camera and stored in a database. The area where work releasees enter and leave a jail is equipped with an iris scanner that checks via infrared light whether a particular inmate can leave, recording both exit and entry times. There may soon be a national iris database, so identity information could be checked across states or against other facilities within a state.

Source: Kamp, Chase. 2011. PCSO unveils new iris-scanning ID technology. *Today Publications,* May 23, 2011. http://nfcnews.com/2011/05/24/arizona-sheriffs-office-acquires-new-iris-recognition-devices

Work release can also be a useful sentence for first-time offenders, particularly if the offender already has a job or is already going to school at the time the crime is committed. In these specific cases, a judge orders that offenders must reside in jail but be allowed to continue working to pay restitution or to attend school (for example, high school or college classes). This option is sometimes used when restitution centers or halfway houses are not available in an area.

The available evidence for work release programs is scant. Studies evaluating work release from a prison setting found that participating in work release reduced recidivism compared with prisoners who were eligible but did not participate (Drake, 2007). Washington State continues to use work release facilities regularly for about one-fifth of all offenders exiting prison because it is cost effective. Work release recovers 16% of incarceration cost through charging offenders room and board, and the rate of recidivism for new crimes is 2.8% lower than similar offenders who do not participate in work release (Drake, 2007).

Community-Based Work Release: Restitution Centers

Restitution centers are a type of **RCCFs** specifically targeted for work-capable offenders who owe victim restitution or community service, are eligible for minimum custody, and have six months or less until their earliest release date (Drake, 2007). In a work release facility, the emphasis is on gainful employment and payment of rent, child support, restitution, and other court-ordered fees. The center collects from offenders all money earned and dispenses a portion for agency subsistence (rent and food), transportation, victim restitution payments, and child-support payments, and gives the offender a small amount of pocket money. The remainder is saved in an individual account until release.

restitution center
A type of residential community facility specifically targeted for property or first-time offenders who owe victim restitution or community service.

Restitution centers provide some treatment but the focus for offenders is on stable employment and paying back the victim. Some programs will release an offender when restitution is paid in full. As a result, some jurisdictions such as Florida, Texas, and Washington consider work release a type of RCCF or pre-release center (Levin, 2008a). Many work release facilities are coed, and a small number are exclusively for women.

TEXAS RESTITUTION AND TRANSITIONAL TREATMENT CENTERS. Restitution centers are operated by the county for probationers, whereas Transitional Treatment Centers serve parolees and probationers who are released from a residential substance abuse facility. During their stay in either a restitution center or in a transitional treatment center, residents remain employed and develop restitution plans; the centers offer GED, life skills, cognitive restructuring curriculums, and individual and family counseling as needed. Residents may also be required to work at community service projects on weekends and during evening hours. They normally remain at a center until their restitution is completed. About eight out of ten clients remain employed by the time they complete the program (Levin, 2008a). The average cost of a restitution placement costs taxpayers $60 per day, with an additional $10 to $25 a day paid by each offender. Across the state, restitution center clients pay over $4.5 million toward court fees, fines, and victim restitution. In addition, they contribute community service hours that equal approximately $600,000 in labor costs if they were paid for that labor (Levin, 2008a). One internal evaluation of community-based centers in Texas reported that 18.4% of clients were revoked to prison over a two-year period, compared with felony probationers who averaged a 30% prison revocation rate (Texas Legislative Budget Board, 2015).

Clearing roadside weeds is one of many forms of community service.

AP Images/Matt York

FLORIDA WORK RELEASE CENTERS.   In Florida, state prisoners who are minimum-custody inmates are eligible for work release when they have 10 months remaining on their sentence. Inmates usually find a minimum-wage job within one month despite not having any help from anyone within the work release agency. The client is not allowed out of the facility unless he or she is going to look for work or going to an existing job. Once employed, about 75% of a client's paycheck is deducted for various expenses—45% for facility room/board, 10% for restitution, 10% for child support (if applicable), and 10% for savings. The remainder is provided as an allowance every two weeks (Berk, 2008). Staff monitor employment closely, visiting on-site weekly. Berk found that work release inmates had higher employment rates and earned about $400 more per quarter for the first year than a comparison group that did not participate in a work release program. He (2008) concludes:

> I find that work release participation does lower recidivism but that individuals who commit income-generating crimes [such as robbery, burglary, and drug dealing] are responsible for this change. Ex-offenders who commit non-income motivated crimes have improved employment outcomes after work release participation, but their probability of returning to prison does not change. (p. 24)

So it seems that, with restricted bedspace for work release programs, limiting them to property and drug offenders makes sense from a fiscal standpoint.

Work Ethic Camps

work ethic camp
A 120-day alternative to prison that teaches job skills and decision making using a cognitive-behavioral approach, followed by intensive supervision probation.

A **work ethic camp** is a 120-day prison-alternative residential program based on a cognitive-behavioral treatment approach. One program in Nebraska allows inmates to be eligible once they have completed a 90-day intake and assessment period (Siedschlaw & Wiersma, 2005). Once participants have completed the 120-day program, they are released on intensive supervision probation. The work ethic camp is considered a minimum-custody facility, and though it costs nearly $44 per day per person, the duration of the stay is about half that of the cost to incarcerate, which translates into a cost savings. The higher program cost is due to the assistance the program offers in developing job-readiness skills, decision-making skills, and life skills such as money management. A work ethic camp is similar to a halfway house in that it combines work and treatment.

COMBINED WORK RELEASE AND THERAPEUTIC COMMUNITY.   Another program that combines work release with treatment through the therapeutic community concept (initially discussed in Chapter 6) is the CREST program. Clients entering the program from prison must first progress through a significant amount of drug and alcohol education, counseling, and confrontation before they are eligible for the work release phase in the community. Evaluation data indicated that CREST participants have significantly lower relapse and lower recidivism rates than a comparison group. More recently, a study of nearly 20,000 Irish prisoners who participated in combined work and treatment programs (life skills, substance abuse treatment, and other therapeutic services) were significantly less likely to return to prison as a result of program participation (Baumer et al., 2009).

SHOCK INCARCERATION

Shock incarceration refers to a brief period of imprisonment that precedes a term of supervised probation in the hope that the harsh reality of prison will deter future criminal activity. A variety of shock incarceration formats are used that go by a number of names—shock probation, intermittent incarceration, split sentence, and boot camp. The programs vary somewhat in design and organization, but all feature a short jail term followed by supervised release. The target population is young offenders with no previous incarceration in adult prisons.

shock incarceration
A brief period of incarceration followed by a term of supervised probation. Also called shock probation, shock parole, intermittent imprisonment, or split sentence.

In shock probation, an offender is sentenced to imprisonment for a short time (the shock) and then released on probation. It is hoped that incarceration will be so distasteful that the offender will fear returning and will thereafter avoid criminal behavior. Short incarceration periods are praised for making an unforgettable

Courtesy Leanne Fiftal Alarid

Boot camp attempts to break down offenders and then to retrain them to respect authority, increase self-control, and act responsibly.

initial experience without enabling full immersion in an institutional subculture. Another type of shock incarceration is correctional boot camp programs.

Correctional Boot Camps

boot camp
A form of shock incarceration that involves a military-style regimen designed to instill discipline in young offenders.

The idea of **boot camp** programs for offenders first began in 1983 in Georgia, whereby correctional programs borrowed the military concept of breaking existing habits and thought patterns and rebuilding offenders to be more disciplined through intensive physical training, hard labor, drill and ceremony, and rigid structure. This concept multiplied as the most common form of shock incarceration throughout the 1990s. Boot camp programs exist inside state prisons or as stand-alone community facilities:

- *Inside Prison Walls.* Participants are chosen from a prison population by correctional administrators. The boot camp is within prison walls, but boot camp participants remain separate from the general population for the program duration. Offenders are paroled upon graduation from boot camp. Time served is significantly less than with a regular prison sentence.
- *Stand-Alone Community Facilities.* Offenders at time of sentencing are chosen by judges to participate in a facility administered by a county. Following boot camp, offenders graduate to intensive supervision probation or regular probation.

Regardless of whether the boot camp program is inside prison walls or in a stand-alone facility, it operates the same. Correctional boot camp participants live in "barracks," wear military-style fatigues, use military titles, and address their drill instructors by "sir" or "ma'am." Each "platoon" of 45–60 individuals is responsible for the actions of every individual, and many boot camps use group rewards and punishments to encourage participants to work together. The drill instructors attempt to break down old habits and attitudes of the recruits and build them back up into respectful young men and women. Eligible candidates, who volunteer to participate, are young first-time felony offenders who are able to meet minimum physical requirements. Programs typically last 90–180 days before graduation.

The successful correctional boot camps also provide therapeutic and educational activities, such as drug and alcohol education, individual or group counseling, vocational training, anger management, and academic education, which together comprise almost half a day. Boot camps that were therapeutic and voluntary were able to produce positive short-term attitude changes in participants (Meade & Steiner, 2010). Programs that provided counseling had lower recidivism rates than boot camp programs without this component (Wilson et al., 2005). Box 8.4 tells the story of a boot camp participant named Mr. John from his teacher's perspective.

Table 8.1 shows a daily schedule that begins at 5:30 A.M. and is full of hard labor, drills, and confidence-building rope courses along with educational classes and an early bedtime. For many offenders, boot camp is difficult and does not leave much free time. Participants learn respect, leadership, and the program has added medical and weight loss benefits.

It seems, then, that boot camp, despite its denial of television and cigarettes and its requirement of rigorous physical engagement, has provided positive experiences to help offenders and so has increased its legitimacy above that of prison (Franke et al., 2010). See Box 8.5 for what offenders thought about joining the U.S. military as an alternative to prison.

BOX 8.4   **FIELD NOTES**

How Do You Try to Reach and Change the Lives of Young Offenders in Boot Camp?

Despite the troubled and violent lives students at the Harris County Boot Camp have led, the story of Derrick John still seems to catch them off guard. I drag it out and use it to get their attention just once during the few weeks that I will be their teacher. I wait for the precise moment when I feel it will be most effective—sometimes at the beginning of our time together, sometimes at the end. Most of the time, however, I tell the story when I am feeling overwhelmed by the task in front of me.

He was a nice guy with a great smile, I always start. An attractive, lean young man, 6'3" or taller, I often told him he should go to Hollywood when he got out of Boot Camp. I actually looked forward to seeing him in class. This is not always true of the students I teach. While it's easy to like the students, almost all are tough and drain on any teacher caring enough to look into their eyes. Even the smart, easy learners have needs for attention that are so deep they draw energy from you. They have holes in their young lives that have made them hard and violent or else depressed and despairing.

Simple autobiographies the students write their first class take days for me to read because of the harsh existence most have had. And that's just the parts of their lives they are willing to write down. Even joking, these students have affectations that show they are covering up, trying for a resilience to bounce back from family cycles that have led them to crime.

For a while, Mr. John was one of those same draining students who spent the first half of his tenure at Boot Camp with a chip on his shoulder. "Why do we have to do this? I don't understand that," he'd say, without really ever listening or trying to understand in the first place. When his mood was even darker, he'd just lay low and try not to call attention to himself. Those quiet students who try hard to go unnoticed are often the most troubled, I have found. On those quiet days, I worried the most about Mr. John, feeling like he was still fuming, boiling deep inside his youthful outward appearance.

Then, for whatever reason, a light went on inside Mr. John when he was about halfway through the program. I see this reaction to Boot Camp often. The program teaches discipline and respect, and the

students seem to catch on at some point. Either that happens, or they realize they are here for the long haul and should take advantage of the county's services. Whichever is the case, an education immediately reduces their chances of returning to the criminal justice system.

Mr. John started caring, and then he started learning. He finished assignments quickly and made scores higher than I even expected of him. But halfway is often too late for some probationers, especially those who quit school as early as Mr. John. Time and his Boot Camp days were running out. Every day his schoolwork improved. He became an ideal student, working hard and offering me a respect he had never shown before. I began to joke about having him stay in the program long enough to get his G.E.D. We call it "recycling," and it means more time at Boot Camp for probationers. It's the thing they dread the most. "If I could just keep you another three months, Mr. John," I'd say, "I could help you finish this G.E.D." "I think I'll just have to talk someone into getting you recycled." It would make him crazy when I would say this. No one wanted to be recycled. Everyone wanted to go home, even those whose home life had led them to Boot Camp.

Dodging Recycling

No one ever jokes about recycling, either. It's much too serious a subject to the probationers. I was only half joking, though. I would have loved to have kept Mr. John in Boot Camp and still think about the difference it would have made had he stayed there for another three months.

His beaming smile would fade for a moment at my attempt at humor. "You wouldn't do that to me," he'd start. "Would you?" Something in my returned look would tell him I wasn't serious, and his smile would reappear before I even needed to reassure him. Of course, I could never have him recycled at that point. He was now the picture of a perfect student. I knew, however, he had started working too late to finish his G.E.D. in Boot Camp. I emphasized the importance of continuing his education now that he was on the right track. He could still get his G.E.D. in a few more months with the help of the continuing education program at

(Continues)

BOX 8.4   FIELD NOTES (*Continued*)

the Harris County Adult Probation Department. He just had to take more of the responsibility on himself.

Finally, one Wednesday, as is always the case with graduations at Boot Camp, he left the program along with the other 45 members of his barracks. He marched for the crowd of parents and visitors and listened to the graduation speech of hope for the future—now with cleaned slates and new, healthier habits and minds. He was so nervous, like all the probationers are on this day, that he shook my hand quickly with little notice as to whose hand it was. He never let his eyes meet mine, although I tried to impress him with one last remark. "Keep at it, Mr. John. You've come too far to stop," I said.

Nine days later, his last essay still in my briefcase, Mr. John was shot and killed by a police officer after a robbery. He had fallen back in with a peer group that had waited for him back home and outside the secure barbed wire fence of the Boot Camp. At 17 years old, Mr. John never even had a life. With little or no parenting and an unsuccessful school experience, he never had a chance. When he entered Boot Camp, he may have looked like a hardened street thug, but when he left, he looked like the boy he still was.

Story's Impact

I don't know what part of Mr. John's story reaches my other students first. Maybe they see their own vulnerability to death. Maybe they were shocked by his youth. Maybe they are just frustrated that I use him as an example of my desire to keep them out of trouble and into education.

I can't keep them alive just by keeping them locked up, which is what I wish I had done with Mr. John. I know that wouldn't be a life. I know also that if they return to their former habits and former friends, things are going to happen to them anyway. Sooner or later. Prison or death.

I run across Mr. John's math workbook when I'm searching other files. Occasionally, I see an essay he wrote tucked in with other students' school papers. Maybe I run into the newspaper article about his death. I keep all these remembrances intentionally. It always surprises me for that minute; stuns me with reality.

I see his smile and picture his long legs stretching from his desk at the back of the classroom. And his eyes; I can still see the boy that would never live long enough to be a man. I want to be reminded of Mr. John. That's why I keep his schoolwork. I also want my other students to be reminded. I want them to realize that this same probationer could be any one of them. I tell them that I can't have it happen again. The story of Mr. John has broken my heart, and it will never harden to such blows. With this, I'm telling them that I care. I want them to try. I want them out of trouble and into a happy life that does not include violence and death.

Question: What can be done, if anything, to change the life path of individuals who are going in the wrong direction?

Source: Hensley, Denise Bray. 1995. One boy's life. *Houston Chronicle* (September 17). Reprinted with author permission.

Criticisms of Boot Camps

Boot camps have their share of critics. A primary concern is that these stand-alone community-based facilities widen the net, choosing offenders who otherwise would have received a lesser sentence (probation) had boot camp not been available. In net widening, costs increase because offenders who should be on probation undergo a more expensive program. Another concern is that the confrontational style of military-style boot camps, characterized by coercion, stress, and leadership styles likely to reduce self-esteem, can have potentially negative outcomes by increasing the potential for violence and encouraging an abuse of power. Such factors can make boot camps targets for civil lawsuits. For example, one boot camp closed in Tampa after a 14-year-old boy died as

TABLE 8.1   Daily Schedule in a Typical Boot Camp

Time	Schedule
A.M.	
5:30	Wake up and standing count
5:45–6:30	Calisthenics and drill
6:30–7:00	Run
7:00–8:00	Mandatory breakfast and cleanup
8:15	Standing count and company formation
8:30–11:55	Work and school schedules
P.M.	
12:00–12:30	Mandatory lunch and standing count
12:30–3:30	Afternoon work and school schedule
3:30–4:00	Shower
4:00–4:45	Network community meeting
4:45–5:45	Mandatory dinner, prepare for evening
6:00–9:00	School, group counseling, drug counseling, prerelease counseling, decision-making classes
8:00	Count while in programs
9:15–9:30	Squad bay, prepare for bed
9:30	Standing count, lights out

Source: National Institute of Justice. 1994. *Program focus shock incarceration in New York.* Washington, DC: U.S. Department of Justice, National Institute of Justice (August).

BOX 8.5

SHOULD MILITARY SERVICE BE OFFERED AS AN ALTERNATIVE TO INCARCERATION?

Recent studies of military troops coming home from war-torn combat zones indicate that 20% of soldiers who return home may later develop symptoms of post-traumatic stress disorder. There is also a chance that some soldiers may never return. Despite these numbers, a survey of inmates in a minimum-security prison found that six out of ten people favored spending eight years in the military over eight years in prison if given a choice on day for day with no time off for good behavior. The military option was less popular as an alternative to parole, which received the nod from 43%. The main reason for favoring the military option was that it would provide training and a better option over the lack of opportunities in prison. Prisoners with less formal education and a longer criminal history tended to support the military option. A solid 30% of prisoners would not consider the military over prison, even if only four years out of eight would have to be served, primarily because (at the time of the survey) our country was actively deploying troops (Frana & Schroeder, 2008).

Having the military as an alternative to incarceration is not a new idea but more of a controversial one. While one side contends that the military instills self-confidence, discipline, and respect for one self and others, there are legitimate concerns that providing specialized weaponry and combat training to people who have already crossed legal limits set by society is even more problematic (Milburn, 2012).

Sources: Frana, John F. & Schroeder, Ryan D. 2008. Alternatives to incarceration. *Justice Policy Journal 5*(2): 5–25; Milburn, Travis W. 2012. *Exploring military service as an alternative sanction: Evidence from inmates' perspectives.* An unpublished Master's Thesis, Eastern Kentucky University.

a result of a videotaped beating by boot camp staff (Associated Press, 2006). Other camps in at least four other states closed for possible abuses.

Evaluations of Boot Camp Programs

There are over 30 known evaluations of boot camp programs. The vast majority of boot camp research has shown that although attitudes of graduates were more positively adjusted in the short-term (Meade & Steiner, 2010), such attitude changes did not directly translate into long-term reduced recidivism (Gültekin & Gültekin, 2012). Only five or six out of thirty studies showed significant recidivism reduction of boot camp graduates compared to offender groups (Duwe & Kerschner, 2008). The most successful programs offered a treatment component of at least three hours per day mixed with discipline and were characterized by voluntary participation, selection from prison-bound offenders, and longer program duration. Finally, aftercare, or a period of transition after an intense boot camp experience, was important for learning retention (Kempinen & Kurlychek, 2003). The drills, labor, and discipline of the boot camp experience, by themselves, are not enough to reduce recidivism. This is because discipline, drills, physical conditioning, and self-esteem are all noncriminogenic factors that are not related to criminal behavior and recidivism, so it is not surprising that boot camps made so little impact on reducing criminal behavior over the long term. Interest in boot camps has diminished such that, today, fewer than 40 programs remain open in the United States, and their future remains uncertain.

SUMMARY

- RCCF offenders posed a higher risk and had more treatment needs than traditional probationers, but they posed a lower risk than people incarcerated in prison.

- Halfway houses remain a valuable residential community program for reentry of offenders coming out of prison. Overall evaluations of halfway houses show that benefits outweigh the costs, particularly for high-risk offenders.

- By allowing their children to live with them, residential programs for female offenders, aid them in learning better parenting skills and in maintaining close relationships, which in turn prevents recidivism.

- Work release and restitution centers focus offenders on working to pay back victims and learning how to maintain employment. Work release, through offender subsistence payments, helps curb program costs to taxpayers by about 20%.

- Boot camps as a type of shock incarceration program vary in the degree of treatment programs offered. Voluntary participation, selection from a prison population, and intensive aftercare provisions are important elements of the boot camp experience. But because recidivism rates for most boot camps are no different from those for prisoners, the popularity of boot camps has declined in recent years.

DISCUSSION QUESTIONS

1. How are halfway houses similar to and different from work release?

2. What would working in a halfway house be like? What are some of the problems you might face?

3. Should programs like the John Craine House be expanded?

4. Discuss the positive and negative aspects associated with correctional boot camps.

 # WEBSITES, VIDEOS, AND PODCASTS

Websites

University of Cincinnati Research Studies: Halfway Houses
http://www.uc.edu/content/dam/uc/ccjr/docs /reports/project_reports/HH_CBCF_Report1.pdf

The Chickering Foundation
This foundation honors Hannah Chickering, who established the first halfway house for female prisoners and their children, and continues to help fund programs in eastern Massachusetts. http://www.chickeringfund.org/

John P. Craine House
http://www.crainehouse.org

Ohio Community Corrections Association
http://www.occaonline.org/links.asp

Videos/Podcasts

California Department of Corrections and Rehabilitation
This 5-minute video shows an example of a Women's Residential Multiservice Center in California. http://www.youtube.com/user /CACorrections#p/u/31/yI-A6Gq5Gmk

Residential Drug and Alcohol Treatment
Brighton Hospital is a leader in drug and alcohol treatment and counseling services that began in the 1950s in Michigan. The clinic's rehabilitation treatment program includes an adult halfway house. http://www.dailymotion.com/video /xaojt9_drug-rehab-center-crack-brighton -ho_news http://www.dailymotion.com/video/xb5vpa _substance-abuse-treatment-brighton_webcam

Cognitive-Behavioral Therapy for Addicts:
This video showcases Inside Out—a cognitive-based therapy (CBT) program for substance abuse treatment. http://www.youtube.com /watch?v=9zMVFSpJYM8

McGregor Veterans Residential Program
(Length: 6 minutes) New York State Department of Corrections and Community Supervision developed the Incarcerated Veterans Programs that is designed to address the readjustment and reentry needs of veterans returning to society following military service. https://www.youtube .com/watch?v=pUT8NGy-C3A

CASE STUDY EXERCISES

Site Visit to One Community-Based Residential Correctional Program

Visit one community-based correctional program, and use this visit to conduct your own case study. Your visit may be done individually or with a small group. You will likely need to clear the visit ahead of time with your instructor, who may suggest a facility with which he or she has some connection. If this is a group exercise, members can be assigned to each focus on a small section of the paper or presentation. There are four sections, and questions are presented so that each member can ask a few questions during the site visit. Write a paper or make a presentation to include one or more of the following areas:

Section 1: Program Description

- What are the goals of this program?
- What tools or techniques are used to meet these goals?
- What is the capacity (how many clients can be treated at one time)?
- How many contact hours/treatment hours are part of this program?

Section 2: Clients

- Who are the clients being served?
- What does the typical client look like (gender, age, education, and so on)?
- What are the client's perspectives of the treatment program?

Section 3: Staff

- What is the client-to-staff ratio?
- What are the staff backgrounds and qualifications?
- What are the perspectives of the staff about working there (or about program effectiveness)?

Section 4: Evaluation

- How many clients finish the program, and how many drop out or do not complete it?
- What are the reasons for not completing the program?
- What is the daily (or yearly) cost per client served?
- Have any clients been tracked after they leave the program? What were the results?

Nonresidential Graduated Sanctions

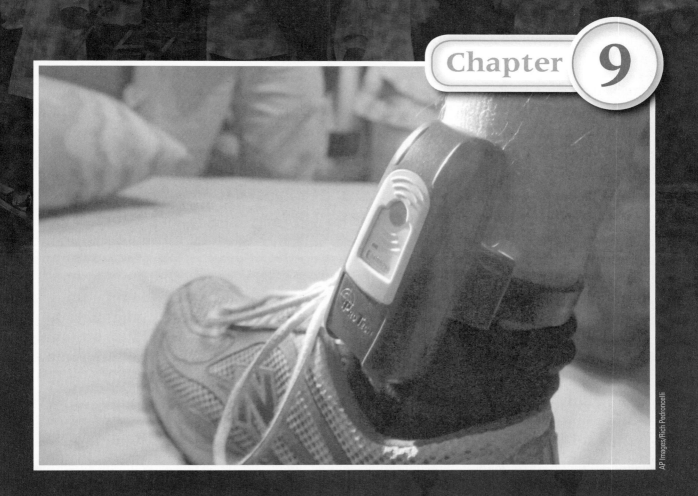

AP Images/Rich Pedroncelli

CHAPTER OUTLINE

CHAPTER LEARNING OBJECTIVES

1. Describe the conditions under which offenders are court-mandated to house arrest.

2. Compare how electronic monitoring has progressed from radio frequency to global positioning systems.

3. Explain the importance of correctional technology as a tool, but not as a replacement, for community supervision.

4. Identify how day reporting centers are unique from other community supervision programs.

KEY TERMS

house arrest
home-based electronic monitoring
electronic monitoring (em)
real-time access
global positioning system (GPS)
active GPS
passive GPS
exclusion zones
inclusion zones
day reporting centers DRC

By the time he was 17 years old, Torrey Dale Grady was found guilty of his first sex offense against a child. Ten years later, he was again convicted of a similar sexual offense for which he served three years in prison in North Carolina. North Carolina is one of only eight states that allow courts to order lifetime electronic monitoring in the community for sex offenders who are recidivists or who are deemed to pose a threat in the future regarding predatory sexual offending behavior. The difference with this situation was that the lifetime monitoring was under the civil side of the law and occurred *after the criminal sentence* had already been served. There are currently 600 offenders in North Carolina being monitored in this manner.

A separate civil hearing in 2013 determined that because Grady repeated the same offense, he must be monitored with a global positioning satellite unit and be subjected to unannounced home visits for the rest of his life. Grady appealed the decision to the U.S. Supreme Court, saying that he had already served his time, and that the continued home visits and monitoring was a violation of his right to privacy. The U.S. Supreme Court ruled that electronic monitoring without consent constituted a Fourth Amendment search because the program collects information when attached to one's physical body. So, this can also be interpreted as saying that the Fourth Amendment applies to both criminal and civil law. However, the Court did not rule on whether Grady's searches were or were not in violation of the Fourth Amendment's prohibition against unreasonable searches. Instead, the Supreme Court remanded the case back down to the North Carolina courts to decide whether these searches as applied to lifetime monitoring after offenders have served their time under criminal law are reasonable or unreasonable (Grady v. North Carolina, 2015).

Question for Discussion: Are unannounced home searches and lifetime electronic monitoring reasonable or unreasonable after sex offenders have finished serving their time? Justify your decision.

INTRODUCTION

This chapter examines community-based sanctions that offenders participate in while living at home. These programs can be sentences by themselves; or they can be combined with other sanctions such as probation; as a phase of aftercare, following a period of time spent in a residential facility; or following confinement in jail and prison. Types of nonresidential programs to be discussed include house arrest, electronic monitoring, and day reporting centers.

HOUSE ARREST

House arrest is an intermediate sanction designed to confine pretrial detainees or convicted offenders to their homes during the hours when they are not at work, attending a treatment program, or visiting a supervising officer. Defendants who cannot afford bail and who do not qualify for release on personal recognizance may be considered for house arrest. House arrest, by itself, literally means being confined to one's home. However, house arrest is frequently paired with a form of technology like a home-based voice verification device or electronic monitoring device (which we discuss later in this chapter).

house arrest
A community-based sanction in which offenders serve their sentence at home. Offenders have curfews and may not leave their home except for employment and correctional treatment purposes. Also called home detention or home confinement.

Purposes of Home Detention

House arrest is otherwise known as home detention or home confinement; it is neither a new concept nor a U.S. innovation. Galileo (1564–1642) was placed under house arrest by church authorities for his heretical assertion that the earth revolved around the sun. House arrest programs have proliferated since the 1990s in the United States as an alternative to incarceration for pretrial detainees and as a means of easing jail overcrowding while ensuring appearance in court. House arrest is also a more restrictive form of probation for convicted offenders insofar as it strictly limits time spent outside the home.

Staples and Decker (2010, p. 7) explain how house arrest technology works:

Offenders sign a three-page, 17-point contract....Clients must develop a daily schedule of approved activities...[consisting of] weekly face-to-face meetings with their house arrest officer...[and] also meet with collateral contacts and make unannounced on-site visits to places of employment and residences.... A Mitsubishi® Electronic Monitoring system device...functions to verify compliance...by recording the offender's voice, taking his or her picture, and collecting breath samples...through a straw inserted into the home monitoring unit. The photograph is displayed on a computer screen in the house arrest office next to a reference photo previously entered into the system....If a client does not respond to phone calls, they have two hours to call the house arrest officer or show up in person.

Through their interviews of people under house arrest, Staples and Decker (2010) observed rigid and repressive conditions that seemed to ignore differences among individuals and increased participants' anxiety over something going wrong. They suggest that discipline should "be productive and not simply repressive" (p. 17).

COMMUNITY CONTROLLEES IN FLORIDA. *Community controllees* are required to maintain employment and to participate in self-improvement programs, such as a general equivalency diploma (GED) program to obtain a high school diploma, drug and alcohol counseling, or other "life skills" programs. Many are required to perform community service as well. When they are not participating in work, self-help programs, or community service, they must be at home. Florida community control officer caseloads are limited by statute to 20 offenders, and the officers work weekends and holidays. They are required to make a minimum of 28 contacts per month with each offender for a period not to exceed 24 months. Officers' schedules vary from day to day, resulting in regular but random visits with offenders. If an offender is not where he or she should be at any particular time, a violation of community control is reported to the court. Some house arrest programs randomly call offenders, and a computer verifies an offender's unique voice electronically. If the voice is that of another person or a tape-recorded voice of the offender, the computer will register an unauthorized absence. Too many unauthorized absences can result in a technical violation of probation and time in jail.

House Arrest Criticisms and Opportunities

A few criticisms are directed at house arrest. First, some argue that staying at home for most people does not seem to be a punishment or a negative experience. This might be true if an offender were not scrutinized so closely, did not receive such frequent visits, and were not awakened in the middle of the night to take a photo. In most jurisdictions, the courts have indeed recognized that home confinement is not the same as jail or prison confinement and that therefore time spent in home confinement awaiting trial as a pretrial detainee cannot be counted as time served toward a conviction, in the way that jail time serves for other pretrial detainees (*People v. Ramos*, 1990). In some jurisdictions, however, time spent on home detention is counted as part of probation. As with probation, if house arrest is revoked, time served in home confinement does not count toward the sentence or toward time served.

Another criticism is that the intrusiveness of house arrest violates a pretrial detainee's constitutional right to privacy in the home, especially one occupied by other family members who are not under supervision. To get around this, house arrest for pretrial defendants is voluntary; offenders sign a contract that they understand the conditions and if they do not agree, they are resentenced to another sanctioning option. A convicted offender's privacy rights, however, are *not* considered to be violated by the use of house arrest and/or electronic monitoring.

A potential risk with house arrest is that offenders can still commit crimes from their residences. For example, pretrial detainees and probationers have been arrested for selling drugs out of their homes. Because customers went to the house of detainees who thus never left home, no house arrest violations were recorded. If it were not for suspicious neighbors calling the police, such probationers might have been able to continue selling drugs without getting caught for some time. Although this is a very real risk, the main purpose of house arrest is to reduce offender movement while being monitored; it does not function to deter crime or to reduce recidivism.

Another challenge of house arrest is that domestic violence incidents can erupt. Because offenders are home all the time and cannot leave their house to "cool off," some take out their frustrations on family members, even while being court-ordered to attend treatment. Several community supervision officers report that it is not unusual for house arrestees to request that they be sent to prison instead of continuing under house arrest (Kilgore, 2012).

In summary, considerable self-discipline is required to comply with house arrest. Although many offenders are impulsive by nature and may be unable to sustain required behavior for long periods, for the right persons with stable employment and supportive families, house arrest allows them to keep working and to support their families without incarceration. Given that house arrest is an enhancement of probation or parole and entails more conditions than routine supervision, offenders under house arrest are highly likely to be revoked for a technical violation. Today, most house arrest programs are paired with some form of electronic monitoring, so let's examine this correctional technology.

ELECTRONIC MONITORING: RADIO FREQUENCY AND GLOBAL POSITIONING SYSTEMS

Imagine this scenario: George was paroled from prison on the condition that for the first year, he must wear an electronic device that fits snugly around his ankle. The ankle device is waterproof and shockproof, and George must wear the device even while showering and sleeping. A transmitter inside George's ankle bracelet emits a continuous signal to his personal receiver, which is attached to the phone lines at his residence. This receiver only transmits to George's ankle device. If the signal is lost for any reason—say, if George moves 500 feet beyond his device—then the transmitter is unable to communicate with the receiver, and the receiver automatically calls in to a centralized computer. The computer checks to see whether the absence of a signal is authorized or unauthorized. The absence is authorized if George has received prior permission from his parole officer, for example, to go out looking for a job or is at work during his scheduled hours. If the absence is unauthorized, his parole officer is automatically notified. George has a curfew, and he still must visit his parole officer, who checks the device to make sure George has not tried to tamper with it or remove it in any way. George must get permission prior to going anywhere, so he has to plan everything in advance.

George's sanction consists of a **home-based electronic monitoring** system, which operates from radio frequencies through phone lines. **Electronic monitoring (EM)** is a correctional technology used in intensive supervision probation, specialized parole, day reporting centers, and house arrest—typically between one and six months. EM can also be applied to pretrial releasees—that is, on defendants who have not yet been convicted but require an elevated level of supervision while out on bond or under pretrial supervision (see Figure 9.1). In the federal system, pretrial releasees are monitored for up to nine months.

History of Radio Frequency Electronic Monitoring

Tracking objects using radio frequency signals has been possible since the 1920s when the U.S. Army monitored airplanes and large ships. Biologists used this technology to track animals, and the first electronic monitoring of humans dates back to the early 1960s when EM was used for checking changes in oxygen levels, body temperature, and other vital signs (Kilgore, 2012). Robert Schwitzgebel at the University of California developed and patented electronic monitoring

home-based electronic monitoring
An intermittent or continuous radio frequency signal transmitted through a landline telephone or wireless unit into a receiver that determines whether an offender is at home.

electronic monitoring (EM)
A correctional technology tool in intensive supervision probation, parole, day reporting, or home confinement, using a radio frequency or satellite technology to track offender whereabouts via a transmitter and receiver.

Ankle monitoring devices can transmit either to home-based receivers using radio frequencies or via global positioning satellite system to a receiver carried around the waist.

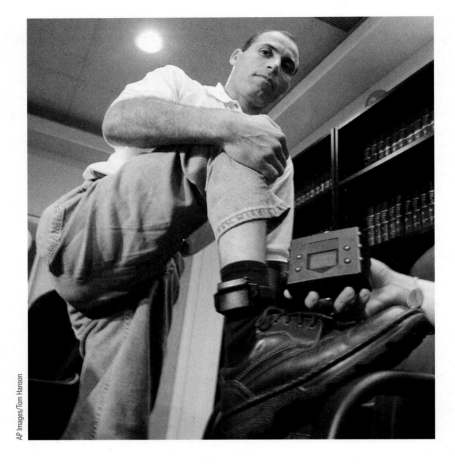

AP Images/Tom Hanson

technology in 1964 to record a parolee's location using a one-way transmitter. When patients were deinstitutionalized from mental hospitals, some were monitored using EM, but the technology was still quite limited to measuring physiological changes rather than actual location.

In the mid-1970s, a two-way transmission system was developed, which led to an idea for the use of EM around the ankle. New Mexico judge Jack

FIGURE 9.1
How Electronic Monitoring Is Used

Source: American Probation and Parole Association. Accessed: http://www.appa-net.org /publications&resources/pubs /electronic_monitoring.pdf.

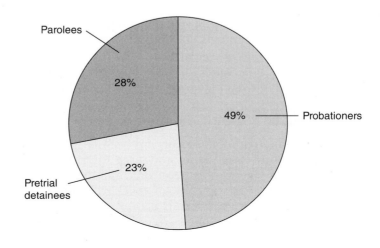

Love saw a picture of a wrist transmitter in a 1977 Spiderman comic book and persuaded a computer salesman to develop the device. The wrist device was first tried in 1983 on offenders convicted of driving under the influence (DUI) and of white-collar crimes at a time when cell phones were not the norm. When a probation office called a house, offenders verified their whereabouts by inserting the wrist device into a receiver that sat next to the telephone. These early units were called home-based radio frequency electronic monitoring systems because they verified whether an offender was at home (Kilgore, 2012).

PROBLEMS OF EARLY HOMEBOUND   Electronic Monitoring Older passive electronic monitoring devices required a connection to a landline telephone within the offender's residence to properly connect the device. Although some electronic monitoring devices have been upgraded for use with digital cell phones, the earliest EM devices require that offenders keep a functioning basic landline that has no special features, such as call forwarding or call waiting.

A second drawback was that passive EM systems were only able to track whether an offender was within a certain number of feet of the receiver connected to his or her telephone. Homebound EM systems were not able to track where offenders went once they left their home. The earliest wrist systems were not customized to the offender, and more than one wrist system could be used on the same monitoring system. Thus, there was no guarantee that a probation office was actually communicating with the correct person. Certain areas such as bathtubs could not receive transmissions, which would ultimately cause false alarms. (See Box 9.1 for the latest updates on EM.)

BOX 9.1   **TECHNOLOGY IN CORRECTIONS**

Advances in Electronic Monitoring

Voice verification monitoring

Monitoring occurs throughout the day and/or night by means of a special pager or random calls made to particular locations at specific times to verify an offender's presence. When the pager beeps, the offender must immediately call the probation or parole office. Through voice and photo verification—that is, checking the voice on the phone against official voice and photo templates created at the probation office—the computer determines a positive match. The computer also records the phone number from which a call originates (Staples & Decker, 2010).

Group monitoring

Individual home-based systems still exist, but now there are ways that a single receiver can monitor up to 75 clients at one time. This makes it possible for community facilities such as halfway houses and group homes to detect the presence or absence of clients within a 300-foot range, which prevents temporary unauthorized absences and allows facilities to better detect a "walk-away" or escape (BI Inc., 2013).

Remote location monitoring systems

Handheld portable receiving devices can intercept an offender's transmitter signals to enable officers to randomly drive by a residence or workplace and verify the location of an offender without stopping to see him or her in person.

Source: BI Inc. 2013. BI products and services. Retrieved at: http://www.bi.com

Global Positioning Systems

The most sophisticated technology for monitoring offenders in the community is a **global positioning system (GPS).** A GPS uses 24 military satellites that orbit the earth and five ground control stations to pinpoint locations anywhere in the world using data coordinates. A one-piece transmitter and GPS receiver containing a microprocessor is worn by an offender. The GPS portable receiver replaces the receiver that is plugged into the landline phone on homebound systems. The transmitter and receiver serve as a medium between the satellite and the central control unit that monitors offender locations (Armstrong & Freeman, 2011). Figure 9.2 summarizes the main differences between home-based EM and GPS.

The way the receiver records data and how often the data are transmitted determines the type of GPS system. In a **passive GPS** system, the tracking point data is temporarily stored throughout the day and downloaded at night through a landline phone while the offender is sleeping. Although major violations are instantaneously reported, most location information can be delayed up to 12 hours. Agencies that use GPS tend to use passive GPS systems because they cost half as much to operate as the more advanced active GPS systems (Pattavina, 2009).

global positioning system (GPS)
A system that uses 24 military satellites orbiting the earth to pinpoint an offender's exact location intermittently or at all times.

passive GPS
A GPS system that temporarily stores location data downloaded through a landline phone once every 24 hours or at specific times when an offender is home.

FIGURE 9.2
How EM and GPS Works

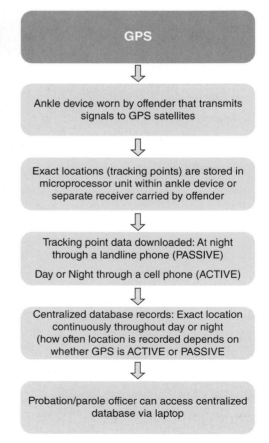

Active GPS systems transmit data through wireless networks used by cell phones. Active systems are also known as **real-time access** units because data can be transmitted with a short lag time. The offender's transmitter emits a radio frequency signal from once per minute to once every 10 minutes. A phone continuously calls a reporting station to update the offender's location, which establishes a tracking point that can be visually seen on a computer or wireless personal digital assistant (PDA). Some companies provide monitoring centers whereas other companies provide officers with web-based capabilities to view on their own. The more frequently the computer reports a tracking point, the more time must be spent examining the data over each 24-hour period. GPS equipment can be leased for around $8 per day for a real-time unit, compared to $4 per day for passive GPS. When the cost of supervision is added to equipment charges, the total cost is between $11 and $20 per day (Yeh, 2010).

HOW DO THE ZONES WORK?   The microprocessor inside the receiver also allows a probation officer to use software to program **exclusion zones** and/or **inclusion zones.** Thus an offender on probation for an offense related to his compulsive gambling habit would not be allowed to enter any casino without the device sounding an unauthorized area alarm. Another exclusion zone could be the residence and workplace of an identified victim. In contrast, an inclusion zone allows an officer to program an offender's work schedule, special appointments, and other events so the computer can verify a location as it is reached. If necessary, an officer is alerted if an offender enters an exclusion zone, as in the case of an assaultive offender who has gone near his or her victim.

Each offender, according to his or her crime and work schedule, has personally defined restricted areas and persons that constitute a violation. Notification methods are different in each GPS system. In some systems, all alerts are transmitted from in-house monitoring centers to a supervising officer's pagers; it is the responsibility of the officer to check each alert to determine what has happened. Reasons for alerts vary widely, and it is not always initially apparent why an alert has occurred. Serious alerts result if an offender enters an exclusion zone, enters an inclusion zone at a time other than what their schedule dictates, or attempts to tamper with or remove a unit. Other reasons for a registered alert could be battery failure or technical failure, such as when through no fault of an offender a signal is blocked and cannot be received. One study reported that *each* offender averages approximately three to four alerts every month (Armstrong & Freeman, 2011). If an officer is supervising 20 offenders, that averages to two alerts per day. Which system registers more false alarms—an active or passive GPS—is open to question. One study in Florida found passive GPS to register three times more false alarms than did active systems (Levin, 2008b), whereas active and passive systems in Arizona seemed to register similar numbers and types of alerts (Armstrong & Freeman, 2011). One concern about a high number of alerts, particularly those for equipment failure, is the reliability and shortcomings of equipment. With a high number of alerts, there may be a tendency for officers to become complacent over time, as if a boy were "crying wolf."

Authorities can potentially use EM and GPS to solve crimes by tracing an offender's whereabouts. In a boat theft case in Tampa, police were able to prove that a suspect was at the scene of a crime at the exact time the theft was committed. The suspect was on EM for felony grand theft (Kalfrin, 2008). As a bonus, some units even allow officers to text message or leave a voice

active GPS
A real-time GPS system that transmits data through wireless networks continuously at a rate of once or twice per minute. A phone line continually calls a reporting station to update an offender's location, which is tracked by a computer.

real-time access
Instant and immediate access via a supervising officer's Internet connection to pinpoint an exact location of an offender using GPS monitoring with a 30-second delay (as opposed to other GPS devices that have a significantly longer delay before a location can be confirmed).

exclusion zones
Exact locations an offender is prohibited from being in or near.

inclusion zones
Exact locations, such as locus of employment, school, or appointment, where an offender is required to be at a certain time.

TABLE 9.1 Electronic Monitoring and GPS for Each Risk Level

Risk Level	Type of System	Contact Frequency	Verification
Low	Home-based, radio frequency EM	Programmed or random	Phone call & voice verification
Medium	Passive GPS	Intermittent	GPS signals emitted once every 15–20 minutes
High	Active GPS	Continuous	GPS signals once every 2–3 minutes; Exclusion/inclusion zones; Video camera at home

Source: © 2015 Cengage Learning

message directly on the receiver worn by an offender. Examples of different GPS companies include:

- VeriTracks by Satellite Tracking of People, LLC, Houston, TX;
- SMART (Satellite Monitoring and Remote Tracking) Ware by Pro Tech Monitoring Inc., Odessa, FL;
- Exacutrac by BI, Inc., Boulder, CO;
- iSecuretrac Corporation, Omaha, NE; and
- G4S Justice Services, LLC, Atlanta, GA.

FOR WHAT TYPE OF OFFENDER IS GPS INTENDED? GPS is authorized in nearly every state in the United States, but most states use GPS for high-risk sex offenders only during the term of supervision. Of these, eight states require that high-risk sex offenders be monitored for life via GPS or EM (Armstrong & Freeman, 2011). The type of technology used, whether EM or GPS, largely depends on a client's risk level (see Table 9.1).

Limitations of GPS

Payne and DeMichele (2011b) caution relying too heavily on EM for a false sense of security. Drawbacks of GPS technology include loss of GPS signal, short battery life, and cost to offenders. Despite advances in technology, in more remote areas where cell phone service is weak or unavailable, radio frequency EM is a more reliable option. Even in urban areas, receivers have trouble picking up signals from satellites in some locations (for example, in the basement of a high-rise office building or between buildings). In addition, in cell phone "dead spots" an offender's receiver is unable to make the repeated cell phone calls to a central station with updates (Turner et al., 2007).

GPS is not completely foolproof. For instance, a motivated offender with specialized tools could cut through an ankle device. Although equipment reliability and data access do not differ among vendors, the primary difference is cost (Blackwell, Payne, & Prevost, 2011). A legitimate concern is offenders who cannot afford to pay the monthly electronic monitoring costs. Some local programs allow subsidies for indigent and low-income families to pay on a sliding scale or for juvenile offenders to substitute community service hours for daily charges, particularly those who are full-time students and do not work. As the cost of using GPS decreases and as cell phone service improves in rural areas, the number of offenders supervised using satellites will increase in the future. Box 9.2 discusses another issue that may be used in the near future: surgically implanted microchips under the skin of offenders under correctional supervision.

BOX 9.2	**TECHNOLOGY IN CORRECTIONS**

Are Surgically Implanted Microchips a Violation of Offender Privacy?

British ministers are considering surgically implanting microchips beneath the skin of offenders supervised in the community. The chips are the same ones that are used to track pets, cattle, luggage, and cars. "The tags, injected into the back of the arm with a hypodermic needle, consist of a toughened glass capsule holding a computer chip, a copper antenna and a capacitor that transmits data stored on the chip when prompted by an electromagnetic reader" (Brady, 2008, p. 1). The tags are reportedly beginning to be used with humans in limited conditions, such as tracking gang members within jails, entry into secure locations, or voluntary usage by customers of exclusive nightclubs (Brady, 2008). The courts have not yet ruled on whether this practice is too invasive or violates privacy under community supervision.

Source: Brady, Brian. Prisoners to be chipped like dogs. *The Independent*, January 13, 2008. Retrieved from: http://www.independent.co.uk/news/uk/politics/prisoners-to-be-chipped-like-dogs-769977.html

Electronic monitoring is being used worldwide. A recent study in Denmark found that for offenders under the age of 25 years, electronic monitoring reduced unemployment and offenders' dependency on social welfare compared to a similar group of offenders who went to prison (Andersen & Andersen, 2014). With technological advances in computers and satellites, the potential for offender tracking is limitless. Box 9.3 examines how electronic monitoring can be combined with less invasive methods to measure alcohol levels of DUI offenders.

HOW DO PEOPLE FEEL ABOUT EM/GPS?   Electronic monitoring has had its share of critics, from those concerned that its widespread use has resulted in net widening to those with ethical concerns that private companies are profiting from correctional supervision technology (Kilgore, 2012). For the most part, as technology has become more precise in tracking an offender's whereabouts, the general public has become more confident in and supportive of its use for offenders.

Although supporting the use of electronic monitoring as a tool for increased field supervision and visits, probation officers have also observed that increased contact means more paperwork. One officer said:

> They're getting seen at least weekly. Sometimes, you know, if people are not compliant or doing what they're supposed to be doing, they're being seen maybe twice a week....There's a lot of requirements by the court...[They get] assessments, and get treatment, and get evaluations, and attend meetings...[and] everything has to be verified. Like grocery shopping, we need to know where they are going. It has to be the closest store. We need to see their receipts the following time....If they got a window [of free time], you're responsible for where they're supposed to be. (Martin, Hanrahan, Travers, 2008, p. 9)

Officers also have said that because of regulations, there is a high probability of violations. Officers are encouraged to use graduated sanctions for technical violators and reserve jail time as a last resort.

Offenders sanctioned by EM preferred it as an alternative to jail in every case, although they reported experiences such as limitations on spontaneity, loss of control and of freedom, the suffering of shame, and family problems from constantly being at home. EM was viewed as both less controlling than jail and as a

BOX 9.3   TECHNOLOGY IN CORRECTIONS

Methods to Measure Blood-Alcohol Content

Only about 10% of all offenders who used alcohol at the time of their offense have been actually ordered to abstain from alcohol while on probation or parole. When the use of alcohol or drugs is revoked for clients, the courts accept testing results solely from urinalysis screenings. When a urine sample is collected from an offender, a staff member of the same sex is typically present to observe the procedure. The sample must be preserved in a cool environment, so logistically it is not realistic to conduct urine tests that often. For the client who is ordered not to drink alcohol, other less invasive methods have been devised to test blood-alcohol content (BAC) levels in the body on a more routine basis. One way is the Secure Continuous Remote Alcohol Monitoring, or SCRAM as first introduced in Chapter 6. SCRAM combines EM with the use of transdermal technology to measure ethanol levels through perspiration. Measurements can occur randomly or continuously, and, as with EM and GPS, ethanol readings can be communicated via a smart modem to a central monitoring station.

A second method is a device called the Sobrietor®. The BI Sobrietor® is a handheld remote device that detects alcohol in the breath through a sample as an individual verifies his or her voice (Reuell, 2008). The unit calibrates to the voice of the person being tested and is compared to a baseline voiceprint already on file.

An ignition interlock system is a third method for testing DUI offenders, now mandatory in some states.

Ignition interlocks are installed in vehicles through the ignition system and require a driver to submit to a breathalyzer before the car will start. Some require the driver to periodically blow into the interlock while driving. Although an ignition interlock will disable a car if alcohol is detected, other systems can measure alcohol levels when an offender is not driving. One concern with all of these systems is whether the correct offender is being tested. Combining the ignition interlock with image transmission and voice verification has improved the validity of the test. In any case, an offender's picture is taken or voice is recorded at the same time he or she submits to a test.

By modifying a glucose monitoring device, tissue spectroscopy is the latest new technological development in measuring BAC levels. This technique "measures a person's BAC [on the inner forearm] through a sensor pad that detects light reflected from capillaries in the middle layers of the skin. The amount of infrared light wavelengths reflected through the skin is affected by alcohol consumption" (Levin, 2008b, p. 6). Tissue spectroscopy is currently being developed for commercial use.

Sources: Levin, Marc A. 2008b. Five technological solutions for Texas' correctional and law enforcement challenges. *Texas Public Policy Foundation Policy Perspective* (June). Retrieved from: http://www .texaspolicy.com; Reuell, Peter. 2008. High-tech device knows when you're not sober. *The Metrowest Daily News*, February 10, 2008. Retrieved from: http://www.metrowestdailynews.com/multimedia/

---

second chance sanction, allowing offenders to remain productive in the community (Martin, Hanrahan, & Bowers, 2009).

Offenders have raised legal and constitutional issues regarding Fourth Amendment concerns with respect to privacy violations, such as the Grady case in the chapter opening story. In *Grady v. North Carolina* (2015), the U.S. Supreme Court ruled that EM/GPS constitutes a search, but has not yet found any Constitutional violations when it is used as a part of the criminal conviction. Stay tuned for whether EM/GPS will be allowed to be used in civil proceedings with regard to sex offenders after time has been served.

Empirical Evaluations of EM and GPS

Completion rates varied between 70% and 92%, with lower completion rates for prison-bound offenders compared to probationers (Roy, 2013). Failure reasons included unauthorized leave of absence (but later return); permanent flight/

absconding; arrest for a new crime; and tampering with EM equipment. Program completion rates began to diminish after 180 days, so 6 months seems an acceptable threshold for how long offenders should be under EM/GPS (Cotter & De Lint, 2009).

Two experiments that compared EM offenders with those under regular community supervision found recidivism rates to be relatively similar. Empirical evaluations support the notion that EM technology makes a difference in how offenders act while under supervision, compared to similar offenders on traditional probation or parole. Florida offenders ($n = 75,661$ total) placed under one of two types of electronic monitoring (home-based and GPS monitoring) were separated into groups by type of sentence (for example, EM as a probation violation sanction, EM as a post-prison sentence, or a direct sentence to EM) and measured while under supervision. Offenders on EM were more likely to complete the terms of supervision and were less likely to commit technical violations and new crimes than those in a comparison group (Padgett, Bales, & Blomberg, 2006). Padgett and colleagues suggest that EM is effective in monitoring serious offenders. In addition, home-based EM was as effective as GPS in significantly reducing the likelihood of technical violation, of committing new crimes, and of absconding while under supervision.

A California study of high-risk sex offenders found that GPS parolees had about the same rate of recidivism as other high-risk sex offenders under traditional parole supervision (Turner et al., 2007). Regarding long-term effects, the use of EM reduces recidivism rates for parolees up to three years after supervision has ended (Marklund & Holmberg, 2009).

Cost-benefit analyses provide mixed results. One analysis determined that EM yielded between 6 and 12 times more benefits through crime reduction than the costs of having parolees and probationers on EM during correctional supervision (Yeh, 2010). With more serious and high-risk sex offenders, however, GPS is not cost effective for parolees. The GPS group cost more per month ($600–$950) than non-GPS parolee group ($200–$400), despite that the two groups committed similar numbers of technical violations (Omori & Turner, 2012).

GENDER DIFFERENCES   It seems that gender and family conditions play a significant role in the outcome of EM sentences. Men who lived with a significant other while on EM reported receiving positive family support and help with dependent children, but female offenders reported that significant others were a source of stress and conflict impacting their success on EM. The female offenders perceived little support from their partners in child care. The lack of freedom to leave home because of EM affected women's primary caretaker role of dependent children. In terms of offenders spending much more time at home, some situations improve whereas other situations worsen.

In summary, success with EM and GPS depends on identifying the type of individual, home, and work situation that creates an ideal environment for completion without causing risk to the public. EM and GPS offer tremendous potential for community supervision, although some caution that perceived expectations of GPS are perhaps greater than its performance capabilities at this time (Armstrong & Freeman, 2011). In a work in progress in which researchers interviewed officers, "agents consistently said that GPS monitoring cannot stop sex offending behavior…[and it is still unclear] whether GPS creates a false sense of security" (Turner et al., 2007, p. 19). GPS technology will become more reliable and less expensive in the future, making EM the method of choice for community-based supervision. Critics caution the overreliance on technology as the only source of supervision—saying there is no substitute for a balance of treatment options and face-to-face contact, while using EM as part of the overall array if supervision tools (Payne and DeMichele, 2011b). There will be, however, a threshold at which we have to decide as a society how much invasion of privacy we are willing to accept for that accuracy.

DAY REPORTING CENTERS

day reporting centers (DRCs)
Nonresidential programs typically used for defendants on pretrial release, for convicted offenders on probation or parole, or for probation or parole violators as an increased sanction. Services are provided in one central location, and offenders must check in daily.

Day reporting centers (DRCs) are a three-phase outpatient program in which offenders live at home but report daily for treatment programs, itinerary, and random drug testing. The centers offer all resources and educational programs in one place. The staff to offender ratio is low, with about one staff member to every fourteen clients served (Craddock, 2009). DRCs are also open extended hours to accommodate offenders who work days and evenings. Some jurisdictions (for example, Nebraska and Indiana) use day reporting for defendants on pretrial release (Kim et al., 2007, 2008), and other states (such as North Carolina and New Jersey) use DRCs as a reentry mechanism for prisoners out on parole (Craddock, 2009) or as an increased sanction for probation or parole violators.

"Day centres" have been popular in England and Wales since the 1970s and began to appear in the United States in 1985. Juveniles were already exposed to day treatment centers established in the United States, so the concept was applied to adults. Connecticut and Massachusetts were among the first states to adopt day reporting centers with the goal of reducing jail or prison crowding and providing a closer level of supervision than traditional probation or parole. Most DRC programs exist in states that do not have intensive probation supervision as a sentencing option. Many DRCs accept high-risk offenders, such as sex offenders, stalkers, mentally ill offenders, developmentally disabled offenders, probation/parole violators, and graduates of therapeutic communities. A large DRC might process up to 2,000 offenders per day whereas smaller centers have a daily capacity of between 40 and 85 offenders.

A typical experience at a day reporting center is depicted in Figure 9.3. Take, for example, Sandra's case. Sandra violated her parole due to continued drug use while on parole for fraud. Eligible for a DRC as a graduated sanction, she was offered this option over jail. For the next three weeks she must report daily to the DRC, where she provides a daily itinerary, attends relapse prevention twice a week, and is drug-tested every third day. When she is not at the center, Sandra must remain at home and answer computer-generated random telephone calls several times during the day and occasionally at night. She must make advance arrangements to leave home to go to a store or on any errands. DRC case managers stop by unannounced at her home later in the week and find her not there. Although she arrives home 20 minutes later, she remains in Phase 1 for an extra week as a consequence of her actions. In the second phase, she can start looking for a part-time job, but Sandra continues to be involved in structured classes and community service and receives computer-generated calls.

After 60 days of good behavior in Phase 2, Sandra begins Phase 3, which requires relapse prevention classes and counseling once a week and reporting to the DRC only once a week. By the time offenders reach Level 3, they must either be employed full time, be going to school full time, or engaged in a combination of both. Assuming that no major violations have occurred, after two

Phase 1 (3 weeks)
- DAILY reporting. At DRC 9:00 A.M.–5:00 P.M.; curfew
- No employment; relapse prevention and drug testing

Phase 2 (60 days)
- Approved to look for a job during day; curfew
- Classes and community service

Phase 3 (60–90 days)
- Full-time employment
- Weekly treatment classes

TRANSFER
- Transfers out of DRC to regular parole or probation supervision

FIGURE 9.3
Phases of Day Reporting Centers.

iStockphoto.com/nicole S. Young

Day reporting centers provide structured group sessions that supervised offenders attend on a weekly basis.

more months in Phase 3, Sandra is transferred from the DRC caseload back to her former parole officer for monthly meetings and continued relapse prevention until the end of her sentence (Kim et al., 2008). For probationers and parolees who do not take their supervision conditions seriously, other DRCs serve to provide enforcement or "muscle" without sending these people to jail or prison.

Treatment-Oriented Versus Supervision-Oriented DRCs

The common theory behind DRCs is that offenders will stay out of trouble if they are occupied, especially with activities that improve their chances for a more normal life—for example, obtaining a GED or finding a job. DRCs all have a requirement of daily itinerary, attendance, and program phases (Kim et al., 2007). Because of the wide variety of clients whom DRCs around the country serve, they also differ in their program goals. Some DRCs are more treatment-oriented and others more supervision-oriented (Craddock, 2009).

Treatment-oriented DRCs provide a wide range of services, all on an outpatient basis. The most common services are job-seeking skills and job placement, drug abuse education and treatment, psychological counseling, life skills training, and GED education classes and literacy. Other services provided by a smaller number of DRCs include parenting, anger management, vocational training, and transportation assistance. Once employed, offenders are still required to attend treatment programs at night or on weekends. Craddock (2009) noted that DRCs that focus on criminogenic needs outlined by risk assessment instruments help increase program completion rates and reduce recidivism. She found that "employment programming is the only component that predicts completion" (p. 130). Her findings also suggest that it is important that housing assistance be incorporated for parolees coming out of prison.

Supervision-oriented DRCs ensure that clients are abiding by the rules, enforce accountability through itineraries, and keep clients busy so they do not have the time or opportunity to engage in criminal activity. Itineraries are important for two reasons. First, clients learn (some for the first time) how to plan their days in advance. Second, DRCs can monitor where clients are when random phone calls are placed via computer. DRCs are authorized to give out Antabuse, a medication that prevents the use of alcohol and is prescribed for alcoholics. Urine screenings and alco-sensor tests ensure that clients have not been using drugs. Another characteristic of DRCs is that many clients are under 24-hour electronic monitoring. As clients remain longer in the program under supervision, DRCs may be able to give them more freedom by removing electronic monitoring devices. Many DRCs use a combination of supervision and treatment approaches.

DRCs are nonresidential versions of halfway houses in terms of providing similar services, except that DRC offenders live at home. Like most halfway houses, most DRCs are private facilities that contract out to state and local entities. Further, contact between program staff and offenders in DRCs is for longer time periods than under intensive supervision probation (ISP). ISP programs include more field visits (in which an officer goes to a home or job site to visit an offender), but DRCs are actually more structured through EM, phone contact, and in-facility time because offenders go to the center (Kim et al., 2007).

Sentences to DRCs range from 40 days to 12 months, with an average of 6 months' duration. DRCs are more costly than traditional probation/parole, and even more expensive than ISP. However, DRCs cost less than residential treatment or incarceration. Many of the treatment program costs are absorbed by the DRC itself or by another agency. In one out of every four DRCs, offenders pay for their own drug treatment.

Evaluations of DRCs

Keep in mind that DRCs serve high-risk clients who have a lot of responsibility in this program. Treatment services in the DRC should be evidence-based (Steiner & Butler, 2013). Also remember that program success is greatly influenced by local policy and practitioner decisions. Rearrest rates, by comparison, are more influenced by actual offender behavior.

DOES TIME SPENT IN THE DRC MAKE A DIFFERENCE?   Most DRCs last 90 days. A group of pretrial detainees who had participated in a DRC for 70 or more days were compared with a group that participated for 10 days or less. Members of these two groups were tracked for three years in terms of their rearrest and reincarceration rates. The longer term group (spending 70 days and over) had lower rearrest and reincarceration rates than the short-term, and also remained free for an average of 122 days longer (Martin, Lurigio, Olson, 2003). However, it seems that the DRC should be limited to no longer than 120 days—spending more time than that contributes to being less likely to complete the program.

COMPLETION RATES   DRC programs seem notorious for lower completion rates compared to those of other community-based programs. Termination rates averaged 50% within four months to six months and ranged from 14% to 86% higher for service-oriented programs than for supervision-oriented DRCs. Failure rates were also higher for programs longer than six months in duration (Craddock, 2009). High failure rates resulted because of the level of supervision intensity and the type of offender admitted to the program. Whereas work release programs accepted lower-risk offenders, DRCs accepted probation and parole violators and higher-risk clients. DRCs that focused on employment and transitional housing increased program completion rates (Craddock, 2009).

RECIDIVISM RATES   Two recent studies examined recidivism of DRC participants compared to another similar group. One experiment used random assignment to a DRC and to regular parole supervision for a period of 90 days for parole violators. Parolees who were randomly assigned to the DRC received employment services to aid them in finding jobs, while the comparison group of parole violators had one or more special conditions imposed such as curfew or drug counseling but remained on regular parole. Both groups were followed post supervision. The DRC group had higher rearrest rates than regular parolees (Boyle, Ragusa-Salerno, Lanterman, & Marcus, 2013).

The findings in the Boyle et al. study do not explain why the DRCs were ineffective at reducing recidivism such as "...whether the DRCs were ineffective at delivering job training, whether the job training delivered was ineffective in helping offenders find employment, whether employment had an impact on recidivism, or all of the above" (Duwe, 2013, p. 146). The differences observed in this study may have been a function of the treatment interventions offered by the DRCs (Steiner & Butler, 2013) or by the variations in program quality—one that we will not know because program fidelity of the DRCs was not assessed (Ostermann, 2013).

Perhaps, evaluation of DRCs is more a matter of who the clients are and whom they are compared against. In comparison to the former study that used a DRC after parolees had already failed, this next study examined how a DRC fares at an earlier point. DRC programs seem to fare well as a reentry program for prisoners, especially when compared with prisoners who are freed under no supervision and compared with parolees under traditional parole. Even after controlling for demographics and prior criminal history, prisoners released with no supervision had a greater volume of arrests and were arrested faster than DRC clients (Ostermann, 2009).

Factors that predicted who would be rearrested include previous criminal history (more prior arrests), and younger aged offenders (Craddock, 2009). In addition, employment was the main component that predicted program completion and reduced the likelihood of rearrest and reincarceration (Craddock, 2009; Kim et al., 2007).

In sum, there is no one right way to operate a DRC or any of the programs discussed in this chapter. Each program has different goals and different kinds of clients. The key is to specifically define the goals of a program (for example, to reduce institutional crowding, to allow a graduated sanction for probationers, and the like) and then measure whether it achieves those goals and contributes to an improved quality of life for society at large, for offenders, and for victims. We discuss these improvements further in the next chapter.

SUMMARY

- House arrest by itself provides cost savings but does not deter criminal misconduct. The level of monitoring is minimal unless house arrest is combined with EM.

- Technological advances in EM include the use of computers and satellites to monitor offenders in the community. No matter what type of EM or GPS is currently used, all offenders must minimally wear an ankle monitoring device, which they cannot tamper or remove without sounding an alarm to a central control station.

- DRCs typically accept convicted offenders or pretrial detainees who require a higher level of supervision than do clients under electronic monitoring or house arrest. DRCs also provide all services in one place and are the most costly type of nonresidential intermediate sanction, although they still cost less than jail or prison.

- All forms of nonresidential programs are more effective when goals are clarified and when target offender populations are more accurately defined to best meet offender needs without unduly compromising public safety.

DISCUSSION QUESTIONS

1. Which of the intermediate sanctions discussed in this chapter are probation or parole enhancements, and which sanctions are true alternatives to prison?

2. How does electronic monitoring support house arrest? What ethical and social criticisms are associated with EM?

3. How do electronic monitoring devices work? What are some of the technical problems associated with them?

4. Do DRCs accomplish their objectives?

 ## WEBSITES, VIDEOS, AND PODCASTS

Websites
Electronic Monitoring of Offenders in Washington, DC
    http://media.csosa.gov/blog/2012/04/gps
    -tracking-of-criminal-offenders-in
    -washington-d-c/

Electronic Monitoring of Offenders in Michigan
    http://www.michigan.gov
    /corrections/0,1607,7-119-1435-5032--,00.html

Effectiveness of Electronic Monitoring Research Report
    http://www.criminologycenter.fsu.edu/p/pdf
    /EM%20Evaluation%20Final%20Report%20
    for%20NIJ.pdf

Evaluation of Maricopa County (Arizona) Day Reporting Center
    http://www.nhtsa.gov/people/injury/alcohol
    /repeatoffenders/eval_dayreport.html

Videos/Podcasts

House Arrest and GPS/Electronic Monitoring System

An in-depth look at how house arrest works using GPS monitoring bracelets. http://www.you-tube.com/watch?v=vznM3y8n9DA

Making Community Supervision Safer Through Electronic Monitoring

(Length: 3 minutes) An NIJ sponsored interview with George Drake, Program Manager of the Community Corrections Technology Center, about electronic monitoring. http://nij.ncjrs.gov/multimedia/video-nijconf2011-drake.htm

Costs and Benefits of Day Reporting Centers

(Length: 7:35 minutes) An overview on the cost and the benefits of day reporting centers. https://www.youtube.com/watch?v=IYde4_38Q3Y

Day Reporting Centers for Youth

(Length: 6 minutes) Kimberly Reeves discusses a Day Reporting Center where young offenders are offered different programs and opportunities that include GED classes or employment services. https://www.youtube.com/watch?v=o15KUQ7Sf5E

CASE STUDY EXERCISES

Intermediate Community Programs

Considering the circumstances provided in the following cases, you are the judge, and you must decide which intermediate sanction or combination of sanctions (using any residential program from Chapter 8 and/or nonresidential options in Chapter 9). Jail is not an option, and you must assume that more is needed beyond traditional probation or parole. After you have made your decision, defend your answer.

CASE A

John is a 29-year-old man who has been twice convicted of fraud by forging checks. His first conviction resulted in a sentence of five years on probation with an order to make restitution in the amount of $2,720. John made three payments of $230 each before absconding supervision. He turned up again after six months and was reinstated on probation by the court after he promised to faithfully fulfill the terms of his supervision and to complete his restitution obligation. During his supervised release, he was in violation of probation conditions regularly and never completed his restitution payments. The current case involves John passing a forged check at a local grocery store in the amount of $624. Due to his previous failure and noncompletion of probation, the court is concerned that he is not capable of following court-ordered probation conditions, yet it does not want to commit him to state prison or to a jail term because his offense is nonviolent. John has a wife and two small children and is their only source of support. He has a high school diploma, he is not mentally ill or disabled, and he is currently employed as a house painter.

CASE B

Ricardo is a 23-year-old identified gang member of the Mexican Mafia, a Latino gang with roots in California. He has a history of criminal offenses including shoplifting, one motor vehicle theft, and three DUIs. Ricardo is not assaultive, but the group in which he is a member has been known to participate in assault and other violent acts. His file does not indicate his rank in the gang, but it shows he has been a confirmed member for at least six years. His current offense is larceny involving theft from his former employer, a local carpet-laying company. The PSI concludes that Ricardo needs more structure than can be gained from probation or intensive supervision, but it does not recommend a prison sentence due to his current nonviolent offense. The PSI reports that Ricardo needs to learn discipline, good work habits, and respect for the rights of others and is concerned about his attitude toward authority.

Economic and Restorative Justice Reparations

CHAPTER OUTLINE

CHAPTER LEARNING OBJECTIVES

1. Examine how restorative principles and practices differ from traditional criminal justice practices.

2. Explain the forms that restorative justice takes, including victim-offender mediation, victim impact classes, family group conferencing, and circle sentencing.

3. Compare and contrast the economic/monetary sanctions used in both restorative and traditional criminal justice systems to include restitution, community service, fines, fees, and forfeiture.

KEY TERMS

community justice
restorative justice
reintegrative shaming
stigmatization
procedural justice
victim-offender mediation
conferencing
sentencing circles
community reparation boards
victim impact panels
restitution
community service
fine
victim compensation fund
fee
forfeiture

Lucinda left her night class at the local university to drive home. She was preoccupied with the exam she just took and wanted to text her friend a quick message to assure her that she passed. The next thing Lucinda heard was a loud screeching sound, and when she looked up from her phone, all she saw were the oncoming headlights of a car coming directly toward her. As she tried to swerve, the phone was knocked out of her hands, and then she felt a very intense impact of metal and she smelled burnt rubber. She couldn't move as she was pulled from the wreckage. As she was taken to the hospital in an ambulance, she later learned that the male driver in the other smaller car, Robert, suffered head and chest injuries so badly that he died on his way to the hospital. At first Lucinda, was in denial about what happened, but once she was released from the hospital, her lawyer convinced her to plead not guilty in the incident.

Robert's family, in their grief at the loss of their son, brother, and father, were deeply devastated and enraged when the prosecutor announced a few weeks later that the female driver who killed Robert was entering a plea of not guilty. Most family members wanted to take revenge, while others talked about turning their grief into stopping more people from becoming victimized by people who text while driving. These family members wanted to honor Robert's memory by assurances that the offender would take responsibility for her actions, would use this experience to change her own life, and to never text and drive again. Robert's family pushed the prosecutor for a mediation meeting and assured the prosecutor that no harm would come to Lucinda. They only wanted the chance to meet with the female driver in a controlled environment, but only if Lucinda first agreed to change her plea and that the family would get a chance to address the court at sentencing.

Lucinda was scared, and at first, in full denial of the pain and loss she caused a family she never met and a victim she never knew. Lucinda was more focused on her own losses and how she had to drop out of school because of her time spent in the hospital. Slowly, through a series of meetings with a mediator, Lucinda's demeanor changed as she became less defensive and more understanding of what Robert's family was going through. And, she began to read the family's written statements and learned that Robert was a person who had dreams, goals, and many talents that positively affected others around him. This was too much for Lucinda to bear and she wondered

Six months after the horrible accident, Lucinda met Robert's family with two mediators present. Lucinda was allowed to express her sorrow and regret for her actions. She profusely apologized and could barely look anyone in the eye. She felt so ashamed. Then, each family member individually shared how the accident and Robert's death affected them personally. The family was allowed to ask Lucinda questions that were important to them, such as why she was texting and what she thought when she learned she had killed Robert. After everyone had spoke, the mediators reached an agreement about what they would recommend to the court at sentencing. The mediation seemed to lessen Robert's family's need for vengeance and start the healing process. Agreeing to the mediation process was difficult for Lucinda, but the court acknowledged her actions and she felt like she could also start to heal from her mistakes and move on with her life once she served her two-year prison sentence.

Discussion: Should face-to-face meetings like this one be encouraged by the criminal justice system? Why or why not?

INTRODUCTION

When an offender is punished for a crime, the public may feel short-term satisfaction and the victim may find some closure, but many might still be left wondering how the punishment will actually affect the offender's future attitude and behavior. In a traditional criminal justice system, the state acts on behalf of victims to punish an offender. It should be no surprise that even following offender sentencing, victims can still feel angry, unsupported, more socially isolated, and more distrustful of a system that was designed to punish on their behalf. Many come to realize that government-sanctioned retribution achieves a form of justice or revenge but does not necessarily heal. Traditional criminal justice strategies and the "get tough" movement may not be as effective as we once thought in dealing with the harm, social isolation, and destruction of community trust that result when crimes are committed. Separating predatory and violent offenders from the general public is necessary, but incarceration is not a magic bullet for most offenders, the majority of whom will be released one day. Incarcerating more people for longer periods of time does not necessarily make our communities safer.

Community Stakeholders

The concept of **community justice** entails using community stakeholders to control and reduce crime and to rebuild community relationships through community policing, community courts, and restorative justice. Examples of community stakeholders can be found in Figure 10.1. Although some authors use the terms *community justice* and *restorative justice* interchangeably, community justice is actually a broader concept that describes a philosophy encompassing the whole criminal justice system (police, courts, and corrections), whereas

community justice
A philosophy of using community—through community policing, community courts, restorative justice, and broken-windows probation—to control and reduce crime.

FIGURE 10.1
Community Stakeholders.

restorative justice
Various sentencing
philosophies and practices
that emphasize an offender's
taking of responsibility
to repair harm done to a
victim and to a surrounding
community. Includes forms
of victim-offender mediation,
reparation panels, circle
sentencing, and monetary
sanctions.

restorative justice is concerned with alternative dispute resolution and contains a corrections component.

In Chapter 1 we introduced the concept of **restorative justice** as a sentencing philosophy and practice that emphasizes an offender taking responsibility to repair the harm done to a victim and surrounding community. Restorative justice is most often used during pretrial proceedings as an alternative in the civil justice system. However, restorative justice may also be used as a part of and/or following traditional criminal sentencing. Restorative justice is more victim-centered than traditional methods of criminal justice, involving the victim and the community throughout the entire process of justice. It is practiced worldwide in both juvenile and adult systems, and the form it takes is largely dependent on cultural factors (Umbreit & Armour, 2010). The form that restorative justice has taken in the United States is termed "Western" as opposed to "aboriginal," which refers to that practiced by indigenous peoples in countries such as Canada, New Zealand, and Australia. Canada recognizes both forms insofar as Western restorative justice speaks to the dominant Canadian majority and aboriginal initiatives honor the traditional values and legal principles of the aboriginal people. In the United States, Western restorative justice is community-based and combines mainstream American criminal justice with the indigenous justice practiced by Native Americans long before European settlers colonized North America (see Table 10.1). Let's begin by discussing restorative justice principles and comparing them with traditional criminal justice sentencing practices.

TABLE 10.1   Roots of Restorative Justice in the United States

MAINSTREAM AMERICAN JUSTICE	INDIGENOUS NATIVE AMERICAN JUSTICE
Imported from Anglo-American models	Indigenous, shared views of the community and victims*
Written codified laws, rules, procedures*	Unwritten/oral customs, traditions, practices
Crime is a violation of the state	Crime is a violation of one person by another
Justice is administered*	Justice is part of the life process*
Offender is focal point; privilege against self-incrimination	Victim is focal point*; offender is obligated to verbalize accountability
Adversarial (fact-finding) process; victim and offender have no contact	Communal*; victim and offender are involved in the whole process and decide action jointly
Conflict settled in court; focus on establishing guilt and blame	Conflict settled through mediation and repairing relationships*
Public defender or lawyer representation*	Extended family member representation
Retributive and deterrence	Restorative or holistic; connects everyone involved*
Incarceration, so criminal can pay debt to society	Community service, restitution, reconciliation*
Criminals who break the law deserve to be punished	Criminal acts are a part of human error, which requires correctional intervention by the community*
Church and state are separated	Spiritual realm is cohesive with justice*
Stigma is difficult to remove	Forgiveness is possible and encouraged

Note: *Applies to restorative justice

PRINCIPLES OF RESTORATIVE JUSTICE

Restorative justice, with roots in a variety of faith traditions, moves from a philosophy of vengeance and retribution to one of healing, reconciliation, and forgiveness. In contrast to mainstream criminal justice that focuses on punishment of the offender, restorative justice focuses on victim, offender, and community throughout the whole process of restoring justice.

Reintegrative Shaming Theory

Due to its focus on reintegration, restorative justice is best applied through community-based corrections or to prisoner reentry. One of the earliest theories that forms the foundation of restorative justice is **reintegrative shaming**, which assumes that after a crime is committed social bonds are weakened and must be repaired in order for an offender to change future behavior. Reintegrative shaming allows the victim and the community to *reject the criminal behavior* rather than the individual, while also relying on them to later forgive the offender (Braithwaite, 1989). Techniques include treating the offender respectfully, encouraging the offender, and focusing on present associations and behaviors rather than past criminal acts (Dollar & Ray, 2015). Reintegrative shaming is thus seen as more reintegrative and more effective in the long run than the traditional justice system use of **stigmatization**. Stigmatization only serves to reject the individual by permanently labeling him/her a criminal and preventing them from becoming fully functioning and productive societal members (Kim & Gerber, 2012).

reintegrative shaming
A process that occurs after an offense has been committed whereby an offender initially experiences reproach from significant others and social disapproval from a community but then is later forgiven, welcomed back into society and provided an opportunity to start anew.

Procedural Justice Theory

Another theory that is related to restorative justice and was developed at exactly the same time as reintegrative shaming is called **procedural justice** theory. Procedural justice is based on the idea that individuals who perceive that they have been fairly treated and respected are more likely to comply with court expectations (Tyler, 1990). Perceived fairness of the legal process and/or case outcome can be measured subjectively with the actual offender and victim participants, and objectively using outside observers. Barnes et al. (2015, p. 108) further define procedural justice as the degree to which:

stigmatization
A process, in effect long after an offense has been committed, whereby an offender continues to experience social disapproval and bias and is never fully welcomed back into society nor provided an opportunity to start anew.

1. citizens are able to exercise some control over the decision-making process/final outcome from that process;
2. procedures are used consistently with similar cases;
3. procedures operate without bias to race/ethnicity, gender and other extra-legal factors;
4. procedures use the most accurate information whenever possible;
5. citizens are able to appeal the results; and
6. citizens are treated respectfully and as valued societal members.

Trained objective observers found that restorative justice proceedings were "... characterized as respectful and as less dominating than traditional court hearings. Offenders contributed more to the outcomes of their conferences and were less coerced into accepting those results. Finally, offenders had more members of the public, more supporters from their own community of care, and more participants for whom they had respect attend their conferences than [traditional] court" (Barnes et al., 2015, p. 126).

procedural justice
A theory that assumes that individuals who perceive that they have been treated fairly and respectfully during legal proceedings are more likely to comply with court and/or contractual expectations.

As you can see, restorative justice attempts to *strengthen* the community by drawing on the participation of the victim, the victim's social support network, the offender, the offender's social support network, and the community. Restorative justice asks: What or who was harmed? Who is responsible for the harm done? What needs to happen to repair the harm? All forms of restorative justice have the following commonalities:

1. The victim/victim's social support network has an opportunity to communicate how the crime affected him or her physically, emotionally, financially, and socially.
2. To develop a reparative plan, accepted by both the victim and the offender, in which the offender will repair the harm caused.
3. Victim and offender participation is voluntary, and conditions of each community meeting are defined with respect to all parties.
4. The parties rely on community partners and volunteer organizations.
5. Offenders must accept full responsibility for their criminal behavior. This means admitting guilt and being willing to comply with restoration agreements.
6. Although restorative justice efforts can take place within jails and prisons (for example, via victim impact panels), most forms are community-based as alternatives to traditional court processing or as a part of diversion.

Using these six common principles and through dialogue, relationship building, and open communication, it is determined who is responsible, how harm can be repaired, and how the victim can be provided closure and healing (Shih-Ya et al., 2010).

RESTORATIVE JUSTICE PRACTICES

We previously discussed that restorative justice is most often used during pretrial proceedings as a diversionary alternative in the civil or juvenile justice systems. Restorative justice practices discussed below include victim-offender mediation, conferencing, and sentencing circles. Other types including reparation boards and victim impact panels may be used as a part of and/or following traditional criminal sentencing. Restitution and community service are restorative in nature and are also discussed among the economic sanctions later in the chapter.

Victim-Offender Mediation

victim-offender mediation a series of structured face-to-face meetings between an offender and a victim in the presence of a trained mediator with the goal of developing a written contractual agreement to address how the offender will repair the harm he or she caused the victim.

Victim-offender mediation (VOM) has existed since the early 1980s, with an estimated 300 programs in the United States and thousands of programs around the world. This type of mediation is different from that traditionally found in civil courts because in the former there is no dispute about liability. The various phases of VOM are depicted in Figure 10.2. A mediator first meets with offender and victim separately to discern each party's willingness to cooperate. Assuming that both parties volunteer, the mediator is present in the same room with them (and if the offender is a juvenile, the parents are invited). After the facts of the offense are described, the focus is on repairing the harm done to the victim, which is quite emotional for both sides. Shaming plays a part in releasing hurtful emotions, such as sadness, anger, and resentment that the victim may feel (Kenney & Clairmont, 2009). The parties, in one or more sessions, reach a mutually desirable written agreement that is later filed with the courts.

The Victim-Offender Mediation (VOM) Process

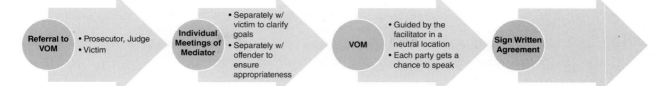

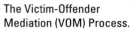

FIGURE 10.2
The Victim-Offender Mediation (VOM) Process.

The primary reasons victims chose to participate were to seek restitution or repayment, to oversee punishment, and to share their grief with offenders. The ability of the mediator and the face-to-face format are key variables in victims' satisfaction. Victims who participate in VOMs report satisfaction with case outcomes and less fear of being revictimized. Victims were also more likely to receive restitution payments than with traditional court cases. Victims were more satisfied when their pain and loss was acknowledged, and they were compensated by the offender, compared to victims whose perpetrator was incarcerated (Laxminarayan, 2012). Another strength of VOM is its overall ability to reduce offender recidivism. A meta-analysis of over 9,000 juveniles at 21 different sites around the United States found that VOM contributed to a 34% reduction in recidivism for juveniles who were involved (Umbreit et al., 2006).

There are some downsides of VOM. First, there is concern that victims' perspectives have been given too much "free reign whereas offenders have more limited room to maneuver...it lends credence to claims that offenders' perspectives are not sufficiently addressed by RJ" (Kenney & Clairmont, 2009, p. 303). Solutions to this problem include a strong facilitator who can manage emotions on both sides and allow a more balanced view so as not to undermine the restorative part of VOM. Second, there is no strong evidence that restorative justice conferences reduce future juvenile offender recidivism over that of juveniles processed using standard juvenile justice court (Kim & Gerber, 2012).

Conferencing

Conferencing originated in New Zealand through traditional Maori tribes and was mainstreamed in juvenile cases in New Zealand and Australia for use by police. Conferencing in the United States is typically used in juvenile cases, when the victim and offender are students at the same school or when they are part of a close-knit group or even part of the same family. Conferencing is also known as family group conferencing and requires that juveniles take responsibility for their actions and that the victim participates. The goal of conferencing is to strengthen and empower families and peer groups—not to tear them apart. Unlike VOM, which most directly involves just a victim and offender, conferencing involves supporters of all ages of both victim and offender. A larger group of people means there is typically a facilitator and some type of security staff present. The group meets in a location of the family's choice at a specific time to be determined in advance. The conference begins, in a similar fashion as VOM, with the facts of the case. After the offender admits to the charges, each member is given a chance to speak within the group. There may be some time provided for the offender and his or her supporters to discuss solutions before reconvening in the larger group. Other times, the negotiations take place out in the open with the victim present.

conferencing
one or more police officer-led structured face-to-face meetings between the offender, victim, and key supporters (family and friends) to increase the offender's awareness of how the crime affected the victim and to engage key supporters in shaping the offender's future behavior.

School resource officers or police officers organize and facilitate conference meetings at school or at a community resource center after school. The conference includes a reparation agreement wherein all participants jointly decide how the offender can make amends to the victim. For youths who participated in a conference, most sanctions consisted of a "symbolic" apology, community service, offender counseling, or some combination of the three.

Youth offenders involved in conferencing generally reported feeling more respected and had more opportunity to express their feelings than youths who were adjudicated for similar offenses through traditional juvenile courts. While some conferences were as stigmatizing as traditional adjudication methods, conferencing that most closely followed the original principles of fairness, procedural justice and reintegration had lower recidivism rates than youths who were deferred from traditional juvenile court. The conferenced youths who recidivated did so *later* than the youths in the traditional group, which is also important showing that conferencing can be effective at recidivism reduction (Hipple et al., 2014).

The most rigorous experiment was the Reintegrative Shaming Experiments (RISE) in Australia, which randomly assigned youth to conferencing versus traditional court and compared three years of behavior before the conference and three years afterward. Recidivism rates were lower for youth who had committed a violent offense and had experienced conferencing than for violent youth who experienced traditional adjudication. Recidivism, however, did not significantly differ between groups for Australian juveniles who had committed a property- or alcohol-related offense.

Sentencing Circles

sentencing circles
a large community meeting adapted from Native American practices, that involves a tribal elder or spiritual leader, the offender(s), victim(s), key supporters of each, justice workers, and community supporters to develop a sentencing plan outside the traditional court system, but that involves community consensus around healing from a crime that occurred.

Of all the types of restorative justice, **sentencing circles** are based most closely on tribal traditions of the medicine wheel and how an individual's physical, emotional, mental, and spiritual sides are interrelated with their community. The goal of the sentencing circle is soul searching, reestablishing trust, and rebalancing relationships that have been damaged from criminal behavior.

A sentencing circle group consists of one or two facilitators/keepers, the offender(s), the victim(s), family, friends, and coworkers of the offender and the victim, juvenile justice/criminal justice personnel, and interested community members, all of whom gather simultaneously in a circle. The purpose of a sentencing circle is for the group to resolve conflict and ultimately arrive at a consensus of what should be done to achieve justice in a particular situation. Facilitators keep things moving but do not control the outcome. This meeting is therefore not about one side winning and the other side losing; it is about closing the wounds and allowing both sides to come to a mutual understanding about how each will coexist in the future (Pranis, 2005).

A "talking piece" such as a stick or feather is used to keep some sort of order, such that the person holding the talking piece is the only one authorized to speak. The talking piece is passed around the circle until everyone who wants an opportunity to state his or her opinion or to offer advice can do so. The following case describes a circle sentencing session:

Tommy is 16 years old and lives on a small tribal reservation where everyone knows each other. While joyriding in another vehicle one night, Tommy crashed into an uninsured parked car and into a police car. When police discussed

Tommy's case with the juvenile court judge, the judge thought it would be best to try the circle sentencing route first.

> In the circle, the victim talked about the emotional shock of seeing what had happened to his car and his costs to repair it. Then, an elder leader of the First Nations community where the circle sentencing session was being held (and an uncle of the offender) expressed his disappointment and anger with the boy. The elder observed that this incident, along with several prior offenses by the boy, had brought shame to his family....After the elder finished, a feather (the "talking piece") was passed to the next person in the circle, a young man who spoke about the contributions the offender made to the community, the kindness he had shown toward elders, and his willingness to help others with home repairs....The police officer, whose vehicle had also been damaged...proposed to the judge that in lieu of statutorily required jail time for the offense, the offender be allowed to meet with him on a regular basis for counseling and community service. After asking the victim and the prosecutor if either had any objections, the judge accepted this proposal. The judge also ordered restitution to the victim and asked the young adult who had spoken on the offender's behalf to serve as a mentor for the offender. After a prayer in which the entire group held hands, the circle disbanded and everyone retreated to the kitchen area of the community center for refreshments.

Of all four forms of restorative justice, sentencing circles involve the largest number of participants and therefore require the most organization. They may be followed by other circles that attempt to further heal and/or to support crime victims who have experienced trauma, pain, or loss. Circles are more effective in schools to reduce bullying or classroom misconduct, and in response to crimes occurring in smaller communities that have a foundation of respect, consensus and people already know each other (Griffin, 2010).

Reparation Boards and Victim Impact Panels

The three techniques previously discussed (VOM, conferencing, and sentencing circles) intervene in a criminal case before sentencing or instead of traditional court processing. The two techniques discussed in this section are methods that intervene post-conviction. Volunteer **community reparation boards** evolved in 10 states (AZ, CA, CO, FL, NY, LA, MO, NE, VT, WA) as a part of juvenile and adult systems for nonviolent misdemeanants sentenced to probation (Humphrey et al., 2012). Typically, the court judge allows the community board to decide the conditions of probation within a reasonable set of guidelines. Conditions are not as stringent as one would find in regular probation, however. Apology letters, community service, and restitution are the three most typical conditions issued as a contract signed by the offender. When these conditions are fulfilled, the board communicates this and supervision is successfully terminated by the court.

community reparation boards
a volunteer group of trained community members that decides and enforces probation conditions of adjudicated cases deemed eligible by a traditional court.

Each board has a chair who manages the session and 3–5 members are trained prior to serving. Victims are allowed to speak before the board or to submit a written statement. Some boards partner with faith-based organizations who agree to mentor or to assist in supervision of an offender's reparation. The board acts as a probation officer would—reporting back to the court monthly or quarterly on an offender's progress or lack thereof. Should an offender fail to comply with the sanctions, the board makes a recommendation to the court. A study of Vermont's reparative probation program compared misdemeanants who went through traditional court probation with those who went through a community reparation board. Humphrey and colleagues (2012) found that "...reparative probationers were significantly less likely to be charged with a new conviction during the five-year time frame (43.5% vs 47.5%)" (p. 120). Of all forms of restorative justice, reparation boards involve more community than victim participation.

A second post-conviction technique that is considered within the realm of restorative justice is the **victim impact panel**. These meetings occur after an offender has been convicted and sentenced. The meetings are prearranged between willing offenders and a group of people whose lives have been affected by a specific type of such as victims of a drunk driving incident or parents of murdered children. The meetings can take place with an individual offender or with a group of DUI offenders, but they do not necessarily involve the exact same victims of the offender(s) being confronted. The sessions typically involve victims sharing how their lives were changed following the incident, victims' rights, and the overall effects of having a conviction for the offender. The sessions are not meant to condemn or shame offenders but to help them make better decisions in the future (Crew & Johnson, 2011). Victim impact panels that create offender empathy are more effective than ones that try to shame offenders or make them feel bad about themselves (Jackson, 2009).

The effectiveness of victim impact panels have been mixed. The victim impact panels reduced criminal thinking errors and increased emotional/relational skills of juveniles who were exposed to 24 sessions, compared to offenders who were exposed to only one session (Baglivio & Jackowski, 2015). For adult DUI offenders, panel sessions had less of an impact for second-time DUI offenders than for first-time DUI offenders. Offenders who were convicted of their second DUI and attended a victim impact panel did not reduce future DUI convictions compared to second timers who were not at all exposed to victim impact classes (Crew & Johnson, 2011). Victim impact panels seem to be more effective for juveniles and first-time DUI offenders who are still contemplating change, while another approach (e.g., alcohol treatment) may be more appropriate for second-time DUI offenders.

victim impact panels
one or more confrontational meetings that occur post conviction between offenders and people whose lives have been affected by a specific type of crime (drunk driving, murder), but not necessarily the exact same victims of the offender(s) being confronted.

Community reparation boards, similar to the one pictured here, reviews each offender's case in an attempt to help them in the reentry process.

AP Images/Stephen Wilson

Effectiveness of Restorative Justice Methods

Measures of restorative justice include victim satisfaction with the outcome or process, payment of restitution, and cost savings. Restorative justice is most welcomed by victims of property crimes because they are more likely to be compensated for property losses. In traditional criminal justice, the victim is rarely fully compensated. When given a choice, property crime victims indicated they would rather be compensated over demanding incarceration for the offender (Umbreit & Armour, 2010). At this time, however, restorative justice as the sole sanction is less likely to be effective for offenders of violent crimes and less endorsed by victims of violent crimes, who typically desire additional offender sanctions (Shih-Ya et al., 2010). Also, when victim and offender know each other well, such as when both are from the same family, it can be difficult for family members who may want to support both sides.

Evaluation of restorative justice can also be measured using recidivism rates of offenders who have participated in a restorative justice program compared to similarly situated offenders who have gone through traditional court adjudication. Conferencing has been found to be effective for juvenile offenders as discussed previously. However, restorative justice techniques for adult offenders in Canada and New Zealand were less successful in recidivism reduction (Aos, et al., 2006).

Some restorative justice initiatives have been criticized for still being centered around offenders (Bazemore et al, 2012). Another reported problem is that some victims are not able to communicate or advocate on their own behalf, so restorative justice exerts too much pressure on them. Since restorative processes depend on a victim actively participating, the victim takes on a role that is more emotionally draining than simply filing an arrest report with the police. One final point is the use of reintegrative shaming as a core component of restorative justice to invoke empathy within the offender. While this technique seems to help in the change process, we must be careful with avoiding shame in a stigmatizing way that increases future offending (Botchkovar & Tittle, 2008).

Restorative justice sanctions are primarily economic in nature (paying back losses) and labor-intensive (bettering the community). Economic sanctions such as restitution, community service, and fines, used in both restorative and traditional justice systems, are discussed next.

RESTITUTION

Crime victims in the United States suffer tangible losses of over $105 billion every year. Part of that loss is returned or restored by the very people who caused the harm in the first place. **Restitution** consists of court-ordered payment by an offender to a victim (or a victim's family) to cover tangible losses that occurred during or following a crime. Restitution has a long history around the world. The Old Testament specified a fivefold restitution for stealing and then killing an ox, and a fourfold restitution for stealing and killing a sheep. Double restitution was mandated for stealing (Exodus 21). Leviticus stipulated that restitution plus an additional fifth be made by robbers (Leviticus 6). The Code of Hammurabi, developed between 1792 and 1750 BCE, mandated a thirtyfold restitution if the victim was a "god" or a "palace" and a tenfold restitution if the victim was a "villein" (a low-status laborer). British philosopher Jeremy Bentham (1748–1833) prescribed restitution as an essential means of making a punishment fit the crime.

TRUTH OR FICTION?

The victims feel dissatisfied and do not receive justice when their perpetrator does not go to jail.

FICTION

FACT: Victims who decide to participate in restorative justice options report feeling satisfied with the outcomes. Victims are more likely to receive closure on their cases when their pain has been acknowledged and they have been compensated by their offenders.

restitution
Court-ordered payment by an offender to a victim to cover tangible losses that occurred during or following a crime.

FIGURE 10.3
Benefits of Restitution in
Restorative Justice.

Restitution typically refers to money, but it can also encompass an offender working for a victim without pay to provide direct services. The money or services offered by an offender helps a victim financially. Restitution is also designed to be an act of atonement for a criminal (see Figure 10.3 for the benefits of restitution).

Benefits of Restitution in Restorative Justice

Restitution was an important custom in the mid-1800s when Quaker prison reformer Elizabeth Fry viewed repaying a victim as a step toward offender rehabilitation. The authority of courts to grant restitution in the United States originates from federal statutes. From 1925 to 1982, restitution could only be imposed as a condition of probation, and it was strictly discretionary. Thus if an offender went to prison, incarceration was used as punishment in lieu of restitution. Stephen Schafer believed that the criminal justice system had become too centered on the offender and the state's interests, to the point that the crime victim was lost in the process. As the victim rights movement in the 1980s gained momentum, judges had to provide reasons for not ordering restitution in cases with tangible losses and an identified victim. In the 1990s, Congress passed a series of three acts to increase the offenses for which restitution could be collected:

1992	Mandatory provision for courts to impose restitution for back child support
1994	Violence Against Women Act passed to mandate restitution in cases of sexual abuse, sexual exploitation of children, domestic violence, and telemarketing fraud
1996	Mandatory Victims' Restitution Act passed to require that restitution be imposed for violent crimes and Title 18 property offenses, and as a sentencing option in juvenile delinquency cases

As a result of these acts, victims were more likely to receive judgments in criminal and civil cases. The remaining problem was enforcing the court order so that victims could collect their restitution. Victims receive very little information about how to collect restitution through traditional criminal and civil courts. Through restorative justice and presentence efforts, restitution is enforced and collected at greater rates than in the past.

Losses Eligible for Compensation

States have broadened the types of losses eligible for compensation as well as the parties eligible to receive restitution. For example, restitution is available for the purpose of lost income as a result of physical injury or time in court, medical expenses, transportation to and from the courthouse, necessary child care during litigation, expenses involving the investigation and prosecution of the case, counseling sessions, sexual assault exams, human immunodeficiency virus (HIV) testing, occupational and rehabilitative therapy, moving expenses, case-related travel and meal expenses, and burial expenses. Restitution may be ordered for psychological counseling in cases in which a victim has suffered physical injury (*United States v. Laney*, 1999). Restitution is limited to the replacement value of direct or actual losses as a result of a crime and cannot be ordered for losses defined as indirect or consequential, such as victims' attorney fees.

Eligible parties may include a victim or a victim's family (in cases of homicide). Eligible organizations that may receive restitution include those that provided medical care, shelter, or counseling to a victim. Many states authorize the collection of interest on the unpaid restitution amount. Victims typically apply for restitution through the prosecutor's office. To receive restitution, a victim must press charges and agree to testify if necessary. Restitution is declared a victim's right in about half of all state constitutions even when the offender has been incarcerated. Despite the mandatory policy, victims are more likely to be reimbursed if the offender is sentenced to a community sanction so that he or she can work to pay the victim back. In other states where restitution is defined as offender rehabilitation, restitution is forfeited if the offender goes to prison.

Problems Associated with Restitution

Restitution remains underutilized in both misdemeanor and felony cases. Nationally, adult courts have ordered restitution in 21% of felony convictions and only 14% of misdemeanors. For felony crimes, restitution is most commonly ordered in property offenses or public order offenses (Bureau of Justice Statistics, 2013). Restitution was ordered in about 33% of juvenile cases, and this was linked to the juveniles being old enough to have a job and be able to pay the restitution, or court concerns about parents paying the restitution (Haynes et al., 2014).

Restitution has been more often required for probationers than for people sentenced to prison, most likely because people on probation have the means to pay restitution whereas prisoners usually do not. Even though restitution may not often be court-ordered even when it is mandatory by law, a study of restitution-eligible cases determined that restitution was ordered in property crimes more often than person crimes, and ordered more often for females, Caucasian offenders, and those who are older and without criminal history (Haynes, 2011).

One barrier to obtaining restitution is a victim's lack of participation in the justice process and lack of knowledge that restitution is available. Many victims fail to request restitution or have not retained documentation showing their losses. Three other problems associated with restitution are indigence of the defendant, determining the restitution amount, and collecting restitution.

INDIGENT OFFENDERS If a defendant is indigent and cannot pay, courts generally cannot cite that defendant for contempt or send him or her to prison. However, indigence at the time of sentencing does not entitle an offender to immunity from restitution; restitution is more dependent on an offender's future ability to pay (*United States v. Bachsian*, 1993). If a defendant is able to pay but refuses, then incarceration is valid. In the federal system, if an incarcerated prisoner must pay restitution and has the ability to pay, parole release can be contingent upon him or her first paying off the entire restitution amount while incarcerated. There are other standards in some state jurisdictions. For example, an Indiana court ruled that the decision to incarcerate a probationer for failure to pay depends solely on the type of probationary sentence. If restitution is ordered as a suspended sentence, a defendant could be imprisoned for being unable to pay. If restitution is ordered as part of a direct probation sentence, a defendant cannot be imprisoned simply for failure to pay (*Wooden v. State*, 2001).

Declaring bankruptcy no longer excuses offenders from paying restitution. A federal statute declared that restitution orders are not dischargeable in Chapter 13 bankruptcies (11 U.S.C.A., sec 1328(a)(3)). A Texas Criminal Appeals court extended this same line of reasoning to Chapter 7 bankruptcy cases (*Cabla v. State*, 1999).

DETERMINING THE RESTITUTION AMOUNT In restorative justice cases, restitution amounts are determined at a victim-offender mediation session. In traditional criminal or civil cases, the court sets restitution amounts according to harm caused to a victim and a defendant's ability to pay based on full disclosure of assets and liabilities. Probation officers who complete PSI reports can suggest a restitution amount to the sentencing judge. To accurately determine a restitution amount, probation officers consider the harms to the victim that are directly caused by the offense along with which harms qualify for restitution. An offender's existing financial obligations and ability to pay are considered as well as whether or not a victim was insured or was partially at fault. A defendant usually has an opportunity prior to sentencing to challenge a victim's claims or the amount of restitution recommended in the PSI.

Because it is often difficult to accurately establish a fair restitution amount, the government has the burden to prove, based on preponderance of the evidence, that a victim did suffer the harm for which he or she is requesting restitution from an offender. The amount of restitution must be based on expenses a victim incurred by the time of sentencing and can be based only on the offense for which an offender was actually convicted.

Collecting Restitution

Collecting restitution is the responsibility of probation officers, day reporting centers, and restitution centers. The entity responsible for collecting restitution acts as both finance officer and collection agent by determining the weekly or monthly installment payment schedule and making sure the victim receives the money. Less than half of felony offenders had paid restitution in full by the time they completed their sentence. Offenders who get too far behind on payments or who are able to pay but refuse to do so might be reassigned to a formal collection agency.

Three ways that have been used to increase restitution collection rates are by notifying an offender through letters and phone calls, restorative justice techniques, and presentence efforts. One experiment determined that sending an informational letter on what is owed versus what has already been paid achieves

---

TRUTH OR FICTION?

Victims are more likely to receive restitution payments if their offender is given a community corrections sentence than if the offender is sentenced to jail or prison.

TRUE

FACT: Most incarcerated prisoners are unable to pay restitution, as they do not earn wages for working. Restitution payments are more likely to be enforced when an offender is employed at a regular job, which occurs during a community corrections sentence.

| **BOX 10.1** | **COMMUNITY CORRECTIONS UP CLOSE** |

Can Restitution Be Collected *Before* Sentencing?

Given that offenders sentenced to prison have no incentive to make restitution payments and that some offenders would rather go to jail to avoid making payments, the restitution burden is largely left to parole officers who become collection agents. The officers attempt to garnish wages to collect as much restitution as possible from an offender before a sentence expires.

Having become wiser, the federal justice system has changed the way it administers restitution with a more effective method. Once an offender decides to plead guilty, federal plea agreements now require defendants to complete a financial affidavit listing all assets and liabilities, including real estate, vehicles, mutual funds, and any other personal property valued over a certain amount. The financial litigation unit runs a credit report and conducts a search for assets to complete its investigation. Then the defendant is required to pay restitution with those assets, all before sentencing. Having a defendant pay before sentencing gives a prosecutor leverage with the plea agreement. If the defendant has completed restitution payments in full or at least attempted to make good, the prosecutor can make a deal with the defendant for a more lenient sentence, giving him or her an incentive. If the defendant does not pay, sentencing will be harsher and an attempt will be made to collect restitution through the backdoor—as many jurisdictions do now. The collection of presentence restitution has resulted in receipts of $5.25 million in one year.

Source: Stottmann, Jonathan O. 2007. Presentence restitution: When opportunity knocks. *News and Views* 32 (19): September 10.

a better result than a letter that contains additional rationalizations for why they should pay their restitution, which may cause resentment (Ruback et al., 2014). Notification letters seemed to work for employed probationers who wished to avoid prison but had less effect on offenders who were already in prison. However, threats have limited effectiveness and not only will increase resentment, but incarceration for nonpayment is a very costly option. Some systems will not release an offender from parole early until all restitution has been satisfied. Box 10.1 discusses a unique practice that the federal government has been doing to collect restitution.

But what about collecting restitution from a youthful offender? Juvenile court judges are more likely to order in restitution-eligible cases that the youth pay fees than restitution. Judges do not seem to be utilizing restitution fully, especially in youth felony cases in traditional juvenile court (Haynes et al., 2014). Another option of course is VOM, which requires that the victim agrees to meet with the offender, and restitution is made a large part of the incentive for victim participation. Restorative justice sessions increased restitution collection rates, where youth offenders genuinely wanted to pay back the victim and society, but they didn't seem to significantly affect future offending (Kim & Gerber, 2012).

COMMUNITY SERVICE

Community service is one of the most cost effective, yet most underused sanction in the United States. **Community service** is defined as unpaid service to the public to compensate society for harm done by an offender. Community service is typically ordered by a judge as part of probation; the place of work is chosen by either a judge or a supervising officer. Community service might consist of working for a tax-supported or nonprofit agency, such as a hospital, public park, or library,

community service
Unpaid labor on behalf of the public to compensate society for harm done by an offense of conviction.

or for a poverty or public works program. The most frequent type of community service work is picking up roadside litter, doing landscape maintenance, removing graffiti, and painting buildings. Some work assignments have trucks or vans that transport work crews to a site where they are supervised for the day, but most assignments require an offender to take the initiative and report to complete a service order.

History of Community Service

Community service first began in the United States as an organized program in 1966 in Alameda County, California. This initiative was created as a substitute for paying fines for low-income female traffic offenders. The women worked without pay in lieu of their fine and avoided jail for fine nonpayment. Because of the positive attention this program received, hundreds of community service programs were established in the 1970s for juveniles and nonviolent adults. In the United States, community service developed as an alternative to fines or as an additional condition of probation.

THE ENGLISH MODEL? Community service suffices in England and Wales as an acceptable alternative to prison for crimes considered minor, such as petty theft or drug possession. Special community service officers administer the sanction. The English model became popular in other areas of Europe, such as Scotland, Switzerland, and the Netherlands. The United States did not follow the English model, believing instead that community service was not punitive enough to substitute for prison. It is not uncommon to see U.S. judges' order between 100 and 1,000 hours of community service in addition to other probation conditions. This difference in national perceptions of community service demonstrates that, in comparison with most other countries in the world, community corrections sanctions in the United States are more punitive (and are not just reflected in long prison sentences).

Purpose of Community Service

Community service is now used in both traditional and community/problem-solving courts (drug, mental health, DWI). Community service is a good example of a restorative justice program *if offenders work alongside community volunteers* in meaningful projects so that offenders can learn marketable skills. Restorative community service can ultimately result in a high level of community support than the traditional work crews alongside the road (Wood, 2012, 2013). Community service generally serves up to four purposes, depending on the circumstances of each offender:

- Helps nonprofit organizations that serve impoverished individuals, and helps individuals stranded in disaster areas (Restorative)
- Provides an alternative sanction for indigent offenders who are unable to afford payment of fines (Fairness)
- An offender's time and freedom is partially restricted until the work is completed (Punitive)
- Appropriate for wealthy offenders whose financial resources are so great that fines/fees have little punitive effect (Punitive)
- Offenders feel they have helped someone in need and increases their self esteem (Rehabilitative)

Rehabilitation occurs when offenders are allowed to do something constructive, reducing their isolation from society, and knowing that they benefitted someone else through their efforts. In comparison with restitution, community service does not require a victim.

Prevalence of Community Service

According to Table 10.2, community service was used as part of probation sentences for 26% of misdemeanants and 22% of felony probationers nationwide (Bureau of Justice Statistics, 2013). Although community service is used as a jail alternative, it is rarely or ever used as a sole sanction. The number of hours of community service varies depending on the nature and seriousness of an offense. For example, Texas assigns the following community service hours for probation (Texas Code of Criminal Procedure, Art. 42.12, Sec. 22(a)(1)):

PUNISHMENT RANGE	MAXIMUM HOURS	MINIMUM HOURS
First-degree felony	1,000	320
Second-degree felony	800	240
Third-degree felony	600	160
State jail felony	400	120
Class A misdemeanor	200	80
Class B misdemeanor	100	24

Community service orders ranged from 20 to 600 hours, with the average number of hours at 230 for felons and 60 for misdemeanants. In most jurisdictions, an offender's employment status must be considered in determining the community service schedule. Because employed offenders must be able to work and retain gainful employment, they are limited to 16 hours of community service per week. Unemployed offenders can perform up to 32 community service hours per week. Offenders in some jurisdictions may be able to perform community service in lieu of a fine or, with judicial permission, in lieu of incarceration. In some jurisdictions, eight hours of community service is equivalent to one day of jail confinement, regardless of the offense committed.

TABLE 10.2   Probationers Who Were Ordered to Fines, Community Service, Restitution, and Treatment

Most serious conviction/ offense	PERCENT WHOSE PROBATION SENTENCE INCLUDED			
	Fine	Treatment	Community Service	Restitution
All offenses	28%	27%	23%	20%
Felonies	28	29	22	21
Violent offenses	26	29	27	22
Property offenses	19	18	23	37
Drug offenses	36	45	21	7
Public-order offenses	27	16	22	26
Misdemeanors	27	13	26	14

A defendant may have received none of these or more than one of these probation conditions.

Source: Bureau of Justice Statistics. 2013. *Felony Defendants in Large Urban Counties, 2009.* (December). Table 28. Washington DC: U.S. Department of Justice.

Effectiveness of Community Service

Many nonprofit organizations, such as churches, homeless shelters, libraries, and the U.S. Forest Service, have benefited from the labor provided by offenders (see Larry's case featured in Box 10.2). Completion rates vary from 50% to a high of 85%, depending on how community service is tracked or enforced. Rarely are probationers extended on probation because they fail to complete community service hours.

Community service has enjoyed wide public support even though it has only been empirically evaluated by a few researchers. For example, community service is able to lower recidivism over a similar matched group of jailed offenders (Wermink et al., 2010). Bouffard and Muftic (2007) compared community service with fines for DUI misdemeanants. Despite only a 50% successful completion of community service compared to over 90% of offenders who paid their fines in full, community service offenders were less likely to recidivate later (Bouffard & Muftic, 2007).

Killias and colleagues conducted an experiment to randomly assign 240 traffic offenders in Switzerland to community service or to electronic monitoring. Reconviction rates were higher in the community service group (31%) compared to the electronic monitoring group (21%). Social integration was measurably better with the electronic monitoring group as well, favoring electronic monitoring methods over community service as a sole community sanction, although it was difficult to determine the amount of supervision the community service program provided in this instance (Killias et al., 2010).

As the search continues for less costly and more effective methods of dealing with offenders, community service has the potential to be a growing trend in U.S. corrections. One difficult problem with evaluating and expanding community service programs is that most do not have clear goals and objectives. In expanding their use, the following considerations must be delineated:

- Is the purpose of community service to reduce recidivism, to divert offenders, or both?
- Should community service be used instead of or in addition to other sanctions?

BOX 10.2 **COMMUNITY CORRECTIONS UP CLOSE**

Larry's Community Service

Larry worked as a cashier at a local retail store. He had long been suspected of skimming small amounts of money off the cash register and of stealing office products from the store. An investigation led to Larry and two other employees being fired and prosecuted for misdemeanor theft. Larry was ordered to pay a fine and perform 300 hours of community service.

Larry was very close to obtaining his college degree in elementary education. The community service center decided to assign Larry to work a 7-hour shift once a week at an elementary school for 42 weeks.

He was initially assigned to playground and lunchroom duties, but his teaching abilities were so impressive that he became the third-grade reading tutor. Students who were tutored by Larry improved their grades and overall classroom behavior. At the end of his community service, Larry felt he had not only touched the lives of children, but he had received much more in return.

Question for Discussion: What other community service placements would be appropriate for offenders with special skills?

- Should community service be expanded for prison-bound offenders?
- How is the value of community service work calculated compared to days in jail or fine amounts?

There are no easy answers to these questions. The potential for use of community service with careful supervision and program administration without further increasing community risk is promising.

FINES

The English jurist Jeremy Bentham (1748–1832) once said, "A fine is a license paid in arrears." In other words, instead of buying beforehand permission to engage in a certain activity, an offender, if caught, pays a fine later. In modern times, a **fine** is defined as a judge-imposed monetary sanction amount that depends on the severity of the offense. The modern fine is meant to be a penalty for engaging in criminal behavior, but as you will see, fines are discretionary and oftentimes will disadvantage indigent offenders because most state laws in the United States do not require judges to consider an offender's ability to pay the fine (Harris et al., 2011).

fine
A fixed monetary sanction defined by statute and imposed by a judge, depending on the seriousness of a crime.

A fine can be imposed as a sole penalty, as in the case of traffic offenses, or accompanied by probation, an intermediate sanction, or incarceration. Throughout European criminal justice systems, fines are used as a primary sanction, as alternatives to incarceration, and structured according to the offense severity and percentage of an offender's income, or ability to pay. For example, in Germany more than 80% of all crimes committed by adults are punished by a fine as the only penalty. Since the fine is assessed as a percentage of one's income, the penalty is the same regardless of how much money one has or earns. Compared to many other countries, fines in the United States are fixed amounts that are tied to offense severity. Since fines in the United States are fixed amounts, their use is more limited.

Prevalence of Fines

Fines are used in only 25% of all state felony cases, most typically as an addition to probation (Bureau of Justice Statistics, 2013). An average fine amount in Washington State was nearly $1,400 per felony conviction. With the accumulation of other legal debt and interest over a period of years, the true average was closer to $11,500 per person with previous criminal records (Harris et al., 2011). In the federal system, fines are used as the sole means of punishment in nearly one-third of misdemeanor offenses but in less than 1% of all federal felony cases. Organizational or corporate defendants in federal corporate or white-collar crime are the exception—where fines are routinely imposed as a primary and sole sanction. According to the United States Sentencing Commission (2010, p. 510):

> The base fine is determined in one of three ways: (1) by the amount based on the offense [seriousness] level...(2) by the pecuniary gain to the organization from the offense; and (3) by the pecuniary loss caused by the organization, to the extent that the loss was caused intentionally, knowingly or recklessly.

Whichever loss is deemed the greatest of these three types is the one selected. This helps to ensure that organizations seek to detect and report such gains in the future and/or prevent intentional losses from happening again. Organizational fines using these guidelines typically range from $5,000 up to $72 million (*United States Sentencing Commission*, 2010).

Monthly payments of fines or fees are expected from the offender while on probation.

iStockphoto.com/DigitalZombie

When a fine is imposed in individual-level federal felony cases, they have ranged from $28 to as much as $10,000, with an overall average fine of $1,400. State-level judges rarely have information on a defendant's ability to pay, so eligibility rests largely on offense severity and prior criminal record. One study showed "...strong evidence that ethnicity and its interaction with offense type significantly impact imposition of monetary sanctions in Washington State. Latino defendants whose charges are stereotype congruent are penalized most harshly" (Harris et al., 2011, p. 254). Individuals of Latino ethnicity who were convicted of drug offenses were assessed significantly higher fines on average ($1,666) than were Caucasian ($1,458) and African-American offenders ($978). Fixed fines may overly burden an indigent person but be less consequential to an affluent offender. When a financial penalty is too high, however, offenders are significantly less likely to pay, and may opt to get their probation revoked in other ways, such as by using drugs or alcohol.

Revoking Probation for Fine Nonpayment

A substantial number of probationers do not satisfy their entire financial obligation. What happens if a defendant does not pay the whole fine? A defendant can avoid paying a fine, in part or in full, if he or she is demonstrably unable to pay. The U.S. Supreme Court held that probation cannot be revoked solely because of an offender's inability to pay a fine or restitution, because revocation based on indigence violates the equal protection clause of the Fourteenth Amendment (*Bearden v. Georgia*, 1983). The Court distinguished, however, between indigence (inability) and unwillingness (refusal) to pay. Unwillingness to pay court-ordered restitution or fines despite a probationer's ability to do so may result in revocation. Statutes in most states and the federal system allow a flexible payment schedule if a defendant is unable to pay an entire fine immediately, modifying a sentence to reduce the fine and in some cases rescinding the fine and imposing an alternative sanction. For federal prisoners who do not get their fine reduced or rescinded, the federal system requires that a fine must be paid in full prior to release from prison.

Ninety percent of fines paid by offenders go to victim/witness assistance programs or to a **victim compensation fund**, which are operated by state and federal governments that compensate victims of violent crime for losses not covered by restitution (Ruback & Bergstrom, 2006). Since fines are paid to the government and not to private parties, it stands to reason why courts are not authorized to order a defendant to pay fines to private charities, as decided by one federal appellate court (*United States v. Wolff*, 1996).

victim compensation fund
A state fund that dispenses compensation to victims of violent crime, paid for by convicted offenders.

INCREASING PAYMENTS OF FINES AND RESTITUTION   One of the drawbacks of imposing any type of financial obligation is the court response if offenders fail to follow through. Traditionally that response has been "jail therapy" (that is, incarceration). How then do we increase the numbers of probationers who make payments of fines and restitution without increasing incarceration rates? An experiment was conducted for low-risk, work-capable probationers who were court-ordered to pay fines/restitution but who missed three months or more of payments or were 60% or more in arrears of the total amount (Weisburd et al., 2008). Selected probationers were assigned at random to one of three groups: (a) no change in supervision; (b) served with a violation of probation and an upcoming court date; or (c) served with a violation notice, received employment training, and were ordered to complete an additional 15 hours of community service per each week that payments were missed. After six months, the researchers found that probationers in Groups 2 and 3 were more likely to make court-ordered payments than those in the "do nothing" Group 1. It seems that the threat of probation violation was enough of a motivation to increase payment, although undertaking extra community service did *not* contribute to paying fines and restitution (Weisburd et al., 2008). The threat of punishment is only as good as the means to carry out that threat. With low-risk offenders, the threat of incarceration is costly and ensures that the fine/restitution will never get paid.

Box 10.3 discusses how technology has helped probation and parole officers to be more successful in collecting fines, restitution, and fees. Recommendations to increase fine and restitution payments include (a) clearer payment instructions for offenders; (b) positive motivation to encourage payments in full;

| BOX 10.3 | **TECHNOLOGY IN CORRECTIONS** | |

Using Databases to Track Offender Fines, Fees, and Restitution

An important function of a probation and parole officers' job is to ensure that each offender remains current on their payment schedule that can include fines, restitution, and/or fees. In the past, the officers were the ones responsible for collecting the money and keeping track of the balances of each person's payment schedule. Valuable time was being spent on the financial aspects, which took away from time spent on other supervision and rehabilitative tasks. Databases can now track this information automatically to send out reminders to offenders based on a preset payment schedule, and they can also alert the officers if a client has fallen behind on their payments. A database

called Offender Payment Enhanced Reporting Access (OPERA) is used throughout the federal system. A variety of companies offer full service collection services to state and local parole and probation departments, so that officers no longer have to be the collection agents. Two providers include Syscon Justice Systems (www.syscon.net) or Fieldware, LLC, (www.fieldware.com) both of which are full service fee management and collection agencies that contract out with state and local government.

Source: U.S. Courts. 2011. *2010 Annual Report.* Available at: http://www.uscourts.gov/uscourts/federalcourts/annualreport/2010

(c) designation of a central officer or public official to collect fines; and (d) authorization of that official either to file a court order holding an offender in contempt of court or to file a civil lawsuit against that offender for the remaining fine balance (Ruback et al., 2006; Ruback et al., 2014).

FEES AND COURT COSTS

fee
A monetary amount imposed by a court to assist in administering the criminal justice system through an offender's repayment of the debt accrued by an investigation, prosecution, and supervision of a case.

While fines are meant for punishment, a **fee** is a court-imposed reimbursement that an offender pays directly to the courts to help defray administrative costs within the criminal justice system. Fees are also known as "court costs" in other regions of the country. The two terms have the same meaning, so we will use fees in this text. Fees are the government's attempt to recover from individual offenders the expenses incurred in the investigation and prosecution of a defendant's case. One thing is clear: Acquitted defendants do not pay fees. Convicted offenders and even those supervised on deferred adjudication pay fees, although an individual can apply for a fee reduction based on inability to pay. Some fees are mandatory for everyone, while other fees are based only on if a particular service is used. A sample fee schedule is provided in Table 10.3.

TABLE 10.3 Sample Fines and Fee Schedule

FINES	
$200–$10,000	General Victim Compensation Fund* (considered as part of a discretionary fine in some states, *OR* as a fixed mandatory fee in other states)
MANDATORY FEES	
$100	Provide a DNA sample (first-time offenders only—not applicable for repeat offenders who are in the system)
$1,000–$5,000	Repayment of attorney's fees or appointed defense counsel (only for defendants who were later found *not* to be indigent)
DISCRETIONARY FEES (IF APPLICABLE OR ASSESSED WHEN USING SPECIFIC COMMUNITY SUPERVISION PROGRAMS)	
$60 per month	Probation
$20 per month	Radio frequency electronic monitoring
$75 per month	Global positioning system electronic monitoring
$60 per month	Ignition interlock
$80 per month	Antabuse (prescription to prevent alcohol use)
$250	DWI classes (8)
$100	Community service administration fee
$400 per month	Residential Community Corrections Facility (work release or halfway house)
$8 per test	Drug and/or alcohol tests (urinalysis)
$75	Diagnostic testing (mental illness, substance abuse, etc.)
No charge	Inpatient substance abuse treatment
$40–$75 per month	Outpatient treatment (assuming once per week)
$200	Court-appointed attorney for indigent defendants
$200–$1,000	Court costs for defendants who go to trial (for complex investigations, evidence testing, hearings)

A fee is not considered punitive and is therefore subject to different legal standards for nonpayment than a fine, restitution, or payments for court-ordered treatment. Courts have held that it is unacceptable to require an indigent defendant to pay court costs. However, probation departments that are locally operated by a county court (such as those in rural areas) seem to rely more heavily on fees to raise revenue (Ruback & Bergstrom, 2006). Many probation departments keep most of the supervision fees they collect as an incentive to collect the fees, and some even consider fee collection rates when probation officers are evaluated (Peterson, 2012). Thus, county-level probation officers seem to focus more heavily on the collection of fees more so than parole officers or other state-operated probation departments. Most courts will extend probation terms for failure to pay debt. Probationers who miss payments become fearful that they will get automatically revoked due to "...aggressive collection tactics by probation officers deter poor people from showing up to probation meetings if they lack the resources to make a required payment - leading these same probation officers to issue a probation violation for the failure to appear." (Bannon et al., 2010, p. 24) Ironically, probationers can get revoked for missing too many appointments, but cannot get revoked for missing payments as long as they are making an effort to pay. A second related concern is whether compliant probationers (those who can make their payments) are released from supervision early, or whether they are carried longer on a caseload because of the revenue they provide the department.

To what degree does probation serve as a collection agency? Requiring probation or parole officers to collect fees reduces officers to collection agents and would seem to diminish their counseling role. There is also a difference between what happens to fees collected by federal probation versus state and local probation agencies. On the one hand, monthly federal probation fees are no longer separate from the fine; instead, the cost of supervision seems to be rolled into the fine amount, making the two less distinct. Most federal fine monies go to the national crime victims' fund, and it is unclear how much of this money is returned back to federal probation. On the other hand, most states allow local departments to not only keep a higher percentage of the fees collected, but they can also decide debt priority—in other words, which type of debt to focus on to pay first (Peterson, 2012). The problem with fees is that they are recurring so long as the offender remains on supervision, and if they are collected before other types of debt, the balances on child support, fines, and restitution never seem to go down. For that reason, it is recommended that probationer and parolee debt be prioritized as follows:

1. Child support payments
2. Victim restitution
3. Fines
4. Fees

Finally, Peterson (2012) recommends that monthly probation and parole fees be replaced by a different type of fee structure that considers an individual offender's situation/risk level, one that is not tied to officer job performance and one that provides judges with more discretionary authority.

FORFEITURES

When material items are acquired through profit directly resulting from illegal activities, those items are subject to seizure by police and are resold, with those proceeds donated according to state law. This is called **forfeiture** because

forfeiture
A government seizure of property that has been illegally obtained, has been acquired with resources that were illegally obtained, or has been used in connection with an illegal activity.

the government takes away any property used in connection with an illegal activity—namely, from drug trafficking and distribution (Ruback & Bergstrom, 2006). Although any property may be seized, cash, homes, and cars are the most typical items, as part of either a criminal or civil action.

In a criminal case, forfeiture occurs after a conviction. But in a civil case, forfeiture can occur when proof by a preponderance of evidence is met. Preponderance of evidence is a lower standard of proof than the threshold of beyond a reasonable doubt required in criminal court. The purpose of forfeiture is to make certain that offenders do not keep illegal property and make a profit, and to discourage criminals from using houses and businesses to conduct criminal transactions. Unlike a traditional fixed fine, forfeiture is not considered a punishment by the Supreme Court. However, a forfeiture is limited in that it must not be "grossly disproportionate to the gravity of the defendant's offense [or else] the forfeiture would violate the excessive fines clause" of the Eighth Amendment (Ruback & Bergstrom, 2006, p. 257). In the past, about 40,000 forfeitures occurred every year, 80% of which are civil and the remaining 20% from criminal cases. It seems that civil asset forfeitures had become quite prevalent with state and local law enforcement at traffic stops *before* a conviction. Critics question that these traffic stop interdiction efforts may be a violation of due process and an abuse of the purpose of the forfeiture law (http://www.cnn.com/2015/01/21/us /asset-seizures/index.html).

A well-known forfeiture case in recent times was the $17 billion Ponzi scheme of Bernie Madoff's 2009 conviction and subsequent 150-year sentence to federal prison for securities fraud, investment fraud, money laundering, and lying to the Securities and Exchange Commission. The case was in federal bankruptcy court to recover as much of the money as possible for the victims. As of September 2012, only about 9.15 billion of assets and property, representing 53% of the original amount, was recovered. Apparently, Madoff's 1,230 victims have collectively received about one-third of the recovered money, totaling 3.63 billion—nowhere near the money they actually lost (Reuters, 2012).

In reviewing all the different types of economic sanctions in this chapter (restitution, fines, fees, and forfeitures), there are many ways the justice system has added to one's legal debt that impact the ability to pay other necessary bills that were not really discussed, such as child support, alimony, and credit card debt. While credit card debt may be reduced by declaring bankruptcy, and child support payments can be garnished through having a job, legal debt must be paid. Not paying legal debt when the offender has the ability to pay, means the debt continues to accrue interest (even while incarcerated) and cannot be removed through declaring bankruptcy. With an average previous fine amount at nearly $11,500 per person not including fees, child support or credit card debt (Harris et al., 2011), it is conceivable that many offenders risk sinking into greater poverty than they do bettering themselves financially after a conviction. Some former offenders may be unable to climb out of debt and may ultimately be forced to give up their freedom—doing time may seem like an option over paying back a mountain of debt. We discuss more about reentry in the next chapter.

SUMMARY

- Community justice is a philosophy of using the community—through community policing, community courts, and neighborhood-based probation—to control and reduce crime.

- Once a crime has been committed, restorative justice emphasizes an offender taking responsibility to repair the harm done to victim and surrounding community.

- Restorative justice is more victim-centered than traditional methods of criminal justice, involving the victim and the community throughout an entire process of justice.

- Restorative justice programs rely heavily on community partners and volunteers to carry out mediation, reparation boards, face-to-face meetings with victims, and victim impact classes. Present patterns in the use of restitution

vary widely, although observers predict greater emphasis on restitution in the future, particularly in conjunction with other sentences.

- Community service also holds promise, but at present its provision is not well enforced.

- The use of fixed fines is still perceived as either too lenient or too problematic for impoverished offenders, sinking deeper into poverty as a result.

- Fees are a monthly payment by an offender that helps curb the cost of community supervision.

- Forfeitures are material items or property acquired from criminal activities that are seized by police, inspected for contraband, and resold at regulated auctions.

- Collection rates of the various economic sanctions remain fairly low at present.

DISCUSSION QUESTIONS

1. How is restorative justice different from traditional justice approaches?

2. How do monetary restitution and community service differ? How are they alike?

3. How can restitution be used for juveniles who are too young to legally work full time?

4. Is it fair to require that probationers pay court costs but not parolees? Why or why not?

5. Why is the collection of fines treated differently from the collection of fees? Should they be treated the same if they are not paid in full?

6. Why do you think day fines have not caught on in American criminal justice?

 # WEBSITES, VIDEOS, AND PODCASTS

Websites

Restorative justice resources
http://restorativejustice.org

The Center of Restorative Justice and Peacemaking, University of Minnesota
http://www.cehd.umn.edu/ssw/rjp/

The Center for Restorative Justice, Simon Fraser University, Canada
http://www.sfu.ca/crj

Restorative Justice Ministry Network of North America
http://www.rjmn.net

Bridges to Life: Faith-Based Restorative Justice Program
http://www.bridgestolife.org

National Center for Victims of Crime
http://www.victimsofcrime.org/

The purpose of economic sanctions
http://www.econlib.org/library/Enc/Sanctions.html

Videos/Podcasts

Bridges to Life Restorative Justice Program, PBS Video
A video about the Bridges to Life program aired on PBS. http://www.youtube.com /watch?v=Z8HZmD9VckY

Why Restorative Justice Works, Part 1 and 2
http://www.youtube.com/watch?v=yAbn6hhMBLs
http://www.youtube.com/watch?v=nAw2ZfsikGc
&feature=related

Probation and Community Supervision

(Length: 9 minutes) Community service projects are carried out in a number of environments from schools, reserves, churches, wherever there is a community need. https://www.youtube.com/watch?v=rp_aiS7EYOA

CASE STUDY EXERCISES

Restorative Justice

In each of the following scenarios, assume that you are a prosecutor or judge and wish to refer a case to one of the four available restorative justice options. Which restorative justice option is best suited to each case, and why?

CASE A: Cross Burning at a Southern Baptist Church

An 18-year-old male with no prior record has been convicted of a "hate" crime. He, with two juveniles (ages 15 and 16), burned a cross in the yard of a church and painted derogatory racial messages on its front door. Most of the church congregation is African American; the offenders are white, and the 18-year-old is reportedly affiliated with a white supremacist organization. The offender states that he began his involvement with the organization only recently and committed the offense as part of his initiation. The church members are divided on what should be done—half are willing to discuss the issue with the boys while the other half want to press criminal charges. What should the pastor do?

CASE B: Accidental Fire

Anthony and Bernardo, both age 11 are two boys from the neighborhood. They play nearly every day after school at one of the two boys' houses. They can usually find something to do like catching frogs or fishing, or they find other neighborhood kids to start a flag football game. The two boys are bored one day and start snooping around Bernardo's father's workshop. They come across some flammable liquids and matches, which they take out behind the workshop to look at closer, near the next door neighbor's fence. Some of the starter fluid accidentally spills out, and a fire starts on the dried grass. The boys run back to the workshop to find something to put out the fire, but within minutes the

fire spreads to the wooden fence and is licking at the house next door. A neighbor across the street sees smoke and calls the fire department. A corner of the neighbor's siding starts to burn before a fire truck arrives to put out the fire, resulting in about $600 in damages on the house. The neighbor is willing to forgo pressing criminal charges for now, until some restorative justice options can be discussed.

CASE C: Bethany's Bruise

From outward appearances, the Franklins seem like most normal families. Both parents work, the three kids go to school, and the family dog, a German shepherd, stays home. The Franklins keep to themselves after the parents arrive home from work, usually by 7:00 P.M. The kids are usually alone between 4:00 P.M. and 7:00 P.M. Sometimes the neighbors can hear shouting, slamming doors, and loud music blaring from the Franklin home after school, but they assume that with three teenagers inside, that is to be expected. Seeing that Bethany Franklin has a bruised arm, a teacher at school notices handprints on where it appears that Bethany was grabbed. When the teacher asks Bethany what happened, the girl says that it's nothing. A few weeks later, the teacher notices a cut below Bethany's eye and immediately calls Social Services. A Social Service investigation results in interviewing the parents, who deny any wrongdoing. Bethany refuses to reveal how she keeps getting bruises and cuts. The older brother suggests that Bethany probably hurt herself intentionally. However, the younger brother admitted that he saw the older brother grab his sister's arm and twist it. Upon further questioning, the younger brother said this was not the first time he had seen his sister get hurt and proceeded to tell about more incidents involving the older brother. What type of restorative justice response is best in this situation?

Part IV

Special Issues in Community Corrections

The four chapters in this section discuss specialty issues that are paramount to community corrections: challenges offenders face in reentry to the community from prison, the career pathways of community supervision officers, juvenile offenders, and collateral consequences that follow a felony conviction.

Chapter 11 pays particular attention to issues involved in prisoner reentry, which include collateral consequences that affect prisoners when they are attempting to reestablish themselves on parole, types of release from prison, and what a parole board hearing is like. Chapter 12 examines the shortage of probation personnel and pays particular attention to how officers are selected and trained, along with nuances in supervision, such as carrying firearms, legal issues, and privatization of probation. Chapter 13 discusses the juvenile justice system and community corrections programs for juvenile delinquent status offenders and dependent and neglected children who come to the attention of the law. The concluding chapter in the text summarizes the main points of the previous chapters, and also examines possible directions for the future that include how convicted offenders may be able to restore some or all civil rights lost.

Prisoner Reentry: Collateral Consequences, Parole, and Mandatory Release

Chapter 11

CRAIG RUBADOUX/FLORIDA TODAY FILE

CHAPTER OUTLINE

CHAPTER LEARNING OBJECTIVES

1. Examine the preparations needed for reentry while an offender is still incarcerated.

2. Discuss how collateral consequences affect the reentry process.

3. Describe examples of civil rights that are lost as a result of felony conviction.

4. Explain the discretionary parole process of how prisoners become eligible for release.

5. Describe a typical parole board hearing, including legal issues in parole board decisions.

KEY TERMS

reentry
collateral consequences
good moral character
surety bond
subornation of perjury
minimum eligibility date
maximum eligibility date
good time
parole eligibility date
prerelease facility
release plan
parole board
victim impact statement
full board review
reentry courts

B illy Lane, who appeared in reality television shows such as *Monster Garage* and *Biker Build-Off*, is finally able to return to doing what he loves most: building motorcycles. For the past six years, he has been incarcerated in a Florida prison because of a series of poor decisions he made that affected the lives of many around him. The evening of September 4, 2006, Lane was driving his pickup truck along Florida State Road A1A on a suspended driver's license with Erin Derrick in the passenger seat. Lane, who had also been drinking, decided to pass slower traffic ahead of him in a "no pass" zone. Lane's truck didn't get over in time and collided head-on with Gerald Morelock who was riding a Yamaha motorcycle. Morelock was killed, and Lane's passenger was injured. Lane was sued by Morelock's family to pay for medical and funeral expenses, and the parties settled out of court in July 2007 for an undisclosed amount (Sangalang & Gallop, 2014). Because of two pending civil lawsuits, Lane initially pled not guilty in the criminal case and his DUI manslaughter case was scheduled for trial. Following the outcomes from the two civil lawsuits, Lane changed his criminal plea to "no contest" and the charge was reduced to vehicular homicide. In 2009, Lane was sentenced to six years of prison, followed by three years of mandatory post-release supervision. Some of the state prison time was spent in a work release program. In September 2014, Lane was released from prison and his three-year post-release supervision will end in 2017.

Discussion: Do you believe Lane will succeed past his three-year mandatory post-supervision period? Why or why not?

INTRODUCTION

> When he is released, a prisoner is in a real sense cast out into a totally alien society. Overnight he is expected to discard months and years of self-survival tactics, to change his values, to readjust to situations and circumstances that he had long forgotten, and to accept responsibility. More important, he has to overcome, in a society that rejects him, his lack of self-worth; he has to become accepted where he is not wanted. Is it any wonder that so many newly released prisoners feel out of their natural environment, that many first-time, petty offenders leave prison and find someone weak to prey on, or that the recidivism rate is so high? (Grooms, 1982, p. 545)

Although Robert Grooms made this observation over 30 years ago, recently released prisoners today continue to face the exact same challenges. After his own release from prison, Grooms experienced problems finding a job, found he had nothing in common with old friends, and at the same time, felt uncomfortable around "square-johns" (law-abiding people). Female parolees also reported feeling isolated, lonely, and lacking family support but were reluctant to talk to other ex-cons because of the ban against associating with other people with criminal records, such as Alice:

> I know people that used to have the [criminal] life and now they're not in that life. And I would love to be able to talk to them and gain some insight… when I see myself going through troubles that are related to feeling like crap…they know about these things because they're felons. (Opsal, 2015, pp. 199–200)

Grooms did not want to be alone, so he found himself in taverns talking to people about what they had in common: crime, prison, and violence. He wrote:

> I had another problem common among recently released prisoners. I wanted to make up all at once for lost time. I wanted the things that others my age had worked years to achieve, and I wanted them right away. (p. 543)

Lack of mentoring, trying to do too much, not having a concrete plan of employment, and no savings all contribute to a high rate of failure on parole. Issues for female parolees included finding stable housing, finding a job that their parole officer would approve of, resuming the mother role and reconnecting with their dependent children (Opsal, 2015). An added level of complexity is that many parolees return to resource-deprived areas that already lack resources and opportunities and this may also influence recidivism rates (Mears et al., 2008). This chapter discusses the challenges that newly released prisoners face during reentry, including collateral consequences, how prisoners become eligible for release, and what parole board hearings are like.

TRUTH OR FICTION?

Most people go to prison for a long time and rarely get out.

FICTION

FACT: More than 95% of incarcerated prisoners eventually return to their communities—nearly half within a mere two-year period of time.

ISSUES IN REENTRY

More than 95% of incarcerated prisoners eventually return to their communities. Of this number, 80% are released via discretionary or mandatory release (which means they remain under community supervision), while 20% are released after they have served their entire sentence behind bars. Back in Chapter 3, you read about how indeterminate sentencing is tied to discretionary release (at the parole board's discretion), while determinate sentencing is tied to mandatory supervised release in the community through a term defined by statute. For example, Section 3583 (b) of the U.S. Code specifies that Class A and B felons spend a maximum of five years on supervised release following prison, Class C and D felons spend three years, and Class E felons and Class A misdemeanants spend no more than one year being supervised in the community (U.S. Sentencing Commission, 2010).

Regardless of how a prisoner is released, former prisoners fare better when they have been prepared to return through reentry (Wright & Rosky, 2011). **Reentry** is any activity or program dedicated to preparing prisoners for release back into a community as law-abiding citizens using a collaborative approach with parole officers, treatment providers, and citizens.

reentry
A process of preparing and integrating parolees into a community as law-abiding citizens using a collaborative approach with parole officers and treatment providers.

Not only do returning prisoners face daily situations very different from life behind bars but their very identities as to how they define themselves must change, so that over time others no longer see them as a criminal (Opsal, 2011). As ex-offenders begin to realize how others view them, they must be prepared to redeem and heal themselves, shed the prisoner role, resist the stigma associated with being a felon, and resume former responsibilities and roles of parent, spouse, family member, worker, and neighbor, among others (Opsal, 2011). Box 11.1 examines what it is like to get out of prison so you can better understand some of the needs and challenges former prisoners face in coming back to the larger community.

As Box 11.1 illustrates, a number of challenges stand between an offender and successful reentry. First, recently released offenders, though likely indigent, still need an identification card, clothes, and bus pass; up to one-third also need medication for a physical and/or psychological condition. They may not be eligible for certain benefits so their prerelease institution needs to assist them in applying to various programs, which can take a few months for approval.

Second, it is often necessary to actually make appointments for ex-offenders rather than simply handing them a list of referrals. Given federal regulations against openly sharing medical records coupled with the fact that most offenders do not leave prison with medical records in hand, some releasees experience a dangerous lag between the time when their medications run out and when they are able to see a doctor to obtain prescription refills. Because some ex-offenders lack the initiative or education to find a service provider right for their situation, they are more likely to follow through if they are expected to appear for a pre-scheduled appointment.

Third, parolees and other recently released offenders have other survival needs to meet, such as finding and maintaining stable employment, finding suitable housing, and staying clean of illegal drugs (Clark, 2014). They also require transportation to find employment, to go to work, and to attend treatment sessions. Their health care can be overlooked in light of all the other responsibilities that need their attention. In addition to education and employment services, female parolees also have needs for protection from abusive relationships in the community, child advocacy, and assistance with family reunification. Even after incarceration for as little as two months, female releasees experienced shifts in family structure, such as from separation, divorce, and changing location of dependent children (Opsal, 2011).

| BOX 11.1 | COMMUNITY CORRECTIONS UP CLOSE | |

What Might It Be Like to Transition from Prison to the Community?

Imagine that you've just gotten out of prison after spending three years of your life locked up in a boring routine you grew accustomed to. Now that you're out, you want to celebrate, get back with your old friends, and try to catch up on the time you lost. After all, there's a lot of catching up to do. The people and situations you remember seem different, however. When you return to your neighborhood, you realize that the people who were doing well have moved on and all you see there now are those not doing so well. They'll be glad to lend you a couple of bucks or get you drunk so you can celebrate. But those were the same people who participated in this mess to begin with. What now? You burned your bridges with your brothers, who won't talk to you. Your mother will let you stay with her only until you can get on your feet again, but you don't know how long her support will last. You have a daughter who has been living with her (her grandmother); she is now five years old and doesn't even know you. You desperately want to connect with her but don't feel confident you have the skills to make the first move. You also feel guilty for not being able to repay your mom for raising your two sons and are afraid you'll never be able to pay her

back. Although you feel a huge sense of urgency, at the same time fear and depression have set in, and you wonder whether leaving prison early was a mistake.

Like most people who relocate to a new state, offenders need to obtain identification cards, change their address, locate housing, and find a job. If relocation isn't stressful enough, think of the additional challenges of finding a job when you have only a high school education or GED, of having to explain a transient (or nonexistent) employment record, and of bearing the stigma of admitting your felony record. Many people who relocate know when they are moving, whereas often offenders in prison do not know their exact release date very far in advance, which presents an obstacle to plan for anything other than "Who's coming to pick me up?" Other difficulties include overcoming a drug or alcohol addiction, managing stress and anger, and avoiding temptations that lead to the beginnings of bad habits. Most offenders who do not make the transition fall short within the first six months after they leave prison. The reentry process therefore starts while prisoners are incarcerated and attempts to bridge this crucial phase.

Parole officers understood their role in referring parolees on the basis of their needs to community agencies and in assisting ex-prisoners with successful community reentry. When asked to ascertain the most important features of successful reentry programs, steady employment was mentioned by parole officers as the key element, followed by ex-prisoners remaining drug free, having positive social support systems, and experiencing plenty of structure through daily activities.

However, many parolees have a significant amount of apprehension about community reentry—in part due to perceived social alienation, lack of community support, and lack of institutional preparation for release into an environment that requires taking on immediate responsibilities, such as paying rent, looking for employment, sustaining a job, and abiding by supervision conditions—all in a place that limits opportunities to do what is expected. Box 11.2 describes how motivational interviewing (an evidence-based practice introduced in Chapter 5) is used by parole officers to overcome offender resistance to change.

The next section will discuss in more detail the **collateral consequences** that affect people convicted of felonies.

collateral consequences
Civil and/or political rights that are lost temporarily in some cases, or permanently in others, following a felony conviction.

| BOX 11.2 | **EVIDENCE-BASED PRACTICES IN COMMUNITY CORRECTIONS** |

How to Use Motivational Interviewing with Released Prisoners

When paroled and recently released prisoners are ordered to change by a releasing authority such as a parole board, traditional interactions between parolees and their officer required the officer to only focus on whether the offender is following the rules, attending treatment, making progress toward community service hours, and making regular restitution payments. This meant that an officer was only asking supervision-oriented questions, and in dictating to the offender what not to do; the officer never establishes trust with a parolee.

While supervision questions are indeed essential to help the officer complete his or her paperwork, they are not helpful in any way to parolees who struggle daily with staying motivated to change their old habits and behaviors. A communication style called motivational interviewing is essential for officers to learn so that they can build trust and assist an offender in changing and ensuring successful completion of parole (or probation). The community supervision officer creates a positive climate of sincerity and understanding, along with good communication skills to reinforce what the offender is learning in treatment. The key to motivational interviewing is to get offenders to recognize the

cognitive-behavioral problem themselves rather than to argue why they haven't made the strides toward change (Bourgon et al., 2012).

Effective techniques include asking open-ended questions of an offender, demonstrating empathy, and taking a genuine interest by way of follow-up statements and positive recognition (Taxman, 2008). Statements such as "How can we come together on this?" and "It's your choice, but is there anything we can do to help you avoid those consequences?" (Clark, 2005, p. 26) are less confrontational than responding to negative rule-breaking behavior with punitiveness, mandates, threats, and graduated sanctions. Recent research has shown the effectiveness of motivational interviewing techniques in offenders finding employment, paying fees, recognizing drinking behavior, and preparing for substance abuse treatment (Alexander et al., 2008). The more quality time that an officer spends with a client, coupled with regular homework assignments, the more devoted that both the officer and the client become to addressing client needs. These practices translated into helping to lower the recidivism rate (Bonta et al., 2008).

COLLATERAL CONSEQUENCES OF A FELONY

In addition to the challenges of the reentry process previously discussed, ex-felons encounter additional obstacles and regulations called collateral consequences. Most collateral consequences are civil or regulatory in nature and are based on the assumption that a convicted felon has lost credibility because they have engaged in conduct that is questionable to their reputation and makes it difficult for others to trust them (Ewald, 2011). Some consequences are only temporary through the duration of the correctional supervision, but others can last a lifetime. Collateral consequences affects everyone convicted of a felony in some way, but some states specify that losses may be exercised based only on probable cause that criminal activity may be occurring. For example, a landlord in New York City may invoke eviction proceedings based on probable cause that a renter may be engaged in drug activity. Dependent children may be removed from the home if illegal drugs are found inside the home—all are actions that do not require a conviction (Ewald, 2012; Ewald & Uggen, 2012). More than 16 million Americans are estimated to have felony convictions, and are affected in some way by civil rights' losses (Ewald, 2012). Unlike the right to have an attorney for criminal matters, there is no right that offenders have to legal counsel when it comes to addressing *civil* matters (*Turner v. Rogers*, 2011).

The number of collateral consequences varies considerably among how different states formally treat people with felony convictions with regard to voting, public office eligibility; jury service, firearms, employment protections, eligibility for temporary assistance to needy families, eligibility for driver's licenses, and public availability of criminal records (Ewald, 2012). The variation that Ewald found was not only in the number of restrictions but also whether the loss was temporary or permanent and how restorable each loss was. Figure 11.1 depicts a map of the number of legal barriers that each state has imposed upon ex-felons.

There are good reasons for removing some civil rights from offenders. Some argue that doing so is necessary to maintain public confidence in the courts system, public officers, and other areas of government. Thus, some states restrict people from serving on juries, holding public office, and serving as credible witnesses. A second reason is to narrow taxpayer benefits to the law abiding, cutting off those who break the law in the areas of welfare, pensions, student financial aid, and disallowing naturalization privileges to aliens who break the law. More recently, certain rights have been denied to offenders on grounds of increasing public safety and protecting children from harm. These abrogations involve firearm restrictions, sex offender registration, and loss of parental rights.

Figure 11.2 shows the possible civil and political rights restricted or removed following conviction of a felony crime. Note that while some of these rights are

FIGURE 11.1

Number of Legal Barriers During Prisoner Reentry

Source: Legal Action Center. 2011. After prison: Roadblocks to reentry. Available from: http://www.lac.org /roadblocks-to-reentry /main.php?view=national#

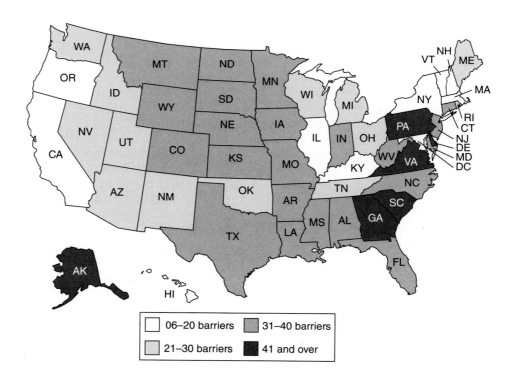

Legend:
- 06–20 barriers
- 21–30 barriers
- 31–40 barriers
- 41 and over

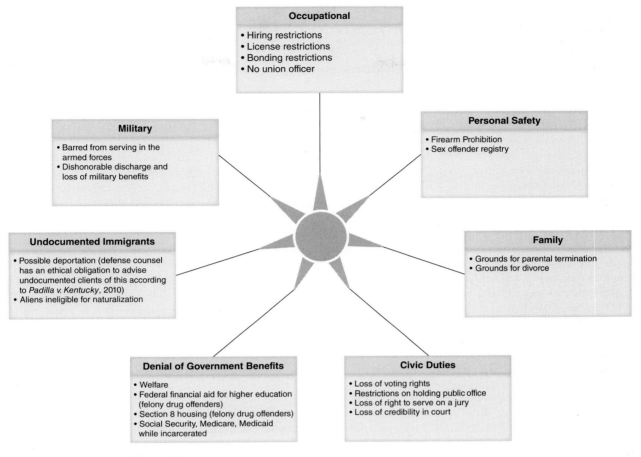

FIGURE 11.2   Possible Collateral Consequences

federal losses that apply across the board, most are left up to each individual state to decide. Also, some rights' restrictions are specific to drug offenses or sex offenses but do not necessarily apply to crimes of violence or property crimes.

This next section discusses six of the most common restrictions in greater detail: employment, firearms, voting, government benefits, parenting, and the courts.

Finding Employment

You have learned in this text that stable employment is a primary way for offenders to reduce their risk of reoffending, yet many current restrictions decrease offender opportunities for jobs. Employment of felons raises issues, including applying for work on-line, restrictions on occupational licenses, and an individual's capacity to be bonded (see Box 11.3).

OCCUPATIONAL LICENSE LIMITATIONS   Many occupations require a license to practice or legitimately work (see Table 11.1 for examples). Obtaining a license requires that a licensee possess **good moral character**. A licensing agency

good moral character
The totality of virtues that form the basis of one's reputation in a community.

BOX 11.3 TECHNOLOGY IN CORRECTIONS

Background Checks Using Publicly Accessible Databases

"Have you ever been convicted of a felony?" is a question that job applicants in most states are asked up front. The entire job search process has changed from employers accepting only online applications, to requiring applicants to offer more information about themselves including taking personality tests with their application (Kelly & Fader, 2012). More employers conduct background investigations and drug testing before the job offer.

While allowing employers to conduct a background check before the job offer is made is not allowed in at least nine states, the amount of information available to employers about a potential applicant is widespread and largely unregulated in most states. Criminal records databases are operated by private companies, and they rely on states to provide them with criminal history and credit report data. Each state regulates the type of data that are released (arrests, deferred adjudications, misdemeanor convictions, and/or felony convictions) to these companies and how far back they will go in time (Ewald, 2012). Fourteen states allowed unrestricted access to all criminal records, including arrests and convictions. Other states restrict access to just convictions or to certain time periods (Ewald, 2011).

Companies required to conduct background checks have been found to be more reluctant to hire former offenders than were companies in which a check was optional (Stoll & Bushway, 2008). For this reason, states like Florida, Hawaii, and Minnesota permit employers to consider convictions only after a conditional offer of employment has been made (Haw. Rev. Stat., Section 378–2.5).

regards a conviction as evidence that a person is not of good moral character, thus restricting entry to many possible jobs. Jobs that tend to be more heavily regulated include union jobs, jobs in the financial industry, insurance, health care, child care, and transportation-related (Ewald, 2011).

State licensing boards have denied ex-convicts an occupational license if a conviction was related to an occupation or if it was too recent. For example, an offender who has served time for robbery may be denied a license to be a bank teller but not to be a land surveyor. For some occupations, such as attorney, any felony conviction is cause for suspension or permanent revocation of an existing certification and disqualifies an applicant from obtaining a license.

Private companies that regulate occupations considered "security-related" (e.g., armed guards, locksmiths, alarm system staff) are even more restrictive. One firm called the Private Security Bureau rejects most crimes above a traffic ticket and ignores whether the applicants' past criminal behavior is work-related, how long ago the crime occurred, or whether there has been any attempt at rehabilitation (Dexheimer, 2007).

A lack of uniformity in the laws and practices of states and localities makes it difficult for people with criminal records to determine where they are allowed to apply their training and skills, whether they have acquired these in or out of prison. This largely explains why former convicts are not able to achieve the same levels of upward economic mobility as their nonincarcerated counterparts (Pew Charitable Trusts, 2010).

LOSS OF CAPACITY TO BE BONDED Jobs in which employees handle money or merchandise can require an employee to be bonded. For example, banks, warehouses, truck-driving companies, collection agencies, bookkeepers, ticket takers,

TABLE 11.1   Examples of Occupations or Fields That Require a License

Accountant/CPA	Acupuncturist	Aircraft dispatcher/mechanic/pilot
Alarm systems	Alcohol server	Appraiser, real estate
Architect	Asbestos removal	Athletic trainer
Attorney/lawyer	Auctioneer	Audiologist
Banking	Barber/hairdresser	Boiler operator
Building codes	Bus driver, school	Charter boat operator
Child care provider	Chiropractor	Collection agency operator
Commercial fisher	Commercial vehicle operator	Concert promoter
Contractor	Cosmetologist	Counselor/therapist
Customs broker	Dentist/dental hygienist	Dietitian/nutritionist
Electrician	Electrology	Emergency medical technician
Engineer	Explosives handler	Forester
Freon technician	Funeral director/services	Geologist
Hearing aid dealer	Home inspector	Insurance occupations
Investment broker/dealer	Land surveyor	Law examiner
Locksmith	Long-term health care	Massage
Medical examiner	Midwife	Mortician
Naturopath	Nursing (LPN, RN)	Occupational therapist
Optician	Optometrist	Osteopath
Painter	Paramedic	Pastoral counselor
Pesticide applicator	Pharmacist/technician	Physical therapy
Physician/surgeon	Plumber	Podiatrist
Psychologist	Real estate	Refrigeration
Residential builder	Respiratory care	Sanitarian examiner
Security guard	Social worker	Speech-language pathologist
Tattooing	Taxidermist	Teacher
Therapeutic recreation	Veterinarian	Water systems operator

Sources: Illinois Department of Professional Regulation (http://www.dpr.state.il.us/); North Carolina Secretary of State Occupational Boards (http://www.secretary.state.nc.us/blio/occboards.asp); South Carolina Department of Labor, Licensing, and Regulation (http://www.llr.state.sc.us/pol.asp); Washington State Department of Licensing (http://www.dol.wa.gov).

and vendors might require a bond before an employee is allowed to work. A bond protects an employer or company from losses caused by dishonest employees. A **surety bond** is signed by an employee and by one or more third parties, known as sureties, who promise to pay money in the event that the employee fails to perform as agreed. A decision to write or deny a bond rests with an insurance company, which in most cases will refuse to bond people with felony records rather than evaluate each case individually. One way around this problem is to apply for fidelity bonding coverage through a state employment office or a local employment service. Because employers and prospective employees seem to lack information about this bonding available through state employment agencies, we highlight this option in Box 11.4.

surety bond
A certificate signed by a principal and a third party promising to pay in the event the assured suffers damages or losses because an employee fails to perform as agreed.

EQUAL OPPORTUNITY COMMISSION POLICY   Due to the numerous problems with former felons finding employment, the Equal Opportunity Commission revised

Former felons convicted of drug offenses can be denied public housing and from receiving other forms of government assistance, especially individuals who have not completed a drug rehabilitation program.

AP Images/Houston Chronicle/Carlos Antonio Rios

their policies in 2012. That directive says that criminal records may be used in making hiring decisions, but employers can no longer use a blanket exclusion policy of all felony applicants. This directive applies to all employers that have 15 or more employees, including private sector, the federal government, and federal contractors. An applicant cannot be excluded solely because of a felony conviction unless those exclusions could be shown to be necessary to that business and that particular job. The felony conviction must bear a direct relationship to the position sought, such as barring a person convicted of burglary from becoming a locksmith. Employers must look at factors such as the nature of the offense, amount of time that has passed since conviction, and the offender's attempts at rehabilitation (Greenhouse, 2012). Some states (MA, NY, WI) prohibit employers from asking about arrests.

At least 10 states have passed "ban-the-box" legislation to regulate what employers can ask about on job applications. For example, Criminal Offender Record Information (CORI) laws in Massachusetts prohibit employers from asking about convictions on the initial job application unless required by a particular job. The employer must receive signed authorization to obtain a copy of the criminal record (CORI report), and then must possess the CORI report before being allowed to question the applicant. If the employer decides against hiring an applicant based on CORI, he or she must provide the applicant written reasons for the decision along with a copy of the CORI report. The applicant can then correct any inaccuracies if they exist and can even find out every 90 days who accessed their CORI report. In Minnesota, employers may not ask about criminal

| BOX 11.4 | COMMUNITY CORRECTIONS UP CLOSE |

How Can Convicted Felons Become Bonded?

Commercially purchased bond insurance serves to protect an employer against employee dishonesty or for loss of money or property as a result of theft, forgery, larceny, or embezzlement. Insurance companies refuse coverage to persons considered *at risk*, such as former offenders, recovering substance abusers, people who have declared bankruptcy, those with poor credit scores, persons with dishonorable discharges from the military, and employees who have behaved with questionable credibility or honesty. As a result, such applicants at risk are routinely denied employment because they cannot be bonded.

The U.S. Department of Labor (USDOL) created the Federal Bonding Program in 1966 as an incentive for employers to hire employees at risk. The bonds issued by the Federal Bonding Program have been:

> designed to reimburse the employer for any loss due to employee theft of money or property with no deductible amount to become the employer's liability (i.e., 100% bond insurance coverage).... Bond issuance can apply to any job at any employer in any State, and covers any employee dishonesty committed on or away from the employer's

work facility. Any full or part-time employee paid wages (with Federal taxes automatically deducted from pay) can be bonded, including persons hired by "temp agencies." However, self-employed persons cannot be covered by these Fidelity Bonds.

Most public or private companies must be preapproved or "certified" to use Fidelity Bonds. Once certified:

- Bonds are issued free of charge effective the day that an applicant is scheduled to start work, and they are self-terminating after six months.
- Bond insurance ranges from $5,000 to $25,000 coverage for an initial six-month period, with no deductible.
- When an initial six-month bond coverage expires, continued coverage can be purchased by an employer if a worker has demonstrated job honesty during that time period.

At-risk job applicants seeking bonding services should call 1.877.872.5627 for the nearest workforce office and should contact a state bonding coordinator for the appropriate state of residence.

Source: U.S. Department of Labor. 2009. *The Federal Bonding Program.* Retrieved from: http://www.bonds4jobs.com/index.html

---

history until after the applicant has been selected for an interview or offered the job (Uggen et al., 2014).

Loss of Right to Vote

Voting is considered a basic right within a democratic society, yet about 5.3 million citizens are not allowed to vote because of a felony conviction (Sentencing Project, 2011). In the 1970s, the U.S. Supreme Court held that it is constitutional for a state to deprive ex-felons of the right to vote, thus giving states a lot of authority, if they so desire, to disenfranchise offenders (*Richardson v. Ramirez*, 1974). The impact of not being able to vote (also called felony disenfranchisement) is quite significant, even though half of persons not allowed to vote have successfully completed their sentences. The Sentencing Project (2011) also found that about 13% of African-American men are disenfranchised, at rates seven times the national average.

At this time, only Maine and Vermont allow incarcerated prisoners to vote through the mail. Most states prohibit felons from voting while they are in prison, on parole, on probation; but once the sentence is complete, most states allow voting rights to be restored. Only four states still prohibit felons from voting after their sentences have been completed.

In the last decade, it appears that public sentiment on the issue of felony disfranchisement is turning toward laws that would either allow more ex-felons to vote or would make the process for felons to have their voting rights restored less cumbersome. For example, Louisiana enacted a bill requiring the Department of Public Safety and Corrections to provide felons with voter registration applications when they leave prison.

Loss of Right to Own or Possess a Firearm

For some individuals, loss of the right to own a firearm is the most restrictive of all civil disabilities incurred by conviction. Federal law prohibits convicted felons from possessing, shipping, transporting, or receiving any firearms or ammunition (18 U.S.C. sec. 921(a)(20)). It also prohibits possession of guns by anybody convicted in any court of domestic violence, which is a misdemeanor crime (18 U.S.C. sec. 922(g)(9)). However, federal law also gave states the opportunities to make their laws more lenient. According to Table 11.2, most states restrict firearm

TABLE 11.2   Firearm Restrictions

No Restrictions	Temporary Restrictions or Restrictions on Handguns Only	Adult Felons Restricted (Same as Federal Ban)	Felons Restricted Indefinitely	Adult and Juvenile Felons and Some Misdemeanants Restricted Indefinitely
Vermont	Idaho	Alabama	Arizona	California
	Montana	Alaska	Colorado	Connecticut
	New Mexico	Arkansas	Delaware	Florida
		Kansas	Georgia	Hawaii
		Maine	Iowa	Illinois
		Michigan	Kentucky	Indiana
		Missouri	Louisiana	Maryland
		Mississippi	New York	Massachusetts
		Nebraska	Ohio	Minnesota
		Nevada	Oklahoma	New Jersey
		New Hampshire	Tennessee	Oregon
		North Carolina	Utah	Pennsylvania
		North Dakota	Washington	Wisconsin
		Rhode Island		West Virginia
		South Carolina		
		South Dakota		
		Texas		
		Wyoming		

Sources: Data taken from information presented in Ewald, Alec (2012) and from the Legal Action Center. http://lac.org/

possession and ownership for people convicted of a felony crime, which is consistent with the federal ban (Ewald, 2012). However, 21 states allow firearm restrictions to be restored; 12 upon passage of time from completion of sentence and 9 following restoration of rights proceedings.

The issue of loss of the right to own a firearm has been litigated in a number of cases, but two deserve mention here. In *Beecham v. United States* (1994), the U.S. Supreme Court held that *federal* felons are held to the federal firearms ban and not to the state they happen to reside. Federal felons are restored through a federal not a state, procedure. This means that "federal felons who have had their civil rights restored by state law or procedure nonetheless are still prohibited by federal law from possessing firearms." This includes state certificates that allow rifles and shotguns but restrict handguns. The U.S. Supreme Court held that when a state certificate bars one type of firearm, it is the same as barring all firearms as far as the federal firearm statute is concerned. Thus, even though Massachusetts state law had permitted the defendant to possess rifles, his restriction of handguns made it illegal for him to possess any firearm—a rifle, a shotgun, or a handgun (*Caron v. U.S.*, 1998). In effect, federal law prevails over state law in firearms regulation for federal offenders.

Loss of Government Benefits for Drug Offenders

A separate database is retained by the Bureau of Justice Assistance to keep track of persons convicted of felony drug offenses, ranging from possession to trafficking. This database keeps track of various government benefits that are denied just to drug offenders (Ewald, 2011). Offenders convicted of drug offenses lose Supplemental Security Income (SSI) and Social Security Disability (SSDI) if their disability is alcohol or drug dependence, according to Public Law 104–121.

DENIAL OF HIGHER EDUCATION FINANCIAL AID College students who are convicted of any state-level or federal-level drug offense (misdemeanor or felony) while receiving federal financial aid for school are ineligible to receive future financial aid. The law does not require a student to report previous convictions years before receiving financial aid. At least 24 states also disqualify students so convicted from state-level aid because receiving such is contingent upon federal eligibility. The period of financial aid denial is one year for a student's first offense of possession of a controlled substance, two years for a second offense, and indefinitely for a third drug-related offense. Financial aid denial becomes indefinite after a second offense for sales of a controlled substance. Even the Internal Revenue Service has become involved by refusing to allow a tax credit claim for tuition during a conviction year. Students who become ineligible for financial aid can have their aid reinstated sooner if they complete an approved drug rehabilitation treatment program, according to Section 483 of the 1998 Amendment to the Higher Education Act (20 U.S.C. sec. 1091 (r)). However, about 15 states are choosing to ignore this amendment's provision for reinstatement altogether. See the report at: http://www.raiseyourvoice.com/statereport/fallingthrough.pdf to see where your state falls on the issue.

DENIAL OF WELFARE Withholding welfare benefits is the most recent form of collateral consequence for convicted drug offenders. When the government overhauled the welfare system with its Welfare Reform Act, the former Aid to Families with Dependent Children (AFDC) program was replaced with a one called Temporary Assistance for Needy Families. The federal act denied food stamps and welfare benefits to anyone convicted of the possession or sale of controlled substances but allowed states to modify the ban as they saw fit. Thirteen states opted out of the ban entirely (thus allowing welfare for drug offenders) so that children of offenders are not negatively impacted. About half of all states have modified the ban to require drug treatment or have placed a time limit on the ban, and 11 states deny welfare benefits altogether to convicted drug offenders (Ewald, 2012).

DENIAL OF PUBLIC HOUSING   The U.S. Department of Housing and Urban Development (HUD) can prohibit the public housing occupancy of any individual who uses drugs or infringes on the health, safety, or right to peaceful enjoyment of such premises. HUD policy bans individuals for three years who have been evicted for "drug-related criminal activity" (which does not even require a conviction). HUD has placed a lifetime ban on two different offenders: sex offenders who must register for the rest of their lives in a sex offender database and individuals who manufacture methamphetamine on public housing property. Aside from these restrictions, HUD allows public housing agencies in each state to set their own admission and termination policies as they see fit. As a result, it has become commonplace for public housing agencies to exclude people with all felony convictions, which was not the intent of the original policy. In June 2011, HUD issued a statement that public housing agencies should, when making screening decisions, consider evidence of rehabilitation and counseling as indication of future positive behavior. Furthermore, evicted occupants and/or those convicted of a drug offense can be readmitted into public housing if they submit proof of completion of drug court or of a supervised drug rehabilitation program (24 CFR 960.204; 24 CFR 966.4; 24 CFR 982.553).

For all felony offenders who become incarcerated, government payments for social security, unemployment, and welfare are temporarily stopped and Medicaid and Medicare benefits are stopped temporarily until release (the loss of which doesn't affect most offenders with a community-based sentence). An offender must reapply upon release to get these benefits reinstated.

Loss of Parental Rights

About 1.5 million children under age 18 have at least one parent serving time in prison. Of the 48 states that allow the termination of parental rights of felony offenders (if other family members wish to take custody), 18 states may terminate such rights solely due to long-term prison confinement. Most states (37) will terminate parental rights for a serious felony conviction against one or more children in a household, which includes murder/manslaughter or felonious assault/battery. If it can be shown to a court that a continuation of a convicted parent's relationship with a child poses a threat to that child's well-being, a conviction can result in permanent loss of parental rights.

Losses in Court

To sustain the integrity of the court system, two common rights that are limited for felons are the right to serve on a jury and the ability to be viewed as a credible witness in any future court proceedings.

SERVING ON A JURY The exclusion of convicted people from jury service has its origin in common law. The federal rule is that citizens are not eligible to serve on a federal grand or petit (trial) jury if they have been convicted of a crime punishable by imprisonment for more than one year and if their civil rights have not been restored (28 U.S.C. sec. 1865). Felons are allowed to serve on a jury in Colorado and Maine without restriction, but 25 states permanently ban felons from serving on juries. The remaining states permit felons to serve on juries after they have completed their sentences or after a passage of time.

LOSS OF CREDIBILITY AS A WITNESS Absolute disqualification to be a witness in court applies to people convicted of perjury (telling a lie under oath) or of subornation of perjury (inducing another person to take a false oath). The justification of absolute disqualification for those convicted of perjury is that such people cannot be trusted to give truthful testimony. The usual situation, however, is that a person convicted of a crime other than perjury or **subornation of perjury** is permitted to testify. However, the fact of any previous conviction can be used to discredit a witness's testimony, with a court or jury allowed to take this record into account. A witness asked whether he or she has been convicted of a felony or other crime must answer truthfully. Opposing counsel may then argue, and usually does, that because a witness is a convicted offender, his or her testimony should not be believed. Whether a witness who is an ex-offender is entitled to full credibility or no credibility at all is up to a judge or jury to decide.

For civil rights that are not restored after the sentence has already been served, ways to restore rights will be discussed in the final chapter of this book.

subornation of perjury
The criminal act of persuading another person to commit perjury.

THE REENTRY PROCESS

The first step in the reentry process is that an offender be eligible for release consideration. Those permanently ineligible for release include offenders on death row, offenders serving life without parole, and some habitual offenders sentenced under statutes such as "three strikes and you're out."

Time Sheets and Eligibility Dates

For the remainder of inmates (those with mandatory or discretionary releases), a computer keeps track of all good time earned and number of days served to determine minimum and maximum eligibility dates. The **minimum eligibility date** is the shortest amount of time defined by statute, minus good time earned, that must be served before an offender can go before a parole board. The **maximum eligibility date** is the longest amount of time that can be served before an offender must, by law, be released (whereupon an offender has "maxed out" his or her sentence).

Good time was originally introduced as an incentive by prison authorities for institutional good conduct. Good time reduces the period of sentence an inmate must serve before parole eligibility. Now good time is automatically granted (in states that offer it) unless an inmate commits a disciplinary infraction. That is, good time is lost for misbehavior in prison rather than awarded for good behavior. Good-time credits vary greatly from state to state, ranging from 5 days per month to as many as 45 days per month. In recent years, large amounts of good time have been temporarily awarded by correctional

minimum eligibility date
The shortest amount of time defined by statute, minus good-time earned, that must be served before an offender can go before a parole board.

maximum eligibility date
The longest amount of time that can be served before an inmate must be released by law.

good time
Sentence reduction of a specified number of days each month for good conduct.

authorities (e.g., 120 days for every month served) to reduce prison overcrowding and avoid lawsuits. When jail and prison crowding subsides, good time is decreased to the regular amount.

Typically, a prison case manager submits good time earned (or in some cases submits good time lost for misbehavior) to a parole board or division within the Department of Corrections that prepares status or time sheets. Offenders receive an updated time sheet every six months to one year so they know when to expect their first parole hearing.

parole eligibility date
The point in a prisoner's sentence in which he or she becomes eligible for parole. If an offender is denied parole, a new parole eligibility date is scheduled in the future.

Prisoners generally become eligible for release upon completion of their minimum sentence. The manner in which a **parole eligibility date** is established varies from state to state. Mandatory minimum states require that between 50% and 85% of an entire sentence be served before a prisoner first becomes eligible. Other discretionary parole states require a prisoner to have served one-third of an imposed sentence to be eligible for consideration for early parole. However, most statutes allow further reductions in an eligibility date through credit for time served in jail before sentencing and good-time credits. Federal law provides release for a minimum of one year when an offender has served two-thirds of a term of five years or longer, unless he or she has amassed serious disciplinary infractions in prison or there is a high probability of recidivism (U.S. Sentencing Commission, 2010).

Some states credit good time to an offender upon arrival in prison and calculate eligibility date by subtracting credited good time from the maximum sentence. A prisoner who is serving a 15-year sentence and receiving standard good time of 20 days per month (i.e., 50 days' credit on his or her sentence for each 30 days served) would thus be eligible for parole consideration after 40 months. As a first parole eligibility date approaches, institutional case managers (also called institutional parole officers in some states) prepare an individualized release plan for a parole board.

Prerelease Preparation Within the Institution

prerelease facility
A minimum-security prison that houses inmates who have earned such a privilege through good institutional conduct and who are nearing their release date.

Some prisoners are fortunate to be transferred to a prerelease program within the criminal justice system in preparation for their release. A **prerelease facility** is a minimum-security residential program that houses prisoners who have earned this privilege through good institutional conduct and are within two years of their release date. Prerelease facilities provide increased opportunities for job readiness, education, housing assistance, and furloughs. Faith-based volunteer programs (e.g., *Welcome Back* programs) educate offenders about networks of social support agencies that can assist with the release process in their locale.

Halfway houses and work release are also types of residential prerelease facilities used prior to parole. Recently released prisoners experience pressure when they are charged for rent the moment they arrive at the halfway house. Financial pressure builds not only from daily living expenses but also from having to set aside money for paying court costs, fees, victim restitution, and back child support that accumulated while behind bars. Despite this some states, such as Washington, believe in the importance of work release and prerelease centers, sending between 30% and 40% of all prisoners there before parole release. This rate is considered quite high compared with most other states surveyed.

release plan
A case-management summary of offender institutional conduct and program participation as well as plans for housing and employment upon release, which is submitted to a parole board in cases of discretionary parole or to a parole officer in cases of automatic release.

Prison institutions prepare a **release plan** while an offender is still incarcerated. This includes a summary of institutional conduct and program participation as well as plans for housing and employment upon release. Some states employ case hearing officers to interview each prisoner, prepare a case summary, and report directly to a parole board with their recommendation. Other states submit case summaries and written reports along with a case file. Preparing some form of release plan in advance of a scheduled parole hearing has three main advantages:

1. A release plan increases an offender's chances of parole because it solidifies living arrangements and work opportunities.
2. A release plan saves time during a parole board hearing.
3. Positive support systems will likely increase an offender's success on parole and make it less likely that this offender will return to crime.

An institutional case manager interviews a prisoner to document exactly where he or she will be living and the names of any household members. A different (local) field parole officer interviews household members to ensure that an address is valid and checks whether it is an acceptable place for an offender to live. Positive family relations increase the likelihood of parole. Offenders are usually discouraged from paroling to themselves, which means living and supporting themselves without any assistance. However, one study suggested that former prisoners who moved far away from their homes after release (due to forced relocation because of Hurricane Katrina) were 14% less likely to be reincarcerated over three years than released inmates who returned to their original neighborhood (Kirk, 2012). Because most offenders at time of release from prison do not have the money required for rent and utility deposits, the vast majority must parole to an existing household of a friend or relative. In an effort to assist in community reintegration, paroling employable offenders to a halfway house or community residential center is helpful.

An institutional case manager documents the amount of money an ex-prisoner has in savings and any job leads or specific employment plans he or she has. Most offenders leave prison without any savings and with few solid job prospects. The case manager then summarizes any programs an offender has attended or completed (e.g., general equivalency diploma courses) while in prison and lists all disciplinary infractions (write-ups) received during the entire period of incarceration.

Reentry Risk Assessment

Essentially the case manager brings together official data (e.g., current conviction, current age, amount of time served for current conviction, number of prior prison incarcerations, number and type of prior convictions) and data about an offender's education level, employment history, and substance abuse history. All of the information is scored in a systematic way, and a report is provided to a parole board for a parole hearing. This report is prepared according to predefined state parole guidelines and is used by a parole board much like a probation officer's presentence investigation report by a judge at time of sentencing. Time is saved during the hearing because the parole board does not have to search through offender files (many of which are fairly thick) to find what they need to know.

Like with assessments at the beginning of a sentence, reentry decisions are now quantitative using many of the same criteria (age, offense seriousness, and prior institutional commitments) that were used in measuring risk while on community supervision. Over 80% of releasing authorities now use some type of decision-making instrument or risk assessment that includes numeric scoring. Although some risk assessments have been developed in house by a state's Department of Corrections, many states now use the Ohio Risk Management System (see Figure 11.3).

FIGURE 11.3 Ohio Risk Management System

OHIO RISK ASSESSMENT SYSTEM — REENTRY TOOL (ORAS-RT)

Name: _____   Date of Assessment: _____

Case#: _____   Name of Assessor: _____

_____ Age at Time of Assessment
    0 = 24+
    1 = 18–23

1.0 CRIMINAL HISTORY

1.1. Most Serious Arrest Under Age 18
    0 = None
    1 = Yes, Misdemeanor
    2 = Yes, Felony

1.2. Age at First Arrest or Charge
    0 = 26+
    1 = 16–25
    2 = 15 or younger

1.3. Prior Commitment as a Juvenile to Department of Youth Services
    0 = No
    1 = Yes

1.4. Current Offense Drug Related
    0 = No
    1 = Yes

1.5. Number of Prior Adult Felony Convictions
    0 = None
    1 = One
    2 = Two or More

1.6. Number of Prior Adult Commitments to Prison
    0 = None
    1 = One
    2 = Two or More

1.7. Ever Received Official Infraction for Violence While Incarcerated as an Adult
    0 = No
    1 = Yes

1.8. Ever Absconded from Community Supervision as an Adult
    0 = No
    1 = Yes

Total Score in Criminal History:

(Continues)

FIGURE 11.3 *(Continued)*

2.0 SOCIAL BONDS

2.1. Ever Suspended or Expelled from School
  0 = No
  1 = Yes

2.2. Employed at the Time of Arrest
  0 = Yes
  1 = No

2.3. Ever Quit a Job Prior to Having Another One
  0 = No
  1 = Yes

2.4. Marital Status
  0 = Married or Cohabitating with a Significant Other
  1 = Single, Married but Separated, Divorced, or Widowed

Total Score in Social Bonds:

3.0 CRIMINAL ATTITUDES AND BEHAVIORAL PATTERNS

3.1. Criminal Pride
  0 = No Pride in Criminal Behavior
  1 = Some Pride in Criminal Behavior
  2 = A lot of Pride in Criminal Behavior

3.2. Believes That It Is Possible to Overcome Past
  0 = Yes
  1 = No

3.3. Uses Anger to Intimidate Others
  0 = No
  1 = Yes

3.4. Walks Away from a Fight
  0 = Yes
  1 = Sometimes
  2 = Rarely

3.5. Problem-Solving Ability
  0 = Good
  1 = Poor

3.6. Expresses Concern About Other's Misfortunes
  0 = Concerned About Others
  1 = Limited Concern
  2 = No Real Concern for Others

3.7. Believes in "Do Unto Others Before They Do Unto You"
  0 = Disagree
  1 = Sometimes
  2 = Agree

Total Score for Criminal Attitudes and Behavioral Patterns:

TOTAL SCORE:

(Continues)

FIGURE 11.3   *(Continued)*

Risk Categories for MALES			Risk Categories for FEMALES		
Scores	Rating	Percent of Failures	Scores	Rating	Percent of Failures
0–9	Low	21%	0–10	Low	6.5%
10–15	Moderate	50%	11–14	Moderate	44%
16+	High	64%	15+	High	56%

Domain Levels

1.0 Criminal History

	Score	Failure
_____	Low (0–3)	23%
	Med (4–6)	45%
	High (7–12)	65%

2.0 Social Bonds

	Score	Failure
_____	Low (0–3)	32%
	Med (4–5)	45%
	High (6–7)	62%

3.0 Criminal Attitudes and Behavioral Patterns

	Score	Failure
_____	Low (0–2)	30%
	Med (3–5)	51%
	High (6–11)	58%

Professional Override:

Reason for Override

(note overrides should not be based solely on offense)

Other Areas of Concern. Check all that Apply:

_____ Low Intelligence*
_____ Physical Handicap
_____ Reading and Writing Limitations*
_____ Mental Health Issues*
_____ No Desire to Change/Participate in Programs*
_____ Language
_____ Childcare
_____ Transportation
_____ Cultural Barriers
_____ History of Abuse/Neglect

*If these items are checked it is strongly recommended that further assessment be conducted to determine level or severity.

Source: In the public domain through the University of Cincinnati's Center for Criminal Justice Research.

THE PAROLE BOARD AND RELEASING AUTHORITY

The prison releasing authority is a group of individuals that have authority to release prisoners prior to completion of an indeterminate sentence. Traditionally this group has been known as a **parole board**, but as determinate sentencing replaced indeterminate sentencing for crimes of violence or for all felonies in some states, the name attached to the releasing authority has varied by state. This text uses the more traditional term of parole board to apply to *any* prison releasing authority, regardless of its sentencing framework, for two reasons: (a) most states have a mixed sentencing structure with elements of both determinate and indeterminate sentencing and (b) even in states with determinate sentencing structures, 75% still retain a releasing authority group with discretionary release (Caplan & Kinnevy, 2010).

Parole boards have four basic functions:

1. to decide when individual prisoners should be released;
2. to determine any special conditions of parole supervision;
3. to successfully discharge a parolee when conditions have been met; and
4. to determine whether privileges should be revoked if release conditions are violated.

Some parole boards have additional functions, such as granting furloughs, reviewing pardons and executive clemency decisions made by a governor, restoring civil rights to ex-offenders, and granting reprieves in death sentence cases. Each state establishes the extent of its own parole board's authority.

Although most parole boards are independent entities, they are appointed by a governor or director of the Department of Corrections for a term that ranges from three to seven years (average of five years). Only two states (Ohio and Wisconsin) have appointed members for life. The size of the group ranges from 3 to 19 members, with an average of 7 board members. The chair of the board and all board members in 28 states are full-time salaried employees, and the rest are part-time employees paid per diem (Paparozzi & Caplan, 2009).

A gubernatorial appointment must be confirmed by a legislature. Parole board members must possess integrity, intelligence, and good judgment to command respect and public confidence. Board members should have sufficiently broad academic training and experience to be qualified for professional practice in fields such as criminology, education, psychology, law, social work, and sociology. Each member must have the capacity and desire to learn and understand legal processes, the dynamics of human behavior, and the cultural conditions contributing to crime. Ideally parole board members have previous professional expertise that has given them intimate knowledge of the situations and problems confronting offenders—that is, of the human experience (Paparozzi & Caplan, 2009).

parole board
An administrative body empowered to revoke parole, to discharge from parole those who have satisfactorily completed their terms, and to decide whether inmates shall be conditionally released from prison before completion of their sentence.

The Parole Hearing

Once prisoner eligibility for release has been determined, an offender is scheduled for a parole hearing date. Parole board members have access to an entire offender case file with a summary report completed by the institutional case manager. As previously mentioned, some hearing examiners scrutinize only a case file without interviewing an offender, whereas other parole boards have access to both a case file and an offender in person. In the federal system, a sentencing judge, an assistant U.S. attorney, and a defense attorney can all make written recommendations to a parole board. Federal prisoners can later request a copy of their parole hearing recording under the Freedom of Information Act (U.S. Parole Commission, 2010).

Parole board hearings serve many purposes, which include:

1. resolving inconsistencies in available information directly from an offender, a victim, or other parties;
2. reviewing institutional program participation and institutional conduct to better understand indications of change and behavior while confined;
3. considering an offender's motivation for parole; and
4. considering input from a victim and other interested parties.

Parole board hearings are tape-recorded and conducted in one of three ways: in person, by video teleconference, or by the board viewing a hard-copy paper file without meeting the person. Face-to-face parole board hearings are the most common of the three and take place at the prison in which an eligible prisoner is located. Hearings in person allow a prisoner to be in the same room with a parole board. Some boards conduct parole release hearings using videoconference technology (see Box 11.5), which has greatly reduced a need to travel to each prison while allowing an opportunity to ask and answer questions. File review parole hearings offer no face-to-face contact with a prisoner, and a board makes a decision based only on documents submitted by prison officials.

A video or face-to-face parole hearing is attended by one to three board members (or hearing examiners) who represent an entire board. In a face-to-face hearing, one hearing examiner thoroughly reviews the file and leads with most questions. If other members are present, they review the file less thoroughly and ask supplemental questions from a different angle or ask follow-up questions to those of the leading parole board member. At least two signatures are required to parole a person convicted of a nonviolent crime, but most states average three required signatures (Kinnevy & Caplan, 2008).

BOX 11.5 **TECHNOLOGY IN CORRECTIONS**

Federal Parole Hearings Videoconference

The Parole Commission used to travel to more than 60 facilities all over the United States to conduct parole release and revocation hearings face-to-face. Prisoners facing parole release hearings met with the Commission in a prerelease facility. Prisoners facing revocation hearings traveled by airplane from a local jail to a central transfer facility in Oklahoma or to a detention center in Philadelphia within a 90-day period. Following their revocation hearing, they would again travel to wherever the Commission felt was best to place them.

Using videoconferencing, Parole Commission members can remain in Maryland while prisoners can visibly and audibly interact with them from any federal facility in the United States. The technology was initially tried with parole release hearings. The Commission found that "video and audio transmissions are clear and the hearings are seldom interrupted by technical difficulties… [and] the prisoner's ability to effectively participate in the hearing has not been diminished" (U.S. Department of Justice, 2005, p. 19262). Videoconferencing saves travel time and money for Commission members as well as the travel time, money, and risk involved in transferring prisoners. The practice has been so successful with parole release hearings that it was extended to revocation hearings.

Source: U.S. Department of Justice. 2005. 28 CFR Part 2: Paroling, recommitting, and supervising federal prisoners: Prisoners serving sentences under the U.S and D.C. Codes. *Federal Register 70* (70), April 13, 2005, p. 19262.

Parole Hearing Attendees

Parole boards consider input from other sources to assist them in making their decision. Each state varies as to who can attend a hearing and how that information must be conveyed (whether in person, through written correspondence, by telephone, or videotaped). Some states allow an offender's family at parole hearings, but most do not permit legal representation for an offender. Prosecutors, law enforcement, and victims directly involved in an offender's case are invited to make a statement (Caplan, 2012). Relatives or potential employers may write letters or submit a videotaped statement for use at a hearing. The federal system limits each offender to one representative to make a statement on his or her behalf (U.S. Parole Commission, 2010).

Written correspondence through a victim impact statement is the most common form of correspondence accepted from victims. A **victim impact statement** addresses how a crime has taken a toll physically, emotionally, financially, and/or psychologically on a victim and a victim's family. Victim impact statements cite how the victim continues to experience psychological, physical, and/or financial difficulties as a direct result of the actions of the offender (Caplan, 2012). Most states keep impact statements confidential because of concern that prisoners might attempt to further harm their victim(s) for opposing that offender's release. Other states, such as Arizona and Oklahoma, allow victims to veto a parole release decision if they had requested notification of a hearing but were not given a chance to contribute their opinion.

The Parole Board Decision

The top four factors that releasing authorities use in their releasing decisions are current offense seriousness, parole/reentry risk score, time served on current sentence, and institutional disciplinary record (Morgan & Smith, 2008). Victim input has arguably too much influence on parole decisions, according to some critics (Caplan, 2010). Parole boards today aim to maximize public safety over offender rehabilitation, so not all factors are weighed equally, particularly with sex offenders who seem to be treated differently than non-sex offenders by virtue of their offense (Huebner & Bynum, 2006). Interestingly, all other things being similar, offenders convicted of drug felonies were released sooner than property offenders, leading researchers to conclude that parole boards still function as an equalizer for harsh drug sentences at the front end (Huebner & Bynum, 2008). Although parole board members do consider a number of criteria, there is no evidence to indicate that race or ethnicity has any bearing on release decisions (Huebner & Bynum, 2006; Morgan & Smith, 2008).

A parole board has three possible options: to grant parole, to deny parole, or to defer to a later date. A decision to *grant* parole results in scheduling a conditional release before an expiration of a maximum term of imprisonment. Release decisions require the vote of two out of three board members to grant parole for that region. Crimes of a violent or sexual nature can require a **full board review**—that is, that all members of a parole board review a case. If so, all board members meet with the chair at a central office for a few days out of every month. A violent or sex offender is paroled if the full board decides by a majority or quorum vote (e.g., four of seven members) that he or she should be released.

A parole denial results in continued imprisonment. In the federal system, a denial of parole on a sentence less than seven years in length allows an offender

victim impact statement A written account by a victim as to how a crime has taken a toll physically, emotionally, financially, and/or psychologically on said victim and victim's family. Victim impact statements are considered by many states at the time of sentencing and at parole board hearings.

TRUTH OR FICTION?

Victims have no influence on a parole board's decision to release an offender.

FICTION

FACT: Outspoken victims who appear in person at parole hearings or who send letters to contest a prisoner's release are significantly more likely to convince a parole board to deny release than victims who take no action (Caplan, 2010).

full board review A statutory requirement that all members of a parole board review and vote on an early release from prison of individuals who have committed felony crimes, usually of a violent or sexual nature. Some states require this type of review on every discretionary release.

to automatically go before a board again in 18 months. A sentence longer than seven years delays the next parole board hearing for another two years (U.S. Parole Commission, 2010).

A release deferral means that a parole board has delayed its final decision (to grant or deny parole) until a later time, somewhere between six months and a year. The most common reason for deferrals is that an offender has not yet completed an in-prison treatment program related to his or her offense. For example, a sex offender in some states must complete sex offender treatment before being considered for release, whereas a chronic drug user might have to complete an in-prison substance abuse program. The problem is not that an offender won't complete a program but rather that space available for treatment is limited and an offender must wait for an opening, which many times doesn't occur until after his or her minimum release eligibility date has already passed. The second most common reason for deferrals is administrative delay, such as paperwork is not in order or has not been completed by the Department of Corrections, a victim has not yet provided input (in the 17 states that require a victim impact statement before a board can make a decision), or an offender is at another facility and not available for interview at a scheduled time (Kinnevy & Caplan, 2008).

Legal Issues in Parole Hearings

Prisoners seeking parole have been sentenced to prison and are seeking early privileged release. Insofar as parole is a privilege and not a right, one of the most surprising aspects of the parole process is an inability to challenge parole board decisions. Below are some key court cases in the parole process.

The court long ago ruled that due process is *not* an issue in parole because it is a privilege and not a right (*Menechino v. Oswald*, 1971). Rights afforded at the pretrial process like an attorney, cross-examining witnesses, and so on are not present during a parole hearing. In another case, the U.S. Supreme Court emphasized that parole boards have broad discretion in their decision making. For example, admitting guilt or refusing to admit participation in a crime can be used in some jurisdictions as a reason to deny release (*Silmon v. Travis*, 2000). However, when parole is denied, prisoners are required to be informed how each fell short of qualifying for parole to satisfy minimum due process (*Greenholtz v. Inmates of the Nebraska Penal and Correctional Complex*, 1979). *Greenholtz* also required reasonable notice of one month prior to the parole hearing date.

There are some interesting rulings about what types of information can be used during parole board hearings. For example, hearsay evidence may be used in parole release decisions (*Goldberg v. Beeler*, 1999). Parole boards have even been known to deny parole if DNA evidence matches a parole candidate with an earlier crime for which he or she was never prosecuted (Johnson & Willing, 2008). DNA evidence does not convict or add time to a sentence for such crimes but just allows a parole board to deny early release for crimes for which an offender was convicted. At the same time, a parole board may not deny parole for false, insufficient, or capricious reasons (*Tucker v. Alabama Board of Pardons and Paroles*, 2000), so there seems to be a fine distinction as to what kinds of information are allowed to become part of a decision.

Prisoners seeking parole do not have a right to be represented by counsel. Although a lawyer is welcome to attend in support of a prisoner, that lawyer may not represent nor speak on behalf of the prisoner during a parole hearing (*Franciosi v. Michigan Parole Board*, 2000). Even if a parole board changes its mind about its decision, no due process rights are necessary, provided a prisoner has not actually been released from an institution (*Jago v. Van Curen*, 1981). Unlike sentencing, parole board decisions are not subject to judicial review if made in accordance with statutory guidelines (*Ramahlo v. Travis*, 2002).

COMMUNITY-BASED REENTRY INITIATIVES

You've learned that successful reentry starts with release planning while still inside the institution, such that the transition can be more seamless. Programs that support the reentry of criminal offenders have increased over time, particularly with respect to housing, job placement, mentoring services, and faith-based initiatives. This section describes and evaluates various reentry initiatives that provide community referrals, quick access to benefit programs, and continuity of care between the institution and the new community situation. Reentry partnerships do not necessarily entail more resources—they merely involve using existing resources in a smarter and more holistic way by collaborating with other agencies in criminal justice and in the larger community.

Workforce Development

Workforce development is services provided to offenders to help them search for jobs, prepare resumes, and polish interview skills (McNichols, 2012). Some workforce programs also educate employers on tax breaks and incentives they can receive to hire felony offenders, and may offer career fairs at prerelease facilities that allow offenders to interview and be selected for a job before they leave the prison. For example, programs like the Solution to Employment Problems (STEP) are an effort of manufacturing businesses to provide jobs to convicted offenders. In this program, employers provide equipment and instructors to train offenders while they are in prison and then guarantee them jobs upon their release.

Evaluations of Minnesota programs found that offender participants had improved employment rates and lower rates of reoffending, due not only to having a stable job but also because of higher levels of community and social support (Duwe, 2011, 2012). Similar results between family support, employment, and reduced recidivism were found elsewhere (Berg & Huebner, 2011). Along with workforce development and stable employment, stable housing at work release centers and inpatient treatment facilities will more significantly reduce recidivism over emergency shelters (Clark, 2014). More examples of reentry initiatives require former prisoners to live at home and include reentry courts, day reporting centers, and location monitoring, discussed next.

Reentry Courts

Reentry courts are a collaborative, team-based program that occurs after prison with the aim of improving the link between parole supervision and treatment providers. Reentry court programs initially identify and begin to work with high-risk offenders prior to release. After release, an offender has structured court appointments with a reentry team, which coordinates job training, housing, substance abuse treatment, and transportation. Reentry courts are structured similarly to drug courts in that they use judges, court hearings, and graduated sanctions and incentives to reward positive behavior and predictably punish negative behavior

reentry courts
A collaborative, team-based program that aims to improve the link between parole supervision and treatment providers to help recent parolees become stabilized.

(Vance, 2011a). They also operate on contracts that keep offenders law abiding for fear of returning to prison. The main difference between all the other problem-solving courts discussed in earlier chapters (drug courts, mental health courts, and veteran's courts) and reentry courts is that reentry courts begin after release from prison and are specific to a particular geographic area or neighborhood. Two examples are discussed below.

A reentry court in the western district of Michigan targeted high-risk federal offenders coming out of prison. The offenders are required to participate in Moral Reconation Therapy. The judge, together with the offender and the probation officer meets every month for one year to examine progress thus far and revisit reentry goals. After 12 months of successful hearings, the offender is discharged from reentry court to regular mandatory supervision for one more year. A group of 36 reentry participants were matched with 36 nonparticipants according to risk level, supervising officer, motivation level, and demographic factors. After 12 months, one-quarter of the reentry group and one-half of the comparison group were rearrested for a new crime (Vance, 2011a).

Another reentry court in East Harlem targeted nonviolent felons who had at least two convictions. The program had three phases, which one-third of participants had successfully completed; the other two-thirds were in an earlier stage of the program. Evaluations of court participants compared to a matched group that did not experience reentry court found that participants were less likely to be reconvicted of a new crime three years following release (Hamilton, 2010). Still, researchers need to better understand factors that promote success after prison. Until more is learned about why ex-prisoners return to prison, an increased attention to the need of prisoners for substantial assistance with reentry has certainly been a step in the right direction.

Day Reporting Centers and Electronic Monitoring

Nonresidential programs for parolees released to the community include day reporting centers (DRCs) and electronic monitoring. DRCs were more fully discussed in Chapter 9, and won't be repeated here. Both types of DRCs are similar in that they offer services for the first six months for parolees recently released. While a parolee is looking for a job during the day, classes are offered at night. The focus is on three main areas: substance abuse counseling, anger management, and cognitive-behavioral approaches. In addition, employment assistance classes are offered to help parolees obtain a job.

Electronic monitoring (also more fully discussed in Chapter 9) is widely used for the first 6–12 months of the release of a minimum risk federal prisoner. This program is known as "location monitoring" and allows released prisoners to live at home but pay a portion of the $15 per day to cover the costs. This is significantly less expensive than the $67 per day cost for a federal residential reentry center (Cornish & Whetzel, 2014).

Parole and Mandatory Supervision Effectiveness

To examine the effectiveness of parole and mandatory supervision, recidivism rates of former prisoners who were supervised after prison were compared with ex-cons who were not at all under supervision. Recall that mandatory releases are supervised similarly to parole, but the release decision is made by statute and not by a parole board.

Offenders can effectively integrate back into society when employers are willing to hire them.

AP Images/The Herald-Palladium/ John Madill

The first study examined prisoners on mandatory release compared to those released by a parole board over a 10-year period (Hughes et al., 2001). Unconditional releases were not part of the sample. Discretionary parolees were more successful (50%–56%) than those released on mandatory supervision (24%–33%).

A second study measured rearrest over a two-year period, using a sample of 30,624 prisoners released from 15 states (Solomon, 2006). This time, all three groups of prisoners were compared: unconditional (no supervision), mandatory supervised release, and discretionary parole release. Mandatory supervised releasees and unconditional releasees recidivated at the same rate—61% and 62%, respectively, over the two-year period. A slightly lower rate—54%—of those released on discretionary parole by a parole board recidivated. In interpreting the overall recidivism findings among the three groups, Solomon (2006, pp. 31–32) says:

> Clearly there is a value judgment being made here, in characterizing a four-percentage point difference as "relatively small," differing "only slightly."… Because parole boards take into account factors such as a prisoner's attitude and motivation level, institutional conduct, preparedness for release and connections to the community.… I would expect this group to be substantially, rather than marginally, less likely to recidivate. The suggestion here is that lower rearrest rates may be largely due to who is selected for discretionary release rather than discretionary supervision itself, which is not systematically different than mandatory supervision across states.

Most recently, a third study compared 6,464 prisoners released to parole supervision to 1,372 prisoners released without supervision (voluntary max outs) and tracked recidivism over three years after release (Ostermann, 2012).

The difference with this study is that propensity score matching was used to create more similarity between the two groups. After three years, parolees under supervision had lower rates of rearrest and reconviction than those who maximized their entire prison sentence on the inside, but a portion of this time, the paroled prisoners were under active supervision still (Ostermann, 2012, 2015).

But what about just the time periods when former prisoners (paroled and max outs) are not under any active supervision? Ostermann looked into this question and found that prisoners released on active supervision after prison are temporarily insulated from committing new crimes, and thus at first, will fare better (5% lower rate) than prisoners without any post-release supervision. However, this effect is short-lived—once the mandatory supervision and discretionary parolees are no longer being actively supervised, their recidivism rate difference is only 1% lower than former prisoners without any post-release supervision (Ostermann, 2013). This may be because post-release supervision has a significant recidivism reduction effect for low-risk offenders, but makes no difference for high-risk offenders, who by definition are at high risk for recidivism (Morris et al., 2013). The good news of all of this is that, not considering type of release, about two-thirds of state prisoners will *never* return to prison, according to a recidivism study in 17 states over a 13-year period (Rhodes et al., 2014). How much of that decision is dependent on having previously been on parole or not is likely to be a small one.

In conclusion, the more pressing reentry issue facing society is, to what degree is society going to support community-based transition programs and hiring of ex-offenders so that prisoners do not repeat their criminal cycle? In terms of discretionary parole decisions, the trend continues of replacing subjective assessments with quantitative risk assessments that social scientists show reduce propensity to commit future crime. Parole boards certainly have the potential to assume an important role in the release of prisoners, providing that members have the appropriate education, training, and experience for the job (Paparozzi & Guy, 2009). Until parole board membership is valued as a paid professional position that is merit-based rather than a political appointment, quantitative risk assessment will slowly become the method of choice in the prediction of future criminal behavior instead of relying on the political nature and subjective judgment of board members.

SUMMARY

- Reentry programs include those that take place in a prison setting as well as community-based programs that follow up on the transition process.

- A parolee faces issues related to finding stable employment, locating suitable housing, and reestablishing contact with his or her family. Because most releasees are also under supervision, they face pressure to be careful with whom they associate and to check in with their parole officer.

- Collateral consequences, which take the form of civil disabilities, can deprive a person of civil and political rights and make finding or holding a job difficult.

- The types of civil disabilities resulting from conviction vary widely from one state to another and are governed by federal and state laws.

- Civil and political rights lost after conviction include the right to vote, to serve on a jury, to hold public office, to own and possess a firearm, to receive welfare benefits, and to exercise parental rights.

- There are three types of release from prison—release without any supervision, release under a short period of mandatory supervision by a parole officer, and release under discretionary parole.

- Parole boards have power to decide whether to release prisoners serving sentences with the eligibility for discretionary parole.

- Parole boards determine when revocation of parole and return to prison are necessary.

- Because discretionary parole is defined as a privilege rather than a right, courts have allowed broad discretion and minimal due process protections.

- Reentry initiatives include reentry courts and collaborations between parole agencies and grassroots community organizations or other criminal justice agencies.

- Prisoners released on parole or mandatory supervision after prison will initially fare better than prisoners without any post-release supervision. However, once active supervision ends, their recidivism rate difference is not significantly different than former prisoners who never had post-release supervision.

DISCUSSION QUESTIONS

1. What issues do prisoners face in preparing for their reentry into a community?

2. What issues exist with respect to prisoner reentry and the impact on his or her family?

3. If you were an employer, would you hire a former felon who has been recently released on parole? What about hiring an offender who has finished parole and has stayed out of trouble for two years? Justify your answer.

4. Which civil and political rights, in your opinion, should be permanently prohibited from ALL offenders for the rest of their lives?

5. Which civil and political rights, in your opinion, do not make any sense to limit? If you feel that some civil and political rights should be limited according to offense, identify which should be limited to which type of offender.

6. If you were a victim of a violent crime, would you take time to write an impact statement or attend a parole board hearing, knowing the offender would also be there? Why or why not?

7. What are the primary qualifications of a good parole board member? Why are these qualities important?

8. Why are good public relations between a parole board and its outside community necessary?

9. If you were a parole board member, what factors would you consider in attempting to arrive at a fair and just decision? Why?

10. If you were a prisoner, which method of release from prison would you prefer—discretionary or mandatory/automatic? Why?

WEBSITES, VIDEOS, AND PODCASTS

Websites

National Reentry Resource Center
http://csgjusticecenter.org/nrrc/

The Reentry Policy Council
http://www.reentrypolicy.org

Reentry National Media Outreach Campaign
http://www.outreachextensions.com/portfolio/view/reentry_national_media_outreach_campaign/

Ohio Civil Impacts of Criminal Convictions
http://civiccohio.org/

U.S. Parole Commission
http://www.usdoj.gov/uspc/

Ohio Parole Board
http://www.drc.ohio.gov/web/parboard.htm

Texas Parole Release Guidelines
http://www.tdcj.state.tx.us/bpp/parole_guidelines/parole_guidelines.html

Videos/Podcasts

Long Road Back: Ex-Offenders' Struggle for Acceptance
(Length: 4:14 minutes) Examines the stigma and struggles that ex-offenders must overcome to avoid recidivism.
https://www.youtube.com/watch?v=58T9qc4_xKY

ReEntry Program to Help Ex-Offenders Transition into Community

(Length: 3 minutes) A reentry program helps ex-offenders transition back into the community.
https://www.youtube.com/watch?v=acYMRLwrOLE

Transition from Prison to the Community

(Length: 5 minutes) The Transition from Prison to the Community program has been adopted by the Minnesota Department of Corrections to help offenders readjust to life outside of prison.
https://www.youtube.com/watch?v=oaauPmJ7XcU

Consequences of a Prison Record on Employment

(Length: 9 minute) This video is sponsored by the National Institute of Justice and was released in 2014. This is an interview with Dr. Scott Decker about how a felony record affects chances for employment in the future.
http://www.nij.gov/multimedia/exhibits/pages/video-decker.aspx

Housing and Health at Reentry

This 63-minute video is sponsored by the National Reentry Resource Center.
http://www.youtube.com/watch?v=Jd3sHnzwMWQ

Mentoring Offenders in the Community at Reentry: A Panel Discussion

This 70-minute video is sponsored by the National Reentry Resource Center.
http://www.youtube.com/watch?v=biuWGlo_39I

Reentry of Inmates with Mental Illness

The podcast discusses mental illnesses amid prison populations and how agencies can plan for the release of prisoners with mental illness.
http://www.corrections.com/system/podcast/file/21/media_20031022.mp3

Second Chance Act: What Have We Learned About Reentry So Far?

(Length: 8 minute) This video interviews Ron D'Amico about the Second Chance Act. This is sponsored by the National Institute of Justice.
http://nij.ncjrs.gov/multimedia/video-damico.htm

Going Home: How Residential Change Might Help Former Offenders Stay out of Prison

(Length: 1 hour, 25 minutes) Dr. David Kirk of the University of Texas discusses relocation to a new area after prison to decrease recidivism.
http://nij.ncjrs.gov/multimedia/video-kirk.htm

State Penitentiary Reintegration: Innovator's Focus

A 17-minute video by Ashland Institute about unconditional prison release.
http://www.youtube.com/watch?v=LNLIAuO3pQg

CASE STUDY EXERCISES

Preparing for Prisoner Reentry

Various systems are used to make release decisions about incarcerated offenders. In states in which sentences are indeterminate, a paroling authority often must make a decision to release an offender and decide when that release should occur. Sentencing laws might determine when an offender is eligible for release, but he or she is not granted a release until a parole authority approves.

In the following cases, a paroling authority must determine whether to release an offender to a community. Factors considered often involve probability of recidivism, victim impact, community impact, conduct of offender in an institution, and release plan offered. Consider these cases and determine whether an offender's release has merit.

CASE A

Joseph, age 28, is serving up to 20 years for two counts of armed robbery. He has already served the mandatory minimum of five years and is being considered for release for the first time. Joseph served a previous sentence for burglary and successfully completed a release period before he committed the current crimes. The victims in both robberies were elderly gas station attendants, and very small amounts of money were obtained from the robberies. The victims remain fearful of the offender, and both indicate that their lives were significantly affected by the experience. Neither victim ever returned to work out of fear of similar future events. While incarcerated, Joseph has completed substance abuse treatment for his cocaine dependence, meeting treatment summary calls for his attendance in facility Cocaine Anonymous meetings. He attends such meetings about half of the time they are offered. He has also completed an anger management program, has been assigned to several inmate jobs, and has had no rule violations while incarcerated. Joseph would like to have transitioned to a work release facility, but due to a waiting list he was not able enter its program prior to being considered for release. His community plan is to return to the same community where he committed his crimes, live with his elderly aunt, seek work as a construction laborer, and attend community substance abuse aftercare. He would be under the supervision of a parole officer upon his release, if granted.

CASE B

Fred is a 39-year-old individual serving 14 years for possession with intent to sell a controlled substance. This is his second prison term, having served a six-year sentence for sale of heroin in the 1990s. He was paroled on the first offense after four years and successfully completed parole supervision. However, he was arrested on the current charge within two months of being released from parole supervision. Law enforcement officials reported that he had been under surveillance for several months before the arrest and was suspected of dealing drugs during most of the period under parole supervision. While under supervision, he reported regularly to his parole officer and worked steadily at a job in a warehouse owned by his brother-in-law. There were no known law violations during the period of supervision. Fred's institutional adjustment has been excellent. He attended drug counseling and is a member of the prison Narcotics Anonymous group. He attained his GED certificate and reports that he wants to attend community college when released. He will work for his brother-in-law again when released and live with his sister and her husband until he can afford to rent an apartment. The sheriff in the county in which he would live has protested his parole release, stating that Fred is a manipulative and devious individual who maintains a façade of cooperation and honest living while continuing to sell drugs. Fred has served 5 years of his current 14-year sentence. Institutional counselors recommend his release at this time.

CASE C

Marie is a 55-year-old female who has served 30 years of a 20 years-to-life sentence for murder. She was convicted of killing her two young children (ages two and four years). She reported that her live-in boyfriend would not agree to stay with her as long as she had children. She chose to kill the children to maintain that relationship. She has maintained a near-perfect prison record and is considered by authorities a model inmate. She reports great remorse for her actions. The prison chaplain has counseled her for many years and states that she has been "born again" and "forgiven" for her crimes and sins. Marie works as a chaplain's assistant in the institution and is well thought of by both prisoners and prison officials alike. If paroled, she will work for Prison Ministries in her hometown and will be provided with a place to stay by her employers.

Career Pathways in Community Corrections

Lisa F. Young/Shutterstock.com

CHAPTER OUTLINE

CHAPTER LEARNING OBJECTIVES

1. Understand how community corrections staff are selected and trained.

2. Identify the types of knowledge, skills, and abilities that staff needs to work with offenders in community-based corrections.

3. Compare and contrast various arguments in support of and against carrying firearms on the job.

4. Learn to identify and respond to various stressors inherent in most community corrections jobs.

5. Discuss the positive growth and criticisms of private probation agencies and treatment providers.

KEY TERMS

preservice training
in-service training
peace officer state training
role ambiguity
role conflict
negligence
absolute immunity
qualified immunity
private probation
private service provider
section 1983

John Doe was driving home from work in Atlanta, Georgia, when he noticed that a police cruiser was behind him with its siren and lights to pull him over. The officer said, "I've stopped you for speeding; I clocked you at 40 miles per hour in a 30 MPH zone. May I see your driver's license and insurance please?" Mr. Doe obliged willingly and didn't seem concerned about the stop—10 miles over wasn't a lot, he thought.

The officer returned 10 minutes later and said, "I was going to let you go, but Sir, I must instead place you under arrest. The probation department has a hold placed on you for violating probation." Mr. Doe was confused because it was over a year since he completed his 12-month probation period with a private probation company for reckless driving and illegal lane change. He was originally placed on probation because at that time, he was unemployed and could not afford the $500 fine for the traffic violations. He hadn't been in trouble since his initial misdemeanor arrest and he felt that there must be some mistake.

When he went to court, the judge said that there was no mistake. Mr. Doe had failed to pay his $500 fine in full and all the required fees of $40 per month before his probation ended, so the probation department requested that the court extend his sentence. Mr. Doe responded that while on probation, he had problems finding a job, and instead of working with him, the private probation department kept adding late "tolling" charges of an additional $30 per month (in addition to the $40 per month he already owed for "supervision"). Mr. Doe ignored the late charges and eventually paid the $500 fine and the $40 monthly fees.

The private probation company representative argued that of the $980 that Mr. Doe paid, $840 went to pay the monthly fees and the late charges, so Mr. Doe not only still owed the court $360 in fines, his probation had been extended and he also owed an additional $840 for the last 12 months that he had been on extended probation. Mr. Doe was furious, saying that he paid his fine and original monthly fees in full. Furthermore, Doe argued that he has never received any "services" from the private probation department and cannot believe that the county court allowed such hefty late charges and extended his probation for traffic violations—violations that most other people

In November 2014, the Georgia Supreme Court ruled that private probation companies are not allowed to collect "tolls" or add late charges to probationer fees. The Georgia Supreme Court also ruled that private probation companies are not allowed to request an extension of a probation sentence if the probationer is not paid in full, as long as he or she has been attempting to make payments when possible (Salzer, 2014). While John Doe was freed from jail and his probation sentence was completed in full, three questions remain:

Why are traffic violations in Georgia considered misdemeanors that are eligible for private probation supervision? Why is the rate of people being supervised for misdemeanors in Georgia more than four times the national average? Why are there so many private probation agencies in Georgia?

INTRODUCTION

People are initially attracted to probation and parole careers because of dual desires to help people and to protect the community, but ultimately it's helping others that motivates new trainees to stay in the profession (Deering, 2010). As you've learned, community supervision officers generally engage in five main functions:

1. Enforcing supervision conditions by means of monitoring with home visits, employment checks, and meetings with offenders;
2. Motivating offenders to find/maintain employment, remain sober, and continue with the change process;
3. Referring offenders to drug and alcohol treatment, anger management programs, parenting classes, and other community-based services according to their individual needs;
4. Conducting investigations and write reports regarding any significant violations and new criminal activity;
5. Working with crime victims and the community to ensure offender restitution payments and community service obligations are met, if applicable.

In implementing these functions, Carl Klockars (1972) developed a classic typology of probation supervision officers that designated four basic types: law enforcer, time-server, therapeutic agent, and synthetic officer. Klockars argued that these four styles are defined by an officer's professional beliefs about crime causation, the kind of training they received, and each department's orientation. Box 12.1 Orientation to system goals considered important (rehabilitation, deterrence, reentry, monitoring, etc.) affects the strategies officers use to ensure that offenders fulfill conditions of supervision. However, such orientation does not necessarily affect the amount of time spent in treatment and supervision activities (Payne & DeMichele, 2011a). This is because orientations are not rigid and opposing in nature but, rather, are flexible, applicable to offenders on a case-by-case basis. Furthermore, in supervising juvenile delinquents, officers over the age of 40 tended to hold less punitive attitudes than younger officers (Ward & Kupchik, 2010).

Most officers believe that the synthetic officer is the most effective because it entails a healthy combination of monitoring and therapeutic components (Lutze, 2014). Such officers apply punishment and treatment on a case-by-case basis and are involved in evidence-based practices—that is, holding offenders accountable for their behavior while being engaged in setting boundaries and motivating offenders to change. As you read this chapter, think about how these varied roles and working styles are influenced by officer beliefs, selection, and training.

SELECTION AND APPOINTMENT OF PROBATION OFFICERS

Initial selection of probation or parole officers is similar to that of other public employees. In addition to holding a baccalaureate degree, probation and parole officers must not have any felony convictions and must undergo a criminal background check. Most states also require parole and probation officers to be American citizens. Officers are appointed, selected on merit, or chosen by some combination of the two.

| BOX 12.1 | **EVIDENCE-BASED PRACTICES IN COMMUNITY CORRECTIONS** |

Which Officer Style Is Most Likely to Engage in EBP?

Carl Klockars (1972) designated four basic types of community supervision officers, each having a different emphasis. The four types are the law enforcer, therapeutic agent, synthetic officer, and time-server. These four types are based on Daniel Glaser's idea that community supervision is a dichotomy between power and authority over an individual and an expectation that officers assist offenders during their sentence. *Law enforcers* emphasize monitoring, authority, and enforcement aspects of their job, conveying that firmness and obeying the laws are essential. Of prime importance to such officers are following court orders, consistency, and making all decisions by the book. Law enforcers favor swift jail punishments over counseling and graduated sanctions for revocations (Steiner et al., 2011). The law enforcer may be effective in certain situations, but this officer has a low tolerance for misbehavior which contributes to low client rapport and ultimately a high client revocation rate.

Therapeutic agents see their role as administering treatment, assisting a probationer or parolee, providing guidance and support, and rewarding offenders when they had completed supervision goals (Steiner et al., 2011). They tend to spend a great deal of time and emotional investment on establishing a therapeutic alliance with each individual—respecting clients, demonstrating concern, and a huge degree of optimism. A therapeutic agent may hesitate or even wait too long to file a revocation in hopes that the client will change in the future. As a result, other staff may consider the therapeutic agent "too soft" or even a pushover at times—not establishing boundaries and letting their clients get away with too much negative behavior.

Synthetic officers are a hybrid style that balances treatment/rehabilitation with components of surveillance and control. Their philosophy is to help individuals understand how their old behavior has been problematic (places and people to avoid that put them at risk of offending) and how offenders can establish new supportive relationships and ways of behaving. Synthetic officers use motivational interviewing and positive rapport, but are also firm and fair with offenders. The officers seek community partnerships and support from offender's family members but are not afraid to create boundaries and enforce the rules when necessary (Miller, 2015). Synthetic officers favor graduated sanctions over jail for revocations and may view sanctions as mechanisms that enhance the change process (Steiner et al., 2011). They may encounter role conflict in combining an authoritarian model with a therapeutic one (Skeem & Manchak, 2008).

Time-servers have an immense amount of experience, but manifest little aspiration to improve their skills or change their ways. Their conduct on the job is that of abiding by the rules and meeting minimal job responsibilities, but time-servers are likely experiencing burnout and no longer strive to excel. They want to do as little paperwork as possible with as little probationer resistance to get through each day. The time-server has been criticized by clients as being not helpful or perhaps a bit callous, but clients also realize that a time-server may tolerate more technical violations than a law enforcer (Klockars, 1972).

Discussion: Which officer working style is most likely engage in evidence-based practices and why? Does the working style of an officer potentially affect the success or failure of an offender? If so, how? If not, why not?

Sources: Klockars, Carl B. 1972. A theory of probation supervision. *Journal of Criminal Law, Criminology and Police Science* 63(4): 550–557.

Appointment System

Jurisdictions that appoint probation officers are run by a judicial selection committee that appoints its chief probation officer. The chief probation officer can then hire new assistant probation officers and/or terminate assistant probation officers from the former chief's tenure. The system of politically appointing agency heads has received criticism because the leaders may not have the experience necessary and are accountable to judges who put them in that position to run the agency as the judges see fit (Paparozzi & Guy, 2013). Politically appointed leaders may be able to change personnel, but seem less able to change policy within their organizations (even if they wanted to), and as a result, may be behind agencies in which leaders are selected from the ranks for their ideas and vision.

Merit System

Merit, or civil service, systems were developed to remove public employees from political patronage. In a merit system, applicants who meet minimum employment standards are required to pass a competitive exam. Those who score above a specified minimum grade are placed on a ranked list. Candidates are selected from the list according to their order of rank. In some systems, applicants are also graded on the basis of their education and employment history. The merit system is used to determine promotions such that mid-range supervisors and chief probation officers are more likely to be hired from within the ranks of a department than in the appointment system.

OFFICER QUALIFICATIONS, SALARY, AND TRAINING

What does it take to be a good probation or parole officer? A female parole officer named Jane who made a career out of community correctional work remarked:

> We have to be able to recognize volatile situations; and you have to be able to know how to handle those situations using your communication skills. I have been involved in situations that could have easily turned volatile, but my manner, my demeanor, my communication skills, and the manner in which I dealt with these individuals has made a very big difference in the way they have responded to me. (Ireland & Berg, 2008, p. 483)

From his experience as an adult probation officer, Eladio Castillo provides his opinion in Box 12.2 on core competencies—desirable knowledge, skills, and abilities that officers should possess to supervise offenders in an EBP community.

Generally, individuals should possess confidence, integrity, sound knowledge about human behavior as well as good oral and written communication skills to be able to interview offenders, provide testimony to judges, and correspond with offenders' employers and family members. Relationship building and establishing rapport is key, along with knowing local programs and resources that exist in the area in which clients are referred. Knowing how to treat people fairly, consistently, firmly, and with respect is of utmost importance, especially when in the presence of an offender's family or employer (Ireland & Berg, 2008). It is helpful for officers to be knowledgeable about different cultures and to be good managers of time.

Education and Experience

Most juvenile and adult probation and parole officers must have a baccalaureate degree. The degree can be in any area, including criminal justice, criminology, social work, and psychology. As you can see from the sample job posting in Box 12.3, knowledge of crime causation and criminal law is important. Subjects that students can learn more about while they are taking classes and getting their

| BOX 12.2 | **FIELD NOTES** |

What type of knowledge, skills, and abilities do you believe are important to be a probation or parole officer?

The most important knowledge, skills, and abilities that I believe are important for students to acquire before looking for a job involve the use of critical thinking and professional interpersonal skills. The ability to identify and analyze information and observations swiftly to determine the validity of a judgment is a skill used on a daily basis. Students must learn to condition their mind to set aside assumptions, mindsets, and biases, and evaluate evidence to substantiate which hypothesis of a question has the least amount of inconsistencies.

Furthermore, working professionally and collaboratively with others is a skill that must be acquired. Knowing how to work with different offenders is important. You must learn to identify problems by focusing on the risk and needs of each individual. Understanding social learning, social bonding, mental disorders, substance abuse, finances, and criminal tendencies will facilitate your decision on how much time you should spend on the individual, whether in treatment or socioeconomic assistance. Whatever the

Courtesy of Leanne Fiftal Alarid

Eladio D. Castillo,
M.S. Former Adult Probation Officer

problem(s) may be, you must learn to identify it at the initial appointment or early in the probation term to avoid potential noncompliance.

Also, time and stress management are important skills. As is the case in many jobs, the number of offenders on a probation officer's caseload is often more than policy recommends. Nonetheless, you must learn to manage your time to accomplish specific tasks, projects, or goals. Time management depends on the individual, and you must learn to prioritize activities. You will feel the weight of stress over time, but adapting and coping with the stress is key.

Lastly, understanding and communicating in a secondary language is an asset. Executives consider secondary languages when hiring, and some agencies even provide incentive pay. If the offenders feel comfortable with you, their compliance increases from my experience. Although a secondary language is not required, it would be beneficial to acquire the skill, not only for probation but in any of your future aspirations.

degree include understanding antisocial personality disorder and detecting thinking errors, fully appreciating causes of substance abuse and treatment modalities, identifying which strategies work effectively with certain types of offenders; and understanding what it takes to change habits and behaviors (e.g., motivational interviewing, relapse prevention). To learn more about these topics, courses outside of criminal justice that are helpful to take include those in social work and psychology:

- Abnormal psychology
- Drug use and abuse
- Mental health treatment
- Developmental psychology

Officer Salary

Based on positions advertised nationwide in 2013 (www.payscale.com), an entry-level probation officer or correctional treatment specialist with less than one year of experience can expect a median salary of $35,000. With five to nine years of experience, the median salary for the same job is $40,000; with 10 to

| BOX 12.3 | COMMUNITY CORRECTIONS UP CLOSE |

Two Sample Job Advertisements

JOB #1: U.S. PROBATION OFFICER

A career position for presentence and investigation/supervision officer in U.S. Probation. Minimum requirements: BS/BA degree in criminal justice, criminology, or psychology *and* three years related corrections experience; or MA/MS degree and one year related corrections experience (local or state pretrial, probation, parole). Computer skills required. Under age 37 (OPM Reg. SCRF842.803A).

Starting salary $55K. Send cover letter, resume, and AO78 application (www.ohsp.uscourts.gov)

JOB #2: STATE PAROLE/PROBATION OFFICER (PPO)

Wages: $17.81–$28.32/hr (depends on grade)
Union: United Auto Workers

Job Description: Employee of this position follows the policies, procedures, Directors Office Memorandums (DOMs), and guiding principles of the Department of Corrections to provide background information to the courts on offenders convicted in Circuit Court and to supervise those convicted.

Minimum Education: Possession of a bachelor's degree in criminal justice, correctional administration, criminology, psychology, social work, counseling and guidance, child development, sociology, school social work, social work administration, education psychology, family relations, human services, or theology.

Minimum Experience:
   PPO 9: None required.
   PPO 10: One year of professional experience working with adult offenders equivalent to a PPO 9.
   PPO 11: Two years of professional experience working with adult offenders equivalent to a PPO 9 or 10.

Special Requirements: Possession of a valid driver's license and the availability of an automobile for business. Possession of a cell phone listed in the name of the employee. Residence is required in the area where employed. Passing a criminal background check and substance abuse test.

How to Apply: Interested applicants must submit a cover letter, resume, copy of official college transcript and Reference Authorization form. All required forms must be submitted at the time of application for further consideration. Application materials must be postmarked by the deadline date.

Source: http://www.careerbuilder.com. Retrieved on May 11, 2015.

19 years, the salary is $46,000, and with 20 years or more on the job, the salary rises to $58,000. Another salary website reported overall average for probation and parole officers as $46,000 (www.indeed.com/salary/). Probation officers in urban areas working for local government agencies tended to earn higher salaries than when a department was situated in a state government.

Another general trend is that parole officers in stand-alone departments had a higher starting salary. They also earned higher salaries over their career than did parole or probation officers in combined departments. The differences in salary could be due to fewer turnovers of probation officers in stand-alone departments or from earning better raises over time than those provided by combined departments. Probation and parole administrators earned considerably more than did field officers. The average salary for parole administrators was $161,435 and for probation administrators $101,109. In combined departments, probation and parole administrators earned an average of $84,442 (Camp et al., 2003).

preserve training
Fundamental knowledge and/or skills for a newly hired officer in preparation for working independently.

in-service training
Periodic continuing education training for seasoned officers.

Community Supervision Officer Training

Staff training is separated into two basic types: preservice and in-service. Once a new officer has been selected and hired, he or she begins **preservice training** to provide the basic knowledge, skills, and abilities that newly hired officers need before they begin working independently. Probation and parole departments normally require between 120 and 200 hours of preservice training before officers assume their duties. No national training standards exist for training juvenile probation officers, so officers who work with youths received only an average of 100 hours—significantly less training than officers who work with adults. Table 12.1 shows an example of a training curriculum for probation and parole officers that provides 150 hours of basic training.

In-service training consists of continuing education training that occurs annually for all seasoned officers following their first year of employment. This allows officers to keep current with new laws and new developments in the field or to repeat important topics from initial training. In-service training may include cultural competency, peace officer training to become certified to carry a weapon

TABLE 12.1   Example of Probation/Parole Officer Basic Training Topics and Hours

I.	OVERVIEW of Community Corrections Programs:	4 Hours
II.	LEGAL ISSUES:	14 Hours
	Presentence Investigation and Report (4)	
	Technical Violations, Sanctions, Hearings (4)	
	Search, Seizure, and Arrest Procedures (6)	
III.	OFFICER–CLIENT RELATIONS:	38 Hours
	Understanding Offender Behavior (4)	
	Cognitive-Behavioral Counseling (6)	
	Crisis Intervention and Home Visits (4)	
	Offenders with Drug Addictions, Mental Health Issues (12)	
	Motivational Interviewing (4)	
	Evidence-Based Practices (4)	
	Community Resources (2)	
IV.	CASE MANAGEMENT:	44 Hours
	Targeting Offender Risk and Needs (8)	
	Treatment Plans and Offender Supervision (20)	
	Parole/Probation Violations and Revocations (6)	
	Report/Technical Writing (10)	
V.	DEFENSIVE PROTECTION:	18 Hours
	Controls, Restraints, Defensive Techniques (8)	
	Verbal De-escalation (10)	
VI.	PROFESSIONAL CONDUCT AND ETHICS:	20 Hours
	Scenario-Based Role Plays and Ethics (12)	
	Courtroom Demeanor and Testifying (8)	
VII.	OTHER:	12 Hours
	Drug/Alcohol Identification (2)	
	Gang Identification (2)	
	Employee Wellness/Stress Reduction (2)	
	Written and Oral Exams (6)	
	Total Number of Training Hours	**150 Hours**

(discussed in next section), in-depth cognitive-behavioral treatment techniques, recognizing child abuse/neglect, and empathy training. In empathy training, probation officers become sensitized to what juvenile probationers endure during arrest and detention (Hartzler & Espinosa, 2011). Other examples of in-service training include bringing in outside trainers or "peer coaches" for three-day refresher workshops, such as one out of Canada called "Strategic Training Initiative in Community Supervision." Another workshop series is called "Effective Practices in Community Supervision" out of Cincinnati and one for federal probation officers called: "Staff Training at Reducing Re-Arrest" (Bourgon, 2013, p. 31). These training modules seem to provide officers with evidence-based tools that help offenders reduce criminal thinking patterns, cognitive distortions, and behavioral change. In turn, the training also helped officers develop tolerance for the change process (Labrecque et al., 2013).

The American Correctional Association recommends that seasoned officers receive 40 hours of annual training. For officers supervising juveniles, only 30 states require some annual training of about 30 hours per year. A recent study was able to show that when juvenile probation officers were trained with peer coaches in evidence-based techniques such as reflective listening, affirmations, and motivational interviewing, the training itself was tied directly to officers responding differently to juveniles. The officers with enhanced training through in-house peer specialists had lower rates of surveillance-oriented and punitive referrals, which in turn, lowered the recidivism rates of juvenile probationers (Young et al., 2013).

As officers' job expectations have risen, the amount of training and responsibility has also increased. One example of increased responsibility is that many officers are authorized to carry firearms—an issue we discuss next.

FIREARMS' POLICIES FOR PROBATION AND PAROLE OFFICERS

One of the most significant and controversial changes that has occurred over the last few decades in probation and parole is the increased prevalence of officers who carry concealed firearms on the job. In the federal system, 85 out of 94 judicial districts allow federal probation officers to carry firearms of .40 caliber and above. At the state and county levels, officers in 35 adult probation jurisdictions and in 40 adult parole jurisdictions carry firearms (see Table 12.2). Although these numbers might seem as if most officers carry a weapon, only about half of all firearm-carrying jurisdictions in the adult system are mandatory. The other half of jurisdictions have authorized firearms, but their use is either voluntary or the policy is limited only to the small number of officers who supervise specialized caseloads or who make evening home visits.

In comparison with those officers supervising adults, the vast majority of juvenile officers do not carry firearms. In the juvenile system, 15 states mandate that officers carry firearms, two give officers the option, and two states narrow firearms only to certain counties or to officers who supervise serious juvenile offenders. If an officer carries a firearm, most departments require officers to purchase and maintain all their own equipment (weapon, holster, bullets, etc.) without reimbursement. Officers are allowed to carry a firearm only when working on the job (they are not authorized to carry off the clock as an officer, but may if they have also received a permit to carry as a private citizen).

TABLE 12.2   Firearms' Policies for Probation and Parole Officers

	PROBATION		PAROLE	
Firearms' Policy	Adult	Juvenile	Adult	Juvenile
Officers not armed statewide	17	40	12	43
Mandatory arming statewide	17	4	25	3
County specific	6	5	2	2
Optional choice	9	2	9	2
Job specific (Intensive)	3	2	4	1

Source: American Probation and Parole Association. 2006. *APPA Adult and Juvenile Probation and Parole National Firearm Survey*, 2nd ed. Lexington, KY: APPA. Accessed: http://www.appa-net.org/eweb/Resources/Surveys/National_Firearms /docs/NFS_2006.pdf

Peace Officer State Training
Specialized and standardized training that officers are required to complete before they may carry a firearm on a job.

Officers can typically use their firearm only in self-defense, or if the officer believes he/she, or a fellow officer, is in imminent danger of death or serious bodily injury. Departmental firearms' policies do not usually allow a probation or parole officer to use a firearm to come to the aid of any other third party. In states in which probation and parole officers carry firearms, they must first complete **Peace Officer State Training** (POST), which may be as much as 500 hours in a separate training facility where they learn about mental preparedness, psychological testing, proper decision making, responsible gun use, and must score 80% or higher on firearms proficiency. Once trained, officers must requalify every year to remain current on their license according to state peace officer regulations.

A trainee takes aim at a simulated gunman projected onto a screen of the Firearms Training System (FATS). FATS helps officers who carry guns make better decisions during confrontations.

AP Photo/Rick Rycroft

Arguments in Support of Carrying Firearms

Most officers, particularly those who made late-night home visits and specialized units who supervised gang members and violent offenders, reported feeling safer when carrying a firearm. Officers who favored firearms while on duty tended to be individuals who favored law-and-order case management strategies than those who favored counseling or treatment-oriented approaches. Guns seem to satisfy a psychological need for safety independent of an actual threat (Roscoe et al., 2007). At the same time, another study found that carrying firearms did not seem to change the way that parole officers supervised their clients, nor did it change the rapport they had with their clients (Lopez, 2007).

An interesting viewpoint came from female parole officers who noted that in a male-dominated occupation emphasizing safety, security, and physical prowess, female parole officers acquired more respect from male parole agents by making a decision to carry a weapon even if they never intended to use it (Ireland & Berg, 2008). However, not all female officers felt the same. Teressa Price provides her first-hand experience about carrying a firearm when working with juveniles on probation in Pennsylvania (see Box 12.4). Pennsylvania is a state that leaves the decision open to each individual agency, does not allow officers to take the county-issued weapons home, and funds the cost of equipment and training through a $5 fee paid by all convicted offenders (Learn-Andes, 2014). As of 2014, 78% of the counties in Pennsylvania opted for their officers to carry, and 22% of counties were not authorized for any officer to possess a firearm (Halpin, 2014).

Arguments Against Carrying Firearms

Arming probation and parole officers seem to be an American phenomenon that is not shared by other countries, such as those in the United Kingdom. "I have yet to meet an English or Welsh officer who has expressed the slightest wish to carry firearms" (Teague, 2011, p. 326). U.S. jurisdictions in which probation is under the judicial branch have tended to oppose the carrying of firearms, contending that doing so is a function under the executive branch of powers and not appropriate for employees of the judicial branch. The New Jersey Supreme Court upheld this, ruling that judicial officers performing an executive branch function unconstitutionally violated the separation of powers (*Williams v. State of New Jersey*, 2006) and might conflict with rehabilitation objectives and traditional casework strategies.

Officers opposed to carrying a firearm question whether a threat is real or perceived. Such opponents argue that not every probation officer needs to carry a deadly weapon, especially if that officer supervises misdemeanants or juveniles. Rita explains that carrying weapons can change how situations are handled:

> When I was first a parole agent, we did not carry weapons. When I left, it was an option [*pause*]; it was also a part of my decision to leave. I did not feel that carrying a weapon was good for the job. We had not done that; you learned to talk your way through things; you learned to look at things differently [*pause*] in order to resolve your problems. I was not for weapons, although I was comfortable with them. [*thoughtful pause*]....When I came back, it was mandatory to carry a weapon. It was required. I became comfortable with it. I've never had to use it for protection or because I was in fear. (Ireland & Berg, 2008, p. 484)

Probation officers who carried a firearm experienced more incidents of confrontation than did officers not carrying a firearm. This might have been due either to a higher volatility of an offender or the way in which an officer

| BOX 12.4 | **FIELD NOTES** |

Did carrying a firearm change the way you approached community supervision of juveniles? If so, how? Do you think the policy is a good idea?

As a juvenile probation officer (JPO), I feel it is important that I am equipped with everything necessary to maintain my safety, as well as the safety of those around me. I was a JPO for eight months before becoming certified to carry a firearm. For those eight months, I was stationed at a local high school and was required to visit the homes of juveniles on my caseload on a weekly basis from 6 P.M. to 10 P.M. I had to be out after dark, wearing a visible vest with "Probation Officer" in big letters on the back. Anyone could spot me easily and all I had was mace and a baton, not enough to protect myself from a kid with a gun.

I received my certification on a Friday and began carrying my firearm the following Tuesday. I would not say that it necessarily changed how I supervised the juveniles on my caseload, but it did change my comfort level in that I knew that I had the training and ability to react in the unfortunate situation that anyone, not just a juvenile, should open fire either at the school or in the community.

Detaining juveniles, sending them to placements and boot camps or treatment centers, along with placing them on electronic monitoring sometimes are a part of supervising juveniles. All of the above things came at a monetary cost to the parents who, often times, could not afford the burden of paying child support to a placement for their child resulting in the government garnishing their wages. And I was the one making the decision to

Teressa Price
Former Juvenile Probation Officer

recommend these things to the court. All it would take is one upset juvenile, or parent for that matter, to get their hands on a firearm and see me as a target.

With violence among juveniles increasing, I believe it is a good policy that juvenile probation officers have all the equipment necessary to protect them. If someone opens fire randomly, or at me specifically, I would not be able to do much with a can of mace. With being stationed at a school, it is especially important because I, along with the school resource officer, would also have the ability to protect the students and faculty of the school. While I would not say that school shootings are the norm, I would say that these things do happen occasionally. Juveniles are receiving charges for bringing a weapon on school property—anything from a small baseball bat to an AK-47. In the crucial minutes it would take for someone to call 911 and the police to respond, many could be wounded or dead. School probation officers and school resource officers could respond immediately to the threat whether that threat is another student, or an intruder in the school.

I know that juvenile probation officers carrying firearms is a controversial subject and that not everyone agrees that it is a necessary part of supervising children in the community. I, however, am grateful to have every protection possible, along with the knowledge and training on how and when to use it in the event that I need it.

handled a situation—or both. Furthermore, if a probationer or parolee is carrying a weapon, an armed officer's safety is at greater risk compared with that of an unarmed officer.

From a more practical viewpoint, carrying firearms entails ongoing liability and training costs. One jurisdiction in which adult probation officers did carry firearms later prohibited all officers from carrying weapons. The moratorium resulted from concern about the department's ability to pay for proper training within its budget (Chasnoff, 2006). Some jurisdictions favor a policy of carrying

| BOX 12.5 | **TECHNOLOGY IN CORRECTIONS** |

Interactive Firearms Video Training

The Firearms Training Simulator (or FATS®) uses interactive video technology to enhance the training in firearms of any peace officer, including probation, parole, and pretrial services officers. FATS is different from shooting at traditional fixed targets, in that a video image projected onto a screen is connected to a computer, speakers, and firearm replicas that spray liquid peppermint when a trigger is pulled.

Each unique scenario requires trainees to choose which action to take. After a variety of scenarios, trainees discuss and justify their actions to an instructor. The training is effective both to mentally prepare individuals and assure them how to make better split second decisions.

Source: http://www.meggitttrainingsystems.com/Commercial -ranges/Commercial-simulation-equipment/FATS-L7.aspx

firearms but simply can't afford to implement it. Other effective options include use of chemical agents, stun guns, self-defense/pressure point training, and home visits by two officers.

As probation and parole officers increasingly carry firearms on the job, they are also considered a type of law enforcement officer, particularly if they have completed peace officer training. Should officers be authorized to carry weapons, decisions must be made as to actual need, proper training, liability issues, and selection procedures that minimally include physical and psychological examinations. All officers who choose to carry a firearm receive training, such as the *Firearms Training Simulator* (see Box 12.5).

One of the strongest indicators of a department's overall philosophy of offender supervision is symbolized by its firearms policy. One study found that as the percentage of armed officers' increases, the more enforcement-oriented the department (Roscoe et al., 2007). Carrying a firearm also creates more legal liability for a department and puts a heavier burden on the individual. Thus, making the decision to carry firearms is very much an individual choice that should be carefully considered. When deciding where to work, new applicants may wish to research what kind of firearms' policy exists in their state or at that agency (mandatory, optional, no firearms allowed) and determine what is most consistent with their own individual philosophies about offender supervision and treatment.

STRESSORS ENCOUNTERED IN PROBATION AND PAROLE

> …[T]he officer is charged with the responsibility to make the right decisions about the offender: when to trust, when to violate, and when to simply hope that nothing goes wrong with the supervision plan. If something does go wrong, officers undergo administrative scrutiny that although legitimate, is also designed to be critical—and, when something goes seriously wrong, legislators, advocates, judges, and juries often have something to say about what happened. (Severson & Pettus-Davis, 2013, p. 19)

Probation and parole supervision is centered around managing people rather than on processing information. Building professional relationships and "achieving successful outcomes with offenders who have managed to make changes in their life" (Annison et al., 2008, p. 266) is an art, and when officers can impact the lives of even one person for the better they are rewarded with a great deal of satisfaction.

Jobs that are people-centered also tend to demand higher levels of risk-taking and result in greater burnout than do jobs that are data-oriented. This is in part because caring officers "often connect emotionally (whether in a positive or negative way) with our clients or the victims, and this can in turn cause us emotional turmoil" (Catanese, 2010, p. 37). Further, the emotional attachment to the job that comes from working with clients is different from connecting with the working conditions of one's department. Client-centered employees who do not feel a positive emotional connection or sense of belonging were more likely to leave, and organizational factors were found to contribute more to employee turnover than did the nature of the work itself (Lee et al., 2009). Although most jobs are stressful to some degree, situations that place unreasonable demands on one or that take a person outside his or her comfort zone can exacerbate stress. This section seeks to inform readers realistically about community corrections supervision so that those interested in this profession are more fully aware of the demands this line of work presents. Studies of officer stress certainly apply to any position involving community corrections supervision.

Sources of Stress

How do officers manage the pressures of maintaining a caseload, what with its work of supervising clients' contacts and drug tests and of filing reports within a specific time period? Researchers have uncovered the following sources of stress for community supervision officers (Drapela & Lutze, 2009; Vicini, 2013):

- Excessive paperwork
- Lack of control over high caseload sizes
- Lack of promotional opportunities
- Role ambiguity/conflict (treatment vs. punishment)
- Perceived court leniency on offenders
- Agency failure to recognize accomplishments
- Perceived lack of supervisory support
- Fear of being sued

Sometimes feeling overly stressed can simply mean that a job is not a good fit for a person. In criminal justice, written documentation is an important part of taking legal responsibility for the supervision and treatment of another person. Federal officers in particular spend a lot of time documenting matters on every client they supervise, which accounts for complaints of what some officers refer to as "excessive paperwork" (Slate & Johnson, 2008). Time spent on paperwork coupled with heavy caseloads has led to officers feeling like they lack time for the actual supervision or treatment of clients.

In fact, caseloads that were too high were a major source of job discontent. Although caseload sizes averaged 140 offenders, they ranged widely between a low of 30 to nearly 4,000 individuals for one officer to supervise. As caseload size increased, officers were less tolerant of technical violations and more likely to write a court report to support a violation (Kerbs et al., 2009). To the extent that writing a report entails more work, this finding may seem counterintuitive, but it is possible that officers hope to receive a temporary reprieve by way of a replacement with a different client. Experts have consistently recommended that caseload sizes be reduced to an appropriate level to allow officers meaningful contact with offenders while also reducing their stress and turnover (Drapela & Lutze, 2009; Ireland & Berg, 2008).

ROLE AMBIGUITY   **Role ambiguity** refers to the fact that community supervision officers have broad discretion and authority over offenders. The degree of independent decision making that community correctional officers have has been equated with that of a police lieutenant (Ireland & Berg, 2008). People accustomed only to following the lead of others and uncomfortable making their own decisions can experience a sense of uneasiness with this kind of authority. This is why setting boundaries, using common sense, and behaving ethically and consistently are so important. Further, "professionals may become too involved with their work, not setting proper boundaries with individuals on their caseload. They may find themselves staying at work longer or not being able to separate work from their personal lives" (Catanese, 2010, p. 37). Time management is especially important when officers must conduct home visits in the field.

ROLE CONFLICT   **Role conflict**, a common source of stress, can arise from playing "good cop/bad cop"—constantly switching from trying to gain trust and increase motivation, to having to recommend revocation. Officers must be empathetic, and understanding enough to help offenders, yet be firm, consistent, and objective enough to make those tough decisions of graduated sanctions, or revocation of clients who do not follow the conditions of their supervision.

Finally, supervising offenders can all too often mean ignoring basic principles of behavior modification: to reward positive behavior and to discourage negative behavior. Officers in community corrections supervision frequently take action on negative behavior while downplaying positive or prosocial behavior.

role ambiguity
The discretion inherent in the role of a probation and parole officer to treat clients fairly, consistently, and according to individual circumstances.

role conflict
The two functions of a probation and parole officer that are sometimes contradictory and difficult to reconcile: (1) enforcing rules and laws and (2) providing support and reintegration.

Home visits and searches are important tools that probation and parole officers use to ensure that conditions are being followed.

CIRO CESAR/LA OPINION/Newscom

Such practices are enough to make a behavioral psychologist shudder and might explain, at least in part, why so many offenders "fail" under supervision. A policy of rewarding offenders for positive behavior can help officers feel good as well.

Alleviating the Fear of Being Sued: Types of Immunity

Given the large amount of discretion officers have, the fear of being named in a civil lawsuit is a concern for some (Drapela & Lutze, 2009). One way to decrease stress is for officers to know the general limits of the law regarding actions and inactions on the job. First, it is important for officers to minimize risk by keeping track of the people they are supervising and responding professionally to inappropriate behaviors. No matter how accomplished and competent an officer is, officers cannot control the actions of another person at all times.

The best that officers can do is to follow departmental policy, follow the orders of a court or a parole board, justify their actions with accurate paperwork, and *avoid* being negligent. **Negligence** is a failure to do that which a reasonably prudent person would do in similar circumstances. For example, if an officer finds out through credible sources that one of her probationers is planning to commit a crime and therefore is in a position to prevent it but fails do so, she is likely negligent. An officer can be held liable (or responsible) if the negligence was gross or willful. Though such terms depend on the meaning assigned by a judge or jury, gross or willful negligence generally means that a person must have intentionally or maliciously failed to act.

Because probation and parole officers are government officials (as are police, judges, and prosecutors), they are entitled to different types of legal protection so that they are comfortable exercising discretion without fear of being personally sued over the actions of clients under their supervision. The type of immunity that officers have depends on what function they are performing (Drapela & Lutze, 2009).

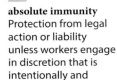

negligence
The failure of an officer to do what a reasonably prudent person would do in like circumstances.

absolute immunity
Protection from legal action or liability unless workers engage in discretion that is intentionally and maliciously wrong.

ABSOLUTE IMMUNITY FOR QUASI-JUDICIAL FUNCTIONS   **Absolute immunity** protects government officials from any legal action unless they engage in acts that are intentionally and maliciously wrong. Absolute immunity provides the highest level of protection for anyone who officially acts in a legislative, quasi-judicial, or prosecutorial function. For example, parole board officials have absolute immunity in decisions to grant, deny, or revoke parole (*King v. Simpson*, 1999). Probation and parole officers have absolute immunity only when they are acting in a quasi-judicial function, such as in the preparation and submission of a presentence investigation report, even if there are errors later found in the report (*Spaulding v. Nielsen*, 1979). Recall that every defendant has an opportunity to review and make changes to any errors in his or her PSI before it is submitted to a judge. State statutes, however, must define PSI reports as a quasi-judicial function—otherwise a probation officer is eligible for a lower level of protection called *qualified immunity*. Another important thing to remember is that even though absolute immunity protects individuals from being sued (even if there was harm caused), it does not protect them from being tried in criminal court if criminal behavior occurred.

QUALIFIED IMMUNITY FOR ADMINISTRATIVE FUNCTIONS   Compared with absolute immunity, qualified immunity is much more narrow and is limited to compliance with agency policy for employees in the executive branch or workers performing administrative functions, such as offender monitoring and supervision.

In **qualified immunity**, workers are not liable for wrongdoing when their actions are found to be "objectively reasonable" and within the scope of agency directives and/or policies at that time, given limited information. The legal standard of being "objectively reasonable" is ironically quite subjective. Given that most functions of probation and parole officers are administrative, such officers have qualified immunity even when involved in a disciplinary or probation revocation hearing, which is considerably different from a court hearing whose outcome results in conviction.

Community supervision officer functions are defined differently from jurisdiction to jurisdiction. In New York, for example, parole officers have only qualified immunity when recommending an issuance of a revocation warrant. This is because under New York law issuing a revocation warrant is considered investigatory, and not a prosecutorial function (*Best v. State*, 1999). In another state the same activity—initiating a parole revocation proceeding and presenting a case during parole revocation hearings—was identified as a quasi-judicial function and was therefore subject to absolute immunity.

The biggest problem arises when there is an absence of policy for various activities, such as for neighborhood-based supervision activities like those integrated with police substations in which probation officers build relationships with agency leaders and work toward solving problems endemic to a community (Drapela & Lutze, 2009). Despite fears of lawsuits, the reality is that officers who do their job well and follow agency policy are protected by qualified immunity. In cases in which no policy exists for a particular activity, policy needs to be drafted and officer training must occur. The most important thing an officer can do is to always act in an ethical and responsible manner.

Despite these potential stressors, many people find community corrections very rewarding and have spent their entire career in this field. Agencies that encourage social support among officers and providing debriefing or counseling for traumatic events are essential to maintain a positive work environment (Severson & Pettus-Davis, 2013). Catanese's (2010) recommendation for individuals is to "maintain a light and humorous work environment…steer clear of negative people and form relationships with colleagues who have positive attitudes…surround themselves with others who are not in the same profession… [and] avoid negative coping skills such as alcohol consumption, risky behaviors, or isolation" (p. 38).

PRIVATE PROBATION

Because of a limited number of staff available to supervise a growing number of probationers, states are increasingly contracting with private probation agencies to assist with supervision. **Private probation** agencies contract with local or state government to provide misdemeanor probation supervision. According to Alarid and Schloss (2009), private probation refers to both supervision and/or treatment services, so a more generic term for a private probation company is a **private service provider**. Such a provider is "any for profit or nonprofit private organization that contracts with county-level or state-level government to provide probation supervision, independent probation treatment services, or both probation supervision and treatment under one roof" (Alarid & Schloss, 2009, p. 5).

At least 18 states currently use the private sector for some form of supervision. Ten states grant private agencies sole responsibility for supervising misdemeanor and low-risk clients, relying on a state agency to focus on felony

qualified immunity
Protection from liability in decisions or actions that are "objectively reasonable."

private probation
An agency owned and operated by a private business or nonprofit organization that contracts with state, local, or federal government to supervise clients convicted of a misdemeanor.

private service provider
Any for-profit or nonprofit, private organization that contracts with county-level or state-level government to provide probation supervision, independent probation treatment services, or both probation supervision and treatment.

probationers (Schloss & Alarid, 2007). Of states that rely on the private sector for misdemeanor supervision (AL, AR, AZ, CA, FL, GA, MO, TN, UT), Georgia uses private probation agencies significantly more than all other states. More than half a million people were on misdemeanor probation last year in Georgia, which is four times the national average (Salzer, 2014). The number of probationers does not include the thousands of probationers who are court-ordered to attend outpatient treatment centers (many of which are private) and the thousands of offenders in residential community correction facilities.

The privatization debate is centered on two main arguments. The first assumes that continued growth in the correctional system ensures survival of private agencies that depend on outside referrals and fees collected from offenders, but that some level of supervision or service must still be provided. The second suggests that because government cannot adequately function as effectively as private companies, services for lower-risk individuals must be redistributed out of necessity, so that the government can refocus its efforts on higher risk clients.

Staff in the United Kingdom who worked for public probation agencies and left to work for private agencies reported that private agencies were more innovative and responded to change faster than public agencies that created "…the need to provide quality and to achieve targets and goals set for them in order to win further contracts and hence protect their future employment; they also emphasized the need to perform as poor performance would not be tolerated" (Deering et al., 2014, p. 245).

Services Provided by Private Probation and Private Treatment Companies

Private nonprofit entities have been involved in community supervision of offenders for quite a long time—since the 1800s, in fact. The Salvation Army has a long history of providing such services. Over time, state codes and statutes were formulated to permit the provision of private agencies for ancillary treatment services to state and local probationers, such as for mental health, driving-while-intoxicated classes, drug treatment, and anger management (see Figure 12.1). There are even fee-based companies that will write a presentence investigation report to be used at sentencing, which reportedly favors financially affluent offenders (Teague, 2011).

As state and local governments look to trim costs in their budgets, they have increasingly turned to private companies for a wide array of services, from drug testing to electronic monitoring. A privatized probation system allows probationers to choose from a variety of contractors, who would compete on the basis of cost for services provided and location. Private providers are fined by the state for not providing an agreed-upon level of services. The state can choose not to renew their contract if the agency is under performing (Hucklesby, 2011).

Many private contractors do not have face-to-face contact with any low-level probationers but rather assist in monitoring community service compliance via phone, mail, and email. Georgia has 32 different private probation companies throughout the state; reduced from 41 companies in 2006. One such private company providing misdemeanor probation services is Providence Community Corrections, which operates in Florida, Georgia, South Carolina, Tennessee, and Washington. Providence Community Corrections is a subsidiary of Providence Service Corporation, which provides substance abuse treatment and is involved with drug courts and adult community corrections (see www.provcorp.com).

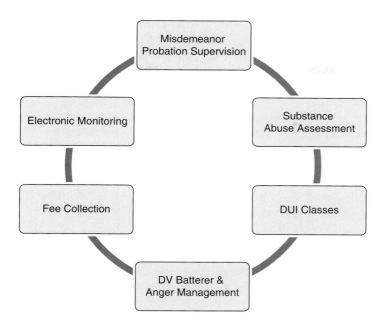

Statutes Authorizing Private Probation

The American Legislative Exchange Council has developed model legislation related to probation privatization. Regulating the private sector has generally been slow, with some jurisdictions operating in a grey area of unclear or nonexistent standards concerning the awarding of contracts to private providers, staff hiring requirements, and curricula for outpatient treatment services (Schloss & Alarid, 2007). Statutes examined by Schloss and Alarid (2007) in seven states that authorized private probation (Alabama, Arkansas, Florida, Georgia, Missouri, Utah, and Tennessee) found that most required agencies to sign a formal contract with the government outlining the scope of services to be provided, the responsibilities of the contractor, and the obligations of the court. For example, private agencies in Missouri wishing to provide services must make application with a circuit judge, prove financial ability to operate a probation office, and provide liability insurance. However, Missouri has few standardized guidelines for private agency approval other than that an agency cannot be related in any way to a judge. Once agencies are approved for a three-year term, there are no requirements to provide verification of fees collected.

Criticism of Probation Privatization

Critics of privatization argue that the need to provide effective correctional services is at odds with a profit-making agenda. Private probation may be viewed as intruding upon and competing with government's traditional, core responsibility to carry out punishment in a fair manner. Furthermore, the private sector is not equipped to be a full-service organization and thus might only be able to take on low-risk offenders who require little, if any monitoring. Private-sector services generally have no uniform method of monitoring probation conditions or of ensuring that victim restitution is collected.

Also, state statutes stipulate a range of requirements for hiring officers as employees. There is concern that employees in private companies, compared with those in the public sector, receive less training, have less opportunity for career advancement, and show higher staff turnover (Hucklesby, 2011).

Another concern relates to a lack of standardization for agencies that wish to become probation program providers. Some states have no requirement that providers demonstrate such qualifications as licensing and experience (Schloss & Alarid, 2007). This is particularly disconcerting given that the U.S. Supreme Court ruled in the case of a private prison that the same level of qualified immunity protection should not be provided to employees of private correctional companies as to government employees (Richardson v. McKnight, 1997). This is because private companies can include into their contracts those conditions under which they will indemnify employees found liable for their actions on the job. In *Correctional Services Corp vs. Malesko* (2001), the Supreme Court ruled that in such a **Section 1983** case the harmed individual must sue the person responsible for the harm, but that a private company is not considered a person. Therefore a private company cannot be sued under Section 1983, and a plaintiff must go after individuals deemed to be responsible. These two U.S. Supreme Court decisions indicate that individual employees working for private companies are by far the least protected individuals in the criminal justice system, especially if a company has not fully outlined an indemnification clause.

Georgia has been under intense scrutiny for its illegal use of tolling, which was adding late fees to financially strapped probationers, causing them to incur more charges to the company and ultimately end up in jail for failure to pay. Critics contended that the money has been used for company profits and expansion, and not for the betterment of probationers who were initially placed on probation because they could not afford their court fine. The Georgia Supreme Court ruled in 2014 that private probation companies are not allowed to collect "tolls" or late charges on probationers, nor is the court allowed to extend a probation sentence if not paid in full, as long as the probationer has been attempting to make payments when possible (Salzer, 2014).

In the process, audits were done on various private probation companies to ensure that they were fulfilling their contractual obligations. The audits uncovered misconduct that went beyond tolling practices, which likely caused the number of private probation agencies in Georgia to be reduced from 41 in 2006 to 32 in 2015 (Georgia County and Municipal Advisory Council, 2015). For example, one company failed to conduct criminal background checks of employees, submit a current employee roster, and may have falsified employee training hours. For new employees of private probation companies, Georgia requires that new employees complete 40 hours of training and a criminal background check within 10 days of hiring. Once hired, a current list of employees is to be kept on file with the Advisory Council. Employees are to receive 20 hours of in-service training after their first year. Ultimately, the company lost its license in 2013. Georgia's use of private probation is predicted to continue, but it is unclear to what extent traffic violators who cannot afford their fine will be allowed by the court to be supervised under

Section 1983
A federal lawsuit alleging that a government official violated one or more of an individual's civil rights afforded them in the U.S. Constitution.

private probation supervision. The Georgia Governor appointed panel of experts to study the issue and make recommendations for changes (Salzer, 2014).

Views on Privatization

Recommendation of community supervision as a sanction is partly dependent upon the perception of courtroom attorneys—that is, whether they accept probation as a viable alternative. During a case screening process, prosecutors decide whether sufficient evidence exists to charge a defendant with a crime. If enough evidence exists, prosecutors also decide the level or severity of an offense. They are in a unique position to assess defendant eligibility for probation and/or to connect defendants with private probation agencies. Because of this, prosecutors and defense attorneys were surveyed on the use of private treatment providers. Private agency accountability to courts was of primary concern for prosecutors, whereas defense attorneys were more concerned about treatment costs for their clients (Alarid & Schloss, 2009).

In contrast with traditional probation in which a court orders a client to report to his or her probation officer after sentencing, private service providers station a representative in court to make initial contact with a client upon sentencing. In this way an offender's initial appointment and intake are completed immediately after sentencing rather than following the seven- to fourteen-day time period it takes to start traditional probation. Court attorneys generally supported having a private representative present in court (Alarid & Schloss, 2009). Attorneys also believed that qualifications for offering supervision and treatment services were important, such as utilizing identical curricula statewide, in order that treatment offered by private providers would be uniform.

SUMMARY

- Probation or parole officers are selected by appointment, by merit, or by a combination of the two. In most states necessary qualifications include U.S. citizenship, being at least 21 years of age, possessing a baccalaureate degree, passing a drug test, and not having a felony record.

- Issues continually evolving are provisions for preservice and in-service training and the effect of firearms' policies on probation and parole supervision.

- Applicants should find out about the firearms' policy of the department to which they are applying and also determine whether carrying a firearm is suitable to them, insofar as this is very much an individual decision.

- The future of probation supervision aims to give line-level officers more decision-making opportunity and responsibility, which in turn will likely decrease job stress and burnout.

- Workers in corrections enjoy absolute immunity when acting in a quasi-judicial or prosecutorial function but have only qualified immunity when performing administrative or other discretionary functions.

- Private service providers (PSPs) are growing in number and seem to be accepted by court attorneys who work with PSP representatives.

- Some private community corrections organizations have the potential to effectively supervise low-risk clients, but requirements range widely by jurisdiction.

DISCUSSION QUESTIONS

1. What type of knowledge, skills, and abilities are necessary for a community supervision officer to possess?

2. Why are college degrees required for probation and parole officers but not necessarily for entry-level police officers? What advantages might a college education provide in the field of community correctional supervision?

3. Do probation officers receive enough training for the responsibilities they have? Why or why not?

4. What are the advantages and disadvantages regarding probation and parole officers carrying firearms?

5. Would you carry a weapon on the job? Why or why not? If so, explain under what conditions you would carry it.

6. Out of the possible sources of stress identified, which ones can be controlled by an officer and which ones are inevitable to the job? Discuss innovative ways that work-related stress can be effectively managed.

7. How can probation and parole officers minimize the chances that they will lose a civil lawsuit if they are ever sued?

8. Agree or disagree with the following statement: Private probation supervision and treatment services should be expanded.

9. Which limitations or controls would you place on private probation agencies? Why?

 WEBSITES, VIDEOS, AND PODCASTS

Websites

Careers in Corrections
> http://www.discovercorrections.com/resources /types-of-positions

Community Corrections Connect
> http://www.appa.cequick.com/data/appa /ccconnect_homepageinstructions.pdf /Instructions on how to register and subscribe to the American Probation and Parole Association blog for professional development and networking with other community corrections' professionals.

Pennsylvania Firearm Education and Training Commission
> http://www.fetc.pa.gov

Georgia County and Municipal Private Probation Advisory Council
> http://www.cmpac.gaaoc.us

Tennessee Private Probation Services Council
> http://www.tn.gov/regboards/privatepro/

Videos/Podcasts

Firearms Training Simulation
> http://www.youtube.com/watch?v=2_3Sf8_5szU

Federal Judiciary Careers: Probation and Pretrial Services
> (Length: 6 minutes) Federal offices of Probation and Pretrial Services assist in the administration of justice and promote community safety. They work on the frontlines of federal offender supervision. https://www.youtube.com/ watch?v=QYgIfmqXMFE

Working in Corrections: Correctional Peace Officers point of view
> (Length: 3 minutes) Hear about why Canadian correctional peace officers chose to work in corrections. https://www.youtube.com /watch?v=uI-EVBwxHTw.

Working in Washington Prisons as a Corrections Officer
> (Length: 1:34 minutes) The Washington Department of Corrections employs correctional officers who act as positive role models for offenders and use good communication skills to counteract criminal thinking of offenders while maintaining safe environments until reentry. https://www.youtube.com/watch?v=0rqozgmicpi

Correctional Officer Stress
> This podcast interviews a former officer. The discussion focuses on the stress of working in the field of criminal justice and corrections. http://www.corrections.com/system/podcast /file/38/media_20050602.mp3

CASE STUDY EXERCISE

Decisions of a Community Corrections Administrator

In these scenarios you are a community correctional administrator tasked with making policy changes, changes in the way things are done and, if need be, personnel adjustments. You also have control over a budget and how allocated money is spent.

CASE A: Adjusting Probation Caseloads

Charles is chief probation officer in Pleasant County, a position he has held for 10 years. Prior to becoming chief, he served as a middle manager in the same department for 6 years and as a probation officer for 10 years. The county has 4,500 probationers total, of which 1,500 are on probation for a felony and 3,000 are misdemeanants. Of the 1,500 felony offenders, 275 are defined as specialized cases. Of the 3,000 misdemeanants, 1,500 are Class A and the other half are Class B and Class C.

If all positions are full, the county can support a total of 30 probation officers (15 felony and 15 misdemeanor officers), two middle managers (one supervising all officers with misdemeanor cases and another supervising all officers with felony cases), and a chief probation officer. All probation officers currently conduct pre-sentence investigations and write reports on a rotating basis. Right now cases are assigned based only on whether they are a felony or a misdemeanor, and a new client is given to the officer handling the least amount of cases.

There is currently a hiring freeze due to economic difficulties and budget shortfalls facing Pleasant County for at least two more years, but this could last longer. As a result, if a probation officer leaves there is no replacement, and clients on his or her caseload are divided among existing officers. Currently Charles has 2 middle managers, 13 misdemeanor officers, and 14 felony officers, so he is down by 3 positions. The morale in his department has been decreasing due to remaining officers doing more work for the same amount of pay, so Charles must act fast. He is considering a number of options:

Option 1: Move 4 of the misdemeanor officers over to felony caseloads, so there will be 18 felony officers and 9 misdemeanor officers. All officers still rotate on the PSIs.

Option 2: Move 5 of the misdemeanor officers over to felony caseloads, so there will be 19 felony officers and 8 misdemeanor officers. One of those felony officers will be assigned to write all felony presentence investigation reports for the county and not do any supervision.

Option 3: Keep caseload numbers the same (100 for felony and 200 for misdemeanor), and geographically separate offenders by zip code so it is easier for an officer to visit clients in a smaller area.

Option 4: Have smaller felony caseload sizes for specialized types like sex offenders, offenders with mental illnesses, etc. (e.g., 55 for specialized felony caseloads and 100 for general felony caseloads).

Option 5: Allow Class B and Class C misdemeanants electronic check-in and mail-in options (this affects 1,500 offenders), so only one officer has to supervise Class B and Class C while 7 officers supervise Class A misdemeanants at 214 offenders each).

Which options should Charles select and why? You may choose as many as you think are cumulatively effective. Is there another option that might be better than the ones listed, without hiring new staff?

CASE B: Responding to a Civil Lawsuit

Simon is a federal prisoner with a documented heart condition who was transferred to your halfway house. You are the halfway house manager of a private facility that contracts with the federal government. You decide to give authorization to allow Simon to use the staff elevator instead of the stairs so he will not overexert himself. You communicated your decision in writing and at a recent staff meeting to all employees, so everyone knows. One night, two months later a brand new employee begins working the evening shift. Everyone else has gone home except another senior staff member who is occupied with another client. The new employee catches Simon trying to use the staff elevator. Simon tries to convince the new employee that he has been approved to use it, but the employee thinks this is a con job by someone trying to pull one over on her, and instead of verifying authorization with the senior staff member she makes Simon use the stairs. At the top of the stairs Simon goes into cardiac arrest, and an ambulance is called. He suffers a heart attack but lives due to the fast-acting new employee. Alas, Simon sues the new employee, you, and your facility in a Section 1983 case, asserting that the new employee is at fault for denying access and that you, the administrator, are at fault for not conveying the necessary information to train her appropriately. The facility overall is at fault because the event occurred inside it, Simon contends.

Can your facility be sued? For what? Can you be sued as an administrator? For what? Can the new employee be sued? For what? How would the courts likely rule on this one?

Juvenile Justice, Probation, and Parole

Chapter 13

BRENDAN SMIALOWSKI/AFP/Getty Images

CHAPTER OUTLINE

CHAPTER LEARNING OBJECTIVES

1. Understand how the corrections system for juveniles has changed over time from diversionary individualized treatment to options resembling those for adults.

2. Analyze the similarities and differences between the juvenile and adult criminal justice systems.

3. Describe how a juvenile offender is processed and supervised in corrections.

4. Identify the unique options that still exist for juveniles, such as teen court and school-based probation.

KEY TERMS

parens patriae
mens rea
juvenile delinquency
conduct in need of supervision
transfer
statutory exclusion
judicial waiver
concurrent jurisdiction
intake
delinquency petition
adjudication
youth courts
disposition
opportunity-focused supervision
school-based probation

Freddie Gray was a 25-year-old man who was known to the police for being involved in selling drugs in Baltimore, Maryland. He had a prior criminal history for drug possession and he was in an area that was widely known to be an area where illegal drugs were openly sold. The Baltimore police arrested Gray in April 2015 on suspicion of drug charges and put him in a van in handcuffs and leg irons. Gray suffered severe head injuries while inside that van, and it took up to 25 minutes before police called for medical assistance. Gray died of a severed spinal cord and a broken neck and six police officers were suspended.

Residents in the Baltimore community rioted over the way the police treated Gray. The riots caused businesses, nonprofit organizations, schools, and even the courthouse to close while back-up law enforcement were brought in to control looters and vandals. A 10:00 P.M. curfew was enforced by the National Guard. The riots intensified after Gray's funeral, whereby hundreds of people were arrested and held in the county jail. Of those arrested over eight days, 60 of them were juveniles—many of whom were local high school students throwing rocks and bricks at police. One of the hundreds of youths that was in the area was 16-year-old Michael Singleton who was dressed in a hoodie and a mask. Michael's mother, Toya Graham, was watching from the crowd and just happened to notice her son from across the street. Without even thinking, she walked right over to him and started yelling at her son and hitting him publicly in reaction for him taking part in these riots and putting himself at risk. Toya Graham replied: "That's my only son and at the end of the day I don't want him to be a Freddie Gray" (CBS News, 2015). Michael went home with his mother, and avoided arrest. Mrs. Graham was called a responsible parent and "mother of the year" by many for intervening at a critical moment in her son's life.

About one-third of those who were arrested from the incident site had no criminal records, and were held longer in jail even if they met release standards, because the courts were closed for safety reasons and no one was present to determine release eligibility (Laughland, 2015). Since that time, a grand jury indicted the six police officers for reckless endangerment related to Freddie Gray's death.

How should have the Baltimore police and the courts responded to the 60 youths who were arrested following the riots in Baltimore? Should anything happen to these youths? What about their parents?

INTRODUCTION

The juvenile justice system becomes involved when juveniles engage in behaviors that violate family codes/civil law (status offenses) or violate criminal law (delinquency). It also becomes involved when juveniles need to be protected from abuse or neglect by their parents as neglected or dependent children. Sometimes a juvenile has a history of all three situations.

In the last decade, juvenile crime has decreased. Many state and county juvenile justice systems have lessened their use of detention for misdemeanants and status offenders. While cracking down on staff abuse of juveniles in detention, such systems have committed to serving youths in the least restrictive environment possible. With secure facilities costing an average of nearly $280 per day for one juvenile (Levin, 2010) and mounting evidence that community corrections options are more effective, the latter option has become the preferred choice for most offenses involving juveniles. This has meant more alternatives to detention, better methods of screening youths for risk, and increased community-based services, more created in the last few years than ever before.

These responses have decreased the rate of juvenile delinquency overall since the 1990s. Yet juvenile arrests still account for 17% of all violent crimes and 26% of all property crimes (when added in with adults) each year in the United States (Snyder, 2008). Delinquency concerns center around how to handle juveniles who violate laws, particularly those who commit serious and violent felony crimes. Answers do not come easily, partially because there are philosophical differences regarding juvenile offending. On the one hand is recognition that many status offenses and delinquent acts are committed by at-risk youth who originate from abusive families, unhealthy peer groups, school failure, life in high-crime areas, and other deeply rooted social problems and failures of social control. "At-risk" is often used to describe youth who show signs of emotional or behavioral problems and who lack the support to navigate pro-social developmental tasks successfully. Various risk factors such as substance use, predisposition for mental health disorders, family violence, low parental involvement, poor school performance, and deviant peers put youth at risk for involvement in the juvenile justice system (see Figure 13.1).

FIGURE 13.1
Risk Factors Connected with Juvenile Delinquency

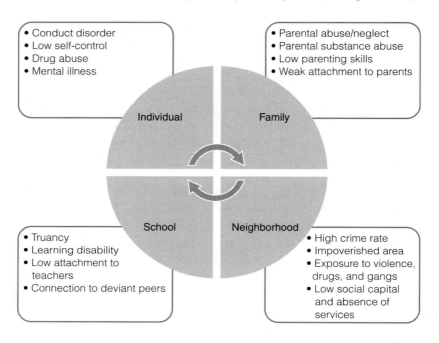

- Conduct disorder
- Low self-control
- Drug abuse
- Mental illness

Individual

- Parental abuse/neglect
- Parental substance abuse
- Low parenting skills
- Weak attachment to parents

Family

- Truancy
- Learning disability
- Low attachment to teachers
- Connection to deviant peers

School

Neighborhood

- High crime rate
- Impoverished area
- Exposure to violence, drugs, and gangs
- Low social capital and absence of services

At the same time, "protective factors" such as supportive relationships, positive recognition in school and friends committed to conformity shielded or counteracted the risk factors. The belief is that if the ratio of risk factors was higher than the number of protective factors, an individual is more likely to drop out of school, be unemployed, and potentially engage in substance abuse and criminality later in adulthood. A long line of research on the risk factors of delinquency have determined that abusive family relationships contribute to girls' pathways to delinquency, while peer associations seem more influential for boys. Prematurely dropping out of high school, however, has no causal effect on later delinquency or criminal behavior (Sweeten, Bushway, & Paternoster, 2009).

Risk Factors Connected with Juvenile Delinquency

On the basis of the original concept of **parens patriae**, the juvenile justice system seeks to do what is best for the welfare and safety of a minor child who is unable to support him or herself. The theory of just deserts advocates societal protection and the accountability of youth offenders based on the seriousness of the current act committed and the youth's prior record. During the mid 1980s until mid 2000, legal precedent drifted juvenile courts further from the original parens patriae philosophy of treatment and individualized sentencing. This movement ignored significant differences in the development of juveniles and adults. Then, between 2005 and 2012, the U.S. Supreme Court recognized that:

parens patriae
Latin term meaning that the government acts as a "substitute parent" and allows the courts to intervene in cases in which children, through no fault of their own, have been neglected and/or are dependent and in which it is in their best interest that a guardian be appointed for them.

1. Juveniles have a "lack of maturity and underdeveloped sense of responsibility": (*Roper v. Simmons*, 2005, at 569) and are impulsive, reckless, and oblivious to obvious risks;
2. Juveniles are more vulnerable to "negative influences and outside pressures" (*Roper v. Simmons*, 2005, at 569);
3. Juveniles' personalities and temperaments are not as established and are less likely to be irretrievably depraved.

These developmental differences mean that the traditional goals in the adult system of retribution, deterrence, and incapacitation are not necessarily going to be as effective for juveniles (see Figure 13.2).

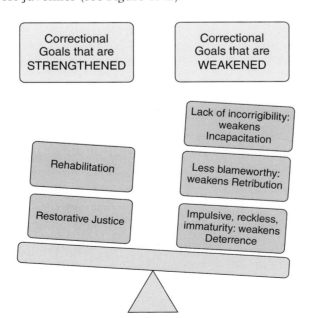

FIGURE 13.2
The Strength of Correctional Goals in Juvenile Justice

Source: Bennett, Katherine. 2013. Analysis of *Miller v. Alabama*, 567 U.S. __ 2012. An unpublished paper presentation at the annual conference of the Academy of Criminal Justice Sciences, Dallas, Texas, March 20–23, 2013. Reproduced with permission.

In the next section, we examine how the juvenile justice system compares with the adult criminal justice system.

JUVENILE JUSTICE AND ADULT CRIMINAL JUSTICE SYSTEMS COMPARED

Despite a growing similarity between juvenile and adult criminal proceedings, some differences persist. One of the most notable differences is the support and participation of family and schools, which may require a slightly different style of community supervision and treatment that teaches youths how to reduce their exposure to criminal opportunities (Miller, 2014). Another difference is that a juvenile court judge takes a more active part in proceedings. He or she is expected to act as a wise parent rather than as an impartial arbiter, the latter of which is a judge's role in adult criminal cases. A juvenile court judge may initiate questioning of an alleged offender, cross-examine witnesses, bring up a juvenile's background, and actively admonish or counsel him or her. While juvenile intake officers have more discretion than at adult intake, judges are increasingly experiencing more statutory guidelines that limit initial case decisions to dismiss, to divert through informal probation, or to use community sanctions.

Another difference between juvenile and adult justice is in the severity of punishment imposed. For instance, most juveniles spend limited time in institutions because they are released upon reaching a maximum age specified by state law, or they reach an age by which they must be transferred to the adult system to finish their sentence. In contrast, adult criminals can be made to spend life in prison, a sanction that cannot be administered to juveniles unless they are tried as adults through a waiver or certification process. The differences between adult and juvenile proceedings are summarized next:

ADULT PROCEEDINGS	JUVENILE PROCEEDINGS
1. Arrested	1. Taken into custody by police
2. Charged	2. Prosecutor petitions court
3. Accused of crime under the criminal penal code	3. Violation under the juvenile code or family code (civil)
4. Trial	4. Adjudication
5. Formal, public trial	5. Quasi-civil and private hearing
6. Right for case to heard by either a judge or jury	6. No right to a jury (although some states do provide a jury if requested)
7. Sentenced if found guilty	7. Disposition hearing
8. Community-correction options residential facilities	8. Community-based placements, gender-specific services, family counseling
9. Incarcerated in prison	9. Secure facility as last resort
10. Release determined by statute	10. Aftercare determined by sentence, by parole board authorities, or when age of majority is reached

In reality the previous differences are more terminological than substantive and are, therefore, more symbolic than real. They have minimal impact on process because the procedures are similar regardless of the term used. For example, adults who are arrested and juveniles who are taken into custody are deprived of liberty while under control of the justice system. Because both processes lead to hearings, a prosecutor petitioning a court for a juvenile to be adjudicated is very similar to an adult suspect being charged. Sentencing and disposition both subject an offender to lawfully prescribed sanctions, including incarceration. Whether an adult is on parole or a juvenile is in aftercare, the degree of supervision and the results of violation are similar.

Jurisdiction of Juvenile Courts

The types of cases that proceed to juvenile courts are defined by state law. Jurisdiction, or the authority to try cases in juvenile courts, varies from state to state, and is based on the age of an offender and the act committed.

BASED ON AGE   Criminal liability is based on the concept of **mens rea**, which is Latin for "a guilty mind" (Garner, 2014). Without intent, an act is generally not considered criminal. A guilty mind implies that a perpetrator knows what he or she is doing; therefore, an act is punishable because the perpetrator intended an injury to occur. Children under six years old are presumed by law to be unaware of the full consequences of their actions. Absent mens rea, those of six years and under cannot be formally punished by the juvenile justice system. Instead, juveniles under age 6 who commit criminal acts are usually processed informally or placed in the care of social services.

mens rea
Latin term meaning "guilty mind" that addresses the level of mental intent to commit a crime.

Most states process youths who have committed delinquent acts until their 18th birthday, but a small number of states have a lower age at which an individual (e.g., at age 17) are routinely processed in the adult system *for all acts of delinquency*. As the political tide is turning in favor of less severe punishment for youths, policymakers in the remaining states have been discussing raising the age of juvenile jurisdiction in line with over 40 other states, so that all 15-, 16-, and 17-year-olds remain in the juvenile justice system (except a small percentage of waived cases, which are discussed later in the chapter). The minimum and maximum ages refer to the age at which an act was committed, not when an offender was caught or tried in court.

BASED ON ACTS COMMITTED   Juvenile cases that trigger court intervention are of three types: **juvenile delinquency**, conduct in need of supervision (CINS), and juveniles as victims. About six in ten of all juvenile justice cases are delinquency proceedings, which center upon criminal actions committed by juveniles. Another two in ten cases are for conduct in need of supervision, which includes status offenses (related to school misconduct, truancy or runaway) that would not be illegal if committed by an adult. Many delinquent and status offense cases concern child victims of abuse or neglect (Griffin, 2010).

juvenile delinquency
Acts committed by juveniles that are punishable as crimes under a state's penal code.

Each state, by law, determines which acts come under each category. In general, juvenile delinquents are those who commit acts that are punishable under a state's penal code. Examples are murder, robbery, burglary, and any act considered criminal in a particular state. Every year juvenile courts in the United States handle an estimated 1.7 million juvenile delinquency cases (Knoll & Sickmund, 2010). More than eight out of ten delinquency cases have been referred by law enforcement. The percentage of boys and girls adjudicated for each type of offense is presented in Table 13.1, which indicates that about 73% of all

TABLE 13.1   Delinquency and Gender Differences

Most Serious Offense	Girls	Boys
Total delinquency	27%	73%
Person	30%	70%
Property	27%	73%
Drugs	18%	82%
Public order	28%	72%

Source: C. Knoll, and M. Sickmund. 2010. *Delinquency cases in juvenile court, 2007.* Washington, DC: OJJDP.

delinquency cases that come to a court's attention involve boys, while about 27% involve girls.

In contrast, **conduct in need of supervision**—also known in some jurisdictions as CHINS (children in need of supervision), MINS (minors in need of supervision), or JINS (juveniles in need of supervision)—are juveniles who commit status offenses that would not be punishable if committed by adults. These include truancy, running away from home, tobacco use, inhalant abuse, curfew violation, and underage drinking (Snyder, 2008). The most common status offense for girls is running away, which is tied to parental abuse or neglect. Law enforcement agencies refer fewer CINS cases to court than they do delinquency cases—just over half of all CINS cases have been referred to juvenile courts by police. The rest have reached the courts through reports from social services agencies, victims, probation officers, county attorneys, schools, or parents (Snyder, 2008).

Waiver to Adult Court

For the most serious and violent juvenile cases, all states have provisions to move a case from juvenile courts to adult courts based on case seriousness and the age of the offender. **Transfer**, also known as a waiver or certification, can be accomplished in a variety of possible ways (Griffin Addie, Adams & Firestine, 2011):

- **Statutory exclusion**. State legislative statutes automatically exclude certain juvenile offenses from juvenile court jurisdiction and require that cases be filed directly with criminal courts.
- **Judicial waiver**. Authority to transfer a case to criminal court is given to a juvenile court judge, who certifies, remands, or binds over for criminal prosecution following a formal hearing to determine case appropriateness.
- **Concurrent jurisdiction/Prosecutorial waiver**. Original jurisdiction is shared by both criminal and juvenile courts, in either of which a prosecutor has discretion to file without a court hearing. This process is also known as prosecutorial waiver, prosecutor discretion, or direct file.

Statutory exclusion has outpaced judicial waivers as the most commonly used transfer decision, insofar as prosecuting violent offenses is mandatory. Other states allow a discretionary waiver as appropriate to the situation. Most waiver decisions follow an intake decision, or an initial decision to formally file a case before a court. Once transferred, a juvenile ceases being a juvenile and becomes an adult in the eyes of the law, including for the purposes of trial proceedings and sentencing.

conduct in need of supervision (CINS)
Acts committed by juveniles that would not be punishable if committed by adults; status offenses.

transfer of jurisdiction
The transfer of a juvenile from juvenile court to adult court for trial.

statutory exclusion
An automatic exclusion of certain juvenile offenders from juvenile court jurisdiction by state statute, requiring a case to be filed directly with an adult criminal court.

judicial waiver
Transferring a juvenile case from a juvenile court to an adult court.

concurrent jurisdiction
Original jurisdiction for certain juvenile cases that is shared by both criminal and juvenile courts, with a prosecutor having discretion to file such cases in either court.

A juvenile appears before a juvenile judge at a disposition hearing in which he received six months' probation and 80 hours of community service for shoplifting.

Out of every 1,000 petitioned delinquency cases, less than 1% were actually waived or transferred over to adult court (Griffin et al., 2011). Waived/transferred cases that were swept directly into the adult system through prosecutorial discretion or statutory exclusion are not accurately tracked or reported as well as cases that originated in juvenile court and a formal transfer hearing was held. No single data source exists at the federal level to accurately estimate the actual number of waived cases, so the following information is based on larger jurisdictions in 13 reporting states such as Arizona, California, and Florida that do keep records. Of these jurisdictions, the total number of waived/transferred cases average around 14,000 per year, not counting the mandate that all youths in nine states, aged 15, 16, and/or 17 must go into the adult system by law. Waived/transferred cases are most often for violent crimes (63.5%), and then a smaller number are for property (18%), drug (15%), and public order (3.5%) crimes (Griffin et al., 2011, p. 12). A decision to transfer is, in theory, based on a juvenile's severity of offense, prior record, prior responses to supervision or treatment in the juvenile justice system, and level of danger he or she might pose in the future. Wide variation on waivers exists among states, resulting in inconsistency.

Only about 21% of waived cases are supervised on adult probation, with the rest serving time in jail or prison. Incarcerating juveniles with adults increases the juveniles' rate of violence and later recidivism. Although waivers are indeed a symbol of "get tough" policies, the reality is that few youths are truly a public safety threat and most youths will age out of crime anyway. Thus, the rest of this chapter presents options for the vast majority of youths within the juvenile justice system.

AN OVERVIEW OF THE JUVENILE JUSTICE PROCESS

We have discussed general differences between juvenile justice and the adult criminal justice systems thus far. The civil or quasi-civil process of juvenile justice casts a wider net than that of the adult system. Juvenile behavior that sets the

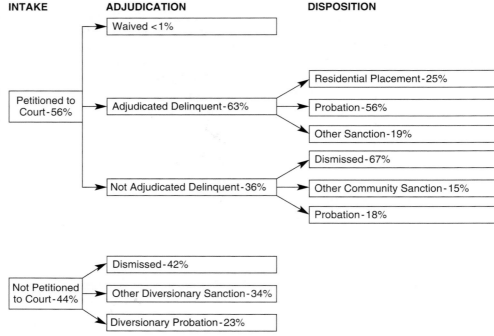

FIGURE 13.3
Case Flow of Delinquency
Cases After Arrest

Source: C. Knoll and
M. Sickmund. 2010.
*Delinquency cases in juvenile
court, 2007.* Washington, DC:
Office of Juvenile Justice and
Delinquency Prevention, p. 4.

justice process in motion can come to attention by way of the general public, probation officers, victims, parents, neighbors, school authorities, and/or the police. Most state statutes encourage police officers to release juveniles to a parent or guardian. In practice, police officer decisions include release, warning, referral to a community agency for services, referral to a citizen hearing board, and referral to court intake. Figure 13.3 details the three stages of the juvenile justice process: intake, adjudication, and disposition.

Intake

intake
A process whereby a juvenile is screened to determine whether a case should proceed further in the juvenile justice system or whether alternatives are better suited for said juvenile.

delinquency petition
An intake officer's formal request to a juvenile court judge to hear a juvenile case in family court or probate court and determine whether the juvenile is to be declared delinquent.

A juvenile taken into custody by police usually goes through an **intake** process—a case screening process that determines whether that juvenile should proceed further through the juvenile justice system or whether alternatives are more suitable. Intake officers are experts in crisis intervention, in gathering information, and in assessing risk and needs. Considered one of the most crucial points in the juvenile justice system, intake involves a probation officer interview of a youth and his or her parents or guardians. To determine potential causes of delinquency, intake questions pertain not only to a pending incident but also to juvenile home life, school problems, peers, mental health, drug abuse, and physical health. According to Figure 13.4, an intake officer can decide whether to handle a case informally (non-petitioned) or formally through a petition. If a case is to be handled formally, a **delinquency petition** is filed to request either an adjudicatory hearing (in which a case proceeds through juvenile courts) or a waiver hearing (in which a case is further screened to see whether it should proceed through adult courts). If a case is to be handled informally through diversion, a petition will not be filed. Intake officers can decide whether to counsel parents and child and just close a case, even against a police officer's recommendation for formal adjudication.

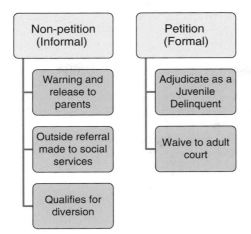

FIGURE 13.4
Possible Decisions at Intake

Slightly less than half of all juvenile cases were either dismissed or diverted from the system at intake (Knoll & Sickmund, 2010). Cases were dismissed at intake because of lack of evidence. The diverted cases were documented in a written agreement known as a consent decree. Juvenile diversion works identically to adult diversion and includes a period of supervision with such conditions as school attendance, community service, drug counseling, curfew, and restitution, if applicable. Diverted cases that were successfully completed resulted in later dismissal (Knoll & Sickmund, 2010).

Intake is considered highly subjective, involving very little collateral investigation or checking of sources. The intake process has been criticized for its lack of formal guidelines and a possibility of inconsistency from one intake officer to another (Lindner, 2008). As a result, prosecutors have replaced probation officers in some jurisdictions in an attempt to correct such inconsistency.

Intake can also involve detention screening, crisis intervention, and other procedures if mandated by a court. A juvenile may be detained by police but only up to 24 hours. Federal law stipulates that juveniles be separated from adult offenders by "sight and sound." This assures that juveniles are detained in facilities separate from those used for adults. The U.S. Supreme Court has held that preventive detention of juveniles, due to a likelihood that they will commit other offenses, is constitutional (*Schall v. Martin*, 1984).

If an intake officer decides to refer a case to court, the prosecutor petitions the court for the juvenile in question to be adjudicated. A summons is issued directing the juvenile to appear before the court at a specified time and place for an initial appearance on the petition. An arraignment is then held, and the juvenile is given an opportunity to admit or deny the allegations.

Adjudication

adjudication
Juvenile justice equivalent of a trial in adult criminal cases.

Adjudication is the formal processing of a juvenile delinquency case through the juvenile courts. Some juvenile courts fall under the jurisdiction of family courts/family law that also handle status offenses, dependency and neglect, adults who contribute to the delinquency of a minor, child support, child custody, divorce, and alimony. In both family court and juvenile court, proceedings are less formal, and a judge takes a more active part in the hearing—including asking questions of juveniles, their parents or guardians, and witnesses. Most states appoint counsel for a juvenile if their parents are indigent and the youth might face jail time, and Michigan courts require counsel regardless of indigent status (Brown, 2012). Although rules of evidence are present in juvenile court, juveniles have less procedural due process rights—such as, they have no right to a jury trial or to bail. Status offenses are only rarely (if ever) adjudicated in a formal hearing. Status offenders get diversionary conditions that eventually lead to no case dismissal and no permanent record.

For delinquent behaviors, an adjudication hearing attempts to establish responsibility for a criminal act. About 64% of cases that go to family court are adjudicated delinquent, which is the same as a finding of guilt. The other 36% of cases not adjudicated delinquent will be dismissed unless a youth and his or her parents can be convinced to voluntarily take part in a sanction (Knoll & Sickmund, 2010). Table 13.2 illustrates the "big picture" outcomes of actual number of cases that were adjudicated in juvenile court versus cases that were not adjudicated.

youth courts
Community-based programs in which youths sentence their peers for minor delinquent and status offenses. Also known as teen, peer, and student courts.

YOUTH COURTS FOR NON-ADJUDICATED CASES Most states have established **youth courts** to respond to youths who have no prior record and who have been involved in school misconduct (status offenses) or misdemeanors such as vandalism, theft, disorderly conduct, and minor possession of alcohol. Most youth courts do not hold hearings to determine guilt; rather, they require ahead of time that the youth admits guilt and the youth court is involved in the sentencing aspect (Norris, Twill, & Kim, 2011). The philosophy behind teen courts is twofold. First, youth courts tap into the primary group of influence for young kids—other peers. The thinking here is that youths who have made bad choices are more likely to listen to other youths than to their parents or to other people they view as authority figures. Youth volunteers act as a panel or as jurors, usually under the supervision of an adult coordinator or adult judge (Smith & Blackburn, 2011). The second reason that youth courts became so popular was that schools had increasingly more punitive sanctions for dealing with misconduct such as tardiness, truancy, disrespect, and created zero tolerance policies for bullying. The traditional juvenile justice courts lacked the personnel to handle these additional cases, so youth courts were created to respond to status offenses that occurred on school grounds. Youth courts handle about 12%

TABLE 13.2 Case Outcomes of Adjudicated vs. Non-adjudicated Cases in Juvenile Court

Case Outcome	Adjudicated	Not Adjudicated	Total Juvenile Court Cases
Placement	148,603	0	148,603
Probation	327,425	234,194	561,619
Fines, restitution, community service	110,207	302,908	413,115
Dismissed after a warning or counseling	0	534,260	534,260
Waived to adult court	0	8,467	8,467
TOTAL	586,234	1,079,829	1,666,064

Source: M. Sickmund, A. Sladky, and W. Kang. 2010. Easy access to juvenile court statistics: 1985–2007.
Available online: http://ojjdp.ncjrs.gov/ojstatbb/ezajcs/

of non-adjudicated cases that would have otherwise gone through the juvenile courts (Norris, Twill, & Kim, 2011). Youth court records never become part of a juvenile's criminal record.

The National Youth Court Association reported that youth courts are most often tied to juvenile courts (42%) or sponsored by a school (36%) or by a private community agency (22%) (Cole & Heilig, 2011). Through these leadership roles, the teen court concept also allows prosocial youths an opportunity to become involved as positive mentors in their community and to learn about legal principles and their application.

Youth courts are a good example of restorative justice because many of their creative sentences involve a youth offender taking responsibility for his or her behavior and redressing harm to a victim and community. The most frequent youth court outcomes are community service, written apology or essay, and restitution. Other consequences include victim offender mediation, tutoring sessions, peer mentoring, and to serve as jurors for future cases that come before the youth court (Cole & Heilig, 2011).

Evaluation studies of youth court participants showed no significant differences in recidivism compared to similar youths who were placed on diversion through the juvenile court (Norris, Twill, & Kim, 2011). Even though there were no significant differences between the two groups, having youth courts is necessary to take some of the burden off of the juvenile court, which would be handling these cases. The researchers found that increasing the sanctions too much in youth court had the opposite effect of causing youths to drop out or reoffend. Youth court was more effective for 15–18 year olds than for 11–14 year olds (Norris, Twill, & Kim, 2011). The National Youth Court Association is the central clearinghouse of information related to programs and effectiveness studies (see www.youthcourt.net).

Disposition

If a juvenile is found to have engaged in conduct alleged in a petition, the **disposition** stage follows. For less serious misdemeanors and nonviolent felonies, a juvenile court judge wields greater discretion than do judges in adult criminal court. Rehabilitation is an integral part of juvenile corrections, so a judge typically has a wide choice of available dispositions, including oral reprimand, probation, drug court, mental health court, and community service. Although most youths are still able to live at home on probation, some youths with too many problems at home or who show evidence of parental abuse or neglect require residential placement in a community-based facility. Most placements have an indeterminate commitment, which means that the youth is given a minimum length of stay before he or she is eligible for early release to parole.

For violent offenses, a prosecutor can choose to pursue conventional delinquency proceedings with an indeterminate commitment or to pursue a determinate commitment which allows for sentences (in one state as an example) up to 40 years for first degree violent felonies, 20 years for second degree, and 10 years for third degree felonies. A judge's decision depends on the severity of the current offense and the youth's prior record (Applegate, Cullen, & Davis, 2008).

BLENDED SENTENCES Blended sentences came about due to a concern that a 17 year old, who is nearing adulthood is no longer under juvenile court

disposition
Juvenile justice equivalent of sentencing in adult cases.

jurisdiction and the courts have no authority once a certain age is reached (usually 18 years). About half of all states allow an opportunity for juvenile judges to extend a juvenile sentence past the age of 18. In other words, the juvenile judge may impose *both* juvenile and adult correctional sanctions to allow for maximum flexibility for when a juvenile case starts in the juvenile courts, and then the juvenile turns the age considered to be an adult. Blended sentences provide an incentive for older youths to participate in treatment so that the juvenile judge may suspend the adult portion. In states such as Colorado, Massachusetts, Rhode Island, South Carolina, and Texas, a sanction starts under juvenile jurisdiction but when a juvenile comes of age, the case is transferred to the adult system. For example, if a 17-year-old female juvenile is sentenced to probation, she begins supervision under a juvenile probation officer. Just before reaching her 18th birthday, a progress hearing is held to see if her case can be terminated, should remain in the juvenile system until her 21st birthday, or should continue into the adult system until her 21st birthday.

Other states (Arkansas, Connecticut, Iowa, Kansas, Minnesota, Missouri, Montana, and Virginia) allow for imposition of both juvenile and adult sanctions but suspend the adult sanction unless a juvenile violates the juvenile sanction. Blended sentencing laws thus create a middle ground between traditional juvenile and adult sanctions, but they also narrow the gap between juvenile and adult punishments. Currently, nearly half of all states have some form of blended sentencing laws with limits for certain juvenile offenders (Snyder & Sickmund, 2006).

Most recently, the U.S. Supreme Court banned the use of life without parole sentences for any felony crime including murder, committed when a defendant is under the age of 18. The court based its decision on the fact that a life without parole sentence does not allow any opportunity for release despite the fact that a juvenile will mature and change over time. The court agreed that a life without parole sentence for anyone under the age of 18 is cruel and unusual punishment. The decision in this case seems to indicate that the court has re-emphasized once again that juveniles need to be treated and punished differently than adults, even for crimes when juveniles are charged as adults. Other major U.S. Supreme Court cases that have affected juveniles over the last 50 years are summarized in Table 13.3.

RESIDENTIAL PLACEMENTS FOR JUVENILES

For more serious offenses, some states invoke determinate sentencing laws that require confinement in a secure institution for a minimum number of years (such as 1–10 years for a third-degree felony, 2–10 years for a second-degree felony, 3–10 years for a first-degree felony, and 10–40 years for a capital felony). Although most adjudicated delinquency cases have resulted in formal probation, about 25% of youths have been placed in residential settings such as (in order of most to least secure): training school, detention, reception or diagnostic center, inpatient drug treatment, boys' or girls' ranch, shelter, and private group home (Hockenberry, 2011; Sickmund, Sladky, & Kang, 2008). Very few delinquents end up in a secure locked facility, such as a large training school or detention, which is designated for youths who have committed a felony offense and are considered to be a danger to a community. An ongoing concern is the overrepresentation of African American and Latino youths in confinement facilities. Research has found

TABLE 13.3 Major United States Supreme Court Decisions in Juvenile Justice

CASES THAT RECOGNIZE CONSTITUTIONAL RIGHTS FOR JUVENILES	CASES THAT LIMIT CONSTITUTIONAL RIGHTS FOR JUVENILES
Kent v. United States (383 U.S. 541 [1966]) Juveniles must be given due process rights when transferred from juvenile to adult court. These rights consist of a hearing, counsel representation, access to court records, and a statement of reasons in support of a waiver order.	*McKeiver v. Pennsylvania* (403 U.S. 528 [1971]) Juveniles have no constitutional right to trial by jury even in juvenile delinquency cases in which a juvenile faces possible incarceration.
In re Gault (387 U.S. 1 [1967]) Juveniles must be given four due process rights in adjudication proceedings that can result in confinement in an institution in which their freedom would be curtailed. These rights consist of notice of charges, counsel (appointed if juvenile is indigent), ability to confront and cross-examine witnesses, and privilege against self-incrimination.	*Davis v. Alaska* (415 U.S. 308 [1974]) Despite confidentiality laws, the fact that a juvenile is on probation may be elicited by an opposing lawyer in a cross-examination of a juvenile witness.
In re Winship (397 U.S. 358 [1970]) Proof beyond a reasonable doubt, not simply by a preponderance of the evidence, is required in juvenile adjudication hearings in cases in which an act would have been a crime if committed by an adult.	*Smith v. Daily Mail Publishing Co.* (443 U.S. 97 [1979]) A state law making it a crime to publish the name of a juvenile charged with a crime is unconstitutional because it violates the First Amendment right to freedom of the press.
Breed v. Jones (421 U.S. 517 [1975]) Juveniles are entitled to a constitutional right against double jeopardy in juvenile proceedings.	*Fare v. Michael C.* (442 U.S. 707 [1979]) A request by a juvenile to see his probation officer is not equivalent to asking for a lawyer. Moreover, there is no probation officer-client privilege, meaning that any information a juvenile gives to a probation officer may be divulged in court.
Roper v. Simmons (543 U.S. 551 [2005]) It is unconstitutional to execute juveniles who committed their crime before the age of 18.	*Schall v. Martin* (467 U.S. 253 [1984]) Preventive detention of juveniles is constitutional.
Graham v. Florida (08-7412) *and Sullivan v. Florida* (08-7621) 560 U.S. __ [2010] Life without parole is a cruel and unusual sentence for a non-homicide felony committed by anyone under age 18.	*New Jersey v. T.L.O* (469 U.S. 325 [1985]) Public school officials need reasonable grounds to search students; they do not need a warrant or probable cause.
Jackson v. Hobbs, (10-9647) *and Miller v. Alabama,* 567 U.S. ___ 2012 (10-9646). Life without parole is a cruel and unusual sentence for any homicide committed by anyone under age 18.	

that youth perceived to be at a higher risk of reoffending originated from economically disadvantaged neighborhoods, and that certain residential areas were used as proxies for risk which unfairly biased minority youths which disproportionately originated from disadvantaged neighborhoods (Rodriguez, 2013).

Table 13.4 compares the percentage of various secure and community-based facilities that confines its residents, uses mechanical restraints on juveniles, locks juveniles in their rooms for four or more hours, and allows unauthorized departures. Large training schools and detention facilities are considered to be classic lockdown facilities in which youths are most likely to experience isolation, mechanical restraints, and other confinement measures. Some youths are being temporarily held in detention centers until their cases are adjudicated and disposed.

Table 13.4 also shows group homes, shelters, and wilderness camps, which are community-based facilities where youths are for the most part, not locked in their rooms. About 70% of residential facilities are publicly operated settings in which youths from 15 to17 years old have been placed by the courts. One of the larger private companies is Youth Services International, which operates 13 residential facilities and aftercare programs in five different states. The reality is that the youths in community-based (nonsecure) residential placements pose little threat to the community; youths are placed there because there may be some problems with their parents, guardians, or a situation at home that needs to be addressed before the youth is allowed to return home.

Wilderness Challenge Programs

Wilderness Challenge programs provide residential placement along with outdoor skill-based activities that rely on learning survival skills and teamwork in a group approach to problem solving. Program lengths varied widely from 3 days to 25 weeks. Activities like canoeing, backpacking, and rock climbing are among

TABLE 13.4 Characteristics of Residential Facilities for Juveniles (percentages reflect facilities that reportedly engaged in a particular practice if necessary [$N = 2,458$])

Type of Facility	Locked Youth in Isolation for 4 + Hours	Other Confinement Features (Other Than Locked Sleeping Rooms)	Used Mechanical Restraints	Had Unauthorized Youth Departures
Secure Facilities				
Training school ($n = 210$)	51%	93%	69%	6%
Detention ($n = 734$)	45%	96%	42%	3%
Reception/diagnostic center ($n = 64$)	31%	75%	52%	10%
Community-Based Facilities				
Residential treatment center ($n = 847$)	10%	46%	16%	29%
Wilderness camp/ ranch ($n = 85$)	6%	26%	20%	38%
Shelter ($n = 167$)	4%	30%	4%	37%
Group home ($n = 661$)	1%	13%	2%	39%
TOTAL FACILITIES ($N = 2,458$)	21%	53%	23%	22%

Source: S. Hockenberry, M. Sickmund, and A. Sladky. 2011. *Juvenile residential facility census, 2008: Selected findings.* Washington, DC: Office of Juvenile Justice and Delinquency Prevention.

the mentally rigorous and physically challenging exercises that attempt to improve a youth's self-esteem and help them learn how to resolve interpersonal conflict in a different way (Wilson & Lipsey, 2000). Eligibility criteria were similar to boot camps, in that youths between 10 and 21 years who had substance abuse problems were targeted. Youths who exhibited low self-control and poor decision making skills were also good candidates for experiential and active learning by doing.

Structured program length (less than 6 weeks vs. 10 weeks or more) did not have any difference of an effect on later delinquency. In general, Wilderness Challenge programs are *not* among the best programs to decrease recidivism—they are not harmful, they just generally do not decrease recidivism as much as other interventions. However, the programs that produced some decrease in re-offending were the programs that had "defining experiences that result from the challenges a participant must meet" (Wilson & Lipsey, 2000, p. 10). These defining experiences included family therapy and nightly group counseling sessions in the context of physically challenging activities like group backpacking (Wilson & Lipsey, 2000).

Group Homes

Group homes, home-like settings with sitting areas, a kitchen, and bedrooms, are considered among the least restrictive residential placements for youths unable to live with their own families. Group homes are structured environments that cost $115 per day per person, compared to $162 for a secure placement (Deitch, 2009). There are typically 10–20 youths of the same sex between the ages of 12–17 living together under 24-hour supervision. They attend school together, participate in weekly family counseling and in community activities like field trips, and are assigned to an individual counselor. Most group homes are privately owned and operated by contracting out to state and county government. One example of such a company is ResCare Youth Services. ResCare is headquartered in Louisville, Kentucky, but owns and operates group homes and emergency shelters for at-risk youth in 23 states. In addition, ResCare offers foster care placements and is a job corps operator for employable youths aged 16–24 years old.

The current trend has been to decrease the percentage of detained youths in larger facilities, especially given that secure institutions are located in remote areas and tend to have issues related to safety. The alternative is to employ a continuum of sanctions using smaller community-based facilities and other community options, such as group homes, multidimensional treatment foster care, and family therapy modalities depicted in Figure 13.5.

Mentoring At-Risk Youth

Tied with residential placement is the idea that at-risk youths need connections to healthy relationships with mentors—older peers or other adults who are supportive and trustworthy outside the youth's nuclear family. A national program like Big Brothers/Big Sisters is well known for screening, matching, and training eligible adult volunteers with at-risk youth. The matching process is based on a long-term commitment of a stable volunteer of the same gender who ideally shares similar interests with a youth. The mentor not only spends time with the youth in fun activities, but is also there to listen, to help solve problems, and to

FIGURE 13.5
Community
Correctional Program
Options for Juveniles

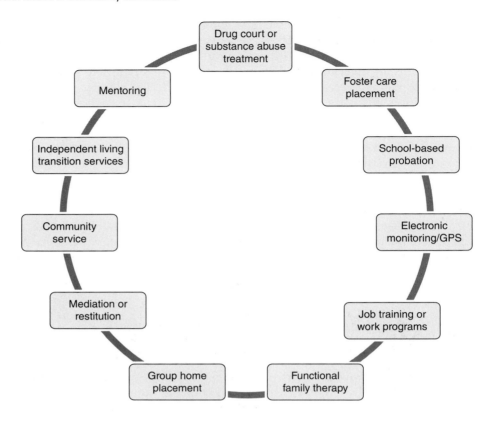

encourage youth on how to pursue goals and opportunities. School-based mentoring programs target students who are struggling academically or who have exhibited disruptive problems on school grounds.

There are currently 5,000 mentoring programs serving about 3 million youths throughout the United States. Mentoring programs generally improve youth academic achievement and social development compared to similar youths who do not participate in mentoring (DuBois, Portillo, Rhodes, Silverthorn, & Valentine, 2011). Most mentoring program evaluations have been conducted with youths who are at-risk of delinquency, but have not yet entered the juvenile justice system with very few mentoring program studies of youths who are being actively supervised within the juvenile justice system.

Family Therapy

Parental participation and support plays a primary role in youth community supervision and treatment. The **opportunity-focused supervision** style is more conducive to supervising youth than adults on probation and parole. Opportunity-focused supervision teaches youths and their parents how to reduce youth exposure to criminal opportunities through changing peer associations and using time after school in a productive manner (Miller, 2014). Parents are encouraged to become an active participant in transporting their children to probation officer appointments and community service, but they may also be involved in therapeutic interventions. Two interventions include functional family therapy and multisystemic therapy, which are discussed in Box 13.1. We introduce each and discuss the differences between these two types of therapy.

In a meta-analysis of CBT programs, generic CBT programs that had components such as anger control and interpersonal problem-solving skills were just as effective as brand-name CBT programs in reducing juvenile recidivism (Lipsey, 2009).

JUVENILE PROBATION

Probation is the disposition most often used in juvenile delinquency cases, with youth property offenders aged 14–16 accounting for the largest share of probationers. Juvenile probation can be formally adjudicated (60%) or informally non-adjudicated (40%). Formal probation takes place through court action after an adjudication hearing in which a juvenile is found to have committed a delinquent act. Informal probation occurs when a juvenile voluntarily (or with prior consent from his or her parents) agrees to be placed on probation, but the case is

BOX 13.1	EVIDENCE-BASED PRACTICES IN COMMUNITY CORRECTIONS

Facilitating Prosocial Family Networks Through Community-Based Family Therapy

Parental support and consistency is a key component in healthy youth development and success on probation. Two prominent therapies that involve parents and youth probationers in this endeavor are functional family therapy and multisystemic therapy. Both of these therapies involve the youth and his/her parents in a home-based intervention.

Functional Family Therapy (FFT)

FFT helps delinquent youth, siblings, and their parents to develop problem-solving skills, increase communication, and aids parents in following strategies for controlling youth misbehavior. FFT involves three distinct phases over three–four months. Agencies that use this method must agree to track clients using a centralized database to help with ensuring consistency in how the modules are implemented. FFT sessions are one hour in duration, and cost between $1,350 for 8–12 sessions, or up to $3,750 for 30 sessions, depending on the severity of the problem (Hinton, Sims, Adams, & West, 2007). FFT has been shown to be cost effective when the cost of therapy is compared to an average cost of $33,000 for detaining a juvenile. Most importantly, FFT is an effective way of decreasing youth recidivism (Darnell & Schuler, 2015).

Multisystemic Therapy (MST)

The goals and participants of MST are very similar to FFT, but MST therapy is considered to be more intense for higher risk youths. MST clinicians work as a team, treatment is more intense involving 60 contact hours over four months, and treatment sessions are conducted right at the youth's home. MST empowers caregivers with skills on how to handle more chronic family problems or violent, uncontrolled youth behaviors. About 4–6 MST clinicians rotate being on-call for up to six families at one time. When on-call, one clinician is available to the six families anytime, 24 hours a day, so the cost of MST intervention is about twice that of FFT. The reductions in recidivism with MST are also very promising (Hinton, Sims, Adams, & West, 2007).

One recent study compared FFT and MST with matched comparison groups (who were matched on risk level, gender, and other factors) and found "… few significant differences in the effectiveness of the two modalities" (Baglivio, Jackowski, Greenwald, & Wolff, 2014, p. 1050). When just high-risk youths were examined, the FFT resulted in better recidivism outcomes than the MST, which goes against the established view that MST is better for high-risk youths.

not adjudicated. If he or she adheres to the conditions imposed, nonadjudicated charges are dropped and nothing appears in the juvenile's record, similar to diversionary cases for adults (Livsey, 2012).

Conditions of Probation

Juvenile court judges have considerable discretion when imposing probation conditions because very few states specify which conditions should be imposed. Instead, setting conditions is left to the sound discretion of a juvenile court, usually upon recommendation of a probation officer acting as a wise parent. Typically conditions include provisions designed to control as well as to rehabilitate a juvenile. Juvenile probation conditions are either mandatory or discretionary. Mandatory conditions for juveniles are nearly identical to conditions for adults, with an addition of curfew and mandatory school attendance. If a juvenile is unable to live at home, he or she is placed in a foster home, group home, or other residential setting. Discretionary conditions may include family therapy, mental health treatment, and drug treatment. In all cases, the probation officer provides the referrals to the parents who are expected to follow through with scheduling and attending appointments with their child (Holloway, Brown, Suman, & Aalsma, 2012).

Gender-Specific Services for Girls

The gender split of youths on probation is roughly 73% male and 27% female (Livsey, 2012). Girls are generally charged with less serious offenses than boys, and have different needs. The term "gender-specific programming" was first introduced back in Chapter 5 to allow girls to participate in community-based services that are more suitable for them. For example, girls are significantly more likely to report sexual trauma/victimization, substance abuse, lack of healthy relationships, and have a misunderstanding of living independently. Some girls said that getting pregnant is a way to create a meaningful identity as a mother or to gain legal independence (Garcia & Lane, 2013). Others mentioned the economic role that boyfriends played. Interestingly, the top three things that girls in the juvenile justice system mentioned wanting the most were: to have a voice/be understood, staff who were fair and caring, and to learn independent living skills (Garcia & Lane, 2013).

Gender appropriate treatments for girls should foster a sense of community to address raising self-esteem, focusing on self-worth, resolving trauma, and developing healthy and positive relationships (Walker, Muno, & Sullivan-Colglazier, 2012). In the past, there seemed to be a lack of knowledge and training for probation/parole officers, as well as very few program choices for girls on probation (Gaarder, Rodriguez, & Zata, 2004). That environment seems to be radically improving as more services are available for girls that equip them with the skills necessary to live independently.

Change as an Integral Process

Changing attitudes and behaviors is a difficult and sometimes painstaking process, but this is an integral part of growing from a youth into an adult. Encouraging youths to be open to change in the maturation process is the essence of juvenile probation/parole. Youths who were confident, more open to change, and had well-defined strategies about how to resist negative peer influences were more motivated to take action and more likely to succeed (Abrams, 2012). An important part

BOX 13.2	**FIELD NOTES**

Question: When you worked as a program director at a boys' ranch, when did youth offenders begin to make changes in their lives and who was instrumental in that process?

In juvenile corrections success is measured by the future behaviors of the youths. As program director my charges were urban youth who were knockin' on prisons' door due to repeated offenses and probation violations. To succeed I needed to learn how to create the conditions where most of the boys would make the decision to change and how to make that happen as early as possible.

Mark Masterson, M.Ed., NCC
Director of Corrections, Sedgwick County, Kansas

Courtesy of Leanne Fiftal Alarid

To help learn what worked I conducted an exit interview with every boy that successfully finished the program and tracked recidivism. The most significant discovery was boys that changed could always discuss when they made the decision! They could easily talk about what was happening at the time, who was helpful to them in deciding to make the change, and how they went about it. These decisions were usually made alone, thinking about their situation and deciding to try a technique taught in a skills group on anger management, problem solving, or assertiveness. The usual time frame for making the decision was three to five months. There were some 30-day wonders and some hardheads at 9 to 10 months, but they were not the norm.

After hearing about their decision to change, my focus in the interview shifted to asking if there was anything we could have done to get them to make the decision earlier. The short answer is that resistance to change varies widely between individuals. When asked if the reason for such a late decision was "on us" or "on you," the latter was the case. The usual answer was, "It was on me because I wasn't ready to change."

The interviews helped me realize that reducing resistance to change first requires feeling safe in your environment. That doesn't happen fast in a juvenile offender facility. For this reason I sequenced programming to include cognitive skills curricula on problem solving, anger management, and refusal skills during the first three months. It worked well and was like "planting seeds" to grow when the time was right.

Decisions to change ingrained antisocial thinking, attitudes, and behaviors are hard work and most likely to be made during times of pain and frustration. Each setback or crisis translates into an opportunity for self-reflection and supportive intervention. Interestingly, not a single youth reported making the decision during a scheduled counseling session. For this reason all direct care staff needed to be trained to watch for and effectively use these moments and to be included as members of the treatment teams.

The conditions for change are ripe when the youth is "tired of being tired" of the risks and consequences of their behavior and they decide to reach out to a staff member they feel cares about them. I found maximizing these opportunities was the key for youths to make a decision to change in less time. Staff members that are able to connect with youths and make themselves available at these times are critical to the change process. Many times when told of their helpfulness, the staff member did not realize the significance of the moment for the youth. It was their usual practice of doing their jobs, having a caring attitude, being approachable and then available to the youth that separated the most effective staff from the rest. This became a cornerstone of our training program and helped improve youth success and reduce recidivism.

---

of change consists of a realization that it is a process involving some minor victories and also some setbacks. Change is not like a light switch that can be turned on and off at will; rather, it occurs over time. A frequently asked question about the change process is whether change can be forced or whether its undertaking is completely up to each individual. If change is self-induced, when does it occur and how do people know when they've changed? Box 13.2 addresses these very important questions from a former director of a boys' ranch for at-risk youths.

Juvenile Probation Officers as "Superheroes"

The job of a juvenile probation officer is often more demanding than that of an adult probation officer. Playing multiple roles of hard-nosed cop, confessor, teacher, problem solver, crisis manager, and community resource specialist, this officer has a difficult job made even more challenging by changing system philosophies, programs that won't accept particular youths, and an increasingly high-risk clientele.

Mark Jacobs (1990) observed the drama and genuine passion that juvenile probation officers exhibited in their jobs as advocates for youths who had never had anyone else stand up for them. Jacobs describes such barriers as unsupportive parents and sometimes the narrow criteria of the system itself, with its agencies often screening out the very youths who most needed help. The paperwork situation is frustrating, along with the inordinate amount of time spent in court appearances, investigations, and furnishing necessary documentation, all of which take away from counseling and helping functions. Despite these drawbacks, juvenile probation officers remained optimistic, believing that change is possible. Validated by Jacobs as modern-day "superheroes," these officers display a noteworthy creativity and sacrifice in their jobs despite systemic barriers (Jacobs, 1990). A juvenile probation officer who prioritizes rehabilitation as part of system accountability is the last hope for a juvenile (Ward & Kupchik, 2009).

It is therefore recommended that, when developing individualized case plans, probation officers consider equally the juvenile offender, the victim, and the community. This standard further requires that a probation officer, in conjunction with a juvenile and his or her family, assesses medical needs, individual capacity to benefit from a program, transportation availability, and availability of a community placement.

School-Based Probation

school-based probation
A type of probation wherein probation officers move out of traditional district offices into middle, junior high, and high school buildings, supervising their caseloads right in schools.

A comparatively new but increasingly popular concept in juvenile probation supervision is **school-based probation**. In school-based probation supervision, juvenile probation officers have their offices right in one of the school buildings and are able to observe and meet with kids throughout the school day or immediately after school. School-based probation is good for parents who do not need to drive their child to see a probation officer. Probation officers are also able to get access to student attendance records, grades, and progress reports, which is information unavailable to most traditional juvenile probation officers (Alarid, Sims, & Ruiz, 2011b). Benefits of school-based probation include:

- *Frequent contact between probation officers and youth.* More frequent contact with juveniles can lead to heightened awareness of potential problems at school and with peers.
- *Increased school success.* Incentive to attend school regularly and to try hard increases the youth's overall chances of succeeding in school.
- *Reduced school misbehavior.*

The idea behind school-based probation is based on the two central ideas: first, that juvenile delinquency peaks during school hours (Soulé, Gottfredson, & Bauer, 2008). School-based probation programs can thus enforce probation conditions at school in an attempt to decrease delinquency (Alarid, Sims, & Ruiz, 2011a). The second reason for school-based probation relates to school districts taking stronger measures to reduce school truancy, particularly in states that receive funding dollars based on the percentage of student attendance. One controversial method that has been tried is using GPS devices to keep track of truant students, as featured in Box 13.3.

Legal Issues in Juvenile Probation

The only case ever to be decided by the U.S. Supreme Court on juvenile probation supervision is *Fare v. Michael C.* (1979). This important California case helps to define the relationship between a probation officer and a probationer

---

BOX 13.3   **TECHNOLOGY IN CORRECTIONS**

Tracking Truants Using GPS

School districts in Texas, California, and Maryland that receive state funding based on the number of students who attend class can actually lose money because of absentee students. For every student who misses one day of school, a district in Anaheim, California, loses $35. Texas had long used fines for habitual truancy, but once truancy became a Class C misdemeanor, youth involvement with the juvenile courts increased so much so that youths were being referred to adult court and even jailed for failure to pay fines. Critics contended that habitually truant youths were missing school for financial hardship reasons than for being irresponsible or criminal. For example, youths stayed home from school to care for ill dependent children when the family could not afford daycare, or the car broke down on the way to school, and so forth. The response to truancy unfairly discriminated against indigent families who were not able to pay the fine. In 2015, Texas law limited truancy fines to $100 with graduated amounts not to exceed $500 and truancy incidents that were paid before September 1 were expunged. Parents could still be charged with a Class C misdemeanor (Associated Press, 2015).

As a diversionary alternative to juvenile hall and payment of fines, some districts have turned to GPS devices to track youths who repeatedly skip school. California youths need to miss only four days of school before they are deemed a chronic truant and court-ordered to wear

School-based probation officers have partnered with school resource officers to reduce truancy and keep a closer eye on kids already on probation.

a GPS device (Matisons, 2014). Truant students are required to carry a GPS device and to enter a code at key times during the day to track their exact location, such as going to and from home and school during lunch and just before an 8:00 P.M. curfew. Such youths receive an automated wake-up call and an adult "coach" calls them three times per week for progress reports. School district officials report that they received initial grant funding to help pay for each GPS device, which costs between $300 and $400 to purchase, with an operational cost of $8 per day. Programs reportedly decreased absentee rates from 23% to 5% (Carpenter, 2011). Once the grant funds ran out, some school districts were unable to afford continual purchasing of new equipment. Districts such as the one in Austin, Texas, decided against renewing their contract (Salazar, 2014).

Critics of these practices contend that lack of privacy and extreme control measures outweigh this otherwise minor offense. The tracking is not for the betterment of youth, but merely so that schools can get funding for student attendance. A second related concern is cost—the cost of truancy tracking software and GPS devices come from public tax dollars. Since school funding is such an issue, students who do not wear GPS devices are tracked using software installed on the student's own cell phone (Matisons, 2014). So far, there has been surprisingly little public debate about truancy tracking for dollars and for protecting student privacy.

during probation supervision. Michael C., a juvenile, was taken into police custody because he was suspected of having committed a murder. He was advised of his *Miranda v. Arizona* (1966) rights. When asked whether he wanted to waive his right to have an attorney present during questioning, he responded by asking for his probation officer. He was informed by police that his probation officer would be contacted later but that he could talk to them if he wanted.

Michael C. agreed to talk to police and during questioning made statements and drew sketches that incriminated himself. When charged with murder in juvenile court, he moved to suppress the incriminating evidence, alleging it was obtained in violation of his Miranda rights. He said that his request to see his probation officer was, in effect, equivalent to asking for a lawyer. However, the evidence was admitted at trial, and Michael C. was convicted.

On appeal the U.S. Supreme Court affirmed the conviction, holding that the request by a juvenile probationer during police questioning to see his probation officer, after having received the Miranda warnings, is not equivalent to asking for a lawyer. Evidence voluntarily given by the juvenile probationer after asking to see his probation officer is therefore admissible in court in a subsequent criminal trial.

The *Fare v. Michael C.* case is significant because the Supreme Court laid out two principles that help define the supervisory role of a juvenile probation officer. First, the Court stated that confidentiality of communication between a probation officer and a juvenile probationer is not equivalent to lawyer-client privilege. This means that information given by a probationer to a probation officer may be disclosed in court, unlike the information given to a lawyer by a client that cannot be revealed to anyone unless the right to confidentiality is waived by both client and lawyer. Said the Court:

> A probation officer is not in the same posture [as a lawyer] with regard to either the accused or the system of justice as a whole. Often he is not trained in the law, and so is not in a position to advise the accused as to his legal rights. Neither is he a trained advocate, skilled in the representation of the interests of his client before police and courts. He does not assume the power to act on behalf of his client by virtue of his status as advisor, nor are the communications of the accused to the probation officer shielded by the lawyer-client privilege.

Second, the *Fare v. Michael C.* case is also significant because the Court emphasized that a probation officer's loyalty and first obligation are to the State, despite any obligation owed to a probationer. The Court said:

> Moreover, the probation officer is the employee of the State which seeks to prosecute the alleged offender. He is a peace officer, and as such is allied, to a greater or lesser extent, with his fellow peace officers. He owes an obligation to the State notwithstanding the obligation he may also owe the juvenile under his supervision. In most cases, the probation officer is duty bound to report wrongdoing by the juvenile when it comes to his attention, even if by communication from the juvenile himself.

This statement defines where a probation officer's loyalty lies. Professionalism requires that an officer's loyalty must be with the state and not with a probationer, regardless of the sympathy that officer might have for the juvenile.

SUPERVISING HIGH-RISK JUVENILES IN THE COMMUNITY

A high-risk juvenile is one who is likely to recidivate or continue criminal behavior at a higher rate than peers of the same age. This section discusses home visits of high-risk youth probationers, youth who are known gang members and youths who reenter the community on aftercare as three examples.

Home Visits and Curfew

Opportunity-focused supervision in practice can involve intensive surveillance aimed at reducing criminal conduct by limiting opportunities. Strategies vary from one state to another, but there are some common features in intensive supervision of juveniles:

- unannounced visits at home, school, known hangouts, and job sites;
- collateral contact of family members, friends, teachers, and neighbors;
- geographic restrictions; and
- curfew enforcement.

Historically, this kind of program was called "Operation Night Light" in many jurisdictions because it involved juvenile probation officers and police officers who traveled together making evening home visits of probationers. The probation officer would conduct home visits one evening shift every week, and a police officer was present for any security and safety issues. The idea behind home visits was for a designated probation officer to visit probationers in their own environment at a time when immediate family members were present. The partnership involved police and probation officers each stepping out of their traditional roles to take a collaborative interest in the juvenile's progress (Alarid, Sims, & Ruiz, 2011a). Interviews of youths and their parents revealed that juvenile probationers spent more time at home, more quality time with family, and less time out drinking and using drugs with friends. Home visits had more perceived benefits with high-risk youth than with adults on probation (Alarid, 2015).

In an empirical study of two groups of youth probationers (regular probationers and youth who experienced home visits) who were tracked for 24 months, officers supervising youth on home visits were more likely to detect new crimes and technical violations during probation supervision. However, the recidivism rate was significantly lower after probation supervision ended for youth who had the home visits, leading researchers to suggest that opportunity-focused supervision through home visits, curfew, and involvement of the parents and family members is effective at interrupting youth rearrest (Alarid & Rangel, 2015).

Youth Gang Members

Most gang members are young offenders, either juveniles between 12 and 17 years old, or young adults in their early to mid-twenties. Gang members pose a challenge for probation and parole officers. While under supervision, gang members are significantly more likely than nongang members to be rearrested for drug and violent crimes. Gang members have more extensive criminal histories and associate with other people who have themselves been involved in criminal activity. This situation creates a high propensity for recidivism, making it necessary to assign active gang members to intensive supervision caseloads.

Probation/parole officers routinely interact with local law enforcement as a secondary source of information gathering and education. Some officers attend workshops and are members of gang task forces to further specialize and keep current as new groups emerge and as codes and signs change. Probation and parole officers must keep current within the online community, including social networks, discussion boards and chat rooms, to determine information about gang activity, parties, and local hangouts (Bennish, 2008).

Juvenile Parolees

Juveniles who are confined in a state institution or in community residential placement are released to the community on **aftercare**, which is the equivalent of parole. Juvenile aftercare dates back to the 18th century when youths were released to "masters" for additional training. Today, about 100,000 youths are released every year after having been away from home for about one year. Aftercare provides transition back into the family, regular school environment and pursuing employment for youths 16 and older. Aftercare workers help with the transition, while probation or parole officers monitor progress with the court. Aftercare workers have little leverage on which to require their clients to attend meetings or accomplish anything, unless enforced by the probation or parole officer (Dum & Fader, 2013).

In reality, many youths have not completed school and lack the necessary developmental skills to obtain a job or to survive independently. Instead, they return to "families struggling with domestic violence, substance abuse, unresolved mental health disabilities, and extremely low income. Many youths return to neighborhoods with few supportive programs, high crime rates, poverty, and poorly performing schools" (Youth Reentry Task Force of the Juvenile Justice and Delinquency Prevention Coalition, 2009, p. 9). The health of that community is indeed an influential component in the success of reentry.

In juvenile corrections, the release decision is left to the discretion of institutional officials, with the exception of a few states that have juvenile parole boards. If released on aftercare, a juvenile is supervised after he or she reaches the age of majority—generally 18 years of age. In some jurisdictions juvenile officers supervise both juvenile probationers and parolees. The conditions of probation and parole are the same in many jurisdictions, the most common being not committing violations of the law, getting gainful employment, meeting curfew, submitting to electronic monitoring and drug testing, reporting regularly, and allowing home visits. Juvenile aftercare presents similar challenges to that of adult parolees in Chapter 11, with the added complexity of stifled emotional and social development that youth experience on their way to adulthood (Dum & Fader, 2013).

To overcome these challenges, a federal reentry model called intensive aftercare program has a structured module of prerelease planning that includes developing a sense of positive self esteem, preparing youth to live and work independently, assist them with interacting with the community, work with the youth's family, and monitor the youth's progress. In addition, Congress passed the Chafee Foster Care Independence Act, which provides monetary assistance to states to develop programs and provide vouchers to former foster care youths between the ages of 16 and 21. The act, administered through the U.S. Department of Health and Human Services, attempts to help at-risk foster care youths to achieve self-sufficiency as adults. This act affects 30,000 foster care youths, out of the nearly half a million youths currently in foster homes, who emancipate every year (Youth Reentry Task Force of the Juvenile Justice and Delinquency Prevention Coalition, 2009).

For youths coming from secure correctional institutions, housing, mental health care, and employment are chief concerns. Youths who received mental health care within their first three months after release were significantly less likely to recidivate than were delinquents who did not receive such services (Bouffard & Bergseth, 2008). Task forces call for a federal policy to strengthen funding for reentry to assist vulnerable youths with the integration process of finding appropriate housing, continuing to receive medical and mental health services, and benefitting from some sort of transition mentoring (Youth Reentry Task Force of the Juvenile Justice and Delinquency Prevention Coalition, 2009).

Juvenile Parole Boards and Parole Officers

Most release decisions are made by a committee at an institution or else a youth is released when he or she ages out of the juvenile justice system. Only five states have a separate juvenile parole board (California, Colorado, New Jersey, South Carolina, and Utah), whose memberships vary from five to nine members. Some members serve full time, others part time; most are appointed by a governor while others are elected; some are paid, others unpaid (Frendle, 2004).

Juvenile parole officers have duties and responsibilities similar to those of adult parole officers. Juvenile parole officers:

- conduct predisposition investigations of juvenile delinquents;
- prepare written reports and recommendations for a court or juvenile parole board, including reporting alleged violations;
- supervise and provides mentoring for juveniles to ensure compliance with release terms;
- coordinate specialized drug and/or mental health treatment with community-based treatment providers; and
- coordinate suitable out-of-home care and transportation if needed.

Probation and parole officers use both confrontational and client-centered approaches with juveniles. Confrontational strategies were used more frequently with younger clients and included informing youths of potential consequences ahead of time in order to obtain compliance. Rapport, motivational interviewing, and the art of persuasion were used as well to decrease revocation (Schwalbe & Maschi, 2011).

Revocation of Juvenile Probation or Parole

The revocation rate of delinquent youths is quite high. Between one-third and one-half of youths commit a new offense while under supervision, and more are revoked for technical violations (Schwalbe & Maschi, 2011). The revocation process works the same way as it does for adults (discussed in Chapter 7). Most delinquents have committed an offense similar to a misdemeanor or a status offense, for which probation is the maximum sanction. If probation is revoked, however, a juvenile can then be classified as a delinquent because of violation of a court order. Revocation for delinquent offenses categorized as felonies can result in a juvenile being sent to an out-of-home community placement or a secure institution for juveniles (Leiber & Peck, 2013). Revocation of a blended sentence can result in imposition of a sentence that continues into adulthood.

THE FUTURE OF JUVENILE JUSTICE

The juvenile justice system has undergone a huge transformation from its original vision in 1899. The juvenile system we have today is more balanced with elements of both rehabilitation and the protection of public safety. There is a greater distinction with respect to adolescent psychosocial development and competency which recognizes that are impulsive and immature by nature, but that doesn't mean they will continue to commit crimes as adults (Brown, 2012). Consistent with those distinctions are more diversion options such as drug courts and mental health courts to keep children out of the juvenile system. The use of assessment tools is important for the prevention of and early intervention in youths with substance abuse and mental health problems. An emphasis on restorative justice is ideal for facilitating a stronger family unit and increasing institutions of social control through schools, peer groups, and communities. Evidence-based practices and use of technology to increase data gathering and information sharing have filtered into juvenile agencies.

Community based correctional programs that emphasize fear, instilling discipline, and surveillance to catch youth at behaving badly are the *least effective* at helping youth change their old habits and reducing recidivism. Thus, programs like Scared Straight, correctional boot camps, and electronic monitoring are among the least effective. The same thing holds true with punishing parents of delinquent youth. While it is important for all parents of delinquent youth to be held responsible for being part of the solution and to attend therapy sessions, threatening and/or jailing parents for failing to perform does very little at helping the parent learn how to be a better parent.

Wilderness camps are in the neutral category, as they are somewhat effective. The most effective community-based programs for juvenile offenders appear to be those that involve the youth and parents in home-based family therapy, involve the youth in skill-building programs (social skills, academic, vocational, and problem-solving), and restorative justice techniques. If youth must be in residential placement, small residential facilities that offer individual cognitive-behavioral therapy as well as family counseling, quality education classes, and aftercare support are the best model (Howell & Lipsey, 2012). There is no doubt that quality therapeutic interventions with high-risk offenders are the most effective of all (Lipsey, 2009). With the implantation of evidence-based practices in juvenile corrections, we believe the future of juvenile justice looks bright.

SUMMARY

- Juvenile justice in the United States was originally influenced by parens patriae, but that influence has greatly diminished over time.

- Juvenile court jurisdiction is based on age and acts committed. Minimum and maximum ages for juveniles vary from state to state.

- Juvenile delinquency refers to acts that, if committed by adults, are punishable under a state's penal code; conduct in need of supervision comprises acts committed by juveniles that, if committed by adults, would not be punishable at all.

- After a juvenile is taken into custody, the processing sequence for juveniles consists of intake, adjudication, and disposition.

- Juveniles may be transferred for trial from a juvenile court to an adult court. Once transferred to an adult court, a juvenile is tried and punished like an adult. Juveniles are allowed parole as an option for all non-homicide offenses and cannot be sentenced to death for homicide.

- Probation is the most common disposition used in delinquency cases.

- School-based probation is a mechanism to decrease delinquency during school hours and decrease reliance on parents for transportation.
- Gang members pose a special challenge to probation and parole officers in that they are more

likely to be rearrested for violent crimes and are feared by the public.
- Most release decisions are made by a committee at an institution or youths are released when they age out of the juvenile justice system.

DISCUSSION QUESTIONS

1. Do you think the juvenile justice system should become even more like the adult criminal justice system, or should it go back to its original idea of individualized treatment? If so, for which types of offenses? If not, why not?

2. Provide examples illustrating the main difference between juvenile delinquency and conduct in need of supervision. Can both apply to the same juvenile?

3. Do the intake, adjudication, and disposition stages unfairly label children as delinquent?

4. Pick one effective method of supervising a juvenile in a community and discuss the characteristics of the program, concluding with why you believe it to be effective.

5. Is school-based probation an effective means of supervision? Why or why not?

6. Does the case of *Fare v. Michael C.* damage the relationship between probation officers and their clients? If so, how can officers gain rapport?

7. In the most recent juvenile justice case that have been decided by the U.S. Supreme Court, what general trend or direction do you see the Court going?

8. What specific strategies are most effective for working with offenders who are active gang members?

9. If you could change anything about the juvenile justice system, what would it be and how would your change make an improvement?

 ## WEBSITES, VIDEOS, AND PODCASTS

Websites

The National Youth Court Association
http://www.youthcourt.net/

National Council of Juvenile and Family Court Judges
http://www.ncjfcj.org

National Council on Crime and Delinquency
http://www.nccd-crc.org/

Juvenile ISP Programs
http://www.nicic.gov/library/018875

National Youth Gang Center
http://www.iir.com/nygc

ResCare Youth Services
http://www.rescare.com

Youth Services International
http://www.youthservices.com

South Dakota Juvenile Aftercare
http://doc.sd.gov

Texas Juvenile Justice Department
http://www.tjjd.texas.gov/

Center for Children and Family Futures
http://www.cffutures.org

Videos/Podcasts

Juvenile Delinquency Court Orientation
This 13-minute video provides an educational overview of a delinquency court in California.
http://www.youtube.com/watch?v=rRXKIZTKJ-w

San Diego Juvenile Delinquency Court Video
(Length: 14:31 minutes) This video is a basic overview of the juvenile court process and how they provide with treatment and assistance for the parents or guardians.
https://www.youtube.com/watch?v=dRuL3gpvPQ4

San Diego County Probation Department Video 1–3
This is a series of three videos that examines probation and the juvenile court system in San Diego County.

http://www.youtube.com/watch?v=ZSLTeyfcQW
s&feature=related
http://www.youtube.com/watch?v=
Q3WFV2Vlmkc
http://www.youtube.com/watch?v=qFk51TkAJG
Q&feature=related

Inside Juvenile Detention: Court Day

This eight-minute video shows a real juvenile justice court hearing to determine the best placement for two brothers.
http://www.youtube.com/watch?v=diXmUvZb_eg

Addressing the Needs of Juvenile Status Offenders and Their Families

This two-hour educational video is sponsored by the Office of Juvenile Justice and Delinquency Prevention, the American Bar Association Commission on Youth at Risk, and the Department of Health and Human Services Families/Youth Services Bureau.
http://www.youtube.com/watch?v=1wh1TKc_I2Q

Trying Children as Adults Panel, Florida (1 hour, 50 minutes)

http://www.mainsailcom.com/ABA/

Girls in the Correction System

This is a podcast of an interview with the CEO of Girl Inc. about girls in the correctional system.
http://www.corrections.com/system/podcast/file/16/media_20050201.mp3

Juvenile Reentry

A podcast discussion about the juvenile offender and reentry programs
http://www.corrections.com/system/podcast/file/47/media_20030717.mp3

San Francisco's Juvenile Reentry Court

(Length: 3:29 minutes) At San Francisco's Youth Guidance Center, Judge Kathleen Kelly presides over the Juvenile Reentry Court, a collaborative model that is one of a few in the nation where the juvenile court is directly involved with the juvenile probation department, the public defender's office, and the Center on Juvenile and Criminal Justice to provide reentry case planning and aftercare services for youth returning to the community from out-of-home placements.
https://www.youtube.com/watch?v=Mi8LMqWB1l8

CASE STUDY EXERCISE

Juvenile Justice, Probation, and Parole

You are a juvenile probation officer attempting to decide what to do about each of the court referrals before you in order to make recommendations to a judge. Should a case be dismissed? Should a case be diverted to another program (e.g., to teen court)? Should a case be adjudicated? If so, should a case be adjudicated within the juvenile justice system, or should the case be waived to adult court?

CASE A

Brian is a 13-year-old male who has come to the attention of a court for an offense of vandalism. He and a friend "tagged" a school building with graffiti and broke several windows in the school gymnasium. The school principal estimated the total damage and cleanup costs to be approximately $1,300. Brian resides with both natural parents and two younger siblings. The family income is $65,000 annually. Brian admits to the offense but refuses to identify his co-offender to authorities. The family has agreed to pay complete restitution. Brian has no prior juvenile record although he has been disciplined several times in school in the past year for minor violations

of school rules. His grades, which were formerly As and Bs, have fallen off to Cs and Ds.

CASE B

Quint is a 17-year-old male who has been referred to a court for aggravated robbery. He is accused of robbing a convenience store and assaulting the clerk. He is a high school dropout with a lengthy history of arrests including robbery, burglary, car theft, and larceny. Quint was adjudicated delinquent for burglary 10 months before the current offense and placed on probation. His probation officer reports that he has been uncooperative and hostile toward supervision. He lives off and on with his mother and three younger siblings. His mother reports that she has little control over his behavior and that he spends many nights away from home. She suspects that he is using drugs.

CASE C

Carlos is a 15-year-old male who was referred to a court for truancy. He has missed 34 school days in the past 90 days and is failing in all his classes. His parents report that they send him to school every day, but he never stays. Even when they take him to the front door of the school, he leaves immediately after they do. Carlos is of average intelligence and relates well to his peers. He has no other involvement with illegal activity, and until this past school year he did well in school, attending regularly. His parents have no explanation for the change in his behavior.

CASE D

Cathy is a 14-year-old female who has been referred to a court for running away. Her parents report she is a chronic runaway, having left home on more than 10 occasions since age 12. She is in the seventh grade. She has been held back twice and is thus two grade levels behind her peers. Cathy was diagnosed with Attention Deficit Disorder at age 7. She is currently taking Ritalin under a physician's supervision. Her parents have attempted to get help for Cathy on many occasions, but nothing seems to be effective. She has been referred once for shoplifting, three times for truancy, and three times previously for running away.

Bringing It All Together: Practical Solutions for Community-Based Corrections

CHAPTER OUTLINE

CHAPTER LEARNING OBJECTIVES

1. Understand how the principles of correctional intervention lead to the use of evidence-based practices (EBP), and why EBP is important to sustain in corrections.

2. Identify top-tier community-based correctional programs that reduce recidivism as well as ineffective programs that do not work.

3. List risk factors that predict the likelihood that an offender will return to crime in the future.

4. Compare and contrast the focus of community supervision solutions with restorative solutions.

5. Explain how former offenders can apply to have their rights restored and/or their records kept from public access.

KEY TERMS

desistance
Justice reinvestment
pardon
absolute pardon
conditional pardon
automatic restoration
certificate of rehabilitation
certificate of discharge
expungement
petition for nondisclosure
sealing of records
restricted access

Actor Mark Wahlberg recently celebrated the release of the *Transformers* movie for which he was reportedly paid $16 million. He has also been involved in a reality-based television show called *Wahlbergers,* which involves building a family-owned business with his mother and brothers in his home town of Dorchester, Massachusetts, and expanding to another location in California. When Wahlberg applied for a concessionaire's license in California for the California restaurant, he was denied because of a violent felony assault for an incident that happened way back when Mark was 16 years old, but he was tried and convicted as an adult.

The attack happened when Wahlberg was under the influence of cocaine and alcohol and was attempting to steal two cases of beer from a convenience store owned by a Vietnamese man in his own neighborhood, and was shouting racial slurs. To avoid arrest, Wahlberg assaulted a second Vietnamese man. Wahlberg's prior criminal history and racially motivated attacks on African American school children (based on a civil rights lawsuit in 1986) caused him to be charged as an adult, and sentenced to two years in prison, of which he served only 45 days (Forry, 2014). The only way to get that concessionaire's license was to get the Massachusetts governor to issue a full and unconditional pardon, which would restore his right to get the license, but the conviction record would remain.

In 2001, Wahlberg started a foundation to help youth in his local community. Between 2001 and 2012, the foundation has provided over $7 million in grants to youth-based organizations such as the Boys and Girls Club, among others (Forry, 2014). Wahlberg also is a frequent visitor in his old neighborhood to hang out with the kids.

Now at age 44, having never been in trouble again and with four children of his own, Wahlberg's pardon petition to the governor has generated considerable controversy. Wahlberg has received the support of the first convenience store victim (who says that Wahlberg didn't hurt him too bad), as well as two people who knew Wahlberg as a 16-year-old and throughout his life: a Catholic priest named Jim Flavin and the Executive Director of the Boys and Girls Club of Dorchester, Bob Scannell. A petition circulated among the Dorchester neighborhood residents has secured over 1,865 signatures against his pardon (Forry, 2014).

In his own words, Wahlberg wrote: "I am deeply sorry for the actions that I took on the night of April 8, 1988, as well as for any lasting damage I may have caused the victims.... Since that time, I have dedicated myself to becoming a better person and citizen so that I can be a role model to my children and others" (Leopold, 2014). The pardon petition is expected to be reviewed by the parole board who will make a recommendation to Massachusetts Governor Deval Patrick (Leopold, 2014).

Do you think Mark Wahlberg should be pardoned? Why or why not?

INTRODUCTION

desistance
The gradual process by which prisoners change dysfunctional and criminal behaviors into new habits that keep them out of the criminal justice system.

We began this text with a discussion of why it is important to have community supervision within the array of correction system options. Mass incarceration in jails and prison is an extremely costly response and does *not* make communities safer (Barlow, 2013). The ultimate goal of community corrections is crime **desistance**, by which prisoners change dysfunctional and criminal behaviors into new habits that keep them out of the criminal justice system (McNeill, Farrall, Lightowler, & Maruna, 2012). In reality, desistance is more of a gradual process rather than a sudden event, but we seem to expect desistance to occur automatically as a result of involvement in supervision and treatment. The single most common measure of desistance is recidivism rates, but there are many other ways to measure the desistance process (see Figure 14.1).

The three objectives to achieving crime desistance are a combination of rehabilitation through effective treatment, protecting the public through consistent supervision methods and deterrence, and restoration of victims, offenders, and communities. This chapter brings together the main points of the book by developing a *solution-based agenda* that addresses each of these three objectives, including specific strategies for restoring individual civil rights and investing in communities.

REHABILITATION SOLUTIONS

First, rehabilitation as a correctional goal corrects root causes of criminal behavior such as drug or alcohol addiction or lack of emotional control. Rehabilitation can also provide necessary skills and abilities such as education, vocational training, parenting, and stabilizing a mental illness or developmental disability. Practicing the art and science of rehabilitation requires that the community corrections' profession return to one that emphasizes human services (Lutze, Johnson, Clear, Latessa, & Slate, 2012). One important point to remember is that if offenders are provided with an opportunity to change, even if a little at a time, change is possible. Timing of the treatment must be right, as offenders will not respond to treatment unless they are ready to change.

FIGURE 14.1
Ways to Measure Success of Community Corrections' Programs

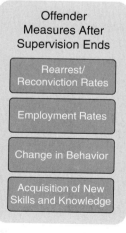

Offender Measures While on Supervision	Offender Measures After Supervision Ends	External Measures
Rule Compliance Rates	Rearrest/Reconviction Rates	Victim Satisfaction
Revocation Rates	Employment Rates	Positive Family Support
Treatment Completion	Change in Behavior	Cost Savings/Less Reliance on Prisons
Payment of Restitution and Fees	Acquisition of New Skills and Knowledge	Partnerships and Treatment Providers

What Programs Work to Reduce Recidivism?

The theory of risk/need/responsivity (RNR)—otherwise known as the principles of correctional intervention—helps to identify program characteristics that will produce the greatest reduction in recidivism. These concepts are tied to EBPs, which not only use the principles of correctional intervention, but EBP interventions have also been rigorously evaluated to determine how much of an effect on recidivism there will be.

The principles of correctional intervention suggest that rehabilitation efforts are most effective when cognitive-behavioral methods are used for a long enough duration—three to nine months is ideal. Treatment programs operating in the community have greater effectiveness—day for day—than the same treatment program operating within a prison setting. Much of the reason is that treatment involves practicing new techniques and ways of thinking after each session—similar to doing homework. Practicing new techniques, ways of thinking, and ways of behaving are better in a more realistic environment such as one's home, than in an artificial institutional setting, which may be overrun by hostility, anger, and bullying behaviors that are anti-rehabilitative.

Treatment aimed at treating high-risk offenders, matched with each person's individual criminogenic needs, and addressed to his or her particular learning style will have the greatest effect on reducing recidivism, over programs that do not adhere to these standards (Andrews & Bonta, 2010).

Brand-name programs for juveniles that have the largest reductions in recidivism include life skills training for substance use, multisystemic therapy, functional family therapy, multidimensional treatment foster care, and Big Brothers Big Sisters mentoring programs (Greenwood, 2010). Many of these programs were covered in detail earlier in the text. On the other hand, juvenile programs that are considered "ineffective" because they do not reduce recidivism, tend to be those with too heavy of a discipline or deterrence component, and do not teach enough new useful skills. These ineffective programs include drug abuse resistance training (DARE); boot camps, scared straight, and intensive probation/parole supervision without treatment (Greenwood, 2010). Community corrections programs can no longer afford to be using programs that are deemed ineffective.

One solution is to require that all community corrections programs be evidence-based and that all community corrections staff (judges, prosecutors, probation officers, and treatment providers) are trained in evidence-based principles (Lutze, 2014). Furthermore, each of the available community-based programs should be predefined via a written summary sheet according to the types of offenders that fare best in each program. This written summary will ensure that both court and corrections staff not only know about available sentencing options that work, but also that the appropriate offender is matched with the most effective program for his or her situation.

Valid Risk/Needs Assessments

One of the central components of this text is emphasizing the importance of using valid assessments that quantitatively measure offender risk of recidivism and offender treatment needs based on characteristics and deficiencies tied to criminal behavior. These assessments should be completed and routinely used at all decision-making points in corrections. There are many assessment instruments that exist, but the Ohio assessment instrument (reproduced in this book) features valid and empirically tested questions that can be used at every decision-making point starting with the diversion decision, sentencing, probation supervision, and reentry.

COMMUNITY SUPERVISION SOLUTIONS

Finally, crime desistance and specific deterrence is achieved through consistent supervision practices, unannounced visits, and letting offenders know in advance what the consequences will be for their actions. While it is important for the courts and paroling authorities to stand behind these policies, we also discussed how having progressive and graduated sanction alternatives to incarceration will allow offenders to face consequences without crowding the county jails.

Craig Schwalbe's (2012) participation process model was also introduced at the beginning of Chapter 1 as a framework to help understand how community correctional supervision practices can influence successful outcomes. This model pointed out that supervision practices must strive toward helping offenders remain compliant with their conditions and helping offenders remain actively engaged in treatment participation on community supervision. As depicted in Figure 14.2, offender compliance and participation are achieved through communication, casework methods, and leverage.

Communication

Communication includes listening, clarifying expectations, and the use of motivational interviewing to give praise and encouragement for desirable behavior (Schwalbe, 2012). Part of motivational interviewing includes using more positive reinforcement and incentives than has been used traditionally. Successful community supervision depends, in part, on the attitudes that offenders encounter during supervision. Personal familiarity with offenders seems to reduce stigmatizing views about crime and criminals, which in the end, help to reintegrate offenders (Hirschfield and Piquero, 2010).

FIGURE 14.2
How Community Correction Supervision Can Influence Successful Outcomes: The Participation Process Model

The figure is author created. The three concepts identified in the figure are borrowed from: Schwalbe, Craig S. 2012. Toward an integrated theory of probation. *Criminal Justice and Behavior* 39(2): 185–201.

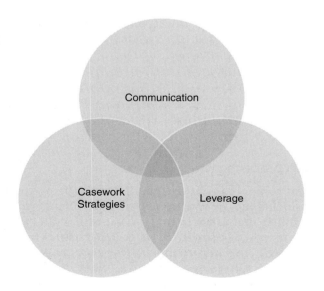

Many offenders recidivate when they feel overwhelmed by the sheer number of conditions and responsibilities they are faced with on probation or parole, and the lack of support to accomplish these goals. Many offenders have felt that very few people are interested in helping them succeed and a limited number of potential employers provide offenders a chance to demonstrate their reliability as an employee. Faced with a perceived "no-win" situation that is more than they can handle, going to jail removes all the immediate financial and employment responsibilities, and the escape they are seeking. While attitude and behavior on the offender's part is instrumental to success, the supervision officer must also be willing to help the offender succeed. However, the supervision officer should not be working in isolation. The officer should have a wide range of community partnerships and resources that he or she can access, such as treatment providers, faith-based organizations, social services, volunteers, and the police (Lutze, 2014). These partnerships should be developed and sustained by the Probation Chief or Parole Director and/or upper management. Upper management also has the responsibility of ensuring that existing programs are routinely measured and that line officers are provided with a reliable data base that can be shared with partners. Finally, upper management has the responsibility of communicating with the media, of broadcasting positive messages, and ensuring the general public that the department is working with them in a collective vision of community safety.

Casework Strategies

Community corrections supervision attends to two major groups of offenders: it serves as a sentence in itself for offenders whose circumstances are such that a community sentence is the best option (probationers); and it serves as a path to reentry for incarcerated prisoners (parolees). People on probation have more lengthy criminal histories and serious offenses of conviction now than they did in the past. More and more probation and parole (P&P) departments have recognized this reality; not only with combined P&P departments, but the nature of the supervision of both groups has also become more similar.

For individuals on probation and parole, casework strategies include assessing criminogenic problems, scoring risk and needs accurately, establishing long-range treatment goals, and assisting the client with implementing action steps to meet these goals (Schwalbe, 2012). Some of these strategies include the officer becoming aware of problematic places, times of the day, or particular people that present an opportunity for each individual probationer to make the wrong decision or that would increase the risk that the individual probationer might get into trouble (Miller, Copeland, & Sullivan, 2015). There is such an abundance of prediction instruments and discussion on risk that it sometimes is difficult to determine key factors in the likelihood of recidivism. However, it is up to the supervision officer to help probationers learn how to make better decisions (Miller, Copeland, & Sullivan, 2015). Box 14.1 discusses some of the major impediments to fully implementing evidence-based practices.

Most major risk factors can be altered over time during the change process. For some offenders, change begins on probation—for others, change begins in the penitentiary and continues on reentry.

BOX 14.1	# EVIDENCE-BASED PRACTICES IN COMMUNITY CORRECTIONS

Impediments and Challenges to EBP

Throughout the text, we have discussed some practical ways to integrate evidence-based practices during community-based supervision. One of the main ways is that community supervision can reduce the main risk factors that will increase recidivism during and after probation or parole. To reiterate, the eight main risk factors identified by Andrews, Bonta, and Gendreau include:

1. *criminal identity*—attitudes and beliefs that are supportive of crime;
2. *antisocial personality disorder*—lack of concern for others or for rules, blaming others, irritable, aggressive;
3. *early and persistent involvement in law-breaking behavior* (conviction record, number of incarcerations, number of parole or probation revocations);
4. *significant others or close associates are antisocial;*
5. *lack of nurturing and supportive parental relationships;*
6. *alcohol and/or drug abuse;*
7. *low levels of performance in school and employment* (education level, reading ability, work history); and
8. *lack of interest in legitimate leisure, hobbies, and recreational pursuits.*

However, the top four areas that probation officers reported that they focused on in their meetings with probationers were employment, housing, payment or fines/fees, and physical health. Family/relationships and treatment attendance (including mental health and/or substance abuse) were discussed, but less often. Perhaps the most interesting was the finding that *none* of the largest threats to recidivism identified in the list given earlier

(criminal personality, associating with criminal friends, prior criminal record, and criminal thinking) were addressed in probation and officer interactions because most probation officers believe that these things were either beyond their expertise or impossible to change, like one's past criminal record (Viglione, Rudes, & Taxman, 2015).

Many probation officers would initially assess an offender but it rarely informed their ongoing meetings and interactions while under supervision. The way that "risk" is assessed in many departments is based on keeping communities safe and protecting the probation and parole departments from liability. Thus, "managing risk" still remains a numbers game of how many visits were done and not on the quality of the visits or the content of the interaction. Managing risk in many departments is still more about telling offenders what not to do, and threatening them with negative sanctions instead of assisting them in what to do, and rewarding them with positive reinforcement (Viglione, Rudes, & Taxman, 2015).

Training officers in evidence-based practices is effective but only to a point. Departments that reward staff who develop EBP skills and proficiencies will assure that EBP's are being integrated by both senior and junior officers. Department leaders must develop policy that mandates the use of EBP and redefines risk. These changes must be communicated to other entities such as the courts, parole boards, and funding sources such as legislative budget boards and state department of corrections (Lutze, 2014).

PREPARING FOR REENTRY   For incarcerated prisoners, the best ways that a prisoner can prepare for success on the outside while still confined are:

1. to complete meaningful treatment interventions before release—that is, to change thinking patterns, take responsibility for actions, and stop blaming others;
2. to maintain contact with positive and supportive family members via mail, phone, or in-person visits; and
3. to develop a solid prerelease plan, which includes living arrangements and job leads.

Parole officers should not wait until after an individual is released to develop a supervision plan. Neither should offenders. Reentry preparation must move beyond the contemplation stage to actual goal setting and carrying out the plans for release and desistance. Every reentry ledger should have a plan for setbacks when they occur and how an offender will respond. Once a prisoner is released, there are a number of factors shown to reduce recidivism while on parole. According to the National Research Council (2008), these factors include:

- concentrated treatment services combined with parole supervision over the first few weeks of release (e.g., day reporting center);
- cognitive-behavioral treatment programs for high-risk offenders;
- strong employment ties and assistance in finding employment;
- stable relationships with significant family members;
- assistance in obtaining identification, clothing, and medication; and
- mentors available at time of release.

Research shows that the most vulnerable time for recidivism is the first 60 days after release. Reentry will be more successful if recent parolees are provided with resources up front, particularly when parolees live in areas marked by concentrated disadvantage (Hipp, Petersilia, & Turner, 2010). These resources include transportation/bus passes, temporary housing, and help with job placements. For example, partnerships with employers could be developed in various industries that historically have a problem recruiting new applicants because of their low pay and seasonal fluctuations. Radisson Hotels in Wisconsin have had positive experiences with employing recently released felons from various work release programs who are near the end of their sentences (Waldo, 2012).

Finally, parolees should not be inundated with too many conditions too soon. As parolees complete one parole condition such as finding employment and stable housing, they can start something else, such as paying restitution or community service.

Leverage

Using leverage appropriately means that officers must continuously confront offenders for undesirable behavior, and then carry out the consequences consistently when rule-violating behavior persists (Schwalbe, 2012). There are of course times when a probationer or parolee has been suspected or arrested for a new crime and must be incarcerated temporarily to determine whether a new charge will be filed for that new offense. If convicted of a new crime, incarceration (or in some cases, a return to prison) might be the best alternative. However, most offenders on community supervision commit technical violations rather than new crimes. Therefore, as detailed earlier in the book, responses to technical violations should be swift, consistent, and fairly applied. However, consequences for a pattern of technical violations should never start with incarceration. Sanctions should be graduated according to the offender's pattern of violations, risk score, and levels of cooperation and motivation thus far. The goal should be to help teach offenders to make better decisions, learn from their mistakes, facilitate continued progress, and not to set up an offender for more failure. One officer provided an example:

> I have a kid who has specific people who he continues to get into trouble with. I ask them to submit a friends' list. We talk about people who might be concerns. Then, those people are off limits. If it's just an association, I talk about solutions and give them a consequence like community service, or if it continues to be a problem, they could go to court and it becomes an official order. (Miller, Copeland, & Sullivan, 2015, p. 189)

Tied to the idea of monitoring progress is the value of problem-solving courts (drug courts, mental health, veterans, and DWI) to help steer offenders on the right path and motivate them to continue treatment even during the tough times. Research in this area shows that problem-solving courts are effective in part, because of the relationships that develop between offenders and court staff, especially with the judges.

SUPPORT FROM SIGNIFICANT OTHERS.   The change process is certainly mediated by the amount of motivation the offender starts with, the level of support from a parent or significant other, and the quality of the officer-client relationship. Part of gaining leverage is minimizing time the offender spends with problematic people and instead seeking support from the offender's family (Miller, Copeland, & Sullivan, 2015). Families should be encouraged to remain supportive when offenders are convicted or become incarcerated, by helping them find a job and a place to live. Families can effect a positive change away from drug use and other dysfunctional habits to healthier, socially acceptable lifestyles (Miller, Copeland, & Sullivan, 2015). Friends have been found to be less supportive than families because of the former's tendency to influence an offender to return to unproductive and illegal behavior (Bahr et al., 2005).

INEFFECTIVE SUPERVISION STRATEGIES OR THOSE LEADING TO HIGHER RECIDIVISM RATES.   "Unsupervised supervision" is ineffective and unnecessary. Unsupervised supervision is a situation by law in which some people must remain on probation or parole for years (sometimes even permanently), but they are not actively reporting in person. They are considered inactive or on unsupervised supervision because they report only by mail or email. This form of supervision serves absolutely no purpose because there is no measurable benefit to either the offender or the general public.

Another ineffective supervision strategy is high caseload sizes, whereby the ratio of offenders to one officer makes it nearly impossible for officers to effectively provide the services and supervision required of them, particularly with medium and high risk offenders (Lutze et al., 2012). This situation has no measurable benefit for the offender who is not receiving quality officer contacts, and only serves to increase staff burnout and a higher turnover rate with officers who are inundated with too much paperwork (Lutze, 2014).

RESTORATIVE SOLUTIONS

Restorative justice provides offenders opportunities to be accountable for their actions and repay the harm they caused to their victims and their communities. As we discussed in Chapter 10, restorative justice is most effective at repairing victim harm when used for nonviolent crimes. Practices such as community boards, victim offender mediation, and sentencing circles can strengthen community life, evoke victim compassion, and provide the victim with more compensation and ultimately more satisfaction with the outcome than many forms of traditional sentencing (Umbreit & Armour, 2010). Since we discussed ways to make the victim whole in Chapter 10, the solutions we discuss in this section involve restoring disadvantaged communities and restoring individual civil rights lost (see Figure 14.3).

FIGURE 14.3
Restorative Justice
Solutions

Justice Reinvestment in Disadvantaged Communities

The *strength* of the community in which individuals are released into has more of an impact in their later success or failure, than how much time an individual has spent in prison (Clear, 2010). Adding to this, a large number of ex-offenders originate from and return to disadvantaged and economically impoverished areas that have a high amount of unemployment, open drug use, and community instability and disorganization. When a community is marginalized, distressed by few legitimate economic opportunities, and its members feel powerless to engage in informal social control of its members, individuals living within this community are more likely to engage in criminal and disorderly behaviors. These resource-deprived areas add to the likelihood that residents will be arrested or reincarcerated (Mears, Wang, Hay, & Bales, 2008). Over time, these areas actually become less cohesive and more unstable, with the potential to become more criminogenic (Wright, Pratt, Lowenkamp, & Latessa, 2013).

Strengthening the number and quality of residential community correctional facilities in disadvantaged areas is an excellent recommendation that also helps former prisoners relocate closer to their families and be able to keep the job they had at the halfway house instead of having to find another job when they leave the facility to go to their permanent home (Wright et al., 2011).

Another positive idea to help disadvantaged communities and to encourage states to save money on incarceration expenses is called **Justice Reinvestment** (Barlow, 2013; Schwartz, Brown, & Boseley, 2012). States that indicate (and can later show evidence) that they will reduce their prison populations are eligible to receive federal funding to be used for employment programs, libraries, schools, and public housing in high-crime neighborhoods. Data must show measurable declines in prison population without indicating subsequent increases in public safety problems (Clear, 2011). Justice reinvestment is a civic engagement model of bettering the community and providing new resources for neighborhoods that have suffered years of neglect. To be successful, the initiative must overlap with workforce development, family or social policy, and health policy (Barlow, 2013).

Justice Reinvestment
Federal funding available for employment programs, libraries, schools, and social services in disadvantaged neighborhoods if states can show evidence that they have reduced their prison populations with no increase in the crime rate or increased safety issues.

BOX 14.2	COMMUNITY CORRECTIONS UP CLOSE

Legal Assistance to Reduce Collateral Consequences for Former Felons

As you read in Chapter 11, persons with felony records experience a wide range of civil losses called collateral consequences that vary by state, and can influence one's ability to move on with their life or may restrict someone from making a living. These consequences include the denial of occupational licenses, suspended driving privileges, past due child support payments because of incarceration, and receiving federal assistance for financial aid or public housing, to name a few. Some of these consequences such as voting are only temporarily lost and regained over time, while others are lost permanently.

Some collateral consequences are restorable or mediated through legal action, but many of these actions would require hiring an attorney. Former offenders are unlikely to have the resources to hire an attorney, so various legal aid offices and teams exist throughout the country to help in this endeavor. However, legal aid offices that receive federal funding through a program called Legal Services Corporation are prohibited by federal law from working with people in prison (Henry, 2008). Initiatives that exist to help former prisoners tend to come from private, not-for-profit organizations, or local sources that include public defender offices in Washington, DC; Philadelphia, PA: Las Vegas, Nevada; and in New York City. For example, the Neighborhood Defender Services in Harlem, the Bronx Defenders, and San Francisco's "Clean Slate" program provides representation in civil court to expunge convictions and seal arrest records, among other services (Henry, 2008).

The Rutgers Federal Prisoner Reentry Project was founded to help ex-offenders with various situations, and to help their own law students gain legal experience on civil matters, such as child support, occupational licensing appeals, and immigration cases (Berger & DaGrossa, 2013). Second- and third-year law students at Rutgers are assigned to cases where they interview their clients to identify the need, prepare the legal brief, and represent their clients in civil court, all for free. The law students will research the law in their state, and through the court, advocate for working out payment plans and presenting their client in the best light.

For example, for past due child support, the law students have worked out payment plans that are significantly less than the rate of 55%, so that the offender is also able to meet his or her other financial obligations. Another law student may attempt to reinstate the former offender's revoked driver's license if the law student can demonstrate the offender's need for the license as a job requirement, and will arrange a payment plan with the court for the offender to pay unpaid traffic fines with the new job. A final example is an appeal of a denial for an occupational license. In cases where the offender's conviction had nothing to do with occupational duties or responsibilities, but the license was denied solely on the basis of the offense being categorized as a felony, the law student helps their client demonstrate successful rehabilitation or challenges the appeal in state or federal court (Berger & DaGrossa, 2013).

Another way of reinvesting in economically-deprived communities is for law schools to provide legal assistance for felony offenders who transition out of prison, and need assistance to restore some of their civil rights they lost through their felony conviction (see Box 14.2) by helping former offenders apply for pardons, expungement, or sealing—all discussed in the next section of this chapter.

Restoring Former Offenders Through Pardons

pardon
An executive act of clemency that serves to mitigate or set aside punishment for a crime.

A **pardon** is defined as "the act or an instance of officially nullifying punishment or other legal consequences of a crime" (Garner, 2009, p. 1144). Historically in England, the power to pardon belonged to the king and was an act of personal forgiveness. Given that crimes are now viewed as a wrong against the government, Article II,

Section 2 of the U.S. Constitution gives the president executive clemency, which is the power to pardon or commute in all federal cases except impeachment. In most states today, executive clemency authority to pardon state felony cases belongs to the governor, acting alone or in conjunction with the board of pardons. In some states, a pardon can be given at any time after a person is charged for a crime, while in other states, a pardon can be granted only after conviction. Still, in other states, a pardon is forbidden until a certain length of sentence has been served or until a specific number of years of successful parole has been completed (Love, 2010).

KINDS OF PARDONS.   Pardons are either absolute (full) or conditional. An **absolute pardon** unconditionally absolves an individual from the legal consequences of his or her conviction and cannot be revoked. By contrast, a **conditional pardon** does not take effect until certain conditions are met, and can be revoked for violation of the conditions imposed. For example, a public officer who commits an offense while in office and is convicted might be pardoned if he or she shows remorse, apologizes to the public, and resigns from public office. A conditional pardon generally does not restore full civil rights of an offender unless express language to that effect is stated in its proclamation (Love, 2010). An offender might opt to serve out his or her sentence rather than accept conditions deemed onerous attached to the pardon.

LEGAL EFFECTS OF A PARDON.   Being pardoned restores civil rights, but the conviction remains on record. Being pardoned at the federal level restores "the right to vote, to serve on a jury, and to hold public office, and generally relieves other disabilities that attach solely by reason of the commission or conviction of the pardoned offense" (Federal Statutes Imposing Collateral Consequences Upon Conviction, 2000, p. 13).

   State laws or a state court decision defines the procedures and determines the effects of a pardon for state felony convictions. Some rights are automatically restored by statute upon sentence completion. States without an **automatic restoration** option require initiative on the part of an offender to remove the disabilities that follow a conviction. Typically, a **certificate of rehabilitation** or a **certificate of discharge** is furnished that specifies the rights that are restored. Check how your state restores various rights at the following website: http://www.abacollateralconsequences.org

OBTAINING A PARDON OR CERTIFICATE.   For federal pardons, the Office of the Pardon Attorney in the Department of Justice receives applications from all over the country. Federal prosecutors are responsible for making recommendations to the president, and this administrative change has led to a decrease in the number of pardons overall (Love, 2010). Federal offenders should wait at least five years after they have completed their sentence to apply.

   The procedures for obtaining state pardons or certificates of discharge are fixed by statute or by regulations of a pardoning authority. Generally a convicted offender must apply for a pardon and furnish references on his or her behalf. There might be limitations on repeated application for pardon, such as a minimum time interval (Love, 2010).

Restoring Former Offenders Through Expungement of Records

Expungement erases or destroys a record and limits public availability to arrest records and conviction records. A distinction must be made between arrest

absolute pardon
A pardon that freely and unconditionally absolves an individual from the legal consequences of his or her conviction.

conditional pardon
A pardon that becomes operative when the grantee has performed some specific act(s) or that becomes void when some specific act(s) transpire(s).

automatically restored
Reinstatement of some or all civil rights upon completion of sentence. The extent of restoration varies by state and by offense type.

certificate of rehabilitation
A certificate furnished upon completion of proceedings that specifies the rights have been restored.

certificate of discharge
Official written document signifying that an offender has completed his or her sentence.

expungement of record
An erasure. Process by which a record of criminal conviction (or juvenile adjudication) is destroyed or sealed after expiration of time.

Hundreds of pardon applications are submitted and reviewed through the Office of the Pardon Attorney, but only a small number make it to the President's desk.

records and court records that did not lead to conviction versus court records of conviction. Arrest records are defined and handled by law enforcement officers according to the number of police contacts resulting in an arrest, regardless of case outcome (e.g., dismissal, diversion, plea of guilty, trial). A record of conviction is one in which a defendant pleaded guilty or was found guilty and was formally sentenced by a court. Each state expunges arrest and conviction records differently, and some states use the term *sealing of records* when they are describing the action of expungement (by the definition given earlier), so comparisons across states can be confusing.

Forty states allow people to expunge or seal arrest records, and if an applicant is successful in expunging, 30 of those same states also allow a denial that such arrest records exist. Fewer than half the states allow expungement for convictions, however. For felony offenses, one source reports that 21 states have expungement procedures (Legal Action Center, 2004, p. 6), while another source says that 26 states, the District of Columbia, Puerto Rico, and the Virgin Islands have such procedures (Bureau of Justice Statistics, 2004). However, in all but 10 of these states, even if a record is expunged its information is still accessible to law enforcement, courts, and other government agencies. The meaning of the word *expungement* can be misleading because some expungement statutes only remove a court decision but not evidence of a case itself. So if expungement is allowable, a defendant must specify the expungement of both arrest records and conviction records, or must first expunge a decision and then seal the rest of a record. Other states do not automatically remove the legal action from a public criminal record. Four states featured next provide examples of expungement statutes.

EXPUNGEMENT IN WASHINGTON.   Washington's version of expungement is called vacating a conviction. Upon completion of sentence an applicant must wait from three years (for misdemeanors) up to 10 years (for Class B felonies). Vacating a record in Washington takes a conviction off the record and gives a person the right to deny having a criminal record; however, the arrest or other court records of a case remain without a finding of guilt. Once a conviction is vacated, it cannot be used as part of one's criminal history in any future conviction to determine a sentence. For all purposes, including responses to questions of employment and on housing applications, a person whose conviction has been vacated may state that he or she has never been convicted of that crime. An expunged conviction also results in a restoration of all civil rights, except for the right to own a firearm.

EXPUNGEMENT IN OHIO.   After a period of three years for nonviolent first-time felonies and after one year for misdemeanors, offenders in Ohio pay a fee of $50 for their records to be considered for expungement. If a judge agrees to do so, at least 13 agencies must be notified, which makes it quite difficult to actually clear a person completely. Such expunged records include complaints, arrests, warrants, institutional commitments, photographs, fingerprints, judicial docket records, and presentence reports. In addition, offender records are sealed rather than destroyed, and state law permits sealed records still to be viewed by some employers, such as agencies that work with children or the elderly (Horn, 2000).

EXPUNGEMENT IN OREGON.   In Oregon an offender seeking expungement must pay an applicant fee of $80 and not be currently under any form of supervision. After a waiting period of one year from arrest and three years or more following any misdemeanor or Class C felony conviction, only one conviction may be expunged every 10 years. Offenders whose cases are dismissed do not have to wait to apply for expungement. Traffic cases, Class B felonies, and Class A felonies are ineligible (Or. Rev. Stat. §137.225(1) through (12)).

EXPUNGEMENT IN NEW JERSEY.   In New Jersey a person may apply to expunge an indictable offense after 10 years, a disorderly people offense or a juvenile adjudication five years later, a municipal ordinance two years later, and a charge of juvenile possession of a controlled substance one year after a sentence is completely served. Types of offenses that cannot be expunged include murder, manslaughter, kidnapping, sexual assault, crimes against children, arson, perjury, robbery, motor vehicle offenses, sale or distribution of large quantities of drugs, and occupational crimes committed by people holding public office. Even after records are expunged, certain occupations involving fields such as law enforcement, the judicial branch, and corrections agencies still require applicants to report in detail information about any expunged arrests and/or convictions (Marain, 2005).

Restoring Former Offenders Through Sealing of Records

A more significant issue concerns the easy access to criminal records on the Internet. In some jurisdictions defendants who have had their conviction expunged complain that evidence of an offense still appears online (e.g., an offense appears with no decision or verdict, leaving employers to question its status). Extra steps might still need to be taken by a defendant to ensure that expunged information is not disclosed in public databases. In some states this requires an additional step known in some areas as sealing or a petition for nondisclosure. A **petition for nondisclosure** is a court order prohibiting public disclosure of a defendant's criminal history record. Other states call this **sealing of records**; it is an act or practice of officially preventing access to particular (especially juvenile) criminal records, in the absence of a court order (Garner, 2014, p. 1377). Sealing differs

petition for nondisclosure
A court order prohibiting public disclosure of a defendant's criminal-history record.

sealing of records
The legal concealment of a person's criminal (or juvenile) record such that it may not be opened except by order of a court.

from expungement in that the latter erases a record, whereas in sealing specifically defined records are closed and can only be opened by a court order. Sealing of records usually applies to juvenile adjudications or to adult arrests or diversion not resulting in a conviction.

As with expungement, a sealing process must be initiated by an offender. An applicant must establish that his or her desire to seal these records outweighs the right of the public to access their information. Sealed records restrict public access to everyone (including the applicant who wants the records sealed), and such an applicant is not obligated to disclose any information to any employer, governmental agency, or official. Legally, an applicant who has his or her records sealed can say that no such records exist. Note that sealed records are retained and not physically destroyed. The only way sealed records can be examined is if the original applicant or a prosecutor files a court order to unseal them and a court grants the order, insofar as public interest outweighs the original justification to seal.

It appears that in the state of Washington, convictions must first be vacated, and then an applicant may apply to request that a record be sealed. Washington's sealing law was designed primarily to petition the courts to seal arrest or court records that have not led to a conviction. Record sealing is an option for dismissed cases but is more difficult to obtain for deferrals and convictions (Washington Law GR-15, Chapter 10.97.060).

Massachusetts permits the sealing of convictions, but sealing must be initiated through the Office of the Commissioner of Probation. The Massachusetts CORI reform reduced the waiting period that begins at time of release from custody (for prison or jail sentences) or at disposition for probation sentences down to 10 years for felonies and 5 years for misdemeanors (Chapter 256, Sec 128).

Are Juvenile Records Confidential?

Youths who have been arrested, taken into custody, or been adjudicated as delinquents in a juvenile court for a Class A or Class B misdemeanor or for any felony also have a juvenile record. Generally juvenile records can be made available nationwide to any law enforcement or court personnel at any time as well as to licensing agencies, employers, and educational institutions under certain circumstances and upon request. The fact that a juvenile is on probation is a matter of public record in most states. Court personnel can disclose such information, but because the details of juvenile probation in case files are confidential, nothing more can be disclosed (such as offense committed, conditions and length of probation, and treatment programs prescribed).

In Texas, for example, juvenile records are automatically eligible for **restricted access** when an individual turns 21 years old. Restricted access is important not only because employers are blocked from information but because an individual has a right to legally deny the existence of a juvenile record (i.e., any juvenile arrest, adjudication, or disposition prior to age 17). Juvenile crimes ineligible for restricted access include crimes of violence and offenses that have been waived to adult court. To become eligible for restricted access, there must be no deferred adjudications, convictions for felonies, or Class A or Class B misdemeanors between the ages of 17–21. When offenders whose juvenile records have been restricted commit a crime after their 21st birthday, their records are subsequently removed from restricted access and made available to potential employers again. Given that their records are no longer restricted to criminal justice personnel, an individual must openly claim that he or she has a juvenile

restricted access
Juvenile arrest, adjudication, and disposition records are accessible to law enforcement or criminal justice personnel for a criminal justice-related purpose (hiring for potential employment at any law enforcement agency, investigation of a future crime, sentencing for a future crime, etc.) but are not accessible to anyone else for any other purpose.

record if asked. Restricted access is different from having a record sealed. A juvenile record in Texas can be sealed only if an offense is eligible for sealing by law and a petition is filed in court to have that record sealed (Texas Juvenile Justice Department, 2011).

The confidentiality of juvenile records, however, is not a constitutional right and may be lifted by state law or agency policy. Over the years, confidentiality has gradually diminished. Juvenile codes in most states allow names of juveniles involved in delinquency proceedings to be released to the media. In 16 states juvenile court records or proceedings (including probation records) are now public. The general rule, however, still is that in the absence of state law or an agency policy allowing disclosure, juvenile records are confidential.

Should Former Felons Be Less Stigmatized?

Society expects former offenders to have learned their lesson and to change their ways, becoming responsible and productive members of a community. Most people want former felons to stop committing crimes and to become taxpayers with conventional jobs. Yet our laws and restrictions do not fully permit ex-offenders to live where they want and to have a decent job for which they are qualified, and they are restricted from civic responsibilities. Blumstein and Nakamura (2009) estimated that redemption for property crimes averaged between 4.2 and 4.8 years and 7–8 years before employers were willing to overlook past violent crimes. With all the limitations to which former felons are subjected, it is no wonder they face seemingly insurmountable challenges to becoming part of a community and gaining a sense of belonging.

The majority of people under correctional supervision certainly intend to remain out of trouble in the future. Even though those with the best of intentions do not always remain crime free, the likelihood of committing criminal behavior decreases over a person's lifetime as he or she ages. Crime desistance refers to a gradual process of establishing self-control and of resisting old habits even in the face of disappointing setbacks. The most vulnerable period of recidivism is within the first six months of offender release, but recidivism risk decreases with the passage of time. One study found that after seven years, the risk of an ex-offender reoffending was nearly identical to that of a person who had never committed a crime (Kurlychek, Brame, & Bushway, 2007). This is important to keep in mind when we consider lifetime bans of civil and political rights.

Yet the removal of civil disabilities remains an open question. On the one hand, rehabilitated ex-offenders have the right to start their lives over using the tools they have developed through treatment efforts. Conversely, the public has a right to know of a previous criminal record to protect itself against a recidivist offender. However, given that most offenders do not intend to recidivate, how can genuine desisters be distinguished from those at risk of public endangerment? When has an offender paid his or her debt to society? If our society were serious about reducing recidivism and allowing former offenders to move beyond their past, we would create opportunities for them to change, we would reinforce civic participation as part of reentry preparation, and we would revisit the collateral consequences that continue to marginalize former offenders to permanent outcast status (Ewald, 2011, 2012).

In closing, there are no quick and easy solutions to complex social problems such as crime and recidivism. We discussed the importance of collaboration and partnerships, effective treatment interventions with offenders, and graduated

TRUTH OR FICTION?

Offenders don't deserve more chances. Once a criminal, always a criminal. If they wanted more chances, they should have thought about all of that before they committed their crime.

FICTION

OPINION: Everyone deserves chances to correct mistakes, errors of judgment, and harm caused to others. The form these chances take should vary by individual, but completely stifling too many opportunities results in continued suffering to more people than the good we think we're creating by having those limits. Chances are opportunities that are a part of learning, maturation, emotional development, and spiritual growth that are a part of life, what makes us human, and might be among the reasons why we are here.

responses to technical violations. The important part of community-based correctional solutions is that they provide options without the use of incarceration, or in the reduction of time spent incarcerated, they allow offenders to continue to be employed and contributing members of society, and if done using the solutions outlined throughout this book, work toward contributing to the goal of crime desistance and socially cohesive communities.

SUMMARY

- To achieve crime desistance, rehabilitation, community supervision, and restoration must occur in combination with each other.

- Rehabilitation solutions include the principles of correctional intervention, the use of cognitive-behavioral approaches, and using evidence-based practices to decide which programs work, and discarding programs that do not work.

- Programs that reduce recidivism are life skills training for substance use, multisystemic therapy, functional family therapy, multidimensional treatment foster care, and Big Brothers Big Sisters mentoring programs.

- Ineffective programs include drug abuse resistance training (DARE); boot camps, scared straight, and intensive probation/parole supervision without treatment.

- Good community correctional supervision techniques include the use of risk and needs assessments at every decision point, positive communication, motivational interviewing, case management techniques, and the appropriate response to consequences along a graduated sanction model.

- Risk factors that predict the likelihood that an offender will return to crime in the future are most likely to be attitudes/beliefs that support criminal identity; antisocial personality disorder; early and persistent involvement in crime; significant others are also antisocial; lacks supportive relationships; alcohol and/or drug abuse; low performance in school or employment; and no interest in legitimate hobbies/pursuits.

- Restorative solutions include that the offender must repair the harm caused to the victim. Restoration cannot be complete without attention paid to the community with justice reinvestment and restoring the lives of former offenders.

- The effects of a pardon vary from one state to another. In some states it erases guilt; in others it does not.

- Expungement, if allowed, destroys arrest records and limits public availability.

- Sealing, if allowed for a particular offense, closes existing records and limits access except by court order. Sealing is not a right, but a privilege, so access can be lifted if state law allows.

DISCUSSION QUESTIONS

1. The three objectives to crime desistance are rehabilitation, community supervision, and restoration. Rank order (from 1 to 3) the importance of these objectives to the ideal goal of crime desistance for the offender. Fully justify your choices.

2. Rank order the principles of correctional intervention according to importance in which principle will affect the most offender change and justify your choices.

3. Risk and needs assessments are recommended to be used at each major decision point in corrections. Examine the three assessment tools presented in the

book and compare and contrast the assessments as to which factors are used at which decision points. Which factors are common to all three assessments?

4. There are other promising programs that have worked to reduce recidivism, but they are not necessarily at the top tier. Of the community-based programs and intermediate sanctions listed throughout the book, which do you think are more promising?

5. Which rights would you agree to restore to a property offender who has stayed out of trouble for five

years after completing her sentence? Under what conditions?

6. Should an ex-felon be allowed to own or possess a firearm? Would you ban all guns or would you make exceptions for hunting rifles?

7. Assume you are given a choice between expungement of and sealing of a conviction. Which would be more appropriate and why?

8. Which rights would you agree to restore to a sex offender who has stayed out of trouble for five years after completing his sentence? Under what conditions? Which rights would you not restore under any circumstances?

 ## WEBSITES, VIDEOS, AND PODCASTS

Websites

Justice Atlas of Sentencing and Corrections (Interactive mapping tool and statistics from the Justice Mapping Center)
http://www.justiceatlas.org

American Bar Association Interactive Map and Listing of Collateral Consequences by State
http://www.abacollateralconsequences.org

Federal Office of the Pardon Attorney
http://www.usdoj.gov/pardon/readingroom.htm

Restoration of Rights for Ex-Felons
http://www.aclu.org/votingrights/exoffenders/index.html

Labor Market Information for Community Supervision Officers to Help Offenders Obtain Employment
http://nicic.gov/library/024136

Council of State Governments Justice Center
http://www.csgjusticecenter.org

Videos/Podcasts

What Works in Probation and Parole
Contains a series of audio files that are related to the concluding chapter.

http://nij.ncjrs.gov/multimedia/audio-nijconf2009-probation-plenary.htm

The Continuing Cycle of Reincarceration
Michelle Alexander discusses a wide variety of issues related to the cycle of incarceration, including racial discrimination, collateral consequences, shame, and stigma.
http://www.youtube.com/watch?v=4BSwEYyFu2E&feature=share

Race, Crime, and Punishment Research
(Length: 30 minutes) This presentation by Dr. Lawrence Bobo of Harvard University discusses the effect of racialized punishment on communities.
http://nij.ncjrs.gov/multimedia/video-nijconf2011-bobo-keynote.htm

Hiring People Under Community Supervision Program: Employers' Perspectives
This podcast is an employer's perspective about hiring ex-convicts.
http://www.corrections.com/system/podcast/file/118/CSOSA118_3_.mp3

CASE STUDY EXERCISES

Should Rights Lost Be Automatically Restored, or Should an Offender Apply for This Privilege?

This chapter presents controversial issues on the loss of rights as a result of conviction for a crime. States differ on which specific rights are lost upon conviction, the duration of the loss, and whether rights lost should automatically be restored after a sentence is served or restored only upon application by an ex-offender. There are no authoritative national answers to these hypothetical case studies because laws, court decisions, agency rules, and practices in the private sector vary. The aim here is to make the reader think about what he or she would do if given final decision on what the law, court, agency chief, or private employer should say or do in such cases. Each decision must be justified based on the reader's personal opinion instead of on what established law or practice says. In sum, disregard the law in these cases and simply give your well-considered opinion.

CASE A: The Right to an Occupational License

Dr. Davis, a medical doctor in the community in which you reside, was convicted of shooting one of his neighbors after the two had a big fight. The fight ensued because Davis had carried on an affair with his neighbor's wife, which the neighbor later discovered. Davis was placed on probation for five years after a plea bargain to a charge of terroristic threats. Assume you are a legislator and are asked the following questions by reporters: **(a)** Should Davis be allowed to practice medicine while he is on probation? **(b)** Should Davis be denied an occupational license if after he violates the terms of his probation he then serves two years in prison for the offense?

CASE B: Would You Hire This Applicant?

You are the owner of a big grocery store in town and run a successful business. One day an applicant comes to you and applies for any job he might obtain in your store. He says he did not finish high school and smoked marijuana in the past, but no longer uses now. He further tells you that he was confined in a state institution for juveniles when he was 16 years old because he took part in a robbery with the wrong crowd. He is now 20 years old, is no longer a part of that crowd, and has been clean from drugs for six months. You desperately need someone to help bag groceries, shag carts from the parking lot, and do general clean-up when needed, but have not been able to find someone who will work for minimum wage. As sole owner of the store, you have the final decision to hire or not to hire. **(a)** What will you do? **(b)** And why?

CASE C: The Right to Own a Firearm

Mr. Tate is an avid hunter and a member of the local gun club. In his house Tate has all kinds of firearms, which he uses to hunt. One night he had a serious quarrel with one of his neighbors. In a fit of great anger, Tate went inside the house, pulled out one of his guns, and shot and seriously injured the neighbor. This was his first offense ever involving a firearm. Tate was convicted and sentenced to serve five years in a state prison. While in prison he was a model prisoner, and he was released on parole after only two years. Assume that both state and federal laws provide for Tate to be deprived of his right to own firearms. **(a)** Should he be allowed all his firearms back? If so, when? If not, why not? **(b)** What firearm restrictions would you place upon him?

CASE D: The Decision to Pardon

Ferguson, one of your former classmates, while under the influence of drugs was convicted of rape, based mainly on the testimony of three witnesses who claimed to have been at the same fraternity party when the crime was committed. Ferguson is currently serving a 10-year sentence in a state prison. New DNA evidence now shows that he did not commit the rape and instead proves that somebody else at the party did it. The same three witnesses, however, say they stand by their court testimony and that for them nothing has changed. **(a)** Should Ferguson be pardoned as soon as possible by the governor (who is the only person authorized in the state to grant a pardon)? **(b)** If a pardon is given, should it restore Ferguson's good moral character and all other rights he lost as a result of conviction?

CASE E: The Decision to Seal

Andrea Jacobs is a juvenile who was 15 years old when she committed a burglary and received two years of juvenile probation which she completed. Before that, at age 14, she received deferred adjudication for the sale of drugs. She is now 18 years old and wants all her juvenile records permanently sealed. Assume you are the juvenile court judge before whom Miss Jacobs's request is made. Assume further that your state law gives you, as judge, discretion to seal juvenile records. **(a)** Will you grant Miss Jacobs' request? Why or why not? **(b)** If so, would you agree to seal just one or both offenses?

absconder   An offender under community supervision who, without prior permission, escapes or flees the jurisdiction he or she is required to stay within.

absolute immunity   Protection from legal action or liability unless workers engage in discretion that is intentionally and maliciously wrong.

active GPS   A real-time GPS system that transmits data through wireless networks continuously at a rate of once or twice per minute. A phone line continually calis a reporting station to update an offender's location, which is tracked by a computer.

adjudication   Juvenile justice equivalent of a trial in adult criminal cases.

Alexander Maconochie   A British naval captain who served as governor of the penal colony on Norfolk Island, off the coast of Australia. He instituted a system of early release that was the forerunner of modern parole. Maconochie is known as the "father of parole."

amercement   A monetary penalty imposed arbitrarily at the discretion of a court for an offense.

antabuse   A prescription medication that causes someone to experience severe nausea and sickness if mixed or ingested with alcohol.

assessment   Structured interview of an offender using a validated quantitative instrument that identifies an offender's risk of recidivism and criminogenic needs to address during treatment.

automatically restored   Reinstatement of some or all civil rights upon completion of sentence. The extent of restoration varies by state and by offense type.

bail   Monetary payment deposited with a court to ensure a defendant's return for the next court date, in exchange for said defendant's release.

boot camp   A form of shock incarceration that involves a military-style regimen designed to instill discipline in young offenders.

brokerage of services   Supervision that involves identifying the needs of probationers or parolees and referring them to an appropriate community agency.

caseload   The number of individuals or cases for which one probation or parole officer is responsible.

casework   A community-supervision philosophy that allows an officer to create therapeutic relationships with clients through counseling and behavior modification, assisting them in living productively in a community.

certificate of discharge   Official written document signifying that an offender has completed his or her sentence.

certificate of rehabilitation   A certificate furnished upon completion of proceedings that specifies the rights have been restored.

child safety zones   A condition of probation or parole whereby the offender is not allowed within a certain range of places where children typically congregate such as schools, day care centers, and playgrounds.

chronos   A chronological account of detailed notes written by a probation or parole officer and organized by date, about any client contact and/or case information that becomes a permanent part of the offender's case file.

civil disenfranchisement   Loss of the right to vote by felony offenders.

clear conditions   Conditions that are sufficiently explicit so as to inform a reasonable person of the conduct that is required or prohibited.

clemency   An act of mercy by a governor or president to erase consequences of a criminal act, accusation, or conviction.

cognitive-behavioral therapy   A therapeutic intervention for helping a person to change that is a blend of two types of therapies—cognitive therapy of the mind and behavioral change of the body.

collateral consequences   Civil and/or political rights that are lost temporarily in some cases, or permanently in others following a felony conviction.

collateral contacts   Verification of a probationer or parolee's situation and whereabouts by means of an officer's speaking with a third party who knows the offender personally (such as a family member, friend, or employer).

community corrections   A nonincarcerative sanction in which offenders serve all or a portion of their sentence in a community.

community corrections act   Formal written agreement between a state government and local entities that funds counties to implement and operate community corrections programs on a local level.

community justice A philosophy of using community—through community policing, community courts, restorative justice, and broken-windows probation—to control and reduce crime.

community reparation boards A volunteer group of trained community members that decides and enforces probation conditions of adjudicated cases deemed eligible by a traditional court.

community resource management team model A supervision model in which probation or parole officers develop skills and linkages with community agencies in one or two areas only. Supervision under this model is a team effort, each officer utilizing his or her skills and linkages to assist an offender.

community service Unpaid labor on behalf of the public to compensate society for harm done by an offense of conviction.

commutation Shortening sentence length or changing a punishment to one that is less severe, as from a death sentence to life in prison without parole.

completion rates Individuals who are favorably discharged from drug court as a percentage of the total number admitted but who are not still enrolled.

concurrent jurisdiction Original jurisdiction for certain juvenile cases that is shared by both criminal and juvenile courts, with a prosecutor having discretion to file such cases in either court.

conditional pardon A pardon that becomes operative when the grantee has performed some specific act(s) or that becomes void when some specific act(s) transpire(s).

conduct in need of supervision (CINS) Acts committed by juveniles that would not be punishable if committed by adults; status offenses.

conferencing One or more police officer-led structured face-to-face meetings between the offender, victim, and key supporters (family and friends) to increase the offender's awareness of how the crime affected the victim and to engage key supporters in shaping the offender's future behavior.

continuity of care Ensuring that a newly released prisoner has access to receiving necessary mental health medication and medical services in the community as were provided in jail or prison.

conviction A judgment of a court, based on a defendant's plea of guilty or *nolo contendere* and on the verdict of a judge or jury, that said defendant is guilty of the offense(s) with which he or she has been charged.

criminogenic needs Problems, habits, or deficits that are directly related to an individual's involvement in criminal behavior.

criminogenic needs-based supervision A community supervision style emphasizing motivational interviewing and meaningful professional relationships between clients and officers in a dual role as a therapeutic change agent and an enforcer.

day fines Fines calculated by multiplying a percentage of an offender's daily wage by the number of predefined punishment units (the number of which depends on the seriousness of a crime).

day reporting centers Nonresidential programs typically used for defendants on pretrial release, for convicted offenders on probation or parole, or for probation or parole violators as an increased sanction. Services are provided in one central location, and offenders must check in daily.

deferred adjudication An offering made by a court to a defendant during the pre-adjudication stage to allow the said defendant to complete community supervision and/or a community-based treatment program. Successful completion of pre-adjudication supervision or program results in dropped charges and no formal conviction. Also known as *diversion*.

delegated release authority Statutory authority that allows pretrial services officers to release a defendant before an initial court appearance in front of a judge.

delinquency petition An intake officer's formal request to a juvenile court judge to hear a juvenile case in family court or probate court and determine whether the juvenile is to be declared delinquent.

desistance The gradual process by which prisoners change dysfunctional and criminal behaviors into new habits that keep them out of the criminal justice system.

determinate sentencing A sentencing philosophy that focuses on consistency for a crime committed, specifying by statute or sentencing guidelines an exact amount or narrow range of time to be served in prison or in a community and mandating a minimum amount of time before an offender is eligible (if at all) for release. Also known as a *presumptive*, *fixed*, or *mandatory sentence*.

diminished constitutional rights Constitutional rights enjoyed by an offender on parole that are not as highly protected by the courts as the rights of nonoffenders.

disclosure The right of a defendant to read and refute information in a presentence investigation report prior to sentencing.

discretionary release Conditional release while still remaining under supervision of an indeterminate sentence, which is granted because members of a parole board have decided that a prisoner has earned the privilege.

disposition Juvenile justice equivalent of sentencing in adult cases.

diversion An alternative program to traditional criminal sentencing or juvenile justice adjudication that provides first-time offenders with a chance or addresses unique treatment needs, with a successful completion resulting in a dismissal of current charges. Also known as *deferred adjudication*.

drug courts   A diversion program for drug addicts in which a judge, prosecutor, and probation officer play proactive roles and monitor the progress of clients through weekly visits to a courtroom, using a process of graduated sanctions.

due process   A recognition that laws must be applied in a fair and equal manner. Fundamental fairness.

dynamic factors   Correlates of the likelihood of recidivism that can be changed through treatment and rehabilitation (drug and alcohol abuse, anger management, quality of family relationships, and so forth).

early termination   Termination of probation at any time during a probation period or after some time has been served.

electronic monitoring   A correctional technology tool in intensive supervision probation, parole, day reporting, or home confinement, using a radio frequency or satellite technology to track offender whereabouts via a transmitter and receiver.

evidence-based practices (EBP)   Correctional programs and techniques shown through systematically evaluated research studies to be most effective with offenders.

exclusion zones   Exact locations an offender is prohibited from being in or near.

Expiration   A form of release from prison after 100% of the sentence has been served behind bars and there is no post-prison supervision.

expungement of record   An erasure process by which an arrest, adjudication and/or conviction record is destroyed and public availability to these records are limited. Each state sets its own guidelines.

failure to appear   A situation in which a defendant does not attend a scheduled court hearing.

fee   A monetary amount imposed by a court to assist in administering the criminal justice system through an offender's repayment of the debt accrued by an investigation, prosecution, and supervision of a case.

field contact   An officer's personal visit to an offender's home or place of employment for the purpose of monitoring progress under supervision.

final revocation hearing   A due-process hearing that must be conducted before probation or parole can be revoked.

fine   A fixed monetary sanction defined by statute and imposed by a judge, depending on the seriousness of a crime.

forfeiture   A government seizure of property that has been illegally obtained, has been acquired with resources that were illegally obtained, or has been used in connection with an illegal activity.

full board review   A statutory requirement that all members of a parole board review and vote on an early release from prison of individuals who have committed felony crimes, usually of a violent or sexual nature. Some states require this type of review on every discretionary release.

full pardon   A pardon without any attached conditions.

global positioning system (GPS)   A system that uses military satellites orbiting the earth to pinpoint an offender's exact location intermittently or at all times.

gender-specific programming   Treatment that holistically addresses previous victimization experiences and life circumstances that most often pertain to girls and women offenders, delivered in a collaborative and nonconfrontational manner.

good moral character   The totality of virtues that form the basis of one's reputation in a community.

good time   Sentence reduction of a specified number of days each month for good conduct.

halfway house   The oldest and most common type of community residential facility for probationers or parolees who require a more structured setting than would be available if living independently.

harmless error   One or more types of error made in the pretrial and/or trial process that does not change the outcome of a case

hearsay   Information offered as a truthful assertion that does not come from personal knowledge but rather from a third party.

home-based electronic monitoring   An intermittent or continuous radio-frequency signal transmitted through a landline telephone or wireless unit into a receiver that determines whether an offender is at home.

house arrest   A community-based sanction in which offenders serve their sentence at home. Offenders have curfews and may not leave their home except for employment and correctional treatment purposes. Also called home detention or home confinement.

inclusion zones   Exact locations, such as locus of employment, school, or appointment, where an offender is required to be at a certain time.

indeterminate sentence   A sentencing philosophy that encourages rehabilitation and incorporates a broad sentencing range in which discretionary release is determined by a parole board, based on an offender's remorse, insight into his or her mistakes, involvement in rehabilitation, and readiness to return to society.

in-service training   Periodic continuing education training for seasoned officers.

institutional corrections   An incarcerative sanction in which offenders serve their sentence away from a community in a jail or prison institution.

intake   A process whereby a juvenile is screened to determine whether a case should proceed further in the juvenile justice system or whether alternatives are better suited for said juvenile.

intensive supervision probation/parole   A form of probation that stresses intensive monitoring, close supervision, and offender control.

intermediate sanctions   A spectrum of community supervision strategies that vary greatly in terms of supervision level and treatment capacity, ranging from diversion to short-term duration in a residential community facility.

interstate compact   An agreement signed by all states and U.S. territories that allows for the supervision of parolees and probationers across state lines.

Irish system   Developed in Ireland by Sir Walter Crofton, a system that involved graduated levels of institutional control leading up to release under conditions similar to modern parole. American penitentiaries are partially based on the Irish system.

John Augustus   A Boston bootmaker who was the founder of probation in the United States.

judicial waiver   When a juvenile judge agrees that an eligible juvenile case should be transferred to and prosecuted in adult court. Eligibility initially determined by offense and age at time crime was committed.

just deserts   The concept that the goal of corrections should be to punish offenders because they deserve to be punished and that punishment should be commensurate with the seriousness of an offense.

justice model   A correctional practice based on the concept of just desserts and even-handed punishment. The justice model calls for fairness in criminal sentencing so that all people convicted of a similar offense receive a like sentence. This model of corrections relies on determinate sentencing and/or abolition of parole.

Justice Reinvestment   Federal funding available for employment programs, libraries, schools, and social services in disadvantaged neighborhoods if states can show evidence that they have reduced their prison populations with no increase in the crime rate or increased safety issues.

juvenile delinquency   Acts committed by juveniles that are punishable as crimes under a state's penal code.

laid on file   When an indictment is held in abeyance with neither dismissal nor final conviction, in cases in which the judge wishes to defer adjudication or suspend the sentence.

law violations   When an offender commits a new misdemeanor or felony while being supervised on probation or parole for another offense.

liberty interest   Any interest recognized or protected by the due process clauses of state or federal constitutions.

mandatory release   Conditional release to a community under a determinate sentence that is automatic at the expiration of a minimum term of sentence, minus any credited time off for good behavior.

marks system   A system of human motivation organized by Alexander Maconochie that granted credits for good behavior and hard work and took away marks for negative behavior. Convicts used the credits or marks to purchase either goods or time (a reduction in sentence).

maximum eligibility date   The longest amount of time that can be served before an inmate must be released by law.

medical model   The concept that, given proper care and treatment, criminals can be cured to become productive, law-abiding citizens. This approach suggests that people commit crimes because of influences beyond their control, such as poverty, injustice, and racism.

medical parole   Otherwise known as compassionate release, a prisoner's conditional release from prison to the community if (s)he has a terminal illness or needs long-term medical care and does not pose an undue risk to public safety.

mens rea   Latin term meaning "guilty mind" that addresses the level of mental intent to commit a crime.

mental health courts   A diversion program for mentally-ill defendants in which a judge, prosecutor, and probation officer play proactive roles and monitor the progress of clients through weekly visits to a courtroom.

minimum eligibility date   The shortest amount of time defined by statute, minus good-time earned, that must be served before an offender can go before a parole board.

motion to quash   An oral or written request that a court repeal, nullify, or overturn a decision, usually made during or after a trial.

motivational interviewing   A communication style in which a community-supervision officer creates a positive climate of sincerity and understanding that assists an offender in the process of change.

needs assessment   The use of a validated quantitative instrument to identify those characteristics, conditions, or behavioral problems that limit an offender's motivation or that might be linked with their criminal behavior.

negligence   The failure of an officer to do what a reasonably prudent person would do in like circumstances.

neighborhood-based supervision   A supervision strategy that emphasizes public safety, accountability, partnerships with other community agencies, and beat supervision.

net widening   Using stiffer punishment or excessive control for offenders who would ordinarily be sentenced to a lesser sanction.

Norfolk Island   A notorious British "supermax" penal colony a thousand miles off the coast of Australia that housed the most incorrigible prisoners.

offense-based presentence report   A report submitted to a court before sentencing focusing on the nature of the current offense and prior criminal history, while minimizing coverage on background of the offender and mitigating circumstances.

opportunity-focused supervision   A style of probation or parole supervision that teaches youths and their parents how to reduce youth exposure to criminal opportunities, such as changing peer associations and using time after school in a productive manner.

pardon   An executive act of clemency that serves to mitigate or set aside punishment for a crime.

parens patriae   Latin term meaning that the government acts as a "substitute parent" and allows the courts to intervene in cases in which children, through no fault of their own, have been neglected and/or are dependent and in which it is in their best interest that a guardian be appointed for them.

parole   Early privileged release from a penal or correctional institution of a convicted offender, in the continual custody of the state, to serve the remainder of his or her sentence under supervision in a community.

parole board   An administrative body empowered to revoke parole, to discharge from parole those who have satisfactorily completed their terms, and to decide whether inmates shall be conditionally released from prison before completion of their sentence.

parole conditions   The rules under which a paroling authority releases an offender to community supervision.

parole d'honneur   French for *word of honor*, from which the English word *parole* is derived.

parole eligibility date   The point in a prisoner's sentence in which he or she becomes eligible for parole. If an offender is denied parole, a new parole eligibility date is scheduled in the future.

participation process model   An integrated theory of community supervision that suggests that offender compliance and active participation, along with officer supervision strategies of communication, casework, and leverage are necessary to achieve offender accountability, offender risk/need reduction, and public safety. Change is mediated by offender motivation, parental/significant other support, and officer-client relationship quality.

passive GPS   A GPS system that temporarily stores location data downloaded through a landline phone once every 24 hours or at specific times when an offender is home.

Peace Officer State Training   Specialized and standardized training that officers are required to complete before they may carry a firearm on a job.

penile plethysmograph   A device that measures erectile responses in male sex offenders to determine level of sexual arousal to various types of stimuli. This device is used for assessment and treatment purposes.

petition for nondisclosure   A court order prohibiting public disclosure of a defendant's criminal-history record.

post-adjudication   The state in which a defendant has been sentenced by a court after having either pleaded guilty or been found guilty by a judge or jury. Being adjudicated is equivalent to a conviction.

post-sentence report   After a defendant has pleaded guilty and been sentenced, a report written by a probation officer in order to aid probation and parole officers in supervision, classification, and program plans.

pre-adjudication   The state in which a defendant has not yet pleaded guilty or been found guilty by a judge or jury. Said defendant is either in a pretrial stage or has been offered deferred adjudication.

preferred rights   Rights more highly protected than other constitutional rights.

preliminary hearing   An inquiry conducted to determine whether there is probable cause that an offender has committed a probation or parole violation.

preponderance of evidence   A level of proof used in a probation revocation administrative hearing by which a judge decides guilt, based on which side presents more convincing evidence and its probable truth or accuracy, and not necessarily on amount of evidence.

prerelease facility   A minimum-security prison that houses inmates who have earned such a privilege through good institutional conduct and who are nearing their release date.

prerelease program   A program in a minimum-security, community-based or institutional setting for offenders who have spent time in prison and are nearing release. Its focus includes transitioning, securing a job, and reestablishing family connections.

presentence investigation   An investigation undertaken by a probation officer for the purpose of gathering and analyzing information to complete a report for a court.

presentence investigation (PSI) report   A report submitted to a court before sentencing describing the nature of an offense, offender characteristics, criminal history, loss to victim, and sentencing recommendations.

preservice training   Fundamental knowledge and/or skills for a newly hired officer in preparation for working independently.

presumptive sentencing grids   A statutorily determined sentence that judges are obligated to use. Any deviations (mitigating or aggravating circumstances) must be provided in writing and may be subject to appellate court review.

pretrial release   While preparing for the next scheduled court appearance following arrest, a defendant's release into a community as an alternative to detention.

pretrial supervision   Court-ordered correctional supervision of a defendant not yet convicted whereby said defendant participates in activities such as reporting, house arrest, and electronic monitoring to ensure appearance at the next court date.

principles of effective intervention   Eight treatment standards that, if practiced, have been shown to reduce recidivism below that of other methods and that constitute the theory behind evidence-based correctional practices.

prisoner reentry   Any activity or program conducted to prepare prisoners to return safely to a community and to live as law-abiding citizens.

private probation   An agency owned and operated by a private business or nonprofit organization that contracts with state, local, or federal government to supervise clients convicted of a misdemeanor.

private service provider   Any for-profit or nonprofit, private organization that contracts with county-level or state-level government to provide probation supervision, independent probation treatment services, or both probation supervision and treatment.

probation   Community supervision of a convicted offender in lieu of incarceration under conditions imposed by a court for a specified period, during which it retains authority to modify those conditions or to resentence said offender if he or she violates those conditions.

procedural justice   A theory that assumes that individuals who perceive that they have been treated fairly and respectfully during legal proceedings are more likely to comply with court and/or contractual expectations.

public employment   Paid employment at any level of government.

public office   An uncompensated government position, either elected or appointed.

qualified immunity   Protection from liability in decisions or actions that are "objectively reasonable."

real-time access   Instant and immediate access via a supervising officer's Internet connection to pinpoint an exact location of an offender using GPS monitoring with a 30-second delay (as opposed to other GPS devices that have a significantly longer delay before a location can be confirmed).

reasonable conditions   Probation conditions with which an offender can reasonably comply.

receiving state   Under the interstate compact, the state that undertakes a supervision.

recidivism   A return to criminal behavior, variously defined in one of three ways: rearrest; reconviction; or reincarceration.

recognizance   Originally a device of preventive justice that obliged people suspected of future misbehavior to give full assurance to the court that a future offense would not recur. It is used today in pretrial release decisions to allow a defendant to remain at liberty in the community until their next court date court. The defendant promises to show up at the next court date and to remain law abiding.

reentry   A process of preparing and integrating parolees into a community as law-abiding citizens using a collaborative approach with parole officers and treatment providers.

reentry courts   A collaborative, team-based program that aims to improve the link between parole supervision and treatment providers to help recent parolees become stabilized.

reflective justice   A form of justice whereby each defendant's case is considered by a judge, parole board, or a decision-making authority according to its subjectivities, harms, wrongs, and contexts, then measured against concepts such as oppression, freedom, dignity, and equality.

rehabilitation   A primary goal of the corrections system, and the process in which offenders are exposed to treatment programs and skills training in order to change their thinking processes and behaviors.

reintegrative shaming   A process that occurs after an offense has been committed whereby an offender initially experiences reproach from significant others and social disapproval from a community but then is later forgiven, welcomed back into society and provided an opportunity to start anew.

relapse   When an offender with a substance-abuse problem returns to abusing alcohol and/or drugs.

release plan   A case-management summary of offender institutional conduct and program participation as well as plans for housing and employment upon release, which is submitted to a parole board in cases of discretionary parole or to a parole officer in cases of automatic release.

remote-location monitoring   When a supervising officer uses a handheld remote receiver to wirelessly verify an offender's physical location.

reprieve   Postponing or interrupting a sentence (for example, a prison term or an execution).

residential community correctional facilities   A community sanction in which a convicted offender lives at a corrections facility and must be employed, but can leave the said facility for a limited purpose and duration if pre-approved. Examples include halfway houses, prerelease centers, restitution centers, drug-treatment facilities, and work-release centers.

restitution   Court-ordered payment by an offender to a victim to cover tangible losses that occurred during or following a crime.

restitution center   A type of residential community facility specifically targeted for property or first-time offenders who owe victim restitution or community service.

restorative justice   Various sentencing philosophies and practices that emphasize an offender's taking of responsibility to repair harm done to a victim and to a surrounding community. It includes forms of victim-offender mediation, reparation panels, circle sentencing, and monetary sanctions.

restricted access   A procedure for keeping eligible non-violent juvenile arrests, adjudications, and dispositions that occurred prior to age 17 from being accessed by publicly available criminal background checks, provided that there were no subsequent adjudications or convictions between the ages of 17–21.

retention rates   The combined total of successful program completers and active program enrollees compared to the total number admitted to drug court.

revocation   The process of hearings that results when a probationer is noncompliant with a current level of probation. Revocation results either in modifying probation conditions to a more intensive supervision level or a complete elimination of probation, with a sentence to a residential community facility, jail, or prison.

risk   A measure of an offender's propensity to commit further criminal activity that also indicates the level of community supervision required.

risk/need/responsivity (RNR)   A theory of rehabilitation that suggests focusing on treating high-risk offenders, matching correctional interventions with criminogenic needs, and implementing treatment according to offenders' learning styles and personal characteristics.

role ambiguity   The discretion inherent in the role of a probation and parole officer to treat clients fairly, consistently, and according to individual circumstances.

role conflict   The two functions of a probation and parole officer that are sometimes contradictory and difficult to reconcile: (1) enforcing rules and laws and (2) providing support and reintegration.

scarlet letter conditions   A condition of community supervision that attempts to invoke shame in an offender by requiring him or her to publicly proclaim guilt.

school-based probation   A type of probation wherein probation officers move out of traditional district offices into middle, junior high, and high school buildings, supervising their caseloads right in schools.

sealing of records   The legal concealment of a person's criminal (or juvenile) record such that existing records remain, but may not be opened except by order of a court.

Section 1983   A federal lawsuit alleging that a government official violated one or more of an individual's civil rights afforded them in the U.S. Constitution.

security for good behavior   A recognizance or bond given to a court by a defendant before or after conviction, which allows the defendant to go free conditioned on his or her being "on good behavior" or on keeping the peace for a prescribed period.

sending state   Under the interstate compact, the U.S. state in which a conviction is based.

sentencing   The post-conviction stage, in which a defendant is brought before a court for formal judgment pronounced by a judge.

sentencing circles   A large community meeting adapted from Native American practices that involves a tribal elder or spiritual leader, the offender(s), victim(s), key supporters of each, justice workers, and community supporters to develop a sentencing plan outside the traditional court system, but that involves community consensus around healing from a crime that occurred.

sentencing commission   A governing body that monitors the use of sentencing guidelines and departures from recommended sentences.

shock incarceration   A brief period of incarceration followed by a term of supervised probation. Also called *shock probation, shock parole,* or *split sentence.*

Sir Walter Crofton   An Irish prison reformer who established an early system of parole based on Alexander Maconochie's experiments with a mark system.

special conditions   Probation or parole conditions tailored to fit the offense and/or needs of an offender.

specific deterrence theory   The theory that an offender on community supervision will refrain from committing technical violations and/or new crimes if, after considering the costs and benefits, the consequences for misbehavior are certain and severe enough that the sanctions outweigh the benefits.

split sentence   A court imposed sentence that involves a short time in jail, followed by a longer period of probation. Also known as *shock incarceration.*

staffing   A bi-monthly meeting of key staff members to discuss the progress and/or outcomes of probationers or parolees on a particular caseload or who are enrolled in a specific community corrections program.

standard conditions   Probation or parole conditions imposed on all offenders regardless of the offense.

standard of proof   The level of proof, measured by strength of evidence, needed to render a decision in a court proceeding.

static factors   Correlates of the likelihood of recidivism that, once they are set, cannot be changed (such as age at first arrest, number of convictions, and so forth).

statutory exclusion   An automatic exclusion of certain juvenile offenders from juvenile court jurisdiction by state statute, requiring a case to be filed directly with an adult criminal court.

stigmatization   A process, in effect long after an offense has been committed, whereby an offender continues to experience social disapproval and bias and is never fully welcomed back into society nor provided an opportunity to start anew.

subornation of perjury   The criminal act of persuading another person to commit perjury.

supervision   The oversight that a probation or parole officer exercises over those in his or her custody.

surety   An individual who agrees to become responsible for the debt of a defendant or who answers for the performance of a defendant, should said defendant fail to attend the next court appearance.

surety bond   A certificate signed by a principal and a third party promising to pay in the event the assured suffers damages or losses because an employee fails to perform as agreed.

surveillance   A method of community monitoring that ascertains offender compliance through one or more of the following means: face-to-face home visits, curfew, electronic monitoring, phone verification, and drug testing.

suspended sentence   An order of a court after a verdict, finding, or plea of guilty that suspends or postpones an imposition or execution of sentence during a period of good behavior.

technical violations   Multiple violations that breach one or more noncriminal conditions of probation.

therapeutic communities (TCs)   Residential community facilities specifically targeted to drug-addict and alcoholic offenders and/or drug addicts amenable to treatment.

ticket-of-leave   A license or permit given to a convict as a reward for good conduct that allowed him or her to go at large and work before expiration of sentence, subject to certain restrictions and revocable upon subsequent misconduct. A forerunner of parole.

transfer of jurisdiction   The transfer of a juvenile from juvenile court to adult court for trial.

transportation   The forced exile of convicted criminals. England transported convicted criminals to the American colonies until the Revolutionary War and afterward to Australia.

unconditional release   A type of release from prison without correctional supervision because a full sentence has been served behind bars. Also known as *maxing out* or *killing your number.*

victim compensation fund   A state fund that dispenses compensation to victims of violent crime, paid for by convicted offenders.

victim impact panels   One or more confrontational meetings that occur post conviction between offenders and people whose lives have been affected by a specific type of crime (drunk driving, murder), but not necessarily the exact same victims of the offender(s) being confronted.

victim impact statement   A written account by a victim as to how a crime has taken a toll physically, emotionally, financially, and/or psychologically on the said victim and victim's family. Victim impact statements are considered by many states at the time of sentencing and at parole-board hearings.

victim-offender mediation   A series of structured face-to-face meetings between an offender and a victim in the presence of a trained mediator with the goal of developing a written contractual agreement to address how the offender will repair the harm he or she caused the victim.

widening the net   Sentencing an offender who should have received probation to a harsher, intermediate sanction only because such sanction is available, not because said offender requires more intensive supervision.

work ethic camp   A 120-day alternative to prison that teaches job skills and decision making using a cognitive-behavioral approach, followed by intensive supervision probation.

work release   A program in which offenders who reside in a facility (a community facility, jail, or prison) are released into a community solely to work or attend education classes, or both.

youth courts   Community-based programs in which youths sentence their peers for minor delinquent and status offenses. Also known as teen, peer, and student courts.

Zebulon R. Brockway   An American prison reformer who introduced modern correctional methods, including parole, to Elmira Reformatory in New York, in 1876.

Abrams, Laura S. 2012. Envisioning life on the outs: Exit narratives of incarcerated male youth. *International Journal of Offender Therapy and Comparative Criminology* 56 (6): 877–896.

Administrative Office of the U.S. Courts. 2006. *The presentence investigation report* [Monograph 107]. Washington, DC: Administrative Office of the U.S. Courts.

———. 2007. *The supervision of federal offenders* [Monograph 109]. Washington, DC: Administrative Office of the U.S. Courts.

———. 2012. *2011 Annual Report of the Director: Judicial Business of the United States Courts.* Washington, DC: Administrative Office of the U.S. Courts.

Alarid, Leanne F. 2015. Perceptions of probation and police officer home visits during intensive probation supervision. *Federal Probation* 79 (1): 11–16.

Alarid, Leanne F., Leslie A. Hernandez, and Christine S. Schloss. 2009. Utilization of community-based programs: Which sanctions do attorneys recommend? *The Criminal Law Bulletin 45* (5): 847–860.

Alarid, Leanne F. and Carlos D. Montemayor. 2010a. Attorney perspectives and decisions on the presentence investigation report: A research note. *Criminal Justice Policy Review 21* (1): 119–133.

———. 2010b. Legal and extralegal factors in attorney recommendations of pretrial diversion. *Criminal Justice Studies 23* (3): 239–252.

Alarid, Leanne F., Carlos D. Montemayor, and Summer Dannhaus. 2012. The effect of parental support on juvenile drug court completion and post program recidivism. *Youth Violence and Juvenile Justice 10* (4): 354–369.

Alarid, Leanne F. and Luis M. Rangel. 2015. *Completion and recidivism rates of at risk youth on probation: Home visits and regular probation compared.* An unpublished manuscript.

Alarid, Leanne F. and Maureen Rubin. 2013. *The challenges of having a mental illness and a criminal record: Can outpatient mental health services reduce recidivism?* An unpublished paper presented March 22, 2013, at the Academy of Criminal Justice Sciences, Dallas, Texas.

Alarid, Leanne F. and Christine S. Schloss. 2009. Attorney views on the use of private agencies for probation supervision and treatment. *International Journal of Offender Therapy and Comparative Criminology 53* (3): 278–291.

Alarid, Leanne F., Barbara A. Sims, and James Ruiz. 2011a. Juvenile probation & police partnerships as loosely coupled systems: A qualitative analysis. *Youth Violence and Juvenile Justice 9* (1): 79–95.

———. 2011b. School-based juvenile probation and police partnerships for truancy reduction. *Journal of Knowledge and Best Practices in Juvenile Justice and Psychology 5* (1): 13–20.

Alarid, Leanne F. and Shonna Webster. 2013. *The effect of community-based drug treatment intensity and participation on probationer recidivism.* An unpublished manuscript.

Alarid, Leanne F. and Emily Wright. 2014. Becoming a female felony offender. Chapter 6 in *Sisters in Crime Revisited: Bringing Gender into Criminology in Honor of Freda Adler*, edited by Francis T. Cullen, Pamela Wilcox, Jennifer L. Lux, and Cheryl L. Jonson. London: Oxford University Press.

Alexander, Melissa, Scott W. VanBenschoten, and Scott T. Walters. 2008. Motivational interviewing training in criminal justice: Development of a model plan. *Federal Probation 72* (2): 61–66.

Alexander, Ryan. 2010. Collaborative supervision strategies for sex offender community management. *Federal Probation 74* (2): 16–19.

———. 2014. A difficult position: A feasibility analysis of conducting home contacts on Halloween. *Federal Probation 78* (1): 32–36.

American Probation and Parole Association. 2006. *APPA adult and juvenile probation and parole national firearm survey 2005–2006.* Lexington, KY: APPA. Retrieved from: http://www.appa-net.org/information%20clearing%20house/survey.htm.

American Probation and Parole Association, National Center for State Courts, and Pew Charitable Trusts. 2013. *Effective responses to offender behavior: Lessons learned for probation and parole supervision.* Retrieved from: http://www.appa-net.org/eWeb/docs/APPA/pubs/EROBLLPPS-Report.pdf.

Andersen, Lars H. and Signe H. Andersen. 2014. Effect of electronic monitoring on social welfare dependence. *Criminology & Public Policy 13* (3): 349–379. doi:10.1111/1745-9133.12087.

Anderson, Amy L. and Lisa L. Sample. 2008. Public awareness and action resulting from sex offender notification laws. *Criminal Justice Policy Review 19*: 371–396.

Andrews, Don A. and James Bonta. 2010. Rehabilitating criminal justice policy and practice. *Psychology, Public Policy and Law 16*: 39–55.

Andrews, Don A., James Bonta, and J. Stephen Wormith. 2006. The recent past and near future of risk and/or need assessment. *Crime and Delinquency 52* (1): 7–27.

Andrews, Sara and Linda S. Janes. 2006. Four-point strategy reduces technical violations of probation in Connecticut. *Topics in Community Corrections: Effectively Managing Violations and Revocations.* Longmont, CO: National Institute of Corrections.

Annison, Jill, Tina Eadie, and Charlotte Knight. 2008. People first: Probation officer perspectives on probation work. *Probation Journal 55* (3): 259–271.

Aos, Steve, Marna Miller, and Elizabeth Drake. 2006. *Evidence-based adult corrections programs: What works and what does not*. Olympia, WA: Washington State Institute for Public Policy. Retrieved from: http://www.wsipp.wa.gov/rptfiles/06-01-1201.pdf

Applegate, Brandon K., Francis T. Cullen, and Robin King Davis. 2008. Reconsidering child saving: The extent and correlates of public support for excluding youths from the juvenile court. *Crime & Delinquency 55* (1): 51–77.

Armstrong, Gaylene S. and Beth C. Freeman. 2011. Examining GPS monitoring alerts triggered by sex offenders: The divergence of legislative goals and practical application in community corrections. *Journal of Criminal Justice 39*: 175–182.

Associated Press. 2006. The truth is out with second autopsy: Boy's boot-camp death now said to be result of beating. *The Kansas City Star*, March 17, A7.

Associated Press. 2015. Texas decriminalizing students' truancy. *USA Today* (June 20). Retrieved from: http://www.usatoday.com/story/news/nation/2015/06/20/texas-truancy-absent-students-criminalized/29047285/

Auerhahn, Kathleen. 2007. Do you know who your probationers are? Using simulation modeling to estimate the composition of California's felony probation population, 1980–2000. *Justice Quarterly 24* (1): 27–47.

Augustus, John. 1852/1972. *A report of the labors of John Augustus, for the last ten years, in aid of the unfortunate*. Montclair, NJ: Patterson Smith.

———. 1939. *First probation officer*. New York: National Probation Association.

Babchuk, Lauren C., Arthur J. Lurigio, Kelli E. Canada, and Matthew W. Epperson. 2012. Responding to probationers with mental illness. *Federal Probation 76* (2): 41–48.

Baber, Laura. M. and James L. Johnson. 2013. Early termination of supervision: No compromise to community safety. *Federal Probation 77* (2): 17–22.

Baber, Laura M. and Mark Motivans. 2013. Extending our knowledge about recidivism of persons on federal supervision. *Federal Probation 77* (2): 23–27.

Baglivio, Michael T. and Katherine Jackowski. 2015. Evaluating the effectiveness of a victim impact intervention through the examination of changes in dynamic risk scored. *Criminal Justice Policy Review 26* (1): 7–28. doi:10.1177/0887403413489706.

Baglivio, Michael, Katherine Jackowski, Mark A. Greenwald, and Kevin T. Wolff. 2014. Comparison of multisystemic therapy and functional family therapy effectiveness: A multiyear statewide propensity score matching analysis of juvenile offenders. *Criminal Justice and Behavior 41* (9): 1033–1056. doi:10.1177/0093854814543272.

Bahr, Stephen J., Anita Harker Armstrong, Benjamin Guild Gibbs, Paul E. Harris, and James K. Fisher. 2005. The reentry process: How parolees adjust to release from prison. *Fathering 3* (3): 243–265.

Bandy, Rachel. 2011. Measuring the impact of sex offender notification on community adoption of protective behaviors. *Criminology and Public Policy 10* (2): 237–263.

Bannon, Alicia, Mitlali Nagrecha, and Rebekah Diller. 2010. *Criminal justice debt: A barrier to reentry*. New York: Brennan Center for Justice.

Barlow, Melissa. 2013. Sustainable justice: 2012 Presidential address to the Academy of Criminal Justice Sciences. *Justice Quarterly 30* (1): 1–17.

Barnes, Geoffrey, Lindsay Ahlman, Charlotte Gill, Lawrence W. Sherman, Ellen Kurtz, and Robert Malvestuto. 2010. Low-intensity community supervision for low-risk offenders: A randomized, controlled trial. *Journal of Experimental Criminology 6* (2): 159–189.

Barnes, Geoffrey C., Jordan M. Hyatt, Caroline M. Angel, Heather Strang, and Lawrence W. Sherman. 2015. Are restorative justice conferences more fair than criminal courts? Comparing levels of observed procedural justice in the reintegrative shaming experiments (RISE). *Criminal Justice Policy Review 26* (2): 103–130. doi:10.1177/0887403413512671.

Baumer, Eric P., Ian O'Donnell, and N. Hughes. 2009. The porous prison. *The Prison Journal 89* (1): 119–126.

Bazemore, Gordon, Michael J. Gilbert, and Jung Jin Choi. 2012. Review of research on victims' experiences in restorative justice: Implications for youth justice. *Children and Youth Services Review 34* (1): 35–42.

Bazemore, Gordon and Shadd Maruna. 2009. Restorative justice in the reentry context: Building new theory and expanding the evidence base. *Victims and Offenders 4* (4): 375–384.

Bazemore, Gordon and Mark Umbreit. 2001. A comparison of four restorative conferencing models. *Juvenile Justice Bulletin* (February). Washington, DC: U.S. Department of Justice, Office of Juvenile Justice and Delinquency Programs. Accessed: https://www.nttac.org/views/docs/jabg/balancedRestoreJustice/comparison_four_rc_models.pdf

Bechtel, Kristin, Christopher T. Lowenkamp, and Alex Holsinger. 2011. Identifying the predictors of pretrial failure: A meta-analysis. *Federal Probation 75* (2): 78–87.

Bennett, Katherine. 2013. Analysis of *Miller v. Alabama*, 567 U.S. __ 2012. An unpublished paper presentation at the annual conference of the Academy of Criminal Justice Sciences, Dallas, Texas, March 20–23, 2013.

Bennish, Steve. 2008. Technology helps gangs go hi-tech. *Dayton Daily News*, February 18.

Benson, Michael L., Leanne F. Alarid, Velmer S. Burton, and Francis T. Cullen. 2011. Reintegration or stigmatization? Offenders' expectations of community reentry. *Journal of Criminal Justice 39*: 385–393.

Berenson, Steven. 2010. The movement toward veterans' courts. *Clearinghouse Review: Journal of Poverty Law and Policy 44*: 37–42.

Berg, Mark T. and Beth M. Huebner. 2011. Reentry and the ties that bind: An examination of social ties, employment, and recidivism. *Justice Quarterly 28* (2): 380–410. doi:10.1080/07418825.2010.498383.

Berger, Todd A. and Joseph DaGrossa. 2013. Overcoming legal barriers to reentry: A law school-based approach to providing legal services to the reentry community. *Federal Probation 77* (1): 3–8.

Berk, Jillian. 2008. Does work release work? Retrieved from: http://client.norc.org/jole/SOLEweb/8318.pdf.

Berry, William W. 2009. Extraordinary and compelling: A re-examination of the justifications for compassionate release. *Maryland Law Review 68* (4): 115–141.

Bhati, Avinash S., John K. Roman, and Aaron Chalfin. 2008. *To treat or not to treat: Evidence on the prospects of expanding treatment to drug involved offenders.* NCJ 222908. Washington, DC: U.S. Department of Justice.

Blackwell, Brenda S., Brian K. Payne, and John Prevost. 2011. Measuring electronic monitoring tools: The influence of vendor type and vendor data. *American Journal of Criminal Justice 36*: 17–28.

Blumstein, Alfred and Kiminori Nakamura. 2009. Redemption in the presence of widespread criminal background checks. *Criminology 47* (2): 327–359.

Bonta, James S., Tanya Rugge, Terri-Lynne Scott, Guy Bourgon, and Annie K. Yessine. 2008. Exploring the black box of community supervision. *Journal of Offender Rehabilitation 47*: 248–270.

Bosker, Jacqueline, Cilia Witteman, and Jo Hermanns. 2013. Agreement about intervention plans by probation officers. *Criminal Justice and Behavior 40* (5): 569–581.

Botchkovar, Ekaterina V. and Charles R. Tittle. 2008. Delineating the scope of reintegrative shaming theory: An explanation of contingencies using Russian data. *Social Science Research 37*: 703–720.

Bouffard, Jeffrey A. and K. J. Bergseth. 2008. The impact of reentry services on juvenile offenders' recidivism. *Youth Violence and Juvenile Justice 6*: 295–318.

Bouffard, Jeffrey and Lisa R. Muftic. 2007. The effectiveness of community service sentences compared to traditional fines for low-level offenders. *The Prison Journal 87* (2): 171–194.

Bouffard, Jeffrey and Katie A. Richardson. 2007. The effectiveness of drug court programming for specific kinds of offenders: Methamphetamine and DWI offenders versus other drug-involved offenders. *Criminal Justice Policy Review 18* (3): 274–293.

Bourgon, Guy. 2013. The demands on probation officers in the evolution of evidence-based practice: The forgotten foot soldier of community corrections. *Federal Probation 77* (2): 30–34.

Bourgon, Guy and James Bonta. 2014. Reconsidering the responsivity principle: A way to move forward. *Federal Probation 78* (2): 3–10.

Bourgon, Guy, Leticia Gutierrez, and Jennifer Ashton. 2012. The evolution of community supervision practice: The transformation from case manager to change agent. *Federal Probation 76* (2); 27–35.

Bowker, Art. 2012. *Cybercrime handbook for community corrections: Managing offender risk in the 21st century.* Springfield, IL: Charles C. Thomas.

Boyle, Douglas J., Laura M. Ragusa-Salermo, Jennifer Lanterman, and Andrea Fleisch Marcus. 2013. An evaluation of day reporting centers for parolees: Outcomes of a randomized trial. *Criminology & Public Policy 12* (1): 117–143. doi:10.1111/1745-9133.12011.

Brady, Brian. 2008. Prisoners to be chipped like dogs. *The Independent*, January 13. Retrieved from: http://www.independent.co.uk/news/uk/politics/prisoners-to-be-chipped-like-dogs-769977.html

Braithwaite, John. 1989. *Crime, shame, and reintegration.* New York: Cambridge University Press.

Brown, Sarah A. 2012. Trends in juvenile justice state legislation: 2001–2011. *National Conference of State Legislatures.* Retrieved March 6, 2015, from http://www.ncsl.org/documents/cj/TrendsInJuvenileJustice.pdf.

Bulman, Philip. 2013. Sex offenders monitored by GPS found to commit fewer crimes. *NIJ Journal* (NCJ 240700) *271*: 22–25.

Bureau of Justice Statistics. 2013. *Felony defendants in large urban counties, 2009.* (December)- Table 28. Washington DC: US Department of Justice.

Burke, Peggy. 2011. *The future of parole as a key partner in assuring public safety.* (NIC Accession #024201). Longmont, CO: National Institute of Corrections. Retrieved from: http://static.nicic.gov/Library/024201.pdf

Byrne, James. 2013. After the fall: Assessing the impact of the great prison experiment on future crime control policy. *Federal Probation 77* (3): 3–14.

Byrne, James and Jacob Stowell. 2007. The impact of the Federal Pretrial Services Act of 1982 on the release, supervision, and detention of pretrial defendants. *Federal Probation 71* (2): 31–38.

Cadigan, Timothy P. 2007. Pretrial services in the federal system: Impact of the Pretrial Services Act of 1982. *Federal Probation 71* (2): 10–15.

Cadigan, Timothy P., James L. Johnson, and Christopher T. Lowenkamp. 2012. The revalidation of the federal pretrial services risk assessment (PTRA). *Federal Probation 76* (2): 3–9.

Cadigan, Timothy P. and Christopher T. Lowenkamp. 2011. Preentry: The key to long-term criminal justice success? *Federal Probation 75* (2): 74–77.

Caplan, Joel M. 2010. Parole release decisions: Impact of positive and negative victim and nonvictim input on a representative sample of parole-eligible inmates. *Violence and Victims 25*: 225–242.

———. 2012. Protecting parole board legitimacy in the 21st century: The role of victims' rights and influences. *Victims and Offenders 7* (1): 53–76.

Caplan, Joel M. and Susan C. Kinnevy. 2010. National surveys of state paroling authorities: Models of service delivery. *Federal Probation 74* (1): 34–42.

Carpenter, Eric. 2011. Kids who skip school are tracked by GPS. *The Orange County Register* (February 17, 2011). Available at: http://www.ocregister.com/common/printer/view.php?db=ocregister&id=288730

Carson, E. Ann. 2014. *Prisoners in 2013.* NCJ 247282. Washington, DC: U.S. Department of Justice.

Castillo, Eladio D. and Leanne F. Alarid. 2011. Factors associated with recidivism among offenders with mental illness. *International Journal of Offender Therapy and Comparative Criminology 55* (1): 98–117.

Catanese, Shiloh A. 2010. Traumatized by association: The risk of working sex crimes. *Federal Probation 74* (2): 36–38.

CBS News. 2015. Baltimore mom who smacked son during riots: I don't want him to be a Freddie Gray. *CBS News* (April 28, 2015). Available at: http://www.cbsnews.com/news/.

Chasnoff, Brian. 2006. Unarmed probation officers fret. *San Antonio Express News*, October 21, 1A.

Clark, Michael D. 2005. Motivational interviewing for probation staff: Increasing the readiness to change. *Federal Probation* 69 (2): 22–28.

Clear, Todd R. 2010. Policy and evidence: The challenge to the American society of criminology: 2009 presidential address to the American society of criminology. *Criminology* 48 (1): 1–24.

———. 2011. A private-sector , incentive-based model for justice reinvestment. *Criminology & Public Policy* 10 (3): 585–608.

Clark, Valerie A. 2014. Predicting two types of recidivism among newly released prisoners: First addresses as "launch pads" for recidivism or reentry success. *Crime & Delinquency:* 1–36. doi:10.1177/0011128714555758.

Cohen, Thomas H. 2012. *Pretrial release and misconduct in federal district courts, 2008–2010.* NCJ 239243. Washington, DC: U.S. Department of Justice.

Cole, Heather A. and Julian V. Heilig. 2011. Developing a school-based youth court: A potential alternative to the school to prison pipeline. *Journal of Law and Education* 40 (2): 305–321.

Cornish, Trent and Jay Whetzel. 2014. Location monitoring for low-risk inmates – a cost-effective and evidence-based reentry strategy. *Federal Probation* 78 (1): 19–22.

Cotter, Ryan and Willem De Lint. 2009. GPS-electronic monitoring and contemporary penology: A case study of U.S. GPS-electronic monitoring programmes. *The Howard Journal of Criminal Justice* 48 (1): 76–87.

Council of State Governments. 2008. *Mental health courts: A primer for policymakers and practitioners.* Washington, DC: Bureau of Justice Assistance.

Craddock, Amy. 2009. Drug reporting center completion. *Crime and Delinquency* 55 (1): 105–133.

Craun, Sarah W. and Poco D. Kernsmith. 2006. Juvenile sex offenders and sex offender registries. *Federal Probation* 70 (3): 45–49.

Crew, Benjamin K. and Sarah E. Johnson. 2011. Do victim impact programs reduce recidivism for operating a motor vehicle while intoxicated? Findings from an outcomes evaluation. *Criminal Justice Studies* 24 (2): 153–163.

Dalley, Lanette P. 2014. From asylums to jails: The prevailing impact on female offenders. *Women & Criminal Justice* 24: 209–228. doi:10.1080/08974454.2014.924352.

Daly, Kevin, Tiffany Brooks, and Chrysanthi S., Leon. *Work release as economic stimulus: Overview of current and potential usage in the 50 States (Working paper).* Retrieved from: http://dx.doi.org/10.2139/ssrn.1458551

Darnell, Adam J. and Megan S. Schuler. 2015. Quasi-experimental study of functional family therapy effectiveness for juvenile justice aftercare in a racially and ethnically diverse community sample. *Children and Youth Services Review* 50: 75–82.

Davidson, Janet T., Richard Crawford, and Elizabeth Kerwood. 2008. Constructing an EBP post-conviction model of supervision in United States probation, district of Hawaii: A case study. *Federal Probation* 72 (2): 22–28.

Deering, John. 2010. Attitudes and beliefs of trainee probation officers: A new breed? *Probation Journal: The Journal of Community and Criminal Justice* 57 (1): 9–26.

Deering, John, Martina Feilzer, and Tim Holmes. 2014. The transition from public to private in probation: Values and attitudes of managers in the private sector. *Probation Journal* 61 (3): 234–250.

Deitch, Michele. 2009. Keeping our kids at home: Expanding community-based facilities for adjudicated youth in Texas. *Texas Public Policy Foundation Policy Perspective* (May). Retrieved from: http://www.texaspolicy.com

DeMichele, Matthew T. 2007. *Probation and parole's growing caseloads and workload allocation: Strategies for managerial decision making.* Lexington, KY: American Probation and Parole Association.

DeMichele, Matthew and Nathan C. Lowe. 2011. DWI recidivism: Risk implications for community supervision. *Federal Probation* 75 (3): 19–24.

Dexheimer, Eric. 2007. Locked out of their livelihoods. *Austin American-Statesman*, February 18. Retrieved from: http://www.statesman.com.

Dollar, Cindy B. and Bradley Ray. 2015. The practice of reintegrative shaming in mental health court. *Criminal Justice Policy Review* 26 (1): 29–44. doi:10.1177/0887403413507275.

Drake, Elizabeth. 2007. *Does participation in Washington's work release facilities reduce recidivism?* Olympia, WA: Washington State Institute for Public Policy. Retrieved from: http://www.wsipp.wa.gov/rptfiles/07-11-1201.pdf

Drapela, Laurie A. and Faith E. Lutze. 2009. Innovation in community corrections and probation officers' fears of being sued. *Journal of Contemporary Criminal Justice* 25 (4): 364–383.

Dubois, David L., Nelson Portillo, Jean E. Rhodes, Naida Silverthorn, and Jeffrey C. Valentine. 2011. How effective are mentoring programs for youth? A systematic assessment of the evidence. *Psychological Sciences in the Public Interest* 12 (2): 57–91.

Dum, Christopher P. and Jamie J. Fader. 2013. "These are kid's lives!": Dilemmas and adaptations of juvenile aftercare workers. *Justice Quarterly* 30 (5): 784–810.

Duriez, Stephanie A., Francis T. Cullen, and Sarah M. Manchak. 2014. Is project HOPE creating a false sense of hope? A case study in correctional popularity. *Federal Probation* 78 (2): 57–70.

Durose, Matthew R., Alexia D. Cooper, and Howard N. Synder. 2014. *U.S. Department of Justice.* Retrieved March 3, 2015, from http://www.bjs.gov/content/pub/pdf/rprts05p0510.pdf.

Durose, Matthew R. and Patrick A. Langan. 2007. *Felony sentences in state courts, 2004.* Washington, DC: Bureau of Justice Statistics.

Duwe, Grant. 2011. The benefits of keeping idle hands busy: An outcome evaluation of a prisoner reentry employment program. *Crime & Delinquency:* 1–28. doi:10.1177/0011128711421653.

———. 2012. Evaluating the Minnesota comprehensive offender reentry plan (MCORP): Results from a randomized experiment. *Justice Quarterly 29* (3): 347–383. doi:10.1080/07418825.2011.555414.

———. 2013. What's inside the "black box"? The importance of "gray box" evaluations for the "what works" movement. *Criminology & Public Policy 12* (1): 145–152. doi:10.111/1745-9133.12012.

Duwe, Grant and Deborah Kerschner. 2008. Removing a nail from the boot camp coffin: An outcome evaluation of Minnesota's challenge incarceration program. *Crime and Delinquency 54* (4): 614–643.

Eggers, Amy, Doris L. MacKenzie, Ojmarrh Mitchell, and David B. Wilson. 2012. Assessing the effectiveness of drugs on recidivism: A meta-analytic of traditional and non-traditional drug courts. *Journal of Criminal Justice 40* (1): 60–71.

Englebrecht, Christine. M. 2012. Where do I stand? An exploration of the rules that regulate victim participation in the criminal justice system. *Victims and Offenders 7:* 161–187. doi:10.1080/15564862012.657290.

Evjen, Victor H. 1975. The federal probation system: The struggle to achieve it and its first 25 years. *Federal Probation 39* (2): 3–15.

Ewald, Alec C. 2011. Collateral consequences and the perils of categorical ambiguity. Pp. 77–123 in *Law as punishment: Law as regulation,* edited by Austin Sarat, Lawrence Douglas, and Martha Merrill Umphrey. Stanford, CA: Stanford Law Books.

———. 2012. Collateral consequences in the American States. *Social Science Quarterly 93* (1): 211–247. DOI: 10.1111/j.1540-6237.2011.00831.x.

Ewald, Alec and Christopher Uggen. 2012. The collateral effects of imprisonment on prisoners, their families, and communities. Pp. 83–103 in *The Oxford handbook of sentencing and corrections,* edited by Joan Petersilia and Kevin R. Reitz. New York: Oxford University Press.

Fennessy, Matthew and Matthew T. Huss. 2013. Predicting success in a large sample of federal pretrial offenders: The influence of ethnicity. *Criminal Justice and Behavior 40* (1): 40–56.

Ferrigno, Lorenzo and Ray Sanchez. 2014. Dying defense lawyer Lynne Stewart released from jail. *CNN,* January 1. http://www.cnn.com/2013/12/31/justice/lynne-stewart-compassionate-release/.

Fogel, David. 1979.... *We are the living proof ... The justice model for corrections,* 2nd ed. Cincinnati, OH: Anderson.

Forry, Bill. 2014. Mark Wahlberg's pardon appeal relies on good he does in Dot. *Dorchester Reporter* (December 10, 2014). Available at: http://www.dotnews.com/2014/

Fortune, Clare-Ann, Tony Ward, and Gwenda M. Willis. 2012. The rehabilitation of offenders: Reducing risk and promoting better lives. *Psychiatry, Psychology and Law 19:* 646–661.

Franke, Derrick, David Bierie, and Doris Layton MacKenzie. 2010. Legitimacy in corrections: A randomized experiment comparing a boot camp with a prison. *Criminology and Public Policy 9* (1): 89–117.

Frana, John F. and Ryan D. Schroeder. 2008. Alternatives to incarceration. *Justice Policy Journal 5* (2): 5–25.

Frendle, Julie Wesley. 2004. *An overview of juvenile parole boards in the United States.* Prepared for the New Mexico Sentencing Commission.

Gaarder, Emily, Nancy Rodriguez, and Marjorie S. Zata. 2004. Criers, liars, and manipulators: Probation officers' views of girls. *Justice Quarterly 21* (3): 547–578.

Garcia, Crystal A. and Jodi Lane. 2013. What a girl wants, what a girl needs: Findings from a gender-specific focus group study. *Crime & Delinquency 59* (4): 536–561. doi:10.1177/0011128709331790.

Garner, Bryan A. 2014. *Black's law dictionary,* 10th ed. Eagan, MN: Thomson Reuters.

Gendreau, Paul. 1996. The principles of effective intervention with offenders. In *Choosing correctional options that work: Defining the demand and evaluating the supply,* edited by Alan T. Harland. Thousand Oaks, CA: Sage. Pp. 117–130

Georgia County and Municipal Advisory Council, 2015. *Private probation providers approved to provide services to the courts of Georgia (Updated: January 30, 2015).* Retrieved from: http://w2.georgiacourts.gov/cmpac/files/2014%20Approved%20Private%20Probation%20Providers_feb%202015.pdf

Gies, Stephen V., Randy Gainey, Marcia I. Cohen. Eoin Healy, Dan Duplantier, Martha Yeide, Alan Bekelman, Amanda Bobnis, and Michael Hopps. 2012. *Monitoring high-risk sex offenders with GPS technology: An evaluation of the California supervision program, final report.* NCJ 238481. Washington, DC: U.S. Department of Justice. Available at: https://www.ncjrs.gov/pdffiles1/nij/grants/238481.pdf

Glaser, Daniel. 1969. *The effectiveness of a prison and parole system.* New York: Bobbs-Merrill Company.

Glaze, Lauren E. 2011. *Correctional population in the United States, 2010,* NCJ 236319. Washington, DC: U.S. Department of Justice.

Glaze, Lauren E., Thomas P. Bonczar, and Fan Zhang. 2010. *Probation and parole in the United States, 2009.* Washington, DC: Bureau of Justice Statistics, U.S. Department of Justice.

Glaze, Lauren E. and Seri Palla. 2005. *Probation and parole in the United States, 2004.* Washington, DC: Bureau of Justice Statistics, U.S. Department of Justice.

Glaze, Lauren E. and Erika Parks. 2012. *Correctional population in the United States, 2011,* NCJ 239972. Washington, DC: U.S. Department of Justice.

Golden, Lori S., Robert J. Gatchel, and Melissa A. Cahill. 2006. Evaluating the effectiveness of the National Institute of Corrections' 'thinking for a change' program among probationers. *Journal of Offender Rehabilitation 43* (2): 55–73.

Gottfredson, Denise C., Brook W. Kearley, Stacy S. Najaka, and Carlos M. Rocha. 2007. How drug treatment courts work: An analysis of mediators. *Journal of Research in Crime and Delinquency 44* (1): 3–35.

Grattet, Ryken, Jeffrey Lin, and Joan Petersilia. 2011. Supervision regimes, risk, and official reactions to parolee deviance. *Criminology 49* (2): 371–400.

Greenhouse, Steven. 2012. Equal opportunity panel updates hiring policy. *New York Times* (April 25, 2012). Available at: http://www.nytimes.com/2012/04/26/business/equal-opportunity-panel-updates-hiring-policy.html

Greenwood, Peter. 2010. *Preventing and reducing youth crime and violence: Using evidence-based practices.* Sacramento, CA: Governor's Office of Gang and Youth Violence Policy. Available at: http://www.nursefamilypartnership.org/assets/PDF/Journals-and-Reports/CA_GOGYVP_Greenwood_1-27-10

Griffin, Patrick. 2010. Models for change: Innovations in practice. *National Center for Juvenile Justice*. Pittsburgh, PA: NCJJ.

Griffin, Patrick, Sean Addie, Benjamin Adams, and Kathy Firestine. 2011. Trying juveniles as adults: An analysis of state transfer laws and reporting. *Office of Juvenile Justice and Delinquency Prevention*. Retrieved March 16, 2015, from https://www.ncjrs.gov/pdffiles1/ojjdp/232434.pdf.

Grooms, Robert M. 1982. Recidivist. *Crime and Delinquency* 28: 541–545.

Grubesic, Tony H., Elizabeth Mack, and Alan T. Murray. 2007. Spatial analysis for evaluating the impact of Megan's law. *Social Science Computer Review* 25: 143–162.

Gültekin, Kübra and Sebahattin Gültekin. 2012. Is juvenile boot camp policy effective? *International Journal of Human Sciences* 9 (1): 725–740.

Guydish, Joseph, Monica Chan, Alan Bostrom, Martha A. Jessup, Thomas B. Davis, and Cheryl Marsh. 2011. A randomized trial of probation case management for drug-involved women offenders. *Crime and Delinquency* 57 (2): 167–198.

Halpin, James. 2014. County probation officers can now carry guns. *Citizens Voice* (April 3, 2014). Available at: http://citizensvoice.com/news/county-probation-officers-can-now-carry-guns.

Hamilton, Zachary K. 2010. *Do reentry courts reduce recidivism? Results from the Harlem parole reentry court*. New York: Center for Court Innovation. Retrieved from: http://www.courtinnovation.org/

Hamilton, Zachary K. and Christopher M. Campbell. 2013. A dark figure of corrections: Failure by way of participation. *Criminal Justice and Behavior* 40 (2): 180–202.

———. 2014. The Impact of New Jersey's halfway house system. *Criminal Justice and Behavior* 41 (11): 1354–1375. doi: 10.1177/0093854814546132.

Hansen, Chris. 2008. Cognitive-Behavioral interventions: Where they come from and what they do. *Federal Probation* 72 (2): 43–49

Harden, Alicia N. 2012. Rethinking the shame: The intersection of shaming punishments and American juvenile justice. *University of California Davis Journal of Juvenile Law and Policy* 16: 93–112.

Harris, Alexes, Heather Evans, and Katherine Beckett. 2011. Courtesy stigma and monetary sanctions: Toward a socio-cultural theory of punishment. *American Sociological Review* 78 (2): 234–264.

Hartney, Christopher and Susan Marchionna. 2009. *Attitudes of US voters toward nonserious offenders and alternatives to incarceration*. Oakland, CA: NCCD. Available at: http://nccd-crc.issuelab.org/research/5/filter/title

Hartzler, Bryan and Erin M. Espinosa. 2011. Moving criminal justice organizations toward adoption of evidence-based practice via advanced workshop training in motivational interviewing: A research note. *Criminal Justice Policy Review* 22 (2): 235–253.

Hawken, Angela and Mark Kleiman. 2009. *Managing drug-involved probationers with swift and certain sanctions: Evaluating Hawaii's HOPE* (NCJ # 229023). Washington, DC: National Institute of Justice. Retrieved from: https://www.ncjrs.gov/pdffiles1/nij/grants/229023.pdf

Haynes, Stacy Hoskins. 2011. The effects of victim-related contextual factors on the criminal justice system. *Crime and Delinquency* 57: 298–328.

Haynes, Stacy H., Alison C. Cares, and Barry R. Ruback. 2014. Juvenile economic sanctions: An analysis of their imposition, payment, and effect on recidivism. *Criminology & Public Policy* 13 (1): 31–60.

Haynes, Stacy Hoskins, Barry Ruback, and Gretchen R. Cusick. 2010. Courtroom workgroups and sentencing: The effects of similarity, proximity, and stability. *Crime and Delinquency* 56 (1): 126–161.

Helmond, P., Greetjan Overbeek, Daniel Brugman, and John C. Gibbs. 2015. A meta-analysis on cognitive distortions and externalizing problem behavior. Associations, moderators and treatment effectiveness. *Criminal Justice and Behavior* 24 (3): 245–262. doi:10.1177/0093854814552843

Henry, Jessica S. 2008. Closing the legal services gap in prisoner reentry programs. *Criminal Justice Studies* 21 (1): 15–25. doi:10.1080/14786010801972654.

Henry, Thomas. 2007. Reflections on the 25th anniversary of the pretrial services act. *Federal Probation* 71 (2): 4–6.

Hensley, Denise Bray. 1995. One boy's life. *Houston Chronicle* (September 17).

Herberman, Erinn J. and Thomas P. Bonczar. 2014. *Probation and parole in the United States, 2013*, NCJ 248029. Washington, DC: U.S. Department of Justice.

Hill, Brian J. 2006. Four-point strategy reduces technical violations of probation in Connecticut. *Topics in community corrections: Effectively managing violations and revocations*. Longmont, CO: National Institute of Corrections.

Hindman, Jan, and James M. Peters. 2001. Polygraph testing leads to better understanding adult and juvenile sex offenders. *Federal Probation* 65 (3): 8–15.

Hinton, W. Jeff, Patricia L. Sims, Mary Ann Adams, and Charles West. 2007. Juvenile justice: A system divided. *Criminal Justice Policy Review* 18 (4): 466–483.

Hipp, John R., Joan Petersilia, and Susan Turner. 2010. Parolee recidivism in California: The effect of neighborhood context and social service agency characteristics. *Criminology* 48 (4): 947–978.

Hipple, Natalie K., Jeff Gruenewald, and Edmund F. McGarrell. 2014. Restorativeness, procedural justice, and defiance as predictors of reoffending of participants in family group conferences. *Crime and Delinquency 60* (8): 1131–1157. Doi: 10.1177/0011128711428556

Hirschfield, Paul J. and Alex R. Piquero. 2010. Normalization and legitimation: Modeling stigmatizing attitudes toward ex-offenders. *Criminology 48* (1): 27–56.

Hockenberry, Sarah, Melissa Sickmund, and Anthony Sladky. 2011. *Juvenile residential facility census, 2008: Selected findings*. Washington, DC: Office of Juvenile Justice and Delinquency Prevention.

Hoefer, Friedrich. 1937. Georg Michael Von Obermaier: A pioneer in reformatory procedures. *Journal of Criminal Law and Criminology 28* (1): 13–51.

Hoffman, Peter B. and James L. Beck. 2005. Revocation by consent: The United States' Parole Commission's expedited revocation procedure. *Journal of Criminal Justice 33* (5): 451–462.

Holloway, Evan, James R. Brown, Phillip D. Suman, and Matthew C. Aalsma. 2012. Aqualitative examination of juvenile probation officers as gateway providers to mental health care. *Criminal Justice Policy Response 24* (3): 370–392. doi:10.1177/0887403412436603.

Homant, Robert J. and Mark A. DeMercurio. 2009. Intermediate sanctions in probation officers' sentencing recommendations: Consistency, net widening, and net repairing. *The Prison Journal 89* (4): 426–439.

Horn, Dan. 2000. Offenders find records hard to erase. *Cincinnati Enquirer*, December 18.

Howell, James C. and Mark W. Lipsey. 2012. Research-based guidelines for juvenile justice programs. *Justice Research and Policy 14* (1): 17–34.

Hucklesby, Anthea. 2011. The working life of electronic monitoring officers. *Criminology & Criminal Justice 11* (1): 59–76.

Hudson, Barbara. 2006. Beyond white man's justice: Race, gender, and justice in late modernity. *Theoretical Criminology 10* (1): 29–47.

Huebner, Beth M. and Timothy S. Bynum. 2006. An analysis of parole decision making using a sample of sex offenders: A focal concerns perspective. *Justice Quarterly 44* (4): 961–992.

———. 2008. The role of race and ethnicity in parole decisions. *Justice Quarterly 46* (4): 907–938.

Hughes, John M. 2008. Results-based management in federal probation and pretrial services. *Federal Probation 72* (2): 4–14.

Hughes, Timothy A., Doris James Wilson, and Allen J. Beck. 2001. *Trends in state parole, 1990–2000*. Washington, DC: U.S. Department of Justice, Bureau of Justice Statistics.

Humphrey, John A., Gale Burford, and Meredith Huey Dye. 2012. A longitudinal analysis of reparative probation and recidivism. *Criminal Justice Studies 25* (2): 117–130.

International Community Corrections Association. 2015. Retrieved from: http://iccalive.org/icca/

Ireland, Connie and Bruce Berg. 2008. Women in parole: Respect and rapport. *International Journal of Offender Therapy and Comparative Criminology 52* (4): 474–491.

Jackson, Arrick L. 2009. The impact of restorative justice on the development of guilt, shame, and empathy among participants in a victim impact training program. *Victims & Offenders 4* (1): 1–24.

Jacobs, Mark D. 1990. *Screwing the system and making it work: Juvenile justice in the no-fault society*. Chicago IL: University of Chicago Press.

Jannetta, Jesse, Brian Elderbroom, Amy Solomon, Meagan Cahill, and Barbara Parthasarathy. 2010. *An evolving field findings from the 2008 parole practices survey*. Bureau of Justice Assistance U.S. Department of Justice. Retrieved from: http://www.urban.org/uploaded-pdf/411999_parole_practices.pdf.

Johnson, James L. 2014. Federal post-conviction supervision outcomes: Arrests and revocations. *Federal Probation 78* (1): 3–10.

Johnson, Kevin and Richard Willing. 2008. New DNA links used to deny parole. *USA Today*, February 7. Retrieved from: http://www.usatoday.com/news/nation/2008-02-07

Jones, Mark and John J. Kerbs. 2007. Probation and parole officers and discretionary decision-making: Responses to technical and criminal violations. *Federal Probation 71* (1): 9–15.

Kalfrin, Valerie. 2008. Ankle device foils boat burglar's plan, police say. *The Tampa Tribune*, January 9.

Killias, Martin, Gwladys Gilleron, Izumi Kissling, and Patrice Villetaz. 2010. Community service vs. electronic monitoring: What works better? *British Journal of Criminology 50:* 1155–1170.

Karuppannan, Jaishankar. 2005. Mapping and corrections: Management of offenders with geographic information systems. *Corrections Compendium 30* (1): 7–9, 31–33.

Keller, Oliver J. and Benedict S. Alper. 1970. *Halfway houses: Community-centered correction and treatment*. Lexington, MA: D.C. Heath.

Kelly, Christopher E. and Jamie J. Fader. 2012. Computer-based employment applications: Implications for offenders and supervising officers. *Federal Probation 76* (1): 24–29.

Kempinen, Cynthia A. and Megan C. Kurlychek. 2003. An outcome evaluation of Pennsylvania's boot camp: Does rehabilitative programming within a disciplinary setting reduce recidivism? *Crime and Delinquency 49* (4): 581–602.

Kenney, J. Scott and Don Clairmont. 2009. Using the victim role as both sword and shield: The interactional dynamics of restorative justice sessions. *Journal of Contemporary Ethnography 38* (3): 279–307.

Kerbs, John J., Mark Jones, and Jennifer M. Jolley. 2009. Discretionary decision making by probation and parole officers: The role of extralegal as predictors of responses to technical violations. *Journal of Contemporary Criminal Justice 25* (4): 424–441.

Kilgore, Jack. 2012. Progress or more of the same? Electronic monitoring and parole in the age of mass incarceration. *Critical Criminology* (On-line version) DOI 10.1007/s10612-012-9165-0.

Kilgour, D. and S. Meade. 2004. Look what boot camps done for me: Teaching and learning at Lakeview Academy. *Journal of Correctional Education 55*: 170–185.

Killias, Martin, Gwladys Gillieron, Izumi Kissling, and Patrice Villettaz. 2010. Community service versus electronic monitoring-What works better? *British Journal of Criminology 50*: 1155–1170.

Kim, Dae-Young, Hee-Jong Joo, and William P. McCarty. 2008. Risk assessment and classification of day reporting center clients. *Criminal Justice and Behavior 35* (6): 792–812.

Kim, Dae-Young, Cassia Spohn, and Mark Foxall. 2007. An evaluation of the DRC in the context of Douglas County, Nebraska. *The Prison Journal 87* (4): 434–456.

Kim, Hee Joo and Jurg Gerber. 2012. The effectiveness of reintegrative shaming and restorative justice conferences: Focusing on juvenile offenders' perceptions in Australian reintegrative shaming experiments. *International Journal of Offender Therapy and Comparative Criminology 56* (7): 1063–1079.

Kinnevy, Susan C. and Joel M. Caplan. 2008. *Findings from the APAI international survey of releasing authorities.* Center for Research on youth and social policy. Retrieved from: http://www.apaintl.org/pdfs/final_apai_survey_10222008.pdf

Kirk, David S. 2012. Residential change as a turning point in the life course of crime: Desistance or temporary cessation? *Criminology 50* (2): 329–358.

Klockars, Carl B. Jr. 1972. A theory of probation supervision. *Journal of Criminal Law, Criminology and Police Science 63* (4): 550–557.

Knoll, Crystal and Melissa Sickmund. 2010. *Delinquency cases in juvenile court, 2007.* Washington, DC: Office of Juvenile Justice and Delinquency Prevention.

Krauth, Barbara and Larry Linke. 1999. *State organizational structures for delivering adult probation services.* Longmont, CO: LIS, Inc. for the National Institute of Corrections.

Kurlychek, Megan C., Robert Brame, and Shawn D. Bushway. 2007. Enduring risk? Old criminal records and predictions of future criminal involvement. *Crime and Delinquency 53* (1): 64–83.

Kyckelhahn, Tracey. 2012. *State corrections expenditures, FY 1982–2010.* NCJ 239672. Washington, DC: U.S. Department of Justice.

Labrecque, Ryan M., Paula Smith, Myrinda Schweitzer, and Cara Thompson. 2013. Targeting antisocial attitudes in community supervision using the EPICS model: An examination of change scores on the criminal sentiment scale. *Federal Probation 77* (3): 15–20.

Lamet, Willemijn, Anja Dirkzwager, Adriaan Denkers, and Peter Van Der Laan. 2013. Social bonds under supervision: Associating social bonds of probation with supervision failure. *Criminal Justice and Behavior 40* (7): 784–801. doi:10.1177/0093854812471659.

Landenberger, Nana A. and Mark W. Lipsey. 2005. The positive effects of cognitive-behavioral programs for offenders: A meta-analysis of factors associated with effective treatment. *Journal of Experimental Criminology 1:* 451–476.

Langan, Patrick A. and David J. Levin. 2002. *Recidivism of prisoners released in 1994.* Washington, DC: U.S. Department of Justice, Bureau of Justice Statistics (June).

Latessa, Edward J., Lori Brusman Lovins, and P. Smith. 2010. *Follow up evaluation of Ohio's community based correctional facility and halfway house programs-outcome study.* Cincinnati School of Criminal Justice, University of Cincinnati. Retrieved on March 3, 2015 from http://www.drc.ohio.gov/public/UC%20Report.pdf.

Latessa, Edward J., Paula Smith, Richard Lemke, Matthew Makarios, and Christopher T. Lowenkamp. 2009. *The creation and validation of the Ohio Risk Assessment System final report.* Cincinnati, OH: University of Cincinnati, Center for Criminal Justice Research.

Laughland, Oliver. 2015. Baltimore unrest: 49 children were arrested and detained during protests. *The Guardian* (May 7, 2015). Available at: http://www.theguardian.com/us-news/2015/may/07/baltimore-children.

Laxminarayan, Malini. 2012. The effect of retributive and restorative sentencing on psychological effects of criminal proceedings. *Journal of Interpersonal Violence 20* (10): 1–18.

Learn-Andes, Jennifer. 2014. County probation officers will carry guns. *Times Leader* (April 1, 2014). Available at: http://www.timesleader.com/news/local-news-news/1295719/county-probation-officers.

Lee, Won-Jae, James R. Phelps, and Dan R. Beto. 2009. Turnover intention among probation officers and direct care staff: A statewide study. *Federal Probation 73* (3): 28–39.

Leiber, Michael J. and Jennifer H. Peck. 2013. Probation violations and juvenile justice decision making: Implications for Blacks and Hispanics. *Youth Violence and Juvenile Justice 11* (1): 60–78.

Leopold, Todd. 2014. Mark Wahlberg asks Massachusetts for pardon in 1988 crime. *CNN* (December 6, 2014). Available at: http://www.cnn.com/2014/12/05/showbiz/celecrity-news-gossip/.

Levenson, Jill S. 2008. Collateral consequences of sex offender residence restrictions. *Criminal Justice Studies 21* (2): 153–166. doi:10.1080/14786010802159822.

Levin, Marc A. 2008a. Work release: Con job or big payoff for Texas? *Texas Public Policy Foundation Policy Perspective* (April). Retrieved from: http://www.texaspolicy.com

———. 2008b. Five technological solutions for Texas' correctional and law enforcement challenges. *Texas Public Policy Foundation Policy Perspective* (June). Retrieved from: http://www.texaspolicy.com

———. 2010. In juvenile justice, less is often more. *Texas Public Policy Foundation Policy Perspective* (May 7). Retrieved from: http://www.texaspolicy.com

———. 2011. Breaking addiction without breaking the bank: Cost-effective strategies for Texas lawmakers to reduce substance abuse. *Texas Public Policy Foundation Policy Perspective* (April). Retrieved from: http://www.texaspolicy.com

———. 2012. Public safety and cost control solutions for Texas county jails. *Texas Public Policy Foundation Policy Perspective* (March). Retrieved from: http://www.texaspolicy.com

Lindner, Charles. 2007. Thacher, Augustus, and Hill: The path to statutory probation in the United States and England. *Federal Probation 71* (3): 36–41.

———. 2008. Probation intake: Gatekeeper to the family court. *Federal Probation 72* (1): 48–53.

Lindner, Charles and Margaret R. Savarese. 1984a. The evolution of probation: Early salaries, qualifications, and hiring practices. *Federal Probation 48* (1): 3–10.

———. 1984b. The evolution of probation: The historical contributions of the volunteer. *Federal Probation 48* (2): 3–10.

———. 1984c. The evolution of probation: University settlement and the beginning of statutory probation in New York City. *Federal Probation 48* (3): 3–12.

———. 1984d. The evolution of probation: University settlement and its pioneering role in probation work. *Federal Probation 48* (4): 3–13.

Lipsey, Mark W. 2009. The primary factors that characterize effective interventions with juvenile offenders: A meta-analytic overview. *Victims and Offenders 4*: 124–147.

Lipton, Douglas, Robert Martinson, and J. Wilks. 1975. *The effectiveness of correctional treatment*. New York: Praeger.

Little, Gregory L. 2005. Meta-analysis of moral recognition therapy: Recidivism results from probation and parole implementations. *Cognitive-Behavioral Treatment Review 14* (1/2): 14–16.

Livsey, Sarah. 2012. *Juvenile delinquency probation caseload, 2009*. Washington, DC: Office of Juvenile Justice and Delinquency Prevention.

Lopez, John S. 2007. *Have perceptions changed among staff regarding parole officers' carrying firearms? A description of changes in safety perceptions and supervisory styles at the Texas Department of Criminal Justice Parole Division*. An unpublished Master's Thesis. Texas State University, San Marcos, Texas.

Love, Margaret Colgate. 2010. The twilight of the pardon power. *Journal of Criminal Law and Criminology 100* (3): 1169–1212.

Lowenkamp, Christopher T. and Kristin Bechtel. 2007. The predictive validity of the LSI-R on a sample of offenders drawn from the records of the Iowa Department of Corrections data management system. *Federal Probation 71* (3): 25–29.

Lowenkamp, Christopher T., Alexander M. Holsinger, Charles R. Robinson, and Francis T. Cullen. 2012. When a person isn't a data point: Making evidence-based practice work. *Federal Probation 76* (3): 11–21.

Lowenkamp, Christopher T. and Edward J. Latessa. 2005. Increasing the effectiveness of correctional programming through the risk principle: Identifying offenders for residential placement. *Criminology & Public Policy 4* (2): 263–290.

Lowenkamp, Christopher T., Richard Lemke, and Edward Latessa. 2008. The development and validation of a pretrial screening tool. *Federal Probation 72* (3): 2–9.

Lowenkamp, Christopher T., Matthew Makarios, Edward Latessa, Richard Lemke, and Paula Smith. 2010. Community corrections facilities for juvenile offenders in Ohio: An examination of treatment integrity and recidivism. *Criminal Justice and Behavior 37* (6): 695–708.

Lutze, Faith E. 2014. *Professional lives of community corrections officers*. Thousand Oaks, CA: Sage.

Lutze, Faith E., W. Wesley Johnson, Todd R. Clear, Edward J. Latessa, and Risdon N. Slate. 2012. The future of community corrections is now: Stop dreaming and take action. *Journal of Contemporary Criminal Justice 28* (1): 42–59. doi:10.1177/1043986211432193.

Mack, Julian W. 1909. The juvenile court. *Harvard Law Review 23*: 102–109.

Mador, Jessica. 2010. New veterans court aims to help soldiers struggling at home. *Minnesota Public Radio News*, March 22, 2010. Retrieved from: http://minnesota/publicradio.org/display/web/2010/03/22/veterans-court/

Malloch, Margaret and Gill McIvor. 2011. Women and community sentences. *Criminology & Criminal Justice 11* (4): 325–344. doi: 10.1177/1748895811408839.

Manchak, Sarah M., Jennifer L. Skeem, Kevin S. Douglas, and Maro Siranosian. 2009. Does gender moderate the predictive utility of the Level of Service Inventory-Revised (LSI-R) for serious violent offenders? *Criminal Justice and Behavior 36* (5): 425–442.

Marain, Allan. 2005. Expungement of criminal proceedings. *New Jersey Lawyer Magazine 232*: 18–21. Retrieved from: http://www.njsba.com/images/content/1/0/1002002/February_05.pdf.

Marklund, F. and S. Holmberg. 2009. Effects of early release from prison using electronic tagging in Sweden. *Journal of Experimental Criminology 5* (1): 41–61.

Martin, Brian and Steve Van Dine. 2008. *Examining the Impact of Ohio's Progressive Sanction Grid*. NCJ 224317. Washington, DC: National Institute of Justice. Accessed at: https://www.ncjrs.gov/pdffiles1/nij/grants/224317.pdf

Martin, Christine, Arthur J. Lurigio, and David E. Olson. 2003. An examination of rearrests and reincarcerations among discharged day reporting center clients. *Federal Probation 67* (1): 24–30.

Martin, Jamie S., Kate Hanrahan, and James H. Bowers. 2009. Offenders' perceptions of house arrest and electronic monitoring. *Journal of Offender Rehabilitation 48* (6): 547–570.

Martin, Jamie S., Kate Hanrahan, and Teah M. Travers. 2008. *Probation officers' assessment of electronic monitoring as an intermediate sanction*. Paper presented at the annual meeting of the Academy of Criminal Justice Sciences, March 11–15, 2008. Cincinnati, OH.

Martinson, Robert. 1974. What works? Questions and answers about prison reform. *Public Interest 35* (Spring): 22–35.

Maruna, Shadd and Anna King. 2008. Selling the public on probation: Beyond the bib. *Probation Journal 55* (4): 337–351.

Maruschak, Laura and Erika Parks. 2012. *Probation and parole in the United States, 2011*. NCJ 239686. Washington, DC: U.S. Department of Justice, Bureau of Justice Statistics.

Matisons, Michelle. 2014. School districts using GPS, ankle bracelets, and smartphone racking on truant kids. *MintPress News* (October 7, 2014). Available at: www.mintpressnews.com

McNeill, Fergus, Steve Farrall, Claire Lightowler, and Shadd Maruna. 2012. Reexamining evidence-based practice in community corrections: Beyond a confined view of what works. *Justice Research and Policy 14* (1): 35–60.

McNichols, Kelley B. 2012. Reentry initiatives: A study of the Federal workforce development program. *Federal Probation 76* (3): 37–42.

Meade, Benjamin and Benjamin Steiner. 2010. The total effects of boot camps that house juveniles: A systematic review of the evidence. *Journal of Criminal Justice 38* (5): 841–853.

Mears, Daniel P., Xia Wang, Carter Hay, and William D. Bales. 2008. Social ecology and recidivism: Implications for prisoner reentry. *Criminology 46* (2): 301–340.

Melton, Ada, Kimbly Cobb, Adrienne Lindsey, R. Brain Colgan, and David J. Melton. 2014. Addressing responsivity issues with criminal justice-involved Native Americans. *Federal Probation 78* (2): 24–30.

Mennel, Robert M. 1973. *Thorns and thistles: Juvenile delinquents in the United States, 1825–1940*. Hanover: University Press of New England.

Messina, Nena, Stacy Calhoun, and Umme Warda. 2012. Gender-responsive drug court treatment: A randomized controlled trial. *Criminal Justice and Behavior 39* (12): 1539–1558.

Milburn, Trevis, W. 2012. *Exploring military service as an alternative sanction: Evidence from inmates' perspectives* (Unpublished Master's thesis). Eastern Kentucky University). Retrieved from http://encompass.eku.edu/cgi/view content.cgi?article=1081&context=etd.

Miller, Joel. 2014. Probation supervision and the control of crime opportunities: An empirical assessment. *Crime & Delinquency 60* (8): 1235–1257. doi:10.1177/0011128712443186.

———. 2015. Contemporary modes of probation officer supervision: The triumph of the "synthetic" officer? *Justice Quarterly 32* (2): 314–336.

Miller, Joel, Kim Copeland, and Mercer Sullivan. 2015. Keeping them off the corner: How probation officers steer offenders away from crime opportunities. *The Prison Journal 95* (2): 178–198.

Minton, Todd D. and Daniela Golinelli. 2014. *Jail inmates at midyear 2013-Statistical Tables*. NCJ 245350. Washington, DC: U.S. Department of Justice.

Miyashiro, Carol M. 2008. Research 2 results (R2R): The pretrial services experience. *Federal Probation 72* (2): 80–86.

Moreland, D.W. 1941. History and prophecy: John Augustus and his successors. *National Probation Association Yearbook* (pp. 1–23). Presentation delivered at the 35th Annual Conference of the National Probation Association, Boston, Massachusetts, May 29, 1941.

Morgan, Kathryn D. and Brent Smith. 2008. The impact of race on parole decision-making. *Justice Quarterly 25* (2): 411–435.

Morris, Norval. 2002. *Maconochie's gentlemen: The story of Norfolk Island and the roots of modern prison reform*. New York: Oxford University Press.

Morris, Robert G., J. C. Barnes, John L. Worrall, and Erin A. Orrick. 2013. Analyzing the presence and consequences of unobserved heterogeneity in recidivism research. *Crime & Delinquency:* 1–24. doi:10.1177/0011128713495952.

Narag, Raymund E., Sheila Royo Maxwell, and Byung Lee. 2013. A phenomenological approach to assessing a DUI/DWI program. *International Journal of Offender Therapy and Comparative Criminology 57* (2): 229–250.

National Institute of Corrections (n.d.). *Classification in probation and parole: A model system approach–A supplemental report: The Client Management Classification System*. Washington, DC: U.S. Government Printing Office.

National Law Enforcement and Corrections Technology Center. 2009. Field search. *TechBeat* (Winter). Retrieved from: http://www.justnet.org

National Research Council. 2008. *Parole, desistance from crime, and community integration*. Washington, DC: National Academies Press.

Neff, Tom. 2006. *Chances: The women of Magdalene*. Video documentary, The Documentary Channel, February 26, 2006.

Nelson, William F. 2004. Prostitution: A community solution alternative. *Corrections Today* (October): 88–91

New York State Division of Parole, Office of Policy Analysis and Information. 1993. Overview of the parole revocation process in New York. In *Reclaiming offender accountability: Intermediate sanctions for probation and parole violators*, edited by Edward E. Rhine. Laurel, MD: American Correctional Association.

Norris, Michael, Sarah Twill, and Chigon Kim. 2011. Smells like teen spirit: Evaluating a Midwestern teen court. *Crime & Delinquency 57* (2): 199–221.

North Carolina Sentencing and Policy Advisory Commission. 1994. *Structured sentencing for felonies-training and reference manual*. Raleigh, NC: Author.

Office of the Attorney General. 2007. *Texas penal code offenses by punishment range*. Austin, Texas.

Office for the Victims of Crime. 2015. *Engaging communities: Empowering victims*. Washington, DC: U.S. Department of Justice, Office for Victims of Crime. Retrieved from: http://ovc.ncjrs.gov/ncvrw2015/pdf/FullGuide.pdf

Oleson, James C., Christopher T. Lowenkamp, John Wooldredge, Marie VanNostrand, and Timothy P. Cadigan. 2014. The sentencing consequences of federal pretrial supervision. *Crime & Delinquency*, 1–21. DOI: 10.1177/0011128714551406

Oleson, James C., Marie VanNostrand, Christopher T. Lowenkamp, Timothy P. Cadigan, and John Wooldredge. 2014. Pretrial detention choices and federal sentencing. *Federal Probation 78* (1): 12–18.

Omori, Marisa K. and Susan F. Turner. 2012. Assessing the cost of electronically monitoring high-risk sex offenders. *Crime & Delinquency:* 1–22. doi:10.1177/0011128712466373.

O'Malley, Pat. 2008. Theorizing fines. *Punishment and Society 11* (1): 67–83.

Opsal, Tara D. 2011. Women disrupting a marginalized identity: Subverting the parolee identity through narrative. *Journal of Contemporary Ethnography 40* (2): 135–167.

———. 2015. "It's their world, so you just got to get through": Women's experiences of parole governance. *Feminist Criminology 10* (2): 188–207.

Ostermann, Michael. 2009. An analysis of New Jersey's day reporting center and halfway back programs: Embracing the rehabilitative ideal through evidence-based practices. *Journal of Offender Rehabilitation 48*: 139–153.

Ostermann, Michael. 2012. Recidivism and the propensity to forgo parole release. *Justice Quarterly 29* (4): 596–618.

———. 2013. Active supervision and its impact upon parolee recidivism rates. *Crime & Delinquency 59* (4): 487–509. doi:10.1177/0011128712470680.

———. 2013. Using day reporting centers to divert parolees from revocation. *Criminology & Public Policy 12* (1): 163–171. doi:10.1111/1745-9133.12013.

———. 2015. How do former inmates perform in the community? A survival analysis of rearrests, reconvictions and technical parole violations. *Crime & Delinquency 61* (2): 163–187. doi:10.1177/0011128710396425.

Padgett, Kathy G., William D. Bales, and Thomas G. Blomberg. 2006. Under surveillance: An empirical test of the effectiveness and consequences of electronic monitoring. *Criminology & Public Policy 5* (1): 61–92.

Panzarella, Robert. 2002. Theory and practice of probation on bail in the report of John Augustus. *Federal Probation 66* (3): 38–42.

Paparozzi, Mario A. and Joel M. Caplan. 2009. A profile of paroling authorities in America: The strange bedfellows of politics and professionalism. *The Prison Journal 89* (4): 401–425.

Paparozzi, Mario A. and Paul Gendreau. 2005. An intensive supervision program that worked: Service delivery, professional orientation, and organizational supportiveness. *The Prison Journal 85* (4): 445–466.

Paparozzi, Mario A. and Roger Guy. 2009. The giant that never woke: Parole authorities as the lynchpin to evidence-based practices and prisoner reentry. *Journal of Contemporary Criminal Justice 25* (4): 397–411.

———. 2013. The trails and tribulations of implementing what works: Training rarely trumps values. *Federal Probation 77* (2): 36–42.

Pattavina, April. 2009. The use of electronic monitoring as persuasive technology: Reconsidering the empirical evidence on the effectiveness of electronic monitoring. *Victims and Offenders 4*: 385–390.

Payne, Brian K. and Matthew DeMichele. 2008. Warning: Sex offenders need to be supervised in the community. *Federal Probation 72* (1): 37–42.

———. 2011a. Probation philosophies and workload considerations. *American Journal of Criminal Justice 36*: 29–43.

———. 2011b. Sex offender policies: Considering unanticipated consequences of GPS sex offender monitoring. *Aggression and Violent Behavior 16*: 177–187.

Perez, Deanna M. 2009. Applying evidence-based practices to community corrections supervision: An evaluation of residential substance abuse treatment for high-risk probationers. *Journal of Contemporary Criminal Justice 25* (4): 442–458.

Petersilia, Joan. 2000. Parole and prisoner reentry in the United States, Part 1. *Perspectives 24* (Summer): 32–46.

Peterson, Liz Austin. 2009. A potential at ease: Harris County youth boot camp may replace rigorous drills with therapy. *Houston Chronicle*, January 28.

Peterson, Paul. 2012. Supervision fees: State policies and practice. *Federal Probation 76* (1): 40–45.

Pew Charitable Trusts. 2010. *Collateral costs: Incarceration's effect on economic mobility*. Washington, DC: Pew Charitable Trusts.

Pimentel, Roger and Jon Muller. 2010. The containment approach to managing defendants charged with sex offenses. *Federal Probation 74* (2): 24–26.

Pogarsky, Greg. 2007. Deterrence and individual differences among convicted offenders. *Journal of Quantitative Criminology 23*: 59–74.

Porter, Nicole D. 2015. *The state of sentencing 2014: Developments in policy and practice*. Washington, DC: The Sentencing Project. Retrieved from: http://sentencingproject.org/doc/publications/sen_State_of_Sentencing_2014.pdf

Pranis, Kay. 2005. *The little book of circle processes: A new/old approach to peacebuilding*. Pennsylvania: Good Books.

President's Commission on Law Enforcement and Administration of Justice. 1967. *The challenge of crime in a free society*. Washington, DC: U.S. Government Printing Office.

Redlich, Allison D., Siyu Liu, Henry J. Steadman, Lisa Callahan, and Pamela C. Robbins. 2012. Is diversion swift? Comparing mental health court and traditional criminal justice processing. *Criminal Justice and Behavior 39* (4): 420–433.

Rendleman, Doug. 2011. Measurement of restitution: Coordinating restitution with compensatory damages and punitive damages. *Washington and Lee Law Review 68*: 973–1006.

Reuell, Peter. 2008. High-tech device knows when you're not sober. *The Metrowest Daily News*, February 10. Retrieved from: http://www.metrowestdailynews.com/multimedia/

Reuters. 2012. Madoff victims to receive 2.48 billion payout. *Daily News* (September 20, 2012). Available at: http://www.nydailynews.com/new-york/madoff-victims-receive-2-48-billion-payout-article-1.1163551

Rhodes, William, Gerald Gaes, Jeremy Luallen, Ryan Kling, Tom Rich, and Michael Shively. 2014. Following incarceration, most released offenders never return to prison. *Crime & Delinquency:* 1–23. doi:10.1177/0011128714549655.

Rikard, R.V. and Ed Rosenberg. 2007. Aging inmates: A convergence of trends in the American criminal justice system. *Journal of Correctional Health Care 13* (3): 150–162.

Rodriguez, Nancy. 2013. Concentrated disadvantage and the incarceration of youth: Examining how context affects juvenile justice. *Journal of Research in Crime and Delinquency 50* (2): 189–215.

Rojek, Dean G., James E. Coverdill, and Stuart W. Fors. 2003. The effect of victim impact panels on DUI rearrest rates: A five-year follow-up. *Criminology 41* (4): 1319–1340.

Roscoe, Thomas, David E. Duffee, Craig Rivera, and Tony R. Smith. 2007. Arming probation officers: Correlates of the decision to arm at the departmental level. *Criminal Justice Studies 20* (1): 43–63.

Roth, Tanya. 2010. Thief sentenced to hold shaming sign for 6 years. Available at: http://blogs.findlaw.com/legally_weird/2010/10/thief-sentenced-to-hold-shaming-sign-for-6-years.html

Rousseau, Caryn. 2015. Jesse Jackson Jr. leaves federal prison for halfway house. *ABC News*, March 26, 2015. Retrieved from: http://abcnews.go.com/US/.

Roy, Sudipto. 2013. Exit status of probationers and prison-bound offenders in an electronic monitoring home detention program: A comparative study. *Federal Probation 77* (3): 26–30.

Ruback, R. Barry and Mark H. Bergstrom. 2006. Economic sanctions in criminal justice: Purposes, effects, and implications. *Criminal Justice and Behavior 33* (2): 242–273.

Ruback, R. Barry, Andrew S. Gladfelter, and Brendan Lantz. 2014. Paying restitution: Experimental analysis of the effects of information and rationale. *Criminology & Public Policy 13* (3): 405–436.

Ruback, R. Barry, Stacy N. Hoskins, Alison C. Cares, and Ben Feldmeyer. 2006. Perception and payment of economic sanctions: A survey of offenders. *Federal Probation 70* (3): 27–31.

Rubin, Maureen, Leanne F. Alarid, and Mary Jo Rodriguez. 2014. A partnership to develop a utilization-focused evaluation plan for a criminal justice diversion program. *Psychiatric Services 65* (1): 8–10. DOI: 10.1176/appi.ps.201300411.

Russell, Robert T. 2009. Veterans treatment court: A proactive approach. *New England Journal on Criminal and Civil Confinement 35*: 357–372.

Sabol, William J. and Heather Couture. 2008. *Prison inmates at midyear 2007*. Washington, DC: U.S. Department of Justice, Bureau of Justice Statistics.

Sabol, William J. and Todd D. Minton. 2008. *Jail inmates at midyear 2007*. Washington, DC: U.S. Department of Justice, Bureau of Justice Statistics.

Sachwald, Judith, Ernest Eley, and Faye S. Taxman. 2006. Four-point strategy reduces technical violations of probation in Connecticut. *Topics in Community Corrections: Effectively Managing Violations and Revocations*. Longmont, CO: National Institute of Corrections.

Salzer, Adan. 2014. Student GPS tracking program halted in some Texas schools. *Infowars* (March 14, 2014). Available at: www.infowars.com

Sangalang, Jennifer and J.D. Gallop. 2014. Social media's buzzing over celebrity motorcycle builder Billy Lane's release from prison. *Florida Today* (September 22, 2014). Available at: http://www.floridatoday.com

Savage, Charles. 2013. More releases of ailing prisoners are urged. *New York Times*, May 1, 2013.

Schloss, Christine S. and Leanne F. Alarid. 2007. Standards in the privatization of probation services: A statutory analysis. *Criminal Justice Review 32* (3): 233–245.

Schultz, E.J. 2007. Female inmates: Jammed behind bars? *Sacramento Bee*, July 9. Retrieved from: http://www.november.org/stayinfo/breaking07/Jammed.html

Schwalbe, Craig S. 2012. Toward an integrated theory of probation. *Criminal Justice and Behavior 39* (2): 185–201.

Schwalbe, C. S., Robin E. Gearing, Michael J. MacKenzie, Kathryne B. Brewer, and Rawan Ibrahim. 2012. A meta-analysis of experimental studies of diversion programs for juvenile offenders. *Clinical Psychology Review 32*: 26–33.

Schwalbe, Craig S. and Tina Maschi. 2011. Confronting delinquency: Probation officers' use of coercion and client-centered tactics to foster youth compliance. *Crime and Delinquency 57* (5): 801–822.

Scott, Elizabeth S. and Laurance Steinberg. 2008. *Rethinking juvenile justice*. Cambridge, MA: Harvard University Press.

Sentencing Accountability Commission & the Statistical Analysis Center, 2005. *First year assessment of the 2003 probation reform law's impact on the administration of justice in Delaware. Delaware Senate Bill 50 and 150*. Retrieved from: http://cjc.delaware.gov/pdf/sb50-sb150.pdf.

Sentencing Project. 2011. *Felony disenfranchisement laws in the United States*. Retrieved from: http://www.sentencing-project.org/doc/publications/fd_bs_fdlawsinusMar11.pdf at the following website: http://www.sentencing-project.org/template/page.cfm?id=133

Severson, M. and Carrie Pettus-Davis. 2013. Officers' experiences of the symptoms of secondary trauma in the supervision of sex offenders. *International Journal on Offender Therapy and Comparative Criminology 57*: 5–24.

Shaffer, Deborah Koetzle. 2011. Looking inside the black box of drug courts: A meta-analytic review. *Justice Quarterly 28* (3): 493–520.

Shaffer, Deborah Koetzle and Terance D. Miethe. 2011. Are similar sex offenders treated similarly? A conjunctive analysis of disparities in community notification decisions. *Journal of Research in Crime and Delinquency 48* (3): 448–471.

Shih-Ya, Kuo, Dennis Longmire, and Steven J. Cuvelier. 2010. An empirical assessment of the process of restorative justice. *Journal of Criminal Justice 38* (3): 318–328.

Sickmund, Melissa, T.J. Sladky, and Wei Kang. 2008. *Census of juveniles in residential placement databook*. Washington, DC: Office of Juvenile Justice and Delinquency Prevention. Retrieved from: http://www.ojjdp.ncjrs.org/ojstatbb/cjrp/

Siedschlaw, Kurt D. and Beth A. Wiersma. 2005. Costs and outcomes of a work ethic camp: How do they compare to a traditional prison facility? *Corrections Compendium 30* (6): 1–5, 28–30.

Skeem, Jennifer L., Paula Emke-Francis, and Jennifer Eno Louden. 2006. Probation, mental health, and mandated treatment. *Criminal Justice and Behavior 33* (2): 158–184.

Skeem, Jennifer L. and Sarah Manchak. 2008. Back to the future: From Klockars' model of effective supervision to evidence-based practice in probation. *Journal of Offender Rehabilitation 47* (3): 220–247.

Slate, Risdon N., Jacqueline K. Buffington-Vollum, and W. Wesley Johnson. 2013. *The criminalization of mental illness: Crisis and opportunity in the justice system*, 2nd ed. Durham, NC: Carolina Academic Press.

Slate, Risdon and W. Wesley Johnson. 2008. *A comparison of federal and state probation officer stress levels*. Paper presented at the annual meeting of the Academy of Criminal Justice Sciences, Cincinnati, OH .

Smid, Wineke J., Jan H. Kamphuis, Edwin C. Wever, and Maud C.F.M. Verbruggen. 2014. Risk levels, treatment duration, and drop out in a clinically composed outpatient sex offender treatment group. *Journal of Interpersonal Violence 30* (5): 727–743.

Smith, Kenneth S. and Ashley G. Blackburn. 2011. Is teen court the best fit? Assessing the predictive validity of the teen court peer influence scale. *Journal of Criminal Justice 39:* 198–204.

Snyder, Howard. 2008. *Juvenile arrests 2006*. Washington, DC: Office of Juvenile Justice and Delinquency Prevention.

Solomon, Amy L. 2006. Does parole supervision work? Research findings and policy opportunities. *Perspectives* (Spring): 26–37. Retrieved from: http://www.urban.org/uploadedpdf/1000908_parole_supervision.pdf.

Soulé, Dave, Devise Gottfredson, and Erin Bauer. 2008. It's 3 P.M. Do you know where your child is? A study on the timing of juvenile victimization and delinquency. *Justice Quarterly 25* (4): 623–646.

Sperber, Kimberly G., Edward J. Latessa, and Michael D. Makarios. 2013. Examining the interactions between level of risks and dosage of treatment. *Criminal Justice and Behavior 40* (3): 338–348.

Staples, William G. and Stephanie K. Decker. 2010. Between the home and institutional worlds: Tensions and contradictions in the practice of house arrest. *Critical Criminology 18:* 1–20.

Steiner, Benjamin. 2004. Treatment retention: A theory of post-release supervision for the substance-abusing offender. *Federal Probation 68* (3): 24–29.

Steiner, Benjamin and H. Daniel Butler. 2013. Why didn't they work? Thoughts on the application of New Jersey day reporting centers. *Criminology & Public Policy 12* (1): 153–162. doi:10.1111/1745-9133.12014.

Steiner, Benjamin, Rhys Hester, Matthew D. Makarios, and Lawrence F. Travis III. 2012. Examining the link between parole officers' bases of power and their exercise of power. *The Prison Journal 92* (4): 435–459. doi: 10.1177/0032885512457546.

Steiner, Benjamin, Matthew D. Makarios, Lawrence F. Travis, and Benjamin Meade. 2012. Examining the effects of community-based sanctions on offender recidivism. *Justice Quarterly 29* (2): 229–257.

Steiner, Benjamin, Lawrence F. Travis III, Matthew D. Makarios, and Taylor Brickley. 2011. The influence of parole officers' attitudes on supervision practices. *Justice Quarterly 28* (6): 903–927.

Stemen, Don. 2007. *Reconsidering incarceration: New directions for reducing crime*. New York: Vera Institute of Justice.

Stickels, John. 2007. A study of probation revocations for technical violations in Hays County, Texas, USA. *Probation Journal 54* (1): 52–61.

Stoll, Michael A. and Shawn D. Bushway. 2008. The effect of criminal background checks on hiring ex-offenders. *Criminology and Public Policy 7* (3): 371–404.

Stottmann, Jonathan O. 2007. Presentence restitution: When opportunity knocks. *News and Views 32* (19): September 10.

Stucky, Thomas D. and John R. Ottensmann. 2014. Registered sex offenders and reported sex offenses. *Crime and Delinquency:* 1–20. Available at: DOI10.1177/001112871456738.

Sundt, Jody, Renee Vanderhoff, Laura Shaver, and Sarah Lazzeroni. 2012. Oregonians nearly unanimous in support for former prisoners. *Research in Brief, August*. Portland State University, Criminal Justice Policy Research Institute.

Sung, Hung-En. 2011. From diversion to reentry: Recidivism risks among graduates of an alternative to incarceration program. *Criminal Justice Policy Review 22* (2): 219–234.

Sweeten, Gary, Shawn D. Bushway, and Raymond Paternoster. 2009. Does dropping out of school mean dropping into delinquency? *Criminology 47* (1): 47–92.

Taxman, Faye S. 2008. No illusions: Offender and organizational change in Maryland's proactive community supervision efforts. *Criminology and Public Policy 7* (2): 275–302.

———. 2014. Second generation of RNR: The importance of systemic responsivity in expanding core principles of responsivity. *Federal Probation 78* (2): 32–40.

Taylor, Scott and Ginger Martin. 2006. Four-point strategy reduces technical violations of probation in Connecticut. *Topics in Community Corrections: Effectively Managing Violations and Revocations*. Longmont, CO: National Institute of Corrections.

Teague, Michael. 2011. Probation in America: Armed, private and unaffordable? *Probation Journal 58* (4): 317–332.

Texas Juvenile Justice Department. 2011. *A Juvenile's guide to understanding automatic restriction of access to records.* (August). Austin, TX: Texas Juvenile Probation Commission.

Texas Legislative Budget Board. 2015. *Statewide criminal and juvenile justice recidivism and revocation rates*. Austin, TX. Retrieved from: http://www.lbb.state.tx.us/Documents/Publications/Policy_Report/1450_CJ_Statewide_Recidivism.pdf.

Thompson, Mark and Nancy Gibbs. 2012. More U.S. Soldiers have killed themselves than have died in the Afghan war: Why can't the Army win the war on suicide? *Time* (July 23, 2012): 23–31.

Travis, Lawrence F. and James Stacey. 2010. A half century of parole rules: Conditions of parole in the United States, 2008. *Journal of Criminal Justice 38*: 604–608.

Schwartz, Melanie, David B. Brown, and Laura Boseley. 2012. The promise of justice reinvestment. *Social Science Research Network*. Retrieved from: http://papers.ssrn.com/sol3/papers.cfm?abstract_id=2078715.

Turner, Susan, Jesse Janneta, James Hess, Randy Myers, Rita Shah, Robert Werth, and Alyssa Whitby. 2007. *Implementation and early outcomes for the San Diego high-risk sex offender GPS pilot program* (Working paper). Center for Evidence-Based Corrections, University of California, Irvine.

Tyler, Tom R. 1990. *Why people obey the law*. New Haven, CT: Yale University Press.

Uggen, Christopher, Mike Vuolo, Sarah Lageson, Ebony Ruhland, and Hilary K. Whitham. 2014. The edge of stigma: An experimental audit of the effects of low-level criminal records on employment. *Criminology 52* (4): 627–654. doi:10.1111/1745-9125.12051.

Umbreit, Mark S. and Marilyn P. Armour. 2010. *Restorative justice dialogue: An essential guide for research and practice*. New York: Springer.

Umbreit, Mark S., William Bradshaw, and David Roseborough. 2006. The effect of victim offender mediation on juvenile offender recidivism: A meta-analysis. *Conflict Resolution Quarterly 24* (1): 87–98.

U.S. Bureau of Prisons. 2008. *Guidelines manual* (November 1, 2008). Section 7B1.4, p. 488.

U.S. Department of Justice. 2005. 28 CFR Part 2: Paroling, recommitting, and supervising federal prisoners: Prisoners serving sentences under the U.S. and D.C. codes. *Federal Register 70* (70), April 13, 2005: 19262.

———. 2013. *The Federal Bureau of Prisons' compassionate release program*. (I-2013-006). Washington, DC: U.S. Department of Justice. Accessed at: http://www.justice.gov/oig/reports/2013/e1306.pdf.

U.S. Department of Labor. 2009. *The federal bonding program*. Retrieved from: http://www.bonds4jobs.com/index.html

———. 2014. *Occupational outlook handbook, 2014–15 edition*. Probation officers and correctional treatment specialists, Bureau of Labor Statistics. Retrieved from: http://www.bls.gov/

U.S. Parole Commission. 2010. *Rules and procedures manual*. Washington, DC: U.S. Parole Commission. Retrieved from: http://www.justice.gov/uspc/documents/uspc-manual111507.pdf

U.S. Sentencing Commission. 2010. Federal sentencing guidelines manual Chapter 5, Part A. (Updated November 1, 2010). Available at: http://www.ussc.gov/guidelines/2010guidelines/manual_pdf/Chapter5.pdf

VanBenschoten, Scott. 2008. Risk/needs assessment: Is this the best we can do? *Federal Probation 72* (2): 38–42.

Vance, Stephen. 2011a. Federal reentry court programs: A summary of recent evaluations. *Federal Probation 75* (2): 64–73.

———. 2011b. Looking at the law: An updated look at the privilege against self-incrimination in post conviction supervision. *Federal Probation 75* (1): 33–37.

Van der Geest, Victor R., Catrien C.J.H. Bijleveld, and Arjan A. J. Blokland. 2011. The effects of employment on longitudinal trajectories of offending: A follow-up of high-risk youth from 18 to 32 years of age. *Criminology 49* (4): 1195–1234.

VanNostrand, Marie and Crime and Justice Institute. 2007. *Legal and evidence-based practices: Applications of legal principles, laws, and research to the field of pretrial services*. Washington, DC: National Institute of Corrections.

Van Wormer, Katherine S. 2010. *Working with female offenders: A gender-sensitive approach*. Hoboken, NJ: Wiley.

VERA Institute of Justice. 2010. *The continuing fiscal crisis in corrections: Setting a new course*. New York: VERA Institute of Justice.

Vicini Jr. James M. 2013. Officer stress linked to CVD: What we know. *Federal Probation 77* (1): 33–35.

Viglione, Jill, Danielle S. Rudes, and Faye S. Taxman. 2015. Misalignment in supervision: Implementing risk/needs assessment instruments in probation. *Criminal Justice and Behavior 43* (3): 263–285. doi: 10.1177/0093854814548447.

Visher, Christy A., Nicole Smolter, and Daniel O'Connell. 2010. Workforce development program: A pilot study of its impact in the U.S. probation office, District of Delaware. *Federal Probation 74* (3): 16–21.

Vito, Gennaro F., George E. Higgins, and Richard Tewksbury. 2012. Characteristics of parole violators in Kentucky. *Federal Probation 76* (1): 19–23.

Von Hirsch, Andrew. 1976. *Doing justice: The choice of punishments*. New York: Hill and Wang.

Vose, Brenda, Francis T. Cullen, and Paula Smith. 2008. The empirical status of the level of service inventory. *Federal Probation 72* (3): 22–29.

Vose, Brenda, Christopher T. Lowenkamp, Paula Smith, and Francis T. Cullen. 2009. Gender and the predictive validity of the LSI-R: A study of parolees and probationers. *Journal of Contemporary Criminal Justice 25* (4): 459–471.

Waldo, Margaret. 2012. Second chances: Employing convicted felons. *HR Magazine 57* (3): 36, 38, 48.

Walker, Donald R. 1988. *Penology for profit*. College Station, TX: Texas A&M University Press.

Walker, Sarah C., Ann Muno, and Cheryl Sullivan-Colgazier. 2012. Principles in practice: A multistate study of gender-responsive reforms in the juvenile justice system. *Crime & Delinquency*: 15–19. doi:10.1177/0011128712449712.

Ward, Geoff and Aaron Kupchik. 2009. Accountable to what? Professional orientations towards accountability-based juvenile justice. *Punishment and Society 11* (1): 85–109.

———. 2010. What drives juvenile probation officers? Relating organizational contexts, status characteristics, and personal convictions to treatment and punishment orientations. *Crime and Delinquency 56* (1): 35–69.

Weisburd, David, Tomer Einat, and Matt Kowalski. 2008. The miracle of the cells: An experimental study of interventions to increase payment of court-ordered financial obligations. *Criminology and Public Policy 7* (1): 9–36.

Wermink, Hilde, Arjan Blokland, Paul Neiuwbeerta, Daniel Nagin, and Nikolaj Tollenaar. 2010. Comparing the effects of community service and short-term imprisonment on recidivism: A matched samples approach. *Journal of Experimental Criminology 6:* 325–349.

Whetzel, Jay, Mario Paparozzi, Melissa Alexander, and Christopher T. Lowenkamp. 2011. Goodbye to a worn-out dichotomy: Law enforcement, social work, and a balanced approach. *Federal Probation 75* (2): 7–12.

White, Michael D., Jeff Mellow, Kristin Englander, and Marc Ruffinengo. 2011. Halfway back: An alternative to revocation for technical parole violators. *Criminal Justice Policy Review 22* (2): 140–166.

White, Michael D., Philip Mulvey, Andrew M. Fox, and David Choate. 2012. A hero's welcome? Exploring the prevalence and problems of military veterans in the arrestee population. *Justice Quarterly 29* (2): 258–286.

Wilson, David B., Doris L. MacKenzie, and Fawn Ngo Mitchell. 2005. Effects of correctional boot camps on offending. A Campbell collaboration systematic review. Available at: http://www.aic.gov/au/campbellcj/reviews/titles.html

Wilson, Holly A. and Robert D. Hoge. 2012. Diverting our attention to what works: Evaluating the effectiveness of a youth diversion program. *Youth Violence and Juvenile Justice 11* (4): 313–331.

Wilson, James A., Wendy Naro, and James Austin. 2007. *Innovations in probation: Assessing New York City's automated reporting system.* Washington, DC: JFA Institute.

Wilson, Sandra Jo and Mark W. Lipsey. 2000. Wilderness challenge programs for delinquent youth: A meta-analysis of outcome evaluations. *Evaluation and Program Planning 23:* 1–12.

Wines, Fredrick H. 1919. *Punishment and reformation: A study of the penitentiary system.* New York: T.Y. Crowell.

Wolf, Isaac. 2011. States balk at tighter sex offender rules. *Scripps Howard News Service* (June 30). Available at http://www.scrippsnews.com

Wood, William R. 2012. Correcting community service: From work crews to community work in a juvenile court. *Justice Quarterly 29* (5): 683–711.

———. 2013. Soliciting community involvement and support for restorative justice through community service. *Criminal Justice Policy Review:* 1–25. doi:10.1177-0887403413499580.

Wooditch, Alese, Liansheng Larry Tang, and Faye S. Taxman. 2014. Which criminogenic need changes are most important in promoting desistance from crime and substance use? *Criminal Justice and Behavior 41* (3): 276–299. doi:10.1177/0093854813503543.

Wright, Kevin A., Travis C. Pratt, Christopher T. Lowenkamp, and Edward J. Latessa. 2011. The systemic model of crime and institutional efficacy and analysis of the social context of offender reintegration. *International Journal of Offender Therapy and Comparative Criminology 57* (1): 91–111.

Wright, Kevin A., Travis C. Pratt, Christopher T. Lowenkamp, and Edward J. Latessa 2013. The systemic model of crime and institutional efficacy: An analysis of the social context of offender reintegration. *International Journal of Offender Therapy and Comparative Criminology 57:* 92–111.

Wright, Kevin A. and Jeffrey W. Rosky. 2011. Too early too soon: Lessons from Montana department of corrections early release program. *Criminology & Public Policy 10* (4): 881–908. doi:10.1111/j.1745-9133.2011.00765.

Yeh, Stuart S. 2010. Cost-benefit analysis of reducing crime through electronic monitoring of parolees and probationers. *Journal of Criminal Justice 38:* 1090–1096.

Young, Douglas. W., Jill L. Farrell, and Faye S. Taxman. 2013. Impacts of juvenile probation training models on youth recidivism. *Justice Quarterly 30* (6): 1068–1089.

Youth Reentry Task Force of the Juvenile Justice and Delinquency Prevention Coalition. 2009. *Back on track: Supporting youth reentry from out-of-home placement to the community.* Washington, DC: Youth Reentry Task Force of the Juvenile Justice and Delinquency Prevention Coalition.

Zandbergen, Paul A., Jill S. Levenson, and Timothy C. Hart. 2010. Residential proximity to schools and daycares: An empirical analysis of sex offense recidivism. *Criminal Justice and Behavior 37:* 482–502.

CODES

Code of Federal Regulations, 24 CFR 960.204, 24 CFR 966.4, 24 CFR 982.553; Drug convictions and public housing.

Hawaii Revised Statutes, sec. 378-2.5; Conditional employment offer post conviction.

Massachusetts Chapter 256 of Acts of 2010, sec. 19, 21, 23, 35–37, 101, 128, 130; Criminal Offender Record Information (CORI).

Oregon Revised Statutes, sec 137.225(1)–(12); Expungement eligibility.

Oregon Revised Statutes, Corrections and Crime Control Administration and Programs, Chapter 423.505 (2009).

UNITED STATES CODES

Title 11, U.S.C, sec. 1328 (a)(3), Restitution in Bankruptcy cases.

Title 18 U.S.C., Part II, Chapter 227, Article 3564, Early termination of probation.

Title 18 U.S.C. sec. 921 (a)(20), Prohibits firearm possession for felons.

Title 18 U.S.C. sec. 922 (g)(9), Prohibits firearm possession for domestic violence misd.

Title 18 U.S.C. sec. 3561, Probation as a federal sentence.

Title 18 U.S.C. sec. 3583 (e)(3), Supervised release after imprisonment.

Title 18 U.S.C. sec. 3606, Arrest of a probation violator.

Title 20 U.S.C. sec 1091 (r), Denial of financial aid, Higher Ed Amendment Act.

Title 28 U.S.C. sec. 1865 (b)(5), Exclusion from jury service for felony convictions

United States Constitution, Article II, Section 2, Power to pardon allocated to president.

Washington Law GR-15, Chapter 10.97.060, Sealing eligibility.

COURT CASES

Bearden v. Georgia, 461 U.S. 660 (1983).

Beecham v. United States, 511 U.S. 368 (1994).

Belk v. Purkett, 15 F.3d 803 (8th Cir. 1994).

Benton v. State, 2003 WL 22220501, Ala. Crim. App. (2003).

Best v. State, 264 A.D.2d 404, 694 N.Y.S.2d 689 (2nd Dept. 1999).

Boling v. Romer, 101 F.3d 1336 (10th Cir. 1996).

Breed v. Jones, 421 U.S. 517 (1975).

Brown v. Plata, 131 S. Ct. 1910 (2011), 570 U.S. ___ (2013).

Bruggeman v. State, 681 So.2d 822 (1996).

Cabla v. State, 6 S.W.3d 543 (Tex. Crim. App. 1999).

Caron v. United States, 524 U.S. 308 (1998).

Commonwealth of Massachusetts v. Talbot, 444 Mass. 586, 830 N.E.2d 177 (2005).

Commonwealth v. Chase, in Thacher's Criminal Cases, 267 (1831), recorded in Vol. 11 of the Records of the Old Municipal Court of Boston, 199.

Connecticut Department of Public Safety v. Doe, 538 U.S. 1 (2003).

Correctional Services Corp v. Malesko, 534 U.S. 61 (2001).

Davis v. Alaska, 415 U.S. 308 (1974).

Ex parte United States, 242 U.S. 27 (1916).

Fare v. Michael C., 442 U.S. 707 (1979).

Fields v. State, 2002 WL 126972, Ala. Crim. App. (2002).

Franciosi v. Michigan Parole Board, 461 Mich. 347 (2000).

Gagnon v. Scarpelli, 411 U.S. 778 (1973).

Goldberg v. Beeler, 82 F.Supp.2d 302 (1999).

Grady v. North Carolina, 575 U. S. ___ (2015) No. 14–593. Per Curiam On petition for Writ of Certiorari to the Supreme Court of North Carolina.

Graham v. Florida, 560 U.S. ___ (2010). (08-7412)

Greenholtz v. Inmates of the Nebraska Penal and Correctional Complex, 442 U.S. 1, 99 S. Ct. 2100, 2107, 60 L. Ed. 2d 668 (1979).

Griffin v. Wisconsin, 483 U.S. 868 (1987).

Hampton v. State, 786 A.2d 375 (R.I. 2001).

In re Gault, 387 U.S. 1 (1967).

In re Winship, 397 U.S. 358 (1970).

Jago v. Van Curen, 454 U.S. 14 (1981).

Kent v. United States, 383 U.S. 541 (1966).

King v. Simpson, 189 F.3d 283 (2d Cir. 1999).

McKeiver v. Pennsylvania, 403 U.S. 528 (1971).

McKune v. Lile, 536 U.S. 24 (2002), 224 F. 3d. 1175.

Menechino v. Oswald, 430 F.2d 403, 407 (2nd Cir. 1970), cert. denied, 400 U.S. 1023, 91 S. Ct. 588, 27 L. Ed. 2d 635 (1971).

Miller v. Alabama, 567 U.S. ___ (2012).

Miranda v. Arizona, 384 U.S. 436 (1966).

Morrissey v. Brewer, 408 U.S. 471 (1972).

New Jersey v. T.L.O., 469 U.S. 325 (1985).

Newsom v. State, 2004 WL 943861, Miss. Ct. App. (2004).

Padilla v. Kentucky, 130 S. Ct. 1473 (2010).

Pennsylvania Board of Probation and Parole v. Scott, 524 U.S. 357 (1998).

People v. Colabello, 948 P.2d 77 (Colo. App. 1997).

People v. Meyer, 176 Ill. 2d 372, 680 N.E. 315 (1997).

People v. Price, 24 Ill. App. 2d. 364 (1960).

People v. Ramos, 48 CrL 1057 (Ill.S.Ct.) (1990).

Perry v. State, 778 So. 2d 1072 (Fla. Dist. Ct. App. 5th Dist. 2001)

Ramahlo v. Travis, 737 N.Y.S.2d 160 (3d Dept 2002).

Reyes v. Tate, 91 Ohio St. 3d 84, 742 N.E.2d 132 (2001).

Richardson v. McKnight, 521 U.S. 399 (1997).

Richardson v. Ramirez, 418 U.S. 24, 94 S. Ct. 2655, 41 L. Ed. 2d 551 (1974).

Roper v. Simmons, 543 U.S. 551 (2005).

Rothgery v. Gillespie County, 128 S. Ct. 2578 (2008).

Samson v. California, 547 U.S. 843 (2006).

Schall v. Martin, 104 S. Ct. 2403 (1984).

Silmon v. Travis, 95 N.Y.2d 470 (2000).

Smith v. Daily Mail Publishing Co., 443 U.S. 97 (1979).

Smith v. Doe, 538 U.S. 84 (2003).

Spaulding v. Nielsen, 599 F.2d 728 (5th Cir. 1979).

State of Missouri v. Anthony Williams, CR 2000-00704 (2000).

State v. Bourrie, 190 Or. App. 572, 80 P.3d 505 (2003).

State v. Faraday, 69 Conn. App. 421 (2002).

State v. Graham, 30 P.3d 310 (Kan 2001).

State v. Gropper, 888 P.2d 12211 (Wash. App. 1995).

State v. Pizel, 987 P.2d 1288 (Utah Ct. App. 1999).

Sullivan v. Florida, 560 U.S. ___ (2010). (08-7621).

Summers v. State, 817 So. 2d 950 (Fla Dist. Ct. App. 2d Dist. 2002).

Turner v. Rogers, 564 U.S. ___ (2011).

Tucker v. Alabama Board of Pardons and Paroles, 781 So.2d 358 (2000).

United States v. Bachsian, 4 F.3d 288 (1993).

United States v. Booker, 125 S. Ct. 738, 160 LED 2d 621 (U.S. 2005).

United States v. Gordon, 4 F.3d 1567 U.S. (10th Cir. September 1993).

United States v. Knights, 534 U.S. 112 (2001).

United States v. Laney, 189 F.3d 954 (9th Cir. 1999).

United States v. Lockhart, 58 F.3d 86 (4th Cir. June 1995).

United States v. McCormick, 54 F.3d 214 U.S. (5th Cir. 1995).

United States v. Pettus, 303 F.3d 480 (2nd Cir. 2002).

United States v. Riviera, 96 F.3rd 41 (2nd Cir. September 1996).

United States v. Salerno, 481 U.S. 739 (1987).

United States v. Thurlow, 44 F.3d 46 U.S. (1st Cir. 1995).

United States v. Washington, 11 F.3d 1510 U.S. (10th Cir. November 1993).

United States v. Wolff, 90 F.3d 191 (7th Cir. 1996).

Walrath v. Getty, 71 F.3d 679 (7th Cir. 1995).

Williams v. New York, 337 U.S. 241 (1949).

Williams v. Oklahoma, 358 U.S. 576 (1959).

Williams v. State of New Jersey, 2006 NJ Lexis 389, (2006).

Wooden v. State, (2001).

CASE INDEX

NAME INDEX